Unceasing war on poverty:

Beatrice and Sidney Webb and their world

Unceasing War on Poverty Beatrice and Sidney Webb and their world

Published by The Conrad Press in the United Kingdom 2024

Tel: +44(0)1227 472 874
www.theconradpress.com
info@theconradpress.com

ISBN 978-1-915494-61-0

Typesetting and Cover Design by: Charlotte Mouncey, www.bookstyle.co.uk
Jacket includes image attributed to Bertha Newcombe, 'Problems of Trade Unionism', 1881. Wellcome Collection. (CC BY 4.0)

The Conrad Press logo was designed by Maria Priestley.

Printed and bound in Great Britain by Clays Ltd, Elcograf S.p.A.

Unceasing war on poverty:
Beatrice and Sidney Webb
and their world

Michael Ward

By their work, Sidney and Beatrice Webb, more widely than any others of their generation, changed for the better the condition of the masses of the people. In field after field of social endeavour we are today reaping the fruits of the seed which they sowed in the minds and hearts of men and women. They declared an unceasing war on poverty.

(Address by Clement Attlee, 12.12.1947, when the ashes of Beatrice and Sidney Webb were interred in Westminster Abbey).

Contents

List of Plates
PREFACE
Chapter One: Introduction
    PROPHETS   10
    BEGINNINGS   10
    THREE INSTITUTIONS   12
    FROM PERMEATION, VIA SOCIAL DEMOCRACY, TO A NEW CIVILIZATION 12
    IDEAS   14
        The Webbs and the State   15
        The National Minimum   19
        Political Leadership   22
    ARTS, MUSIC, AND CULTURE   23
    BEATRICE AS FEMINIST   28
    MARRIAGE AND THE MORAL CODE   29

Notes to Preface and Chapter One   34

PART ONE: APPRENTICESHIPS 1858 - 1892

Chapter Two: Beatrice Potter 1858-1890
    BEATRICE 1858 - 1875   38
    'IRRESPONSIBLE GIRLHOOD' 1875-1882   44
    SOCIAL APPRENTICE 1882-1890   47

Chapter Three: Sidney Webb 1859-1890
    SIDNEY 1859-1880   62
    'THE ABLEST MAN IN ENGLAND'   66

Chapter Four: Joseph and Sidney
    FRIENDSHIP AND THE READING ROOM   75
    'DANCING IN A DREAM TOWARDS SOME PRECIPICE'   81
    SOCIALISM, UNEMPLOYMENT, AND THE DOCK STRIKE 1887-1889   93
    'A LONDON RETAIL TRADESMAN WITH THE AIMS OF A NAPOLEON'   103

Notes to Part One   133

PART TWO: PERMEATION 1892 - 1912

Chapter Five: The firm of Webb 1892-1899

MARRIAGE AND HONEYMOON	146
'LITTLE HOME ON THE BANKS OF THE THAMES'	147
THE WEBBS' YEAR	150
THE TRADE UNION BOOKS	154
THE LONDON COUNTY COUNCIL AND LONDON EDUCATION	159
'SOLID WORK IN ECONOMIC AND POLITICAL PRINCIPLES'	163

Chapter Six: Grosvenor Road 1899-1905

THE WEBB MYTH	170
THE SOULS, THE SALON, AND THE NETWORK	176
HISTORY OF ENGLISH LOCAL GOVERNMENT	184
EDUCATION	187
THE BOER WAR	193

Chapter Seven: The disease of destitution 1905-1912

'THAT NASTY OLD POOR LAW'	202
'OUR TRUSTY AND WELL-BELOVED BEATRICE': THE POOR LAW COMMISSION 1905-1909	206
'THE GOLDEN TIME': THE FABIAN SOCIETY 1905-1912	229
'RAGING,TEARING PROPAGANDA'	253
ENDGAME:1910-1912	271

Notes to Part Two	286

PART THREE: SOCIAL DEMOCRACY: 'A POOR THING BUT OUR OWN': 1912 - 1931

Chapter Eight: Peace and war 1912-1918

A NEW ENGLAND	304
A NEW POLITICAL WEEKLY	308
FABIANS AND GUILD SOCIALISTS	311
THE COMING OF WAR 1914-1916	315
THE WEBB NETWORK AND THE WAR	317
THE MOVEMENT	323
THE WEBBS AND THE WOOLFS	328
WAR EMERGENCY WORKERS NATIONAL COMMITTEE	331
IMPACT OF THE RUSSIAN REVOLUTION	333
REMAKING LABOUR	337
RECONSTRUCTION	340

Chapter Nine: Inevitable gradualness 1919-1924

THE COAL CRISIS AND THE SANKEY COMMISSION 349
SIDNEY, LABOUR, AND SEAHAM 358
THE LSE AND THE NEW STATESMAN AFTER THE WAR 362
THE FIRST LABOUR GOVERNMENT 367

Chapter Ten: Passfield Corner 1924-1929

'THE HOME OF THE AGED WEBBS' 382
'AN AUTOBIOGRAPHY WITH THE LOVE AFFAIRS LEFT OUT' 385
COAL AND THE GENERAL STRIKE: 1924-1926 388
'THE OLD WEBBS CHUCKLING OVER THEIR CHICKENS': POLITICS 1926 –
1929 391
'WHO IS COMING FORWARD AMONG THE YOUNG MEN?' THE NEXT
GENERATION 393
LIFE AT PASSFIELD CORNER 396
'THE BEVERIDGE-MAIR DICTATORSHIP': LSE 1924-1929 409

Chapter Eleven: The second Labour Government: 1929-1931

EAST AFRICA 412
PALESTINE 431
THE ECONOMY, UNEMPLOYMENT, AND THE FALL OF THE LABOUR
GOVERNMENT 447

Notes to Part Three 473

PART FOUR: A NEW CIVILIZATION? 1931 - 1947

Chapter Twelve: Soviet Communism

'WITHOUT DOUBT, WE ARE ON THE SIDE OF RUSSIA' 488
'A NEW KIND OF ROYALTY' 496
THE WEBBS AND LABOUR AFTER MACDONALD 504
LABOUR'S INTERNATIONAL POLICY 1931-1937 510
'A REAL GOOD SORT': BEVERIDGE LEAVES LSE 516

Chapter Thirteen The last years 1937-1947

AGEING 521
'ONE MAN DISGUISED AS A COMMITTEE': BEVERIDGE AFTER 1937 524
THE WEBBS AND THE SHAWS 531
IVAN AND AGNIYA MAISKY 534
APPEASEMENT AND THE NAZI-SOVIET PACT 1937-1939 536
PHONEY WAR 1939-1940 548
BEATRICE AND SIDNEY, 1941-1947 557

Notes to Part Four   570

                        ANNEXES

Annexe One: Acknowledgements and Thanks   578
Annexe Two: Biographical Index   581
Annexe Three: Bibliography   633
Annexe Four: The Potter Sisters   644
Annexe Five: Abbreviations and acronyms   645

                         INDEX

List of Plates

1. The Potter family 1865. Left to right: Georgina, Mary, Lawrencina Potter, Margaret, Beatrice, Richard Potter, Teresa, Blanche.

2. Charles Webb, Sidney's father, in his Westminster Rifle Volunteer uniform.

3. Elizabeth Webb, Sidney's mother

4. Beatrice in the late 1870s

5. Beatrice in ball gown, 1885

6. Leaflet for a course of lectures by Sidney, 1883

7. Sidney 1885

8. The British Museum Reading Room in the 1880s

9. 1889 Dock Strike – one of the daily demonstrations led by John Burns

10. Katherine Buildings, Cartwright Street, Aldgate, East London. Beatrice and Ella Pycroft worked here as housing managers in 1885-86

11. *Fabian Essays* -1889 first edition cover design by Walter Crane

12. Sidney & Beatrice, 1890s/1900s

13. Sidney & Beatrice, 1903-4 – picture by HG Wells

14. 41 Grosvenor Road SW, the Webbs' home from 1892 until the 1920s

15. Beatrice 1908

16. *Disease of Destitution* poster, designed by Gerald Spencer Pryse for the National Campaign for the Prevention of Destitution

17. Beatrice – chalk drawing by Jessie Holliday. ?1909?

18. Sidney – chalk drawing by Jessie Holliday. ?1909?

19. Labour's Medical Advisers cartoon by Will Dyson. Frontispiece to The *World of Labour* by GDH Cole (1913); one of very few cartoons showing both Sidney and Beatrice.

20. The Sankey Commission on the Coal Industry, 1919, in session at the House of Lords. Sidney and R H Tawney on the right. Beatrice compared it to a 'revolutionary tribunal'.

21. *The Webb of Destiny*: Punch cartoon published the week after Sidney's Labour on the Threshold speech, 1923

22. Sidney, 1932, takes a day return to London to talk at LSE. Beatrice wrote: We have shared the glory and the income of Cabinet office, but he takes the title and I travel first class! A concession so I tell myself to old age!

23. Sidney and Beatrice at Passfield Corner, with Maynard Keynes, September 1926

24. Beatrice & Sidney, 1926

25. 1937 party invitation: Beatrice and Sidney *on the threshold of their ninth decade*.

26. Sidney, at Passfield Corner, August 1941

27. Beatrice, at Passfield Corner, August 1941

28. Interment of ashes, December 1947; Two vergers at Westminster Abbey carry the ashes of Beatrice and Sidney to their resting place.

Endpaper map The Webbs' London

The endpaper map was designed by Charles Foster. It is derived from The New Map of London, drawn & engraved by G W Bacon & Co 127 Strand London. Downloaded under a Creative Commons Attribution-Non-Commercial 2.5 License, from the collection of McMaster University.

PREFACE

They made a striking couple.

Beatrice Potter was tall and slim; Sidney Webb short and stout. Beatrice was one of the nine daughters of Richard Potter (sometime chairman of the Great Western Railway) and his wife Lawrencina. Sidney's mother, Elizabeth, ran a hairdressing salon off London's Leicester Square; his father, Charles, kept the books for the business.

Together Beatrice and Sidney formed an enduring partnership. They wrote books together; they travelled the world together. Sidney supported Beatrice when she sat on government committees; Beatrice supported Sidney when he became a County Councillor, a member of parliament, a cabinet minister, and finally a peer. In 1909, in their fifties, they launched a two-year, raging, tearing propaganda campaign for the abolition of the Poor Law.

Early in their relationship, Beatrice noted in her diary that:

We are both second-rate minds: but we are curiously combined – I am the investigator, and he the executor. [1]

After both had died in the 1940s, their ashes were placed in Westminster Abbey. Their extensive papers were deposited in the archives at the London School of Economics (LSE), which they had established in 1894.

While researching this book, I often worked in the LSE archives. I would travel on the London Underground Northern Line to Leicester Square – arriving in a neighbourhood the Webbs knew well. I would leave the station by the Cranbourn Street exit; immediately facing me was the Westminster City Council green ceramic plaque which marks the site of Sidney's mother's hairdressing business, and where he was born.

Turning left along Cranbourn Street, I would cross St Martin's Lane, where Sidney first went to school, and continue along Long Acre, on to Great Queen Street, past the original offices of the *New Statesman*, started by the Webbs in 1913.

On the corner of Great Queen Street and Kingsway stands the Kingsway Hall Hotel. This replaces Kingsway Hall, built in 1912; in the Webbs' lifetime it was often used for Fabian lectures. After Sidney died in 1947, it was the setting for his memorial meeting.

Then I would turn on to Kingsway itself – a wide street, constructed by the London County Council (LCC) in its first flush of municipal confidence and pride before 1914. Sidney was an LCC member from 1892 to 1910. Projects like Kingsway were funded through 'betterment' – acquisition of more land than was required for the road itself, so that sites on Kingsway could be sold on long leases for commercial development.

Walking down Kingsway, after a few hundred yards I would arrive at Aldwych, and at LSE itself. The School now occupies a large site, with some buildings fronting on to Kingsway. Sidney secured the original LSE site (on permanent loan, for a peppercorn rent) on Clare Market, a side street, as part of the LCC improvement scheme.

The Fabian Society – the left of centre political think-tank, of which Sidney was an early member and Beatrice also became a leading member – was based nearby. The first Fabian office (from 1891) was at 276 The Strand; later, they moved to Clifford's Inn, close to LSE.

Many of the regular Fabian meetings were held at Essex Hall, a Unitarian chapel just off the Strand; Fabian members would gather in local cafes before meetings. One evening in February 1906 two recent Fabian recruits, Arthur Colegate and his friend Clifford Sharp (later the first editor of the *New Statesman*) celebrated Colegate's 22nd birthday:

> ...*dinner at the Strand Cabin and then went on to Essex Hall, Strand to hear a paper by H.G. Wells on* The Faults of the Fabian ... [2]

When in 1909 the Webbs set up the National Campaign for the Prevention of Destitution (NCPD), campaigning for the implementation of their Minority Report on the Poor Laws, offices were rented in nearby Norfolk Street. The campaign was unsuccessful, and in 1911 Beatrice and Sidney took a sabbatical year and travelled round the world. When they got back, the Fabians organized a welcome home dinner and soiree, at the Holborn restaurant on the corner of Kingsway and New Oxford Street. [3]

The first meeting of the *New Statesman* board took place in the NCPD office. The Fabian Research Bureau – established by Beatrice in 1912 – was also based there.

Sidney and Beatrice themselves lived a mile away, in a house overlooking the Thames. In the years before 1914 this small corner of London was the heart of their political world. Beatrice wrote in her diary in 1913 that their lives were centred on

> ...*the three offices, of the Fabian, the National Committee and Research Department, and the New Statesman; and it is with the inhabitants of these that we spend our outdoor life...* [4]

Their relationship was both personal and political; Beatrice called it a working comradeship or the *firm of Webb*. Their friend Bertrand Russell said that they became

> ...*the most completely married couple I have ever known...*

The newspaper editor Alfred Gardiner said that Sidney and Beatrice were the ablest couple in London. He thought they had virtually abandoned their separate identities. Either could speak for both: they spoke, not of 'I' but of 'we'. H G Wells, who caricatured the Webbs in his novel *The New Machiavelli*, observed the same behaviour.

Their talk of 'we' was not confined to their work and their opinions: it applied also to their personal lives, their food, and their health. For Russell, Beatrice's indiscriminate use of 'we'

> ...*was one of the delights of their friends.* [5]

For much of her adult life Beatrice ate very little. An obsessive dieter and a borderline anorexic, she experienced several nervous breakdowns. Despite their closeness, her success in enforcing her dietary regime on Sidney was limited.

In September 1903. Beatrice and Sidney, and Bertrand and Alys Russell, went on a cycling holiday together in Normandy. Tensions were emerging between the Russells, which would lead before long to their separation. But both Webbs enjoyed themselves; the mixture of exercise and sightseeing left them rested and fit rather than tired.

Russell noticed that Beatrice did not stop trying to manage Sidney's diet. According to Russell, Beatrice stayed in her room in the mornings; she could not bear the sight of the others eating breakfast. Sidney came down for rolls and coffee but was not allowed butter. Beatrice sent the chambermaid down to the breakfast room with a stern warning:

> *We do not have butter for Sidney's breakfast.* [6]

I first heard this anecdote from my parents; it was the first I knew of the Webbs. The source is Russell's autobiography, the first volume of which appeared in 1967. Maybe my parents borrowed the autobiography from the library; maybe they saw the story in a review. I was in my teens, about to go and study philosophy, politics and economics. They must have thought it was the sort of thing I would appreciate – perhaps even remember – anyhow, they passed it on.

By the time I came to research this book my mother was in her mid-90s; she would ask what I was doing; I would bring her up to date with my latest discoveries about Sidney and Beatrice and their world. Her invariable response would be

> *We do not have butter for Sidney's breakfast.*

I next came across the Webbs as an undergraduate student. One of my final year papers in 1972 was 'Industrial Relations and Labour Economics'; I was taught by Bill McCarthy, who also chaired the Fabian Society's research committee. Bill told his students to read the Webbs' *Industrial Democracy*, with its clear exposition of trade union methods. More than 70 years after its first publication, it remained, (and still remains) an authoritative source.

After I graduated, my first job was based at Toynbee Hall, the East London settlement established by Canon Samuel Barnett and his wife Henrietta in 1884. Sidney and Beatrice knew the Barnetts well; their protegee, and lifetime friend, William Beveridge, became Sub Warden of Toynbee in 1904, after leaving Oxford. Clement Attlee became Secretary of Toynbee in 1909. Toynbee Hall has been – and remains – a great incubator for social policy. Later, I studied in the evenings – as Sidney had done – at Birkbeck, where I completed an MA in Economic and Social History.

In 1981 I was elected to the Greater London Council (GLC) – successor to the LCC. I had a grand office in the 1920s splendour of County Hall, which Beatrice had called

...the LCC palace on the river. [7]

Sidney was a role model: where he had built the Council's education role from scratch, my job was to create an economic development programme. My methods were like Sidney's: close study of arcane corners of local government legislation and careful exploitation of little-known sources of local government finance, all backed up as necessary with Counsel's Opinion, provided in accordance with meticulously drafted instructions.

One of my tasks at County Hall was to identify, and sell off, assets the Council no longer required, in order to generate funds to support new investment programmes. By then the Council had owned the freeholds of the office blocks on Kingsway for eighty years or more. Selling those freeholds to the firms that occupied the offices raised a lot of money to support the capital programme of the 1980s GLC.

Gradually, over the years, I collected copies of the Webbs' books. It was always interesting to see which individuals or institutions now considered they could manage without the Webb canon. My copies of the *History of Local Government* had belonged to the Inner London Education Authority, which had inherited them from the education library of the London County Council. A copy of *Problems of Modern Industry* came from the library of the *Manchester Guardian*. The two-volume *Soviet Communism: a new civilization* was from Transport House Birmingham – regional headquarters of the Transport and General Workers Union. My copy of Beatrice's first book, *The Cooperative Movement in Great*

Britain, had belonged to Rochdale Public Libraries.

I have a couple of books from the Webbs' own library. The first is one of the printed evidence volumes for the Royal Commission on the Poor Laws, embossed in gold letters 'Mrs Sidney Webb'. The other is the First World War diary of Beatrice's sister Kate – printed privately in 1927. I found my copy in an Oxfam shop, a few hundred yards from Grosvenor Road, the Webbs' London home. An inscription on the flyleaf tells me that it had been given away by the Webbs at a big family party in 1937.

Before the party, Beatrice had spent weeks sorting their library:

...the books had overflown onto tables and chairs so that those I sought were hopelessly out of sight – whilst those we did not want were piling up in front. [8]

So she sorted out the duplicates to give away at the party.

Another sister, Georgina, wrote a history of the Potters, their father's family; what is now my copy carries the bookplate of Stafford and Isobel Cripps.

I acquired the books; sometimes I read them. After Mrs Thatcher abolished the GLC in 1986, I moved to Manchester. I continued to work on local economic development, establishing and running the Centre for Local Economic Strategies (CLES). I stayed 13 years in Manchester; my two children were born there. In 2000 we all moved to London; I spent the next three and a half years setting up and leading the London Development Agency – the Mayor of London's economic development agency, part of the restored fabric of London government, taking over where the LCC and the GLC had left off.

In 2009, the centenary of Beatrice's *Minority Report* on the Poor Law, I heard, through the Smith Institute (named after John Smith, not Adam) of an opportunity to produce a commemorative pamphlet for the Webb Memorial Trust. I was commissioned to write it; the result, *Beatrice Webb, her quest for a Fairer Society,* was launched at LSE in 2011. The Trust then generously supported my proposal to write a new biography.

But why a new life of the Webbs?

A new appraisal of the Webbs and their role is overdue. Much has been written about them, little of it recent. The most recent general life of both Sidney and Beatrice is that by Lisanne Radice, published in 1984. (*Beatrice and Sidney Webb: Fabian Socialists*). Attempts by the Webbs' executors, the Passfield Trustees, to commission a comprehensive official biography were unsuccessful. With the passage of time, there is important material on the Webbs now available that was either closed to, or not easily accessible to previous writers.

But the overriding reason for a fresh appraisal of Sidney and Beatrice Webb and their work must be that the world has changed out of all recognition since they died in the 1940s, and since earlier biographies appeared.

Previous writers – whether from the Webbs' own circle like Mary Agnes Hamilton, or Margaret Cole, or writers from within the Fabian tradition – tended to see one great achievement: the Webbs' role in the evolution of Britain's welfare state – and one great error: their uncritical stance towards the Soviet Union in the 1930s.

Beveridge wrote that

The Webbs did much to make Britain as we know it today. [9]

Radice, in her 1984 study, concludes that

With Lloyd George and Beveridge, Beatrice and Sidney Webb can justly be said to be the founders of the modern welfare state. [10]

The excuses and explanations offered for the Webbs' devotion to the Soviet Union in their later years are many and various. Radice pleads in mitigation that Sidney and Beatrice were very old at the time, arguing that *Soviet Communism* was

…the work not of two ruthless totalitarians but of two gullible septuagenarians. [11]

Others point out that the Webbs were not unique in turning away from social democratic reformism in the 1930s: many others on the British left travelled the same route. After the 1917 Bolshevik revolution, Russia, wrote Margaret Cole, had become *…the hope of the world.* [12]

The Webbs had not been early enthusiasts for the Bolsheviks. Their faith was rooted in the gradual, nonviolent transformation of society. What changed was their overwhelming disappointment at the record of the second MacDonald minority Labour government, its failure to deal with mass unemployment, and its ultimate collapse in the financial crisis of August 1931. By 1931 they had begun to doubt, not just the *inevitability of gradualness*, but even the *possibility* of gradualness. [13]

Sidney and Beatrice inspired many of the reforms of the 1945 Labour government. At the reinterment of their ashes in 1947, Prime Minister Clement Attlee said that the Webbs, more than any others of their generation

…changed for the better the condition of the masses of the people. [14]

It was Attlee's 1945 Labour government that finally abolished the Poor Law, forty years after the Minority Report. Attlee's own first job in politics had been as a young organiser for the Webbs' Poor Law campaign. Sidney and Beatrice inspired a generation of young people, moving the issues of poverty and destitution to the centre of the political agenda. Their ideas contributed to the development of policies for full employment and the establishment of the

National Health Service. They helped develop the form in which public owner-ship of major industries was established.

George Dangerfield, in *The Strange Death of Liberal England* (1935) iden-tifies the young poet Rupert Brooke (who died of septicaemia, in April 1915, on the way to fight at Gallipoli) as a central figure in the political changes of the Edwardian period. Dangerfield describes how Brooke fell under the spell of Beatrice and Sidney. Brooke – and many of his generation – were inspired by their arguments

> *...the strong prose, the vigorous thought, the feeling that infuses the whole of lives given up to the betterment of mankind...* [15]

Dangerfield suggests that the Webbs' conclusions were meagre – but it was the language and advocacy that mattered to their audience. By the time war came, Brooke's own socialism had faded. While it lasted, he put his faith in the *goodness of man*.

Seventy-five years after Sidney's death, the legacy of 1945 is far from intact. In the 1960s and 1970s, the insistent voices of a new generation of campaign-ers – many linked to LSE or the Fabian Society, with the *New Statesman* as a ready platform – forced public attention on the fact that poverty had not been abolished for all time, and demanded new reforms.

In the 1980s, many of the industries that had been nationalised in the 1940s were returned to the private sector. Others have shrunk or even vanished, in the face of environmental and economic change.

This is not to diminish the scale of the achievements of the 1945 government. But few political problems – poverty, destitution, economic efficiency – are solved for all time. 1945 was not the end of history; returning to the 1945 programme would not be an adequate or appropriate response to the challenges of the twenty first century.

The Webbs built their career and their reputation on a readiness to investigate the facts – tiresome, difficult, awkward facts. Their successors must investigate new problems, develop new solutions – and not be afraid to recognize that the world has changed. There is a strong and important radical tradition of campaigning and protest. But Sidney and Beatrice were willing to face the diffi-cult problems of the real world.

And the Soviet Union, extolled by the Webbs, has now been gone for more than thirty years. Like Sidney and Beatrice, there were many who, in the 1930s, 40s and 50s closed their eyes to the brutality of the regime.

So it must be time to move on from a simplistic verdict on the Webbs: 'welfare state good, Soviet Union bad'. Instead, I have tried to examine their lives as a whole, looking at the families, backgrounds, relationships, and friendships that shaped them, and the institutions they created – the Fabian Society, the London School of Economics, and the *New Statesman*. All three institutions have, after all, outlasted, not just their founders, but the 1945 social programme and the Soviet Union. I consider their research work and their writing, and Sidney's record in local government and as a minister.

Sidney and Beatrice were ready to challenge received ideas, including those on the left – what Beatrice called the *shibboleths of collectivism*. When they were planning the establishment of LSE in 1894, she noted:

> ...*reform will not be brought about by shouting. What is needed is* hard thinking. [16]

Sidney and Beatrice made provision for their executors to commission an official biography. This project started, but was never completed. Beatrice thought the Trustees might select some *unemployed intellectual*. In fact, in 1948, they chose the LSE historian (and old friend of the Webbs) R H Tawney.

Tawney started work, but was soon disillusioned. He found out that one of the trustees, Margaret Cole, was producing her own book – *The Webbs and their Work*. Tawney complained that this

> ...*made the work of the contemporary biographer both more difficult and less useful.* [17]

Harold Laski, another trustee, supported Tawney, assuring him that he had

> ...*deep loyalty and affection to the Webbs, and I feel as though Mrs Cole has taken over their legacy as a permanent source of income.* [18]

The efforts of supportive trustees to persuade Tawney to reconsider were unsuccessful, and he withdrew from the project.

There the question of the authorised biography rested for nearly twenty years. The Trustees controlled access to the Webb papers; Eric Hobsbawm, writing his PhD thesis on the Fabians, was not permitted to use the papers; the policy, only slowly relaxed, was that the papers would not be available to other researchers until the official biography had been published. [19]

Margaret Cole, with Beatrice's niece Barbara Drake, edited Beatrice's second autobiographical book, *Our Partnership*, published in 1948. She also edited two sets of extracts from Beatrice's diaries, which appeared in 1952 and 1956.

In the 1980s a much fuller (though still selective), 4 volume, edition of the diaries was published, edited by Norman and Jeanne MacKenzie; the MacKenzies also complied a three-volume edited selection of letters by Sidney and Beatrice.

In the 1960s, the Trustees returned to the official biography, appointing the social historian Royden Harrison to write it. Harrison's experience paralleled

Tawney's: the trustees did not tell Harrison about the Tawney episode – he read about it in the archives. Harrison then learned that Beatrice's niece Kitty Muggeridge was working on a life of Beatrice. When he asked the trustees why they had not told him about the Muggeridge project, they told him he had never asked. He also learned that another book, Jeanne MacKenzie's, *A Victorian Courtship*, was under way. Harrison wrote that

> *Amidst these numerous challenges, I felt the Webbs to be less pressing than others might have done.* [20]

Harrison completed his first volume, taking the story up to 1905; it was published in 2000. It is scholarly, thoroughly researched, and objective. Paul Foot (no Fabian) praised the book's

> *…deep historical understanding and its rich sense of humour.* [21]

Harrison died, aged 75, in 2002, without completing the second volume. Neither attempt by the Passfield Trustees to produce an official biography of both succeeded. No other life of both has appeared since Radice's book in 1984, although a study of their ideas and their contribution to sociology, economics and politics was published in 2022. (Reisman, D *Sidney and Beatrice Webb, An academic biography*; Cham, Switzerland, Palgrave Macmillan, 2022.)

Arundel, December 2023

Chapter One: Introduction

PROPHETS

Beatrice and Sidney Webb were at the heart of British politics from the 1880s to the 1940s. Their lives were committed to building a political movement capable of challenging for, and holding, national power. They developed the ideas, conducted and encouraged the research, designed the organisational structures, wrote the policies, and identified the people to staff and run that movement. They played a significant part in reshaping British politics, away from a Liberal-Conservative two party system to one dominated by Labour and the Conservatives. They shaped and inspired the political generation that assumed power in 1945.

In the seventy-five years since their ashes were interred together in Westminster Abbey (the first, and so far the only couple to be commemorated together in this way), their reputations have fluctuated. As in their lifetimes, they have drawn criticism from left and right. They have been seen as dour; insensitive to culture, art, and music; incurably bureaucratic; authoritarian; and committed above all to the expansion of the state.

Each formidable as an individual, Sidney and Beatrice made an extraordinary couple. George Bernard Shaw (GBS) said theirs was a perfect collaboration. One contemporary described them as

> ...*two typewriters that clicked as one...* [22]

The Liberal Herbert Samuel said that Sidney and Beatrice's partnership

> ...*developed over the course of years into a kind of dual personality.* [23]

BEGINNINGS

They grew up in different worlds, he in central London, she in Gloucestershire. Both families – the capitalist Potters, the tradespeople Webbs – could just about be called middle class – but they were at distant extremes of the bourgeois spectrum.

Sidney and Beatrice met in January 1890. In the years before they met, Beatrice worked, in East London and elsewhere, as a social reformer, a housing manager, and a writer. She described herself as a *social investigator*, and contributed to Charles Booth's monumental study of the *Life and Labour of the people of London*. At first, she was close to the Charity Organisation Society (COS), originators of the division of the poor into deserving and undeserving, before rejecting COS orthodoxy in the late 1880s. As a young woman, she built up a circle of close women friends of her own generation, among them her cousin, the novelist Margaret Harkness, Carrie Darling and Ella Pycroft.

In the 1870s Beatrice spent a year at school with Harkness, who subsequently trained as a nurse before becoming a writer. Harkness introduced Beatrice to the world of the British Museum Reading Room, workplace and home-from-home for other young women writers. Carrie Darling cared for the children of Beatrice's sister Mary and later became a teacher. Ella Pycroft worked alongside Beatrice in East London, afterwards working in Gloucestershire, teaching young women cookery and domestic economy.

This group of friends travelled together. They shared their accommodation, and their secrets. They confided in each other and counselled each other. In times of emotional crisis, they supported each other. What the four had in common was that each was trying to establish an independent working life, depending neither on their parents or a husband for support.

In summer 1888 Ella Pycroft stayed with Beatrice; both read a magazine article about glorified spinsters – a

…new race of women not looking for or expecting marriage. [24]

The article drew a distinction between glorified spinsters and old maids: the *glorified spinsters* were young, middle-class women, following independent careers of their own. Beatrice began to use the expression *glorified spinster* to describe her own economic and social position and that of her close women friends.

Sidney started work as a clerk in the City when he was 16. He attended night schools, passed examinations, and won prizes. He competed successfully in the Civil Service examinations, joining the War Office as a Man Clerk in 1878, when he was 19. He rose rapidly through the ranks; in 1881, through further examinations, he reached the senior civil service – at the same age as his contemporaries who arrived at this point via Oxford or Cambridge.

In 1880s Britain a new wave of socialist organisations emerged; Sidney joined one of them, the Fabian Society. His friendships were drawn from work colleagues and from the Fabians; in the 1880s his closest companion was the Fabian writer, George Bernard Shaw (GBS). Sydney Olivier was a civil service colleague who became a Fabian; Graham Wallas was an Oxford friend of Olivier's.

Beatrice and Sidney's emotional experiences before they met were as different as their social origins. In the mid-1880s, Beatrice went through a long, tortured, unhappy relationship with the Liberal – later Unionist – MP and minister Joseph

Chamberlain. Sidney had known his own disappointments; GBS told Margaret Cole that whenever Sidney fell in love, he would come out in spots.

From their first meeting in 1890, Sidney ardently pursued Beatrice; she, scarred by her experience with Chamberlain, was more cautious. Their courtship lasted two and a half years; for the first eighteen months the outcome was uncertain. But they eventually married in July 1892. Some of their friends – like Liberal MP Richard Haldane – congratulated them; others – including Ella Pycroft and Charles Booth – disapproved.

THREE INSTITUTIONS

From the 1880s, Sidney worked to grow the Fabian Society as a policy organisation; later, Beatrice also took a leading role on the Fabian Executive Committee. In 1894, they used a bequest left to the Fabians to found the London School of Economics (LSE) as a social sciences university. In 1913 they started the weekly left journal, the *New Statesman*. Beatrice sometimes referred to the LSE and the *New Statesman* as their children.

These three institutions – the think-tank, the university, and the newspaper – provided the background against which the new political movement could grow. All three continue to flourish in the 21ˢᵗ century – long after the deaths of their founders.

Around those institutions, they cultivated a network of people to sustain and develop the movement. That network was nurtured by the Webbs' generous, if frugal, hospitality at their homes, first in London, subsequently in Hampshire.

FROM PERMEATION, VIA SOCIAL DEMOCRACY, TO A NEW CIVILIZATION

Their approach to politics evolved. Up to 1912 their method was *permeation* – achieving change through existing political parties. Before 1906, Sidney worked with leading Conservatives and Liberals to achieve major reform and expansion of secondary education. When in 1905 Beatrice was appointed to a Royal Commission on the Poor Laws, she and Sidney hoped to repeat this success. Beatrice and her allies produced a substantial Minority Report, calling for the break-up of the Poor Law. They hoped for the same success on welfare policies as Sidney had achieved on education. But there was no Poor Law legislation in the years before the First World War.

Acknowledging this defeat, they took a break, and then announced that permeation was finished. They decided to back the emerging Labour Party;

Beatrice called it

...a poor thing, but our own...[25]

In the years that followed they worked to grow Labour's capacity, to the point where it could form a government for the first time. With the leading trade union MP Arthur Henderson ('Uncle Arthur'), who led the party in the war years, Sidney wrote Labour's constitution and its policies.

After the war, Sidney became an MP, and in 1923 Chairman of the Party. He thought that, before long, Labour would gain the support of a majority of the electorate. He spoke of the *inevitable gradualness* of Labour's programme of change.

But Labour did not win a majority at any of the 1920s general elections. It did form minority governments in 1924 and from 1929 to 1931, under Prime Minister Ramsay MacDonald; Sidney was a Minister in both. The dominant political issue was mass unemployment; the 1924 government had no answer – and the party did not develop a policy response while in opposition from 1924 to 1929.

In the second MacDonald Labour government (1929-1931), Sidney, (now in the House of Lords as Colonial Secretary), was a diligent and effective departmental minister. But politics was dominated by the persistence of mass unemployment, and the lack of any serious policy to deal with it. Trade declined after the 1929 Wall Street crash; crisis followed upon crisis; government report followed upon government report.

Neither the Cabinet, nor the Webbs, knew what to do. In August 1931, faced with calls for deep cuts in public spending, the Government split apart. MacDonald formed a National Government with Conservatives, Liberals, and a handful of Labour defectors. Sidney and Beatrice had long been ambivalent towards MacDonald. Bertrand Russell thought they had hated him from very early days.[26] Even before the government collapsed, they began to doubt *inevitable gradualness*. The ideas they had developed over the previous twenty years were no help; no new thinking was taking place. Their belief in gradual change wavered. Like many others in the west, they convinced themselves that a new civilization was emerging in the Soviet Union.

Their enthusiasm for Russia did not lead them to support the Communist Party of Great Britain; in Britain, the Webbs still backed Labour. The August 1939 pact between Hitler and Stalin shook their faith. They welcomed Churchill's emergence as Prime Minister in May 1940, and believed Britain should (and would) fight on after France had fallen. In 1941 they were relieved when Hitler's invasion of Russia made Britain and the Soviet Union allies.

IDEAS

Beatrice and Sidney Webb made a significant contribution to political thought – but they were, above all, political practitioners. Sidney began as a civil servant, later becoming a politician, serving as a county councillor, an MP, a peer – and twice as a cabinet minister. Beatrice was a social investigator, and a caustic chronicler of her times in her diaries and in her two autobiographical books; she served, indefatigably, on government committees and commissions. Both analysed problems, then proposed institutional, practical remedies and policies.

I like the kitchen of life,

wrote Sidney to Beatrice, before they were married

T. Unions and details of administration are more to me than art or literature and I am keenly and absorbingly interested in their work. [27]

Leonard Woolf – who both Webbs knew well, and with whom they worked closely from 1913 – wrote that liberty,

…and all large vague political ideas and ideals (except, perhaps, those concerned with equality) …meant very little to them. [28]

The partnership of Beatrice and Sidney, starting in 1892, lasted 50 years. From their early years together, they worked in close harmony and evolved their ideas jointly. Their first biographer, Mary Agnes (Molly) Hamilton watched them working; they would review their notes together, reading and discussing them. Then Beatrice's

…eyes would light up. She would spring to her feet and pace up and down, waving her cigarette. 'That implies…' She would then start off on a chain of argument, he swiftly writing the while, using his matchless power of finding appropriate and exactly fitting words… [29]

Before they met, Beatrice had studied cooperation; together they researched and published books on trade unionism, and on local government.

Over those 50 years, their views evolved. While they did not develop a unified, unchanging body of thought, they returned to a few key themes. These included:

• The role of the state;

• The idea of a National Minimum;

• The nature of political leadership

The Webbs and the State

In 2015, two business journalists, John Micklethwait and Adrian Wooldridge, wrote, in a study of the changing nature of the state, that

Beatrice Webb was the godmother of the welfare state. [30]

They argue that, in designing a blueprint for a new form of government intended to provide citizens with a defined, universal minimum of services, Beatrice created.

…a ratchet towards ever bigger government. [31]

Bertrand Russell thought Beatrice worshipped the state. [32]

The Webbs' efforts – and they were the efforts of both Sidney and Beatrice – were not confined to social welfare – although social policy was a major field for their work.

Differing views about the proper role of the state separated the rising generation of Liberal politicians in the 1890s from their predecessors. Similar arguments distinguished the Webbs from their antagonists on the 1905 Poor Law Royal Commission. Their friend the historian R H Tawney wrote in 1914 that future social policy issues would turn on the relations between society and the state:

No one now believes in pure individualism. Few are contented with pure collectivism. [33]

In 1889, before Sidney and Beatrice had met, Sidney was one of the group responsible for the book *Fabian Essays in Socialism*. The six authors declared that, as social democrats, they were convinced of the necessity of

…vesting the organization of industry and the material of production in a State identified with the whole people by complete Democracy. [34]

In his chapter, Sidney pointed to the growing role of the state in economic regulation, and to the expansion of government employment. The largest employer of labour in Britain was a government minister – the Postmaster-General. And

…almost every conceivable trade is , somewhere or other, carried on by parish, municipality, or the National Government itself without the intervention of any middleman or capitalist. [35]

The Webbs saw state action, collective action, and common ownership as components of a process of continual, gradual change. We do not see, they wrote in their 1920 *Constitution for the Socialist Commonwealth of Great Britain,*

…any sudden and simultaneous transformation of the Capitalist System. [36]

At the LCC Sidney oversaw major expansion of secondary and technical education. This experience helped them develop their view of public services. Services like public health, or universal education

…involved enterprises to which no profit making could usually be attached… [37]

They saw this as a new form of state; they called it the *housekeeping state*.

They suggested that an alternative to the profit motive already existed and had evolved over many years at local level. That alternative was to provide services, according to need, through local institutions – councils and Poor Law Guardians. Gradually, feudal structures had been superseded, and the local electorate had become wider and more representative – no longer restricted by property qualifications, but becoming, in Beatrice's words

…practically inclusive of all adult inhabitants. [38]

So they decided to study the development of local government, and to show how local responsibilities – backed by national legislation as necessary – had expanded to cover land drainage, sewers, highways, street lighting, policing, the relief of destitution and the suppression of vagrancy.

They believed that public services should be run by employed, salaried, disinterested experts

…rewarded not by the making of private fortunes, but by public honour and special promotion. [39]

Those experts would be guided by

…accurately ascertained and authoritatively reported facts. [40]

The performance and efficiency of public services would be measured: the results would be publicized. Measurement and Publicity would undermine and eliminate any tendency to autocratic decision making.

The deliberate intensification of this searchlight of public knowledge we regard as the cornerstone of successful democracy. [41]

When in the 1930s Sidney and Beatrice visited the Soviet Union to assess progress under communism, they concluded that measurement and publicity were essential tools to judge the success of change; they thought the Communist government understood this.

During the First World War, Sidney's energies were concentrated on the War Emergency Workers National Committee – set up by trade unions and other labour organisations to monitor the impact of the war on the living conditions of families. After the government had introduced conscription into the armed services, some committee members called for conscription of wealth as well as conscription of labour: the government should seize bank accounts, savings, land, and investments.

Sidney argued that the tax system could be used instead of outright seizure – a graduated levy, like the already-existing Death Duties, on capital wealth. He thought this preferable to the government taking over all 300,000 farms, or local councils managing 500,000 shops.

While the wartime coalition did not adopt this proposal, as the capital levy it became central to Labour Party policy between the wars. It was a new and different insight into how social democrats might use the power of the state, with taxation as the main instrument of redistribution.

There were many contemporaries who did not share the Webbs' faith in the role and potential of the state.

Hilaire Belloc – Catholic writer, poet, and from 1906 to 1910 a Liberal MP – was critical of the expansion of the state in the Edwardian period. Some of the proposals Belloc opposed were supported by the Webbs – like minimum wage legislation; others – such as the 1911 National Insurance Act – they also opposed. Belloc became directly critical of the Webbs, arguing that there was a drift towards a new serfdom, a *servile state*:

> *That arrangement of society in which so considerable a number of the families and individuals are constrained by positive law to labour for the advantage of other families and individuals as to stamp the whole community with the mark of such labour we call THE SERVILE STATE.* [42]

Belloc's position was not just that he disapproved of the expansion of the state. He also identified a superior, patronising, authoritarian strand in the Webbs' ideas. In the Edwardian years Belloc frequently contributed to the *New Age* – a radical weekly magazine, run by Alfred Orage and Arthur Penty. Opposing the Minority Report, Belloc described the Webbs' proposals as

> *…a scheme drawn up by Mr Sidney Webb, the statistician, with the aid of his wife, for dealing with the lives of people much poorer than themselves.* [43]

By the early 1920s, supporters of this critique of the state had divided into two groups. Orage and Penty had been early supporters of the Guild Socialist movement, in which GDH Cole later played a leading role, and which had a divisive impact on the Fabian Society. Belloc worked closely with GK Chesterton; Shaw, with whom they frequently debated, nicknamed them the Chesterbelloc.

Together, Chesterton and Belloc formed the Distributist movement – later the

Distributist League – which stressed the importance of individual proprietors. Some Fabians – among them Hilary Pepler and, later, Henry Slesser – became Distributists.

In a poem published in 1924, Pepler summarized his differences from the Webbs:

> *We are for the PLEBS*
> *Said the Webbs,*
> *The Mess they are in*
> *Wants organisin'*
> *They shall toil while we spin*
> *Any number of webs.* [44]

This criticism, blending opposition to the role of the state with attacks on the perceived authoritarianism of the Webbs' approach, was shared, not only by the Chesterbelloc, but also by some of the Guild Socialists. In the First World War period, GDH and Margaret Cole, (later enthusiastic Webb supporters) and the young research group around them, caricatured the Webb position in a Gilbert and Sullivan parody:

> *Hey, dee, hey, dee, for Measurement and Publicity*
> *We'll thoroughly regiment everybody,*
> *And send up the stock of the State, O!* [45]

Not everyone agreed that the Webbs were focused exclusively on the expansion of the state. In 1920, John Squire, (a Cambridge Fabian; later one of the original *New Statesman* editorial team), reviewing a new edition of the Webbs' *History of Trade Unionism*, wrote that Sidney and Beatrice, while they did not see eye-to-eye with Guild Socialists.

> *…still less do they see eye-to-eye with that fabulous monster who stalks through the writings and speeches of both Revolutionaries and Conservatives – the bureaucratic Fabian Webb, harbinger of the Servile State.* [46]

After the deaths of both Webbs, R H Tawney, delivering a memorial lecture, said that the conventional portrait of Sidney and Beatrice

> *…conspiring to submit every human activity to the centralized control of an omni-competent State…* [47]

was a caricature. Very little of their research and writing was about the central state; they concentrated on local, decentralized institutions and agencies such as the cooperative movement, trade unions, and local government. Later generations used the expression 'civil society' to describe such institutions

The National Minimum

In *Industrial Democracy* (1897), their second trade union book, Sidney and Beatrice floated the concept of the National Minimum. They showed that a central trade union objective was the establishment of the 'common rule' for each industry or sector – a floor level for wages, hours and working conditions. Employers would remain free to exceed that level, but not to fall below it. Unions had various methods at their disposal to achieve that objective, including negotiation with employers or groups of employers, and using parliamentary legislation to regulate the sector.

Having established the idea of the common rule, Sidney and Beatrice then suggested that it should be extended to the community as a whole, thus establishing a National Minimum. Legislation already restricted and controlled working conditions in particular industries – but, they argued, issues like child labour would be better regulated across the entire economy. A policy for child labour should have two aspects – statutory controls on pay, working hours, and physical conditions, but educational and welfare provision as well

> *...we must regard the boy or girl, not as an independent wealth-producer to be satisfied by a daily subsistence, but as the future citizen and parent, for whom, up to twenty-one, proper conditions of growth and education are of paramount importance.* [48]

The idea of a National Minimum, first developed by Sidney and Beatrice, was taken up by the Fabians, then by the Trades Union Congress (TUC), and then by the Labour Party. It began with wages and working conditions – but from the start was about more than simply a minimum wage.

At first, Beatrice and Sidney, when they were trying to influence or permeate all political parties, saw the National Minimum as a policy to be advocated for the Liberals and Conservatives. When, from 1912, they began to concentrate more and more exclusively on Labour, it became a central element of the programme they urged on Labour.

The Webbs lost no opportunity to make the case for the National Minimum. In December 1900, they spent a *delightful* Sunday with Bertrand and Alys Russell, and the rising Liberal MP Richard Haldane, when, Beatrice wrote, they pressed for the

> *...policy of a National Minimum of Health, Education and Efficiency.* [49]

The Boer War revealed that much of the British working population was in poor physical condition; this raised questions of national efficiency. In 1902 the Webbs established a group, the Coefficients, to discuss

...the aims, policy and methods of Imperial Efficiency at home and abroad. [50]

As well as Russell (who soon resigned) and Haldane, members of the group included H G Wells, and the Conservative Leo Amery. A year after the Coefficients began to operate, Sidney led a discussion on

...how far is it possible by legislative regulation to maintain a Minimum Standard of National well-being? [51]

At first, the Webbs had advocated a National Minimum as a matter of social justice; after the Boer War they began to justify it also on grounds of efficiency. Writing in 1904, Beatrice described it as the policy of

...creating an artificial bottom to society by collective regulation and collective expenditure... [52]

In 1905 the Fabians established a committee to work out how to implement a minimum wage. Sidney argued that the Committee should take a wider approach to its brief, arguing for

...the Legal Enforcement of a Minimum Standard of Life... [53]

He pointed out that minimum legally enforceable standards already existed for education (ages 5-14); sanitation; leisure; and subsistence – for children and, through the Poor Law, for poor people. The Committee recommended that a minimum wage should be introduced, with the participation of trade unions and employers, area by area and sector by sector.[54]

Sidney returned to the issue with a lecture in May 1908, subsequently published under the title *The Necessary Basis of Society*. He argued that any modern industrial society – socialist or individualist – must formulate and enforce a National Minimum

...below which the individual, whether he likes it or not, cannot, in the interests of the well-being of the whole, ever be allowed to fall. [55]

Regulation of working time would enforce a national minimum of leisure; public health action, and if necessary, municipal construction, would enforce a national minimum of sanitation – covering water, drainage, and housing. There should be a National Minimum of Child Nurture – not just schools, but

...everything required for the healthy, happy rearing of the citizen that is to be. [56]

Their evangelism for the National Minimum had some impact; in September

1912, Beatrice went to the TUC conference. Overall, she found it not very different from the conferences she had attended twenty years before. But there was a new outlook. Beatrice noted, in the lofty tone she sometimes adopted, that

> *The ordinary Trade Unionist has got the National Minimum theory well fixed in his slow solid head – it has taken twenty years to mature...* [57]

During the 1914-1918 war, Sidney became close to the Labour leadership; for the first time, a Labour government seemed a real possibility. He led the work of drafting Labour's first, comprehensive, national policy statement – *Labour and the New Social Order.* [58] This *systematic plan* for social reconstruction was based on four principles – the first of which was the universal enforcement of the National Minimum. (The others were democratic control of industry, a revolution in national finance, and surplus wealth for the common good). The National Minimum now meant

> *...the securing to every member of the community, in good times and bad alike (and not only to the strong and able, the well-born or the fortunate, of all the requisites of healthy life and worthy citizenship.* [59]

The Labour governments of the 1920s had neither the resources, nor the political headroom, to legislate for the National Minimum. Nor had they any serious policy response to mass unemployment. The Webbs now came to understand that Labour needed a broader economic policy and must draw on a wider range of advice.

In the mid-1920s, Sidney and Beatrice came to know Maynard Keynes, who in a 1926 article called for greater cooperation between Labour and the Liberals. Beatrice saw the piece, and followed it up with a letter to Keynes; the approach upon which the Webbs and the Fabians had been working since the 1890s

> *... the working out of a national minimum of civilized life, so far as regulation and public services can secure it, is now exhausted...* [60]

New research was needed on the control of capitalist enterprise; Beatrice thought that she and Sidney were too old for this *entirely new task.*

Perhaps, even if the Webbs had felt equal to the task, it was just too soon.

Philip Snowden – Labour's financially orthodox Chancellor in 1924 and again between 1929 and 1931 – had little interest in new approaches. Keynes continued to advise Lloyd George's Liberals; he did become a member of the 1929 government's Economic Advisory Council, but his views were little heeded.

Political Leadership

The Webbs – especially Beatrice – took a close interest in political leadership. They argued consistently that public services should be run by educated, trained experts. But leaders were needed as well as experts. Beatrice wrote of a *vocation of leadership*.

Often she referred to her elite of leaders as *Samurai*. This was less an allusion to Japanese history than a reference to a futuristic novel by HG Wells, *A Modern Utopia (1905)*, in which Wells described an ideal society run by the Samurai – a disinterested governing elite. Wells and the Webbs were close while he was writing the book. In April 1905, Wells stayed overnight with Sidney and Beatrice; he sent a copy of the book in advance, and Beatrice congratulated him on it.

In *A Modern Utopia*, Wells describes the Samurai as a voluntary, non-hereditary nobility. Drawn from both men and women, they were rational, advanced and scientifically trained., and would live an austere life. In Wells' novel, a traveller from earth arrives at this ideal society – this modern Utopia. Hearing about the Samurai, he wonders

Will they be a caste? A race? an organization in the nature of a church? [61]

The religious parallels particularly appealed to Beatrice. In 1908, visiting a Salvation Army colony for unemployed people, Beatrice compared the Salvationists to a Samurai caste. For her the most interesting fact was the Salvation Army itself:

In respect to personal character all these men and women constitute a Samurai caste – that is they are men and women selected for their power of subordinating themselves to their cause, most assuredly a remarkable type of ecclesiastic… A beautiful spirit of love and personal service… [62]

The other religious group towards which Beatrice turned as a potential model for the vocation of leadership was the Jesuits. In 1908, Beatrice was impressed by the *fervent, brilliant* Cambridge students who had recently joined the Fabians. One was Hugh Dalton, the future Labour Chancellor of the Exchequer, who she thought astute and thoughtful,

…a sort of lay Jesuit – preparing for political life. [63]

One aspect of the Soviet Union that attracted Beatrice in the 1930s was the leadership provided by the Communist Party. She had always been interested in religion; she thought, before their journey to Russia and Ukraine in 1932, that the Party was becoming like a religious order:

…it has its Holy Writ, its prophets and its canonised saints; it has its Pope, yesterday Lenin and today Stalin; it has its code of conduct and its discipline; it has its creed and its inquisition. [64]

In their book, *Soviet Communism: a new civilisation*, Beatrice and Sidney devote a chapter to the vocation of leadership. They again compare the role of the Communist Party to the role of a religious order, like the Jesuits, in a catholic country.

In Moscow in May 1932, they had a formal interview in the Communist Party headquarters with Stetzky, the Secretary responsible for cultural policy. Beatrice thought him a *very Jesuitical personage*, who

…gave me the answers that were for my own good and did not necessarily express the facts or his opinion of the facts. [65]

ARTS, MUSIC, AND CULTURE

Anthony Crosland, a Labour cabinet minister in the 1960s and 1970s, thought the Webbs were indifferent

…to all forms of art or culture, their lack of temptation towards any of the emotional or physical pleasures of life, the consequent priggish puritanism…
No, I shouldn't have liked the Webbs. [66]

Crosland was not the first person to see the Webbs as lacking in culture, taste, or judgment. Beatrice's sister Rosie thought she

had little or no taste for art and did not care for poetry. [67]

H G Wells, a frequent guest at their London home in the Edwardian years, lampooned Sidney and Beatrice as Oscar and Altiora Bailey in his novel *The New Machiavelli*, writing that, at least sometimes, they seemed

…to prefer things harsh and ugly. [68]

Even Margaret Cole – who as a young woman had been an opponent of the Webbs, later coming to admire them – described Sidney as a *contented philistine.*[69]

In fact, their engagement with art and culture was more complex. Beatrice knew her own limitations; before their marriage, she wrote to Sidney:

Dearest, we will try to have a little culture – but it will be difficult and I fear you will not have the wife to favour the growth of it. I am supremely ignorant, except in my own subjects. All I do bring is a humble reverence for those other subjects… [70]

Later, Beatrice wrote that, in their early years together, they had not the time, the energy, or the means for music, drama, literature, picture galleries, or architecture. Their experience of beauty came from their walking and cycling trips at home and abroad. Otherwise, they got their culture at one remove, through their friendship with Shaw.

Beatrice was certainly capable of expressing sharp aesthetic judgments. The first time she visited the Chamberlain family home, in Birmingham, Beatrice concluded that there was

...much taste and all very bad.[71]

The luxury was ostentatious; it made Beatrice

...long for a bare floor and a plain deal table. [72]

Ten years later Sidney and Beatrice set about creating their own London home, at 41 Grosvenor Road, on the Thames embankment. They stayed there 30 years, moving in 1923 to Passfield Corner, in Hampshire. They chose a pre-Raphaelite, arts and crafts look. Beatrice worked hard to decorate and furnish the house, aiming for beautiful surroundings, but without self-indulgence.

Beatrice's wallpaper and furniture came from William Morris; political differences were not permitted to override aesthetic choice. She *spent days over my curtains* and toured second hand shops looking for *charming* pieces of furniture. She tried to persuade herself that she needed beautiful things to work with; Sidney's view was that they must work in order to deserve the choices they had made.

In 1919 Rosie stayed with them at Grosvenor Road for a week. She found Beatrice

...a strange mixture of idealism and practical common sense, of asceticism and love of luxury. [73]

Sidney was more appreciative of poetry than Beatrice; during their courtship, he read aloud to her. They lay on the grass in Epping Forest while Sidney read her poems by Dante Gabriel Rossetti. In a letter, he asked

Did you credit me with knowing my Rossetti? [74]

Sidney's first present to Beatrice was an edition of Rossetti's poems.

Years later, recalling Rupert Brooke's time as an active Fabian, Beatrice wrote that she was

poetry blind...like some persons are colour blind. [75]

Margaret Cole thought Beatrice never *grasped* poetry: Beatrice's closest approach to poetry was when Cole came upon her

...swaying in time to the voice of James Joyce reading Anna Livia Plurabelle. [76]

Early in their relationship, on a long, late night train journey, Sidney read her William Morris' *Dream of John Ball*, as she gradually fell asleep.

Before they met, Sidney and Beatrice were both widely read in English and European literature; both had read Goethe – aged 16, Beatrice started translating *Faust*. And she enjoyed Hugo's *Les Miserables*

The description of the Bishop and of the criminal is simply splendid... [77]

She spent the winter of 1880/81 on a long trip to Italy. Among other authors, she read George Eliot

...I know no author who is so sad and so uncynical... [78]

And Balzac

...an utter cynic and complete disbeliever in the progress of human nature... [79]

In 1887 she discovered Zola's *Au Bonheur des Dames* –

...a work of true genius. [80]

In 1895 Beatrice thought about following her cousin Margaret Harkness, and writing a novel herself:

...after we have ended our stiff work on Trade Unions I would try my hand at pure 'Fiction'... The truth is, I want to have my 'fling'! I want to imagine anything I damn please without regard to facts as they are... I want to try my hand at artists work instead of mechanics. I am sick to death of trying to put hideous facts, multitudinous details, exasperating qualifications, into a readable form. [81]

But the fling never materialised.

They kept up to date with contemporary writing – especially when they knew the authors. When HG Wells caricatured them, they laughed. Beatrice did not approve of DH Lawrence. Sidney and Beatrice read novels by both Leonard and Virginia Woolf; in 1915, after reading two by Leonard, they donated their copies to the Fabian club room. Beatrice respected Virginia as

...fastidiously intellectual with great literary artistry, a consummate craftsman [82]

But she struggled with Virginia's writing: she recognised that the stream of consciousness was the *latest fashion in the technique of novel-writing* – but found the method objectionable

...it assumes that the author can see into and describe another's mind... [83]

Rosie's second husband, George Dobbs, was in the travel business; they spent long periods abroad. Beatrice on occasions would ask Rosie to obtain copies of foreign editions of English-language books that were banned in Britain. Examples included Radclyffe Hall's *The Well of Loneliness* and D H Lawrence's *Lady Chatterley's Lover*. Beatrice read them – but was not impressed.

Sidney and Beatrice both carried on reading in old age. After Sidney suffered a stroke in 1938, he read novels incessantly: Beatrice ordered them from the London Library, in fortnightly batches of fifteen.

And they were theatregoers; they appreciated works with a social or political theme. They were loyal fans of the plays of GBS, to which they sometimes brought guests – including on one occasion Arthur Balfour as Prime Minister. Shaw would read drafts of his plays to Beatrice and Sidney; they would comment and make suggestions.

But they did not always like Shaw's plays. In December 1933 Shaw came to Passfield Corner and read his recent play *On the Rocks* – about a political crisis, set in 10 Downing Street. Beatrice thought it

...a picture of British society in catastrophic decadence, portrayed by an aged cynic, who had outlived his genius. [84]

The actor, playwright and director Harley Granville Barker joined the Fabians, serving for a time on the Executive Committee. In 1910, Sidney and Beatrice saw Barker's *Madras House* shortly after seeing Shaw's *Mésalliance*. Beatrice thought both writers were obsessed with sex:

...the rabbit-warren aspect of human society.

GBS is brilliant but disgusting; Granville Barker is intellectual but dull. [85]

A few days after seeing *Madras House*, both Webbs went to John Galsworthy's play, *Justice*. Beatrice thought it a great play,

...worked in with the philosophy of the Minority Report. [86]

Rosie thought Beatrice was not very musical, but

...enjoyed listening to good music... [87]

The Potter sisters had not grown up in a musical household. In general, their father had no ear for music, although the family's Gloucestershire home would be filled with guests in the years when the Three Choirs festival was in Gloucester Cathedral. In September 1886, Beatrice noted

…those two days at Gloucester listening to that delightful music. [88]

After the move to Passfield Corner music began to play a more significant role in their lives. Beatrice had always appreciated choral works; two circumstances now encouraged them to develop wider musical tastes. The first was broadcasting: from the start of BBC broadcasting in 1923, programmes included music. Two years after their move, Beatrice noted that the wireless was teaching her to listen to music. In 1927, Virginia Woolf wrote that

…Mrs Webb listens in and prefers Mozart to Handel, if I may guess. [89]

The wireless became a source of delight for the Webbs.

Secondly, there were opportunities to hear music locally. The local music society in nearby Haslemere ran regular concerts. Beatrice attended some, and also went to London performances. She thought she had attended as many concerts in the second half of 1925 as she had in the previous twenty years; music had become her main recreation.

When, in spring 1929, Sidney and Beatrice toured Turkey, Austria and Germany, they ended with three days at Munich, where they enjoyed a concert by the Berlin Philharmonic Orchestra. In 1931, Beatrice went once more to the Three Choirs Festival at Gloucester – partly out of nostalgia, but mostly

…to hear music direct and not over the ether. [90]

At the 1931 festival, she was entranced by the first performance of Holst's *Choral Fantasia.*

The cellist Juliette Alvin – later a pioneer of music therapy – was married to the LSE professor William Robson, who, with Beatrice and Leonard Woolf had been one of the founders of the *Political Quarterly.* Neither of the Webbs was keen on Robson; Sidney found him *quite intolerably boring.* [91] Beatrice, however, liked Juliette and their children. They became regular visitors to Passfield Corner – Beatrice wrote, in 1938,

The Robsons, owing to the charming wife who played to us on her cello, were far more agreeable than I had foreseen. [92]

There were more such visits in Beatrice's final years; Beatrice would invite Juliette to come and play for her. According to Margaret Cole, Beatrice hinted that she would herself have liked to be a musician, if she had had the gift. [93]

BEATRICE AS FEMINIST

From middle age, Beatrice was one of the best-known women in British public life. She became the first woman fellow of the British Academy (in the Economic Section); she was well known as a radio broadcaster.

Beatrice's own version of feminism was idiosyncratic. As a glorified spinster, she was committed to her personal economic emancipation. For a young, middle-class woman in the 1880s, building an independent career was a radical act. But she was not at first a supporter of the suffrage campaign. In 1889, she signed a public petition opposing women's suffrage. Personally, Beatrice felt, she had not experienced any disadvantage as a woman; she wrote that her father, Richard Potter

> *…was the only man I ever knew who genuinely believed that women were superior to men.* [94]

If she had been a man, Beatrice thought, she would have been pushed into a money-making profession, but

> *…as a mere woman I could carve out a career of disinterested research.* [95]

Beatrice's friend and cousin Margaret Harkness became involved in London social reform and radical politics; she introduced Beatrice to the secularist and Fabian Annie Besant. Beatrice heard her speak; she thought Besant was the only woman she had ever heard who was a real orator and could persuade her hearers. But Beatrice did not approve; she thought Besant's behaviour was not womanly.

Beatrice did not want to be seen as concerned only with women's issues. Before she began her research into the cooperative movement, the Cambridge economist Alfred Marshall tried, unsuccessfully, to persuade Beatrice to work on the

> *…unknown field of female labour.* [96]

30 years later, Beatrice did study women's employment: towards the end of the First World War, she was appointed to a government Committee on Women in Industry. She produced another Minority Report, concluding that the existing inequalities in the employment conditions of women and men were bad for women, bad for men, and detrimental to efficiency and national productivity.

After signing the anti-suffrage document in 1889, Beatrice soon concluded that she had made a mistake. Early in their relationship, Sidney told her so. But she did not make a public commitment to the suffrage cause until 1906.

MARRIAGE AND THE MORAL CODE

Rosie Potter thought that

As regards all matters of sex Beatrice is a Puritan and quite out of touch in sympathy with modern views of sexual relationship. [97]

Like her politics, Beatrice's attitude to sex and morality evolved. The Potter sisters were born into a world of settled values: they were expected to 'marry well'- to a man of substance, sustained by assets, income, and a profession. Most of her sisters made such marriages.

That success required participation in the rituals of the marriage market and the London season. Beatrice describes the

...pleasurable but somewhat feverish anticipation of endless distraction... [98]

Beatrice's glorified spinster friends talked about their relationships, continually exchanging ideas about love and marriage. Around Beatrice's twentieth birthday, Margaret Harkness wrote

Dear Beatrice

I think the idea of the matrimonial market if properly faced anything but ghastly. If you want such an article as a husband or such an article as a wife, surely, you should if possible go to the <u>best</u> market. [99]

Some contemporaries lived outside the narrow boundaries of the conventional moral code – among them some of the male Fabian founders. GBS was a serial philanderer. Beatrice knew this from her own experience: she once told a nephew that, the first time she found herself alone with Shaw, he

...simply flung himself on me. [100]

Hubert Bland, the Fabian treasurer, lived in South East London in a *ménage à trois* with his wife – the writer Edith Nesbit – and Alice Hoatson, a member of the Fabian Executive Committee, and their children.

In May 1883, Beatrice was introduced to Eleanor, youngest daughter of Karl Marx. Beatrice concluded, with regret, that Eleanor's *irregular lifestyle* – the combination of her *peculiar* views on love, and her *natural* relations with men – ruled out any closer friendship between them.

Beatrice met Joseph Chamberlain for the first time a few days after her encounter with Eleanor Marx. Emotionally, she was overwhelmed, later writing in her diary that Chamberlain had, for several years, absorbed the whole of her sexual feeling. Chamberlain's family warned Beatrice that he took a very conventional view of the role of women. Margaret Harkness supported Beatrice during the

Chamberlain relationship; they shared accommodation, in East London and in Cheyne Walk; in summer 1884, they took a long holiday together in Bavaria.

At the same time, as a housing manager in East London, Beatrice was a moral enforcer; in summer 1885 she wrote to her father that she had to *wage incessant war* against drink and immorality. That week, Beatrice wrote, she had evicted two women for *leading bad lives*; one of them was a favourite with the local police:

> *The constable on duty watched 3 of his inspectors go upstairs (This was confidentially told me by our policeman's wife).* [101]

Any possibility of marriage to Chamberlain ended in November 1888, when he married an American heiress. In her first autobiographical volume, Beatrice wrote that the

> *…rumour of marriage to a great political personage would be followed by a stream of invitations: if the rumour proved unfounded the shower stopped with almost ridiculous promptitude.* [102]

In later years, when Chamberlain was in the news, Beatrice would occasionally glance backwards. But, just over a year after Chamberlain's third (and last) marriage, Margaret Harkness introduced Beatrice to Sidney Webb.

Beatrice had fallen in love with Chamberlain; she did not at first fall for Sidney. She told him his photograph was hideous; she wanted a picture just of his head – it was the head alone she was marrying. [103] It was reason, not love, that won her. [104]

After this uncertain start, she and Sidney formed a close and enduring bond. Beatrice noted in 1893 that she was *triumphantly happy*.[105] Marriage had worked for Beatrice; she thought it ought to work for other people. In 1918 she told Virginia Woolf that marriage was a waste pipe for the emotions. Beatrice also said to Virginia that people should only have one great relationship in life – or at most two: marriage and parenthood.

By 1905 the Fabian Society had become middle aged, if not wholly respectable. An influx of new, younger members – some of them the children of the founders, some of them students or recent graduates – changed all that. The Liberal landslide of 1906 created a new climate for radical ideas. Some were inspired by the novels of H G Wells, who stormed into and through the Fabians, and out again on the far side.

In 1908, Beatrice watched the new young recruits at the Fabian Summer School in North Wales, startling Methodist Wales with their unconventional clothes, leading their unconventional lives, the women without their customary chaperones.

'Is dancing sexual?' I found three pretty Cambridge girl graduates discussing with half a dozen men. [106]

Beatrice also noticed *a somewhat dangerous friendship* growing up between Amber Reeves, one of the Cambridge young women and HG Wells:

...if Amber were my child, I should be anxious. [107]

The following year, Amber had a child with Wells. Early in the pregnancy, a marriage was quickly arranged with one of the younger Fabian men. Amber's father was outraged; Beatrice was scandalized. She called Wells a blackguard; her sympathy for Amber was limited. She tried to help and advise Amber, but told her bluntly she must choose between her husband and Wells.

Over time, Beatrice's old certainties gave way to a hesitant agnosticism – no one knew anymore, she wrote in her diary

...what exactly is the sexual code we believe in... [108]

This remained her position. Beatrice did not think that the

...lack of any fixed sexual code... [109]

was a good thing. She instinctively believed in

...monogamy tempered by divorce and remarriage...[110]

She thought the old scale of values, based on Christian morals, had completely vanished.

Beatrice's agnosticism about a moral code was all very well in theory; it provided limited guidance in practice. Sidney and Beatrice both liked William Beveridge; in 1919 Sidney appointed him Director of LSE. At LSE, Beveridge was soon joined by Janet Mair, who was married to his cousin David Mair. Beveridge and Mrs Mair had worked closely together during the war. Mrs Mair soon became the most senior administrator at LSE. Her efficiency was formidable – but both Sidney and Beatrice, and the LSE academic staff, thought it inappropriate for both to occupy these senior posts. There was plenty of gossip; for a long time, Beatrice convinced herself that the relationship was platonic – but nevertheless *far too romantic* for one to be Director, the other, Secretary of LSE. Beveridge, she wrote,

...was obviously infatuated, and everyone sees it. [111]

Beatrice worried whether she should condone

...sexual irregularity in one's associates? [112]

She thought the Beveridge/Mair relationship another example of

…complete anarchy in opinion about sex relations. [113]

In her diary, Beatrice combined public toleration with private censure She thought there was

…too much strong drink and free-love-making in Labour circles, especially among the younger folk. [114]

She described Barbara Ayrton Gould, Labour Women's Officer in the 1930s, as

…the last word in vulgarity in her relations with men. [115]

She described how the philosophy professor C E M Joad was

…refused admission to the Fabian Summer School…as he would come with a different lady every time… [116]

By 1931, Beatrice thought there were few celibate women left in public life –

…a type of which there were many in my young days in the philanthropic world. [117]

That summer the Labour MP Ellen Wilkinson, staying with the Webbs, asked Beatrice what she thought: must a woman, who did not want to marry, stay celibate

…if she found a congenial friend who happened to have an uncongenial wife?

Beatrice answered that she remained a puritan, but that she was not

…dogmatically opposed to extra-matrimonial arrangements as long as they were not promiscuous. [118]

Most of the Potter sisters had complied with the dominant 19th century moral code and made conventional, 'good' marriages. This did not guarantee that they would all live happily ever after.

In 1905 Blanche, who had married the surgeon Willie Cripps, hanged herself, after Willie had introduced his mistress into the family home. The next year, the eldest sister, Lallie (Lawrencina), died after years of cocaine addiction brought on by extreme family divisions.

The least conventional sister was Rosie (Rosalind), the youngest. The others often criticized her. In 1888 Rosie had married Dyson Williams, a young barrister. At the time, Beatrice dismissed him as inferior to the other brothers-in-law. Dyson was already sickly when he and Rosie married; five years later, he died of tertiary syphilis. The sisters encouraged Rosie to re-marry, putting on the pressure when suitable prospects appeared, and in 1899 she married George Dobbs. She had one child with Dyson; she had five more with George. Rosie had other lovers both before and after the wedding; George and Rosie did not always did not always live together.

Beatrice and the other sisters were censorious. But in the end, Beatrice concluded that Rosie had the laugh over her 'prudish' sisters:

> *She shocked us with her free ways during her widowhood. Today her free ways are a la mode. From first to last she has maintained there is no harm in free love...Meanwhile I have been compelled to shift my position and to tolerate and accept conduct in the younger generation which twenty years ago I should have boycotted. The decay of religion has completely undermined sexual morality.* [119]

In July 1931 the Webbs returned to a hotel near Beachy Head, where they had stayed before. Beatrice talked to the hotel keeper's wife, who told her that there was *no sexual morality left*

> *Even the clergy were not above suspicion. Eastbourne clergymen would bring different girls to tea; and other clergy would bring them out to dine.* [120]

How would society ever get another sexual code? There was no agreement.

Notes to Preface and Chapter One

All references to Beatrice Webb's Diary are to the complete, digital version of the typescript diary held by LSE Library (Archives and Special Collections)

Preface

1   Beatrice Webb Diary 7 July 1891
2   LSE Library; Colegate Diaries; LSE Coll Misc 741/1; 9 February1906
3   LSE Library; Fabian Society Executive Committee minute book, 10 Mar 1911 - 24 Jan 1913; 19 April 1912
4   Beatrice Webb Diary 13 July 1913
5   Russell, B; *Autobiography*; London, Unwin, 1978; p 75
6   Russell, B; *Autobiography*; London, Unwin, 1978; p 75
7   Beatrice Webb Diary, 30.06.1938
8   Beatrice Webb Diary, 05.05.1937
9   Cole, Margaret, Editor; *Beatrice Webb's Diaries 1912 – 1924*; introduction by Lord Beveridge, p vi; London, Longmans Green, 1952
10 Radice, L; *Beatrice and Sidney Webb: Fabian Socialists;* London, Macmillan, 1984; p 7
11 Radice, L; *Beatrice and Sidney Webb: Fabian Socialists;* London, Macmillan, 1984; p 309
12 Cole, Margaret; *Growing up into revolution*; London, Longmans, 1949; p 96
13 See Beatrice Webb Diary, 04.02.1931
14 *Daily Herald*, 13.12.1947
15 Dangerfield, George; *The strange death of Liberal England, 1910-1914*; New York, Capricorn Books, 1961; p430
16 Beatrice Webb Diary 21.09.1894
17 R H Tawney to Alexander Carr Saunders, 22 December 1948; LSE Library TAWNEY 24/2
18 Harold Laski to RH Tawney, 24 March 1949; LSE Library TAWNEY 24/2
19 See Evans, Richard J; *Eric Hobsbawm, a life in history*; London, Little Brown, 2019; p245; and Goldman, Lawrence; *The life of R H Tawney*; London, Bloomsbury, 2013
20 Harrison, R J; *The Life and Times of Sidney and Beatrice Webb; 1858-1905: the formative years;* London, Macmillan, 2000; p xi
21 Foot, Paul; review in *The Guardian*, 4 March 2000

Chapter One

22 E T Raymond; quoted in Hamilton, Mary Agnes (Molly); *Sidney and Beatrice Webb*; London, Sampson Low, 1933; p 86
23 Samuel, Viscount; *Memoirs;* London, The Cresset Press, 1945; p29
24 Beatrice Webb Diary 03.09.1888
25 Beatrice Webb Diary Christmas 1912
26 Russell, B; *Autobiography*; London, Unwin, 1978; p 75
27 Sidney to Beatrice, 09.12.1891 in Webb, B & Webb, S; *The Letters of Sidney and Beatrice Webb; Vol I;* Cambridge; CUP; 1978; ed Mackenzie, N; p 347
28 Woolf, L; *Political Thought and the Webbs*; in Cole, M ed. The Webbs and their Work   London, Frederick Muller, 1949; p 263
29 Hamilton, Mary Agnes (Molly); *Sidney and Beatrice Webb*; London, Sampson Low, 1933; p 75
30 Micklethwait, John and Wooldridge, Adrian; *The Fourth Revolution: the global race to reinvent the state*; London, Penguin Random House, 2014; p 65
31 Micklethwait, John and Wooldridge, Adrian; *The Fourth Revolution: the global race to reinvent the state*; London, Penguin Random House, 2014; p 65
32 Russell, B; *Autobiography*; London, Unwin, 1978; p 74
33 Tawney, Richard H; *R H Tawney's Commonplace Book*; edited and with introduction by J M Winter and D M Joslin; Cambridge; Cambridge University Press; 1972; p79
34 Preface to Shaw, George Bernard, ed; *Fabian Essays in Socialism;* 1920 edition with introduction by Sidney Webb; London, Fabian Society and George Allen and Unwin, 1920; p 3
35 Webb, Sidney; *Historic*; in Shaw, George Bernard, ed; *Fabian Essays in Socialism;* 1920 edition with introduction by Sidney Webb; London, Fabian Society and George Allen and Unwin,

1920; p 47

36 Webb, S & B; *Constitution for the socialist commonwealth of Great Britain, A;* London; Longmans; 1920; p 318

37 Webb, B; *Our Partnership;* ed. Cole, M & Drake, B; London, Longmans, 1948; p149

38 Webb, B; *Our Partnership;* ed. Cole, M & Drake, B; London, Longmans, 1948; p 151

39 Webb, B; *Our Partnership;* ed. Cole, M & Drake, B; London, Longmans, 1948; p150

40 Webb, S & B; *Constitution for the socialist commonwealth of Great Britain, A;* London; Longmans; 1920; p 191

41 Webb, S & B; *Constitution for the socialist commonwealth of Great Britain, A;* London; Longmans; 1920; p196

42 Belloc, Hilaire *The Servile State;* London, T N Foulis, 1912; p 16

43 *New Age,* 14 April 1910

44 Pepler, Harry Douglas Clarke [Hilary]; *Libellus Lapidum;* Ditchling, St Dominic's Press, 1924

45 In Cole, George Douglas Howard (GDH) and Cole, Margaret, editors; *The Bolo Book;* London; 1921; The Labour Publishing Company Ltd, and George Allen and Unwin; p 52

46 *London Mercury,* Vol 1 No 5 March 1920, p 614

47 Tawney, Richard H; *The Webbs in Perspective;* Webb Memorial Lecture 1952; University of London Athlone Press, 1952; p 8

48 Webb, S & B; *Industrial Democracy;* Vol II; London, Longmans, Green & Co; 1897; pp 770-771

49 Beatrice Webb Diary, 09.12.1900

50 Sidney to H G Wells, 12.09.1902; in Webb, B & Webb, S; *The Letters of Sidney and Beatrice Webb; Vol II;* Cambridge; CUP; 1978; ed Mackenzie, N; p170

51 LSE Library; Minutes of Coefficients, 09.11.1903; Coefficients Minutes LSE ASSOC 17 (microfiche)

52 Beatrice Webb Diary 08.06.1904

53 LSE Library; Fabian Society; paper by Sidney with the papers for meeting of the Minimum Wage Committee, 13.04.1905

54 *The case for a legal minimum wage;*

Fabian Tract No 128, by W S Sanders; London, the Fabian Society, 1906

55 *The Necessary Basis of Society;* Fabian Tract No 159, by Sidney Webb; London, the Fabian Society, 1911

56 *The Necessary Basis of Society;* Fabian Tract No 159, by Sidney Webb; London, the Fabian Society, 1911; p 10

57 Beatrice Webb Diary 05.09.1912

58 *Labour and the New Social Order, a report on reconstruction;* London, The Labour Party, 1918.

59 *Labour and the New Social Order, a report on reconstruction;* London, The Labour Party, 1918; p 5

60 Beatrice to Maynard Keynes, 22.02.1926; in Webb, B & Webb, S; *The Letters of Sidney and Beatrice Webb; Vol III;* Cambridge; CUP; 1978; ed Mackenzie, N; p 256

61 Wells, Herbert G; *A Modern Utopia;* London, Penguin, 1905; p91

62 Beatrice Webb Diary 02.02.1908

63 Beatrice to Mary Playne, September 1908; in Webb, B & Webb, S; *The Letters of Sidney and Beatrice Webb; Vol II;* Cambridge; CUP; 1978; ed Mackenzie, N; p 316

64 Beatrice Webb Diary 05.1932

65 Beatrice Webb Diary 05.1932

66 C.A.R; Crosland Common place book; quoted in Crosland, Susan; *Tony Crosland;* London, Coronet Books (Hodder and Stoughton); 1982; p 47

67 Dobbs, Rosie; typescript *autobiography,* (BL Add MS 50657); p 116

68 Wells, Herbert G; *The New Machiavelli;* London, Penguin, 2005; pp 172-173

69 Cole, Margaret; *The story of Fabian Socialism;* London, Heinemann, 1963; p 256

70 Beatrice to Sidney, 12.12.1891, in Webb, B & Webb, S; *The Letters of Sidney and Beatrice Webb;* Vol I; Cambridge; CUP; 1978; ed Mackenzie, N; p 352

71 Beatrice Webb Diary 16.03.1884

72 Beatrice Webb Diary 24.01.1884

73 Dobbs, Rosie; typescript *autobiography,* (BL Add MS 50657); p123

74 Sidney to Beatrice, 14.05.1890, in Webb, B & Webb, S; *The Letters*

	of Sidney and Beatrice Webb; Vol I; Cambridge; CUP; 1978; ed Mackenzie, N; p 136	105	Beatrice Webb Diary 25.12.1893
		106	Beatrice Webb Diary 15.09.1908
		107	Beatrice Webb Diary 15.09.1908
75	Webb, B; *Our Partnership*; ed. Cole, M & Drake, B; London, Longmans, 1948; p 415n	108	Beatrice Webb Diary Early August 1909
		109	Beatrice Webb Diary 20.08.1925
76	Cole, M; *Beatrice Webb;* London, Longmans, 1945; p 180	110	Beatrice Webb Diary 20.08.1925
		111	Beatrice Webb Diary 20.08.1925
77	Beatrice Webb Diary 15.06.1878	112	Beatrice Webb Diary 18.08.1933
78	Beatrice Webb Diary 02.02.1881	113	Beatrice Webb Diary 20.08.1925
79	Beatrice Webb Diary 20.03.1881	114	Beatrice Webb Diary 19.03.1932
80	Beatrice Webb Diary 22.01.1887	115	Beatrice Webb Diary 19.03.1932
81	Beatrice Webb Diary 01.02.1895	116	Beatrice Webb Diary 21.05.1939
82	Beatrice Webb Diary 01.04.1931	117	Beatrice Webb Diary 28.06.1931
83	Beatrice Webb Diary 28.05.1928	118	Beatrice Webb Diary 28.06.1931
84	Beatrice Webb Diary 08.12.1933	119	Beatrice Webb Diary 05.10.1929
85	Beatrice Webb Diary 13.03.1910	120	Beatrice Webb Diary 25.07.1931
86	Beatrice Webb Diary 15.03.1910		

87   Dobbs, Rosie; typescript *autobiography*, (BL Add MS 50657); p 116

88   Beatrice Webb Diary 14.09.1886

89   Virginia Woolf Diary, 03.02,1927; Woolf, Virginia; *Selected Diaries*; abridged and edited by Anne Olivier Bell; London, Vintage, 2008

90   Beatrice Webb Diary 10.09.1931

91   Beatrice Webb Diary 17.10.1936

92   Beatrice Webb Diary 06.12.1938

93   See Cole, M; *Beatrice Webb*; London, Longmans, 1945; p 181

94   Webb, B; *My Apprenticeship*; London, Longmans, 1926; p10

95   Webb, B; *My Apprenticeship*; London, Longmans, 1926; p355

96   Beatrice Webb Diary 08.03.1889

97   Dobbs, Rosie; typescript *autobiography*, (BL Add MS 50657); p130

98   Webb, B; *My Apprenticeship*; London, Longmans, 1926; p 48

99   Margaret Harkness to Beatrice Potter, late 1877 or early 1878.; LSE Library; PASSFIELD 2/1/2/2

100 See Muggeridge, K & Adam, R; *Beatrice Webb: A life 1858-1943*; London, Secker & Warburg, 1967; p136

101 Beatrice to Richard Potter ?August 1885, in Webb, B & Webb, S; *The Letters of Sidney and Beatrice Webb*; Cambridge; CUP; 1978; Vol I p 40

102 Webb, B; *My Apprenticeship*; London, Longmans, 1926; p 52

103 Beatrice Webb Diary 20.08.1891

104 Beatrice Webb Diary 24.05.1897

PART ONE:
APPRENTICESHIPS 1858 - 1892

Chapter Two: Beatrice Potter 1858-1890

BEATRICE 1858 - 1875

Beatrice was born Beatrice Potter on 22 January 1858, the eighth child of Richard and Lawrencina Potter. The Potters were an affluent family: in later life Beatrice described them as

...a typical nineteenth-and twentieth-century upper-middle-class family, rising in the government of the country... [1]

Richard's father (also Richard) was one of three Potter brothers (the others were William and Thomas). In 1802 they had moved from Tadcaster in Yorkshire, where the family had been farmers, to establish a cotton warehouse in Manchester. Richard and Thomas, both Unitarians, were members of the Little Circle, radical nonconformist Manchester business people who established the *Manchester Guardian* in 1821. The brothers also played an active part in the campaign for the 1832 Reform Act; Thomas became Manchester's first Mayor, following the 1835 Municipal Corporations Act. Richard Potter senior, known as 'Radical Dick', was MP for Wigan from 1832-1839.

Beatrice wrote that the Potter brothers were

...energetic pioneers of Manchester radical politics...founders of the civic life of the town. [2]

The younger Richard Potter attended University College London, and qualified as a barrister, though without any intention of practising. As the son of an MP, he was welcome in London political society, *associating with the elite of the radical world of the day* [3], sometimes attending the great Whig *salon* of Holland House.[4]

When Richard Potter senior died in 1842, he left his son Richard with a substantial fortune. Richard junior intended to lead the leisured life of a country gentleman. But when stock markets crashed after the revolutions of 1848 he lost most of his inheritance.

Beatrice thought this episode had been the making of her father. She thought he was naturally indolent, and

...would never have worked unless he had been stimulated by his passion for his wife and children – and by his ambition for a place in the world.[5]

So Richard Potter became a successful businessman in his own right: partner in a timber company, and a railway director, in Britain and overseas. He went on to chair the boards of the Great Western Railway and the Canadian Grand Trunk Railway.

Lawrencina Heyworth, Beatrice's mother, came from a similar background. The Heyworths had worked in cotton weaving on the Lancashire – Yorkshire border, rising to become small-scale employers. Lawrencina's father, Lawrence, became a merchant in Liverpool, trading with Latin America. In 1820 Lawrence Heyworth had married Elizabeth Aked, who had grown up in a weaver's household in Bacup, Lancashire. At the time of their marriage Elizabeth was working as a power loom operator in a factory. Like Richard Potter, Lawrence Heyworth had become an MP.

Richard Potter and Lawrencina Heyworth met in Rome; both were making the Grand Tour with other members of their families. Among others accompanying Lawrencina was her servant, Martha Jackson, known in the family as Dada. Richard and Lawrencina married in 1844; their first child, Laurencina, (Lallie), was born the next year. Laurencina was followed by eight more daughters: Catherine (Kate) in 1847; Mary in 1849; Georgina in 1850; Blanche in 1851; Theresa in 1852; Margaret in 1854; Beatrice; and Rosalind (Rosie) in 1865. The Potters hoped for a son; but the only boy, another Richard, arrived in 1862, and lived just two years.

Beatrice was born at Standish House, in Gloucestershire – a substantial mansion with extensive grounds, not far from the timber company's main yard at Gloucester. The Potters rented Standish from 1853; it was a rambling house, its main rooms at the front, and at the back the girls' bedrooms and nurseries, the school room, and the billiard room.

Standish was not their only home. There were more timber yards in Westmorland, where the family had another house, Rusland Hall. They spent several weeks every year at The Argoed, a Jacobean farmhouse in Monmouthshire, overlooking the Wye Valley. Every spring from 1864 Richard Potter rented a furnished house in London for the season. Beatrice remembered that, during her childhood and adolescence, the family were always on the move;

...the restless spirit of big enterprise dominated our home life.[6]

She described her childhood as

...creeping up in the shadow of my baby brother's birth and death...I was neither ill-treated nor oppressed: I was merely ignored.[7]

She thought the birth and death of her brother had been
...the crowning joy and devastating sorrow of my mother's life...[8]

The Potter sisters – Beatrice in particular – were closer to their father than their mother. Beatrice found Lawrencina

...a source of arbitrary authority whose rare interventions in my life I silently resented. I regarded her as an obstacle to be turned... [9]

As the girls grew older, Lawrencina became withdrawn. She read widely and studied languages, saying that she wanted to know twelve languages before she died. She studied religion. She wrote one novel; its success was limited, and she did not attempt another. Her involvement with her children was distant.

Instead the sisters relied on their father. They loved and admired him; he had great faith in the ability and potential of women in general, and his own daughters in particular. Looking back, Beatrice remembered that he had worshipped his wife, and admired and loved his daughters; he was

...the only man I ever knew who genuinely believed that women were superior to men, and acted as if he did; the paradoxical result being that all his nine daughters started life as anti-feminists. [10]

In the 1870s, Richard Potter's North American business interests were at their height; every year he spent several months in Canada and the United States. He usually took two of his daughters with him – though never their mother. In 1873 he travelled with Beatrice and her sister Kate, visiting New York, Niagara, Chicago, Utah, and California. It was on this journey that Beatrice first kept a diary.

The nine sisters turned to the servants for company and sympathy. All her life Beatrice depended on domestic servants. She befriended, and was befriended by, the laundry maids and the coachman, and above all by the children's nurse, Dada – Martha Jackson, who had been with Lawrencina at the start of her courtship in Rome and was a distant relative.

Beatrice thought Dada was a saint. Her sister Mary wrote later that Dada was their real mother, on whom they could depend:

Our own mother never near to us, at least never to me, and never seemed quite natural. [11]

Beatrice would curl up, chattering, in the laundry-room, dozing and dreaming amid tablecloths and bed sheets, or in the hayloft, with a big tabby cat.

The sisters had little formal education outside home. Lawrencina doubted whether Beatrice would have benefitted from more schooling:

'Beatrice', she wrote in a diary while I was yet a child, is the only one of my children who is below the average in intelligence', which may explain her attitude of indifference. [12]

Instead of school, there was the schoolroom, and governesses – English, French, and German. They made little impression on Beatrice; she liked them, they liked her

But after a few weeks or months of experimenting with regular schoolroom hours, and disagreeable tussles with arithmetic or grammar, I always took to my bed, the family doctor prescribing 'no lessons, more open-air exercise, if possible a complete change of scene'. [13]

Beatrice only spent one year at school; in 1875, aged 17, she was sent to Stirling House, a Bournemouth boarding school. She was unwell, and preoccupied with religious doubts: it was not a happy experience. Even home seemed better: returning to school after the summer break, she felt

…wrenched from a home which for the first time this year agreed with me and where I have been thoroughly happy, and a family who I was beginning to appreciate and love. [14]

She was irritated by the gossip of the other girls and

…the continual din of the pianos…

She made one friend among the other boarders: her cousin Margaret Harkness, four years older than her. Margaret's father was rector of a country parish near Salisbury. The friendship lasted for the next 15 years.

So Beatrice educated herself, mostly by reading. She could not remember ever learning to read. The Potter household was bookish: parcels arrived from booksellers and circulating libraries; spending on books

…was perhaps the only expenditure unregulated or unrestricted by my mother…

When we complained to my father that a book we wanted to read was banned by the libraries: 'Buy it, my dear', was his automatic answer.[15]

When she was thirteen, Beatrice asked her father whether she should read Fielding's *Tom Jones*.

By all means read it if it interests you…[16]

He would have hesitated to recommend it had she been a boy

…but a nice-minded girl can read anything; and the more she knows about human nature, the better for her… [17]

In later life, Beatrice recollected

…no curiosity about sex: my knowledge of the facts always outrunning my interest in the subject. [18]

By her early twenties, Beatrice had read extensively in both English and European fiction – including the Brontes (she did not like *Jane Eyre*), George Eliot, (*eagerly read and discussed in the family circle*[19]) Balzac, Zola, and Victor Hugo. *Les Miserables* she thought *a glorious drama.* [20] But she never appreciated poetry.

She was a sickly, depressive child

…almost continual illness, bouts of neuralgia, of indigestion, of inflammation of all sorts and kinds, from inflamed eyes to congested lungs, marred my happiness…[21]

When she went to America in 1873 Beatrice was ill for a month, with scarlet fever, measles, and rheumatism. At Stirling House she suffered from headaches. All her life she had insomnia, often writing her diary in the middle of the night. There were many crises of physical and emotional health.

Two, at least, of the Potter sisters had more troubled adolescent years. Rosie recorded that Teresa, shortly after puberty, became

…extremely thin and emaciated, grew hysterical, and refused to eat…[22]

And Rosie herself, after a period of unusually intensive schooling, was, for a time, highly neurotic. [23]

As well as Beatrice's reading, and her brief experience of boarding school, a third element in her intellectual development was her contact with the writer and social theorist Herbert Spencer – *the old philosopher,* as she later referred to him. For Beatrice and her sisters, Spencer filled the roles of a tutor or mentor; Spencer's friendship with Beatrice lasted until his death in 1903. Rosie thought him

…by far the most important influence on the intellectual life of our family…[24]

Spencer was a long-standing friend of both Richard and Lawrencina –

…my father's ardent admirer and my mother's intellectual associate. [25]

Like Richard Potter, Spencer became less radical as he grew older. When the Potter children first knew him, in the 1860s and 1870s, he was seen as the prophet of evolution and progress, opposing clericalism, militarism, and superstition. He is credited with coining the phrase *survival of the fittest.*

Richard Potter had little time for Spencer's ideas, saying to Beatrice

'Poor Spencer, he lacks instinct my dear, he lacks instinct — you will discover that instinct is as important as intellect.' And then, taking out his engagement book, he added, in a more sympathetic tone 'I must see whether I can't arrange another day's fishing with him — poor man.' [26]

For the girls, however, Spencer was a liberator. He derided the governesses as *stupid persons who taught irrelevant facts in an unintelligible way.* He declared *submission not desirable.* [27]

Spencer subverted the governesses. He argued that the curriculum was irrelevant: science was what mattered — and science meant exhilarating outside expeditions, searching for fossils, flowers, and insects. What fascinated Beatrice was to watch him collect illustrations for his theories.

He was also a serious hypochondriac; he talked to Beatrice about her own health

...constantly suggesting this or that remedy for my ailments. [28]

Throughout her life Beatrice was preoccupied with religion. During her adolescence, Spencer was one of four adults, with quite different spiritual approaches, who influenced her. Born into a Methodist family, he had become agnostic; he argued with Lawrencina about the origins of religion.

By middle age Richard Potter had abandoned his father's Unitarianism — Beatrice called Unitarianism an *arid creed* — and joined the Church of England. Lawrencina pursued her own theological studies:

Her soul longed for the mystical consolations of religious orthodoxy. She spent hours studying the Greek Testament and the Fathers of the Church. [29]

Martha Jackson, the faithful Dada, was a Particular Baptist. Beatrice thought the teachings of the Particular Baptists *primitive if not barbaric* [30] — but Dada did not try to convert the household. In the country the Potters attended Anglican services; in London, their observance was more fluid; they looked for stimulating preachers, Anglican, Catholic or Nonconformist.

Beatrice had a restless spirituality, writing, aged 16, that

I cannot accept the belief of my Church without inward questioning. [31]

In 1875, at Stirling House, she *sought mental security in traditional Christianity.* [32] She decided to be confirmed in the Church of England, and to take Communion regularly. But this did not mean she had overcome her doubts. In particular, she would not accept the doctrine of the Atonement:

The idea that God demanded that some innocent person should die for the sins of men... is repugnant to me. [33]

'IRRESPONSIBLE GIRLHOOD' 1875-1882

For the Potter sisters, the London season, and presentation at court, formed part of the transition from girlhood to adult life. Beatrice left school at Christmas 1875; later, she referred to the time that followed as

...six years of irresponsible girlhood. [34]

In her first autobiographical book, *My Apprenticeship*, (1926), Beatrice writes about London society, and the spring and summer London season. From February, the social season and the parliamentary session overlapped for three months. She describes the various elites – the Court, the cabinet, the financial elite, the racing set. Her older sisters had been presented at Court; Lallie, the eldest, in 1864. Beatrice was both fascinated by, and ambivalent towards, the rituals involved.

In 1874, aged sixteen, Beatrice had enjoyed her first ball.

It was the first dance I had ever been at as a grown-up lady, and I felt considerably satisfied with myself, as I had two or three partners for each dance. Ah vanity! vanity! unfortunately for me my ruling passion...[35]

Then, in her year at school, she went through a period of intense religious commitment. By December 1875 she did not want

...to 'come out', and I hope I shall have enough determination and firmness to carry my point...[36]

That mood did not last; there was a round of house parties and dances

...at the conventional age of eighteen I joined my sisters in the contemporary pursuits of girls of our class, riding, dancing, flirting and growing up...[37]

This frenetic social life was directed towards one end:

...the business of getting married; a business carried on by parents and other promoters, sometimes with gentle surreptitiousness, sometimes with cynical effrontery.[38]

On the whole, the process worked for the Potter sisters: before their mother died in 1882, six of them had made more-or-less conventional 'good' marriages. The eldest, Lawrencina, met Robert Holt, of a Liverpool shipping dynasty, in 1865; she married him two years later. Mary married a Gloucestershire landowner, Arthur Playne, in 1870. Georgina married the banker Daniel Meinertzhagen in 1873. Two of the Potter sisters married two brothers, Willie and Charles Alfred Cripps. Blanche married Willie, a surgeon, in 1877. Four years later Theresa married Charles Alfred – a lawyer, later an MP. Surgery, as a profession, was not yet wholly respectable, and Richard Potter never really took to Willie Cripps. But he warmed to Charles Alfred, nicknaming him *the little jewel of an advocate*. [39]. By 1882 only Kate, Beatrice and Rosie were still single.

Outside the formal season, Beatrice travelled, read widely, and enjoyed the company of her sisters – at least until they got married. In 1878 there was a five-month tour of Germany and Hungary with her sister Mary, Mary's husband Arthur Playne – and Carrie Darling, then governess for Mary's children.

Carrie became a close friend; in 1878, Beatrice called her ...*a dear little woman.*[40] In Germany, at Wiesbaden, Beatrice and Carrie had adjoining rooms,

...we used to sit late into the night with our feet cocked high on the china stove... smoking cigarettes and talking philosophy... [41]

Once, when Beatrice and her sisters were

...in full swing of seeing men with a view to marriage...

she went for a London walk with Carrie. Beatrice described

...a week's round of riding in the Row, dinners and balls and the Sunday calls from eligible young men... [42]

Carrie, now teaching in Dulwich, South London, was not impressed

Oh! Beatrice, I would rather lead my life – hard though it be – than yours. [43]

Over winter 1880-1881, Beatrice went to Italy with two of her sisters – Margaret and Theresa. In 1880 Margaret had married Henry Hobhouse, a Somerset landowner, and, later, MP. Beatrice had become close to Margaret; when Margaret married, Beatrice noted,

...I lost my one intimate friend. [44]

Beatrice continued to be fascinated by spirituality and religion. She thought that she had resolved her doubts in the year at Stirling House; the resolution did not last:

The London season of 1876 came and went, and with it disappeared my feeble hold on orthodox Christianity... [45]

Her interest extended to Eastern religions, including Buddhism, and the *religion of science*, inspired by the ideas of Herbert Spencer. In 1878, she visited a Prague synagogue; in 1880, she went to mass in St Peter's in Rome. She tried, unsuccessfully, to reconcile Catholicism and agnosticism. She was attracted to Catholicism:

...the temptation to commit this intellectual (and perhaps moral) suicide is strong, to one whose life without a religious faith is unbearable.[46]

Margaret Harkness shared Beatrice's religious uncertainties. After Stirling House, Harkness returned to her father's country rectory. She told Beatrice it was

...life in a High Church dolls house.[47]

Margaret's relations with her immediate family were strained:

My people mean well, but they make me feel a very devil. They worry me to death. Oh Beatrice, Beatrice, I feel inclined to drown it all in amusement or drink. [48]

In 1877 she decided to become a nurse and moved to London. Her family did not approve; Margaret herself was uncertain, writing, in August 1878 to Beatrice

I do not think I have any love of nursing in my constitution

...and yet, Beatrice, I long for something more...[49]

Harkness became ill and left London for a while; when she returned, she switched from nursing to working in the hospital dispensary.

Margaret and Beatrice corresponded frequently – about religion, love, and marriage; in August 1878, Margaret wrote to Beatrice

I wonder very much if you will fall in love with anyone. I suppose you will live above the herd, & never do anything so vulgar.[50]

Later that year she added

I think marriage is a woman's natural career

So few women have enough character to live an unmarried life, and not sink back into a nobody.[51]

Margaret now turned to writing. In 1880 she obtained a ticket for the British Museum Reading Room; her first article was published in 1881.

Although Margaret was turning away from nursing, she told Beatrice

Remember, if you are ill, I will come and nurse you.[52]

It was not Beatrice but her mother who fell ill, in spring 1882. Lawrencina became unwell at The Argoed on 6 April. Richard Potter moved her back to Standish, where the family assembled. The illness quickly became serious. A nurse was taken on, but Lawrencina did not like her, so the Potters sent for Margaret Harkness, who nursed Lawrencina until her death on Thursday 13 April.

Wednesday was the blackest day. None of us went in to her. Maggie Harkness and the nurse stayed with her. There was really no hope, but it was thought wiser to avoid exciting her in any way.[53]

The following Sunday the Potters went to church. Beatrice yearned

...for some religion by which to console grief and stimulate action.[54]

Rationally she was still agnostic – but

...a new and wondrous faith has arisen within me – a faith in goodness, in God. I must pray; I do pray and I feel better for it...[55]

At the end of June they took a family holiday. Richard Potter, Beatrice, her youngest sister Rosie, and Herbert Spencer went to Germany and Switzerland. Carrie Darling saw them off from Victoria Station. Carrie had been offered a headteacher post in Australia; for Beatrice it was a *sad parting...probably for ever.*

In January 1883, Beatrice reviewed the past year. The first quarter of 1882 had been

...the last of the inactive and irresponsible part of my youth... typical of the many years I passed in self-contemplation and self-commiseration. [56]

SOCIAL APPRENTICE 1882-1890

The death of my mother revolutionised my life [57]

wrote Beatrice. She became her father's hostess, business manager, and confidant.

I became a principal, a person in authority, determining not only my own but other people's conduct; the head of a large household perpetually on the move.[58]

She wanted more. In *My Apprenticeship*, Beatrice describes her search for a creed – her religious crises, and her emergence as a socialist – and her choice of a craft: becoming a social investigator. In 1884 she wrote

Social questions are the vital questions of today: they take the place of religion. I do not pretend to solve them. [59]

Beatrice focussed on London, which, in the 1880s, was undergoing profound social and economic change. The labour market and the housing market were in crisis; acute poverty was growing. Commercial and civic redevelopment and construction displaced poor people from their homes. The central London poor could not afford to move far; overcrowding and rents increased. The labour market was characterised by low paid, casual, short term, seasonal employment.

Awareness of these conditions was rising. Forty years later Beatrice called that awareness

...a new consciousness of sin among men of intellect and men of property...[60]

She listed, as among those newly aware, philanthropists like Shaftesbury, artists and writers like Ruskin and Morris, and church leaders like Samuel Barnett, Cardinal Manning, and General Booth of the Salvation Army.

In 1883 the London Congregational Union published *The Bitter Cry of Outcast London*, a pamphlet on London housing. The *Bitter Cry* referred to pestilential human rookeries

...where tens of thousands are crowded together amidst horrors which call to mind what we have heard of the middle passage of the slave ship. To get into them you have to penetrate courts reeking with poisonous and malodorous gases arising from accumulations of sewage and refuse scattered in all directions and often flowing beneath your feet... [61]

This was the world in which Beatrice chose to work. There was no shortage of ideas on how to resolve the crisis: philanthropists, churchmen, socialists, and others all had their proposed solutions. Beatrice's cousin Mary Booth wrote:

People's minds were very full of the various problems connected with the position of the poor, and opinions the most diverse were expressed, remedies of the most contradictory nature were proposed. [62]

Beatrice first turned to the Charity Organisation Society (COS). The C.O.S. had been established in 1869 as the 'Society for Organising Charitable Relief and Repressing Mendicity', to campaign against uncoordinated and indiscriminate charitable giving to the poor. They opposed state intervention, including any state relief of unemployment, and proposals for the introduction of old age pensions. Early COS members included Octavia Hill, Samuel Barnett and his wife Henrietta, and Charles Stewart Loch. The COS and similar organisations, wrote Jose Harris

...formed a powerful and articulate pressure group against local or central government intervention...[63]

In spring 1883 Beatrice, looking for practical, useful opportunities, joined a local COS committee, becoming one of its visitors in Soho.

Beatrice first met Octavia Hill, the housing reformer, in 1886

...a small woman, with large head finely set on her shoulders...the attractiveness of mental power. [64]

Hill had been influenced by John Ruskin (for whom she had worked, copying pictures) and by Christian Socialists, who she met through her mother. In 1865 Ruskin bought three houses for Octavia to manage; she went on to manage more. She set out both to improve living conditions for poor people, and to earn a 5% return. Her approach was based on a weekly visit, by a lady housing visitor, to collect rent. Most of the early lady visitors were volunteers.

Samuel (later Canon) Barnett became Rector of St Jude's Whitechapel in 1873, after six years as a curate in London's West End. St Jude's was not sought-after: offering Barnett the parish, the Bishop of London wrote

Do not hurry in your decision. It is the worst parish in my diocese, inhabited mainly by a criminal population... [65]

The same year, Barnett married Henrietta Rowland, herself a lady visitor (they had met at Hill's 1870 birthday party).

Barnett was not much to look at; Kate Potter described him as

...plain and insignificant... [66]

Writing after his death in 1913, Beatrice said Barnett was

Small in stature and unpretentious in manner, with no great oratorical gift or literary talent... [67]

But she regarded Barnett as the virtual, often unrecognised, leader of the social reform movement. His work had the merit of

...linking up the Individualist works of yesterday with the Collectivist work of today. [68]

Beatrice recalled Barnett saying, frequently, that

The sense of sin has been the starting-point of progress. [69]

Charles Stewart Loch, as Secretary, was the public face of the COS from 1875 to 1914. Loch developed and articulated the COS analysis of poverty; he was hostile to anything that sounded like socialism. Samuel Barnett was a leading advocate of old age pensions; Loch was a die-hard opponent.

Loch first noticed Beatrice at a COS committee in 1886:

I have heard of her before, perhaps met her. I suppose she would do things well. Dark haired, dark-eyed, pale complexion and striking-looking... [70]

In its early years the COS campaigned for stricter enforcement of the 1834 Poor Law, dividing the poor into deserving and undeserving. Beatrice described how the first step for the COS was detailed investigation of each case

...to save themselves from being taken in by the plausible tales of those who hastened to prey on their credulity. [71]

Once the investigation was complete, and need established, they aimed

...to eliminate those whose evil state could be plausibly ascribed to their own culpable negligence or misconduct. All enlightened philanthropy was to be concentrated on 'the deserving', the others being left to a penal Poor Law.[72]

Later Beatrice called the COS *my friend the enemy*; in the 1880s she thought they were *...an honest though short-circuited attempt...* to help the poor, using evidence and reasoning. [73]

In summer 1883 Beatrice threw herself into COS work – committees, debate, and home visiting. But she soon realised that through the COS she would meet only people in extreme destitution

...who could no more be regarded as a fair sample of the wage-earning class then the 'sporting set' of London society could be considered as representative, either in conduct or in intelligence, of the landed aristocracy and business and professional class...[74]

Beatrice acknowledged her

...utter ignorance of the manual-working class, that is, of four-fifths of my fellow-countrymen. [75]

She had seen destitution; now she wanted to understand the lives of working people: the world of Nonconformist chapels, trade unions and friendly societies. She mused:

Were the manual workers what I was accustomed to call civilised? [76]

The COS could not answer that question. Beatrice turned instead to her own roots. Her mother's family, the Heyworths, had been Lancashire cotton weavers; Beatrice's grandmother, Elizabeth Aked, had operated a loom before her marriage. Some relatives still worked as weavers in Bacup.

Martha Jackson, 'Dada', the children's nurse, (who was in fact a distant cousin) had come from Bacup with Elizabeth Aked, staying to work for Lawrencina. Beatrice's mother had talked to the children about Bacup life; after Lawrencina's death, Dada drew on the same memories:

...of chapel and Sunday school and long walks along dirty lanes to prayer meetings in weavers' cottages. [77]

Dada agreed to take Beatrice next time she visited Bacup; and so, in November 1883 they went for two weeks, staying with family members. Beatrice pretended to be *Miss Jones, a farmer's daughter from Monmouth* rather than one of the affluent Potters.

For Beatrice, that two week visit to Bacup was transformative; it was her *first step as a social investigator* – though she recognised it was

...more of a sentimental journey than a scientific exploration.[78]

She was welcomed; she felt accepted. She learned about work, mills, nonconformism, and cooperation. She went back twice, in 1886 and 1889, at the end of the second visit telling her hosts her true identity.

After her first visit Beatrice wrote that at Bacup

...I felt as if I was living through a page of puritan history; felt that I saw the actual thing, human beings governed by one idea; devotion to Christ, with no struggle or thought about the world; in every action of their daily life giving unto God.[79]

Samuel Barnett, as well as helping to found the COS, established Toynbee Hall, the first university settlement. Barnett outlined the idea in a talk to Oxford students in 1883: he believed middle class professional volunteers should live within sight of the poor. This idea went down well at Oxford. Plans were made, funds raised, and a site (next to St Jude's Rectory) acquired. Barnett became the Warden; the building included living accommodation for the Barnetts and other residents. The historian Gareth Stedman Jones describes the initial vision as

...urban manor houses from which a new squirearchy would lead the poor to virtue...[80]

Other settlements followed, in British cities and in the United States. Their purpose evolved, becoming training grounds and laboratories for reformers. Many of the architects and builders of the twentieth century welfare state had

...settlement house experience and continuous settlement house contact in their background. [81]

Barnett followed Hill's lead in seeking to improve housing conditions. Overcrowded dwellings were taken over; the tenants were trained in thrift, punctuality, and responsibility by 'lady visitors' or rent collectors. The system depended on a continuing supply of visitors; the Barnetts called them *the Canon's ladies.*

Beatrice's sister Kate became a lady visitor. Kate had not enjoyed the London season and the marriage market; in 1875 she decided

> ...*to leave home and go to Miss Octavia Hill to be trained for her work in London.* [82]

In 1876, Kate moved to work for the Barnetts; years afterwards, Kate told Beatrice that Samuel Barnett

> ...*was my guide in the East End work – far more than Octavia Hill with whom I lived for a year but who never liked me.* [83]

Beatrice stayed with Kate while she was a lady visitor, later writing that it was at this time that she

> ...*first became aware of the meaning of the poverty of the poor.* [84]

In 1883 Kate did marry. Her husband was Leonard Courtney, Liberal MP for Liskeard. He was 51, Kate 36. Beatrice thought

> *Marriage at their ages is rather a leap in the dark – curious to see how it turns out.*[85]

The wedding, at St Jude's, was conducted by Barnett; Beatrice thought it

> ...*the pleasantest wedding I have ever been at...*[86]

Afterwards Barnett wrote

> *This year we lose Miss Potter.* [87]

Kate's departure was Beatrice's opportunity. In December 1884 she wrote to her sister Mary

> *Kate has some building she is taking over in the City, perhaps I shall take to that.* [88]

Beatrice now became a lady visitor in Katherine Buildings – named after Kate. Newly constructed and run by the East End Dwellings Company, Katherine Buildings was a five-storey block of flats, in Cartwright Street, near the Tower of London, with 281 rooms and about 600 residents. Henrietta Barnett described Beatrice:

> ...*so strong in mind, graceful in limb, and noble in feature, yet fearlessly, in her search for facts, working in sweating-shops and living as a lone girl in block dwellings.* [89]

The other collector in Katherine Buildings was Ella Pycroft:

Daughter of country doctor and one of two families, stepmother died. Plain, very strong-looking and unattractive except for sincerity of expression. [90]

Ella, with Carrie Darling and Margaret Harkness, became part of Beatrice's circle of women friends of her own generation. All came from middle class families and were looking for careers outside the home. They did not necessarily intend, or expect, to marry.

Beatrice and Ella managed Katherine Buildings from its opening in January 1885; Beatrice worked there intensively until November 1885, and for shorter periods after that. The block represented a new venture, attempting to rehouse

...without financial loss, in a manner both sanitary and cheap, the poorest of the poor: in particular, the dock labourers... [91]

Before Beatrice started, she and Kate met the directors of the company. They discussed practicalities: rent levels, stoves; why are all the rooms painted the same? Kate mildly suggests that the tenants do have taste. One of the directors

...cut and dried philanthropist, with little human nature, determined that tenants should *like nothing but what was* useful.[92]

Katherine Buildings was intended to combine profitability and hygiene. Beatrice described the bleak result:

Right along the blank wall ran four open galleries, out of which led narrow passages, each passage to five rooms, identical in size and shape, except that the one at the end of the passage was much smaller than the others. All the rooms were 'decorated' in the same dull, dead-red distemper, unpleasantly reminiscent of a butcher's shop. Within these uniform, cell-like apartments, there were no labour-saving appliances, not even a sink and water-tap! [93]

Sixty rooms shared three sinks and six taps; for toilets

...behind a tall wooden screen were placed six closets on the trough system... [94]

Beatrice immersed herself in detail. Barnett encouraged her to get information about all the public officials for the area. In March she was vetting prospective tenants:

All is chaos at present. Long trudges through Whitechapel after applicants and references, and tenants tumbling in anyhow. [95]

She was depressed by the sheer scale of what she had taken on

When I look at those long balconies and think of all the queer characters – occupants, would-be occupants ... I feel rather dizzy. [96]

In April 1885 Beatrice wrote to her sister Mary, saying it would be *a hard pull to make those Buildings successful.* [97] A few days later, she was exhausted, and took a break at The Argoed

My work takes a great deal out of me…Feel so utterly done when I come back from Whitechapel. Too tired to think or feel…[98]

In June Beatrice was still working hard; she found the Buildings unsatisfactory, the caretaker inadequate. The tenants were a rough lot –

…the aborigines of the East End…[99]

Beatrice and Ella came under pressure to change the policy of housing the poorest. Peabody – the London housing provider backed by American philan-thropic capital – only housed those in regular employment. Should the East End Dwellings Company become more selective?

There were also practical management issues:

May have some rough work to do, but am gaining experience. When over-tired, the tenants haunt me with their wretched, disorderly lives.[100]

Writing to her father, Beatrice explained what she meant by *rough work*

I have turned out two women this week for leading bad lives and I am quite certain there are ½ dozen more… A young married woman, whose husband is a sailor and away, I found out is a well-known character among the sailors – and also a favourite with the inspectors at Leman Street Police Station… [101]

When they started, Ella and Beatrice were given accommodation at Katherine Buildings; they agreed they did not want any other workers on the block. They did not stay there all the time; Beatrice stayed some nights at York House, her father's London base for the season, or at Kate and Leonard Courtney's house on Cheyne Walk when they were away during the parliamentary recess. Beatrice explained to her father that she was at the Buildings from Monday to Friday

…and sleep here on Monday – I think it would really pay to sleep here oftener…[102]

For some months in 1885-86 Beatrice and Ella were joined at Katherine Buildings by Margaret Harkness. Margaret's writing career was beginning to succeed. She had spent some time in Germany; on her return, she stayed both at Katherine Buildings and with Beatrice at Cheyne Walk. Her first novel, *A City Girl*, was partly set in Katherine Buildings – renamed Charlotte Buildings. In *A City Girl*, Margaret describes the Buildings; they

...were not beautiful to look upon; they might even have been termed ugly. Their long yellow walls were lined with small windows; upon the rails of their stiff iron balconies hung shirts, blankets and other articles fresh from the wash-tub. Inside their walls brown doors opened into dark stone passages; and narrow stone staircases led from passage to passage up to the roof. [103]

She introduced the lady visitors:

Several times in the week ladies arrived on the Buildings armed with master-keys, ink-pots and rent-books. A tap at the door was followed by the intrusion into the room of a neatly-clad female of masculine appearance. If the rent was promptly paid the lady made some gracious remarks, patted the heads of the children and went away. If the rent was not forthcoming the lady took stock of the room (or rooms) and said a few words about the broker. [104] [i.e., pawnbroker]

The ladies were not always appreciated by the tenants:

'She takes the bread out of a man's mouth, and spends on one woman what would keep a little family,' grumbled a tenant to his neighbour... [105]

In autumn 1885, Beatrice and Margaret both stayed at Kate Courtney's home on Cheyne Walk, Chelsea. Beatrice commuted to Whitechapel by Thames river boat.

...once back in that perfect house, Maggie Harkness fresh from her novel-writing to greet me to chat on all subjects, human and divine, and to play snatches of good music on the parliamentary piano; I, lying the while on the sofa, watching the river and the barges on it creeping by. [106]

By November, Beatrice was thinking about improving the management of the Buildings, and coordinating the work of different housing agencies. This demanded better information; she decided to produce

...a book of all the tenants, past and present, with description of occupation, family, etc., and statement of income and previous history – cause of leaving or ejectment. [107]

She also wanted information on income, race, religion, and whether born in London. Beatrice immediately started work on the book; four hours work on 10 November; seven on 13 November.

Beatrice was unable to concentrate on her research for long: on 26 November 1885 Richard Potter had a stroke. Beatrice soon became his main family carer. She found accommodation for him in Bournemouth. After that, until her father's death on 1 January 1892, Beatrice spent long periods out of London with him, returning for short bursts of work while one of her sisters took over her caring duties. She took over the management of his finances, including sometimes countermanding his instructions to his brokers to invest funds speculatively.

'The book' became a joint project for Beatrice and Ella. Some were sceptical about its value; Octavia Hill told Beatrice she *did not see the use of it*:

...there was already too much 'windy talk'...[108]

Beatrice felt penitent but not convinced.

Ella and Beatrice began by collecting information on work. They recorded 161 male occupations. There were 40 dock and waterside labourers – 16 permanent, 24 casual. Another 24 were carmen or porters; there were 4 sailors, a ship's cook, and a Customs House Officer. Many of the remainder were low-skilled – labourers, scavengers, shoeblacks, messengers, and costermongers – but there were also 6 carpenters, 2 plasterers, 2 engineers, a policeman and 2 musicians.

They established the occupations of 109 women, 47 of whom had living husbands. The largest groups were cleaners – 23; and 'tailoresses' – 24. Otherwise, the range covered a variety of needle trades – dress makers, frill makers, and mantle makers; shopkeepers, old clothes dealers, and fruit sellers. One occupation was recorded as 'beggar'.

They made detailed notes, dwelling by dwelling; this example probably by Ella:

The Fisher family – husband, wife and four children – occupied no 150 Katherine Buildings, a double room at a weekly rent of 5 shillings. They moved in on 25 May 1885 and were evicted again on 6 September 1886, owing 13 shillings. James Fisher was a carman earning £1.00 a week; his wife was an 'untidy, rowdy, goodhearted woman'.

Some of the lowest people on the Buildings. Irish Catholics. Fisher and his wife fight sometimes. Mostly on account of wife's brother who being out of work from ill health lodged with them. I said he must go because of overcrowding. He went but returned in a fortnight unknown to me. One day Mrs F upbraided him for his laziness (he was strong again she said) and he smashed all her ornaments and pitched into her. Neighbours sent for Fisher to defend his wife, and the two men fought on the balcony. I separated them, and got Fisher into his room, only let him out on his promising not to go on with the fight. The men shook hands ferociously over my shoulder, if I hadn't been between them they would have fought again. If I could have knocked the man down without making a row on D Buildings I should have liked it. Mrs F's mother keeps house for Mrs Levy (late 144) and used to sleep in 150.

Ejected for rowdiness and arrears.[109]

Ella and Beatrice included tongue-in-cheek portraits of themselves – occupants of apartments 97 and 98:

> *Ella Pycroft*
> *Rent collector of Katharine* [sic] *Buildings*
> *Beatrice Potter, ditto. Shares the two rooms.*
> *E Pycroft b. in Devonshire. Daughter of Physician (single woman)*
> *Came to London in 1883 in search for work.*
> *B Potter, daughter of timber merchant, born in Gloucestershire*
> *Came to London for family reasons and with the hope of work. (single woman)*
> *Income; In religious opinion they are doubtful and differing. Energetic and*
> *functional in professional duties. Not absolutely accurate in accounts.*
> *BP especially deficient. EP takes the lead in management, BP in observation.*
> <u>*Both*</u>*? of them are professionally ambitious.*[110]

In November 1886 Beatrice returned to London, after time caring for her father, and after her second Bacup journey. Ella was now managing Wentworth Dwellings, a nearby block. Beatrice took over Ella's duties to give her a break. She told her father

> *I found Ella Pycroft very much overdone and worried so I thought the least*
> *I could do would be to offer to take her work for a fortnight and let her go*
> *home.*[111]

Beatrice was becoming disillusioned:

> *These buildings are to my mind an utter failure. In spite of Ella Pycroft's heroic*
> *efforts, they are not an influence for good.*[112]

Samuel Barnett agreed, writing in 1887 that he now thought it a false economy,

> *…as it is false benevolence, to provide for fellow creatures things acknowledged*
> *to be ugly. In the long run such things will be rejected…* [113]

The long run was a long time coming: Katherine Buildings survived until the 1970s.

In the 1880s, the Liverpool shipowner Charles Booth came to share the growing middle-class anxiety about the condition of England. Booth was from an established Liverpool nonconformist (Unitarian) business family. When he was twenty-two, Charles formed a partnership with his brother Alfred which became the Booth Steamship Company.

In 1871 Booth had married Mary Macaulay, a cousin of Beatrice Potter (Mary's mother was a sister of Richard Potter). When growing up, Mary had frequently spent holidays with her Potter girl cousins at Standish and at the Argoed. Mary and Charles met at the home of Beatrice's sister, Lawrencina – who had married into another Liverpool ship owning family, the Holts. In later life Charles largely based himself in London, and at his country home, Gracedieu, in Leicestershire.

Beatrice first knew Booth in the 1870s; she was struck by his

…unselfconscious manner and eager curiosity to know what you thought and why you thought it. [114]

In 1879, Mary Booth had found Beatrice

…as odd as ever but a good sort of girl. [115]

Samuel Barnett thought Booth *…a noble fellow…* [116]

Both Mary and Charles Booth were concerned about poverty; they were influenced by the Barnetts. From the early 1880s, Charles set out to establish the facts; he wrote later that the lives of the poor

…lay hidden from view behind a curtain on which were painted terrible pictures: starving children, suffering women, overworked men; horrors of drunkenness and vice, monsters and demons of inhumanity; giants of disease and despair. [117]

Booth was a successful businessman; he believed in individual effort, and was wary of increased government activity encroaching on individual freedom. He disliked any form of socialism.

Booth's concern to establish the facts about poverty and the labour market led him to establish – and fund from his own resources – the research project that eventually became the seventeen volume *Life and Labour of the People of London*. To carry out the study he gradually assembled a team, drawn from his contacts at Toynbee Hall, the Royal Statistical Society, the COS, and elsewhere. Beatrice was an early member of that team.

In summer 1885 Beatrice stayed with the Booths; they talked about the study. Charles wanted to avoid a shallow, superficial approach.

The following spring, Beatrice wrote to Mary about the research plan:

…the scheme is very ably worked out in theory – it remains to be seen how far it can be carried out in practice. [118]

Beatrice offered to conduct the research in East London and the docks when she was in London; she joined the board Booth established to manage the survey. In April 1886, the board agreed the aim – to get a fair picture of the whole of London society by district and by employment – and a detailed work plan. At that stage Beatrice noted that, apart from her offer of help, Booth was the only person working on the study.

Charles and Beatrice exchanged ideas about methods. From Joseph Chamberlain's Birmingham experience came the suggestion of using the records of the School Board Visitors, who monitored school attendance. Booth noted

Every house in every street is in their books, and details are given of every family with children of school age. [119]

In September, two researchers began interviewing the visitors.

Beatrice's caring responsibilities made contact with Booth intermittent. She had dinner with Charles and Mary during a London visit in October 1886. They talked till midnight. She saw them again in December and made a further commitment:

I have promised to undertake the docks in my March holiday.[120]

Beatrice now counted the Booths as among her closest friends or relations.

They become each year more near to me. Perhaps they are the only persons who really love me.[121]

In January 1887 Ella Pycroft did the Katherine Buildings fieldwork for the Booth survey:

Katharine [sic] *Buildings*

Miss Pycroft

30.01.1887

32   Says she makes very little and is poor

38   very poor indeed just now – work slack

40   husband in Germany. Sends very little money

44   decidedly poor

45   miserably poor

50/51   very respectable and now comfortably off

69   deals in hotpot and sausages at docks, but says charitable dispensation of these articles has ruined her trade

79   drinks a little

89   iron worker. Travels about putting up iron roofs. Prob gets good money, but living expensive.

105/106   might do better if he liked – does almost nothing

111 ill. A mystery how they manage – must get help somewhere.

122 Army pension. Has bad health and can do very little.

133 plasterer. Had no work for many months – wife keeps him

*191 Army pension. Was in docks – met with a severe accident & got £60
compensation – has quite recovered, but had no work since- doesn't seem to try
much – is demoralized.*

*205/206   Was a policeman, but discharged for borrowing a little money from
a publican to pay the carriage of some furniture. A hard case.* [122]

While Ella had work on the survey, Margaret Harkness complained to Beatrice

*By the way, why did not Mr. Booth employ me on his enquiry into the work of
women in the East End? I know more than...?...* [123]

Beatrice returned to London in February 1887 to study the docks. She wanted
to understand both the business and the organisation of labour: the different
docks, the various commodities, and the payment systems. She interviewed dock
managers, trade unionists, and School Board Visitors. Working on the Booth
study, Beatrice came to appreciate the relationship between casual, insecure,
intermittent labour and poverty.

Her notes were extensive, sometimes acerbic:

*Mr. Birt, the General manager of the Millwall, is a self-important man, who
considers himself an authority on dock labour...* [124]
London and St C [Katherine] Docks
Mr Cox, Superintendent, a gentle and courteous minded man... [125]

In March, she reflected,

This book leaves me fairly launched in social diagnosis. [126]

Beatrice looked for local colour as well as dry statistics; the Limehouse School
Board Visitor, Kerrigan, was an invaluable source:

*Describes his casuals (about 900) as 'hereditary casuals'. London born; the worst
scoundrel is the cockney born Irishman – the woman is the chinaman of the place,
and drudge as the woman of the savage races. She slaves all day and all night.* [127]

Another worker on Booth's study was Hubert Llewellyn Smith; Beatrice
worked with him in 1888, researching the London Jewish community. She
described Llewellyn Smith as

...a Toynbee man and fellow statistician... [128]

On a cold December morning in 1888, waiting at the docks for the possible
arrival of a boat bringing new immigrants, Beatrice and Llewellyn Smith chatted
over their coffee and buns: Beatrice said he was

...a clever ambitious young Oxford graduate...generous in his helpfulness to others working on the same line...He and I are good friends and working Camarades... [129]

Chapter Three: Sidney Webb 1859-1890

SIDNEY 1859-1880

Elizabeth Webb, Sidney's mother, ran a hairdressing business at 45 Cranbourn Street, off Leicester Square in central London. She was born Elizabeth Stacey in 1825; her father was a sea captain from Wivenhoe, near Colchester. In 1848 a family member lent her the money to start her business. In 1854 she married Charles Webb, of Pimlico, at St George's Hanover Square; they lived over the shop in Cranbourn Street.

Charles Webb's father, James, had kept a pub at Petham, near Canterbury, for fifty years; Beatrice described him as a *vigorous old Radical*. [130] Charles himself was the accountant for the salon and for other local businesses. He was also a sergeant in the Queen's Westminster Rifle Volunteers, a vestryman, and a Poor Law guardian. His health was fragile; probably most of the family income came from the hairdressing business. Charles, like his father, was a political radical, supporting John Stuart Mill in his successful Westminster election campaign in 1865.

Beatrice described Sidney's family as

…neither rich nor poor, neither professional brain-workers nor manual workers, neither captains of industry nor hired hands. [131]

George Bernard Shaw knew both mother and father; he wrote to Sidney in old age:

You had wonderful parents: I have never met a more gentle, conscientious, + thoroughly likeable pair in my life. [132]

Beatrice never met Sidney's father; by the time she met his mother, Elizabeth was already *old and crippled*. Sidney's friend and colleague Graham Wallas had known Elizabeth before her health collapsed; he said she was

…wise and witty, with a remarkable memory [133]

Beatrice thought the family possessed

…the charm of essential goodness, of honesty, personal kindliness and public spirit. [134]

Sidney was born in Cranbourn Street on 23 July 1859; he had an older brother, Charles, and a younger sister, Ada. Another sister had died aged seven. As a child, Sidney wrote

I wandered endlessly through the miles of streets, in which I do not remember ever being molested or robbed. [135]

He learned to read roaming the streets

...very largely from the books and notices displayed in the shop windows, a source of endless interest. [136]

His favourite book was *Kelly's Directory*.

The two boys went to a local school – St Martin's Collegiate, in St Martin's Lane, run by a Mr. Pincher. Sidney was there between the ages of 8 and 13. Charles described St Martin's as

...a first class middle class day school... [137]

Sidney wrote in 1881 that the school had long since ceased. [138]

The hairdressing business must have prospered; advised by a customer, Elizabeth sent the boys abroad to finish their schooling. Many years later, Sidney explained to Virginia Woolf that he

...came too early to profit from secondary education. My parents were lower middle class shopkeepers, with a blind determination to educate their sons somehow, but without a ghost of a notion how to set about it. They hit on the plan of sending me and my brother abroad to France and Germany... [139]

From April 1872 to March 1873, they stayed at Pension Morgenthaler, in Neuveville in Switzerland, learning French and German. Charles remembered that, after three months, Sidney could hold his own against the French-speaking Swiss boys in French dictation lessons. They lived well; the school had a vineyard running down to the Lac de Rienne. When the grapes were ripe the boys could eat all they wanted.

They then spent eighteen months at Wismar, in Germany, lodging with a Lutheran clergyman, Dr Massmann, who taught them German. In 1890, Sidney told Beatrice that he and Charles had *run wild* at Dr Massman's. [140]

The brothers returned to London in February 1875 and started work. Charles joined Marshall and Snelgrove, the department store, living on their premises. Eventually, with his languages, he became their Foreign Correspondence clerk.

In April 1875 Sidney, now aged sixteen, started as a clerk, with an annual salary of £90, with a colonial broker in the City of London – Thomas Stiff & Co, of Harp Lane – a narrow street of tall, ancient warehouses, in the tea and spice district of the City, in the days when the City still handled and traded in physical commodities.

Sidney stayed three and a half years at the brokers. When he left, the head of the firm offered him a stake in the business when he was twenty one if he stayed. He later, however, told Beatrice that he had been

Disgusted with the petty cheating of a low class broker...

Instead, he aimed for the Civil Service, the higher grades of which had not long been opened up to recruitment on merit via competitive examination. His education continued at night schools; between 1875 and 1880 he enrolled at five different institutions – the City of London College, the Society for the Extension of Further Education, the Society for the Extension of University Teaching, the Society for the Encouragement of the Arts, Manufactures and Commerce, and the Birkbeck Literary and Scientific Institution. He secured a wide range of qualifications and was awarded a number of prizes. He joined the London Library, and obtained a ticket for the Reading Room at the British Museum.

Sidney first applied to the Civil Service in January 1878, entering the competition for Men Clerkships, Lower Division. He was unsuccessful, despite a mark of 96% in the arithmetic exam, and coming 6th out of all the candidates. He applied again that August, reminding the Civil Service Commissioners of his strong performance earlier in the year. This time he came 3rd and was successful. In November, he wrote to the Commissioners:

I am prepared promptly to enter upon the situation offered me, but as my home is in London, I should much prefer a situation here. [141]

He joined the War Office as a Man Clerk on 2 December 1878; he then progressed rapidly through the ranks. The following November, he moved to the Inland Revenue as an Assistant Surveyor of Taxes – a higher grade. A reference from the War Office stated that his conduct and efficiency had been 'excellent' and his health had been very good. According to Molly Hamilton, the Webbs' first biographer, one taxpayer he assessed was Robert Browning – who argued, successfully, that he did not earn enough from his poetry to come into the tax paying bracket. [142]

In 1881 he entered the competition for the senior Civil Service – Class I; he was placed second. This enabled him to choose from the available vacancies; he wrote to the Commissioners on 8 March 1881 to say that he had selected one of the vacant clerkships in the Colonial Office. Alfred Apthorpe, the Surveyor of Taxes to whom Sidney reported at the Inland Revenue, wrote in his reference that Sidney was

...painstaking, industrious, exact in his work, and performs his duties in a thoroughly satisfactory manner. [143]

First place in the Class I clerkships competition went to Sydney Olivier, who also chose the Colonial Office. Olivier, son of a clergyman, was the same age as Sidney Webb. He arrived in the senior civil service by the conventional route of Tonbridge School and Oxford. George Bernard Shaw described Olivier as

...handsome and strongly sexed, looking like a Spanish grandee in any sort of clothes, however unconventional... [144]

Sidney and Sydney both became 'resident clerks', staying overnight at the office, monitoring telegrams from the Empire. Although they were required to attend the office, their duties were not onerous. Olivier described how

In the afternoons, exercise was provided in the large First-class clerks room of the Eastern Department in the form of cricket, played with a paper ball tightly lashed with string and a long tin map case for a bat. [145]

In the 1880s, with both sons in employment, Elizabeth Webb gave up hairdressing. The family moved less than a mile, to Keppel Street, behind the British Museum. In 1889 they moved again to Park Village East, on the edge of Regent's Park.

Sidney carried on studying; he took a law degree, and read for the bar. And he played chess. One evening Graham Wallas, an Oxford friend of Sydney Olivier, then teaching in North London, turned up at the office to meet Olivier. Olivier was not there – so Wallas spent the evening playing chess with Sidney Webb.

Like Olivier, Graham Wallas was the son of a vicar; also like Olivier, his religious belief was fast disappearing. This soon brought his career as a schoolteacher to a close. Later he taught at LSE. In his twenties, however, Wallas was short of money, sometimes in debt, and undecided about his future. Writing in 1887, Sidney advised him to qualify as a barrister, as he had done. Among other reasons

It qualifies you for several things which might come your way in afterlife, when <u>we</u> all get into power. [146]

Later, when Beatrice was getting to know Sidney, she also met Wallas:

A strange, warm-hearted young man with a bright intelligence, not much beyond commonplace except in its social fervour. [147]

Sidney Webb, Sydney Olivier, and Graham Wallas became friends; the friendship endured. They developed their political ideas together, travelled together, corresponded frequently, and shared their hopes and disappointments.

In 1920, Sidney wrote about the life they had shared in the 1880s:

We were young in those days...and I suppose as eagerly presumptuous as young people ought to be. We spent what free time we had, after earning our daily bread, in reading and talking – in studying everything from blue-books to art, from history and politics to novels and poetry, and perpetually discussing and lecturing, among ourselves, and before anybody who would listen to us. [148]

'THE ABLEST MAN IN ENGLAND'

After a long period of inactivity, socialist politics revived in Britain in the 1880s.

Sidney wrote that, after the collapse of Chartism in the 1850s

...all serious agitation of a Socialist character came to an end... [149]

Pressure for radical political change came only from small, isolated groups. In the absence of a broad political movement, effort went into trade unions, cooperatives, friendly societies, building societies and secularist or ethical groups. Most trade unionists put their political trust in the Liberal Party. Socialist ideas had survived in London's radical clubs and union branches.[150] Club members included Chartist veterans, and European political refugees – among them, after 1871, survivors of the Paris Commune.

The American land campaigner, Henry George, generated great enthusiasm with two British speaking tours. These attracted new members to the recently established Democratic Federation. The Federation's leader was Henry Hyndman: a Cambridge graduate, a barrister, and a cricketer. Hyndman was rich; he dressed accordingly, in frock coat and top hat. He had known Marx (who died, in London, in 1883). *Capital* was not yet available in English; Hyndman summarized Marx's views in his own book, *England for All* (1881) – but alienated Marx by not crediting him.

Marx's daughter Eleanor joined the Federation; so did William Morris. Another early member was the engineer John Burns. Born in Battersea, south London, to Scottish parents, Burns started work locally, aged 12, at Price's Patent Candle Factory. In 1873 he began an engineering apprenticeship, working alongside Victor Delahaye, communard exile and Marxist; Burns described Delahaye as

One of the formative influences of my own life, a centre of inspiration... [151]

Burns spoke in defence of free speech at meetings on Clapham Common. By 1884 he was a leading light of the Battersea Branch of the Federation. He was teetotal, and a strong temperance advocate.

In 1884 the Federation changed its name, becoming the Social Democratic Federation (SDF). Then, in December 1884, the SDF split – largely over Hyndman's autocratic leadership. Eleanor Marx, her lover Edward Aveling, Morris, and others formed the Socialist League. Morris wrote to George Bernard Shaw about Hyndman

I have done my best to trust him, but cannot any longer. [152]

Eleanor said one issue was

...whereas we wish to make this a really international movement...Mr Hyndman... has endeavoured to set the English workman against 'foreigners'. [153]

Another was the question of standing for parliament; Morris and the Socialist League were against, the SDF in favour. Burns sided with Hyndman and the SDF.

W Stephen Sanders, a secularist, joined the Battersea SDF in 1888, aged 17. The branch met in the Sydney Hall,

Situated above a waxwork show of an inferior kind...flanked by a yard in which gypsy caravans found temporary sojourn... [154]

Sanders wrote later that Burns was the branch's dominant and best-known member. Burns' voice, his energy and his strength, and his power to sway an audience, marked him out as

...a man likely to become the great working-class leader of his generation. [155]

Hyndman, who was scathing about Burns' subsequent career, acknowledged that in the 1880s, Burns did *very useful work for socialism*:

He was, I think, on the whole the best stump orator I have ever heard [156]

Other radical networks emerged: local parliaments, local debating societies, and self-improvement groups. Sidney joined the Lambeth and Charing Cross parliaments, and regularly lectured to a wide range of audiences.

In 1879 he joined the Zetetical Society, which aimed

...to search for truth in all matters affecting the interests of the human race; hence no topic, theological or otherwise, discussed with decorum, is excluded from its programme. [157]

Another 'Zet' recruit was George Bernard Shaw. Two years older than Sidney, GBS had arrived in London from Dublin in 1876, hoping to become a writer. His workplace was the British Museum Reading Room. He lived nearby on Fitzroy Street, with his mother. He passed his evenings at literary and debating societies; he wanted to learn to speak in public. He was conspicuously poor; his clothes were tattered and torn.

Shaw's first encounter with Sidney was at a Zetetical meeting; the lecturer

...was about 21, rather below middle height, with small hands and feet, and a profile that suggested an improvement on Napoleon the Third, his nose and imperial moustache being of that shape. He had a fine forehead, a long head, eyes that were built on top of two highly developed organs of speech (according to the phrenologists) and remarkably thick, strong, dark hair. He knew all about the subject of the debate; knew more than the lecturer; knew more than anybody present; had read everything that had ever been written; and remembered all the facts that bore on the subject. He used notes, read them, ticked them off one by one, threw them away, and finished with a coolness and clearness that seemed to me miraculous.

This was the ablest man in England: Sidney Webb. [158]

So their friendship began. In the 1880s they met several times every week. Shaw

...at once recognised and appreciated in him all the qualities in which I was myself pitiably deficient. He was clearly the man for me to work with. I forced my acquaintance on him; and it soon ripened into an enduring friendship. This was by far the wisest step I ever took. The combination worked perfectly. [159]

In September 1882 GBS had heard Henry George speak in London. He read George's book *Progress and Poverty*; he tried – unsuccessfully – to convert Sidney to land nationalisation. He became a candidate member of the SDF. At an SDF meeting Shaw quoted Henry George – and was told to read Marx. So he read *Capital* (still available only in French) in the British Museum.

Sidney and GBS then joined the Karl Marx Society (which later changed its name to the Hampstead Historic Society). This met at a farmhouse on Hampstead Heath, home of Charlotte Wilson. Married to a stockbroker, Wilson had been one of the first Cambridge woman students. She joined both the SDF and the Fabian Society; she was the only woman on the first Fabian Executive Committee. She resigned from the Committee in 1887, to concentrate on the anarchist movement, working with the Russian émigré Peter Kropotkin. Twenty years later she returned, supporting the establishment of the Fabian Women's Group.

In November 1884, Sidney went to a Marx Society meeting without Shaw. Charlotte Wilson

...read a most dense analysis of Ch. I of Marx, in English, over which she must

have spent weeks.[160]

The meeting was chaired by the economist Francis Edgeworth – who held Marx in contempt. Edgeworth and Sidney spent the meeting

...gaily dancing on the unfortunate K.M., trampling him remorselessly underfoot, amid occasional feeble protests and enquiries from Mrs Wilson (who had thrown away her young love upon him) ...[161]

Nevertheless, Sidney and GBS persisted with Marx. Sidney bought Volume II of *Capital* (this time in German), writing to Shaw

We shall find it very dull – in fact, I fear, quite unendurable. But we may as well begin it together if you are in earnest about learning German. [162]

GBS noted that he and Sidney had been reading *Capital* together:

Sat rather late with him and drank some lemonade that resulted in a nightmare. [163]

Neither GBS nor Sidney aligned themselves firmly with Marx or with Henry George; they searched elsewhere for a political home.

In March 1885, Sidney spoke to the Fabian Society; he talked of the condition of England, poverty, and the hypocrisy of blaming the poor for their own misfortunes. The Fabians were a new organisation. GBS had joined in September 1884; Sidney Webb and Sydney Olivier joined in May 1885, Graham Wallas in April 1886.

The first meeting of what became the Fabian Society had taken place in October 1883, at the flat of Edward Pease in Osnaburgh Street, Somers Town. Pease (a Quaker, interested in spiritualism) had previously been active in the Society for Psychical Research. Concluding that this was foolish, he turned to politics. Fifteen people had attended that initial meeting; some were interested in spiritual renewal, others in a political movement. In October they agreed to call themselves the New Life; in November, the Fellowship of the New Life. In December they adopted an objective

The cultivation of a perfect character in each and all. [164]

The Fellowship of the New Life had then split into two parts in January 1884; the more spiritual faction kept the name; the other – *on somewhat broader and more indeterminate lines* [165] – became the Fabian Society. The Fellowship survived until 1898; members included Edward Carpenter.

Some people joined both; one such was James Ramsay MacDonald, who arrived in London in 1886 from Lossiemouth, in North East Scotland, aged 20. MacDonald had left school at 15, then spending four years as pupil teacher. In

1885, he briefly went to Bristol, where he joined the SDF. MacDonald became a Fabian in May 1886; he later became a member of the Fabian Executive Committee (1890-1894). From 1891 – 93 he was Secretary of the Fellowship.

The name 'Fabian' was a reference to a Roman general, Quintus Fabius Maximus, renowned for delaying tactics. A paragraph, which became the Fabian motto, appeared on the front of the first Fabian Tract:

For the right moment you must wait, as Fabius did most patiently, when warring against Hannibal, though many censured his delays; but when the time comes you must strike hard, as Fabius did, or your waiting will be in vain, and fruitless. [166]

When the split came, Pease chose the Fabians. So did another founder, Hubert Bland – a businessman, and the Society's first Treasurer. GBS described Bland's

...fierce Norman exterior and huge physical strength...never seen without an irreproachable frock coat, tall hat and a single eye glass which infuriated everybody. [167]

Bland was the erratic husband of Edith Nesbit, the children's author, another Fabian; they led a Bohemian life at Well Hall, Eltham, south London. Edith wrote

The talks after the Fabian meetings are very jolly. I do think the Fabians are quite the nicest set of people I ever knew. [168]

It was not yet clear what the Fabians would do – they ran talks, they intended to produce pamphlets, but had no programme.

By 1890 Sidney Webb, Bernard Shaw, Sydney Olivier, and Graham Wallas had emerged as the leading Fabians. They were known, variously, as the musketeers, the quartet, and the junta. Later they became known as the Old Gang. For a while all the Society's records were kept in a drawer in the Colonial Office in Downing Street.

In 1887 they adopted the *Fabian Basis* – to be signed by all new members

...not a confession of faith...merely a test of admission, a minimum basis of agreement [169]

The *Basis* stated that

The Fabian Society consists of Socialists.
It therefore aims at the reorganisation of Society by the emancipation of Land and Industrial Capital... The Society accordingly works for the extinction of private property in Land... [170]

Annie Besant, secularist and feminist, joined the Fabians in 1885; she was also close to the SDF. In 1867, aged 20, Besant had married an older Anglican clergyman. She became increasingly agnostic; after six years they separated. She came to London and obtained work with the *National Reformer,* a secularist newspaper, working closely with Charles Bradlaugh, president of the National Secular Society.

There were regular Fabian discussion meetings, which attracted a wide range of participants – among them socialists, anarchists, liberals, and trades unionists. GBS recalled that there were

> *...anarchists, led by Mrs Wilson, who would not hear of anything Parliamentary. There were young ladies on the look-out for husbands, who left when they succeeded. There were atheists and Anglo-Catholics.* [171]

The subjects discussed at the meetings were equally varied, covering economic policy, social reform, and the arts. In February 1887, H M Hyndman, of the SDF, spoke on Marx – Sidney, Sydney Olivier, Shaw, and Annie Besant all contributed to the discussion.

A year later, the young Liberal MP Richard Haldane spoke on *Radical remedies for economic evils.* A Scot, educated in Germany at Gottingen, Haldane was a barrister; when he became a QC in 1890, he was the youngest appointed for 50 years. First elected in 1885, Haldane was one of a group of younger Liberal MPs interested in social reform – others included Asquith, Arthur Acland, and Edward Grey. Haldane had already acquired a reputation as a gourmet and a wine connoisseur.

After his talk at the Fabian meeting, Haldane was attacked by Sidney, GBS, Wallas and Annie Besant.[172] Sidney

> *...sprang to his feet, eager, excited, and anxious to shake the life out of Mr Haldane before anyone else could get at him. He spoke so rapidly that he became at times almost unintelligible.*[173]

An account of the meeting was published under the title *Butchered to make a Fabian holiday.*

From these unpromising beginnings sprang a long term friendship, first with Sidney, soon also with Beatrice. Haldane wrote that in this period he

> *...used to study stimulating ideas with Sidney Webb, Bernard Shaw and other Socialists.* [174]

In July 1888, the artist Walter Crane read a paper on *The prospects of art under socialism.* As well as Shaw, Olivier, Wallas, and Annie Besant, one of the contributors to the discussion was Oscar Wilde. John Burns was there; he thought Wilde

...made a capital speech... [175]

At the start of 1889, Edward Carpenter lectured on *Civilization, its cause and its cure.*

Later that year, Sidney spoke on Charles Booth's *Life and Labour of the people of London.* It was just after he had reviewed the book for the London evening paper, the *Star*, praising Beatrice Potter's contribution. Llewellyn Smith was there.

In September 1888, Besant proposed to the Society that *Socialists should organise themselves as a political party.* This was opposed by William Morris, who argued that *it would be a false step for Socialists to attempt to take part in the Parliamentary contest.* Morris, who was backed up by Charlotte Wilson, lost; Annie Besant was supported by Shaw and by John Burns. It was a repeat of the debate that had already happened within the SDF.

When the SDF had split in 1884, Burns had sided with those who favoured contesting elections. He followed this by standing – unsuccessfully – in Nottingham in 1885. One of his leading supporters there was Harry Snell. Snell, aged 20, had grown up in rural Nottinghamshire, the child of agricultural workers. He had started work, aged 8, as a bird-scarer; when he was 12 years old, he stood for hire in the market place. By 1885 Snell was both a secularist and an SDF member. He thought Burns a magnificent candidate, whose

...power as a popular street-corner orator was probably unequalled in that generation. [176]

From autumn 1886, Burns became a regular attendee at Fabian meetings; he joined in the 1890s. He followed his Nottingham campaign by becoming, in 1889, a Battersea representative on the first London County Council. In 1892 he was elected MP for Battersea. Burns' fellow Battersea SDF member, W Stephen Sanders, worked for the Battersea Labour League, Burns' electoral vehicle. Sanders joined the Fabians in 1890.

As the socialist revival of the 1880s gathered pace, leading speakers from all the organisations – the Fabians GBS and Sidney; Morris, Eleanor Marx and Aveling for the Socialist League; Hyndman, Burns and others for the SDF – were speaking regularly every night of the week across London, at clubs, open air meetings, and other events.

In 1888, J J Dent, secretary of the Club and Institute Union, talked to Beatrice Potter *in tones of mingled admiration and suspicion* about the particular contribution of the Fabians:

...a group of clever young men who, with astonishing energy and audacity, were haranguing the London Radical clubs... [177]

Dent told Beatrice that the group included some very clever speakers

...but the man who organises the whole business, drafts the resolutions and writes the tracts, is Sidney Webb. [178]

While the early Fabian meetings covered a broad canvas, a more focussed approach emerged from Fabian publications, or Tracts. Long afterwards, Shaw explained why he had recruited Sidney:

...I made Webb join. I knew that what these people needed was Facts for Socialists, *and that Webb alone could write it. Marx was at the back of this; for I knew from my own experience that* Das Kapital *had changed the mind of Europe not by Marxist dialectics translated into a pseudo-Hegelian jargon that only philosophers could understand and nobody could read, but by the terrific battery of official facts dug out by Marx in the British Museum Reading Room from the reports of the factory inspectors.* [179]

Facts for Socialists is just that: a 15-page penny pamphlet, crammed with statistics on income and wealth, housing and poverty, and leavened with quotations from economists and commentators. Published in January 1887, by 1890 it had sold 25000 copies; by 1897, 40,000. Successive editions, regularly updated, remained in print until 1955. Sidney battered the reader remorselessly with snippets of information, illustrated with simple diagrams. He dominated the Fabian policy output. He wrote all three of the tracts that appeared in 1889. The Society began to emphasize municipal socialism in a series of twenty-eight pamphlets, nineteen of them written by Sidney.

In 1888 the Fabians organised a lecture series on the basis and prospects of socialism. The lecturers were Sidney, GBS (two lectures), William Clarke, Sydney Olivier, Annie Besant, Hubert Bland, and Graham Wallas. The inspiration came from Sidney. Wallas suggested that the lectures should be published as a book; Shaw was made editor, and made responsible for finding a publisher. He reported that the result was *commercially unproducible* – so the authors decided to shoulder the risk themselves. The initial print run was 1000, at a selling price of six shillings (30p). Walter Crane designed the cover; May Morris, daughter of William, designed the spine (though her father was highly critical of the content of the book).

The book was called *Fabian Essays*: within a month of publication,1000 copies were sold. Within a year, 20,000 copies had gone, and it was still selling at 400 copies a week. Shaw said it *went off like smoke*.

Sidney's own contribution to *Fabian Essays* was a chapter on the historic background. He described the great increase in the nineteenth century both in direct provision by the state, and in regulation, inspection, and control by the state. He equated the provision of services, or the undertaking of activities, by central or local government, under democratic control, with socialism. He noted

...the general failure to realize the extent to which our unconscious socialism has already proceeded. [180]

The largest employer in Britain was a government minister, the Postmaster General, and

...almost every conceivable trade is, somewhere or other, carried on by parish, municipality, or the National Government itself without the intervention of any middleman or capitalist. [181]

Sidney saw this as an inevitable consequence of political reform, the widening of the franchise:

...the unconscious abandonment of the old Individualism, and our irresistible glide into collectivist Socialism. [182]

Every increase in the political power of the proletariat will most surely be used by them for their economic and social protection. [183]

The approach Sidney outlined in his contribution to *Fabian Essays* had a long and powerful influence on British Fabian and Labour thought. GDH Cole wrote that *Fabian Essays* was

The most important single publication in the history of British Socialism. [184]

Henry Pelling suggested that *Fabian Essays* underpinned British socialism for fifty years. In practice, the influence lasted for nearly a century; Sidney also wrote:

No nation having once nationalized or municipalized any industry has ever retraced its steps or reversed its action. [185]

But at the turn of 1889 the possibility of retracing steps lay far in the future.

Chapter Four: Joseph and Sidney

FRIENDSHIP AND THE READING ROOM

In the mid-1880s, while Sidney Webb was making his way in London radical and socialist politics, Beatrice Potter was becoming a social investigator.

In the same period Beatrice became fascinated, even obsessed, by the politician Joseph Chamberlain. Apart from Chamberlain, there is little information on the emotional relationships of either Beatrice or Sidney before 1890.

I was not made to be loved, Beatrice reflected in 1883:
There must be something repulsive in my character. [186]

Beatrice wrote that, as a young woman, she enjoyed dancing and flirting. But she left few details. In Switzerland in July 1882 with her father and Rosie, she met John Main, a young professor from the South Kensington School of Science. Before the holiday, Beatrice had been lonely; now, she found the company of the young professor *delightful.* They walked together; they had long, serious talks. Rosie wrote later that Main *fell violently in love* with Beatrice and *made her an offer* [187] before the Potters left. Rosie was struck by the speed and intensity of his courtship.

But Beatrice was ambivalent: she felt guilty at having *given way to a pleasure, thoughtlessly ignoring what pain might come of it.* She reproached herself with having neglected her father and Rosie.

Eighteen months later, meeting another South Kensington academic, Beatrice learned that Main was consumptive, and had gone abroad for his health

...to the Engadine or Colorado. [188]

Beatrice mused

Two young human beings – on the threshold of life and on the verge of an ever-uniting love. Parted – for ever – one to die – the other to live a life of? [189]

Sidney had also known disappointment. Bernard Shaw said that Sidney

...used to come out in spots when he fell in love, which he did first with a lady who did not reciprocate... [190]

In 1885 Sidney had hoped to marry Annie Adams. Instead, she married Corrie

Grant – a barrister, later a Liberal MP. Sidney shared his sorrows with Wallas, and later with GBS:

Spent the evening with Webb at Colonial Office. He told me about his love affair and disappointment. [191]

In 1888 Edward Pease, the Fabian secretary, became engaged to Marjorie Davidson. Sidney wrote, congratulating Marjorie, but saying that in five years he had lost five close friends to marriage. Pease was another:

Now you are to come in and carry him off from me and others just as our friendship ripens. C'est dur. The loss is irreparable whatever you may intend to say. [192]

The Potter family annual routine, moving regularly from one grand house to another, continued after Lawrencina's death; Beatrice was now in charge. The annual stay in London for the season continued. Rosie Potter described how

Beatrice, seven years my senior, handsome and brilliantly clever, took over the control of the household, and to some extent of myself...

I had a great opinion of her abilities, as she, no doubt, had a contempt for mine... [193]

In February 1883, the Potters rented 47 Prince's Gate Kensington – part of a substantial development in Albertopolis, near the site of the 1851 Great Exhibition. It was a large house, requiring several staff. Leaving Standish for London, Beatrice wrote

I go with a sincere intention of devoting myself to Society and the family, but that familiar 'daemon' desire for self-improvement threatens to overcome intention. [194]

In 1884 Richard Potter gave up Standish, and moved his London base to an even grander address, York House, Kensington Gardens. In old age Rosie Potter recalled that Beatrice made the most of this new opportunity, and

...became, for a time, one of London's fashionable hostesses. [195]

The Potters used York House for three years; after Richard Potter had a stroke in 1885, there was less need for a home on such a scale. After the 1887 season they did not return.

Rosie had been deeply affected by her mother's death. She wrote later that she became preoccupied with her father, and

...intensely jealous of my sisters. [196]

Beatrice thought Rosie was vulnerable; but she was also critical:

No imagination, no spirit of adventure... [197]

she noted in March 1883.

The family arranged for Rosie to spend some time at a French boarding school – Les Ruches, at Fontainebleau, near Paris – run by Marie Souvestre, a pioneer of women's education. The school attracted the daughters of prosperous (and liberal) families from France, Britain, and the United States – including Joseph Chamberlain's daughter, Beatrice, and the daughters of the Strachey family. In 1884 Souvestre gave up the Paris school, and instead started one at Wimbledon, near London; in London she became friendly with Beatrice.

Lacking a Potter London home after 1886, Beatrice began to stay at the Devonshire House Hotel, run by the Quakers and adjacent to their headquarters, near Liverpool Street station.

In the 1880s Beatrice relied on her small group of close women friends. She could talk to them freely and openly – unlike her sisters, who

...secretly condemn my want of success and think my aim absurdly out of proportion to my capacity. [198]

Beatrice regularly listed her friends in her diary; Carrie Darling, Ella Pycroft and Margaret Harkness were always high on the list. These four young women set out to lead independent lives, without necessarily marrying, or continuing to depend on their parents and relations. At times they shared accommodation, or worked together, or travelled together. They talked and corresponded about life, work, and relationships, trying to balance career aspirations against the traditional pattern of marriage and family. Of the four, Beatrice probably came from the most affluent background.

Beatrice wrote informal wills; her 1882 will asked her father to make a settlement for *my only two great friends*, Carrie Darling and Margaret Harkness. Later she added that her father should send her diaries to Carrie

I don't want any of the sisters to see them. [199]

She made another will in 1886

To Margaret Harkness I leave any books that belong to me and any of the pictures in my room she cares for. [200]

Carrie Darling worked as governess to the children of Beatrice's sister, Mary Playne, later becoming a teacher. Unlike Beatrice, she had no choice but to work. She also experienced several personal relationships: in Beatrice's words

*Twice or three times she was engaged or 'kept company'; for her lower middle
class origin showed itself in her love affairs if nowhere else. Jilted or jilting, she
lived through them all, with little display of passion: her whole enthusiasm
centred in learning.* [201]

In 1882, Carrie was offered a headship in Australia and emigrated, taking
her four sisters with her. Carrie's school was successful; the sisters found work.
In October 1882, Carrie wrote

Ah Bee it was right to come. I am needed here and I was not in England. [202]

Complications followed. Carrie became involved with a married male teacher
at a nearby school; after four years of *struggle and misery* he left, to teach in Japan.
Then, Beatrice heard that Carrie had

…thrown up her school: her lover had got a divorce, or was getting one… [203]

Carrie sailed for Japan – but on the way she became engaged to the ship's
captain. Beatrice commented

Oh! Woman, you are passing strange. [204]

Ella Pycroft's father was a doctor; Ella herself worked as a lady visitor with
Beatrice in East London. They regularly confided in each other. Ella had a long,
troubled relationship with Maurice Paul, a medical student, also involved with
Booth's research. Maurice had lived and worked in Katherine Buildings, running
a boys' club.

In autumn 1886, Maurice asked Ella to marry him; then, she turned him
down – but two years later accepted. In 1889 they both stayed with Beatrice at
The Argoed

*A queer pair, absorbed in one another: I see little of them, which suits my
student life: but they serve as 'company' over the afternoon and evening cigarette.*
[205]

A year later it was over: Maurice had gone off with a (much older) nursing
sister; Ella came to stay again. Beatrice was critical:

*For the last two years those two have had daily and hourly companionship: he
lodging opposite her and living in her rooms. Of course his health broke down
under the unnatural relationship: constant love-making without the natural
physical fulfilment… Miserable boy – I warned him 4 years ago against these
unhealthy maudlin friendships… he will go from woman to woman, ruining
other lives and dissipating his own.* [206]

Margaret Harkness turned first to nursing, then to pharmacy, before becoming a writer. Beatrice had known her cousin Margaret for longer than she had known Carrie or Ella; for fifteen years Margaret was probably Beatrice's closest friend of her own generation. And Margaret had nursed Beatrice's mother in her last illness.

Beatrice and Margaret confided in each other, but it was a complex relationship, laced with episodes of competition and suspicion. At first, Beatrice had thought Margaret

...an hysterical egotistical girl with wretched health and still worse spirits. [207]

Later, she wrote that her feeling for Margaret had been

...one of pity not liking... [208]

Once Margaret had loosened her ties with her family, however, and her career was starting to succeed, Beatrice thought she was

...blossoming out into a clever, interested and amusing young woman with much charm of looks and manner. [209]

In 1885, they looked back on their conversations at school, ten years earlier. They had thought they would be talking about cooks and baby-linen:

...who would have thought of our real future – our struggling for our livelihood – with queer experiences of a working-woman's life – of another – with her cook and big establishment – but also absorbed in work outside home duty – both passed through the misery of strong and useless feeling.[210]

Beatrice was fascinated by Margaret's new life, which she called *literary piece-work.* In 1882 Margaret (who had obtained a reader's ticket in 1880) introduced Beatrice to the British Museum Reading Room

The little glimpses into the British Museum life through Maggie Harkness and the Pooles [British Museum Curator who helped Harkness] interested me...they are like the worms, who prepare the soil.[211]

This was Beatrice's first contact with the Reading Room and its regulars. Margaret Harkness and Beatrice remained close through the 1880s.

The Reading Room provided a London base for many aspiring writers. When he arrived in London, GBS found that the Reading Room provided

...all the advantages of communal heating, lavatory accommodation and electric light, with a comfortable seat, unlimited books, and ink and blotting paper all for nothing... [212]

Women writers worked and met there. Beatrice became a regular visitor; in April 1886 she got her own reader's ticket. The poet Amy Levy described the Reading Room in 1888:

For some it is a workshop, for others a lounge; there are those who put it to the highest uses, while in many cases it serves as a shelter,—a refuge, in more senses than one, for the destitute. [213]

In 1887 some of Beatrice's Bacup cousins visited London; Beatrice showed them round:

…the one thing they delighted in was the endless galleries of books in the British Museum. [214]

Among others, Beatrice met Eleanor Marx, the south African exile Olive Schreiner, and Amy Levy, at the Reading Room. Clementina Black – novelist, Fabian, and trade unionist – was another Reading Room regular.

Eleanor (Tussy) Marx, the sixth child of Karl Marx, was another literary pieceworker. From 1884 Eleanor and Edward Aveling lived on Great Russell Street, near the Museum. Beatrice encountered her in May 1883

Went in afternoon to British Museum and met Miss Marx in refreshment rooms. Daughter of Karl Marx, socialist writer and refugee. [215]

They discussed socialism, and religion. But for Beatrice, there was no basis for friendship:

…evidently peculiar views on love, etc, and I should think has somewhat 'natural' relations with men! Should fear that the chances were against her remaining long within the pale of 'respectable' society. Asked me to come and see her. Exactly the life and character I should like to study. Unfortunately, one cannot mix with human beings without becoming more or less connected with them. [216]

Olive Schreiner arrived from South Africa in 1881, intending to train as a doctor. Instead she became a writer, working in the Reading Room. Schreiner's novel, *The Story of an African Farm* (1883) established her reputation as both narrator and feminist. Olive knew both Eleanor Marx and Margaret Harkness. Like Beatrice, she sometimes stayed at the Devonshire House Hotel. They met there in October 1887; Beatrice wrote

She is a wonderfully attractive little woman, brimming over with sympathy and thought. [217]

Next spring Schreiner wrote to Beatrice

I look out always eagerly for whatever you write. You are one of the few women I want to know more of. If you come to London while I am here will you please let me know. [218]

Amy Levy, born 1861, had studied at Newnham College Cambridge. She travelled in Europe, then returned to her parents' home in London. She had some success with her poetry, which was praised by Oscar Wilde and by WB Yeats; she had two novels published.

Success as a writer did not come easily for Margaret Harkness. In 1883-84 she went to Germany – to learn the language, and because she could live there for half the cost of London. She soon came back, turning to the Potters for help:

I am not satisfied with my present position. I have tried literature for nearly three years... My brain is being worn out, and my health too...

But before returning to nursing I want to make one more trial. I want to be able to say, 'I <u>proved</u> I had no real talent, no special worth in literature, otherwise I shall be haunted by the idea in my nursing, & perhaps bitterly reproach [?] myself. [219]

She wanted to borrow money, and asked Beatrice to discuss it with her father:

I hate asking favours, but you know how much I am in earnest about my life, & how much I desire to do what is right...[220]

Margaret's immediate family could not help; support from elsewhere would come with conditions. It is unclear whether Richard Potter lent money to Margaret; some recent writers conclude that he did. [221] In 1887, in a letter to Beatrice mostly about other issues, Margaret wrote

I enclose a note to your father to thank him.[222]

Her first major breakthrough came with the publication of *A City Girl* in 1887.

'DANCING IN A DREAM TOWARDS SOME PRECIPICE'

On 3 June 1883 Beatrice dined with Caroline Williams, a Kensington neighbour. Another guest (and neighbour) was Joseph Chamberlain, 46-year-old President of the Board of Trade. The Potters were seasonal tenants at Prince's Gate; Chamberlain lived in a house there from 1880 until 1882, and then bought a house round the corner in Prince's Gardens. The costs exceeded his ministerial salary.

Chamberlain was the leading radical in Gladstone's Liberal government. In March he had attacked aristocracy in general, and the Conservative leader in particular:

Lord Salisbury constitutes himself the spokesman of a class – of the class to which he himself belongs, who toil not neither do they spin.[223]

Queen Victoria approved neither of the man nor the speech; she had

…greatly deprecated Mr Chamberlain's being in the Cabinet…

The queen now thought her fears justified.[224]

Born in London, Chamberlain came from a nonconformist – Unitarian – family. Aged eighteen, he was sent to Birmingham to run a family business making screws. The business succeeded, and by the 1870s controlled 70% of Birmingham's output of screws.

He switched from business to politics, working with nonconformists and Liberals, opposing the funding of church (Anglican or Catholic) schools from local taxation. In 1869 he became a city councillor. He created the Caucus, a formidable local political machine, which in 1873 achieved Liberal majorities on both the Council and the separate School Board. Chamberlain handed over the business, becoming full-time Mayor.

Under Chamberlain's leadership, Birmingham brought both gas and water under municipal control. Some called it *gas and water socialism*. He then led large scale redevelopment. In 1876 he became a Birmingham MP.

By 1883, Chamberlain had been married twice; both brides had come from West Midlands, nonconformist, business families. Both had died during, or shortly after childbirth. He had six children.

Beatrice was fascinated. Her frank, detailed diary documents the relationship from beginning to end. This is not matched by any record from Chamberlain's side. He left no personal letters; a Chamberlain biographer warns that Beatrice's

…descriptions of Chamberlain and their encounters need to be taken with caution. [225]

Her vignettes of Chamberlain and his household are caricatures, with the truth and distortion of the bold and brilliantly overdrawn descriptive style she develops in her diary. [226]

Beatrice's sister Rosie observed the relationship as it developed, leaving an account of it in her own unpublished autobiography.

She described how Chamberlain

…obviously admired Beatrice and soon fell in love with my beautiful and clever sister and there is little doubt that she was greatly attracted by him and also perhaps by the position he had to offer her, but she had already developed strong views of her own which she felt she could not give up for any man however great. [227]

Some time later, Beatrice was invited to another dinner at Caroline Williams' home. When the day came, Beatrice had a headache, and persuaded Rosie to go instead. Miss Williams asked Chamberlain to take Rosie down to dinner; he was

…disappointed that instead of the brilliant Miss Beatrice Potter it was her insignificant younger sister he had to sit next to during dinner, so after a few perfunctory remarks he turned from me to the lady on his other side. [228]

Beatrice saw Chamberlain again later in June. Herbert Spencer held an annual picnic for his friends; the Potters were always invited. In 1883 the Chamberlains came too (though neither Joseph nor Herbert had much time for each other). Beatrice talked to Joseph's sister Clara

…a really genuine woman who is somewhat perplexed and bored by London Season life. [229]

Joseph arrived later

…and I had much conversation with him. His personality interests me.[230]

In July Chamberlain dined with the Potters;

Curious and interesting character, dominated by intellectual passions *with little self-control but with any amount of* purpose. [231]

She did not understand Chamberlain's passions

How I should like to study that man! [232]

The season was ending. Chamberlain had made a deep impression on Beatrice

He had energy and personal magnetism, in a word masculine force to an almost superlative degree.[233]

Later she called the relationship *the catastrophe of my life*. Nothing like this had ever happened to her before. From her room in Princes Gate, *sleepless from excitement*, she lay awake watching the sunrise. In August she wrote

Alas! Alas! The whirlpool! [234]

Looking back nearly twenty years later, Beatrice tried to explain what had happened

At once, and I think on both sides, there arose the question of marriage. He was seeking a wife, attractive, docile, capable. I was ripe for love, revelling in newly acquired health and freedom, my intelligence wide awake, my heart unclaimed. He absorbed the whole of my sexual feeling, but I saw him at rare intervals and loved him in the imagination, in his absence more than in his presence. [235]

Beatrice spent most of summer 1883 out of London.

In September 1883, the Three Choirs Festival was at Gloucester; the Potters hosted a house party at Standish. Later that month, Beatrice stayed a week with Chamberlain's daughter, another Beatrice. They discussed Joseph; Beatrice Potter reflected

Coming from such honest surroundings he surely must be straight in intention... [236]

Beatrice Chamberlain warned her guest about Joseph's

...very conventional view of women... [237]

Beatrice Potter wrote to her sister Mary that this meant she might be

...saved all temptation by my unconventionality... [238]

In November Beatrice made her first visit to Bacup. Before leaving, she had invited Chamberlain and two of his children to come to Standish after Christmas. She was in a state of indecision:

Alas! the whirlpool. Only two months and I shall be sailing past it for weal or for woe. [239].

She kept Carrie Darling, in Queensland, informed; on 3 November Carrie wrote to her

Beatrice dearest I know you will get married but don't don't say goodbye to me in consequence...You shall not say goodbye to me Beatrice. [240]

The Chamberlain family did come to Standish in January 1884. The Potters gave a ball; the house was full of young people. Beatrice felt as if she had been

...dancing in a dream towards some precipice. [241]

Richard Potter was not welcoming. After greeting Chamberlain, he returned to his patience game looking absent and distressed,

...utterly disgusted at the supposed *intentions of his visitor.*[242]

Rosie Potter said that their father *very much objected to the match*; he did not want a son-in-law who was more distinguished than himself. [243]

Over dinner, and walking in the gardens next morning, Beatrice and Joseph got down to practicalities

...after some shyness, we plunged into essentials and he began to delicately hint his requirements. [244]

Chamberlain talked about his life

Hitherto the well-to-do have governed this country for their own interests; and I will do them this credit, they have achieved their object. Now I think the time is approaching for those who work and have not. My aim in life is to make life pleasanter for this great majority. I do not care if in the process it becomes less pleasant for the well-to-do minority.[245]

Beatrice felt he was watching her to see whether she yielded to his absolute supremacy.

If I objected to or ventured to qualify his theories or his statements, he smashed objections and qualifications by an absolute denial, and continued his assertion.[246]

Beatrice was exhausted; Chamberlain felt as if he had been making a speech. Beatrice thought it was the end; Chamberlain had reached the same conclusion. And this was before they talked about women's role.

The following morning Chamberlain suggested another walk:

'I have only one domestic trouble: my sister and daughter are bitten with the women's rights mania. I don't allow any action on the subject.'
'You don't allow division of opinion in your household, Mr Chamberlain?'
'I can't help people thinking differently from me.'
'But you don't allow the expression of the difference.'
'No'
And that little word ended our intercourse.[247]

That seemed final. But Beatrice was still fascinated

...he is an enthusiast and a despot.
...running alongside this genuine enthusiasm is a passionate desire to crush opposition to his will, a longing to put his foot on the necks of others...[248]

Rosie Potter was at Standish when the Chamberlains came to stay. She recalled that

Chamberlain left without having succeeded in persuading Beatrice to become his wife, for she could not bring herself to give up her own individuality and to merge her own in another's mind. [249]

Then Beatrice Chamberlain invited Beatrice to stay at Highbury, the family home in Birmingham. Beatrice, thinking negotiations were ended, saw no harm in going.

She was not impressed by the house:

Inside there is very <u>much taste</u> and all very bad. [250]

After dinner at there was a rally at the Town Hall. Beatrice described Chamberlain's performance

As he rose and stood silently before his people, his whole face and form seemed transformed. The crowd became wild with enthusiasm. Hats, handkerchiefs, coats were waved frantically as an outlet for feeling…

Perfectly still stood the people's tribune, till the people, exhausted and expectant, gradually subsided into fitful and murmuring cries. [251]

Beatrice thought the audience's relationship to Chamberlain was like that of a woman to a lover:

Perfect response, unquestioning receptivity. Who reasons with his mistress? The wise man asserts his will, urges it with warmth or bitterness, and flavours it with flattery and occasional appeals to moral sentiments. [252]

Chamberlain always wore an orchid; he grew them at Highbury. The morning after the rally, he took Beatrice on a tour of the orchid houses. She did not think he tried to please her; rather, that he had

…an intense desire that I should think and feel like him … [253]

She had thought everything was finished; now it was opaque again. Six weeks later she remained in turmoil

I don't know how it will all end. Certainly not in my happiness. As it is, his personality absorbs all my thought … [254]

In April, the Potters returned to London. Beatrice's mind was still not made up. She had worried over the issue for five months, had

…done little else but think about it; now I am no nearer solving it. [255]

She was torn – between her attraction to Chamberlain, her career hopes, and her responsibility towards her sister Rosie. She became introspective, then depressed.

Parts of her thought the relationship was over; other parts would not let go. In May she wrote

> *The woman's nature in me has been stirred to its depths; I have loved and lost; but possibly by my own willful mishandling possibly also for my own happiness; but still lost…*
>
> *There is glitter all around me and darkness within, the darkness of blind desire yearning for the light of love.*[256]

Carrie Darling thought about Beatrice constantly, but hesitated to write

> *…lest my letters should find you married and so disinclined for a while to talk with me. Your letter tells me how much you have learned of life since I saw you. Woman cannot live* happily *alone. That I know to my bitter cost, but I am determined to show that she can live* usefully *alone.* [257]

In summer 1884 Beatrice saw Chamberlain once or twice:

> *…there was a little flicker of feeling and then it died.*[258]

She wondered if she would hear that he had married someone else.

In August, still brooding, Beatrice travelled to Switzerland and Bavaria with Margaret Harkness:

> *…passion, with its burning heat, and emotion which had for long smouldered unnoticed, burst out into flame, and burnt down intellectual interests, personal ambition, and all other self-developing motives.* [259]

Margaret told Beatrice that for the first time she felt at one with the world; Beatrice appreciated Margaret's company, calling her an intimate friend,

> *…but day and night I cried secretly over the past…* [260]

Back in England in the autumn, Beatrice once more told herself it was finished:

> *The storm has swept over. I can once again go on my way, if I knew only which way to turn.* [261]

But then Chamberlain's sister Clara (who was shortly to marry Frederick Ryland) came to stay, telling Beatrice tales of Joe's childhood. They met again in the new year.

Again Beatrice wrote as if the relationship had ended:

...this morning's talk seemed like the dropping of the curtain over the tragic end... [262]

In July 1885, Chamberlain dined with the Potters. Gladstone's government had been defeated in a vote in June; Chamberlain was no longer a Minister; the Conservative Lord Salisbury was Prime Minister.

Kate's husband, Leonard Courtney, had opposed a Liberal government bill. Chamberlain was blunt about him:

Your brother-in-law is an ass. Proportional Representation lost him his chance of distinction in political life. This has lost him his seat.[263]

He looked intently at Beatrice, trying to gauge her reaction.

A week later the Courtneys arranged a country picnic for Beatrice and Chamberlain to talk. It did not go well:

The day will always remain engraved on my memory as the most painful one of my life. The scene under the Burnham beeches, forcing me to tell his fortune – afterwards, behaving with great rudeness and indifference.[264]

Afterwards Kate wrote to Beatrice:

...to me there was no sign or trace of any other feeling than an intense personal ambition and desire to dominate at whatever cost of other people's rights – I do not even see any room in his nature for such an affection as would satisfy one of us. It would be a tragedy – a murder of your independent nature – just as he and his minions will destroy if they can, and crush out all independent political thought in England... [265]

In letters and in her diary, Beatrice now referred to Chamberlain as *the great man*. She wrote to her sister Mary

...I should think one or other of us would break off this enigmatical relationship this autumn, by refusing to see more of each other.[266]

She also wrote to Mary Booth, probably more explicitly; Mary thought Beatrice was better off without Chamberlain

I can't tell you the feeling of relief that your letter has given me...I do rejoice to know that the decision is 'No'... you never could be happy and would be increasingly unhappy with that man in such a relation to you.[267]

She added in October:

...the more I hear and read of that man, the more satisfied I am of the rightness of your decision and the more thankful I am that you have made it. [268]

Even the picnic did not end Beatrice's contact with the Chamberlains. In October 1885 Clara Ryland invited Beatrice to stay:

What has become of you I wonder? Are you at present inhabiting a Kensington Mansion or a Whitechapel slum, or are you peacefully reposing yourself after the London season on the shores of Windermere?[269]

The visit happened in November. It was another disaster. Beatrice told Clara how she felt about Chamberlain. But

...I broke down utterly and she told me I was mistaken. The brother had never thought of me. And this after she had talked to me and examined me as to my intentions a year since. [270]

Then came Richard Potter's stroke; Beatrice assumed responsibility for his care. Later, Beatrice called this time *the dead point* in her life. Looking back, she thought she suffered from a divided personality, between

...the normal woman seeking personal happiness in love given and taken within the framework of a successful marriage: while the other self claimed, in season and out of season, the right to the free activity of 'a clear and analytic mind'. [271]

In December 1885 there was a general election. Gladstone formed another Liberal government. Chamberlain hoped to be Colonial Secretary. Instead, he became President of the Local Government Board (LGB), responsible for the Poor Law and unemployment – insofar as any department covered unemployment – an emerging political issue with neither an agreed definition, nor any accepted remedy.

In early 1886, Beatrice was gloomy, anxious, and depressed. Matters remained unresolved with Chamberlain. And, after Richard Potter's stroke, Rosie Potter became even more jealous of her sisters, developing

...an almost hysterical and possessive passion for him... [272]

Again, the sisters arranged for Rosie to spend some time abroad.
On 11 February Beatrice wrote one of her most morbid diary entries:

I struggle through each new day, waking with suicidal thoughts early in the morning... When will pain cease? Hopelessness is not yet complete: I look out tonight on the beating of that hateful grey sea, the breaking and vanishing of the surf on the shore; the waves break and vanish like spasms of my feeling, but they return again and again – and behind them is the bottomless ocean of despair. Eight and twenty! Living a life without hope... [273]

That month, there were disturbances in London. A demonstration in support of tariffs clashed with an SDF unemployed march. Beatrice wrote to the *Pall Mall Gazette* about unemployment, based on her experience at Katherine Buildings. The letter was published as a short article. At this point, Beatrice still expressed orthodox COS views, opposing relief works and more generous outdoor relief.

Chamberlain read the article. He wrote to Beatrice suggesting a meeting, saying

> *My Department knows all about Paupers and Pauperism, but has no official cognizance of distress above the Pauper line.* [274]

He thought something should be done, arguing in favour of *some poorly remunerated employment* – which would neither be degrading, nor compete with existing jobs, nor tempt people to stay longer than necessary.

Beatrice was *ominously excited* when she saw Chamberlain's handwriting

> *…I knew it was the old torture coming back again.*[275]

There was no meeting; but Beatrice sent two letters

> *But is it not rather unkind of you to ask me to tell you what I think? I have tried to be perfectly truthful. Still, it* is *a ludicrous idea that an ordinary woman should be called upon to review the suggestion of Her Majesty's ablest minister! especially when I know that he has a slight opinion of even a superior woman's intelligence in these matters (I agree with him) and a dislike to any independence of thought.*[276]

She added a more personal note, which she copied into her diary:

> *Now I see I was right not to deceive you. I could not lie to the man I loved. But why have worded it so cruelly, why give unnecessary pain?…Do not think that I do not consider your decision as* final *and destroy this.*[277]

Chamberlain got his public works programme; on 20 March, the LGB authorised local authorities to run relief work schemes. It was virtually his last act as a Liberal Minister: on 26 March, he resigned in disagreement with Gladstone's policy of Irish Home Rule.

Beatrice watched his resignation speech from the gallery of the House of Commons, noting that his voice was particularly clear, with

> *…that peculiar 'timbre' that gives it its charm…*
>
> *I felt how vastly superior the great man was to me. How unworthy it had been for me to dwell exclusively on the personal side of our relationship. If I had been equal to friendship!* [278]

But she was still fascinated. In May 1886 she saw Chamberlain's daughter Beatrice – who, like Joseph, was depressed.

Beatrice spent summer 1886 at The Argoed with her father and Rosie Potter; Beatrice was writing a paper on economics. At the end of August Beatrice Chamberlain joined them for a week. This was a *painful happiness* for Beatrice, still brooding

I could not have idealized that man, though I loved him so passionately.[279]

At the end of September, she

Spent two days castle-building about the great man at Highbury and reread that episode of six months ago. He either has a cautious wish to show that he has forgotten, or he does not wish to lose all hold on me, for he half asked through Beatrice for an invitation here (which of course he did not get) …For me, it would be happier if I never heard more of that family. They have been black friends for me. But faithfulness, pride, and sentiment hold me from a complete separation.[280]

Beatrice doubted whether she would see Chamberlain again. But in October she again stayed with Clara, at Highbury, in Joseph's absence. Despite everything, she saw Clara as a friend:

…I think she used me badly in her anxiety to give her brother just what he wanted, when he wanted it and to throw it overboard when he found it did not suit. [281]

In December Beatrice read an article about the concept of multiple personality; she seized on the idea and applied it to herself.

My intimacy with the great man brought about a deadly fight between the intellectual and the sensual, the sensual bringing forth the nethernmost being and for a time overwhelming the higher part. But the intellectual has triumphed not by its own strength but by the force of circumstance… The nethernmost being, however, stands there, vain, despondent, grasping, waiting only for physical depression to clutch and strangle the Ego.[282]

Beatrice returned to this analysis in *My Apprenticeship* (1926).

Just before Christmas 1886 Beatrice decided to end contact with the Chamberlains. She would see Clara once more; then it would all be over.

But then, in May 1887 Chamberlain contacted her:

…another act of the old, old story…[283]

Out of government, he again asked her what should be done about East London; he had talked to Charles Booth. He invited her to visit Birmingham again, for another rally – and she did.

Things had changed – a smaller crowd, a different speech:

Sentimental sympathy for the wrongs of the down-trodden masses was exchanged for a determination to preserve law and order. The statesman had overcome the demagogue. [284]

Nevertheless

...after he sat down it was natural our eyes should meet in the old way.[285]

She did not attend the all-male dinner at Highbury, instead meeting Chamberlain at his brother's house. All the old ambivalence reappeared. She accused him of not treating her with simple respect.

But he behaved towards me as the triumphant lover, as a man who is sure of his conquest. [286]

In spite of all that had happened, Beatrice invited him to stay at The Argoed –

...to come and see Father and enjoy bracing air and beautiful scenery. [287]

Chamberlain arrived on 30 July. At last Beatrice told him bluntly how strongly she felt but insisted they should not meet again:

...in another moment of suicidal misery [I] told him I cared for him passionately. This after he had pursued me for 18 months and dragged me back into an acquaintance I had all along avoided. To insist on meeting a woman who had told you she loved you in order to humiliate her further. [288]

Afterwards he wrote offering friendship. Of course, wrote Beatrice

...I was weak and gave way again, weak and romantic. But he did not like the tone of my letter. Perhaps that has saved me from more entanglement.[289]

Rosie had also been at the Argoed during the Chamberlain visit; once more, Beatrice and Joseph

...went for long walks together but it came to nothing and on the Monday morning Chamberlain left and we never saw him again. [290]

This was the final episode. After Chamberlain left, Beatrice was depressed. Mostly she stayed in her room. The wound remained. At Christmas 1887, back with her father at Bournemouth, Beatrice described the previous four years as *misery tempered only by humiliation.*

Beatrice ripped these pages out of her diary and sealed them up. She did not reopen them for three years, noting when she did

I was ready to humble myself by telling frankly of my deep and abiding feeling, how was it possible for a man, bred up in conventions, to see me as I was and to realize all the horrible suffering I was passing through.[291]

Ten years later she added

...in spite of knowing that I loved him desperately, he turned away and left me. [292]

In April 1888 Beatrice saw a newspaper placard: 'Chamberlain's marriage': while in the United States he had become engaged to Mary Endicott, daughter of an American cabinet member

A gasp, as if one had been stabbed, and then it is over.[293]

The wedding was in Washington DC in November: Beatrice's emotions were stirred up once more:

The blow has come. I thought the nerve was killed: it was only deadened, deadened and dying, dying in the life of new and growing interests. [294]

By day she walked about *with a bit of cold steel in my heart*; at night she tossed and turned. She prayed in Westminster Abbey. She brooded on Chamberlain's political future:

He must become a Tory. The tendencies of his life are already set in that direction: hatred of former colleagues, sympathy with the pleasure-loving, attractive class of 'English gentlemen' with which he now associates. [295]

The following Sunday Beatrice took communion at St Paul's, then walked across London to see Margaret Harkness in her Gower Street room, close to the British Museum.

SOCIALISM, UNEMPLOYMENT, AND THE DOCK STRIKE 1887-1889

Once Kate had married Leonard Courtney in 1883, only two of the sisters, Beatrice and Rosie, remained single. After Richard Potter's stroke in late1885, Beatrice carried two family responsibilities: towards her father, as his main carer; and towards her sister Rosie.

Rosie's condition fluctuated: the stays abroad did not resolve everything. In summer 1886 Beatrice thought Rosie

...a changed mortal. Sweet-tempered, modest and unselfish. [296]

But the following December, she described

...poor incapable Rosie, with her heavy face and irritating ways...[297]

In April 1888 Rosie became engaged to Arthur Dyson Williams, the barrister nephew of Caroline Williams, at whose home the couple had met. Dyson was closer to Aunt Caroline than to her sister, his mother; Caroline supported Dyson with an annual allowance of £400. Beatrice said that Caroline Williams was the *fairy godmother* to the young couple.

Rosie wrote later that, from puberty at thirteen,

...my thoughts were largely occupied with the other sex. [298]

She had been, however, like most girls at that time, brought up in

almost complete ignorance of the facts of life... [299]

Rosie thought Dyson was a brilliant, witty talker. She said he was

...the first man who seemed to care for me. [300]

Beatrice was not impressed with Dyson; she thought him respectable, but

...not likely to do brilliantly, with a small income of his own. He is not up to the mark of the other brothers-in-law, but then Rosy is the least gifted, mentally and physically, of the whole sisterhood. [301]

The wedding was in July, at The Argoed.

Afterwards Beatrice again became miserable and introspective. With Rosie married, she was now

...the last and only Potter! [302]

Chamberlain's third marriage had been announced, but the wedding itself had not yet taken place.

Beatrice's sisters Mary and Kate stayed on at The Argoed into August. Their conversation irritated Beatrice, who complained that they talked personalities all day:

...the more I see of other people the more I realise how utterly unintellectual we are as a family considering of course our (great!) ability. [303]

Later in August, Beatrice's friend Ella Pycroft came to stay at The Argoed. Together, they read about glorified spinsters – a newly-identified group in the population, described in an article in *Macmillan Magazine*. A glorified spinster was

…a plainly-dressed woman, clad in an ulster and unmistakeably home-made hat or bonnet.

Her bearing was self-reliant; she had

…an air of having some definite business to perform in a definite time…

She might work as a teacher, a nurse, an accountant, a clerk, or a librarian. The journalist had interviewed one of these women, who declared

An Old Maid is a woman 'minus something'; the Glorified Spinster is a woman 'plus something'. [304]

Beatrice thought it *…a cleverish paper,* which described

A new race of women not looking for or expecting marriage.' 'Self-dependent, courageous and cool-headed. [305]

Beatrice had described Rosie's wedding as *the last marriage of the Potter girls.* In her diary, she imagined what other guests at the wedding party might be saying to each other:

'…for you know that other Miss Potter is a confirmed old-maid – and has taken to writing and statistics etc.; you would hardly have thought it, would you? From looking at her ten years ago. Some say she was the prettiest of the lot; but then she took to queer ways and that never pays.'
'Ah! but it wasn't that (says a spiteful mother of unmarried daughters) she wanted to make a great marriage and failed.' So thinks the world.' [306]

The phrase 'glorified spinster' now entered Beatrice's vocabulary. A week after Ella had left The Argoed, Beatrice noted that Glorified Spinsterhood was at present *gilded by the charm of novelty and youth* [307] – though she was afraid that dark times and depression might return.

In October Beatrice heard that both Ella and Carrie were planning to marry (though Ella's planned marriage, to Maurice Paul, never happened). Beatrice had looked on both as

…settled in 'glorified spinsterhood'…
Ah! woman! she exclaimed. [308]

Beatrice's work, as researcher and reformer, flourished. A pattern developed of intense bursts of work in London, and long periods in the country with her father. She developed an interest in the organisation of work, and in particular with 'sweating': long working hours, combined with casual, uncertain, inter-mittent employment and low wages in insanitary, often dangerous conditions. Such work went largely unregulated by the Factory Acts. Her article on the London docks appeared in the *Nineteenth Century* in October 1887. The editor then suggested further pieces, on sweating, and on the cooperative movement.

Beatrice had already started researching sweated labour in tailoring. Beginning with some training in a cooperative workshop, in spring 1888 she worked for a short period as a *plain trouser hand* in East London sweatshops.

She drew on her diary to produce a vivid picture of life in the sector. This appeared in the *Nineteenth Century*, headlined *Pages from a Work Girl's Diary*, and contributed to her chapters, on tailoring and on London's Jewish community, in Booth's *Life and Labour*.

Before publication Beatrice gave evidence to a House of Lords Committee on sweating. She covered wages, conditions, housing, and the impact of Jewish immigration on the labour market. She dismissed the Committee –

...a set of well-meaning men, but not made of stuff fit for investigation. [309]

Her evidence was reported in the press; the *Pall Mall Gazette* described her as

...tall, supple, dark, with bright eyes... [310]

The following week, Beatrice was challenged by Lewis Lyons, an SDF-supporting trade unionist:

...she came to work (?) at ten o'clock in the morning and went home at three o'clock in the afternoon. That is not twelve hours a day. [311]

Beatrice responded that Lyons had confused the workshop at which she had been trained with those where she had worked incognito. She was upset by this

...detestable mis-statement of my evidence. [312]

She thought Margaret Harkness was responsible

...taking for granted all that the newspapers told of my evidence was true... spreading a report that I had been telling stories. [313]

Beatrice's interest in cooperation had originated with the visits to Bacup; in summer 1885 she had noted

Should like ...to go back to Bacup and learn Cooperative spirit.[314]

Both Charles Booth and the Cambridge economist Alfred Marshall tried to dissuade Beatrice from researching cooperation; Marshall told her that any man could write a history of cooperation; only she could write about women's work – and if she did, her name would be

...a household word two hundred years hence... [315]

But Beatrice, reluctant to be seen as just a specialist in women's issues, persisted. From February 1889 she worked on cooperation for the rest of that year.

She read widely – old copies of *Cooperative News*, old conference reports. She befriended leading cooperators, including Ben Jones, General Manager of the London Cooperative Wholesale Society. Jones was on the board for Booth's research; Beatrice thought him

...a worthy and able little man...began life as a Methodist, became a free thinker... [316]

She began to see cooperation

...with its production for use, and its elimination of the profit-maker... as *...a possible alternative to modern business enterprise...* [317]

Consumer cooperatives Beatrice termed *democracies of consumers*; she saw *democracies of workers* as complementary.

The research on cooperatives took Beatrice to the midlands, the north and Scotland. In March 1889 she was working in Lancashire and Yorkshire. Margaret Harkness was in Manchester, working on a new novel (published in 1890 as *A Manchester Shirtmaker*). After a few days in Hebden Bridge, Beatrice caught a train to Manchester and

...ran up to see Maggie Harkness in her lodgings...

Poor Maggie gets bitterer and bitterer – does foolish and inconsiderate things and then is vexed that she loses friends. Poor Maggie! – with her lonely tortuous life and envious temper. And yet for those in trouble she has plenty of warm sympathy... [318]

Once the cooperative research had been completed, Beatrice decided that her next project would be a study of trade unions.

The worlds of social reform and metropolitan politics overlapped: points of contact included the Fabian Society, Toynbee Hall, and the British Museum Reading Room. Later, Beatrice was surprised that, given the interests of the Fabians, and her own absorption in politics and economics,

...I failed to become known to any of the future Fabian essayists (apart from a slight acquaintance with Mrs Annie Besant, then at the zenith of her power as a great popular orator) until January 1890. [319]

Some reformers became more radical. Samuel and Henrietta Barnett were always high on Beatrice's list of friends. From the mid-1880s, widening divisions emerged between the Barnetts and the leaders of the Charity Organisation Society. Samuel and Henrietta now rejected the division of people into 'deserving' and 'undeserving'; it was

> ...a bad training for workers, and did much to limit the work undertaken as well as alienate the young and generous-hearted. [320]

In 1888 Samuel Barnett met a COS group:

> They were just impossible – refusing to do anything except to clothe themselves in the dirty rags of their own righteousness. [321]

The change mattered to Beatrice

> The break-away of Samuel and Henrietta Barnett in 1886 from the narrow and continuously hardening dogma of the Charity Organisation Society sent a thrill through the philanthropic world of London. [322]

Beatrice did not think the Barnetts were becoming socialists. But she saw that they now advocated socialistic measures, involving increased public administration and expenditure – beginning with their support in 1883 for old age pensions.

Margaret Harkness mixed with both socialists and reformers. Several papers – including the *Pall Mall Gazette* and *Justice*, the SDF paper – published her work regularly. Her first novel, *A City Girl*, was widely reviewed. Some reviews were critical – the *St James's Gazette* declared

> It had been better if this clever but unpleasant little study had never been committed to paper. [323]

But Friedrich Engels, sent a copy by Vizetelly the publisher, appreciated the book, writing to Harkness

> What strikes me most in your tale besides its realistic truth is that it exhibits the courage of the true artist. [324]

By 1890 she had published four novels.

Harkness had good contacts in the socialist movement. Between 1885 and 1887 she was close to the SDF, getting to know leading SDF members, including the trade unionists Tom Mann and John Burns, and Henry Hyde Champion, secretary of the SDF and editor of *Justice*. She was briefly an SDF member – but

> ...discovered it to be a dead body in a few months. Then I left it. [325]

She became critical of the SDF leadership; in October 1888 she went to see John Burns and his wife Pattie in Battersea, telling Burns that she was

...full of regrets for the present poor show of the Socialist movement and almost hopeless of good being done while several men who are now in it exercise the influence they do. [326]

The mid 1880s crisis in the London labour and housing markets galvanized political as well as philanthropic opinion. It reached both established Westminster politics, and the new, growing, socialist movement. This was the London that Booth studied; it was the London that Beatrice brought to public attention in her research and articles, and about which Harkness wrote in her novels.

The crisis formed the background to Beatrice's exchanges with Chamberlain in spring 1886. Since 1884 the SDF had organized demonstrations of unemployed people. Other demonstrations, demanding trade tariffs, were organized by groups on the right. On 8 February 1886, a pro-tariff demonstration in Trafalgar Square clashed with an SDF counter-demonstration, led by Burns, Hyndman, and Champion. Burns, carrying a red flag, led the socialist demonstration towards Hyde Park; some windows were broken and shops looted. Burns, Hyndman, Champion, and another were charged with sedition, but were acquitted.

Burns was less fortunate the following year. A Trafalgar Square demonstration against the government's Irish policy, planned for Sunday 13 November 1887, was prohibited by the police. This action united those opposed to policy in Ireland with those concerned to defend free speech, and the SDF.

The police broke up the demonstration; the day became known as Bloody Sunday. Margaret Harkness describes it in *Out of Work*. Ramsay Macdonald was there; so was GBS. Shaw and Annie Besant were

...swept aside by the front ranks of their own procession in counter-revolutionary retreat. [327]

Writing to William Morris, Shaw described his experience

Running hardly expresses our collective action. We skedaddled and never drew rein until we were safe on Hampstead Heath... [328]

Burns and the radical MP Cunninghame Graham were arrested and charged with

...riotously assembling to the terror and disturbance of Her Majesty's subjects. [329]

In January 1888, Burns and Cunninghame Graham were acquitted on the riotous assembly charge, but convicted of unlawful assembly, and sentenced to 6 weeks imprisonment. On 8 February he celebrated the anniversary of the 1886 riots in his Pentonville cell

…by singing Marseillaise Carmagnole and inscribed on my prison wall. Long live socialism. Ca Ira. [330]

Margaret Harkness was in Scotland in early 1888; she went to support Keir Hardie ahead of the March 1888 Mid Lanark byelection. She wrote to Beatrice, saying that she would not be back in London for some time. Harkness later said that she had paid Hardie's election expenses. Election expenses were a sensitive issue for the SDF: in the 1885 general election, it was alleged that the expenses of two London SDF candidates had been paid with 'Tory gold', and that Champion was implicated.

It was Harkness who introduced Beatrice to Annie Besant – secularist, Fabian, friend of GBS. Beatrice heard Besant talk to a Fabian audience on collective ownership of utilities. For Beatrice, Annie was

…the only woman I have ever known who is a real orator, who has the gift of public persuasion. [331]

But she did not approve:

…to see her speaking made me shudder. It is not womanly to thrust yourself before the world. [332]

In June 1888, the novelist Clementina Black spoke about female labour at one of the regular Fabian meetings. As well as Sidney Webb, Wallas and GBS, Annie Besant and Champion were there. After a discussion, Champion moved a resolution condemning Bryant and May, the East London match manufacturers, for paying starvation wages.

The next day Besant went to the Bryant and May factory and interviewed workers. Her interviews confirmed the low wages; she also documented the health risk of the phosphorus which workers handled. She publicized conditions in an article entitled *White Slavery in London.*

Management then asked the workers to sign a statement that they were happy with their conditions; some refused and were dismissed. 1400 then went on strike; they had no union, so they asked Besant help start one.

The new union campaigned publicly for a boycott of Bryant and May matches. Wallas and Besant reported to the next Fabian meeting, which took a collection in support of the strikers.

After three weeks the company re-employed the strikers. Later, the Webbs wrote that originally, without funds, without organisation, the match workers' struggle had seemed hopeless:

It was a new experience for the weak to succeed because of their very weakness, by means of the intervention of the public. [333]

They concluded that other groups of workers, seeing the match workers success, followed their example.

In 1889 two previously unorganised groups in London – gas-stokers and t dock workers – applied the lesson. They were supported by experienced trade unionists – among them Tom Mann, John Burns, and Ben Tillett – and by socialist activists, including Champion (no longer an SDF member, and now editor of a new paper, the *Labour Elector*), Eleanor Marx, and Annie Besant.

The dock strike began in August; a local dispute developed into a demand for sixpence an hour (the docker's tanner) across the port of London. As well as pay, the dockers' grievances included irregular work and casual employment. The strike committee was based at the Wade's Arms, in Poplar.

The strike captured public attention. Every day for a month, Burns, wearing a distinctive straw hat, led large, colourful demonstrations through the East End and the City. Llewellyn Smith, with Vaughan Nash, another Toynbee Hall resident, described the scene in their 1890 book on the strike

There are in all forty banners of trade and friendly societies; and fish-heads, onions and tiny loaves are carried on pikes as an object-lesson in dockers' fare to the magnates of the city. [334]

Beatrice was at The Argoed, caring for her father. She followed every detail:

The Dock Strike becoming more and more exciting – even watched at a distance. [335]

The hero was

John Burns the socialist, who seems for the time to have the East London working man at his feet... [336]

Beatrice felt depressed by her isolation, and her powerlessness to suggest a way out.

The dockers raised money, including donations from Australia. By 14 September they had won: the employers conceded the dockers' tanner, and some employment improvements. Employers and unions accepted mediation; the key mediator was Cardinal Manning, Archbishop of Westminster.

After the settlement, on 21 September, Samuel Barnett entertained the strike committee to supper at Toynbee Hall – Burns, Champion, Tillett and sixty others.

To begin her trade union study, in September Beatrice went to the annual

Trades Union Congress in Dundee. Burns and Besant stayed in London. Beatrice was struck by the hostility of the older union leaders to the new unionism; on 1 September she had breakfast with George Shipton, Chairman of the TUC General Council:

His view of the dock strike is strongly adverse to the men, and is visibly biased by his antipathy to, I might almost say hatred of, Burns…Clearly, whatever might be his sympathy for dock labour, his dislike of a socialist victory was the stronger feeling. [337]

But victory, when it came, was a socialist victory – which Beatrice celebrated:

The dock strike has ended in a brilliant victory for the men… [338]

While Beatrice had been away during the strike, Margaret Harkness was on the spot. She was close to some of the leaders and played a role in getting Manning to mediate. She wrote

…I happened to be at the Wade Arms when a general strike was suggested. That night I could not sleep. [339]

Next morning Harkness saw Manning; he left his own account:

On 5th September Miss Harkness came to me from the leaders of the strike to tell me that the coal heavers who had returned to work would strike again at noon the next day…If the coal supply had failed, the railroads and the gas factories would have been affected. [340]

Beatrice did not return to London until November. In September, she went to the annual trades union congress in Dundee. In early October, she helped to settle Richard Potter in what was to be his final home, a house at Box, close to the Playnes' home, Longfords.

The day Beatrice arrived back in London, 14 November, Harkness came to supper at the Devonshire House -

Sad to feel that I more and more distrust her. [341]

Beatrice knew that Harkness had been working closely with *the underground labour Party, with Champion, Burns, Mann etc.* Harkness told a complicated tale about Keir Hardie's election expenses and said she would write a book explaining all

I can tell you nothing now, but I shall get out of the whole thing someday – then I can tell you all. [342]

Poor Maggie! wrote Beatrice *A strange weariness and chronic depression adds*

pathos to her curious contortions… [343]

'A LONDON RETAIL TRADESMAN WITH THE AIMS OF A NAPOLEON'

Beatrice's stay in London in November 1889 was cut short abruptly. Her father's condition worsened, and the family were summoned back to Gloucestershire:

Father sinking – he may linger a few days, but Death is waiting…[344]

It was a difficult autumn for Beatrice. A year on from Chamberlain's re-marriage, some of her emotional wounds had healed, but the underlying hurt remained. On the anniversary, as twelve months earlier, Beatrice took communion at St Paul's:

…and prayed earnestly against bitterness and evil feelings.
Many of my thoughts during the last year have been unworthy. [345]

She wondered whether the coming year would be any better.

That September, Amy Levy, who Beatrice knew from the British Museum Reading Room, had taken her own life. Amy had been depressed, and upset by criticism of her novel *Reuben Sachs*. Beatrice did not usually mention the deaths of her friends in her diary; but she was unusually moved:

The very demon of melancholy gripping me: my imagination fastening on Amy Levy's story – a brilliant young authoress in the hey-day of success who has chosen to die rather than stand up longer to live. [346]

Margaret Harkness and Ella Pycroft, Beatrice's close friends, were in the thick of London politics after the Dock Strike. In London,

…strikes are the order of the day, the new trade unionism with its magnificent conquest of the docks…[347]

Beatrice, with her caring responsibility for her father, felt

…exiled from the world of the thought and action of other men and women. [348]

Her own research and writing were beginning to succeed, but her new project, on cooperatives, was proceeding slowly, held back by lack of company and lack of material. Beatrice felt she was

…struggling on day by day alone in the world. [349]

She dreamed of writing novels like Margaret Harkness; she longed

...to create characters and to move them to and fro among fictitious circumstances [350]

She was no longer involved in the conventional marriage market, which had dominated her early adult years. Now, Beatrice and her glorified spinster friends talked about whether they would ever marry – or whether they wanted to marry. Beatrice counselled them on their emotional relationships.

Carrie Darling was still in Australia: in occasional letters she kept Beatrice up to date with the tortuous course of her personal life:

Passionate love: a break: a sudden revival without seeing her lover but under the influence of imaginative pity – and then the whole thing dispelled: engaged to another man... [351]

Beatrice sympathized

God preserve me from a lover between 35 and 45: no woman can resist a man's importunity during the last years of an unrealised womanhood. [352]

Richard Potter rallied after his November crisis. During his illness, he told Beatrice

'I want one more son-in-law.'

'I should like to see my little Bee married to a good strong fellow', and the darling old Father dreams of the 'little Bee' of long ago: he does not realise that she has passed away, leaving the strong form and determination of the 'glorified spinster' bending over him as a mother bends over her sick child. [353]

Beatrice and two of the sisters, Mary and Kate, stayed on at Box over Christmas. The weather was gloomy; Beatrice's research remained slow.

Kate suggested Beatrice should go to London. Robert Browning, the poet, had died; Leonard Courtney was going to his funeral in Westminster Abbey. Beatrice could go too.

Rather a grim diversion, thought I, but I could go to the British Museum and get what I want – I will get Margaret Harkness to introduce me to someone there who will put me on the track. [354]

Forty years later Beatrice remembered Margaret's response

'Sidney Webb, one of the Fabian essayists, is your man. He knows everything: when you go out for a walk with him he literally pours out information.' [355]

So Margaret introduced Beatrice to Sidney early in January 1890. Beatrice had heard of Sidney Webb, but not met him. She had been told by John Dent (Secretary of the Club and Institute Union) *in tones of mingled admiration and suspicion* about a group of young men who were haranguing the London Radical Clubs. Some of them were clever speakers, but

> *…the man who organises the whole business, drafts the resolutions and writes the tracts, is Sidney Webb.* [356]

Fabian Essays was published at Christmas 1889; Beatrice read an early copy. Sending the book to a Coop contact, she wrote

> *. .by far the most significant and interesting essay is the one by Sidney Webb; he has the historic sense.*[357]

At that first meeting, in Margaret's lodgings on Gower Street, near the Museum, Sidney wrote out a reading list; afterwards he sent the latest Fabian pamphlet.

Beatrice went back to Box. Her father lay, half-conscious, motionless

> *…recognizing his children but not realizing ideas or feelings; his life a flickering shadow…* [358]

She felt chained to his side, all her plans were postponed indefinitely. She saw a sharp contrast between her new world of socialists, new unionists and cooperators, and the lives of her *respectable and highly successful* brothers-in-law – lawyer, banker, doctor –

> *…picked men of the individualist system, living in luxurious homes.* [359]

She now hoped for a socialist community with

> *…individual freedom and public property in the stead of class slavery and private possession of the means of subsistence…At last I am a socialist.* [360]

She returned to London in February, for two intensive weeks of meetings, staying as usual at the Devonshire House Hotel. Margaret Harkness also stayed there for two nights; Beatrice thought Margaret's contact with the new unionists had *softened and enlarged* her life, transforming her from a

> *…cold blooded journalist in search of copy to an honourable colleague.* [361]

Margaret passed on the news and the gossip; Beatrice thought her a conspiracy theorist

> *…she represents the society she lives in as a huge whirlpool…* [362]

That same week Beatrice organised a dinner at the Devonshire House with *Sidney Webb the socialist* and Charles and Mary Booth.

She put down her first impression of Sidney

*A remarkable little man with a huge head on a very tiny body, a breadth
of forehead quite sufficient to account for the encyclopaedic character of his
knowledge, a Jewish nose, prominent eyes and mouth, black hair, somewhat
unkempt, spectacles and a most bourgeois black coat shiny with wear; regarded
as a whole, somewhat between a London card and a German professor.
To keep to essentials: his pronunciation is Cockney, his Hs are shaky, his
attitudes by no means eloquent, with his thumbs fixed pugnaciously in a
far from immaculate waistcoat, with his bulky head thrown back and his
little body forward he struts even when he stands, delivering himself with
extraordinary rapidity of thought and utterance and with an expression of
inexhaustible self-complacency. But I like the man. There is a directness of
speech, an open-mindedness, an imaginative warm-heartedness which should
carry him far.*[363]

Beatrice left London at the end of February. She was researching an article
on sweated trades for the *Nineteenth Century* magazine, and travelled back to
Box via the Black Country, where she met chain makers and nail makers. By
late March she was sick of her work:

Was I made for brain work? Is any woman made for a purely intellectual life?
[364]

She was depressed: her father lay there *like a log*. She wanted release, but was
sickened by the thought she wanted her father to die.

In April Beatrice, having finished and despatched her article, took a break.
Her father's illness still made it hard for her to plan her time. Her own ideas
were evolving:

Every day my social views take a more decidedly socialist turn. [365]

She began to feel guilty about her circumstances:

*In this household [there are] ten persons living on the fat of the land in order to
minister to the supposed comfort of one poor imbecile old man...* [366]

Later that month, she invited Sidney to spend a Sunday with her at Box. He
told her his life story – the London childhood, the city brokers, and the Civil
Service – saying that he had

...done everything I intended to do. I have a belief in my own star. [367]

She warned him not to be complacent about small successes. She was in two
minds about him; she told Sidney that he had made her a socialist. But she was

unsure about his future:

His tiny tadpole body, unhealthy skin, lack of manner, Cockney pronunciation, poverty, are all against him. [368]

And she thought him conceited:

This self-complacent egotism, this disproportionate view of his own position is at once repulsive and ludicrous. [369]

This judgment convinced one of Beatrice's biographers, Carole Seymour Jones, that Beatrice found Sidney ...*physically repulsive...* [370]. It is certainly true that, early in their acquaintanceship, Beatrice made, in her diary, a number of negative, disparaging remarks about Sidney's appearance. But her only recorded use of the word 'repulsive' is in this comment on Sidney's estimation of himself, rather than on his body.

Sidney had been powerfully attracted to Beatrice from their first meeting in January. But if he had fallen in love at first sight, she had not. She did warm to him – but gradually, over many months, and with great uncertainty and hesitation. A pattern developed: after showing Sidney some encouragement, Beatrice would step back, and insist on rules – which Sidney would accept. Then he would show excess ardour, which would lead to a rebuke and a fresh crisis. His – ultimately successful – strategy was endless patience.

That April day, Beatrice saw that he was quick, sensitive, and adaptable and had the capacity to learn. She summed him up as

A London retail tradesman with the aims of a Napoleon! a queer monstrosity to be justified only by success. [371]

Above all, he could give her access to the exciting world of London socialism, of which she longed to be part. Sidney Webb offered

...a loop-hole into the socialist party; one of the small body of men with whom I may sooner or later throw in my lot for good and all. [372]

Beatrice's glorified spinster friends already mixed with the London socialists; Beatrice, spending half the year in involuntary exile in Gloucestershire, felt isolated and excluded.

A few days after Sidney's visit to Box, on Sunday 4 May 1890, 200,000 socialists and New Unionists demonstrated in Hyde Park in support of the Eight Hour Day. Eleanor Marx was the star; the Fabian speakers were Graham Wallas and GBS; both George Lansbury and John Burns also spoke.

Engels, delighted, watched from the top of a van:

What would I give if Marx had lived to see this awakening. I held my head two inches higher... [373]

As well as Engels, Ella Pycroft was there, and wrote to Beatrice to tell her about the day's events:

...Tom Mann & Tillett make two very good reasonable speeches. The crowd was perfectly orderly. Maggie [Harkness] was in the van, looking very much worn out, and to my amusement Mrs Barnett presently appeared there too, glad to get a seat on the edge of the van. [374]

Beatrice and Sidney began to exchange letters. For the first year these were cautious, stilted, and formal, following convention. He wrote to *Dear Miss Potter...*; she would reply *Dear Mr Web*b.

On 30 April, Sidney wrote to Beatrice, telling her that the day at Box had made a very deep impression on him; he had warmed to her *frank friendliness*. He asked for her help; he needed

...a Mentor outside the working circle, a looker-on who sees most of the game... [375]

She agreed:

I shall expect to be used; I shall venture to ask help from you if I need it. [376]

Beatrice told Sidney that her friendliness reflected her gratitude to him: at their first meeting in January

...it flashed across my mind that I was, or ought to be, a Socialist...by this sudden self-revelation you saved me months, perhaps years, of study. [377]

Still at Box, Beatrice found work difficult. She could not *grasp and represent the detail of facts*; she felt she had become *absolutely alone and independent*. She thought

...that terrible time of agonising suffering seems to have turned my whole nature into steel – not the steel that kills, but the surgeon's instrument that would save. [378]

Meanwhile, Ella Pycroft had written to Beatrice, telling her that her engagement to Maurice Paul was off:

...his health broke down under the unnatural relationship: constant love-making without the natural physical fulfilment. [379]

On 16 May Miss Potter wrote to Mr Webb. After commenting on some articles on the Poor Law he had sent her, she told him that she was going to a cooperative conference in Glasgow at the end of the month:

> *I am anxious to keep in with the leading Co-operators in view of any future work. Do not you feel inclined to come too?* [380]

She included advice on obtaining cheap train tickets and visitor tickets for the Conference itself.

The next Friday 23 May, Sidney and Beatrice caught the 10.00 from Euston:

> *A long journey up in third class saloon, I in one of the two comfortable seats of the carriage, with SW squatted on a portmanteau by my side, and relays of working men friends lying at full length at my feet, discussing earnestly Trade Unions, Cooperation, and Socialism. SW's appearance among them surprises and on the whole pleases them.* [381]

They travelled in a group which included Vaughan Nash, Hubert Llewellyn Smith, and Ella Pycroft. Nash, who already knew them both, thought Sidney

> *…humbler than I have ever seen him before. Quite a different tone.* [382]

That day, Ella told Beatrice more about the breakdown of her own engagement. Beatrice thought Ella *brave and noble*; about Maurice Paul she was damning:

> *Miserable boy. I warned him 4 years ago against these unhealthy maudlin friendships… The story will of course repeat itself in his life: he will go from woman to woman, ruining other lives and dissipating his own.* [383]

The Glasgow Whitsun cooperative conference was a significant moment in the developing relationship. Beatrice began to unbend towards Sidney: Sidney, ever optimistic, began to assume that Beatrice was open to a closer friendship.

On Friday evening they walked through Glasgow together. Beatrice said that what followed was *a critical twenty-four hours*:

> *…another long walk by glorious sunset through the crowded streets, knocking up against drunken girls, with glory in the sky, and hideous bestiality on the earth – the two Socialists came to a working compact.* [384]

As part of that compact Beatrice warned Sidney about boundaries:

> *You understand, you promise me to realise that the chances are 100 to 1 that nothing follows but friendship. If you feel that it is weakening your life, that your work is less efficient for it, you will promise me to give it all up?* [385]

They shook hands and went back to discussing economics.

Afterwards Sidney lay awake; he read and re read the Book of Job, in the hotel bible. Next day he sent Beatrice a note, pleading with her, and suggesting they should miss the morning session of the conference *to clear up what is more important than all Congresses.*

…this agony is unendurable. You will at any rate not be indifferent to my suffering. I do not know how to face another night such as I have passed. [386]

They did not skip the session; they did not clear things up.

Back in London, Beatrice wrote to him that she was perplexed and miserable. She tried to clarify her position: she was offering friendship plus working cooperation; she was not offering more:

Do not let us misunderstand each other. It is the first time in my life that I have granted friendship to a man who has desired something more.[387]

In reply he asked her to

…simply let things alone, and see what happens? That was our Concordat on Glasgow bridge, when I called the Sunset Glow to witness. Do not go back on that. [388]

Beatrice agreed

Let it be as you say. I will not withdraw my friendship unless you force *me to do so, by treating me otherwise than as a friend … Your letter has touched me deeply;* but it must be the last word of personal feeling. [389]

Now Beatrice reopened the packet of pages about Chamberlain, torn from her diary three years earlier

…to try and rid my mind of the whole story by seeing the actual facts. [390]

Chamberlain still *haunted her day and night*; still she watched his life and his new marriage with *feverish interest.* To some extent she blamed herself for what had happened: her own faults were ample enough

…to account for all the sufferings I passed through. Can I be brave and sensible and once for all vow that I will forgive and forget? [391]

In June Beatrice went on holiday to Bavaria and the Dolomites with Alice Green. Alice, born in Ireland, was the widow of an Oxford historian; after his death she emerged as a historian in her own right. She had befriended Beatrice the previous year:

She has called twice in one week and seems to wish to see me every day – suggests I should live with her. [392]

On their way out, they stopped at Cologne. Beatrice prayed in the cathedral:

I thought of the worship a Man is giving me – not me – but Woman through me – and I prayed again that I might make my life a temple of purity within to receive it. And I so vain, so impure – God help me. [393]

Beatrice and Alice saw the Oberammergau Passion Play; she encouraged Sidney to see it too.

While she was away, Beatrice warned Sidney in a letter from Northern Italy

You are expecting too much from me – if you do not take care – you will frighten me back into acquaintanceship…Remember we are simply friends… [394]

He responded at once:

You cannot realise how much you have changed me

As to the future, let it wait… [395]

For the next few months Sidney and Beatrice tried to live within the framework which she had dictated and he had accepted. It was not straightforward: it was not the conventional rulebook for middle class courtship. The residual pain from Beatrice's relationship with Chamberlain remained; her attempts to support Ella remained fresh.

Beatrice was due back in London early in July; she wrote from Austria, inviting Sidney to dinner on the evening of Saturday 5 July at the Devonshire House

…to talk over methodically(!) sweating, Co-operation, my study and your politics. You can rely that no word you tell me will escape. [396]

They met several times in July. Sidney arranged for her work on cooperation to be published in book form. The dinner on 5 July happened; the next week, Beatrice gave Sidney a birthday present. They spent Saturday 26 July in the Surrey hills. Arriving home that evening, Sidney found a request for a review of Alfred Marshall's *Principles of Economics*. He read the 600 page book that evening – he thought it was great – but it would not re-make economics.

The next day – Sunday – they met again. Beatrice took Communion at St Paul's, then they lunched in the City, and spent the afternoon in Epping Forest

He read me poetry as we lay in the Forest – Keats and Rossetti … [397]

Sidney wrote afterwards

You were so ravissante yesterday, and so angel-good, that I had all I could do not to say good-bye in a way which would have broken our Concordat. I had to

rush away from you speechless to hold my own. Do not punish me either for the impulse or for my self-control. I have no lover's arts...[398]

Perhaps he did break the Concordat. Beatrice referred to

...words of personal feeling which burst from him as we parted. [399]

She told Sidney he could think about her when he would be thinking about himself – but not

...when you have sufficient power to work. I am willing to replace self in your consciousness, but never, never would I oust work or others. I have promised you – that you know is our compact. [400]

Whether or not Sidney had crossed boundaries in what he said in Epping Forest, he made things worse in a pleading letter to Beatrice two days later:

...I do not see how I can go on without you. Do not now desert me. [401]

This was too much for Beatrice; writing on 9 August, she accused him of

...a constant and continuous pressing forward of wishes of your own which you know are distasteful to me...
If you value the continuance of our friendship, exercise a little more self-control
...
Don't provoke me again. [402]

In the same letter, Sidney had written that he had not realised that, one day, Beatrice would be rich

...I had not realised that your father was so rich. This is one more barrier between us. [403]

Beatrice told him he had misunderstood:

...I shall never be rich – only sufficiently well-off to carry out my everyday life on the plan of greatest efficiency possible to my very limited ability. That is all I care for. [404]

Sidney arrived home on 11 August. Beatrice's letter was waiting. It hit him hard

I will not offend again. You shall not need to write me another such letter: a terrible letter. [405]

This restored peace; Beatrice then gave Sidney advice that she would give *If I were your sister*

However old your coat may be…brush it

Take care of your voice and pronunciation: it is the chief instrument of influence

Don't talk of 'when I am Prime Minister', it jars on sensitive ears.[406]

Beatrice stayed at Box, working on the cooperatives book. Progress was good; she began writing in August, and by early October was starting the second chapter. Friends – *journalists, socialists and incipient socialists* – came to stay. Inviting Ella Pycroft, Beatrice told her about the book

Don't tell MH [Margaret Harkness], *it makes her so jealous.* [407]

Another visitor was Graham Wallas:

…one of the knot of Fabians who would 'run the world'… [408]

After Beatrice's death, GBS suggested that she

…quite deliberately sampled the Fabians as possible husbands by inviting them down to Gloucestershire for weekends one after the other. [409]

When, in October, she invited Shaw, he turned her down:

My dear Miss Potter

This is the most unreasonable thing I ever heard of. Why, I find it would cost me seventeen shillings for railway travelling alone…

Never, by Heaven, never will I suffer any created woman to lead me about in this fashion. No: you may reduce the rest of the Fabian to slavery – they prattle from morning to night about Beatrice Potter in a way I despise – but if I am to go through my amusing conversational performances for you, you must come up to town: this lion is untameable …[410]

Later GBS claimed that his real reason for turning down the invitation was that he had learned of Sidney's love for Beatrice.

Sidney and Beatrice corresponded about work and politics. She counselled him not to spend too much time on *political every-day work*; he thought she was too dismissive of political parties. Before she had met Sidney, Beatrice had signed an anti-suffrage manifesto; now Sidney told her he thought, one day, she would feel

…the need of more obviously and actively 'repenting' about Women's Suffrage.
[411]

In September 1890 they attended the economic section of the British Association, in Leeds. They found it dull – apart from a debate on the 8 Hour

Day. Alfred Marshall spoke; since reading Marshall's *Principles of Economics* in July, Sidney had been helping Beatrice with it – but, after the book, they found the man disappointing.

On the train home, Beatrice fell asleep while Sidney read William Morris' *Dream of John Ball* aloud to her:

Fellowship is life, and lack of fellowship is death. [412]

She quoted the phrase in the cooperation book. Beatrice thought the tie between them was becoming stronger.

Another tie was weakening. Margaret Harkness told Beatrice she was leaving Britain permanently. She did not want to meet; it was the end of the friendship.

It could hardly be otherwise – she had lost my respect and confidence – and her feeling for me was undermined by jealousy of my small success.

Beatrice acknowledged Margaret's past support:

…she was as tender to one in one's trouble as she has been traitorous in success. A strange nature – the two dominant impulses, pity and envy, helpfulness and treachery. [413]

In October Margaret denounced the socialist leaders in the *Pall Mall Gazette*. They were incapable of working together: they

…talked Socialism, but practiced Individualism… [414]

Poor girl wrote Beatrice

…another treachery added to the long roll. [415]

Margaret's new heroes were the anarchist Kropotkin, and the Salvation Army

Of all the men I have ever met Prince Kropotkin is the most perfect [416]

She endorsed the Salvation Army's policy of establishing land colonies – residential communities to enable long term unemployed people to resettle in agricultural or horticultural work. The hero of Harkness' third novel (published in 1889) is a Salvation Army officer, Captain Lobe.

Beatrice and Margaret had been close for fifteen years; after autumn 1890, they probably never met again. Beatrice makes few subsequent diary references to Harkness in her diary. Margaret went overseas, to New Zealand and Australia, where she lived and worked until 1904/5. She then spent about ten years in India before returning to Britain during the First World War to nurse her own mother in her final illness. She died in Italy in 1923.

In autumn 1890 the relationship between Sidney and Beatrice seemed to be going well; Beatrice wrote to Sidney

Let us go forward with this fellowship without thought for the morrow – the form it will take is not in our hands, it will grow up as the joint creation of two natures. [417]

Sidney set off on a Fabian provincial speaking tour. That June, Henry Hutchinson, a Derby solicitor, had joined the Fabians. In July he donated £100 for regional campaigning; Sidney started in the north west, then went on to Carlisle and Gateshead.

He sent *diary letters* to Beatrice – little notebooks covering his thoughts, the meetings, the audiences, and their research. Each notebook contained several days' news; Sidney posted each one as the book was filled up. Sidney also sent her his first present – an edition of the poetry of Dante Gabriel Rossetti. He wrote that he was not a fanatic about Rossetti

…but some of his work is very perfect. [418]

He added

I think I am too much in love to be a lover. My whole feelings are so transformed that it does not occur to me to do the ordinary things. [419]

Sidney's audiences on the speaking tour included trade unionists, socialists, and cooperators. In Rochdale, after speaking, he had supper in a beerhouse with twelve gas stokers and sang the Marseillaise with them (in English). The night Sidney spoke in Manchester, Bernard Shaw, having a free evening, turned up as well, and spoke for ten minutes at the end, converting all

…(for the moment) even to the word spoliation or confiscation of the rich. [420]

On Saturday 27 September Sidney again spent a day at Box. Alice Green was there too. Beatrice thought each impressed the other. Alice thought Sidney

A dear little man, one would get quite fond of him…

Sidney said that Alice was

A bright woman, clever of course… [421]

Beatrice thought Sidney *extraordinarily improved.*

Something went wrong. Perhaps Sidney, encouraged by Beatrice's friendliness, began to assume that eventually she would agree to marry him. Somehow he overstepped the mark; another crisis followed. Leaving for Yorkshire on 8 October, Sidney wrote

...Forgive me, it is I who am to blame. You had explicitly warned me that your kindness was only kindness, but you were so kind... Pray forgive me... [422]

His letter made her miserable; she wept. She told Sidney something of her unhappy experience with Chamberlain – though without, apparently, identifying him by name

Remember that I was desperately in love and for six years with another man – and that even now the wound is open ... [423]

...I saw that man again last summer by accident and I felt a horrible certainty that I could care for no-one else. You need not fear – he is married; (as you probably know). I never respected him or thought well of him though I was passionately attached. [424]

Beatrice admitted to Sidney that she had thought their friendship might end in marriage – but she had experienced a

...revulsion of feeling – a sort of panic that I would sooner leave life than enter into any promise. [425]

She told him that marriage was not practical at present, and might not be for another two or three years:

If I were in love it would be different – but I am not in love. [426]

She told Sidney not to be impatient: she would try to love him:

That other man I loved but did not believe in, you I believe in but do not love. [427]

When Sidney received her letter, he was in Barnsley on the next stage of his northern speaking tour. This time he read Isaiah while lying awake. He told Beatrice that he knew perfectly well

...how little likely I am to be personally attractive to anyone; and I know also how all one's bad habits and tricks of manner are apt to be positively repellent. [428]

What he wanted was affection, and hope;

If you marry me, it will be as a means of greater usefulness and helpfulness...I should prefer that you were not a person of station and good connections and some wealth. [429]

Frequent letters passed between them; on 12 October, Sidney wrote

Be careful with me just now, for I am *evidently 'sore all over' and you may hurt me more than you know. Indeed, it seems to me that I am in rather a bad way* ...[430]

When she read this, Beatrice felt wretched:

...do not write like that again – do not 'let yourself go' – it is not fair on me nor wise for yourself.[431]

That week Sidney dined with Charles and Mary Booth. They met to talk about the Poor Law, but the dinner gave the Booths – who had disapproved of Chamberlain – the chance to vet and inspect Sidney. They talked about socialism: on his own admission, Sidney

...forgot to try and make a good impression (!)...[432]

He apologized to Beatrice for not ingratiating himself more. The day after the dinner, Charles wrote to Beatrice, saying that

If there were no special circumstances involved...I should have said that I rather liked him... [433]

Booth thought Sidney earnest, genuine and clever.

I should perhaps have hesitated to use the word 'able' but that might well be because I don't agree with many of the conclusions. [434]

But there were special circumstances:

Do what I will I can't think of him at all in that light. I know you do not ask my opinion in that shape, but the worst of it is, in that concatenation, I find I don't like him at all; & neither Mary nor I can bear to think of you as his wife or of him as your husband.

Our hearts are very consciously filled by love for you, & this love demands a great deal from fate for you. If you cared for him, it might be different – would be very different – but, if you do not, I believe you would make a great mistake if you were to marry him. Don't do it I say. Life has not yet by any means reached its last chapters for you; turn another page and read on! But always remember that whatever you decide you have dear friends in us to whom you will always be something more than a cousin. [435]

Beatrice saw the Booths a week later, on a hectic, brief London visit. They confirmed the judgment made in the letter

Booth's opinion. He is not enough of a man. You would grow out of him. [436]

Beatrice felt low and miserable. She consoled herself – and tried to console Sidney – with the thought that it was

…our work that is important and not ourselves…[437]

As in the previous year, autumn 1890 was tough for Beatrice. Perhaps it was not as bad – she thought it was

…the first November which I have spent without terrible despondency… [438]

She wrote that she was no longer standing on the bank, watching, but

…I am swimming in mid-water with another by my side… [439]

Even so, the anniversary of Chamberlain's remarriage brought back unhappy memories

The *day: and now all that terrible pain is like a passed dream, and even the scar is well nigh imperceptible: has the whole skin hardened?* [440]

On Sunday 30 November Richard Haldane spent the day at Box. Sidney had known Haldane for some time; in July, he and Beatrice had been to a dinner at Toynbee Hall with Haldane and some trade unionists, talking about the Eight Hour Day, cooperation, and socialism. Now Haldane came to Box to explore the scope for an alliance between progressive Liberals and Fabian socialists – and maybe also, thought Beatrice,

…with an arrière pensée *of a suitable wife!* [441]

Haldane had himself become engaged earlier that year – but after only a few weeks his fiancée had broken off the engagement, leaving him depressed.

That day, Beatrice and Haldane spent at least seven hours discussing, even negotiating, the details of a radical socialist programme – and about another three hours

…on the minor business of the wife… [442]

Beatrice dismissed Haldane's suit, in terms which may indicate her state of mind. It was not so much marriage to him that she rejected, as marriage to anyone at all:

'Ah, Mr. Haldane: I will let you into the secret of woman's unmarried life. In my days of deep depression I brood over matrimony – but it is as an alternative to suicide.'

… That is exactly it: marriage is to me another word for suicide. I cannot bring myself to face an act of felo de se *for a speculation in personal happiness. I am*

not prepared to make the minutest sacrifice of efficiency for the simple reason that though I am susceptible to the charm of being loved I am not capable of loving. Personal passion has burnt itself out, and what little personal feeling still exists haunts the memory of that other man. [443]

Charles and Mary Booth, her trusted friends, did not approve of Sidney; her doubts about whether she should marry at all reappeared. Meanwhile, in London, Sidney had fallen ill; in November he developed scarlet fever. He could not go out; he was too sick to see Beatrice when she came to London in early December. He could still write:

…poor Sidney Webb writes me despairing letters from his sick-room, letters which pain me deeply with their strong emotion. [444]

In September Sidney had thought marriage a possibility; early October had been the *…zenith of my life.* [445] Now he wrote that his life was at a crisis. He was sad; he was bitter – though not towards her. He expected

…to remain all my days a clerk in the Colonial Office.

I see that I must forego the hope of your one day consenting to marry me.

Of course, as you once said, it would be so easy if you loved me. But you have let me see only too clearly that you don't.

…I need hardly say that I still love you with all my strength…I still believe that we can do, together, several times as much as we can do separately. [446]

On 6 December he wrote that he was lonely, he had no friends, while she had a wide circle.

Beatrice wept over his letter

…and tossed about the night through feeling how wrong it had been to have been led away from my better judgment last spring and to have granted your request for friendship …

It would suit my work – and therefore me – far better to marry a clerk in the Colonial Office than a leading politician to whose career I should have in the end to sacrifice my own.

But I do not love you. All the misery of the relationship arises from this… Frankly I do not believe my nature is capable of love. I cannot, and never will, make the stupendous sacrifice of marriage. [447]

She wrote that she did at one time

...fancy *that I was beginning to care for you – but I was awakened to the truth by your claiming me as your future wife – then I felt that what I cared for was not* you *but simply the fact of being loved...* [448]

Beatrice assured Sidney that she believed in him

...far more completely than I have ever done before. [449]

She told him not to fail in the crisis of his life, and not to be disheartened. A couple of days later she wrote again, telling him he was not alone in his suffering, adding

...do not think it needful to decide anything till you are quite strong ... [450]

Sidney went off to Bournemouth to convalesce; Graham Wallas came too, to look after him. Beatrice carried on with her research. In London she went to a dockers' meeting; in Leicester she visited production cooperatives. The weather was cold; she was

...cold at heart after my miserable correspondence with SW. [451]

On Sunday 14 December she wrote from her Leicester hotel, proposing a framework for a continuing relationship:

I am willing to remain on friendly (tho' not intimate) terms on these conditions.

1. That any correspondence between us should be so worded that it might be read by anybody...
2. That all the letters written by either to the other up to the end of this year should be returned to the writer thereof in a sealed packet...
3. That I should receive from you, with my letters, a solemn promise that you will break off the friendship if you find it is leading again to hopes ...

The conditions I have given you are the are the 'minimum' and must not be disputed – though of course they may be refused ...
PS Do not think me hard; I am thinking more of you than of myself. [452]

After Christmas Sidney did return her letters, telling her he had burnt some. He wrote
I have taken for my motto 'Be Patient' – that is what your initials shall mean to me. [453]

Beatrice ended the year with her usual review. The coops book was two thirds complete. She said 1890 had been a year of love *accepted but not given*:

The tie that was growing between me and another I have snapped asunder and I am alone again, facing work and the world. Six months trial, and then I felt the chain unbearably fretting me, day by day ...[454]

She still found her responsibility towards her father onerous: she felt she was working with *one foot tied;*

...centring my thought and feeling round a dying man begins to prey on me. [455]

A year after their first meeting, New Year 1891 was the low point in Sidney and Beatrice's relationship. In January, hesitantly, cautiously, they picked up the thread, trying to make their new rules work.

On Saturday 3 January, Beatrice had dinner with Sidney and Graham Wallas; she warned Sidney in advance that

...you will of course remember that in future you must write as a friend, as a friend only. [456]

She found the conversation unsatisfactory: Sidney was *thoroughly weak and miserable.* [457] She did agree to join the Fabian Society – but anonymously, so as not to compromise the independence of her research.

In London she attended a Dockers Union meeting; Tom Mann – ...*a genius in his way, a true reformer of men* – spoke. Beatrice talked to him, but sensed hostility. She asked Vaughan Nash what this meant:

He looks upon you as a schemer, a person with tin-pot schemes as he calls them, possibly it is your cousin Miss Harkness who has given him that idea. [458]

Nash accused Harkness and Champion of *calumny and treachery* towards Burns and Mann. Beatrice reflected

Mrs Besant has always distrusted me: and Tom Mann and John Burns regard me as a schemer! [459]

Just as Sidney and Beatrice were resuming contact, there was a new misunderstanding. Beatrice accused Sidney of telling Alice Green

...that you regarded me otherwise than as a friend.

He had forced her hand

...laid me open to the reflections of being rather a vulgar coquette. [460]

Sidney apologized; it had been hard to conceal from Alice that he

...had had a heavier blow than my illness accounted for, and the intuition of a sympathizing (and intellectually curious) woman made her suspicious. [461]

January 22 was Beatrice's 33rd birthday:

...I feel younger than I have ever done before, except that I feel horribly 'independent', absolute mistress of myself and my circumstances – uncannily so. 'Men may come and men may go, but I go on for ever.' [462]

Beatrice stayed at Box in January, February, and March, working on the cooperatives book. By the end of March it was finished. She and Sidney continued to correspond; their letters covered work, politics, and Sidney's future. He formed a plan to leave his Colonial Office job, and stand for the London County Council (LCC). The first LCC, elected in 1889, had a Progressive (Liberal/ Labour) majority; John Burns was the Progressive LCC member for Battersea.

As Beatrice approached the end of writing the book, (Sidney thought it had taken too long), she began to think in more detail about her planned study of trade unions. At the end of February Hubert Llewellyn Smith spent a weekend at Box

...we wandered into the Longford woods early in the morning, and thrashed out the whole question of a trade union book and found when we returned it was 3 o'clock and we had spent exactly five hours talking. [463]

In April Beatrice stayed with Alice Green in London. She was due to deliver a course of lectures on cooperation; the *Times* asked for a report in advance of the first one. Beatrice asked Alice

How can I write a report of a lecture which I have not given?

Alice replied

Why not ask Mr Webb to do it? [464]

Sidney was summoned by telegram and got to work; Beatrice thought the version of her argument in the *Times* was more lucid than the lecture itself. She felt the lectures had been a success – more successful than she had expected. She was confident the book, too. would succeed.

The lectures brought Sidney and Beatrice together again; then, in May, they travelled, with Alice Green, to the cooperative congress in Lincoln, where Sidney gave a paper. Horace Plunkett, the Irish Cooperative leader, noted in his diary:

Sidney Webb (Socialist) read a paper on how to bring Cooperation to the very poor, of course a Socialistic speech was clothed in cooperative disguise. [465]

Plunkett nevertheless became a long-term friend of both.

Everything began to change after the Lincoln conference. Beatrice noted

I cannot tell how things will settle themselves, I think probably in his way. His resolute patient affection, his honest care for my welfare – helping and correcting me – a growing distrust of a self-absorbed life…all these feelings are making for our eventual union… [466]

Twelve months later she reminisced

A year since our engagement. How well I remember that evening at Devonshire House – in the twilight when we for the first time embraced – how well I remember the happiness tempered by great anxiety. [467]

Writing to Beatrice on 21 May, Sidney could hardly believe what had happened:

…I am still a little in a dream: I have not yet fully realised all your kindness.
[468]

Two days later he wrote again. He sent the proofs of the Coop book. He thought their partnership had enormous advantages, and thought any difficulties were not insuperable:

One – la vie intime *– I want to talk to you about very frankly, or rather, I want you to talk to me, who am more than usually ignorant.* [469]

They did not look back. In June they went to Norway with Graham Wallas. On holiday. Beatrice reflected

The world will wonder. On the face of it, it seems an extraordinary end to the once brilliant Beatrice Potter (but it is just because it is not an end that she has gone into it) to marry an ugly little man with no social position and less means, whose only recommendation, so some may say, is a certain pushing ability. And I am not 'in love', not as I was. But I see something else in him (the world would say that was proof of my love) – a fine intellect and a warm-heartedness, a power of self-subordination and self-devotion for the 'common good'. And our marriage will be based on fellowship, a common faith and a common work. [470]

In Norway, they discussed their future. They talked about their talents and abilities, and what they could or could not achieve. Beatrice thought they were both

…second-rate minds, but we are curiously combined – I am the investigator, and he the executor. [471]

By now Sidney had firmly decided to leave the civil service and stand for the LCC; he told Beatrice that he wanted

...to take part in the government of the country according to socialist principles.
[472]

At the end of September, John Burns met Sidney:

Went to see Sidney Webb who resigns his office today for parliamentary and municipal work. Discussed attitude of Liberals to Labour and general labour questions. [473]

Beatrice had already started the research for her trade union book; it would continue, but with Sidney rather than Llewellyn Smith as collaborator. Together, they plunged into the research. Beatrice spent July and August in London, lodging in Herbert Spencer's house in St John's Wood, examining official documents in the Home Office by day, interviewing trade unionists over dinner in the evenings.

Sunday 11 August they spent together:

Breaking ground in trade unionism. SW comes and works with me. Yesterday being Sunday and wet he came at 11 o'clock. We allowed half an hour for confidential talk and 'human nature' and then worked hard at the Iron Founders records. Then lunch, cigarettes. A little more 'human nature' and then another two hours' work. [474]

The research continued through the autumn 1891 and into 1892. It was substantially completed before their wedding in July.

In December Beatrice wrote from Box:

I had a morning at the Boot and Shoe Society... There is something very pathetic about the records – the struggle with the anarchic spirit in every union. The miserable petty passions which are always threatening to subvert the union; and the crude economics of the leaders. [475]

Sidney replied by return:

No doubt you feel the Boot and Shoe people tedious: it is hard for you shut up there away from anyone sympathetic to talk to. Dearest, I confess to a low taste. I like the kitchen of life. T. unions and details of administration are more to me than art or literature and I am keenly and absorbingly interested in the work .
[476]

When they were apart, they corresponded constantly; the tone of the letters now changed. The formality of *Dear Mr. Webb* and *Dear Miss Potter* gave way to *Dearest* and *Dearest One*; Beatrice would sign herself *Always your loving comrade* or *Ever your devoted comrade*. In October she started addressing Sidney as *My own dear Boy.*

Phrases like *la vie intime,* in Sidney's letter of 23 May, and 'human nature' in various diary entries by Beatrice, appear to provide hints – but only hints – about their personal relations. Another possible insight comes from the memoirs of Elizabeth Longford, a distant cousin of the Chamberlain family. Joseph Chamberlain's third wife, the American Mary Endicott, had once asked Chamberlain's daughter Hilda about the relationship with Beatrice. The response was that the fastidious Joseph

> *...could never have married a woman who rolled about with Sidney on the carpet in front of the fire.*[477]

It is not clear how this tale might have reached Chamberlain's daughter. Sidney told Beatrice he kissed her photograph. Did she kiss his? She was blunt:

> *No, dear, I do not even look at your photograph. It is too hideous, for anything. Do be done in a gray suit by Elliott and Fry and let me have your head only – it is the head only that I am marrying.* [478]

He took this literally, writing a fortnight later that

> *I have ordered the photographs of myself, as you directed. I wish I was more worthy of you – but you will make me so.* [479]

He sent her prints of the final version:

> *Dearest, here is my portrait in its finished form. I fear I can't 'put a better face on it' than that. You will help me to be true to the better part of me and perhaps by upright living I may get some kind of light in my face which will take off its ugliness.* [480]

In December 1891 Beatrice reviewed her list of friends. The friendship with Margaret Harkness was over

> *...her strange ways, deliberate lying, mysterious financial positions have killed all respect on my side.* [481]

They had confided in each other. Margaret had been there when Beatrice's mother died; she had travelled abroad with Beatrice during the troubled Chamberlain years. Through Margaret, Beatrice had discovered the British Museum Reading Room. And Margaret had introduced her to Sidney. But gradually the trust between them had vanished.

Now Ella Pycroft was the only one of the original circle of Beatrice's women friends who was accessible. She was no longer working in London; she had moved to Gloucestershire as Superintendent of the Gloucestershire School of

Cookery and Domestic Economy, established by Beatrice's sister Mary Playne with the county council. Ella was often at Box when Beatrice returned during Richard Potter's last illness.

Ella told Beatrice that Mary hoped Beatrice would marry Haldane (Ella found Haldane repulsive). She also told her that Mary

...detests Mr Webb [482]

Ella told Beatrice she was far too *deliberate* to be womanly; she was shocked at anyone choosing a husband on grounds other than personal attraction. Ella did not hear about the engagement until after Christmas 1891; she sent Beatrice a blunt letter:

I'm just going to tell you the absolute truth Bee – & that is that I should be quite genuinely glad if I thought you cared for him one half so much as he does for you – but you know when we were talking of marriage the other day I felt as if you hadn't the remotest idea of what love meant in my sense of the word – perhaps I'm wrong, & at any rate you may learn to know if you don't know, & then it would be all right- You're quite right one wants intimacy of thought and comradeship, but marriage ought to mean something much more than just that – I'm lecturing you like an old widow, – well, I feel very like one & I do want you to be happy-

No doubt you'll tell me I'm a goose & utterly wrong – I hope I am – You must give my best congratulations to Mr. Webb, he'll forgive me for not thinking him quite good enough for you – yet; but then you see I'm not sure, as I've been explaining, that you are quite good enough for him either- yet. [483]

In old age Beatrice and Ella met for a final time; they were over eighty. Beatrice's recollection then was that Ella had been even more direct:

...her naive response when I suggested I might marry Sidney Webb: 'Oh! Beatrice, you couldn't.' [484]

Richard Potter's condition got worse. In August Beatrice came to Box and read to him. Returning in October, she found him

...in a miserable state – his breathing terrible to listen to and preventing all sleep. He has had two bad nights and his breathing is no better. I cannot believe that he can last long... It is very sad to see this brave old man linger on in this wretched state of discomfort and weariness. [485]

He did not get better; Beatrice was still the main family carer:

Two months here and resting and being the daughter in charge of the poor struggling dying father. His breathing is terribly hard – he has paroxysms in which he seems like one drowning and then intervals of semi consciousness. [486]

By 30 December Beatrice was writing to Sidney that the nurses thought her father was dying;

Happily, he has ceased to suffer. I do not believe he is conscious or barely so. [487]

Beatrice sat with her father most of that day. In the evening she wrote again

We are now keeping him under doses of chloroform to prevent the breathing from being a terrible struggle and tonight the Dr will inject morphia. It is the last duty one has to him to keep as free as possible from suffering. [488]

Sidney, whose own father had died a few months earlier, wrote, on New Year's Eve

Poor dear father-in-law whom I shall never see! I have watched by a father's death bed, happily not prolonged, and I know that it means something, however 'rational' we may resolve to be. [489]

Richard Potter died on New Year's Day. Once the formalities had been completed, wrote Beatrice

...the old life is over – or rather, the old shell is cast off and a new one adopted. Past are the surroundings of wealth, past the association with the upper middle class, past also the silent reserve and the hidden secret. [490]

The funeral was on 5 January; that afternoon, the will was read. Beatrice's share of the estate was £26,000. She wrote to Sidney that it

...ought to bring in a good £1000 a year. That is a high salary to get at the start of our life – let us hope we shall use it well. [491]

The next step was to tell the family about the engagement. They were already curious: in August, Kate had exclaimed, in conversation with Beatrice:

I wonder whether you will marry

She then asked Beatrice whether she liked Sidney Webb

...as much after the tour [the Norway trip] as before. [492]

Immediately after Richard Potter's death, Beatrice's sister Margaret begged her not to cut adrift from the family, and

...implored me not to marry out of my 'class' – 'I believe in a woman marrying someone of her own position, now Haldane would do capitally'. I suggested that I feared Haldane had heart disease and would not live so very long. 'Better marry a man with heart disease than some little fellow with no position'! Poor Maggie, she married 'position' and has had a life of no companionship and of constant distress. [493]

Margaret also told Beatrice it would be improper for her to employ a male secretary; Beatrice told her to mind her own business.

...I feel the weight of Death in the house – and the large assembly of sisters and brothers-in-law asking me questions about the future – and throwing out ominous warnings! [494]

At least the Courtneys were pleasant and sensible, and the Playnes were hospitable.

News of the engagement threatened to leak, so Beatrice sent her eldest sister, Lallie Holt, a letter she had drafted in December, for circulation to the other sisters. Once the family knew, there was a formal meeting with the sisters and their husbands:

The family behaved with benevolence and good grace and received Sidney at a family dinner in London with grave propriety. [495]

Outwardly, the family's reception of Sidney was courteous and correct. Privately, Rosie recorded other reactions. Mary's husband Bill Playne called Sidney

...that seditious little cad... [496]

Alfred Cripps (who thirty years later would end up serving as a cabinet minister alongside Sidney), and who was married to Teresa Potter, was heard to say that he

...could not stand a man who eats peas with his knife. [497]

Following the dinner Sidney set out on the expected round of calls

I am a little afraid of these sisters, with all their kindness and smothering me with invitations. [498]

They could be confusing. Georgina, (married to the banker Daniel Meinertzhagen), sharply reminded Sidney that they had met two years earlier, at Longfords. Sidney had forgotten

(There was a sister who came to tea in the afternoon with Mrs Playne but I had vaguely thought that was Mrs Alf Cripps). She said I totally neglected her, and talked only to you. I said I hoped she had not noted it at the time. But she said she did. [499]

Sidney may have been afraid before he met the sisters, but he was not over-awed. After meeting Lallie and Maggie he wrote

Dearest, my impression is that your sisters are not very able women in the intellectual way. Really, Mrs Holt is the cleverest of the lot: and your trained intellect stands out as quite alien to them all. I have been amused to watch how they all rush at me with futile little arguments, utterly lacking in logic or acumen ... [500]

Beatrice agreed

You are quite right – my sisters are not intellectual women. They are shrewd women of the world with good motherly hearts... [501]

Rosie appears not to have been included in this social round. Dyson Williams was now in an advanced stage of the syphilis that would eventually kill him (Willie Cripps had helped with the diagnosis). In 1891, Beatrice referred to Dyson as *mortally stricken* [502]; in 1893, she said he was a *hopeless morphia and chloroform drunkard.* [503] Mrs Thompson, who had nursed Richard Potter, returned to nurse Dyson; he died in 1896.

There were others to be told. In 1887 Herbert Spencer had asked Beatrice to be his literary executor:

I was taken aback, but it was evident that he had set his heart on it and longed, poor old man, that someone who loved him should complete his life. I was very much touched ... [504]

Spencer disapproved of Sidney even more than he had disapproved of Chamberlain.

I cannot congratulate you – that would be insincere.

It would not do for my reputation that I should be openly connected with an avowed and prominent socialist – that is impossible. Inferences would be drawn ... [505]

The role of literary executor was withdrawn – but with the proviso that she would do the work anyway – just not be acknowledged for it.

Sidney went ahead with his plan to resign from the civil service and stand for the London County Council; the three-yearly LCC elections were due in

March 1892. In September 1891 he told Beatrice he was being asked to stand in Shoreditch or West Islington; a week later, Haggerston seemed likely. There was a lull in November while the School Board election campaign got underway (Sidney resisted all invitations to stand); then came the first approach from Deptford.

In mid-November he told Beatrice he was getting lots of approaches, but preferred Stepney or Deptford. In December he was interviewed for Stepney – but preferred Deptford.

Beatrice had already offered to meet the costs:

Of course, you will let me pay all your expenses – County Council and Parliamentary ... [there had been some talk of him becoming an MP, which did not proceed in the 1890s] [506]

He replied at once:

Yes. You shall give me a cheque for County Council expenses: it won't come to £100 at most – and I shall be the 'Member for Potter'. [507]

On 10 December he told Beatrice that Deptford had agreed virtually unanimously to have him as one of their two LCC candidates; a week later this was confirmed.

Over Christmas he planned the campaign. The legal limit on election expenses was £100, for which Beatrice duly sent him a cheque. On 7 January he wrote that Deptford would be

...a laborious and anxious business and uncertain. But the Conservatives cannot even find a candidate yet, which is hopeful. [508]

Frank Galton, their secretary/researcher, was Sidney's agent.

In February Beatrice was in Manchester, researching the trade union book. She had planned to come to Deptford for the end of the campaign

I will soothe and comfort you – and if you are defeated I will spend the Sunday kissing you. [509]

But she caught flu and could not make it. Others did: Graham Wallas ran the committee room; Emma Brooke also helped.

Sidney won. Before polling day, he expected *horrible confusion* but thought they would muddle through. On the night the two Progressives were comfortably elected.

The result was not declared until after 1 a.m. I made a little speech etc and then was lifted shoulder high by an excited mob, carried downstairs to the

imminent risk of scraping the ceilings with my nose, and so out into the road amid a fearful uproar. [510]

Sidney and Galton *took refuge in a hansom.*

…leaving a howling mob parading New Cross Road, hooting the Conservative Club, etc…I felt inclined to go round by Cannon St in order, like Jack Cade, to smite London Stone with my umbrella, and shout out into the night 'Now is Mortimer Lord of London'. But I went by the Central Telegraph Office instead. [511]

At Easter Sidney and Beatrice had a snowy four-day break at Arundel, with GBS and Graham Wallas.

They settled on a London wedding in July, with a honeymoon in Ireland and Scotland. Beatrice's sister Margaret questioned Sidney about the arrangements:

where will it be, I suppose at the Registry Office, I much prefer the Church. [512]

Sidney investigated the practicalities: they chose St Pancras Vestry Hall, behind the station. They could have chosen the Chelsea Vestry Hall, but Beatrice would have had to stay at Kate Courtney's home in Chelsea for eighteen days.

Sidney described the hall as

…an ordinary 'official' looking place, and the Registrar's office is of ordinary office type, neither better nor worse. I fear the Courtneys will think it 'mean', but you won't mind, dearest? [513]

It was to be a low-key event; but on 5 July, Sidney wrote

I suppose we must let your sisters come to 'the ceremony' if they like! But we will talk about it. [514]

The wedding took place on Saturday 23 July. Lallie's husband Robert Holt thought that the ten-minute ceremony was

…not impressive, but legally it is as binding as if performed by all the clergy. [515]

There was a good turn out from both families:

The party consisted of our two selves, the bride and bridegroom, best man Graham Wallas – Miss Webb – Mr and Mrs Webb (Brother) 2 Courtneys, 2 Alfred Cripps, 2 Chas Booth, Blanche Cripps, Maggie Hobhouse, 2 Dyson Williams (he looking awfully seedy) making 18 of a party. [516]

Afterwards, the Holts entertained the company to a wedding breakfast at a local hotel. The Holts

...had a perfectly cheerful time though there were many criticisms in confidence – the 'happy pair' left by 2 o'clock train for Chester and then our party broke up. Beatrice looked remarkably well being for once tidily dressed. [517]

Beatrice's own diary entry was terse:

Exit Beatrice Potter. Enter Beatrice Webb, or rather Mrs Sidney Webb for I lose alas! both names.[518]

Notes to Part One

All references to Beatrice Webb's Diary are to the complete, digital version of the typescript diary held by LSE Library (Archives and Special Collections)

Chapter Two

1 Beatrice Webb Diary 13.06.1937
2 Beatrice Webb Diary, 26.11.1889
3 Beatrice Webb Diary, 26.11.1889
4 Beatrice Webb Diary, 26.11.1889
5 Beatrice Webb Diary 16.11.1889
6 Webb, B; *My Apprenticeship*; London, Longmans, 1926; p 40
7 Webb, B; *My Apprenticeship*; London, Longmans, 1926; p 58
8 Webb, B; *My Apprenticeship*; London, Longmans, 1926; p 11
9 Webb, B; *My Apprenticeship*; London, Longmans, 1926; p 12
10 Webb, B; *My Apprenticeship*; London, Longmans, 1926; p 10
11 Mary Playne to Kate Courtney, 1896; quoted in Caine, B; *Destined to be Wives; the sisters of Beatrice Webb*; Oxford, OUP, 1986
12 Webb, B; *My Apprenticeship*; London, Longmans, 1926; p 12
13 Webb, B; *My Apprenticeship*; London, Longmans, 1926; p 60
14 Beatrice Webb Diary 21.09.1875
15 Webb, B; *My Apprenticeship*; London, Longmans, 1926; p. 56
16 Webb, B; *My Apprenticeship*; London, Longmans, 1926; p 10
17 Webb, B; *My Apprenticeship*; London, Longmans, 1926 ; p11
18 Webb, B; *My Apprenticeship*; London, Longmans, 1926 ; p11
19 Webb, B; *My Apprenticeship*; London, Longmans, 1926 ; p10
20 Beatrice Webb Diary 15.06.1878
21 Webb, B; *My Apprenticeship*; London, Longmans, 1926; p 59
22 Dobbs, Rosie; typescript autobiography, (BL Add MS 50657); p13.
23 Dobbs, Rosie; typescript autobiography, (BL Add MS 50657); p 35.
24 Dobbs, Rosie; typescript autobiography, (BL Add MS 50657);
25 Webb, B; *My Apprenticeship*; London, Longmans, 1926; p 23
26 Webb, B; *My Apprenticeship*; London, Longmans, 1926 p 24
27 Webb, B; *My Apprenticeship*; London, Longmans, 1926 p 25
28 Webb, B; *My Apprenticeship*; London, Longmans, 1926; p 29
29 Webb, B; *My Apprenticeship*; London, Longmans, 1926; p 14
30 Webb, B; *My Apprenticeship*; London, Longmans, 1926; p 20
31 Beatrice Webb Diary 27.09.1874
32 Webb, B; *My Apprenticeship*; London, Longmans, 1926; p 77
33 Beatrice Webb Diary 27.03.1875
34 Beatrice Webb, *My Apprenticeship*; London, Longmans, 1926; p92
35 Beatrice Webb Diary; 03.08.1874
36 Beatrice Webb Diary 17.12.1875
37 Beatrice Webb, *My Apprenticeship*; London, Longmans, 1926
38 Webb, B; *My Apprenticeship*; London, Longmans, 1926; p 49
39 Beatrice Webb Diary 28.12.1894
40 Beatrice Webb Diary 09.11.1878
41 Beatrice Webb Diary 30.09.1889
42 Beatrice Webb Diary 30.09.1889
43 Beatrice Webb Diary 30.09.1889
44 Webb, B; *My Apprenticeship*; London, Longmans, 1926; p 93
45 Webb, B; *My Apprenticeship*; London, Longmans, 1926; p 83
46 Beatrice Webb Diary 14.11.1880
47 M Harkness to Beatrice, 09.05.1878; LSE Library; Passfield Papers 2/1/2/2
48 M Harkness to Beatrice, 09.1876, LSE Library; Passfield Papers 2/1/2/2
49 M Harkness to Beatrice, 22.08.1878, LSE Library; Passfield Papers 2/1/2/2
50 M Harkness to Beatrice, 24.08.1878, LSE Library; Passfield Papers 2/1/2/2
51 M Harkness to Beatrice, 1878, LSE Library; Passfield Papers 2/1/2/2
52 M Harkness to Beatrice, 03.02.1880, LSE Library; Passfield Papers 2/1/2/2
53 Beatrice Webb Diary undated, April 1882
54 Beatrice Webb Diary 23.04.1882

55   Beatrice Webb Diary 23.04.1882
56   Beatrice Webb Diary, 02.01.1883
57   Beatrice Webb; *My Apprenticeship*; London, Longmans, 1926; p 113
58   Beatrice Webb; *My Apprenticeship*; London, Longmans, 1926; p 113
59   Beatrice Webb Diary, 22.04.1884
60   Beatrice Webb; *My Apprenticeship*; London, Longmans, 1926; p 113
61   London Congregational Union, The; *The bitter cry of outcast London*; London, James Clarke & Co; 1883; p 4
62   Booth, M; *Charles Booth – A Memoir*; London, Macmillan, 1918; pp 13-15
63   Harris, J; *Unemployment and Politics: A study in English Social Policy,1886-1914*; Oxford, Oxford University Press, 1972; p 105
64   Beatrice Webb Diary 22.05.1886
65   Quoted in Barnett, Henrietta; Canon Barnett, His Life, work and friends; London, John Murray,1921; p 68
66   Letter from Kate Courtney to Henrietta Barnett; quoted in Barnett, Henrietta; *Canon Barnett, His Life, work and friends*; London, John Murray,1921; p 37
67   *New Statesman* 26 June 1913
68   *New Statesman* 26 June 1913
69   Webb, B; *My Apprenticeship*; London, Longmans, 1926; p 180
70   Quoted in Mowat, C L, The Charity Organisation Society 1869 – 1913; London; Methuen; 1961
71   Webb, B; *My Apprenticeship*; London, Longmans, 1926; p 212
72   Webb, B; *My Apprenticeship*; London, Longmans, 1926; p 212
73   Webb, B; *My Apprenticeship*; London, Longmans, 1926; p 196
74   Webb, B; *My Apprenticeship*; London, Longmans, 1926 p151
75   Webb, B; *My Apprenticeship*; London, Longmans, 1926 p151
76   Webb, B; *My Apprenticeship*; London, Longmans, 1926 p151
77   Webb, B; *My Apprenticeship*; London, Longmans, 1926 p 153
78   Webb, B; *My Apprenticeship*; London, Longmans, 1926 p151
79   Webb, B; *My Apprenticeship*; London; Longman; 1926; p 171
80   Jones, Gareth Stedman *Outcast London*; Oxford; Clarendon Press; 1971; p 328
81   Gilbert, B; *Evolution of National Insurance in Great Britain*; London, Michael Joseph; 1966; p 44
82   Kate Courtney Diary, 1875; quoted in Caine, Barbara; *Destined to be wives; the sisters of Beatrice Webb*; Oxford, OUP, 1986; p 59
83   Beatrice Webb Diary 12.08.1923
84   Webb, B; *My Apprenticeship*; London; Longman; 1926; p 93
85   Beatrice Webb Diary 17.03.1883
86   Beatrice Webb Diary, 17.03.1883
87   Barnett, Henrietta *Canon Barnett, His life, work and friends*; London, John Murray,1918; p 107
88   Beatrice Potter to Mary Playne; December 1884; in Webb, B & Webb, S; *The Letters of Sidney and Beatrice Webb; Vol I*; Cambridge; CUP; p 32
89   Barnett, Henrietta: *Canon Barnett, His life, work and friends*; London, John Murray,1918; p 106
90   Beatrice Webb Diary 16.01.1885
91   Webb, B; *My Apprenticeship*; London; Longman; 1926; p 261
92   Beatrice Webb Diary 12.1884
93   Webb, B; *My Apprenticeship*; London, Longmans, 1926; p 262
94   Webb, B; *My Apprenticeship*; London, Longmans, 1926; p 263
95   Beatrice Webb Diary 08.03.1885
96   Beatrice Webb Diary 13.03.1885
97   Beatrice to Mary Playne, 09.04.1885. in Webb, B & Webb, S; *The Letters of Sidney and Beatrice Webb*; Cambridge; CUP; 1978; Vol I p 38
98   Beatrice Webb Diary 12.04.1885
99   Beatrice Webb Diary 04.06.1885
100   Beatrice Webb Diary 04.06.1885
101   Beatrice to Richard Potter ?August 1885, in Webb, B & Webb, S; *The Letters of Sidney and Beatrice Webb*; Cambridge; CUP; 1978; Vol I p 40
102   Beatrice to Richard Potter ?August 1885, in Webb, B & Webb, S; *The Letters of Sidney and Beatrice Webb*; Cambridge; CUP; 1978; Vol I p 40
103   Margaret Harkness (John Law); *A City Girl*; Brighton, Victorian Secrets, 2015; p 43
104   Margaret Harkness (John Law); *A City Girl*; Brighton, Victorian Secrets, 2015; p 43

105 Margaret Harkness (John Law); *A City Girl*; Brighton, Victorian Secrets, 2015; p 43

106 Beatrice Webb Diary 15.09.1885

107 Beatrice to Richard Potter early November 1885, in Webb, B & Webb, S; *The Letters of Sidney and Beatrice Webb*; Cambridge; CUP; 1978; Vol I p 47

108 Beatrice Webb Diary 12.05.1886

109 LSE Library Coll Misc 0043

110 LSE Library Coll Misc 0043

111 Beatrice to Richard Potter, October 1886, in Webb, B & Webb, S; *The Letters of Sidney and Beatrice Webb*; Cambridge; CUP; 1978; Vol I p 58

112 Beatrice Webb Diary 08.11.1886

113 Barnett, Henrietta *Canon Barnett, His life, work and friends*; London, John Murray,1918; p 139

114 Beatrice Webb; *My Apprenticeship*; London, Longmans, 1926; p 219

115 Quoted in Thomas and Margaret Simey; *Charles Booth, Social Scientist*; Oxford, OUP, 1960; p 72

116 Samuel Barnett to Frank Barnett, 1890; quoted in Barnett, Henrietta *Canon Barnett, His life, work and friends*; London, John Murray,1918; p 388

117 Booth, Charles *Life and Labour of the People in London*, Third Edition; London, Macmillan, 1902-1903; First Series, Poverty; Volume I p I172

118 Beatrice to Mary Booth, March 1886, in Webb, B & Webb, S; *The Letters of Sidney and Beatrice Webb*; Cambridge; CUP; 1978; Vol I pp 55,56

119 Paper by Booth; quoted in Simey, Thomas & Simey, Margaret; Charles Booth, Social Scientist; Oxford, OUP, 1960; p 81

120 Beatrice Webb Diary 10.12.1886

121 Beatrice Webb Diary 10.12.1886

122 LSE Library; Booth B 19 notebook for Katherine Buildings

123 LSE Library; PASSFIELD 2/1/2/2

124 Beatrice Webb Diary 22.03.1887

125 Beatrice Webb Diary 24.03.1887

126 Beatrice Webb Diary 24.03.1887

127 Beatrice Webb Diary 08.05.1887

128 Beatrice Webb Diary 16.12.1888

129 Beatrice Webb Diary 16.12.1888

Chapter Three

130 Webb, B; *Our Partnership*; ed. Cole, M & Drake, B; London, Longmans, 1948; p 1

131 Webb, B; *Our Partnership*; ed. Cole, M & Drake, B; London, Longmans, 1948; p 1

132 GBS to Sidney, 26.03.1946; quoted in Harrison, R J ; *The Life and Times of Sidney and Beatrice Webb; 1858-1905: the formative years*; London, Macmillan, 2000; p 5

133 Webb, B; *Our Partnership*; ed. Cole, M & Drake, B; London, Longmans, 1948; p 3

134 Webb, B; *Our Partnership*; ed. Cole, M & Drake, B; London, Longmans, 1948; p 3

135 Sidney Webb 'Reminiscences III: The London County Council'; St Martin's Review 1928 p 621

136 Sidney Webb 'Reminiscences III: The London County Council'; St Martin's Review 1928 p 621

137 'Notes on Sidney Webb by his brother Charles Webb'; LSE Library, TAWNEY 24/2

138 The National Archives of the United Kingdom (TNA); CSC 11/62

139 Virginia Woolf Diary, 18 September 1918; in Woolf, V; *Selected Diaries*; abridged and edited by Anne Olivier Bell; London, Vintage, 2008; p 54

140 Beatrice Webb Diary 22.04.1890

141 Sidney to Civil Service Commission, 14.11.1878; TNA; CSC 11/62

142 Hamilton, Mary Agnes (Molly); *Sidney and Beatrice Webb*; London, Sampson Low, 1933; p 20

143 Apthorpe to Civil Service Commissioners, 12.03.1881; TNA; CSC 11/62

144 Quoted in Holroyd, M *Bernard Shaw; Volume 1, The Search for Love, 1856 – 1898;* London, Penguin, 1990; p 176

145 Olivier, Sydney; *Letters and Selected Writings;* Ed. With a memoir by Margaret Olivier; London, George Allen and Unwin, 1948; p 34

146 Sidney to Graham Wallas, 14.06.1887; LSE Library; Passfield 2/2 LSE

147 Beatrice Webb Diary 26.08.1890

148 Webb, S; Introduction; in Shaw, GB,

ed *Fabian Essays in Socialism*, 1920 edition with introduction by Sidney Webb; London; Fabian Society and George Allen and Unwin; 1920; p i

149 Webb, S; *Socialism in England*; London, Swan Sonnenschein & Co; 1893; p 19

150 See Shipley, S; *Club Life and Socialism in mid Victorian London*; History Workshop Pamphlet No 5, London 1971

151 Quoted in Grubb, Arthur Page; *From Candle Factory to British Cabinet; The life story of the Right Hon John Burns, PC, MP*; London, Edwin Dalton, 1908; p 32

152 William Morris to GBS; quoted in Holmes, R *Eleanor Marx, A life*; London Bloomsbury, 2014; p 232

153 Eleanor Marx to William Liebknecht, 01.01.1885; quoted in Holmes, R *Eleanor Marx, A life*; London Bloomsbury, 2014; p 233

154 Sanders, W S, *Early Socialist Days*; London; Hogarth Press; 1927; p14

155 Sanders, W S, *Early Socialist Days*; London; Hogarth Press; 1927; p 24

156 Foreword by Hyndman to Burgess, J; *John Burns: the rise and progress of a right honourable*; C Glasgow; The Reformers' Bookstall Ltd; 1911; p ix

157 LSE Library; Passfield Papers

158 Shaw, George Bernard; *Sixteen Self Sketches* by Bernard Shaw; London; Constable and Co 1949; p 65

159 Shaw, GB, and Cole, M; *Early Days; in* Cole, M, ed; *The Webbs and their work*; London, Frederick Muller, 1949; p 5

160 Sidney to GBS, 04.11.1884; in Webb, B & Webb, S; *The Letters of Sidney and Beatrice Webb; Vol I*; Cambridge; CUP; 1978 p 81

161 Sidney to GBS, 04.11.1884; in Webb, B & Webb, S; *The Letters of Sidney and Beatrice Webb; Vol I*; Cambridge; CUP; 1978 p 81

162 Sidney to GBS, 05.08.1885 in Webb, B & Webb, S; *The Letters of Sidney and Beatrice Webb; Vol I*; Cambridge; CUP; 1978; p91

163 GBS Diary 14.08.1885; in *Bernard Shaw: The Diaries*; ed Stanley Weintraub London; Pennsylvania State University Press; 1986

164 Fellowship of the New Life, Minutes, 06.12.83; LSE Library; Fabian Society/C

165 Frank Podmore to Thomas Davidson, 16.12.1883; quoted in MacKenzie, Jeanne and MacKenzie, Norman; *The Fabians*; New York, Simon and Schuster, 1977

166 Fabian motto, first appearing on the front page of Fabian Tract no 1, *Why are the many poor?*; London, Fabian Society, 1884

167 Shaw to Archibald Henderson, 03.01.1905; in Collected letters, ed D H Laurence, 1972, p494

168 quoted in MacKenzie, N; and MacKenzie, J; The Fabians; New York, Simon and Schuster, 1977; p28

169 Pease, Edward R; *The History of the Fabian Society*; London, Fabian Society and Allen and Unwin; 1925; p72

170 Fabian Basis; in Pease, Edward R; *The History of the Fabian Society*; London, Fabian Society and Allen and Unwin; 1925; Appendix II p 259

171 Shaw, GB, and Cole, M; *Early Days; in* Cole, M, ed; T*he Webbs and their work*; London, Frederick Muller, 1949; p 7

172 LSE Library; Fabian General Meeting minutes, 16.03.1888

173 *Butchered to make a Fabian Holiday* -article by GF Standring in *The Radical*, April 1888.

174 Haldane, Richard B; *An Autobiography*; London, Hodder and Stoughton, 1929; p 93

175 John Burns Diary 06.07.1888; British Library add ms 46310

176 Snell, Lord (Harry Snell); *Men, Movements, and Myself*; London, J M Dent, 1936; p62

177 Webb, B; *My Apprenticeship*; London, Longmans, 1926; p 402

178 Webb, B; *My Apprenticeship*; London, Longmans, 1926; p 402

179 Shaw, GB, and Cole, M; *Early Days; in* Cole, M, ed.; *The Webbs and their work*; London, Frederick Muller, 1949 pp 7-8

180 Shaw, GB, ed *Fabian Essays in Socialism*; 1920 edition with introduction by Sidney Webb London, Fabian Society and George Allen and Unwin, 1920; p 50

181 Shaw, GB, ed *Fabian Essays in Socialism*; 1920 edition with introduction by Sidney Webb London, Fabian Society and George Allen and Unwin, 1920; p 47

182 Shaw, GB, ed *Fabian Essays in Socialism*; 1920 edition with introduction by Sidney Webb London, Fabian Society and George Allen and Unwin, 1920; p 60

183 Shaw, GB, ed *Fabian Essays in Socialism*; 1920 edition with introduction by Sidney Webb London, Fabian Society and George Allen and Unwin, 1920; p 61

184 quoted in Hamilton, M A; *Sidney and Beatrice Webb*, London, 1933, p 36

185 quoted in Fremantle A; *This Little Band of Prophets; the British Fabians*; London, Allen and Unwin; 1960; p 89

Chapter Four

186 Beatrice Webb Diary 01.02.1883

187 Dobbs, Rosie; typescript autobiography, (BL Add MS 50657) p 41.

188 Beatrice Webb Diary 11.03.1885

189 Beatrice Webb Diary 11.03.1885

190 Cole, M; and Shaw; GB; *Early Days*; in Cole, M ed; *The Webbs and their Work* London, Frederick Muller, 1949; p13

191 GBS Diary 03.08.1885; Shaw, George Bernard; *Bernard Shaw The Diaries*; Vol I; Vol II 1885-1897; ed Stanley Weintraub; Pennsylvania State University Press, University Park & London;1986; p 101

192 Sidney Webb to Marjorie Davidson, 15.12.1888; in Webb, B & Webb, S; *The Letters of Sidney and Beatrice Webb*; Cambridge; CUP; 1978; Vol I p 119

193 Dobbs, Rosie; typescript autobiography, (BL Add MS 50657) p 39

194 Beatrice Webb Diary 14.02.1883

195 Dobbs, Rosie; typescript autobiography, (BL Add MS 50657) p 51

196 Dobbs, Rosie; typescript autobiography, (BL Add MS 50657) p 44

197 Beatrice Webb Diary 31.03.1883

198 Beatrice Webb Diary 10.12.1886

199 With Beatrice Webb diary; 13.06.1882; 26.09.1882

200 Beatrice Webb Diary 01.01.1886

201 Beatrice Webb Diary 30.09.1889

202 Carrie Darling to Beatrice, 08.10.1882; LSE Library; PASSFIELD 2/1/2/3

203 Beatrice Webb Diary 30.09.1889

204 Beatrice Webb Diary 30.09.1889

205 Beatrice Webb Diary 12.05.1889

206 Beatrice Webb Diary 05.05.1890

207 Beatrice Webb Diary 24.03.1883

208 Beatrice Webb Diary 30.09.1889

209 Beatrice Webb Diary 24.03.1883

210 Beatrice Webb Diary 15.09.1885

211 Beatrice Webb Diary 13.02.1882

212 Quoted in Holroyd, M; *Bernard Shaw; Volume 1, The Search for Love, 1856 – 1898;* London, Penguin, 1990; p 84

213 Amy Levy, *Readers at the British Museum*, in *The Romance of a Shop*; Atalanta, April 1888, pp. 449–54; quoted in Bernstein, Susan David; *Reading Room Geographies of Late-Victorian London*: Interdisciplinary Studies in the Long Nineteenth Century, 13(2011) <http://19.bbk.ac.uk>

214 Beatrice Webb Diary 14.10.1887

215 Beatrice Webb Diary 24.05.1883

216 Beatrice Webb Diary 24.05.1883

217 Beatrice Webb Diary14.10.1887

218 Olive Schreiner to Beatrice, April 1888; LSE Library Passfield/2/1/2/9

219 M Harkness to Beatrice, 29.02.1884, LSE Library; Passfield Papers 2/1/2/2

220 M Harkness to Beatrice, 29.02.1884; LSE Library; Passfield Papers 2/1/2/2

221 Mutch, D & Elkiss, T; Biography of Margaret Harkness; in Harkness, M; *A City Girl* (ed. Mutch, D); Brighton, Victorian Secrets, 2015

222 M Harkness to Beatrice, undated, 1887, LSE Library; Passfield Papers 2/1/2/2

223 Speech by Chamberlain, 30.03.1883

224 Quoted in Heffer, S; *Age of Decadence;* London, Random House, 2017; p 49

225 Fraser, P; *Joseph Chamberlain; Radicalism and Empire 1868-1914*; London, Cassell, 1966; p112

226 Fraser, P; *Joseph Chamberlain; Radicalism and Empire 1868-1914*; London, Cassell, 1966; p115

227 Dobbs, Rosie; typescript autobiography, (BL Add MS 50657) p 50

228 Dobbs, Rosie; typescript autobiography, (BL Add MS 50657) p 51

229 Beatrice Webb Diary 27.06.1883

230   Beatrice Webb Diary 27.06.1883

231   Beatrice Webb Diary 15.07.1883

232   Beatrice Webb Diary

233   Beatrice Webb Diary 01.01.1901

234   Beatrice Webb Diary 13.08.1883

235   Beatrice Webb Diary 01.01.1901

236   Beatrice Webb Diary 26.09.1883

237   Beatrice to Mary Playne, 10.1883, in Webb, B & Webb, S; *The Letters of Sidney and Beatrice Webb*; Vol I; Cambridge; CUP, 1978; p 17

238   Beatrice to Mary Playne, 10.1883, in Webb, B & Webb, S; *The Letters of Sidney and Beatrice Webb*; Vol I; Cambridge; CUP, 1978; p 17

239   Beatrice Webb Diary 24.11.1883

240   Carrie Darling to Beatrice; 03.11.1883; LSE Library; PASSFIELD 2/1/2/3

241   Beatrice Webb Diary 12.01.1884

242   Beatrice Webb Diary 12.01.1884

243   Dobbs, Rosie; typescript autobiography, (BL Add MS 50657) p 50

244   Beatrice Webb Diary 12.01.1884

245   Beatrice Webb Diary 12.01.1884

246   Beatrice Webb Diary 12.01.1884

247   Beatrice Webb Diary 12.01.1884

248   Beatrice Webb Diary 12.01.1884

249   Dobbs, Rosie; typescript autobiography, (BL Add MS 50657) p 57

250   Beatrice Webb Diary 24.01.1884

251   Beatrice Webb Diary 16.03.1884

252   Beatrice Webb Diary 16.03.1884

253   Beatrice Webb Diary 16.03.1884

254   Beatrice Webb Diary 16.03.1884

255   Beatrice Webb Diary 22.04.1884

256   Beatrice Webb Diary 09.05.1884

257   Carrie Darling to Beatrice; 08.05.1884; LSE Library; PASSFIELD 2/1/2/3

258   Beatrice Webb Diary 28.07.1884

259   Beatrice Webb Diary 15.10.1884

260   Beatrice Webb Diary 15.10.1884

261   Beatrice Webb Diary 15.10.1884

262   Beatrice Webb Diary 01.02.1885

263   Beatrice Webb Diary 12.05.1886

264   Beatrice Webb Diary 12.05.1886

265   Kate Courtney to Beatrice, 23.07.1885, with typescript Diary for Jan 1886

266   Beatrice to Mary Playne; ?late July 1885, in Webb, B & Webb, S; *The Letters of Sidney and Beatrice Webb*; Vol I; Cambridge; CUP; 1978, p 36

267   Mary Booth to Beatrice Potter, 28.07.1885; LSE Library; PASSFIELD

2/1/2/6

268   Mary Booth to Beatrice Potter, October 1885, with typescript Diary for October 1885

269   Clara Ryland to Beatrice, 08.10.1885, with typescript Diary for October 1885

270   Beatrice Webb Diary 06.03.1886

271   Webb, B; *My Apprenticeship*; London, Longmans, 1926; p 279

272   Dobbs, Rosie; typescript autobiography, (BL Add MS 50657) p 57

273   Beatrice Webb Diary 11.02.1886

274   Chamberlain to Beatrice, 28.02.1886; quoted in Harrison, R J ; *The Life and Times of Sidney and Beatrice Webb; 1858-1905: the formative years;* London, Macmillan, 2000; p 121

275   Beatrice Webb Diary 06.03.1886

276   B Potter to J Chamberlain, early March 1986, in Webb, B & Webb, S; *The Letters of Sidney and Beatrice Webb*; Vol I; Cambridge; CUP, 1978, p 54

277   Beatrice Webb Diary 06.03.1886

278   Beatrice Webb Diary 12.04.1886

279   Beatrice Webb Diary 30.08.1886

280   Beatrice Webb Diary 28.09.1886

281   Beatrice Webb Diary 16.10.1886

282   Beatrice Webb Diary 10.12.1886

283   Beatrice Webb Diary 09.06.1887

284   Beatrice Webb Diary 09.06.1887

285   Beatrice Webb Diary 09.06.1887

286   Beatrice Webb Diary 08.08.1887

287   Beatrice Webb Diary 09.06.1887

288   Comment by Beatrice, written on letter by Chamberlain to her, August 1887, quoted in *Harrison, R J; The Life and Times of Sidney and Beatrice Webb; 1858-1905: the formative years;* London, Macmillan, 2000; p 210

289   Beatrice Webb Diary 08.08.1887

290   Dobbs, Rosie; typescript autobiography, (BL Add MS 50657) p 59

291   Beatrice Webb Diary May 1890

292   Beatrice Webb Diary 01.01.1901

293   Beatrice Webb Diary 26.04.1888

294   Beatrice Webb Diary 07.11.1888

295   Beatrice Webb Diary 15.11.1888

296   Beatrice Webb Diary 11.07.1886

297   Beatrice Webb Diary 10.12.1886

298   Dobbs, Rosie; typescript autobiography, (BL Add MS 50657) p 33

299   Dobbs, Rosie; typescript autobiography, (BL Add MS 50657) p 34

300 Dobbs, Rosie; typescript autobiography, (BL Add MS 50657) p 72

301 Beatrice Webb Diary 09.04.1888

302 Beatrice Webb Diary 21.08.1888

303 Beatrice Webb Diary 21.08.1888

304 Quotations from *The Glorified Spinster*; *Macmillan Magazine*, September 1888

305 Beatrice Webb Diary 03.09.1888

306 Beatrice Webb Diary 17.08.1888

307 Beatrice Webb Diary 10.09.1888

308 Beatrice Webb Diary 25.10.1888

309 Beatrice Webb Diary 12.05.1888

310 *Pall Mall Gazette*, 12.05.1888

311 Lewis Lyons, letter in *Pall Mall Gazette*, 18.05.1888

312 Beatrice Webb Diary 25.05.1888

313 Beatrice Webb Diary 25.05.1888

314 Beatrice Webb Diary 22.08.1885

315 Beatrice Webb Diary 08.03.1889

316 Beatrice Webb Diary 31.10.1886

317 Webb, B; *My Apprenticeship*; London, Longmans, 1926; p 393

318 Beatrice Webb Diary 25. 03.1889

319 Webb, B; *My Apprenticeship*; London, Longmans, 1926; pp 403-404

320 Barnett, Henrietta *Canon Barnett, His life, work and friends*; London, John Murray,1918; p 655

321 Samuel Barnett to Frank Barnett, 1888; quoted in Barnett, Henrietta; *Canon Barnett, His life, work and friends*; London, John Murray,1918; p 657

322 Webb, B; *My Apprenticeship*; London, Longmans, 1926; p 207

323 *St James's Gazette* 12.05.1887

324 Engels to Margaret Harkness, April 1888; in Harkness, M (John Law); *A City Girl*; Brighton, Victorian Secrets, 2015; Appendix A, p133

325 Harkness, M; letter to the editor, The Star; 25.09.1889; quoted in Kirwan, B Introduction to Harkness, M; *Out of Work*; London, Merlin press, 1990

326 John Burns Diary 27.10.1888; British Library add ms 46310

327 Holroyd, M *Bernard Shaw; Volume 1, The Search for Love, 1856 – 1898;* London, Penguin, 1990; p185

328 G B Shaw to William Morris; quoted in Holroyd, M *Bernard Shaw; Volume 1, The Search for Love, 1856 – 1898;* London, Penguin, 1990; p185

329 Quoted in Burgess, Joseph; *John Burns: the rise and progress of a Right Honourable*; Glasgow, The Reformers Bookstall, 1911; p103

330 John Burns Diary, 08.02.1888; British Library add ms 46310

331 Beatrice Webb Diary 27.11.1887

332 Beatrice Webb Diary 27.11.1887

333 Webb, S & B; *The History of Trade Unionism*; London; Longmans Green, 1894, 1920; p 402

334 Smith, H Llewellyn & Nash, V; *The Story of the Dockers' Strike* London, T Fisher Unwin, 1890; p 37

335 Beatrice Webb Diary 29.08.1889

336 Beatrice Webb Diary 29.08.1889

337 Beatrice Webb Diary 01.09.1888

338 Beatrice Webb Diary 22.09.1888

339 John Law (Margaret Harkness); The Cardinal as I knew him; *Pall Mall Gazette*, 18.01.1892

340 Manning account taken from Purcell, E S; Life of Cardinal Manning; quoted in Coates, K and Topham, T; *The making of the labour movement;* Nottingham, Spokesman, 1994, p63

341 Beatrice Webb Diary ?14.11.1888

342 Beatrice Webb Diary ?14.11.1888

343 Beatrice Webb Diary ?14.11.1888

344 Beatrice Webb Diary 26.11.1889

345 Beatrice Webb Diary 17.11.1889

346 Beatrice Webb Diary 11.10.1889

347 Beatrice Webb Diary 01.02.1890

348 Beatrice Webb Diary January 1890

349 Beatrice Webb Diary 27.12.1929

350 Beatrice Webb Diary 30.09.1889

351 Beatrice Webb Diary 30.09.1889

352 Beatrice Webb Diary 30.09.1889

353 Beatrice Webb Diary 26.11.1889

354 Beatrice Webb Diary 27.12.1929

355 Webb, B; *My Apprenticeship*; London, Longmans, 1926; p 407

356 Webb, B; *My Apprenticeship*; London, Longmans, 1926; p 402

357 quoted in Webb, B; *My Apprenticeship*; London, Longmans, 1926; p 405

358 Beatrice Webb Diary 01.02.1890

359 Beatrice Webb Diary 01.02.1890

360 Beatrice Webb Diary 01.02.1890

361 Beatrice Webb Diary 12.02.1890

362 Beatrice Webb Diary 12.02.1890

363 Beatrice Webb Diary 14.02.1890

364 Beatrice Webb Diary 29.03.1890

365 Beatrice Webb Diary 22.04.1890

366 Beatrice Webb Diary 22.04.1890

367 Beatrice Webb Diary 26.04.1890
368 Beatrice Webb Diary 26.04.1890
369 Beatrice Webb Diary 26.04.1890
370 Seymour-Jones, C; *Beatrice Webb, Woman of conflict*; London, Pandora, 1992; pp xi, 187
371 Beatrice Webb Diary 26.04.1890
372 Beatrice Webb Diary 26.04.1890
373 quoted in Armstrong, G; *London's Struggle for Socialism*; London, Thames Publications, 1948
374 Ella Pycroft to Beatrice Potter, 04.05.1890; LSE Library; PASSFIELD 2/1/2/7
375 Sidney to Beatrice, 30.04.1890; in Webb, B & Webb, S; *The Letters of Sidney and Beatrice Webb*; Vol I; Cambridge; CUP; 1978; p 132
376 Beatrice to Sidney, 02.05.1890, in Webb, B & Webb, S; *The Letters of Sidney and Beatrice Webb*; Vol I; Cambridge; CUP; 1978; p 133
377 Beatrice to Sidney, 02.05.1890, in Webb, B & Webb, S; *The Letters of Sidney and Beatrice Webb*; Vol I; Cambridge; CUP; 1978; p 133
378 Beatrice Webb Diary 05.05.1890
379 Beatrice Webb Diary 05.05.1890
380 Beatrice to Sidney, 16.05.1890, in Webb, B & Webb, S; *The Letters of Sidney and Beatrice Webb*; Vol I; Cambridge; CUP; 1978; p 137
381 Beatrice Webb Diary 23.05.1890
382 Beatrice Webb Diary 23.05.1890
383 Beatrice Webb Diary 23.05.1890
384 Beatrice Webb Diary 23.05.1890
385 Beatrice Webb Diary 23.05.1890
386 Note from Sidney to Beatrice, 24.05.1890, with Beatrice Webb Diary 24.05.1890
387 Beatrice to Sidney, 29.05.1890, in Webb, B & Webb, S; *The Letters of Sidney and Beatrice Webb*; Vol I; Cambridge; CUP; 1978; p 139
388 Sidney to Beatrice, 30.05.1890, in Webb, B & Webb, S; *The Letters of Sidney and Beatrice Webb*; Vol I; Cambridge; CUP; 1978; p 144
389 Beatrice to Sidney, 31.05.1890, in Webb, B & Webb, S; *The Letters of Sidney and Beatrice Webb*; Vol I; Cambridge; CUP; 1978; p 145
390 Beatrice Webb Diary May 1890
391 Beatrice Webb Diary 29.05.1890
392 Beatrice Webb Diary 11.02 1889
393 Beatrice Webb Diary 01.06.1890
394 Beatrice to Sidney, 22.06.1890; in Webb, B & Webb, S; *The Letters of Sidney and Beatrice Webb*; Vol I; Cambridge; CUP; 1978; ed Mackenzie, N; p 154
395 Sidney to Beatrice, 24,06.1980; Webb, B & Webb, S; *The Letters of Sidney and Beatrice Webb*; Vol I; Cambridge; CUP; 1978; ed Mackenzie, N; p 155
396 Beatrice to Sidney, 22.06.1890; in Webb, B & Webb, S; *The Letters of Sidney and Beatrice Webb*; Vol I; Cambridge; CUP; 1978; ed Mackenzie, N; p 154
397 Beatrice Webb Diary 27.07.1890
398 Sidney to Beatrice, 29.07.1890, in Webb, B & Webb, S; *The Letters of Sidney and Beatrice Webb; Vol I*; Cambridge; CUP; 1978; p 160
399 Beatrice Webb Diary 27.07.1890
400 Beatrice Webb Diary 27.07.1890
401 Sidney to Beatrice, 29.07.1890, in Webb, B & Webb, S; *The Letters of Sidney and Beatrice Webb*; Vol I; Cambridge; CUP; 1978; p 161
402 Beatrice to Sidney, 09.08.1890, in Webb, B & Webb, S; *The Letters of Sidney and Beatrice Webb*; Vol I; Cambridge; CUP; 1978; p 162
403 Sidney to Beatrice, 29.07.1890, in Webb, B & Webb, S; *The Letters of Sidney and Beatrice Webb*; Vol I; Cambridge; CUP; 1978; p 160
404 Beatrice to Sidney, 09.08.1890, in Webb, B & Webb, S; *The Letters of Sidney and Beatrice Webb*; Vol I; Cambridge; CUP; 1978; p 162
405 Sidney to Beatrice, 11.08.1890, in Webb, B & Webb, S; *The Letters of Sidney and Beatrice Webb*; Vol I; Cambridge; CUP; 1978; p 164
406 Beatrice to Sidney, 11.08.1890, in Webb, B & Webb, S; *The Letters of Sidney and Beatrice Webb*; Vol I; Cambridge; CUP; 1978; p 166
407 Beatrice to Ella Pycroft ?mid-August 1890; in Webb, B & Webb, S; *The Letters of Sidney and Beatrice Webb*; Vol I; Cambridge; CUP, 1978, p 177
408 Beatrice Webb Diary 26.08.1890
409 Shaw, GB, and Cole, M; *Early Days*; in Cole, M ed. *The Webbs and their*

Work; London, Frederick Muller, 1949; p 13

410 GBS to Beatrice, 06.10.1890; <u>in</u> Michalos, AC & Poff, DC; editors; *Bernard Shaw and the Webbs*; Toronto, University of Toronto Press, 2002; p10

411 Sidney to Beatrice, 12.10.1890, in *Webb, B & Webb, S; The Letters of Sidney and Beatrice Webb*; Vol I; Cambridge; CUP, 1978, p 211

412 Morris, William; *A dream of John Ball, and A King's Lesson*; London, Longmans Green & Co; 1907; p133

413 Beatrice to Sidney, 17.10.1890, <u>in</u> Webb, B & Webb, S; *The Letters of Sidney and Beatrice Webb;* Vol I; Cambridge; CUP; 1978; p 223

414 '*Salvation'v. Socialism; article by John Law (Margaret Harkness); Pall Mall Gazette,* 21.10.1890

415 Beatrice Webb Diary 22.10.1890

416 '*Salvation' v. Socialism;* article by John Law (Margaret Harkness); *Pall Mall Gazette,* 21.10.1890

417 Beatrice to Sidney, 09.1890, <u>in</u> Webb, B & Webb, S; *The Letters of Sidney and Beatrice Webb*; Vol I; Cambridge; CUP; 1978; p 185

418 Sidney to Beatrice, 19.09.1890, <u>in</u> Webb, B & Webb, S*; The Letters of Sidney and Beatrice Webb*; Vol I; Cambridge; CUP, 1978, p 190

419 Sidney to Beatrice, 19.09.1890, <u>in</u> Webb, B & Webb, S*; The Letters of Sidney and Beatrice Webb*; Vol I; Cambridge; CUP, 1978, p 191

420 Beatrice Webb Diary 02.10.1990
421 Beatrice Webb Diary 02.10.1990
422 Sidney to Beatrice, 08.10.1890, <u>in</u> Webb, B & Webb, S; *The Letters of Sidney and Beatrice Webb;* Vol I; Cambridge; CUP, 1978, p199

423 Beatrice to Sidney, 08.10.1890, <u>in</u> Webb, B & Webb, S; *The Letters of Sidney and Beatrice Webb;* Vol I; Cambridge; CUP; 1978; p 201

424 Beatrice to Sidney, 08.10.1890, <u>in</u> Webb, B & Webb, S; *The Letters of Sidney and Beatrice Webb;* Vol I; Cambridge; CUP; 1978; p 201

425 Beatrice to Sidney, 08.10.1890, <u>in</u> Webb, B & Webb, S; *The Letters of Sidney and Beatrice Webb;* Vol I; Cambridge; CUP; 1978; p 201

426 Beatrice to Sidney, 08.10.1890, <u>in</u> Webb, B & Webb, S; *The Letters of Sidney and Beatrice Webb;* Vol I; Cambridge; CUP; 1978; p 201

427 Beatrice to Sidney, 09.10.1890, <u>in</u> Webb, B & Webb, S; *The Letters of Sidney and Beatrice Webb*; Vol I; Cambridge; CUP; 1978; p 201

428 Sidney to Beatrice, 08.10.1890, <u>in</u> Webb, B & Webb, S; *The Letters of Sidney and Beatrice Webb*; Vol I; Cambridge; CUP, 1978, p 205

429 Sidney to Beatrice, 08.10.1890, <u>in</u> Webb, B & Webb, S; *The Letters of Sidney and Beatrice Webb*; Vol I; Cambridge; CUP, 1978, p 205

430 Sidney to Beatrice, 12.10.1890, <u>in</u> Webb, B & Webb, S; *The Letters of Sidney and Beatrice Webb*; Vol I; Cambridge; CUP, 1978, p 211

431 Beatrice to Sidney, 17.10.1890, <u>in</u> Webb, B & Webb, S; *The Letters of Sidney and Beatrice Webb*; Vol I; Cambridge; CUP; 1978; p 223

432 Sidney to Beatrice, 15.10.1890, <u>in</u> Webb, B & Webb, S; *The Letters of Sidney and Beatrice Webb*; Vol I; Cambridge; CUP, 1978, p 217

433 Charles Booth to Beatrice; 15.10.1890; LSE Library; PASSFIELD 2/1/2/8

434 Charles Booth to Beatrice; 15.10.1890; LSE Library; PASSFIELD 2/1/2/8

435 Charles Booth to Beatrice; 15.10.1890; LSE Library; PASSFIELD 2/1/2/8

436 Beatrice Webb Diary 22.10.1890

437 Beatrice to Sidney, 17.10.1890, <u>in</u> Webb, B & Webb, S; *The Letters of Sidney and Beatrice Webb*; Vol I; Cambridge; CUP; 1978; p 223

438 Beatrice Webb Diary 06.11.1890
439 Beatrice Webb Diary 06.11.1890
440 Beatrice Webb Diary 15.11.1890
441 Beatrice Webb Diary 01.12.1890
442 Beatrice Webb Diary 01.12.1890
443 Beatrice Webb Diary 01.12.1890
444 Beatrice Webb Diary 01.12.1890
445 Sidney to Beatrice, 05.12.1890, <u>in</u> Webb, B & Webb, S; *The Letters of Sidney and Beatrice Webb*; Vol I; Cambridge; CUP, 1978, p 236

446 Sidney to Beatrice, 04.12.1890, <u>in</u> Webb, B & Webb, S; *The Letters of Sidney and Beatrice Webb*; Vol I; Cambridge; CUP, 1978, p 234

447 Beatrice to Sidney, ?07.12.1890, in Webb, B & Webb, S; *The Letters of Sidney and Beatrice Webb*; Vol I; Cambridge; CUP; 1978; pp 238-9

448 Beatrice to Sidney, ?07.12.1890, in Webb, B & Webb, S; *The Letters of Sidney and Beatrice Webb;* Vol I; Cambridge; CUP; 1978; pp 238-9

449 Beatrice to Sidney, ?07.12.1890, in Webb, B & Webb, S; *The Letters of Sidney and Beatrice Webb*; Vol I; Cambridge; CUP; 1978; pp 238-9

450 Beatrice to Sidney, ?09.12.1890, in Webb, B & Webb, S; *The Letters of Sidney and Beatrice Webb*; Vol I; Cambridge; CUP; 1978; pp 240

451 Beatrice Webb Diary 12.12.1890

452 Beatrice to Sidney, ?14.12.1890, in Webb, B & Webb, S; *The Letters of Sidney and Beatrice Webb; Vol I;* Cambridge; CUP; 1978; pp 244-5

453 Sidney to Beatrice, 30.12.1890, in Webb, B & Webb, S; *The Letters of Sidney and Beatrice Webb;* Vol I; Cambridge; CUP, 1978, p 245

454 Beatrice Webb Diary 31.12.1890

455 Beatrice Webb Diary 29.12.1890

456 Beatrice to Sidney, ?01.01.1891, in Webb, B & Webb, S; *The Letters of Sidney and Beatrice Webb;* Vol I; Cambridge; CUP; 1978; p 246

457 Beatrice Webb Diary 04.01.1891

458 Beatrice Webb Diary 13.01.1891

459 Beatrice Webb Diary 13.01.1891

460 Beatrice to Sidney, ?21.01.1891, in Webb, B & Webb, S; *The Letters of Sidney and Beatrice Webb*; Vol I; Cambridge; CUP; 1978; p 250-1

461 Sidney to Beatrice, 22.01.1891; in *Webb, B & Webb, S; The Letters of Sidney and Beatrice Webb;* Vol I; Cambridge; CUP, 1978, p 251

462 Beatrice Webb Diary 22.01.1891

463 Beatrice Webb Diary 02.03.1891

464 Webb, B; *My Apprenticeship*; London, Longmans, 1926; p 411

465 Horace Plunkett Diary, 18.05.1891

466 Beatrice Webb Diary 22.05.1891

467 Beatrice to Sidney, 21.05.1892, in Webb, B & Webb, S; *The Letters of Sidney and Beatrice Webb;* Vol I; Cambridge; CUP; 1978; p 414

468 Sidney to Beatrice, 21.05.1891, in Webb, B & Webb, S; *The Letters*

469 Sidney to Beatrice, 23.05.1891, in Webb, B & Webb, S; *The Letters of Sidney and Beatrice Webb*; Vol I; Cambridge; CUP, 1978, p 271 *of Sidney and Beatrice Webb*; Vol I; Cambridge; CUP, 1978, p 272

470 Beatrice Webb Diary 20.06.1891

471 Beatrice Webb Diary, 07.07.1891

472 Beatrice Webb Diary 09.07.1891

473 John Burns Diary, 29.09.1891 British Library add ms 46310

474 Beatrice Webb Diary 11.08.1891

475 Beatrice to Sidney ? 09.12.1891

476 Sidney to Beatrice, 09.12.1891

477 Longford, Elizabeth *The Pebbled Shore*; Stroud, Sutton Publishing, 2004;p 291

478 Beatrice to Sidney, 20.08.1891, in Webb, B & Webb, S; *The Letters of Sidney and Beatrice Webb*; Vol I; Cambridge; CUP; 1978; p 281

479 Sidney to Beatrice, 07.09.1891, in Webb, B & Webb, S; *The Letters of Sidney and Beatrice Webb*; Vol I; Cambridge; CUP, 1978, p 288

480 Sidney to Beatrice, 23.09.1891, in Webb, B & Webb, S; *The Letters of Sidney and Beatrice Webb*; Vol I; Cambridge; CUP, 1978, p 308

481 Beatrice Webb Diary; 27.12.1891

482 Ella Pycroft to Beatrice, 10.01.1892; LSE Library; PASSFIELD 2/1/2/7

483 Ella Pycroft to Beatrice, 10.01.1892; LSE Library; PASSFIELD 2/1/2/7

484 Beatrice Webb Diary 05.05.1939

485 Beatrice to Sidney, 01.11.1891, in Webb, B & Webb, S; *The Letters of Sidney and Beatrice Webb*; Vol I; Cambridge; CUP; 1978; p 320

486 Beatrice Webb Diary 27.12.1891

487 Beatrice to Sidney, 30.12.1891, in Webb, B & Webb, S; *The Letters of Sidney and Beatrice Webb*; Vol I; Cambridge; CUP; 1978; p 365

488 Beatrice to Sidney, 30.12.1891, in Webb, B & Webb, S; *The Letters of Sidney and Beatrice Webb*; Vol I; Cambridge; CUP; 1978; p 365

489 Sidney to Beatrice, 31.12.1891, in Webb, B & Webb, S; *The Letters of Sidney and Beatrice Webb*; Vol I; Cambridge; CUP, 1978, p 366

490 Beatrice Webb Diary 21.01,1892

491 Beatrice to Sidney, 06.01.1892, in Webb, B & Webb, S; *The Letters*

of Sidney and Beatrice Webb; Vol I; Cambridge; CUP; 1978; p 377

492 Beatrice to Sidney, 20.08.1891, in Webb, B & Webb, S; *The Letters of Sidney and Beatrice Webb*; Vol I; Cambridge; CUP; 1978; p 281

493 Beatrice to Sidney, 03.01.1892, in Webb, B & Webb, S; *The Letters of Sidney and Beatrice Webb*; Vol I; Cambridge; CUP; 1978; p 372

494 Beatrice to Sidney, ?04.01.1892, in Webb, B & Webb, S; *The Letters of Sidney and Beatrice Webb*; Vol I; Cambridge; CUP; 1978; p 372

495 Beatrice Webb Diary 21.01.1892

496 Dobbs, Rosie; typescript autobiography, (BL Add MS 50657) p 88

497 Dobbs, Rosie; typescript autobiography, (BL Add MS 50657) p 114

498 Sidney to Beatrice, 16.03.1892), quoted in Webb, B & Webb, S; *The Letters of Sidney and Beatrice Webb*; Vol I; Cambridge; CUP, 1978, p 394

499 Sidney to Beatrice, 23.03.1892; in Webb, B & Webb, S; *The Letters of Sidney and Beatrice Webb*; Vol I; Cambridge; CUP, 1978, p 396

500 Sidney to Beatrice, 24.03.1892; in Webb, B & Webb, S; *The Letters of Sidney and Beatrice Webb*; Vol I; Cambridge; CUP, 1978, p 400

501 Beatrice to Sidney, 25.03.1892, in Webb, B & Webb, S; *The Letters of Sidney and Beatrice Webb;* Vol I; Cambridge; CUP; 1978; p 402

502 Beatrice Webb Diary 27.12.1891

503 Beatrice Webb Diary 25.12.1893

504 Beatrice Webb Diary 22.04.1887

505 Beatrice Webb Diary 21.01.1892

506 Beatrice to Sidney, ?08.12.1891, in Webb, B & Webb, S; *The Letters of Sidney and Beatrice Webb*; Vol I; Cambridge; CUP; 1978; p 344

507 Beatrice to Sidney, 09.12.1891, in Webb, B & Webb, S; *The Letters of Sidney and Beatrice Webb*; Vol I; Cambridge; CUP; 1978; p 347

508 Sidney to Beatrice, 07.01.1892, in Webb, B & Webb, S; *The Letters of Sidney and Beatrice Webb*; Vol I; Cambridge; CUP, 1978, p 347

509 Beatrice to Sidney, undated, late February 1892, quoted in Webb, B & Webb, S; *The Letters of Sidney and*

Beatrice Webb; Vol I; Cambridge; CUP; 1978; p 390

510 Sidney to Graham Wallas, 06.03.1892, in Webb, B & Webb, S; *The Letters of Sidney and Beatrice Webb*; Vol I; Cambridge; CUP, 1978, p 393

511 Sidney to Graham Wallas, 06.03.1892, in Webb, B & Webb, S; *The Letters of Sidney and Beatrice Webb*; Vol I; Cambridge; CUP, 1978, p 393

512 Sidney to Beatrice, 24.03.1892), in Webb, B & Webb, S; *The Letters of Sidney and Beatrice Webb*; Vol I; Cambridge; CUP, 1978, p 400

513 Sidney to Beatrice, 12.05.1892), in Webb, B & Webb, S; *The Letters of Sidney and Beatrice Webb*; Vol I; Cambridge; CUP, 1978, p.411

514 Sidney to Beatrice, 05.07.1892), in Webb, B & Webb, S; *The Letters of Sidney and Beatrice Webb*; Vol I; Cambridge; CUP, 1978, p 433

515 Diary of Robert Holt; quoted in Muggeridge, K & Adam, R; *Beatrice Webb: A life 1858-1943*; London, Secker & Warburg, 1967; p 129

516 Diary of Robert Holt; quoted in Muggeridge, K & Adam, R; *Beatrice Webb: A life 1858-1943*; London, Secker & Warburg, 1967; p 129

517 Diary of Robert Holt; quoted in Muggeridge, K & Adam, R; *Beatrice Webb: A life 1858-1943*; London, Secker & Warburg, 1967; p 129

518 Beatrice Webb Diary 23.07.1892

PART TWO:
PERMEATION 1892 - 1912

Chapter Five: The firm of Webb 1892-1899

MARRIAGE AND HONEYMOON

The marriage of Beatrice Potter and Sidney Webb in July 1892 marked the start of a fifty-year partnership. In her first volume of autobiography – *My Apprenticeship* (1926) – Beatrice described their relationship as

> *...working comradeship founded in a common faith and made perfect by marriage; perhaps the most exquisite, certainly the most enduring, of all the varieties of happiness.* [1]

She referred to Sidney and herself as the *firm of Webb*. [2]

Alfred Gardiner, editor of the Liberal *Daily News* and a frequent guest at the Webbs' London home, thought their personalities had become almost completely merged; they were *so entirely one*

> *...that they seem to have dropped their separate identities.* [3]

They had lost, he said, the use of the first person singular; they spoke, not of 'I', but of 'we':

> *'We think', says Mr Webb from his end of the table, and 'We venture to take the view,' says Mrs Webb from her end.* [4]

Bertrand Russell thought they were very averse to any romantic view of love or marriage.

In his caricature of the Webbs, H G Wells described a conversation with them:

> *'We have read your book', each began – as though it had been a joint function. 'And we consider-'* [5]

Herbert Samuel thought that the Webb partnership developed into a kind of dual personality, resulting in

> *...an output of literary work on their own special subjects, and of public activity, which has probably never been equalled.* [6]

After their wedding, Sidney and Beatrice took a two month honeymoon. It was largely a working holiday: after an overnight stay at Chester, they travelled on to Dublin and Belfast to study trade union records. They did, however, enjoy

...*two delightful days of real honeymoon*[7], staying with Horace Plunkett, the Irish pioneer of cooperatives, in the Wicklow hills. Beatrice wrote to Wallas

We are very very happy – far too happy to be reasonable[8]

In Belfast Sidney met the local Fabians:

...a good sort of fellows... Well worth encouraging[9]

In August they went on to Glasgow, for more research and the annual Trades Union Congress.

In Scotland they also stayed with Haldane at his home at Cloan. There they met some of the 'Souls' – a cross-party coterie with shared literary and intellectual interests. Beatrice reported to Wallas:

Under Haldane's beneficial gaze Souls looked at us with eager curiosity and we on the Souls with wondering admiration for they were good to look at.[10]

The visit to Haldane was not purely social. There had been a general election in July. Salisbury's Conservatives had lost. Gladstone's Liberals had formed a government, relying on support from the Irish National Party. Keir Hardie was now an Independent Labour MP; Burns had won Battersea with Liberal support. Leading Fabians had campaigned hard; GBS had spoken at two of Burns' meetings. Haldane, re-elected as a Liberal, did not become a minister, preferring to influence education and social policy.

The Webbs had followed politics while they were away, Sidney corresponding with GBS and Pease. They discussed policy with Haldane, including

...the possibilities of reorganizing the Home Office as the Ministry of Labour, perfecting the Factory Department.[11]

Beatrice wrote to Wallas

...we left Haldane with excellent instructions to be handed on to all the ministers.[12]

They arrived back in London in late September. Shaw saw them at a Fabian meeting on Friday 7 October

...Webb and his wife appeared for the first time since their marriage.[13]

'LITTLE HOME ON THE BANKS OF THE THAMES'

They made their home in London. For a year they lived in a Hampstead flat; then, from autumn 1893, they leased 41 Grosvenor Road, on the Thames Embankment. That part of Grosvenor Road is now Millbank. No 41 was damaged in the

Blitz; the Millbank Tower now stands where it stood. It was not beautiful; their first biographer (who knew it well) called it *distressingly ugly.* [14]

What appealed to Beatrice was the *unique interest and beauty* of the location:

To spring out of bed on a summer morning and see, spread out before you, the sun rising behind Lambeth Palace, on clear days the Dome of St Paul's and the spires of the city churches, its rays lighting up the tiny waves breaking the surface of the swift-flowing tidal river, whilst oar-steered barges, some with red or yellow sails, drifting rafts of timber and steaming colliers passed under the Vauxhall and Lambeth bridges, was a joyful greeting to another day. [15]

Neighbours included Alice Green and Frank Costelloe – (an LCC colleague of Sidney's, ex Toynbee Hall). It was a short walk to Spring Gardens, the LCC headquarters.

In summer 1893 the Webbs worked on the trade union book, staying at The Argoed, where GBS, Wallas, and Beatrice's sister Rosie joined them for part of the time.

While they were in Wales they had 41 Grosvenor Road decorated. Their taste was pre-Raphaelite and arts and crafts. Beatrice wanted

…no self-indulgence and show but beautiful surroundings – i.e. the best tack and the best workmanship…So I have gone to Morris's for papers and furniture and spent days over my curtains and in looking up charming old bits of furniture in second-hand furniture shops. [16]

Beatrice spent days choosing curtains, and toured second-hand shops looking for *charming* pieces of furniture

All of which causes the enemy (i.e. my sisters) to blaspheme – saying 'They do not see much socialism in that'. [17]

Beatrice tried to persuade herself that she needed beautiful things to work with. Sidney's answer was that they must work to justify the choices they had made.

While Sidney and Beatrice were away, Kate Courtney (who still lived nearby on Cheyne Walk) monitored progress:

Dear Bee,

I went to 41 this morning: the drawing room paper is not up and I am to go again on Tuesday when it is up and the rail varnished in the ivory colour it is to be. I distinctly prefer the yellowish pale buff for the frieze but want to see it with the tint of the rail as it should be a shade darker, but the green looks very well and safe only colder for winter. [18]

Even when they returned the house was not finished; the work continued into October. GBS, arriving for dinner on 23 September, found them lodging with Costelloe:

We went into the new house together and looked at wallpapers etc. [19]

The novelist H G Wells got to know 41 Grosvenor Road after 1900, calling it *a hard little house*. Its beauty eluded him. On the walls hung

...two or three indifferent watercolours, there was scarcely any furniture but a sofa or so and a chair, and the floor, severely carpeted with matting... [20]

Sidney and Beatrice planned their home for work and hospitality. The ground and first floors were long, narrow East-West through rooms, catching morning and evening sunlight. The lower room, lined with bookshelves, was for meals and work. They worked at the dining table; their meals were served there by the maids. The long, white-painted room above was the drawing room, designed to accommodate the maximum number of guests, standing or sitting; long seats in alcoves, easy chairs, but no sofa.

Their first secretary was Frank Galton – a young engraver, trade unionist and Fabian. Galton worked in a small room off the landing between the ground and first floors. He described their working day; mornings were for writing and research. After breakfast

...we all smoked a cigarette together, and discussed the coming morning's work, while the table was cleared. By nine o'clock, the Webbs had started to work, seated each at one end of the table facing one another with the necessary books and papers at hand. [21]

At 1.00, work was cleared away, and lunch served. Afterwards Sidney would go to Spring Gardens. Beatrice would rest, then go for a walk, or make social calls.

Writing to Sidney during their August 1892 honeymoon, GBS had made an important suggestion:

I am seriously of the opinion that what is wanted here is a salon for the social cultivation of the Socialist party in parliament. Will Madam Potter-Webb undertake it? [22]

Grosvenor Road would become the home of that salon; its beginnings were slow. Old friends dined; the ILP and the Fabians encountered each other; contact with Charles and Mary Booth was hesitantly resumed; but the salon emerged later.

Regular visitors included GBS and Wallas. Beatrice called Sidney, Graham and Shaw *the Fabian Junta*. Shaw referred to their dinner on 23 September 1893 as *the first Junta dinner*. For the next few years GBS ate with the Webbs at least fortnightly, often for a weekend lunch. One Sunday lunchtime in 1895, he noted in his diary *Webbs as usual.*[23]

In their *History of Trade Unionism*, the Webbs called the emerging leadership of the trade unions in the 1860s the 'Trade Union Junta'; a little circle, including

...men of marked character and ability, who were, both by experience and by temperament, admirably fitted to guide the movement...[24]

For Beatrice to use the same word to describe the Fabian leadership was a compliment.

Wallas, noted Beatrice, was

...a constant visitor for Sunday midday dinner and walks on Hampstead Heath.[25]

GBS and Wallas were among Sidney's oldest friends. Beatrice met them during her courtship; in 1893 she noted her impressions. Wallas was

...six foot with a slouching figure, good features and genial open smile, utterly unselfconscious and lacking in vanity or personal ambition.[26]

Shaw a

...marvellously smart witty fellow...An artist to the tips of his fingers and an admirable craftsman.[27]

She assessed the roles of the three:

Sidney is the organizer and gives most of the practical initiative, Graham Wallas imparts the morality and scrupulousness, Bernard Shaw gives the sparkle and flavour.[28]

She thought that if John Burns became a fourth member, they would be invincible. She also thought it would never happen.

Beatrice now, publicly, acknowledged her Fabian membership, which was approved by the Executive Committee on 14 April 1893.

THE WEBBS' YEAR

Sidney and Beatrice intended spending most of their time at home in London. The rest of each year would be research trips, or stays in the countryside. Those stays were part holiday, part work, to get the books written.

For most of the 1890s, Richard Potter's executors retained The Argoed. In 1893, Sidney and Beatrice spent summer and Christmas there, with GBS and Wallas. They returned for the summers of 1895 and 1897, and at Whitsun 1896.

At other times they stayed with family or friends.

In May 1893, Beatrice's sister Theresa died, in her 40s, after a short illness. She had married Charles Alfred Cripps – the *little jewel of an advocate*. Theresa was the first of the Potter sisters to die. Beatrice mourned her – but realised that in life they had not been close. After Theresa's death, Sidney and Beatrice spent several Christmases with Alfred in Oxfordshire. They also stayed with Lallie in the Lake District, and Maggie in Somerset.

Sometimes they stayed nearer London. For summer 1894 they rented Borough Farm, near Godalming; in spring 1895 they spent a week at Beachy Head with Wallas, GBS, and Herbert Samuel – a recent Oxford graduate, a Liberal with Fabian sympathies, who first met Sidney while still a student. He remained a friend of the Webbs for the rest of their lives.

That year, Beatrice said Samuel was one of

...a certain set of young people all more or less devoted to the Fabian Junta.[29]

Others in this group included Ramsay MacDonald, Charles Trevelyan, and Bertrand Russell. Trevelyan, a committed Liberal, was elected to the London School Board in 1896, and became an MP in 1899.

Beatrice described Russell – mathematician, philosopher, Fellow of Trinity College Cambridge – as

...a very young *man with considerable intellectual promise...*[30]

In 1894 Russell married Alys Pearsall Smith, an American Quaker. They lived in a cottage, Friday's Hill, near Haslemere; Beatrice and Sidney frequently stayed with them.

Samuel, Trevelyan, and MacDonald were also involved with another group, the Rainbow Circle – a discussion group aiming to bring together different strands of progressive opinion. Others Rainbow Circle participants included Wallas, Olivier, Frank Costelloe, and William Clarke, (one of the original Fabian Essayists).

Beatrice invited Samuel again in 1896:

We have taken a small rectory in Suffolk five miles from the sea – we should be so glad if you could spend a week with us and bring your bicycle and your work. We work all the mornings and take our exercise in the afternoons. There are four sitting-rooms – some diminutive – so fortunately we can work alone.[31]

In spring 1897 the Webbs and GBS rented a house in Dorking. Alice Green, Wallas, Herbert Samuel, and Russell all came for weekends. So did Pember Reeves – a New Zealand Fabian who had come to London as the country's diplomatic representative – and his wife Maud. In New Zealand, Pember had been a Labour Party minister, while Maud had been active in the campaign for women's suffrage.

In the 1890s Sidney and Beatrice also took two longer trips. In May 1894 they spent three weeks in Italy. In 1898 they went to the United States, New Zealand, and Australia for nine months.

Sidney and Beatrice had always been energetic walkers; in 1895 they and GBS discovered cycling. At Beachy Head, wrote Shaw,

...I have been trying to learn the bicycle; and after a desperate struggle, renewed on two successive days, I will do twenty yards... I will not be beaten by that hellish machine.[32]

For Beatrice, the time at Beachy Head was *jolly*:

...learning the bicycle and sitting out chatting on the cliff.[33]

That summer, at The Argoed, she described their bicycles as *most absorbing new toys.*[34] Cycling had

...brought some 'fun' or 'sport' into my life, an element that was somewhat lacking ...[35]

Russell and GBS were there too. Shaw still found cycling tough; Monmouthshire was *vile country for bicycling*:

The hills are so bad it sometimes takes an hour and a half to go five miles; and each ride ends by shoving the thing up 800 feet through impossible lanes to this Argoed/Ararat.[36]

Then Russell and Shaw collided:

...a most awful bicycle smash – the quintessence of ten railway collisions – dashed into at full speed flying down a hill ...Russell bereft of his knickerbockers but otherwise unhurt.[37]

During the holiday, GBS and the Webbs rode down to Cardiff to attend the TUC; at the end, they cycled back to London in three days.

Before Sidney married, his regular companions had been Wallas and GBS. After the marriage, Beatrice worried about Wallas:

Like many men who live and work alone he is a joyless being... We are probably his nearest and dearest friends with whom he feels perfectly at ease, ...But friends, however dear, are no substitute for a beloved partner ...[38]

Shaw was different. Beatrice thought he lived

...in a drama or comedy of which he himself is the hero – his amour propre *is satisfied by the jealousy and restless devotion of half a dozen women.*[39]

Beatrice doubted whether Shaw would ever marry.

In 1895 the Webbs met Charlotte Payne-Townshend. Aged 38, Irish, she was well-off, single, and politically sympathetic. She joined the Fabians and donated to the Webbs' causes. In January 1896 she met GBS.

That summer, Beatrice invited Charlotte to join them in Suffolk. Beatrice thought her

...a pleasant, well-dressed, well-intentioned woman – I thought she should do very well for Graham Wallas.[40]

But Wallas bored Charlotte. Instead, wrote Beatrice

In a few days she and Bernard Shaw were constant companions.[41]

Shaw wrote to the actor Ellen Terry (to whom he had been close) that he had met a clever Irish millionairess:

I am going to refresh my heart by falling in love with her – I love falling in love...[42]

Charlotte was another cyclist. At the end of the holiday, she rode back to London with Shaw and both Webbs. By the following summer Charlotte and GBS were sharing a tandem. Beatrice watched the relationship evolve; uneasy about Shaw, she doubted if he could be induced to marry:

I see no sign on his side of the growth of any genuine and steadfast affection.[43]

Charlotte began to act as Shaw's secretary; Beatrice thought her restless and unhappy. When the Webbs went to the United States in March 1898, Beatrice invited Charlotte to come too. Instead, she went to Rome; Beatrice thought a study of Italian local government was needed.

Shaw developed a foot infection. It swelled up; soon he was limping and in pain. He wrote to Charlotte in Italy, and at the end of April she came home. She had not previously visited the flat Shaw shared with his mother in Fitzroy Square; she was shocked to discover chaos and squalor. Charlotte nursed him, prescribing rest and fresh country air. GBS agreed; they then decided that, if they were living under the same roof, they should get married.

Shaw had always said he was against marriage; now he wrote to Beatrice

...I changed right about face on the subject and hopped down to the Registrar, who married me to her on one leg...[44]

The wedding was on 1 June; the following week, GBS and Charlotte moved to Haslemere. The Webbs returned in December and immediately visited the Shaws.

Wallas married too (without any further assistance from Beatrice). In 1897 he became engaged to Ada Radford, described by Beatrice as

...a woman of forty or thereabouts and one of a cultivated, public spirited, somewhat aesthetic middle-class family.[45]

She wrote to Graham:

You seem to be making an ideal marriage – just such another as our own! (the highest compliment we can pay you).[46]

Beatrice did not immediately take to Ada

...she looks as if she had tumbled up out of an armchair in which she had spent the night, and her movements are aggressively ugly.[47]

Beatrice thought they would not be friends. But their friendship endured, long after Wallas had left the Fabians. Beatrice also thought there was no prospect of children – in fact, Graham and Ada had a daughter, May, in 1898.

THE TRADE UNION BOOKS

Most of the research for the *History of Trade Unionism* was finished before the Webbs married in July 1892. They began drafting that autumn – partly in London, otherwise during their long stays at The Argoed, with GBS and Wallas. Beatrice found it tough; the first chapter was finished by Christmas 1892, but she was critical:

Not altogether satisfactory. Wants movement.[48]

By March two more chapters were drafted. Beatrice worried; it was hard

...to tell whether one is doing one's level best or becoming complacent with a low level of exertion.[49]

In summer 1893 the Webbs spent six weeks at The Argoed. Beatrice arrived first, and worked on the book by herself. Sidney joined her later; then Wallas, and later GBS, arrived. Wallas read and criticized the first chapter, to the point where Beatrice felt desperate about its shortcomings. She worked out a new outline for the chapter; Sidney redrafted the text.

GBS arrived on 26 August; Graham and Sidney met him at the station. That afternoon, the Webbs and their guests went walking. In the evening Sidney read a chapter of the trade union book to the assembled company.

Shaw stayed three weeks; his time was divided between helping the Webbs with the trade union book, and his new play, on which he began work the morning after his arrival. He walked a mile from the house, lay down on the grass,

...and got to work from 11 to 13 on a new play, Mrs Warren's Profession. [50]

That evening Sidney read out another chapter of their trade union book, while after lunch on Wednesday, Shaw read the first act of his play to Sidney and Beatrice.

The writers supported each other. GBS worked hard on the trade union book; Beatrice noted that

The form of the first chapter satisfied him, and he altered only words and sentences, the second chapter he took more in hand, and the third he is to a large extent remodelling. [51]

In turn, the Webbs helped Shaw with the play. The heroine, Vivie Warren, developed as a gilded spinster; Beatrice suggested that Shaw

...should put on the stage a real modern lady of the governing class – not the sort of thing that theatrical and critical authorities imagine such a lady to be. [52]

John Burns had already earned a reputation as a collector of books and other material on trade unionism. In October 1893 Beatrice spent a morning with him looking at documents. He wrote in his diary:

Mrs Sidney Webb called and I gave her the loan of a cabfull of books – reports, Labour newspapers, pamphlets and documents on trade unionism, Socialism and the Labour movement.[53]

She reflected on their relationship with Burns; it had never been cordial, though

...it promises to be more so in future. [54]

Beatrice's charges against Burns were many; she thought him

...an intriguer who suspected everyone else of intrigue.

He was unfriendly towards Tom Mann; he had been jealous of Sidney as a potential LCC colleague – although Beatrice thought this had lessened. She wanted to be able to think better of Burns; she admired his capacity and straightforwardness. But she thought his 'burning sin' was jealousy, and

...suspicion of rather a mean kind...

A man of splendid physique, fine strong intelligence, human sympathy, practical capacity, he is unfitted for a really great position by his utter inability to be a constant and loyal comrade. He stands absolutely alone. He is intensely jealous of other labour men, acutely suspicious of all middle class sympathisers – while his hatred of Keir Hardie reaches about the dimensions of mania… it is pitiful to see this splendid man a prey to egotism of the most sordid kind… [55]

Beatrice's conclusions about Burns echoed those reached earlier by Margaret Harkness – who had seen him at work during the Dock Strike. In 1891, Harkness had published a series of articles on labour leaders in the *Pall Mall Gazette*. Of Burns, she wrote of his

…deeply-rooted conviction that no one is to be trusted.

And that he

…mistrusts people, and is always on the look-out for a conspiracy… [56]

Unsurprisingly, Beatrice's borrowing of books and journals did not end well. Frank Galton brought most of them back the following February; but neither Galton nor the Webbs could find them all. In particular, Burns thought some issues of a rare 1860s periodical, *The Beehive*, were missing. Recriminations followed; in April, Galton wrote to Burns

Yes; all your Beehives were returned yesterday… [57]

At Christmas 1893, Sidney and Beatrice, with Wallas and GBS, went back to The Argoed. While Beatrice drafted the last chapter, GBS spent Christmas Day

…reading over and revising the Webbs' trade union book. [58]

Some sections went off to the printers. In the new year Sidney and Beatrice corrected proofs.

The *History of Trade Unionism* was published in May 1894. It was the first – and for decades the only – general history of unions. The Webbs invented the language and concepts – starting by defining a trade union as

…a continuous association of wage-earners for the purpose of maintaining or improving the conditions of their employment. [59]

They traced the growth of unions over the past century, including the recent emergence of the New Unionism.

The book was well received. But having finished it, the Webbs realised that they had written the history of the institutions without explaining what they did: they had no

...systematic and definite theory or vision of how trade unionism actually operated, or what exactly it effected.[60]

So in spring 1894 they began the research and interviews that led to the second book, *Industrial Democracy*. Beatrice began planning in spring 1894:

It will be a difficult and delicate piece of work and need a great deal of hard hammering to weld it into anything like form.[61]

Progress was slow; old anxieties reappeared

Not getting on with our book. It is a horrid grind, this analysis – one sentence is exactly like another – the same words, the same construction – no relief in narrative ... I sometimes despair of getting on with the book – I feel horribly vexed with myself for loitering and idling as I do morning after morning, looking on while poor Sidney drudges along. [62]

There were distractions. In December 1894, the Webbs ran an unsuccessful Progressive slate for the Westminster local authority, the Vestry. In March 1895 Sidney was re-elected to the LCC. Work on the book resumed in April 1895

Finishing each chapter now as we go along ready to be typewritten and submitted to Shaw. [63]

Back at The Argoed in August 1895, two chapters were ready for GBS. Beatrice thought her draft unsatisfactory

I wonder whether other brainworkers make as many futile starts as we do... Having wasted four days, I am disconsolate and discouraged.[64]

In the autumn there was more research. In November Beatrice attended a Derbyshire Miners meeting:

...a stupid, stolid lot of men characterised by fairmindedness and kindliness – but oh! how dense ... [65]

They spent Christmas with Charles Trevelyan's family. Beatrice reflected on a satisfactory autumn's work:

Almost every morning we have worked at the elaborate monographs which make up the chapters – planning – writing – re-writing – polishing – each chapter taking about one month.[66]

She feared they would not finish till 1897 – but thought it would be an 'exhaustive and final' study, good for 50 years.

After Christmas Beatrice attended a miners' conference in Birmingham

...five or six hours in a 'stinking' room with an open sewer on one side and ill-ventilated urinals on the other is not an invigorating occupation.[67]

That summer, when Beatrice arrived in Suffolk, she was *miserable and woebegone*, only watching while Sidney wrote. But later

...we worked well together and have really got within sight of the end of our book and the completion of our theory. [68]

It took another year. In October she was *getting on slowly*. At The Argoed in January it was cold and misty. By day they walked over the moors; in the evening, sat by the fire, Sidney read Ibsen to Beatrice. They worked well, together or separately. Beatrice felt well

...so blessedly happy.

...it has been a splendid time for work: have written the best part of two chapters together.

I doubt whether two persons could stand the stress and strain of this long drawn-out work, this joint struggle with ideas, a perpetual hammering at each other's minds, if it were not for the equally perpetual 'honeymoon' of our life together.[69]

Back in London, progress was again *horribly difficult*. Arriving in Dorking in springtime, Beatrice was

...completely absorbed in thinking out the last chapter of our book.[70]

By late May, both Webbs and GBS were working on the book:

Glorious summer days. In excellent working form. Long mornings spent in work, recasting some of the chapters, filling up crevasses and thinking out the last chapter and foreshadowing the preface. Sidney sits at one table and I at another: the sun streams in through the dancing leaves. As fast as I can plan, he criticizes and executes ...

...an astute reader will quickly divine those chapters which Shaw has corrected and those which he has not – there is a conciseness and crispness in parts subjected to his pruning-knife lacking elsewhere. [71]

Industrial Democracy was finished in autumn 1897 and published in January 1898. Where the first book had described structures, the second set out to analyse what those institutions did.

A century later, Royden Harrison called it

...the most original and comprehensive book ever written about the English trade unions. [72]

Sidney and Beatrice identified three methods by which unions achieved their aims:

- *The method of mutual insurance*
  Insurance against sickness, accident, or unemployment

- *The method of collective bargaining*
  (a term first used by the Webbs)

- *The method of legal enactment*
  Promoting legislation to achieve trade union aims.

Central to those aims was what they called the Common Rule – setting a minimum standard (for pay, hours, and working conditions) below which no employer could go. Employers were, however, free to offer wages and conditions above the Common Rule.

The Webbs went on to suggest that the Common Rule ought to be extended, from individual industries to the community as a whole. They argued for a national minimum wage, national (as opposed to sectoral) statutory restrictions on child labour, and consequential improvements in educational provision. The minimum wage would be determined

...by practical inquiry as to the cost of the food, clothing, and shelter physiologically necessary, according to national habit and custom, to prevent bodily deterioration. [73]

This marked the beginning of their advocacy of a National Minimum; over time, the demand would be applied to a wide range of public services, and became the policy of both the TUC and the Labour Party.

On publication day there were two columns about the book in the Times – plus an abusive leader in the Standard, and other supportive coverage:

Altogether a small triumph in its way. [74]

THE LONDON COUNTY COUNCIL AND LONDON EDUCATION

Sidney was one of 84 Progressives elected to the London County Council (LCC) in March 1892. They were opposed by 34 Municipal Reformers – Conservatives. Sidney, already well known among London Liberals, soon joined the Progressives' leadership group, the Policy Committee.

The LCC Progressives included Liberals, socialists, and trades union-ists – among them John Burns and Will Crooks. The Fabians influenced the Progressives, in particular through Sidney's 1891 *London Programme*. LCC members were unpaid, so needed another income source. Sidney's income came from Beatrice's inheritance; Burns was supported by a Wages Fund raised locally.

Salisbury's Conservative government, which had established the LCC in 1889, soon became alarmed by the radical monster they had created. In 1894 Salisbury described the Council as

...the place where collectivist and socialistic experiments are tried... where a new revolutionary spirit finds its instruments and collects its arms. [75]

When it was set up, the LCC had no role in education. Sidney did not mention education in his 1892 election campaign. Once elected, however, it became his main focus.

Since 1870, elementary education (basic schooling for working class children aged under 14) had been provided by the London School Board. Although their curriculum was limited, Board Schools had achieved major advances in literacy. Board Schools could not provide denominational religious education; public funds paid for the running costs (though not the building costs) of church schools.

Education for children over 14 was less advanced. Few girls benefitted. For boys, there were vestiges of an ancient system: the old public schools, the best known of which had been reorganised in the 1860s, with beneath them old, endowed grammar schools. An enquiry in the 1860s found 782 such schools – but also found that two thirds of English towns had no secondary school. In London, in 1892, 12,500 boys attended 36 endowed secondary schools. Other schools were run by private proprietors.[76]

In the 1880s the London School Board and school boards elsewhere in England, established Higher Grade Schools, enabling children to stay on to 15 or 16, studying maths, science or drawing.

Governments worried that technical skills in Britain were lagging behind other countries. In the 1880s a Royal Commission on Technical Instruction was established. Following their report, in 1889, county councils (not school boards) were empowered to spend money on technical education. In the 1890 budget, some of the proceeds of a new tax on alcoholic drink (known as the Whisky Money) were earmarked for this purpose. Before 1892 the LCC had not used its allocation of Whisky Money.

A campaign was launched – the National Association for the Promotion of Secondary and Technical Education (NAPSTE) – by Hubert Llewellyn Smith and Arthur Acland. Acland, a friend of Haldane, and a progressive Liberal MP, had played a key role in securing the Whisky Money for technical education. Beatrice had met him at Alice Green's. In 1892 Acland became Vice President of the Privy Council for Education – in effect, education minister.

NAPSTE criticized the LCC as

...the only county... that has not hitherto aided technical and secondary education out of the funds accruing to it from the Residue of the Beers and Spirits Duties. [77]

Soon after the LCC election, Llewellyn Smith lobbied Sidney

...to talk over a general Technical Education scheme for London. [78]

In May, the Council established an enquiry into Technical Education, chaired by Sidney. He commissioned Llewellyn Smith to write the report.

Based on his research experience with Barnett, Booth, and the Webbs, Llewellyn Smith produced a comprehensive study of the London labour market. It maps the London trades: building in the south and west; metal and engineering in the east and southeast; woodwork and furniture in Bethnal Green and Shoreditch; print in Holborn and Southwark; chemicals on the south bank; clothing in the East End.

The conclusions were powerful: technical education in London was not only behind France and Germany, but also behind regional centres like Manchester. Craft apprenticeship had collapsed. Education in commercial subjects – including languages and bookkeeping – was *lamentably deficient.*

Of the few in secondary education, it was estimated that 85% came from *professional, trading, and middle class* families, and only 15% from *artisans and labourers.* Science teaching was poor:

No attempt seems to be made to give their pupils an idea that chemistry is a science where new facts may be discovered, and no training in the means of discovery appears to be attempted. [79]

Llewellyn Smith proposed establishing a Technical Education Board, (TEB), composed of 20 LCC members and 15 others – drawn from the London Trades Council and professional, voluntary, and examining bodies.

The recommendation was agreed. Sidney was appointed chair; he remained closely involved until 1904.

The report covered technical and secondary education. Technical provision was to be through polytechnics – evening institutions, with facilities for learning and recreation.

Secondary education would be delivered through low fees, and grants to existing schools, not by establishing new ones. Schools accepting LCC money had to accept LCC representation on their governing bodies, and LCC inspection. The curriculum included drawing and science, with wood and metal work for boys, and 'household economy' for girls.

In 1893 Sidney outlined his vision:

> *We want the very poorest child to be able to remain in school until at least thirteen or fourteen. We want him then to have the chance of adequate scholarships for the secondary schools, and so on to the University or Technical College; and the rest we want through evening class instruction brought to their very door and systematically leading on to the same goal.* [80]

The TEB called their approach *capacity catching*. It set up a *scholarship ladder*, enabling successful children from the Board Schools to go on to the existing grammar or continuation schools. Later critics called this 'selection', arguing that funding places at the old, endowed schools had saved them from extinction, perpetuating a two-tier system. On the other hand, TEB support brought with it inspection, supervision, and control.

The definition of 'technical' was broad. Additional subjects required ministerial approval. Sidney asked Acland to approve as *technical instruction in London* any subject that had been approved anywhere in the country. These included all the sciences, the arts, languages, history, economics, geography, commercial education, and domestic economy. Sidney commented

> *We can now lawfully teach anything except ancient Greek and theology.*[81]

'Domestic Economy' became a major field of activity. Ella Pycroft, Beatrice's former colleague at Katherine Buildings, who had been teaching the subject in Gloucestershire, was appointed 'Lady Organiser of Domestic Economy Classes', at an annual salary of £250. Ella started work at once, proposing to the Board that they should hire ten domestic economy teachers.

Beatrice's sister Mary had started the Gloucestershire school where Ella had taught; in 1894 Beatrice reported to Mary that Ella's

> *...absence of conventionality seems to stand her in good stead with the rum and scratch lot of persons whom you have to work with in any London organisation. But I imagine you taught her a good deal of wisdom in Gloucestershire.*[82]

The London polytechnics already existed; Quintin Hogg, who started Regent Street Polytechnic in 1882, was a Municipal Reform LCC member. As well as funding the polytechnics, the Board supported specialized institutions, including the Shoreditch Technical Institute for furniture, the Leathersellers College in Bermondsey, and the Stepney School for Nautical Cooks. Later they put more into commercial education.

The TEB began operations in 1893; that year, they awarded 500 junior county scholarships. These gave the elementary school pupils who won them free education at any approved secondary or higher grade school, and a £10.00 maintenance grant, to partly compensate parents for loss of earnings. By 1903, the 500 junior scholarships had risen to 600. There were also intermediate and senior scholarships and art and science awards.

For the Webbs, this was a success to be celebrated. Certificates were distributed to the scholars at annual ceremonies; a souvenir programme listed all the names. Beatrice described the 1897 event:

> *A great gathering last night in Queen's Hall – nine hundred LCC scholars receiving their certificates from the Prince of Wales…*
>
> *My boy speaks a few words to the nine hundred children at the end – worth all the rest of the speeches put together – urging them to remember that as London as helped them they must seek, in their future lives, to serve London.* [83]

There were wider opportunities for some of those early successes. In 1906, Beatrice wrote:

> *All this while Sidney is giving at least half his time and thought – perhaps more – to the organization of secondary and higher education in London. This year, four wranglers (Camb.) from the LCC scholars selected nine years ago! He is very happy in the success of his unseen work – all his little schemes, or at least the most dearly cherished of them, have come off.* [84]

The sculptor Eric Gill was awarded a £20.00 Artisan Art Scholarship at the Central School of Arts and Crafts. Aged 21, and working on his own account as a letter cutter and sign writer, he was later commended in the examiners' report:

> *The examiners especially point to the stone-cut capitals of A E R Gill as remarkable for the cleanness and delicacy of the classic outline.*[85]

'SOLID WORK IN ECONOMIC AND POLITICAL PRINCIPLES'

In summer 1894 the Webbs spent three months at Borough Farm, outside Godalming. GBS and Wallas joined them. Shortly after arriving, they heard that the Fabian benefactor, Henry Hutchinson, was dead.

In 1893 'Old Hutch', (as Beatrice called him) had made a will, naming his daughter Constance, and Sidney Webb, as executors. He left his widow a small annuity. Everything else was left in trust jointly *to the said Constance and Webb* and other Fabian Trustees (with Sidney as President and Administrator of the Trustees)

> *...that they may apply the same at once and gradually and at all events within ten years to the propaganda and other purposes of the said Society and its Socialism and towards advancing its objects in any way they deem advisable.* [86]

Then, on 26 July 1894, Old Hutch shot himself.

By the morning after the news arrived, Wallas recalled, Sidney and Beatrice knew what they wanted. They had woken early, had a long discussion, and

> *...at breakfast told us that part of the money would be used to found a School in London on the lines of the Ecole Libre des Sciences Politiques in Paris.* [87]

Sidney's plan was

> *...to found, slowly and quietly, a 'London School of Economics and Political Science' a centre not only of lectures on special subjects, but an association of students who would be directed and supported in doing original work.* [88]

Two questions had to be resolved before this could happen:

Was the will valid? Hutchinson's solicitor, William Harvey Whiston, thought possibly not – he doubted whether Old Hutch had been of sound mind. The provision for Mrs Hutchinson was minimal. Sidney warned the Fabians

> *...there is quite a possibility of the will being upset by the family, as there are several awkward points.* [89]

Sidney avoided challenge by doubling Mrs Hutchinson's annuity, and giving Whiston responsibility for probate.

The object of the bequest was the advancement of socialism. Could that include starting a university?

Sidney turned to Richard Haldane for counsel's opinion. Haldane's instructions listed possible activities, asking

> *...whether any or all of the following purposes would be calculated 'to advance the objects of the Fabian Society...'* [90]

One activity was:

> *(f) The provision by the trustees of public instruction in economic and political science either by way of subsidizing or directly engaging lecturers the foundation of scholarships or the establishment of new educational centres.* [91]

Haldane advised that this – like most of the possible activities – was within the competence of the Trustees. The only activity about which he had doubts was paying election expenses.

Later, William Beveridge gave a more colourful, if second-hand, account. When Sidney consulted Haldane, Haldane asked him whether

> ...he remained a convinced Socialist. On the answer 'yes' followed the further question: 'Do you believe that the more social conditions are studied scientifically and impartially, the stronger does the case for Socialism become?' To this, also, came the answer 'yes'. 'Very well, if you believe that you are entitled to use the bequest for the starting of a School for scientific impartial study and teaching.[92]

Then there was the relationship between the Trustees and the Fabians. The funds had been given to further the Fabian Society's objects. Sidney thought the bequest should not be used for the Fabians' ordinary work:

> Even if all goes well, I do not think the Trustees would be wise to do anything which the Society itself is doing. If the Trustees begin to meet deficits, subscriptions will fall off, and there will be no end to it.[93]

The Webbs, at Borough Farm, developed detailed plans. Beatrice thought

> ...mere propaganda for the shibboleths of collectivism is going on at a rapid rate through the ILP...But reform will not be brought about by shouting. What is needed is hard thinking. And the same objection applies to sending nondescript socialists into Parliament. The Radical members are quite sufficiently compliant in their views...
>
> Last evening we sat by the fire and jotted down a whole list of subjects which want elucidating – issues of fact which need clearing up. Above all, we want the ordinary citizen to feel that reforming society is no light matter, and must be undertaken by experts specially trained for the purpose.[94]

The bequest amounted to about £10,000. Sidney's approach was to keep control with the Trustees, consulting the Fabians and making grants to them for specific projects. In November 1894 he asked the Fabians to suggest projects for the Trust, saying it was clear

> ...that this work should be educational in character.[95]

Suggestions included starting a newspaper; studying international policy; and introducing a study course and an examination as a requirement for Fabian membership.

The Trustees met in February 1895. Sidney repeated that the main object should be educational:

> *…not mere propaganda in the parties but solid work in economic and political principles*
> *Ten years of this work might change the whole political thinking of England.* [96]

Two proposals were agreed:

- £500 to start, initially as an experiment, a London School of Economics and Political Science;

- £150 to organize Fabian lectures around the country.

In March, the Trustees rejected a request from Ramsay MacDonald (since spring 1894 on the Fabian Executive) for funding for the *Progressive Review* – a short-lived journal established by the Rainbow Circle.

> *Letter from J R MacDonald received, making application for aid in establishing the* Progressive Review. *It was decided the matter was not one which the Trustees could take up.* [97]

MacDonald was, however, appointed as a 'Hutchinson Lecturer', to deliver some of the country lectures.

With the Trustees' approval, Sidney could proceed to open the LSE.

He offered Graham Wallas the post of Director; Wallas turned him down. In March 1895 he successfully approached William Hewins – an Oxford economic historian, not a socialist, but a disciple of Canon Barnett.

LSE began with £500 from the Trustees, and £500 from Sidney's LCC Technical Education Board. Hewins made an energetic start – renting premises (9 John Street, off the Strand in central London); approaching lecturers; and advertising for students. In May 1895 Beatrice noted

> *The London School looks promising* [98]

A prospectus appeared in July, announcing that the School would open in October, offering courses in economics, statistics, commerce, commercial geography, commercial history, commercial and industrial law, currency and banking, taxation and finance, and political science.

LSE's first administrator was the secularist and former SDF member, Harry Snell. Snell was now aged thirty; he had moved to London, and had worked for the COS before joining the Fabians in 1890. Harry tried to combine his job with study at the School – until Sidney arrived one morning and abruptly switched him to lecturing for the Trust.

LSE opened with 200 students in October 1895. The Webbs were pleased with the early months: in December, Sidney wrote to Bertrand Russell (who was lecturing, and funded scholarships)

The School is progressing most splendidly – the great economic luminaries are most cordial. [99]

The following autumn LSE moved nearby to 10 Adelphi Terrace. Charlotte Payne-Townshend lived on the upper floors of the building before and after her marriage to GBS. She gave money to the School:

We, knowing she was wealthy, and hearing she was socialistic, interested her in the London School of Economics. She subscribed £1,000 to the Library, endowed a women's scholarship... [100]

Both Webbs raised funds for the Library, which was a separate legal entity:

Sidney wrote to all the politicians, I raked up all my old ball partners, and between us we have raked up a most respectable set of contributors, a list which is eloquent testimony to our respectability! [101]

Every Tuesday Hewins lunched at Grosvenor Road; at Whitsun 1896 he went with the Webbs to The Argoed. But when LSE moved in 1896, Beatrice found him

...in a state of nervous collapse threatening serious illness... [102]

She sent Hewins, plus wife and child, away; she and Sidney took direct responsibility for preparing for the coming term:

Poor Sidney trudges over there directly after breakfast and spends his morning with painters, plumbers and locksmiths, would-be students intervening to whom he gives fatherly advice, comes home to lunch and then off to the LCC. [103]

Thomas Jones, from Rhymney, came to LSE for a term in 1900. From 1895 he had studied economics in Glasgow; there, in 1896, he had joined the Fabians, hearing both Sidney and MacDonald speak:

We went about, it was said, unpacking our hopes of a blissful future, with a New Testament in one pocket and a Fabian Tract in the other, seeking to reconcile the otherworldliness of one and the this-worldliness of the other. [104]

Beatrice recalled TJ at LSE:

When first we knew him, he was a raw Glasgow graduate, destined by his family to become a Methodist minister. Losing his faith, he took to philosophy

*and social economics, came to the London School of Economics as a Shaw
scholar...* [105]

*...one of his earliest remarks was, when he had fathomed the School, 'I see what
you have done, you have torn up all the text books.'* [106]

Hutchinson had thought his bequest would last ten years. When the Trustees
reported in 1904, they had spent almost exactly £10,000. They concluded that
the School, with more than 1300 students and over 20 professors, was now

...one of the leading educational institutions of the metropolis [107]

Success was not achieved without difficulty. In 1895 GBS (who had not got
on with Hutchinson) accused the Trustees of *atrocious malversation*: they were
not being sufficiently left-wing:

*...the Collectivist flag must be waved, and the Marseillaise played if necessary,
in order to attract fresh bequests.* [108]

Shaw was easily dealt with. A more stubborn critic was Ramsay MacDonald,
who followed the activities of the Trustees closely.

Beatrice acknowledged that MacDonald was a *brilliant young Scot* and that
his lectures were successful. But in April 1896 she noted that he was

*...discontented because we refused to have him as a lecturer for the London
School. He is not good enough for that work; he has never had the time to do
any sound original work, or even learn the old stuff well.* [109]

In spring 1896 the Trustees made a further grant to the Library. This roused
MacDonald, who wrote to Pease, the Fabian Secretary:

*...experimenting with a School is most excellent so far as it goes, but for the
purposes of the Trust it ought to be recognised as having very distinct & even
somewhat narrow limits.*

He said the Trustees should report to the executive every six weeks, warning
that

*...I do not think the existing lines of work will save the Trustees from coming
into sharp conflict with at least a section of the Executive & perhaps of the
Society sooner or later.* [110]

MacDonald renewed his attack in April. Pease informed him about commitments made by the Trustees; MacDonald replied

...if you mean that the Hutchinson Trustees have practically mortgaged the Trust to £150 a year to the Fabian (£50 going to the office) and the rest to the School of Economics I shall certainly oppose them and carry through the opposition to the Society if need be.[111]

He demanded a discussion at the next Executive meeting and submitted a resolution.

On holiday in April in the Lake District, Sidney and Beatrice received

...furious letters from J R Macdonald on the 'abuse of the Hutchinson Trust'[112]

At the end of April, the Fabian Executive accepted Macdonald's resolution:

This Executive considers that it ought to be informed from time to time of what the Trustees are doing and requests the Trustees to favour it, for the information of its members, with a statement of monies actually spent or voted and an estimate of expenditure during 1896.[113]

Sidney was asked to report to the AGM.

But MacDonald overreached himself He proposed using the Hutchinson fund to promote the Fabian Society: educational lectures in London; advertising; more provincial lectures; and a 'travelling secretaryship' to organize in the provinces. Parts of MacDonald's proposal were approved in principle; the Hutchinson Trustees were persuaded to allocate another £200 a year to the Fabians, but for purely educational purposes. MacDonald was not satisfied: he forced a vote, but lost 7- 4[114]. MacDonald asked Sidney to let him see the Trust deed and Haldane's opinion. Sidney refused.

Chapter Six: Grosvenor Road 1899-1905

THE WEBB MYTH

Sidney and Beatrice returned from their trip to North America, Australia, and New Zealand just after Christmas 1898.

Since their 1892 marriage they had achieved much. The two trade union books had been successful; LSE was up and running, and Sidney had established a new system of secondary and technical education for London.

Politics was at the centre of their lives. But the destination of their political journey was unclear. Both were Fabians; Sidney had served fourteen years on the Fabian Executive. The 1887 Fabian Basis had declared that Fabians were socialists.

Sidney's closest links were with the Liberal Party. He could have become a Liberal MP; his name was mentioned for particular seats. In 1899 he attended a London Liberal dinner, at which, he told Beatrice

...they meant to make a dead set at me.

But Sidney told them

...very decidedly that I would not stand – and that I don't feel in the least inclined to do so.[115]

Instead, the Webbs worked across party lines, aiming to 'permeate' the existing parties – to work with them to deliver change. Beatrice had summed up this approach in 1894:

the truth is that we want the things done *and we don't much care what persons or which party takes the credit.*[116]

Later she referred to the *Webb myth*: a powerful, unseen, cross-party influence, able to deliver reforms whatever party was in power. She attributed this to Haldane, who

...created and fostered the flattering 'Webb myth' that flowered so agreeably and advantageously for us in the first decade of the twentieth century .[117]

The Conservative Party, led by Lord Salisbury, had regained power in 1895; they renewed their mandate at the 1900 'Khaki' election. Joseph Chamberlain finally became Colonial Secretary in 1895; the South African war kept him in the limelight. Salisbury retired as Prime Minister in July 1902; his successor was his nephew, Arthur Balfour. In March 1903 Chamberlain came out in support of tariffs on imports into Britain, and the creation of a tariff union within the empire. Balfour initially tolerated this departure from Free Trade orthodoxy; in November Chamberlain, however, resigned in order to campaign on the issue.

The Conservatives were split on tariffs; the Liberals were split on the South African war. Meanwhile, Labour politics advanced. In February 1900, the trades unions, the Independent Labour Party, and the Fabian Society jointly established the Labour Representation Committee (LRC), chaired by Keir Hardie. Ramsay MacDonald became its secretary.

In 1903 MacDonald negotiated with the Liberal Chief Whip, Herbert Gladstone, to give Labour candidates a clear run at a number of parliamentary seats at the forthcoming General Election. Between 1900 and 1905 the authority of the Conservative Government was steadily eroded, as they lost twenty four seats to Liberals at byelections.

Like the Webbs, the Fabians were committed to permeation. In 1900 Beatrice noted

> *A Conservative government is as good for us as a Liberal government...Our business is to be friendly to men of all parties.* [118]

Their marriage was close, affectionate, and secure. They had no children; the opportunity was receding. In 1901, married for almost nine years, Beatrice reflected on her

> *...good fortune in entering it with such a partner. We are still in our honeymoon and every year makes our relationship more tender and complete. Rightly or wrongly we decided against having children: I was no longer young, he had been overworking from childhood.*[119]

Sometimes she questioned whether they had been right:

> *Are the books we have written together worth (to the community) the babies we might have had? Then again, I dream over the problem of whether one would marry the same man, in order to have babies, that one would select as joint author?*[120]

There were occasional backward glances. In May 1900 she mused about Chamberlain:

… I find my thoughts constantly wandering to the great man and his family, watching his career with sympathy and interest and desiring his welfare. Sometimes I think I should like to meet him again…[121]

That July they did meet, accidentally, at the House of Commons. The Webbs were dining with Haldane; Chamberlain was looking for his dinner guests. After dinner they talked for an hour. Beatrice thought Chamberlain looked wan and tired. She was pleased to have met on friendly terms

…and that I have shown him that I have no grudge against him and that I am happy in my own life. The lines of our lives cannot bring us together. He is old, I am elderly [Beatrice was forty two] *…Still for all that there is a bond of sentiment between us, I for the man I loved but could not follow.*[122]

In November there was a rumour that Chamberlain and his wife had separated; this led to a month of *miserable suspense*:

And to think that I am over forty, and he is over sixty! What an absurdity![123]

Beatrice worried about her health. She had been a sickly child; now the problems re-emerged. 1901, she said, was

…the most unsatisfactory year of my life since I married.[124]

What was physical, what mental or emotional? Beatrice suffered from eczema, flatulence, and indigestion. She thought something serious could be wrong with her heart or her kidneys. She monitored her weight, her urine, and her bowel movements. Later [125] Beatrice referred to her experience at this time as the first of several nervous breakdowns – and to the cure as starvation.

In October 1901 Beatrice met a doctor who warned her against overeating. She adopted a strict approach, limiting herself to

…one pound of food daily, four ounces at 8 o'clock breakfast, six at 1.30 lunch, and six at 7.30 dinner. I have one small cup of tea without milk or sugar at 7 o'clock in the morning, another at 4.30 in the afternoon and a cup of black coffee after dinner. I take very little water with my meals, having a breakfast cup of hot water at noon and another at night. I take no starchy food after breakfast, taking out my quantity in meat, green vegetables and fruit, sometimes a little cheese and butter.[126]

It seemed to work: a mercury ointment cleared up the eczema; the diet dealt with the flatulence. When Beatrice was in London, she would weigh herself on Monday mornings on the public scales at Charing Cross Station, noting the results in her diary. By January 1902, Beatrice could report that she had stopped losing weight and was working better.

But the diet was not enough. Beatrice knew she had to be

...equally watchful of the contents of my mind. For this I can only rely on some spiritual help arising from prayer. [127]

She found reading religious books relaxing.

And yet I cannot bring my faith and my practice into line with the Christian religion. I cannot acquiesce in the claims of Christianity. I should love to worship with others and to feel the support and the charm of a regular and definite ritual...I do not believe in their doctrine. I am not even attracted by their God, whether in the Jewish or the Christian version. My faith is more in spiritual influence... [128]

In fact, despite her lack of belief in doctrine or deity, Beatrice did worship with others:

...about twice a week I walk along the Embankment to St Paul's and listen to the anthem and join in the beautiful liturgy of the evening prayer. [129]

The seasonal pattern of their life continued. Residence in London while the LCC was sitting was balanced by long periods in the country, staying with Beatrice's sisters, with friends, or in rented houses.

They still cycled. In September 1903 they went cycling in Normandy with Bertrand and Alys Russell; Sidney and Beatrice

...thoroughly enjoyed our time. Cycling abroad is a new discovery to us. [130]

This was the occasion, according to Russell, when Beatrice sent her imperious message to the hotel staff, that

'*We do not have butter for Sidney's breakfast*'. [131]

Beatrice's friends delighted in her use of 'we'.

But the Webbs had irritated Russell:

They have a competent way of sizing up a Cathedral, and pronouncing on it with an air of authority and an evident feeling that the LCC would have done it better. They take all the colour out of life and make everything one cares for turn to dust and ashes. [132]

In these years Beatrice lost several links to her earlier life. In May 1900 Carrie Darling – one of her early women friends beyond immediate family – died of peritonitis.

Herbert Spencer died, aged eighty-three, in 1903. Spencer had never approved of Sidney; but Beatrice was aware of her debt to Spencer; in her childhood, he

> *…was perhaps the only person who persistently cared for me – or rather who singled me out as one who was worthy of being trained and looked after.*[133]

In summer 1905 Beatrice's sister Blanche hanged herself. Blanche and Theresa had married two brothers, Alfred and Willie Cripps – Alfred a lawyer, Willie a surgeon. Theresa had died in 1893.

Richard Potter had never liked Willie Cripps:

> *Father, who had an extraordinary instinct about men, always disliked him, suspected him, and, in spite of his eventual success, never believed in him.*[134]

Married twenty years, with six children, Willie had formed an attachment to an Italian singer, Julia Ravogli. He brought Julia to stay at the family home – where, at 4.00 one morning, Willie found Blanche's body in the shower.

In October, Sidney and Beatrice stayed with Willie. To Beatrice's disgust,

> *…there was the Ravogli woman, flaunted in the face of Willie's children still mourning for their mother.*[135]

They left quickly, saying they would neither come back nor invite Willie Cripps to stay with them. Later the surviving sisters met, and took a softer line

> *…we cannot influence Willie for good, we had better not drive him into worse conduct by taking any decidedly hostile line.*[136]

In summer 1904 Beatrice reviewed their circle of friends. Some had drifted away; she was dismissive of pure 'Society folk'. But there were some newcomers, foremost among whom was H G Wells.

The Webbs met Herbert George Wells in 1901; he was thirty-five and beginning to succeed as a novelist. Later he wrote of Beatrice:

> *She went down to the poor to do as the saints do; I came up from the poor in a state of flaming rebellion, most blasphemous and ungainly. Beatrice wanted to socialize the ruling classes and make them do their duty; I wanted to destroy them.*[137]

In 1901 Sidney and Beatrice both read Wells' book of essays *Anticipations*. Beatrice thought it *remarkable*; they sent him *Industrial Democracy*. In 1902 they stayed with Wells and his wife Jane in their home at Sandgate. Wells was excited, writing that he was

> *…going to spend two full days with Sidney Webb next week & I hope to thrash out all sorts of things. I've never met him and I'm tremendously expectant.*[138]

Beatrice found Wells

...an interesting, though somewhat unattractive personality except for his agreeable disposition and intellectual vivacity. [139]

When Wells met the Webbs he already knew both GBS and Wallas. He joined the Fabians in February 1903. Wells and his wife Jane became frequent guests at Grosvenor Road, staying two nights there in April 1904. The Webbs had a *little dinner* for them – the *carefully selected* guests included Arthur Balfour.

Beatrice approved of Wells:

We like him much – he is absolutely genuine and full of inventiveness. [140]

While Sidney and Beatrice were getting to know Wells, he was working on his novel *A Modern Utopia* (1905). This describes an ideal future world state – led by a self-selecting, abstemious, intellectual elite. Wells called them the Samurai. At this time Wells influenced the Webbs, and the Webbs influenced Wells. Beatrice, who believed in the need for a skilled, disinterested governing elite, kept searching over many years for models or examples for such an elite – enthusing at different times about the Salvation Army, the Jesuits, and the Bolsheviks. She saw Wells' Samurai as a parallel.

When Wells stayed at Grosvenor Road in April 1905, he gave the Webbs a copy of *A Modern Utopia*, telling Beatrice

The chapters on the Samurai will pander to all your worst instincts. [141]

Later, after she and Sidney had fallen out with Wells, she wrote that, for a little while,

...I thought we influenced him – at any rate in thought – and the Samurai of the Modern Utopia was the literary expression of this phase. [142]

Another new acquaintance was William Beveridge, who had graduated from Balliol College Oxford in 1903 and gone to work for Barnett at Toynbee Hall. His Oxford friend, the historian R H Tawney, followed him to Toynbee, where he ran the Children's Country Holiday Fund. Tawney subsequently married Beveridge's sister.

At Toynbee, Beveridge specialised in employment policy. He also met several people who helped to shape his career. One was Hubert Llewelyn Smith. Llewellyn Smith, co-author of the book on the 1889 Dock Strike, former campaigner for technical education, was now a senior civil servant at the Board of Trade, where he expanded the Board's role in labour market policy.

Beveridge's cousin, David Mair, was Chief Examiner for the Civil Service Commission. He wrote to Beveridge to introduce himself, inviting him to come and meet himself and his wife, Janet Mair,[143] at their home in suburban Banstead. Beveridge made an immediate impression on Janet Mair:

…loosely built and badly dressed, but he had an air which put him in the interesting class at first sight. [144]

He also encountered the Webbs. At first they were not impressed:

I met them first I think late in 1904, when, among other things, I sought advice about a pamphlet on labour exchanges. They did not like me then, but I met them again in July 1905, still through the Toynbee connection, for a weekend with them, CFG Masterman, and others at Cyril Jackson's home in Limpsfield, and I pleased the Webbs better than before…[145]

Beatrice called Beveridge *a leading Toynbeeite*; she describes the same incidents:

Beveridge, an ugly-mannered but honest, self-devoted, hard-headed young reformer of the practical type, came out well in comparison with Masterman; and from disliking him, as we had formerly done, because of his ugly manners, we approved him.[146]

Sidney and Beatrice became close to Arthur Balfour after he became Prime Minister. Beatrice had first met him in 1887, at dinner with Kate Courtney; he was already a cabinet minister – Chief Secretary for Ireland, where he was labelled 'Bloody Balfour'. Then, she had found him charming:

Tall, good looking and intellectual. Says cynical and clever things, which are cleverer than they turn out to be. Easy and well bred – of the ancient type of gentleman politician, a type fast fading out of existence.[147]

In 1890 she noted that he was the *ideal Tory*:

…every inch a fine gentleman with a big dash of the scholar and dilettante metaphysician… [148]

THE SOULS, THE SALON, AND THE NETWORK

Just after the Webbs got married, Shaw had suggested the socialist movement needed a salon:

Will Madame Potter-Webb undertake it? [149]

After 1900 she did. 41 Grosvenor Road became a centre of political life. The Webbs built a cross-party network; they entertained at Grosvenor Road, they dined out in London, they were guests at country houses. Their friendships with political leaders – especially with Haldane and Balfour – gave them a wide spread of contacts. Those friendships also introduced them to the aristocratic, intellectual network known as the Souls.

Balfour and Haldane – both single, both intellectual – were unusual politicians. Both wrote, lectured, and published on philosophy. They worked across party lines together – and with Sidney – on educational policy. Haldane was the Webbs' main point of contact with leading Liberals. At his London home they dined with Rosebery, the former Prime Minister; Haldane hoped Rosebery would return to front line politics.

Sidney and Beatrice had both known Haldane before they married, and he remained a friend of both up to his death in 1928. In 1902, Beatrice noted that they were both really attached to Haldane – a

...large and generous hearted man...[150]

After an early disappointment, Haldane had remained single. Beatrice thought his energies were divided between

...highly skilled legal work and the processes of digestion – for he is a Herculean eater. [151]

He spent generously on *the good things of life.*

...not least among them choice edibles and the accompanying portions of nicotine and alcohol, also of select quality... [152]

Haldane's diet was nothing like Beatrice's own. Over the years, she worried about his health, noting, in 1910, that it was strange that Haldane went on

...eating himself into the grave, or at any rate, into permanent invalidity.

John Campbell, Haldane's most recent biographer, suggests that Haldane

...bridged the gap between the dying Whigs and the emerging Labour...[153]

He may have bridged that gap. But Robert Ensor – journalist, Fabian Executive Committee member, London County Councillor, and historian – thought Haldane was *the Webbs' evil genius* in their relations with the Liberal Party. Ensor credits Haldane with responsibility for steering Beatrice and Sidney into alliance with the Liberal Imperialist (Limp) faction, supporters of Lord Rosebery and later of Asquith – rather than the more radical, nonconformist, grouping around Henry Campbell Bannerman and David Lloyd George. Many of this latter group opposed the war in South Africa (1899-1902) between Britain and Boer settlers. Opponents of the war became known as pro-Boers.

Haldane was certainly instrumental in introducing the Webbs to the Limps;

in 1902 and 1903 they thought that Rosebery and the Limps were their best hope within the Liberals. Beatrice thought the Limps had

...no prejudice against our views of social reform... Moreover the leaders of the other school of Liberalism are extremely distasteful to us. [154]

Beatrice was fascinated by Haldane and Balfour. In November 1905 she was at a Souls dinner

Why was I dissipating my energy in this smart but futile world in late hours and small talk? Exactly at the moment this feeling was disconcerting me, the door opened, and Mr Balfour was announced. I confess that the appearance of the P.M. dissipated my regrets. It is always worth while, I thought, to meet those who really have the power to alter things... [155]

'The Souls' were a group of smart, clever people,

...presiding over this band of brilliant diverse people was the ever calming and benign presence of Arthur Balfour [156]

It was Haldane who, in 1892, had introduced the Webbs to the Souls – although he himself was on the periphery of the group.

The Souls had existed since the 1880s. The group revolved around hostesses and country houses, assembling for weekend house parties, or 'Saturday to Mondays.' Unlike the traditional pattern of such parties, at Souls weekends men and women mostly socialized together rather than separately. Leading hostesses included Mary Elcho (later Lady Wemyss), whose country home was at Stanway, in Gloucestershire; Ettie Grenfell (later Desborough) of Taplow, on the Thames, and Frances Horner, of Mells, in Somerset. Notionally bipartisan, the Souls were mostly Conservative.

The name came from an 1888 comment by a non-member, Lord Charles Beresford:

You all sit about and talk about each other's souls. I shall call you the 'Souls' [157]

Balfour told Margot Asquith – herself a Soul:

No history of our time will be complete unless the influence of the Souls on society is dispassionately and accurately recorded. [158]

Haldane, however, thought the Souls took themselves too seriously.

Arthur Balfour's country home was at Whittinghame in Scotland. He also used Fisher's Hill, the Surrey house of his brother Gerald, another Soul. Gerald, a Cambridge Apostle, became a Conservative MP in 1885. Gerald was a member of the 1892 Royal Commission on Labour; Sidney met him when giving evidence.

Later, Gerald served as President of the Local Government Board in Arthur's government. Beatrice called him a *medieval and saintly knight*. Gerald's wife Betty, who later supported the suffrage movement, became a friend of Beatrice.

Beatrice was part fascinated, part repelled by the Souls; she part joined them, part created her own alternative. In 1902 Mary Elcho met Sidney and Beatrice at dinner with GBS. She told her husband about the dinner; he replied

I suppose you are going to invite the creatures to Stanway.[159]

Sure enough, when the Webbs were staying in the Cotswolds that summer, they called at Stanway. Beatrice thought Mary was

...a fascinating and kindly woman married to a card-playing and cynical aristocrat, living in the most delightful old house – Stanway.[160]

At their first meeting Balfour had charmed Beatrice; he charmed many women but never married. He was close to Mary Elcho, first meeting her when she was seventeen. Beatrice called it a *courtly devotion*:

It is clearly an old and persistent sentiment – good sound friendship, with just that touch of romantic regret that it could not have been more. [161]

The Souls regarded it as rather more; Nancy Ellenberger describes how

...in the circles around Arthur Balfour, country house parties were seething with secrets, jealousies, sexual tensions and grieving hearts in ways that put enormous strain on the public facades of sociability.[162]

The Webbs drew closer to Balfour. On 5 November 1902, Haldane wrote:

My dear Mrs Webb
The Prime Minister would like to meet you and SW on either the 11ᵗʰ or 13ᵗʰ. He proposes that Mrs Horner should give a very small dinner with Lady Elcho, who can come then, and myself, at 9 Buckingham Gate. Can you manage either date? Dinner will be at 7.45 to let him get back to the House. Please let him know.
Yours
RB Haldane

He is grateful for what you have done for his Bill and has asked me to convey this to you.[163]

The dinner happened later in November:

I took the Prime Minister in to dinner! I say 'took' because he was so obviously delivered over into my hands by my kindly hostess, who wished me to make as much use as possible of the one and a quarter hours he had free from the House.[164]

Beatrice was star-struck. Balfour

…has the charm of genuine modesty and unselfconsciousness…He is delightfully responsive intellectually, a man with ever-open mind…[165]

Beatrice wrote that Frances Horner (who was personally close to Haldane), had been the *High Priestess of the Souls.*

The dinner with Balfour came at the start of a hectic social round:

Three dinners and two evening parties at one's house in eight days is severe! But it seemed desirable to give a Conservative LCC dinner and London University reception; and also a 'Limp' dinner and 'Limp' reception. Then there was a dinner to Lady Elcho to acknowledge her kindness to us in Gloucestershire and her introduction to Balfour; an introduction which may have good results. So I asked her to meet John Burns, the Shaws, HG Wells and Asquith.[166]

Beatrice said that the dinner for Mary Elcho was successful and *thrilling*:

…the new sensation of meeting such strange forms of distinction as Burns, Wells, Shaws 'at the house of the Sidney Webbs'[167]

One pattern for Grosvenor Road hospitality was that dinner for a select group would be followed by a reception for a larger number. Sixty MPs, LCC Progressives, journalists and trade unionists came to the reception following the Limps dinner.

Balfour came to a *brilliant little dinner* in July 1903. Conversation ranged over music, literature, and philosophy, with little politics:

…a strange paradox as Prime Minister of a great Empire. I doubt whether even Foreign Affairs interest him: for all economic and social questions, I gather, he has an utter loathing.[168]

In Gloucestershire again in August, the Webbs cycled to Stanway:

We lunched with the Elchos the other day (a lovely 13-mile ride across the Cotswolds) and met Mr Balfour. He again struck me as the strangest mortal to be Prime Minister – a most attractive 'private gentleman' but with his mind really occupied in all the wrong things. However, he is delightful to talk to…[169]

This could be the occasion later recalled by Mary Elcho's daughter, when

Beatrice shocked other guests, saying:

> *Don't you agree with me, Mr Balfour, that the only excuse for a dinner party is that it should end in a committee?* [170]

Balfour was back at Grosvenor Road again in April 1904, dining with Wells, the Shaws, and Cosmo Gordon Lang, (an early supporter of Toynbee Hall, by now Bishop of Stepney). Balfour

> *...finding himself in a little party of intimates...belonging to a strange world completely detached from party politics, let himself go and, I think, thoroughly enjoyed the mix of chaff and dialectic which flew from GBS to Wells and round the table to Sidney, the Bishop and myself.* [171]

Beatrice told Balfour that the difference between him and the Liberal leaders

> *...was that his attitude towards proposals of social reform could be expressed by Why not? And theirs by a grudging Why?* [172]

So it was not surprising that the following summer Beatrice could note that

> *We have slipped into a sort of friendliness with Mr Balfour. He comes to dinner whenever we ask him and talks most agreeably.* [173]

There was an emotional charge in Beatrice's relationship with Balfour. In September 1906 both Webbs stayed at Whittinghame. *Prince Arthur*, Beatrice called him; a *philanderer*:

> *Too self-consciously Arthur's 'latest friend' to be quite pleasant, the party each night becoming a watched tête-a-tête between us two, the rest of the company sitting round, as Sidney said, 'making conversation'.* [174]

Haldane and Balfour provided the Webbs with their entry to the world of high politics; soon their contacts became wider. Herbert Gladstone, the Liberal Chief Whip, who had negotiated the agreement with MacDonald giving Labour a clear run in certain seats, came to dinner at Grosvenor Road in June 1904.

Another guest that night was Winston Churchill – 29 years old, Conservative MP for Oldham since the 1900 Khaki election. Beatrice had previously met Churchill in July 1903; then, she found him

> *...egotistical, bumptious, shallow-minded and reactionary, but with a certain personal magnetism...* [175]

A year later, her impression was unchanged; Churchill

…drinks too much, talks too much, and does no thinking worthy of the name… He is completely ignorant of all social questions and does not know it…He has no sympathy with suffering, no intellectual curiosity, he is neither scientific nor benevolent. [176]

Churchill, alienated by growing Conservative support for Joseph Chamberlain's tariff campaign, had just crossed over to the Liberals. Beatrice thought this unwise:

I have watched politics and parties for thirty years, Mr Churchill, and I feel warranted in giving you a word of warning…[177]

David Lloyd George – Welshman, Nonconformist, pro-Boer, an MP since 1890 – was also there. Beatrice thought him

…altogether superior both in character and intellect to Winston Churchill or Herbert Gladstone… A worthy little person with intense personal ambition, but with assiduous industry and honest convictions and brilliant parliamentary talents. But he, also, has no notion of national administration or the problems that it involves.[178]

After dinner other guests – including LCC members – came to a reception. Gilbert Chesterton and his wife Frances were there; Frances thought that *nothing but politics* was dull

…an intriguer's life must be a pretty poor affair.

She added that Beatrice

…looked very handsome and moved among her guests as one to the manner born. [179]

There were lunches as well as dinners. Hewins, the first LSE Director, lunched once a week; his successor, Halford Mackinder, also came regularly. The civil servant Robert Morant was a frequent guest. And Beatrice regularly held 'At Homes' – for example, for LSE staff and students.

The catering was frugal: R H Tawney wrote that the Webbs

…pressed their intellectual wares on all willing to receive them at the price of participation in one of the famous exercises in asceticism described by Mrs Webb as dinners.[180]

Molly Hamilton confirms this;

…many visitors to 41 did undoubtedly come away with the impression that they had not had enough to eat…In general, the food was very plain, and you

took what was offered: there were no choices. Food undoubtedly figured in the chapter of economies.[181]

But the guests came to Grosvenor Road to talk rather than to eat.

In 1911 H G Wells caricatured the salon in *The New Machiavelli*; Sidney and Beatrice appear as Oscar and Altiora Bailey. He described their *hard little house* as a centre for *quite an astonishing amount of political and social activity.* He mocked the restricted menu they offered their guests:

She fed them with a shameless austerity that kept the conversation brilliant, on a soup, a plain fish, and mutton or boiled fowl and milk pudding, with nothing to drink but whisky and soda, and hot and cold water, and milk and lemonade.[182]

Wells understood the object of the hospitality:

Her dinners and gatherings were a very important feature in their scheme. She got together all sorts of interesting people in or about the public service, she mixed the obscurely efficient with the ill-instructed famous and the rudderless rich, got together in one room more of the factors in our strange jumble of a public life than had ever met easily before.[183]

R H Tawney's first visit to 41 Grosvenor Road was in the early 1900s. When he left, by mistake, he took John Burns' hat and not his own. Next day he received a scorching letter from Beatrice. For Beatrice, Tawney's error

…confirmed her conviction of the incorrigible incompetence, unreliability, moral laxity and mental imbecility of most products, however insignificant, of the older universities…[184]

Many years later, in her last months, Beatrice reminisced with Herbert Samuel about the salon.

They were all there with a purpose she said of the guests
We knew we were, responded Samuel.[185]

Some guests found the atmosphere overwhelming. Kingsley Martin first lunched there in the 1920s. Martin's pride

…in being entertained by the Great, plus the importance of the conversation, would have satisfied me if the food had been bran and sawdust instead of boiling mutton and rice pudding.[186]

As he was leaving that day, Martin asked Sidney if he could use the lavatory. He left with Harold Laski, who thought his request an extraordinary act of courage

…which no one had ever dared perform before in the Webb household. He said that the week before he had dined there with Ramsay MacDonald, and that he and the Premier had had to make use of a timber yard on the way home… [187]

HISTORY OF ENGLISH LOCAL GOVERNMENT

After trade unions, Sidney and Beatrice turned to the history of local government, aiming to describe the existing system and recommend improvements.

They were developing new ideas on public services, proposing a new form of state

…the 'house-keeping state', as distinguished from the 'police state'. [188]

Services would be provided according to need. The Webbs argued that 'social utilities' – public health, universal education, provision for the sick and destitute

…involved enterprises to which no profit-making could usually be attached… [189]

They began with the nineteenth century, later deciding to go back to 1689. They never did produce a nineteenth century book. By 1929 eleven volumes had been published – covering parishes, counties, manors and boroughs, prisons, roads, and the Poor Law.

Again they divided their time between Grosvenor Road, research trips, and writing sessions outside London. In spring 1899 they visited Leeds and Manchester. Neither impressed Beatrice:

The personalities of Leeds public life are neither interesting nor attractive. Leeds and its inhabitants strike me as equally unlovely. 'Getting on' measured in money is the dominant idea: the rich are conventional and purse proud; the working man dull and without fight or faith. [190]

The Manchester Town Council turns out to be no better than that of Leeds… there is no Head to the concern, no one who corresponds to a general manager of a Railway Company, still less to its paid Chairman. [191]

Often they would set off together on research visits; then Sidney would return to London for LSE or LCC business. Without Beatrice, Sidney became unhappy. In June 1899, he was at Grosvenor Road, Beatrice in Manchester:

I have been horribly impressed all this week with the <u>loneliness</u> of life except when you are there. I can't bear to think of what it would be if there were an accident to your train, or when you were bicycling – which left me really alone.

I get thoroughly nervous and depressed, and am miserable – unable to work, or read in the evening.[192]

There were distractions; progress seemed slow. In the summers of both 1901 and 1902 they spent long periods out of London.

In April 1901 they stayed with Bertrand and Alys Russell at Friday's Hill. Beatrice was

Delighted to get away from London and to look forward to a long spell of work on the Book...It will be a long pull and a strong pull to get through the work.[193]

They returned to Friday's Hill in summer 1902; Beatrice noticed the relationship between the Russells was deteriorating – so she took Alys to Switzerland with her for three weeks. Alys

...turned out a most restful and pleasant companion. [194]

Sidney and Beatrice went to Lulworth, Dorset – where it was cold and wet, and hard to make progress. Nevertheless, they wrote about parishes. In autumn 1901 they stayed at a *most unsatisfactory* inn in Yorkshire – too much noise from children, cattle, and people talking in the street. For a week Beatrice

...gave up the struggle to work and lay out on the heather. [195]

But in Yorkshire they wrote about Justices of the Peace. In Margate, after Christmas, they dealt with municipal corporations. At Crowborough, in Sussex, in April 1902, they had

...a happy and successful time here: writing the chapter on the Commissioners of Sewers...[196]

The rest of 1902 went on Poor Law history.

Beatrice read widely about the eighteenth century – which, she concluded, had been selfish, self-indulgent, corrupt, and slack:

The reactionary and the radical parties were alike against efficiency, the first for corrupt and the second for doctrinaire reasons.[197]

By January 1903 they were working on vagrancy. They went on to cover prisons and pubs. In January 1905 they started work on counties. This took much of the year; Beatrice worked long days at home or at the British Museum.

It was the summer Blanche died; Beatrice found writing hard. She found her work just *mechanical*. Sidney carried on, writing on county administration. In late June Beatrice noted she had to

…pull the whole together – the County must be finished before we leave for Scotland a month hence.[198]

It was – almost – by the end of July, with long writing days and less socializing:

Not dining out, and not entertaining large parties, makes all the difference.[199]

The *History of English Local Government* is detailed and monumental; it is not a casual read. HG Wells questioned the exercise: as far as modern local government was concerned

…a study of the methods of Dogberry and Shallow was as likely to be as valuable a contribution to contemporary problems as a monograph on human sacrifice in Etruria.[200]

Later writers do not try to cover the same ground. It is a unique reference book.

David Marquand probably had the local government series in mind when he wrote:

Thick, heavy books flowed from their pens – learned, solid and mostly indigestible. [201]

Molly Hamilton thought readers would lose sight of the logic:

Sometimes the long roll of the sentences achieves a kind of heavy eloquence; more often one feels crushed by the remorseless regularity of that roll. [202]

Margaret Cole attributed this style to Sidney, rather than Beatrice

…the man whose natural form of expression resembles nothing so much as the slow passing of an infinitely long, laden freight train.[203]

Unlike the trade union books, the local government series did not benefit from the ruthless editing of GBS. At their best, the books are a catalogue of good and bad practice, a collection of case studies. For example, Sidney and Beatrice document the patterns of abuse and corruption that characterised eighteenth century local government.

One example they give is the Mayor and Burgesses of the little Sussex town of Arundel:

We cannot discover that, beyond maintaining a certain Municipal pomp and ceremony, this Company or Society of Burgesses was of any appreciable utility to the inhabitants.

...the Burgesses regarded themselves, not as trustees, but as absolute owners of their revenues, which they shamelessly shared among their members...

The 'feastings' of the little company were almost incessant. At each three-weekly meeting of the Borough Court there was a feast to the Burgesses and their wives and all the officers. At every meeting of the Burgesses there was a dinner. At the annual Court Leet there was a dinner for the Burgesses and Jury. On the annual receipt of a buck from the Duke of Norfolk there was a 'venison feast'. At the 'going forth' of the retiring Mayor there was a 'great feast' [204]

EDUCATION

Sidney's education work in London had been successful; national education policy remained a mess. School Boards and County Councils overlapped; the issue of church schools was unresolved.

A Fabian Tract, largely written by Sidney, described the situation

Some places have two or three public authorities spending rates and taxes on different sorts of schools, whilst others have none at all. [205]

Sidney believed County Councils should be the only local education authorities (except in London and large towns). Education authorities should be able to support church schools, with the right to appoint staff, and to inspect.

Other Fabians disagreed. Stewart Headlam and Graham Wallas were London School Board members. Wallas objected profoundly to funding church schools. In 1903 Beatrice found him depressed; he suspected that

...Sidney is playing false with regard to religious education. He wants all religious education abolished... there is always in Graham's eyes the priest behind the policy. [206]

In 1904 Wallas left the Fabian Society.

In 1899 central government brought previously separate departments together to establish the Board of Education. Its first President was the Duke of Devonshire. Beatrice had a low opinion both of the Duke – who she thought failed

...through inertia and stupidity to grasp any complicated detail... [207]

and of his junior minister, Sir John Gorst. Beatrice thought Gorst *cynical and careless.* [208] Her negative views were not universally shared; Joseph Chamberlain (who disagreed with the Duke on tariffs) nevertheless said that he was a very clever man. [209]

Much of the initiative came from a civil servant, Robert Morant. Morant had graduated from Oxford in 1885. For eight years he worked as tutor to the Crown Prince of Siam, and reorganised Siam's education system. Returning to Britain in 1894, Morant lived at Toynbee Hall, and worked on education policy at the Privy Council Office. There, he soon concluded that County Councils were better at providing secondary education than School Boards – and that the Boards were exceeding their legal powers in providing any secondary education at all.

Morant rose through the ranks, becoming Gorst's Private Secretary in 1899, then Permanent Secretary in 1903. In April 1902 he stayed with the Webbs: Beatrice described him as the *principal person at the Education Department*. She commented on his rise:

> *Taken into the office as a nondescript in a humble capacity some years ago, Gorst picked him out for his private secretary.*[210]

A London art school initiated a test case against the London School Board. All post-elementary education provided by the Board was ruled unlawful. The Board members were surcharged – made to pay personally – the disallowed spending. In April 1901, this judgement was upheld by the Court of Appeal.

The outcome of the case – known as the Cockerton case, after the name of the auditor – meant that new legislation was needed. This came in three instalments:

- The 1901 Education Act, permitting School Boards to keep their secondary schools open for another year;

- The 1902 Education Act

- The 1903 Education (London) Act

Four men steered the process: Balfour, Morant, Sidney, and Haldane. The eventual settlement closely followed Sidney's approach. Robert Ensor wrote

> *As a piece of highly skilled wire pulling, it marked perhaps the summit of Sidney's achievements.* [211]

Balfour as Prime Minister took personal responsibility for education policy. Edward Talbot, bishop of Rochester (a Grosvenor Road regular) introduced Balfour to Morant. Balfour then asked Morant to draft the 1902 Education Bill and invited him to stay at Whittinghame.

Balfour introduced Morant's Bill in the House of Commons in March 1902. It covered England and Wales outside London, and contained three main provisions:

- School Boards abolished; replaced by County Councils;

- Church schools to be supported from the rates;

- Powers for education authorities to *provide* and *fund* secondary education.

The Bill attracted considerable opposition, mostly over church schools. Before this, Board Schools had only been permitted to teach 'non-denominational' Christianity – a position accepted by nonconformists.

The new power, to fund church – mostly Anglican and Catholic schools – was described as *putting Rome on the rates.* Lloyd George called the Bill a device for

...riveting the clerical yoke on thousands of parishes in England. [212]

He said

...the clergyman would come down to the school like a roaring lion, seeing what little Nonconformists he could devour at the expense of the ratepayers... [213]

The London Baptist Minister Dr John Clifford campaigned against the Bill across the country. Few halls were large enough for Clifford's meetings. A Liberal, a Fabian, and a Christian socialist, Clifford had supported the 1889 Dock Strike, and was a pro-Boer.

Opposition came from secularists as well as nonconformists. Ramsay MacDonald tried to align the Labour Representation Committee (LRC) against the Bill. He was rebuffed by the Fabians, who thought the LRC was

...travelling beyond the purpose for which it was appointed. [214]

The Fabians threatened to withdraw from the LRC.

For the Webbs, agreeing funding for church schools was the price of achieving adequate secondary education:

...at that time and probably for many years afterwards, there was no alternative way of securing for every child in the kingdom, irrespective of class or creed, the maximum duration and efficiency of educational facilities that the House of Commons could be induced to afford. [215]

It cost them friendship and support; radical friends became *bitter or sullen.* [216] Sidney's support for the Bill

...offended both the orthodox Liberals and the powerful Nonconformist element in the nascent Labour Party. [217]

The 1902 Education Act received Royal Assent in December. In July Balfour had promised a Bill for London. LCC members began to understand what was happening: on 16 July Sidney wrote to Beatrice

The Council is slowly getting the idea that it will have to be the Education authority – Burns said it would inevitably be so – by a Bill next year.[218]

Although the government was committed in principle to a London Bill, there was no consensus about details. Nonconformists, and many LCC Progressives, wanted to keep the School Board. Conservatives thought the School Board was dominated by nonconformists and teaching unions; they did not much like the LCC. Some Conservatives argued for a joint board based on London's 28 Borough Councils.

Sidney was clear: the LCC should be the sole London education authority; provision for church schools should be the same as elsewhere. The Webbs lobbied intensively. At dinner with Balfour on 28 November 1902, Beatrice

...seized every opportunity to insinuate sound doctrine and information as to the position of London education. Sidney says I managed skilfully, but then he is a partial judge![219]

They cultivated Morant; he confided in them. In December he came to Grosvenor Road, frustrated with his ministers, and

...wearied out with the autumn campaign and the prospect of having to superintend the working out of the new Education Act with a rotten staff and a hostile minority in each district determined to wreck the Act.[220]

After Christmas they worked on the press – the *Times*, the *Telegraph*, and the *Morning Post*. Sidney persuaded Harmsworth, the *Daily Mail* proprietor, to support the LCC:

Very well, Mr Webb, we'll do it. But we don't know anything about the subject. You must come in every night at 11 pm for a week and see that we say everything just right.[221]

In February they deployed Grosvenor Road hospitality:

A succession of dinners re Education Bill, mostly Conservative and Church.[222]

Sidney and Beatrice spent two years negotiating education policy with the Conservatives and the churches. They risked alienating the London Progressives – Sidney's political base.

Gradually wrote Beatrice, *the Progressive Party realised that the Conservative Cabinet was being encouraged by a leading member of the party to go forward with the abolition of the London School Board.*[223]

That risk began to crystallize in spring 1903.

Ramsay MacDonald was briefly an LCC member, from 1901 to 1903. He suggested that the Webbs gained financially from their relationship with LSE, and opposed the TEB's grant to LSE. In 1902 Beatrice noted

J R MacDonald, Sidney's old enemy in the Fabian Society, slipped into the Council at an uncontested byelection and apparently spends his time in working up the feeling against the Technical Education Board and Sidney's administration of it.[224]

Things got worse. In March 1903 Beatrice observed a *slump in Webbs*. She had no doubts about responsibility:

The LCC Progressives or some of them are playing the fool about the London Education Authority…A little clique headed by J R MacDonald are fighting all they know how Sidney's influence on the TEB, and some of the weaker of the rank and file, somewhat jealous of Sidney, are playing into their hands.[225]

Next day, by four votes to three, the progressives voted down Sidney's candidature for the chair of the TEB.

The 'slump' in Webbs proves to be serious. [226]

The Education (London) Bill was introduced in April 1903 and became law in August. The Webbs aimed to secure their preferred outcome, while defending Sidney. He had to persuade the Progressives to accept responsibility for education, and persuade Conservatives not to impose a joint board of the Boroughs.

The lobbying paid off: by the end of May the Webbs had won. They went off to Gloucestershire:

The Education Bill passed through Committee the day before we left in almost exactly the shape Sidney would have given to it: the LCC absolutely supreme, the borough councils relegated to the quite subordinate part of selecting the majority of the local managers. [227]

The LCC Progressives reluctantly accepted their new responsibilities. But the rift between them and Sidney was deep.

Privately, that summer, the Webbs talked about a new party, based on support for the new education settlement. Beatrice thought that most Conservatives, Anglicans, and Catholics would support this. So would some Progressives.

Others, however,

…would be got hold of by the fanatical 'Noncon' Labour man.

To put it bluntly, we want a small *Progressive majority, the rump of the Progressives superseded by good Conservative educationalists.*

We hope to remain throughout on the Progressive side but, if circumstances compelled, Sidney would come out in the open as the avowed organizer of a new party. [228]

Sidney did not become chairman of the new LCC Education Committee. He did chair the subcommittee for post-14 education, so continued working on the scholarship scheme.

Beatrice was not impressed by the calibre of the Progressive Council members:

…the ordinary Progressive member is either a bounder, a narrow-minded fanatic, or a mere piece of putty, upon which any strong mind can make an impression… [229]

Trouble with the Progressives was not over. Without consulting Sidney, the Progressives took a narrow view of cooptions to the new committee. The whip, Edwin Cornwall, told him:

They say you have hitherto led us by the nose, Webb. Now it is your turn to follow. [230]

Eighteen months later Sidney was removed from the party leadership committee.

Opposition to the legislation continued. Dr Clifford led a campaign of passive resistance and non-payment of rates. His household goods were regularly seized and sold by bailiffs. Kingsley Martin's father, Basil, a congregationalist minister in Hereford, was a passive resister. Kingsley remembered

…each year one or two of our chairs and a silver teapot and jug were put on the hall table for local officers to take away. They were auctioned in the market place and brought back to us. [231]

The campaign against the education legislation contributed to the Liberal landslide election victory of 1906. The new government twice tried to amend the education settlement. The first attempt was defeated in the House of Lords; the second was withdrawn.

The Progressives lost their LCC majority in 1907; Sidney left the Council in 1910. Until then, he was mostly left alone to continue his education work.

The Balfour Acts set a framework for education which lasted until the 1944 Butler Act. The key features of the settlement with the churches lasted even longer.

In *Our Partnership*, Beatrice described the passage of the 1903 Act as

…a successful achievement which entailed some consequences that were unpleasant. [232]

In the short term, Sidney was isolated within the London County Council. In the medium term, the education settlement seriously restricted the opportunity for the Webbs to influence the new Liberal government after 1906. Robert Ensor wrote that the impact on Sidney's standing with Liberals was shattering:

> *He failed to realise how genuine was the Nonconformist grievance in regard to the single-school areas; or, again, how much the School Board had meant to a great many Londoners.*[233]

In first establishing a system of secondary education in London, and then working with Balfour and Haldane to create a national system, run by county councils, Sidney made two compromises. The first was to work with the old network of endowed schools; the second was to give the churches (principally the Anglican and Catholic churches) a significant, guaranteed role in the provision of publicly funded education. As far as the issue of church schools was concerned, Beatrice wrote that they were both convinced that,

> *…at that time and probably for many years afterwards, there was no alternative way of securing for every child… the maximum duration and efficiency of educational facilities that the House of Commons could be induced to afford.*[234]

Whether or not the Webbs were right in their belief that there was no alternative, those two compromises continue to shape education in Britain more than a hundred years after the passage of Balfour's Education Acts

The cooperation between Sidney, Haldane, and Balfour, was not limited to secondary education. Together they worked to reorganise the governance of the federal University of London. They were all impressed by the level of technical education in Germany.

THE BOER WAR

The Boer war (1899-1902) was fought between Britain and settlers of Dutch origin – Boers – in South Africa. Later, Beatrice wrote that none of the factions in Britain or South Africa

> *…ever mentioned the claim of the native population whose conditions of life were at stake.*[235]

Years of tension had preceded the war. British rule at the Cape had been established early in the nineteenth century. Boer settlers responded by moving inland, seeking new territory, away from British rule. They established independent republics in the Transvaal (1852) and the Orange Free State (1854).

Everything changed with the discovery of mineral wealth: first diamonds, then in 1886 the world's richest goldfield at Witwatersrand in the Transvaal. Workers came to the gold reef from around the world – especially from Britain. London relished the investment opportunity. The city of Johannesburg grew up. Soon international investors, having made their fortunes on the Rand, arrived back in London. One group of South African mine owners became known in Britain as the Randlords; they included Julius Wernher, Alfred Beit, Hermann Eckstein, and Barney Barnato.

Foreigners who migrated to work on the Rand were called Uitlanders. Their rights were limited; they paid taxes but could not vote. The Transvaal government spent their taxes on arms.

In September 1899 Joseph Chamberlain, Colonial Secretary, demanded voting rights and representation for the Uitlanders. Kruger, the Transvaal president, responded with an ultimatum to Britain to withdraw troops from the borders of the Boer republics.

Two further factors were important. The Cape was a strategic point on the route to India. And Chamberlain saw potential in South Africa for British – white – settlement. The ensuing war was 'Joe's War'.

In October 1899, the Boers attacked the British colonies, winning victories over the winter of 1899 – 1900. Britain sent more detachments – including troops from Australia, Canada, and New Zealand – and relieved the sieges on British garrisons. In May 1900 the siege of Mafeking, which had begun in October 1899, was lifted; Britain then attacked, capturing Pretoria, the Transvaal capital, in June 1900.

The relief of Mafeking created a moment of euphoria in Britain. Encouraged by Chamberlain, Salisbury's government seized the opportunity to call a general election in September and October. Robert Ensor wrote that

>...the dissolution was quite frankly an attempt to capitalize the emotions of military victory in terms of votes for the government. [236]

But the euphoria was premature. The war was not over. The Boers launched a guerrilla campaign which lasted another two years. Britain responded with a 'scorched earth' policy, burning Boer farms, forcing women and children into concentration camps.

The Boers finally surrendered in May 1902; their republics were absorbed into the Empire, but promised self-government – a promise honoured in 1910.

The war divided Britain into supporters of the war and pro-Boers. The Webbs were split; Beatrice wrote to an American friend

...we don't quite agree. Sidney is on the anti-war side of the line, I am on the 'war was inevitable' side: but we are both so close to the dividing line, that we can still go on holding hands! Our habitual attitude! [237]

What made the situation complex was her lingering regard for Chamberlain: she was mortified that she could not think well of him

...puzzled to try and resist the atmosphere of hostile criticism of his action in Sidney's and Leonard's [her brother-in-law Leonard Courtney] minds...I am prey to an involved combination of bias and counter-bias. [238]

The Potter sisters were divided; Beatrice's eight brothers-in-law

...represented every grade of opinion in favour of and against the war, from die-hard Tory imperialists to stubborn pro-Boers. [239]

The anti-war movement was led by a succession of committees. First came the Transvaal Committee, chaired by Passmore Edwards, (newspaper proprietor, LSE benefactor). This gave way to the South Africa Conciliation Committee (chaired by Leonard Courtney), which in turn was replaced by the Stop the War Committee (chaired by Dr Clifford), with its slogan *Stop the War and Stop It Now*. Courtney, a leading pro-Boer, was losing allies:

The Tories regard him as a wholly unendurable person; the vast majority of the Liberals consider him to be a quixotic crank. [240]

His strongest supporters were ILP and SDF members. Local Liberal Unionists deselected him before the Khaki election.

The pro-Boers were a disparate group. Stephen Koss comments that the Stop the War Committee

...had no affiliation with any political party, and, except for the almighty, recognized no higher authority. [241]

Among the pro-Boers were socialists; Gladstonian Liberals; radical MPs like Lloyd George; Lib Labs, like Burns; and Keir Hardie of the ILP.

After the relief of Mafeking in May 1900, crowds in Battersea threw stones at John Burns' family home. He noted on 18 May that the streets were full of

...shouting delirious people over Mafeking. On arrival home find thousands of people outside and passing my house singing God save the Queen etc, ad lib, ad nauseam. Continued this nonsense till 3.30 am. [242]

The following night, the streets were again

… crowded with wildly excited people …a well-organised gang of political
opponents managed to break three of the front windows. [243]

Lloyd George's opposition to the war made him a national figure. In
Birmingham, in December 1901, he was prevented from speaking. A hostile
crowd shouted

Traitor! Traitor! Bloody traitor! Pro-Boer! Kill 'im! Kill the bloody traitor!

One man was killed; Lloyd George escaped disguised as a policeman.

The *Daily News* and the *Manchester Guardian,* and the radical journalists W
T Stead and F W Hirst, were pro-Boer; most other newspapers supported the
war. The established church was imperialist – but Canon Barnett supported the
Conciliation Committee, as did Dr Clifford, and prominent Quakers. There was
no general anti-war movement in universities – but some academics, including
the classicist Gilbert Murray, and the historian J L Hammond, did oppose it.

Almost all the LibLab MPs were pro-Boers – but trade unions did not
campaign on the issue before 1905, when the government proposed bringing
Chinese workers to South Africa to work in the mines.

There was an anti-Semitic current within the pro-Boer movement, articulated
by J A Hobson, who went to South Africa in 1899 as a war correspondent. On his
return Hobson published a book, arguing that the development of the mines had

…thrown the economic resources of the country more and more into the hands
of a small group of international financiers, chiefly German in origin and
Jewish in race. [244]

Hyndman of the SDF used similar language, writing in 1896, in Justice, that
Beit, Barnato and their fellow Jews wanted

…an Anglo-Hebraic empire in Africa stretching from Egypt to Cape Colony. [245]

So did the former SDF member John Burns, who told the Commons in 1900

Wherever we go in this matter there is the financial Jew operating, directing,
inspiring the agencies that have led to this war…The trail of the financial
serpent is over this war from beginning to end. [246]

Burns said the British army had become *the janissary of the Jews.*

The writer Hilaire Belloc, another pro-Boer, friend of Burns (and a Liberal
MP after 1906), held similar views, writing a poem entitled

Verses to a Lord who, in the House of Lords, said that those who opposed the
South African adventure confused soldiers with money-grubbers

The poem mocks the fact that the financiers did not themselves fight:

We also know the sacred height
Up on Tugela side,
Where those three hundred fought with Beit
And fair young Wernher died...
The little empty homes forlorn
The ruined synagogues that mourn
In Frankfort and Berlin... [247]

In winter 1900/1901, Emily Hobhouse, a member of the Conciliation Committee, working with the Courtneys, went to Africa to report on the camps. Her June 1901 report revealed deteriorating conditions and high death rates; the report was effective in mobilising anti-war public opinion.

The war exacerbated already existing divisions in the Liberal Party. Ranged against the pro-Boers were the Liberal Imperialists, or Limps. Key Limps included Haldane, Asquith, Edward Grey, and Lord Rosebery. The Gladstonian Liberal, John Morley, thought Liberal imperialism was only

Chamberlain wine with a Rosebery label [248]

The Webbs remained closer to the Limps than to the pro- Boers; their contact came via Haldane

...to whom we are both really attached... [249]

Rosebery, the previous Liberal Prime Minister, resigned the party leadership in 1896. His successor, from 1898, after a hiatus, was Sir Henry Campbell-Bannerman – a businessman, and an MP since 1868, who had been Secretary of State for War in Gladstone's later governments. He made a poor impression on Beatrice when she met him in 1900:

Met Campbell-Bannerman at Lord Reay's last night. A quite stupid person, well suited to a position of a wealthy squire or a sleeping partner in an inherited business. Vain. [250]

For a while, Sidney had high hopes of Rosebery, thinking him a better prospect for social reform than the traditional, Gladstonian, small-state Liberals. Sidney persuaded Rosebery to become President of the LSE – but although the Limps wanted Rosebery to return to front-line politics, those hopes came to nothing.

Emily Hobhouse's report forced Campbell-Bannerman to choose a side in the Liberal split. He told a Liberal dinner in June 1901 that he was sickened by the policy of sweeping women and children into camps:

'When is a war not a war?'... 'When it is carried on by methods of barbarism in South Africa.[251]

AJP Taylor saw this as a stroke of genius, shifting the argument

...from the causes of the war to the way in which it was being conducted.[252]

Beatrice commented that, while the Limps had been working at the Bar, and enjoying London Society, Campbell-Bannerman had been captured. Grass roots Liberal members were strongly pro-Boer; now the parliamentary party was

...declaring itself definitely against the war, accusing Milner [High Commissioner in South Africa] and the army of gross inhumanity and asserting the right of the Boers to some sort of independence.[253]

Asquith and about thirty other Liberal MPs voted against Campbell-Bannerman in a division. This deepened the split. Haldane and the Limps wanted Sidney's support. He found this difficult: although the Limps were friends, he was *pro- Boer in sentiment.* Both thought that their chances of support on policy were greater with Haldane and the Limps. The divisions persisted; the factions held dinners and counter-dinners, at which the protagonists made partisan speeches; one commentator called this *war to the knife and fork.*[254]

By 1904 another Liberal government seemed possible. The Limps were depressed: old Gladstonians and young radicals were making the running. Beatrice commented

Little Englandism, crude democracy, economy, secularism, are all again to the fore in the official Liberal Party, are in fact the only actively militant forces with a policy to push... Our poor 'Limp' friends are indeed a pitiful spectacle.[255]

The Limps feared they might even be excluded from an incoming Liberal government.

Divisions among the Fabians appeared at the start of the war. Before 1899 the Society had not formed views on imperial policy – or on other international issues. In October 1899 GBS, on holiday in the Mediterranean, wrote to Pease

Don't let us, after all these years, split the society by declaring ourselves on a non-socialist point of policy. To wreck ourselves on the Transvaal after weathering Home Rule would be too silly.[256]

Some Fabians, suspicious of jingoism, agreed with the little-England Liberals; the strongest advocates of this position were Sydney Olivier and Ramsay MacDonald. On 5 November 1899 Olivier's daughters burned an effigy of

Joseph Chamberlain.

Other Fabians – GBS; Sidney, to some extent; and Hubert Bland – took the opposite view. They were not all-out imperialists, but were now further from the free trade, pacifist, temperance, nonconformist axis. Once the war had started, Pease wrote,

The majority of the Society recognised that the British Empire had to win the war, and that no other conclusion to it was possible. [257]

In autumn 1899, pro-Boer Fabians wanted the Society to declare itself against the war. After inconclusive discussions, it was agreed in January 1900, at MacDonald's suggestion, that there should be a postal ballot on the question:

Are you in favour of an official pronouncement on Imperialism in relation to the war being made by the Fabian Society at the present time? [258]

The membership, by 259 to 217, answered 'No'. Thirteen members then resigned, including MacDonald, Walter Crane, and Mrs Pankhurst.

Later, Pease wrote that the Fabians rejoiced at getting MacDonald out:

Somebody said that the Boer War was a great evil, but there was one compensation: for us, it got rid of MacDonald. [259]

In 1900 the Fabians decided to produce a tract on imperialism. Shaw drafted it; the final version was ready for the October election. The result, *Fabianism and the Empire*, rejected the Gladstonian Liberal world view. Shaw argued that

…a Great Power, consciously or unconsciously, must govern in the interests of civilization as a whole. [260]

After the war, the national mood began to change. There was a new preoccupation with efficiency. During the war, the army had had problems finding recruits who were physically fit enough to serve. In 1903 the government appointed a committee to study what was called physical deterioration. Their 1904 report painted a picture of poverty, malnutrition, and disease.

In autumn 1902 Sidney and Beatrice invited a group of men (they were all men) – chosen for their knowledge rather than their party – to form a dining club with ten or twelve members. The focus was national efficiency and imperial policy; the new group was called 'the Coefficients'. Sidney invited Wells to join

I am asked by the half a dozen who have nominated themselves the first members to invite you pressingly to join…

…the subject of all discussions should be 'the aims, policy and methods of Imperial Efficiency at home and abroad'. [261]

Each member brought particular expertise; Wells was the literature special-ist. Two leading Limps were there – Haldane as the lawyer, Grey as the foreign policy specialist. Hewins, still in 1902 LSE Director, was the economist. His two immediate successors – Halford Mackinder the geographer, and Pember Reeves representing the colonies – were also members. Bertrand Russell was the resident philosopher – he did not last long, resigning in the summer of 1903; his place was taken by the educationalist Michael Sadler. Leo Amery, a Fabian at Oxford, whose first job had been with Leonard Courtney, was about to write the *Times* history of the South African War. Amery was becoming a staunch imperialist; he was invited as military specialist. Later Shaw became a member.

The Coefficients also brought a range of opinions to the dinner table: Sidney understood social reform; Hewins was a tariff reformer and imperialist; Amery an increasingly fervent disciple of Joseph Chamberlain. Wells said they included

...the queerest diversity of brains. [262]

Royden Harrison called the Coefficients a bizarre

...shadow Ministry of all the Talents... [263]

Early meetings covered defence, relations within the empire, and relations with the United States. In March 1903, becoming close to Chamberlain, Hewins spoke on tariffs within the empire – attracting support only from Amery and one other.

For Sidney, the Coefficients provided a new platform for his campaign for a National Minimum; in November 1903, he led a discussion on this theme. In 1904, they discussed the monarchy; mostly they thought it necessary for the empire. Wells dissented.

In *The New Machiavelli*, Wells described meetings of the Coefficients, thinly disguised as the Pentagram Club:

The dinner time was given up to desultory conversation, and it is odd how warm and good the social atmosphere of that little gathering became as time went; then over the dessert, so soon as the waiters had swept away the crumbs and ceased to fret us, one of us would open with perhaps fifteen or twenty minutes' exposition of some specially prepared question, and after him we would deliver ourselves in turn, each for three or four minutes. [264]

The three dominant strands in the Coefficients' programme were empire, social reform, and science; other themes – including tariffs, compulsory national military service, and eugenics – were supported by some members, but opposed by others.

Concern about physical deterioration and decline stimulated the growth of the eugenics movement. Social reformers called for improved health care, and better education; eugenicists demanded that the state should incentivise the fit and healthy to have children, and limit the ability of the weak and unfit. In 1907 the Eugenics Education Society (later the Eugenics Society) was formed; Wells became a member.

The Webbs' priority was social reform; their involvement with eugenics was limited, but real. In a 1907 pamphlet, Sidney wrote that, under current social conditions, the only groups in society likely to *make full use of their reproductive powers* were

...the idle and the thriftless, the drunken and the profligate...[265]

Chapter Seven: The disease of destitution
1905-1912

'THAT NASTY OLD POOR LAW'

In December 1905 Beatrice was appointed to a Royal Commission on

...the working of the laws relating to the relief of poor persons in the United Kingdom. [266]

and to review unemployment policy.

For six years the Poor Law dominated the lives of both Sidney and Beatrice. They concluded that the Poor Law should be abolished, not reformed. As the Commission was completing its reports, Beatrice wrote to William Beveridge:

We will break up, once for all, that nasty old Poor Law [267]

The Poor Law dated back to the 1601 Poor Relief Act, the Statute of the 43rd of Elizabeth. This made the churchwardens of every parish, and the substantial householders, the *overseers of the poor* – responsible for setting the poor to work; providing relief for those who were unable to work; and binding their children as apprentices. The Act empowered the overseers to buy materials with which the poor could work, and to *erect, build and set up convenient houses of dwelling for the said impotent poor.* [268]

Poor people were *paupers*; relief for paupers housed in the poor house or workhouse was *indoor relief*; to those outside, *outdoor relief*.

The previous review had been seventy years earlier. Following the industrial revolution and the Napoleonic Wars, the Poor Law had come under great strain. In the 1830s, the government had been particularly concerned about the allowance system – paying outdoor relief to supplement the wages of people in low paid employment in rural areas. So in 1832 they established a Royal Commission on the Poor Laws. That Commission reported in 1834 , and the report led to the Poor Law Amendment Act of 1834, known as the New Poor Law.

The New Poor Law was hated from the outset. Edward Thompson described the 1834 Act, and its administration, as

...the most sustained attempt to impose an ideological dogma, in defiance of the evidence of human need, in English history. [269]

In *English Poor Law Policy* (1910) the Webbs analysed the New Poor Law; they reviewed the 1834 report, the 1834 Act, and the work of the national agencies responsible for the New Poor Law – the Poor Law Commission (to 1847); the Poor Law Board (to 1871) and the Local Government Board.

The 1834 Report itself was sometimes opaque. Sidney and Beatrice explain: the Commissioners' proposals

…were either formal 'recommendations', exceptionally displayed in prominent type, or suggestions scattered among the pages which purport to summarise the evidence.[270]

In the report and the Act, the Webbs identified three key New Poor Law principles:

1. National Uniformity

Relief given to each category of paupers should be the same throughout the kingdom.

There should be a Central Authority (initially the Poor Law Commissioners; from 1847 to 1871 the Poor Law Board, and from 1871 the Local Government Board – the LGB) to make regulations for the whole country, with as little local discretion as possible.

2. Less Eligibility

The situation of the pauper, according to the 1834 Report,

…shall not be made really or apparently so eligible as the situation of the independent labourer of the lowest class.

Every penny that tends to render the condition of the pauper more eligible than that of the independent labourer is a bounty on indolence and vice. [271]

The 1834 Commissioners said outdoor relief for able-bodied people should stop. Any help should be

…in well-regulated workhouses (i.e. places where they may be set to work according to the spirit and intention of the 43rd of Elizabeth).[272]

3. The Workhouse System

There would be at least four 'classes' of workhouse inmates:

- The aged and really impotent;
- The children
- The able-bodied females

- The able-bodied males

Each group would be housed in a separate building; each would have their own treatment.

There were many additional details. Vagrants, it was thought, would not be a *burden* if subject to the rigours of the regime for the able-bodied. The Report assumed that children would accompany their parents, and therefore be educated by a teacher in the workhouse.

A fundamentalist ethic underpinned policy on illegitimacy:

...a bastard will be, what Providence appears to have ordained that it should be, a burden on its mother, and where she cannot maintain it, on her parents.[273]

Implementation of the New Poor Law was delegated to the Poor Law Commission; they never fully implemented all the 1834 Report. The Commissioners started by grouping parishes into Poor Law Unions with Boards of Guardians. Few Boards established the separate workhouses proposed by the 1834 Report: most established General Mixed Workhouses, with old and young, able bodied and non-able bodied living cheek by jowl.

The Report had stipulated that the work done by paupers should be *useful*. This was ineffective. In 1845 a scandal in the Andover workhouse was exposed. The task for the Andover paupers was crushing bones to make fertiliser; some paupers were so hungry they would gnaw the marrow from the bones. Bone crushing was banned; the Webbs wrote

This left practically only stone-breaking, hand-grinding, and oakum-picking at the disposal of boards of guardians – occupations, as it seems to us, combining in the highest degree the characteristics of monotony, absence of initiative, toilsomeness, and inutility...[274]

The New Poor Law aimed to end outdoor relief for able bodied paupers. The Webbs established that this never happened. The Commissioners reassured themselves that the real priority had been to end the allowance system.

The Commissioners succeeded, however, in creating a hostile environment for paupers. No aspect of paupers' daily lives was too small to escape the attention of the Central Authority. Workhouses became known as new Bastilles; the three Commissioners as the *three Bashaws* or *three Kings* of Somerset House (their London office), or the *pinchpauper triumvirate*.

Until 1842 the Commissioners insisted that all married couples in the workhouse, of whatever age, should be accommodated separately. The diet for workhouse residents was laid down from Somerset House, with six model *dietaries* circulated, with minimal variation permitted.

> *No presents of food to individual paupers or classes of paupers were to be allowed, as they would produce inequality and discontent.* [275]

All paupers everywhere in the country – except the sick, the old and infirm, and children – were to keep the same hours. Able-bodied men and women, and boys and girls over the age of seven, should rise at 5.00 a.m. in summer and 7.00 a.m. in winter; work ten hours in summer, nine in winter; eat three meals, all at standard times; all have one hour off, between 7.00 and 8.00 p.m.; and all go back to bed at 8.00.

Paupers were not allowed to go out in the open air; there was no time when it would have been possible to do so. They could only leave the workhouse for *urgent and special reasons.*

There were no books – not even prayer books or bibles; it was unlawful for the Guardians to provide them.

> *No provision was made for playrooms, playthings, or even playing time for children of any age. With regard to adults, well or sick, it was apparently part of the policy to ignore, and even to prohibit recreation. Playing at cards and all other games of chance were absolutely forbidden to all classes of inmates at all hours and seasons.* [276]

This was the Poor Law Dickens described in *Oliver Twist* (published 1837-1839). The story of the New Poor Law after the years of the Commissioners was one of slow relaxation. Gradually the worst inhumanities were reformed. But the Poor Law remained loathed.

Margaret Cole got to know the Webbs at the end of the Poor Law campaign. She wrote:

> ... *'the workhouse' was pretty real to anyone who knew anything of nineteenth century popular literature. I might not have read Beatrice Webb's Minority Report of the Royal Commission on the Poor Law, but I had read and re-read Oliver Twist and Mrs Henry Wood.* [277]

Harry Snell grew up in the shadow of the Poor Law in rural Nottinghamshire. He recalled that

> *No human institution was ever more hated and feared by free men.* [278]

Clement Attlee began helping at a boys' club in East London in 1905, a year after he had graduated. It was a second education:

I soon began to realise the curse of casual labour. I got to know what slum landlordism and sweating meant. I understood why the Poor Law was so hated.[279]

'OUR TRUSTY AND WELL-BELOVED BEATRICE': THE POOR LAW COMMISSION 1905-1909

Beatrice was formally appointed to the Commission on 5 December 1905, by a Royal Warrant, addressed to *our trusty and well-beloved…Beatrice, wife of Sidney Webb, Bachelor of Laws.*

By then Arthur Balfour had resigned. The new Prime Minister was the Liberal Henry Campbell-Bannerman. In 1908 Campbell-Bannerman became seriously ill, resigned, and died. His successor was Herbert Henry Asquith, Chancellor of the Exchequer from 1905 to1908.

Establishing the Commission was almost the final act of Balfour's government. On 28 November Balfour lunched at Grosvenor Road, afterwards going with the Webbs to see Shaw's *Major Barbara*. Beatrice thought Balfour was

…looking particularly calm and happy…[280]

He said finding someone to chair the Commission had not been easy. Eventually, former Conservative minister Lord George Hamilton had been picked. Apologetically, Balfour told Beatrice:

George Hamilton is not the fool he looks[281]

Others differed. The Liberal journalist A G Gardiner, described Hamilton as a

…model of blameless mediocrity.[282]

Shaw thought Hamilton was outmatched by Beatrice. Hamilton

…imagined that he was going to rule the roost and attached no importance to the fact that Mrs Sidney Webb was a member of the Commission. Of course the poor devil has had no more chance against her than if he were a mouse in a python's cage at the zoo. [283]

Later, Beatrice came to appreciate Hamilton, writing that he

…combined exceptional personal charm and social tact with an open mind and a willingness to give free play to the activities of his fellow commissioners.
[284]

The other Commissioners included five Poor Law Guardians; four senior

Poor Law civil servants; two economists; three clergy (two Anglican, one Catholic); a trade unionist, Francis Chandler; Charles Booth; and the Labour MP George Lansbury. Lansbury, who represented Poplar in East London, had been a member of the Social Democratic Federation (SDF) and was now in the Independent Labour Party (ILP). Lansbury was also a Poplar councillor and Poor Law Guardian.

There were six representatives of the Charity Organisation Society (COS) – including General Secretary C.S. Loch, founder member Octavia Hill, and Helen Bosanquet. Beatrice thought them the *ablest* members of the COS. [285]

Bosanquet became Beatrice's main antagonist. She had studied at Newnham College Cambridge, and had been COS secretary in Shoreditch. She and her husband, Bernard Bosanquet, a philosopher turned COS activist, supported COS orthodoxy.

A general election followed the change of government. Polling lasted from 12 January to 8 February 1906; the outcome was a Liberal landslide. 400 Liberals – including 24 'Lib Lab' members – were elected; for most purposes they could count on the 83 Irish Nationalists, and the 29 Labour Representation Committee (LRC) members, the fruit of the talks between Ramsay MacDonald and Herbert Gladstone.

The Conservatives were still divided: between Conservatives and Liberal Unionists, and between supporters of Balfour and supporters of Joseph Chamberlain and his tariff campaign. Both Balfour brothers lost their seats; Arthur soon found another. Austen Chamberlain was also defeated.

Joseph Chamberlain was re-elected. In July 1906 he turned seventy, celebrating with a large party in Birmingham. Returning to London afterwards, Chamberlain was paralysed by a stroke. The family concealed his condition; he was even re-elected in both 1910 elections. But his active political life was over. He died in 1914.

The Liberal government quickly became embroiled in conflict with the House of Lords, which had a strong Conservative majority. In 1906 the Liberals had promised to revise the educational settlement of the Balfour years, addressing the Nonconformist criticisms. They introduced legislation to this end, but were defeated in the Lords. Another government defeat, on a Licensing Bill, followed. Then, in 1909, David Lloyd George's People's Budget proposed significant tax increases to fund the new Old Age Pension, and increased naval expenditure. The House of Lords voted the budget down – overturning a long-standing constitutional convention that the unelected chamber would not overturn the tax decisions of the Commons. In 1910 two General Elections, fought on the issue of the powers of the House of Lords, followed. Both were won by the Liberals – but they lost their overall majority, and for the rest of their term had to rely the votes of the Irish and Labour members. The Lords only gave way when faced with the threat of a mass creation of new peers.

Appointed by Conservatives, the Poor Law Commission now had to report to Liberal ministers. Sidney and Beatrice, having cultivated the Liberal Imperialists over the years, knew some of them well: Asquith, the Chancellor; Grey, Foreign Secretary; and Haldane, Secretary of State for War. Beatrice rejoiced that

> Our friends the 'Limps' have romped in to the leading posts under Campbell-Bannerman.[286]

But a younger, more pro-Boer generation also joined the government.

Lloyd George, now 40, was President of the Board of Trade. He became Chancellor in 1908 when Asquith became Prime Minister.

The President of the Local Government Board (LGB), and therefore the minister for the Poor Law, was John Burns, LibLab MP for Battersea, becoming the first working-class Cabinet Minister. Burns was an old, uneasy colleague of both Webbs. His days as 'the man with the red flag', the hero of Bloody Sunday and the 1889 Dock Strike, were well behind him. According to Burns' biographer (Beatrice tells the same story), when Campbell-Bannerman appointed him, Burns slapped him on the back, saying

> Bravo, Sir Henry, Bravo! That is the most popular thing you have yet done.[287]

Reactions on the left were mixed. Henry Hyndman of the SDF thought Burns was a turncoat.

Others were more welcoming. Sidney wrote

> 41 Grosvenor Road
> 11.12.5
> My dear Burns
> A thousand congratulations!
> It is splendidly courageous of you to accept the L.G.B. – and I don't think it ought to have been asked of you. You will be cruelly denounced for not doing impossibilities; but you have survived this sort of thing before now.
> I am sure I need hardly say that I am always entirely at your service, if there is ever any way that I can help.
> Yours
> Sidney Webb [288]

After his appointment Burns called at Grosvenor Road:

The very day of his introduction to the Cabinet John Burns arrived, childishly delighted with his own post. For one solid hour he paced the room expanding his soul before me......What he and his big officials will do with each other remains to be seen. To listen to him talking one would think he was hopelessly confused in his views and intentions. [289]

Winston Churchill – now a Liberal, though not a pro-Boer – became Under Secretary for the Colonies. Initially he was not involved in social reform. After 1908, when he became President of the Board of Trade, he took a central role in labour market policy.

In 1907, Leo Chiozza Money, a maverick, radical Liberal MP, told the Webbs:

There are two Ministers in this Government who, on account both of their abilities and their comparative youth, must go to the very top. They are Lloyd George and Winston Churchill. You have neglected them both. Cultivate them.[290]

This advice came too late for them to influence Lloyd George, but they did manage to work effectively with Churchill.

Although the Liberal government of 1906 is remembered as a reforming government, they did not start with a social reform blueprint. Instead, three separate processes evolved:

The Poor Law Commission took evidence and commissioned research, dividing into majority and minority factions, and producing two reports in 1909.

Ministers developed their programme of social legislation, to some extent outflanking and marginalising the issue of Poor Law reform, while contributing to the fiscal and constitutional crisis of 1909-1911.

Burns at the LGB pursued a limited programme of purely *administrative* change, within existing Poor Law legislation.

These processes were not coordinated; they were often in competition, even antagonistic. William Braithwaite, an ex-Toynbee Hall Treasury civil servant who worked on National Insurance, described how:

There was personal friction, to use no stronger word, between Lloyd George and John Burns, so that Treasury and Local Government Board were not on speaking terms. [291]

Most of the Webbs' efforts went into the Commission. They saw ministers pursuing other approaches as (at best) misguided. They became increasingly scornful towards Burns.

It was not clear why Arthur Balfour had established the Commission. Beatrice thought a possible explanation was that his brother, Gerald Balfour, LGB

President, was interested in ideas, while the civil servant head of the Poor Law division of the LGB, James Stewart Davy, was newly appointed and energetic – but *intent on reaction*. LGB officials had an uneasy feeling

> *…that there had been, during the last two decades, an unwilling drift away from the principles of 1834, and one which sooner or later had to be decisively stopped.* [292]

In December 1905 Beatrice met Davy, to understand what the LGB wanted from the Commission. They would accept limited change – perhaps abolishing Poor Law Guardians. But the Commission should recommend

> *…reversion to the principles of 1834 as regards policy: to stem the tide of philanthropic impulse that was sweeping away the old embankment of deterrent tests to the receipt of relief.* [293]

Beatrice thought officials intended steering the Commission towards conclusions predetermined by careful selection of evidence and witnesses;

> *… above all, we were to be given* opinions *and not* facts.[294]

After meeting Davy, Beatrice briefed Lansbury and Booth.

Hamilton outlined the proposed procedure at the Commission's first meeting on 2 December:

> *There was no agenda. A cut-and dried scheme was laid before us, and we were not asked to vote on it, only to express our opinion on half-a-dozen points ranging from the hour of luncheon to the appointment of assistant commissioners.* [295]

This was a highly informal way of working; Beatrice thought it was intended to smooth the path to the LGB's foregone conclusions. She challenged the approach; no one backed her up. She reflected

> *I was not over-pleased with my tone this afternoon and must try to do better. Beware of 'showing off' superior knowledge of irrelevant detail.*[296]

She wrote to Robert Duff, the Commission secretary, and arranged to meet Hamilton. Beatrice and Sidney drafted their own procedural proposals: a full agenda, circulation of minutes and draft evidence before each meeting. The Commission should decide on a plan for research and investigations. Witnesses should include all 14 regional Poor Law inspectors, and local people.

Before meeting Hamilton, she noted that it was

...a new experience to have to make myself disagreeable in order to reach my ends. In private life one can only get one's way by being unusually pleasant. In official life, at least as the most insignificant member of a commission overwhelmingly against me in opinion, I shall only get my share of control by quietly and persistently standing on my rights as an individual commissioner and refusing to be overawed by great personages who would like to pooh-pooh a woman who attempts to share in the control of affairs.[297]

They settled the procedural row by establishing committees – one on procedure, others on statistics, documents, and evidence. This enabled the Commission to start work; Beatrice did not think it a satisfactory outcome, later writing that they were

...spending about £12,000 a year: I would undertake to get more information and better verified information for £1,200. We slip and slide along, massing up blue books, always evading difficult points, sprawling all over the place beginning multitudinous and often irrelevant enquiries and completing and perfecting none.[298]

The Commission took oral and written evidence, conducted visits, and undertook or commissioned research. Beatrice also conducted her own studies, funded by Charlotte Shaw and by the Fabian Society, and assisted by Sidney and their own researchers.

Beatrice warmed to Hamilton. In February 1906 he and his wife dined at Grosvenor Road with the cocoa philanthropist Seebohm Rowntree, Canon Barnett, and others. Beatrice noted

...we are all getting fond of our chairman...[299]

In March, the Webbs dined in quick succession with the Asquiths and with the Hamiltons. Asquith they found vulgar:

The large garish rooms, the flunkeys and the superlatively good dinner[300]

They felt

...half-flattered that we had been asked, half-contemptuous of ourselves for having gone...[301]

In contrast, dinner with the Hamiltons was *homely* and *without pretentiousness.* Later they stayed at the Hamiltons' country home

...those two are the simplest-mannered, kindest and most public-spirited aristocrats I have ever come across – not intellectual but quite open-minded and anxious to understand the point of view of other classes of the community.[302]

211

Working relations with Hamilton established, Beatrice's next potential obstacle on the Commission was the LGB Permanent Secretary, Sir Samuel Provis. Provis, a COS sympathizer, and a master of detail, was approaching retirement. Even John Burns called him a *fossil*.[303]

In February 1906 Provis lost his temper when Beatrice requested access to Board documents, asserting that

...he would not have a poking enquiry into L.G.B. policy [304]

She stayed calm, a couple of weeks later having *a most friendly chat* with Provis, and inviting him to dinner *...to meet a carefully selected party*.[305] He agreed to assist the research.

The Commission met regularly through 1906, 1907 and 1908. They started by examining the working of the existing Poor Law, moving on in autumn 1907 to consider unemployment.

The divisions that would result in Majority and Minority Reports soon emerged. The nucleus of the majority grouping included the four LGB civil servants and the six COS members. At the start they were broadly committed to defending the principles of 1834.

The Commission first discussed possible recommendations in October 1906. C S Loch spoke in favour of 1834; Frank Bentham, a businessman who chaired the Bradford Guardians, declared

We must mark off for stigma the dependents on the state – there must be no blurring of the lines between persons who were supporting themselves and those that were being supported out of the rates... [306]

Beatrice gained a reputation for tenacious interrogation of witnesses. A G Gardiner thought there was

...no cross-examiner at the bar more suave or subtle than Mrs Webb. [307]

This irritated Loch; in May 1906 Beatrice noted

C S Loch completely lost his temper yesterday at my cross-examination...[308]

On another occasion

I heard him say 'what cheek' to one of my questions to a witness. [309]

Beatrice joined official Commission visits to Scotland and Ireland. Independently, she visited workhouses in Yorkshire and Lancashire, and labour colonies in Essex and Suffolk.

The Commission hired Special Investigators to undertake research; one was Thomas Jones. After LSE, TJ had returned to Glasgow to teach economics. His departmental head was a Commission member, William Smart. TJ thought Smart was orthodox and conventional – and scared of Beatrice. Nevertheless, when the Commission was appointing investigators, Smart wrote to Beatrice that

> *...no one will serve us for Wales but a Welshman, and I think I should propose him. Your husband knows him – as a Fabian among other things...And he is as straight and fine a chap as walks the earth.* [310]

TJ wrote two reports (one of them jointly with Constance Williams, a COS social worker) on the impact of outdoor relief on wages. They found – counter to the expectations of the COS – that very little outdoor relief went to men. There was virtually no evidence that it led to lower wages.

TJ recommended an end to casual labour:

> *Among the most effective pauperising agencies must be placed casual labour.* [311]

He also argued that

> *The policy of deterrence should be given up for that of supervision.*

And that

> *Sickness should be treated as a problem in health, not as a problem in poverty.* [312]

Meanwhile, Smart employed R H Tawney to cover TJ's Glasgow teaching.

Other Special Investigators included Rose Squire (a senior Factory Inspector) and Arthur Steel-Maitland (a civil servant). They examined *the relation of industrial and sanitary conditions to pauperism*, concluding that casual, irregular employment was the main cause of poverty. Again, this countered the views of the COS.

In addition there were the Webbs' own research projects, of which, by the end of 1906, there were five:

- The policy of the Central Authority, 1834-1907. Sidney worked on this, with two other researchers. It formed the basis for the Webbs' *English Poor Law Policy*;

- A study of the Poplar and Bradford Boards of Guardians;

- A study on decisions to grant or refuse outdoor relief in certain unions;

- A study on the contrast between Poor Law and public health attitudes to medical services;

- An investigation of the position of children on outdoor relief. The researcher for this was Marion Phillips, an Australian, completing her PhD at LSE.

These studies clarified disagreements in the Commission, and helped Beatrice arrive at her conclusions.

At first Beatrice's research went undisturbed. But in December 1906 she noted

...Loch has got on the scent of my various enquiries...I shall be surprised if, sooner or later, I don't get into hot water over my 'special enquiries' and the means I am taking to get the facts. Poor Lord George – what between Charles Booth, C S Loch and me he is going to have a hard time. [313]

The following month, reporting to Pease about the funds raised from Fabians, she wrote

The COS contingent are getting very angry with me as I have forced their hand and C S Loch is always attacking me and they do already resent my separate enquiries and consequent memorandum. [314]

The first storm came at the Evidence Committee in February 1907. Helen Bosanquet raised Marion Phillips' report on children; the committee discussed

...the advisability of allowing individual Commissioners to undertake investigations on a large scale...[315]

The committee disapproved; they resolved

...to ask the Chairman to interview Mrs Sidney Webb in connection with the enquiry which she was said to be undertaking with regard to the out-relief of widows with children.

Hamilton sent Beatrice a

...curt and crude request to stop investigation on my own account... [316]

She fought back, with the outcome that the Commission took over the study and the two researchers (who received a substantial pay rise).

Beatrice was exhausted by the row; Sidney took her to stay at Beachy Head for four days.

...fled here and completely collapsed with sleeplessness and indigestion [317]

At Grosvenor Road the following week Beatrice wrote to H G Wells:

My Commission is responsible for the collapse: 'Eleven more obstinate men I never did know'. Moreover the fact that they are men... [318]

The Webbs' work on the central authority helped build the case against the principles of 1834, showing that outdoor relief had never been eliminated and arguing that the 1834 approach was obsolete. *National uniformity* had been abandoned except for vagrants; *less eligibility* only applied to vagrants; the *workhouse system* only applied to the able bodied.

This contributed to the arguments for breaking up the Poor Law. A first report was ready in July 1907. Hamilton again raised the issue of reports written by individual Commissioners. Beatrice heard in September that Hamilton had proposed that the report should not be circulated to members. In November Loch was still objecting to the report.

At that time there were two, separate, publicly-funded health systems. The public health service, provided through local government, by Medical Officers of Health (MOHs), was responsible for promoting the health of the population as a whole. The Poor Law medical service provided a limited service for destitute people.

In 1906 Beatrice began examining the relationship between the two. Listening to COS witnesses argue that medical relief should be restricted to the technically destitute

> *Suddenly it flashed across my mind that what we had to do was to adopt the entirely contrary attitude and make medical inspection and medical treatment compulsory on all sick persons – to treat illness, in fact, as a public nuisance...*[319]

From this point the Webbs argued that the two services should be unified under the MOHs. They wrote to all 600 MOHs; subsequently, Loch objected to the sending of the letter.

In January 1907 Beatrice noted that the evidence was coming in nicely; a week later

> *The COS members – Loch, Bosanquet, Booth and Octavia Hill are getting very restive at the evidence of the MOH.*[320]

The Commission picked eight MOHs as witnesses; they did not want to hear more. They also appointed their own medical researcher, Dr McVail, a Scots MOH. By April 1907 the witness statements were arriving

> *...long elaborate essays in favour of transference of Poor Law medical relief to Public Health Authorities and free medical assistance by these...*[321]

Beatrice's health report was ready in September 1907. She contrasted the objectives of the public health system and the Poor Law medical service – the first provided curative treatment and prevention; the second, essential medicine and treatment for those already ill (and destitute). She recommended uniting the two services, with prevention the overall objective. She wrote:

> ...*we have two conflicting public medical services, both rate-paid, overlapping, practically without communication, practically without communication with each other, working on diametrically opposite lines, and sometimes positively hindering each other's work.* [322]

In October the Commission discussed unification. Beatrice thought there might even be a majority for uniting the services. Hamilton, who had seen Dr McVail's report, said that

> ...*it corroborates Mrs Webb's conclusions as to the impossibility of maintaining the Poor Law as the medical authority.* [323]

But the matter did not end there; Helen Bosanquet suspected that the MOHs were not as strongly pro-unification as Beatrice suggested. Beatrice wrote:

> *A brilliant idea has struck Mrs Bosanquet: why not ask Mrs Webb for her 'correspondence with the M.O.H.s' upon which she has manifestly based her report on the medical services? Can we not extract something from this correspondence which will discredit her?* [324]

Beatrice sent the letters; she did not send them all, leaving out some that were *compromising to the authors*, and some *stupid conservative ones*. Helen Bosanquet suspected Beatrice had tampered with the evidence.

> *To be frank I had qualms of conscience in making any kind of selection...But it was clear that Mrs Bosanquet was not playing the game fair.* [325]

Sure enough, it was found that, while twenty five Medical Officers of Health supported merging the two systems, forty nine opposed; thirty had expressed no opinion. [326]

Beatrice wrote to Hamilton:

> *Dear Lord George*
> *The Commission has been in an odious state of mind... but you set the baby teething, and you must expect convulsions! – You have only to wait patiently and then convulsions will subside, and you will be left master of the situation. The trouble had to come sooner or later...It seems pretty clear to me that there must be two Reports (I thought last summer there would be three).* [327]

Beatrice then collapsed. She returned to Beachy Head.

All this has meant, on top of a year's hard work, a bad nervous breakdown, and I am here for ten days' absolute quiet – a truce having been proclaimed in my absence on sick leave.[328]

Sidney remained in London and called on Hamilton to negotiate peace. He wrote to Beatrice with the details:

We were throughout on the most friendly terms – I protesting your earnest desire to accommodate yourself, he explaining what a difficult team he had to drive... I found I had been more than an hour with him...[329]

Despite the agreement between Sidney and Hamilton, Beatrice felt *low and disheartened...*

I don't like all this intriguing. I should prefer to play with my cards on the table. [330]

Before the row over the letters, there might have been a majority on the Commission for unifying health services. That possibility disappeared.

In autumn 1907 the Commission turned to unemployment. All the members accepted that economy and society had changed since 1834, and that unemployment in an advanced industrial economy was different from distress in a predominantly agricultural one. Mass urban unemployment had appeared since 1834; no Commissioners had ready-made solutions. The Majority Report refers to the *striking unanimity* (para 315) of the Special Investigators on the importance of casual labour as a cause of unemployment.

Back in 1886, with high winter unemployment, and the SDF campaign, Joseph Chamberlain, as LGB President, had agreed that councils could offer paid work to unemployed people, on condition that

- *the men to be employed should be engaged on the recommendation of the Guardians as persons whom, owing to previous condition and circumstances, it is undesirable to send to the Workhouse, or to treat as subjects for pauper relief.*

- *The wages to be paid should be something less than the wages ordinarily paid for similar work, in order to prevent imposture, and to leave the strongest temptation to those who avail themselves of this opportunity to return as soon as possible to their previous occupations.* [331]

New legislation in 1905 had extended the relief works policy, as well as permitting the establishment of 'colonies', intended to combine employment and training.

No Commissioners supported relief works. Two Special Investigators, (the

Conservative educationalist Cyril Jackson, and John Pringle, a clergyman close to the COS) reported on methods of helping unemployed people outside the Poor Law. Beatrice thought their report

…did little else but discredit relief work… [332]

Instead, discussion focussed on two policy instruments: land colonization, and the provision of labour exchanges.

Colonies were intended to revive agriculture, providing work and training for unemployed people by settling them on underused areas of agricultural land. George Lansbury's Poplar Guardians pioneered the colony approach, establishing colonies at Laindon in Essex, and at Hollesley Bay in Suffolk. In 1905 Hollesley Bay was taken over by the London Central Unemployed Body (which had been established by the 1905 Act). John Burns, sceptical about colonies, approved the necessary loan against his better judgment.

In 1906 Burns visited a colony at Letchworth, describing the London unemployed there as

A picturesque aviary of cranks, foreman called them 'monkey nuts and macaroni' type. Sandals. No hats. Liberty ties etc… [333]

Next year Burns visited Hollesley Bay:

…a costly and foolish experiment as initiated and developed by that prize fanatic G L Lansbury and others. A holiday home for 250 men from London who deteriorate and go soft by a process of coddling… [334]

At Christmas 1907 Beatrice went to Hollesley Bay; she found the residents

…a faint-hearted nerveless set of men – their manner sometimes servile, sometimes sullen, never easy and independent. Both the organisation of their work and the organisation of their leisure was defective. [335]

She was more impressed by the Salvation Army's colony at Hadleigh, near Southend. The salvationists were

…more successful in getting the men to work, there is less foul talk, perhaps less discontent and jeering. The self-devotion of the officers counts for something in raising the tone of the colonists. On the other hand, there is tremendous religious pressure – far more than I had realised. [336]

But she questioned whether it was right

…to submit men, weakened by this suffering, to this religious pressure exercised by the very persons who command their labour? [337]

Beatrice was fascinated (as Margaret Harkness had been) by the Salvation Army -

> ...*quite the most remarkable body of men and women that I have yet come across...a true Samurai class.*[338]

Labour exchanges were intended to create a register of unemployed people, and to bring potential employers in contact with them. They had been developed in Germany, and were tried in London, where William Beveridge, at Toynbee Hall, had taken an interest. In 1905 they became the responsibility of the London Central Unemployed Body, of which Beveridge became a member.

The Commission decided to take evidence from Beveridge. The Webbs spent summer 1907 at Shaw's house at Ayot St Lawrence in Hertfordshire. They invited Beveridge down, and spent an August morning taking him through his evidence, coaching him and rehearsing him. He wrote later of their ... *inexhaustible industry and preparedness:*

> ... *They alone of all the Commissioners thought of going through my evidence with me.*[339]

Some trade unionists – including Burns – were suspicious of labour exchanges, seeing them as potential recruiting grounds for strike breakers.

In October, giving his evidence, Beveridge took the Commission by storm:

> *After my dress-rehearsal at Ayot St. Lawrence, the performance went well. My friend of Charterhouse and Oxford days, L. R. Phelps, then Provost of Oriel, wrote to congratulate me on my evidence. 'It impressed everyone not a little'. The Chairman said, 'I shall keep my eye on that man.*[340]

After that, Beveridge noted,

> ...*when they reported fifteen months later, the whole Commission blessed labour exchanges whole-heartedly.*[341]

The Webbs, and the Commission, were persuaded. Sidney wrote to Beveridge in February 1908 with his own approach, concluding

> *This scheme will be pressed forward, and* in due course *boomed.*[342]

The next week, Sidney had dinner with Winston Churchill. He told Beatrice

> *Winston made me sit next to him and was most obsequious – eager to assure me that he was willing to absorb all the plans we could give him; that he would read anything we sent him and so on.*[343]

In March, Churchill, Beveridge, and the Liberal MP Charles Masterman dined at Grosvenor Road. Beatrice explained to her sister Mary that Churchill was

...dining with me on the 11ᵗʰ to discuss our scheme for dealing with unemployment...He is much improved in appearance – healthier and less bumptious.[344]

Their opinion of Churchill was rising:

He had swallowed whole Sidney's scheme for boy labour and unemployment... he is most anxious to be friendly and we were quite willing to be so...Winston has a hard temperament... But I rather liked the man.[345]

She thought he had

...the American's capacity for the quick appreciation and rapid execution of new ideas whilst hardly comprehending the philosophy beneath them.[346]

Beveridge described the dinner in a letter to his mother:

Mrs Webb had sent their scheme (which is founded on me) to Winston Churchill before and he has been converted and is now at work converting Asquith. I don't think he is at all points clear as to what Labour Exchanges mean – as Mrs Webb says you never know quite what he's going to hand back to you afterwards as his version of your idea – but still so long as he talks about the name it doesn't matter.[347]

Then came Campbell Bannerman's resignation; in April Asquith became Prime Minister. The King, who was spending six weeks at Biarritz, asked Asquith to come to Biarritz for the formal appointment. On the evening of Monday 6 April, therefore, Asquith left Charing Cross Station to go by train to Biarritz. He travelled incognito, wearing

...a thick overcoat and a travelling cap pulled down well over his eyes.[348]

He arrived at Biarritz late on the evening of Tuesday 7 April, and was appointed the next morning.

There were rumours that the new Prime Minister would ask Winston Churchill to take over at the LGB. But Churchill was not enthusiastic; he was said to have replied, refusing

...to be shut up in a soup kitchen with Mrs Sidney Webb.[349]

And so, on the day of his appointment, Asquith wrote to Burns from the Hotel du Palais, Biarritz, asking him to carry on

My dear Burns

I hope I shall have your assent when I ask you to stay at the Local Government Board. It is not a bed of roses, but there is a lot of useful gardening still to be done there.

Yours very sincerely

H H Asquith [350]

Instead, Churchill became President of the Board of Trade, which was leading on labour market policy. According to Beveridge, Beatrice then told Churchill:

If you are going to deal with unemployment, you must have the boy Beveridge.[351]

Churchill took the advice. On Wednesday 1 July Beveridge was invited to a Board of Trade meeting on unemployment with Churchill, Llewellyn Smith, and Sidney. Churchill told them he was serious about labour exchanges, and needed a report. Beveridge was asked to write it; by Friday he had a job; he wrote to his mother:

I have just been offered and have accepted a permanent appointment in the Board of Trade – £600 a year – to begin at once or at any rate within a fortnight.[352]

Beveridge was congratulated by the editor of the Morning Post (he was replaced there by R H Tawney), and by Canon Barnett.

The Commission agreed about labour exchanges, but about little else.

As early as July 1906 Beatrice noted that her relations with other Commissioners were quite pleasant, but she was

…completely detached from them and yet on most agreeable terms. I just take my own line, attending for just as long as it suits me, cross examining witnesses to bring out my points… [353]

She began to think about recommendations, but was undecided whether to compromise with the others. In October 1906 they had talked about the 1834 principles. Beatrice thought most Commissioners

…were still on the old lines of restricting all provision to the technically destitute… [354]

Beatrice told the meeting she did not feel

…sufficiently at one with the Commission…rather giving them to understand that I should have to have my own report. [355]

In January 1907 she had not given up the possibility of a single report – she thought it might be possible to achieve unity on bringing together Poor Law and local authority health services –

But if I am to carry the majority along with me any part of the way, I shall have to be discreet... [356]

...the less I say on abstract questions the better – it only irritates the bulk of my fellow Commissioners. [357]

By April, Beatrice was *wholly indifferent* to the Commission

I merely work as hard as I know how without caring much what happens.[358]

She began drafting and sharing proposals

What I have to aim at is to draw up a rattling good report, vivid in statement of fact and closely reasoned, with a logical conclusion and immediately practicable proposals of a moderate character.[359]

Her draft foreshadowed the eventual Minority Report: break up the Poor Law; transfer its functions to the relevant County Council Committee; unite Poor Law medical services and the public health responsibilities of local government.

Beatrice first showed her proposals to some of the Commissioners – not the COS block, but the Chairman and others in the middle of the Commission – and then to people outside – politicians including the Liberal Haldane, the Conservative Gerald Balfour; Morant; and Canon Barnett.

In July she noted

...so far as I can see everything is working up towards my solution. [360]

When the Commission met in October 1907, Hamilton circulated what Beatrice called an *astonishing memo*, which, she said, would eviscerate the Poor Law. Hamilton proposed taking vagrants, the sick and the elderly out of the Poor Law, putting all health activities under the public health authorities – but setting up new Poor Law authorities to cover every county.

She thought

...the whole scheme is impracticable – but it is all in the right direction, and incidentally sweeps on one side 'the Principles of 1834' [361]

The COS Commissioners did not object in principle –

Loch talked a good deal but no one could gather what his proposals were...[362]

Haldane advised Beatrice to get Burns on side, saying Burns was

...vain and arrogant and in the hands of his officials, and opposes everything...[363]

She tried; she saw Burns a few days later, leaving him her draft:

You read my scheme and if you agree with it you might give a sort of lead-off to your colleagues on the question of Poor Law reform.[364]

Beatrice's meeting with Burns came just before her November 1907 breakdown and stay at Beachy Head. Late in November, she returned to the Commission. The exchanges at the October Commission meeting had shown that perhaps four or five Commissioners agreed with her; others might be brought round. So Beatrice agreed to submit her proposals to the Commission.

Her proposals were discussed in December, alongside a paper by Hamilton suggesting the Poor Law – its responsibilities, ethos, resources, and culture – should be transferred in its entirety to the county councils, under a statutory committee of the council.

Beatrice argued the Poor Law should be broken up – education of poor children should go to the local education authority; the previously distinct sets of health provision should be brought together, and so on.

Her proposals were

...received in stony silence...[365]

The issue had become: should the Poor Law be broken up? Or transferred to County Councils under a new committee? Beatrice forced a vote. She had two supporters – George Lansbury and Francis Chandler; two Commissioners – the two economists, William Sharp and Lancelot Phelps – abstained. All the others who were present supported Hamilton's scheme:

In their hatred of me, all the C.O.S members rallied to him giving up the ad hoc poor law body, the principle of deterrence, the strict administration of outdoor relief – a real stampede from the principles of 1834.[366]

Before, the divide had been about the 1834 principles; now, it became 'do you reform the Poor Law, but keep it as one entity? Or do you break it up?'

This entrenched the division in the Commission over what was now, for Beatrice, the central issue.

Thereupon, I gave them to understand that we considered the issue vital and should have our minority report.[367]

Beatrice thought that, while Hamilton had won, she had achieved great success:

...having dragged the whole Commission so far in my direction while preserving my freedom for a minority report. [368]

and it would be a *...thoroughly Webbian report.* [369] From now on, while the majority would concentrate on the Commission itself,

...my activity will be outside it – investigating, inventing, making an atmosphere favourable to my inventions; and, where possible, getting the persons with right opinions into high places, and persons in high places in the right state of mind. [370]

In January 1908 Hamilton tabled a new statement of the majority position. This led to an inconclusive discussion.

'Mrs Webb comes here only to sow dissension between us' said Mrs Bosanquet angrily. So I shall take the hint and stay away. [371]

The Commission met regularly until May 1908; the meetings concentrated on what would become the Majority Report, discussing Hamilton's drafts on institutional arrangements. Beatrice was passive:

I propose to take little or no part in these discussions – just stand by in a pleasant and kindly attitude, and await events. [372]

In February, the Majority confirmed their decision on structure: abolish Guardians; create statutory Poor Law committees on county councils; keep Poor Law medical relief within the new structure. They renamed the Poor Law 'Public Assistance'.

Then they discussed unemployment. Everyone supported labour exchanges, though Beatrice thought the COS contingent were *really half hearted* about this. She thought they were

...desperately anxious to slur over everything which distinguishes one destitute person from another destitute person – the category of the destitute is to be kept absolutely and separate from the rest of the population. [373]

She wrote to her sister Mary about the majority

Their scheme is quite impracticable but I think they will stick with it. I am rather glad because it just gives me room for a minority report... [374]

The last regular meeting of the Commission was on Friday 15 May 1908. After that the Majority Report was drafted, mostly by Duff, the secretary, Helen Bosanquet, and William Smart – overseen by the chairman. In June, Hamilton wrote that Helen Bosanquet had

...by far the clearest head on the Commission; her information is very great; her judgment very sound, and in addition she wields the ablest pen... [375]

The Commission began to meet again to review the draft report in October. Beatrice planned to intervene *seldom*.

On 16 October she *looked in*:

They were slugging along quite amiably discussing little details... [376]

A fortnight later she noted

The commission gets madder and madder every day [377]

This continued until December. Beatrice thought the Commission was getting old and weary – *if not actually senile.* [378] Their report was in scraps

They play about, altering commas and capitals and changing the name of things, but leaving it to mere chance whether or not the vagrants or the mentally defective are to be dealt with under the Poor Law. [379]

They assembled on 2 January 1909 for the official photograph – and to sign a blank sheet: the Majority report was not finished. Paragraphs were still being drafted.

Beatrice and Sidney spent all 1908 drafting the Minority Report. In December 1907, the Commission had clarified two things: there would be two reports; the issue which distinguished them would be whether the Poor Law remained a single institution, or whether it was broken up.

Beatrice had already circulated versions of her plan; they now had to finalize it. In January Beatrice noted

...we are working at high pressure collecting our information...At present we can barely see the forest for the trees... [380]

They were

...manufacturing the heavy artillery of fact... [381]

They continued campaigning, sending drafts to Balfour, Haldane, and Asquith. They also

...remitted our unemployment scheme to the leading members of the Labour Party (barring MacDonald) ... [382]

They were pleased the Labour members liked their proposals.

By February, Beatrice thought she could not influence the Majority any further:

Clearly I cannot get them any further along my road.[383]

In March Beatrice and Sidney were working hard

Just at present the whole burden is falling on him, as I feel dreadfully tired – habitually tired – not ill, merely physically and mentally weary. [384]

They continued lobbying; in March they stayed at Stanway, where Beatrice gave Balfour the latest version.

Samuel Provis was due to retire as LGB Permanent Secretary; Beatrice tried, unsuccessfully, to persuade both Burns and Asquith that Morant should replace him. Morant came to Grosvenor Road for a long talk on Good Friday 1908, both about the possible move to the LGB, and about the Minority Report. Later in April Morant asked for a copy of the draft report; Beatrice sent proofs, from which Morant had 300 copies printed. In May, Beatrice circulated these to ministers, opposition leaders, and civil servants.

In April Beatrice went to Ireland with the Commission; Sidney stayed with friends, and rewrote the section of the Minority Report covering the unemployed. He wrote to Beatrice:

We shall have definitely to live for the P.L. Scheme, and put aside everything else for nine months. It is as you say a great responsibility and at the same time a magnificent opportunity. [385]

Beatrice looked forward to finalising the report when she returned from Ireland:

It will be High Jinks doing it and we will get to work at once. [386]

They worked solidly, mostly away from London: three weeks with Beatrice's sister Mary in Gloucestershire; three at Luton Hoo, the country house of the Randlord Julius Wernher; and six in Herefordshire (with a short visit to the Fabian Summer School in Wales). They only returned to Grosvenor Road in September; even then they had not finished the section on the able bodied.

Meanwhile, another row with Hamilton had erupted in August. Extracts from the draft Minority Report appeared in the *Times*. The Webbs had given material to Leo Amery – ex-Fabian, ex- Coefficient, now a Times journalist – asking him not to mention their names or refer to the Commission. According to Beatrice, the leak

...roused Lord George Hamilton to fury. [387]

Hamilton accused them of a breach of confidence.
Beatrice thought this

...breaks, I think finally any friendly relations with my colleagues – with all except Chandler, Lansbury and possibly Wakefield. [388]

In October, the Webbs were *...at the highest pressure of brainwork.* [389] Beatrice was *...living upon the most rigorous hygienic basis*: up at 6.30 am, a cold bath, a walk or cycle ride, then work from 7.30 until 1.00.

...bread and cheese lunch, short rest, another walk, then tea and rest until 6 or 6.30...I feel it is too much and am sleeping badly from brain excitement. [390]

In October they began writing about unemployment. Hamilton was forcing the Majority Report through the Commission on a strict timetable, so they only had six weeks left.

The pressure was relentless. What should be the policy on unemployment?

We answer training. But the Labour men laugh at the notion of training adult men. They want employment at good wages... [391]

The same Labour representatives also suggested state unemployed benefit with no restrictions – which Beatrice thought *sheer madness*. She felt oppressed by the problem:

I dream of it at night, I pray for light in the early morning, I grind grind grind... [392]

By January 1909 they had finished. Beatrice wondered how she had managed to survive the autumn; she attributed it to

...sheer will power induced by prayer [393]

She and Sidney planned a month's holiday as soon as possible.

As Beatrice expected, four Commissioners signed the Minority Report: herself, George Lansbury, Francis Chandler, and Russell Wakefield (who that year became Dean of Norwich).

Both reports were substantial[394]: The Majority Report was 908 pages, the Minority 716. Both included reviews of Poor Law history since 1834, and details selected from the research reports and the testimony of witnesses.

The main difference between the reports remained: should the Poor Law, providing services only for the destitute, be kept as one system? Or should it be broken up, and its component parts merged with public services for the wider population?

The Majority recommended transferring all of the Poor Law to County and County Borough councils, rebranding it as Public Assistance, but running it as a distinct, separate service.

The Minority proposed breaking up the Poor Law – services for children merged with the work of education authorities, the Poor Law medical service amalgamated with the public health service, and so on.

Following Beveridge, both Minority and Majority proposed a national network of labour exchanges. There was a difference: the Minority proposed that, for sectors dominated by casual or seasonal employment, it should be compulsory for employers to recruit via the labour exchange, while the Majority stated:

> *There should be no compulsion to use the Labour Exchanges...*[395]

The minority went further, foreshadowing the 1944 Employment White Paper, which committed government to the maintenance of a *high and stable level of employment after the war.*[396]

The Minority Report proposed

> *...that the duty of so organising the National Labour Market as to prevent or to minimise Unemployment should be placed upon a Minister responsible to Parliament, who might be designated the Minister for Labour.*[397]

The labour Ministry would be responsible, not only for labour exchanges, but for counter-cyclical programmes of public works – such as tree planting, coastal protection, and land reclamation, paid at standard rates – to regularise demand for labour in periods of depression; for supporting trade union-based unemployment insurance; and for running training programmes and the detention colonies.

The tone of the reports was different: the Majority saw unemployment as a failure of character. Hamilton wrote to Helen Bosanquet:

> *...I want, if possible, the moral side of unemployment to be drawn carefully and fully. I believe it is not so much material or industrial changes as deterioration in grit and self-reliance...*[398]

The Majority emphasized drink as a cause of pauperism:

> *A great weight of evidence indicates drink as the most potent and universal factor in bringing about pauperism*[399]

The Minority took an opposite line:

> *...the extent to which the Unemployed are men of good or bad character... appears to us, from the standpoint of the prevention of the evil, wholly irrelevant. Whether the men are good or bad, drunken or sober, immoral or virtuous, it is a terrible misfortune to the community as well as themselves that they should be unemployed.*[400]

The Majority defended Poor Law schools (which the Minority wanted to see integrated into the mainstream school system). They wrote warmly of the *esprit de corps* of the schools, of their annual reunions.

> *…abundant evidence is to hand that those educated in these schools carry away with them a memory of happy days spent there…Results like these are the pride and glory of our great public schools, and it goes far to justify the Poor Law school system that it produces, in a smaller measure no doubt and in humbler form, results of the same kind.* [401]

Afterwards, Thomas Jones recalled his time researching for the Commission. Beatrice and Helen Bosanquet, he said

> *…fought politely and at some verbal distance for the minds if not the hearts of their assistants.* [402]

TJ thought that Helen Bosanquet was the

> *…less clever and more honest-in-the-grain of the two; Mrs Webb the more humorous and the greater charmer.*

He quoted Elizabeth Wordsworth:

> *The good are so harsh to the clever*
> *The clever so rude to the good.* [403]

'THE GOLDEN TIME': THE FABIAN SOCIETY 1905-1912

For twenty years four men led the Fabian Society – Sidney, Sydney Olivier, Graham Wallas, and George Bernard Shaw. Beatrice, when she first met them, had called them the Fabian Junta. Later they became known as the Old Gang. Fabian membership was static. The Old Gang were in charge.

Then numbers began to increase: from 730 in 1904 to 2462 in 1909. Beatrice labelled it

> *…the little boom in the Fabian Society…Sidney and I, GBS and HGW, sometimes ask ourselves whether it represents a larger wave than we think – are we, by our constructive thought, likely to attract considerable numbers of followers in the near future?* [404]

Sidney and Beatrice now found themselves working with, and befriending, a younger generation. Among them were people who would campaign against the

Poor Law, run the new welfare state, and staff – later lead – the emerging Labour Party. The Webbs were key in identifying and forming that group.

Why the membership increase? One answer is the changed intellectual climate around the 1906 election. Robert Ensor, elected to the Fabian Executive in 1907, wrote that

Radicalism and socialism alike, released from the suppressions of two decades, were radiant with sudden hopes of a new heaven and a new earth. [405]

Another reason was H G Wells. Rupert Brooke and Henry Schloesser (later Slesser) started reading Wells at school. Margaret Cole (born 1893, so not in the first wave of new recruits) called herself a *Wellsian Socialist*: she was one among many who

...took their hope of the world from that vivid, many-gifted, generous, cantankerous personality... [406]

In 1907 Beatrice thought it was

...mostly the increasing reputation of GBS and H G Wells – perhaps even of 'Sidney and Beatrice Webb' which is leading the young intellectuals to join us in such numbers... [407]

Some new members were second generation Fabians. Sydney Olivier's two older daughters, Margery and Brynhild, joined in 1906. Amber Reeves was the daughter of William Pember Reeves, the New Zealand Labour politician who had come to London in 1896 as the country's representative. Reeves, a Coefficient, and his wife Maud became close to the Webbs and to GBS. Emily Townshend – one of the original Girton College Cambridge students – had joined in 1894; her daughters Caroline and Rachel now also became members. Both Emily and Rachel were radical suffragettes and served time in prison. Caroline, an artist, made the Fabian stained glass window in 1910. Hubert Bland's daughter Rosamund joined in 1906.

Many new Fabians were students or recent graduates. Frederic Hillersdon Keeling, (later known as Ben), from Colchester, joined when he started at Trinity College Cambridge in October 1904. Both Charles Mostyn Lloyd – a 28-year-old Oxford graduate, living at Toynbee Hall – and George Blanco White (Cambridge graduate, bar student) – joined in November 1906. Two University College London engineering graduates, Clifford Sharp and Arthur Colegate, joined in late 1905.

Colegate's membership was approved in January 1906, as the General Election result was becoming clear. On 15 January, he wrote in his diary

Lunched with Sharp and like everyone else discussed the election results. [408]

The new Fabian members were quickly swept into a life of metropolitan political activism. Colegate lived with his parents (who had paid for his articles as a civil engineer) in South London. They worried that he would be distracted from his career. Anxiously, they asked him about churchgoing. In December 1905 he had a row with his father about socialism. [409]

Colegate first came to Beatrice's attention the following year. She wrote that he was a

...penniless youth, of lower middle class extraction, who had scrambled through London University as an engineering student, but who found himself at four and twenty without employment or the prospect of employment.

He was slim and good-looking

...with refined ways and considerable self-culture, agreeable manners and a pliable temper. [410]

Henry Schloesser, a young barrister, became a Fabian in 1907, despite the fact that some of his legal colleagues thought it was foolish for a lawyer to openly declare himself a socialist.

The Fabian world was centred on the Strand. Fabian members' meetings were at the Essex Hall, Essex Street – a large venue, belonging to the Unitarians. Colegate and Sharp attended regularly. Before or afterwards, they would go to cafes frequented by the speakers. One evening, Colegate

...met Sharp at the Strand Cabin (where we sat at the table next to that occupied by Hubert Bland, Cecil Chesterton etc.). [411]

Before joining, in November 1905, Colegate had heard Stephen Sanders speak on the Minimum Wage:

Very good attendance but paper rather dull. However, an excellent discussion followed. Bernard Shaw, Hobson, Bland, Cecil Chesterton, & Sidney Webb being amongst the speakers. The latter made the best speech & I was very pleased with his sound sense and knowledge of the subject. [412]

Sanders – former Battersea SDF member, and secretary of the Battersea Labour League – had joined the Fabians in 1890. He was now a member of both the Fabian Executive Committee, and the London County Council.

The Fabian office – a semi-basement at Clement's Inn – was close to the Essex Hall. Wells described it as a *miserable cellar*; Sidney was proud of having negotiated a good deal.

In 1907 Clement Attlee and his brother Tom

…went to Clements Inn to try to join the Fabian Society. Edward Pease, the Secretary, regarded us as if we were two beetles who had crept under the door, and when we said we wanted to join the Society he asked coldly, 'Why?' we said, humbly, that we were socialists and persuaded him that we were genuine. [413]

The two Attlee brothers attended an Essex Hall meeting together. Clement was struck that, with Sidney, GBS and others, *the platform was full of bearded men.* He whispered to Tom

Have we got to grow a beard to join this show? [414]

Attlee thought Sidney *lucidly explanatory*. He remembered Wells:

…speaking with a little piping voice, he was very unimpressive. [415]

Clement Attlee had graduated from University College Oxford in 1904. In 1905, newly qualified, he began practising as a barrister; he also started voluntary work at Haileybury House, a Limehouse settlement founded by his old school.

As the Fabian membership expanded, so did the range of the society's activities. They decided to run an annual residential summer school, out of London, and the Executive Committee supported the creation of new groupings of members.

The first of these was the Fabian Nursery. In 1906, Pease reported to the Executive that he had been asked by Rosamund Bland to provide facilities for a *society of junior Fabians*. The Committee agreed; the initial meeting took place on 11 April; Arthur Colegate was asked to help, and became Treasurer. He was asked to draw up a list of socialist literature for members. Pease thought the first draft would not do:

…some of the books mentioned are neither socialist nor literature. [416]

Another early member was Amber Reeves. By 1908, Henry Schloesser was on the Fabian Nursery Committee.

The Fabian Arts Group was started in January 1907 by George Holbrook Jackson and Albert Orage, who together had previously run the Leeds Art Group; in 1906 they moved to London and joined the Fabian Society. In December 1906, Jackson wrote to Pease, saying that the Fabians had already created a

…definite Socialist attitude in both Politics and Sociology… [417]

Why should they not do the same for art and philosophy?

The sculptor and typographer Eric Gill also joined the Fabians in 1906; according to his biographer, he immediately began

...to harangue them on the inadequacies of the socialist view of art... [418]

Later that in January 1907, Charlotte Shaw suggested the Fabians should have

...more group organisation on the Art and Philosophy line... [419]

Gill wrote that the Arts Group made

...vague efforts to deprive Fabianism of its webbed feet... [420]

In May 1907 Gill addressed the Fabians on *Socialism and the Arts and Crafts*. The meeting was chaired by the playwright Harley Granville Barker – a Fabian, and friend of GBS. Gill spoke, according to the Fabian prospectus for the evening, about

The Fabian or quantitative point of view versus the qualitative point of view. [421]

At the same time as initiating the Arts Group, Orage and Jackson (helped by money from GBS) bought a weekly magazine, *The New Age*. They subtitled the paper *An Independent Socialist Review of Politics, Literature and Art*, and themselves became editors. Clifford Sharp worked with them on layout and typography. Sidney, Hubert Bland, and HG Wells all sent supportive letters to the first edition of the revived paper in May 1907.

For about eighteen months the Fabian Arts Group flourished. But after the summer of 1908 its activities were no longer listed in the Fabian Society's programme of events. Some of its activists found the *New Age* a more hospitable environment; over time, the *New Age's* politics became closer to Guild Socialism than to Fabianism. Like Belloc and G K Chesterton, they were hostile to state-based structures and solutions.

The Fabian Arts Group was glamorous but ephemeral. The Fabian Women's group was more long lasting. Before 1907, the Fabians had been lukewarm on the suffrage question. In January 1907 a group of women Fabian members secured an amendment to the Fabian Basis

...declaring that one of the objects of the Society is to establish the equal citizenship of men and women. [422]

The amendment was proposed by Maud Pember Reeves and seconded by Beatrice – key supporters included Charlotte Shaw, Emily Townshend and Charlotte Wilson, returning after a twenty-year absence.

Although Beatrice supported the resolution, she was only a recent convert to women's suffrage. Back in 1889, she had signed a document, drafted by the writer Mrs Humphry Ward, opposing the political enfranchisement of women. Beatrice soon saw that this was a mistake, but did not publicly repudiate her statement until much later. She later wrote that

...the root of my anti-feminism lay in the fact that I had never myself suffered the disabilities assumed to arise from my sex. [423]

Sidney did not agree with the position Beatrice had taken, writing early in their relationship, in August 1890,

I think you will one day feel the need of more obviously and actively 'repenting' about Woman's Suffrage. Are you acting quite 'honest' about that? [424]

The moment of recantation arrived in November 1906: Beatrice wrote to Millicent Garrett Fawcett of the National Union of Women's Suffrage Societies (NUWSS)

You once asked me to let you know if I ceased to object to the grant of the electoral franchise to women, The time has come when I feel obliged to do so. [425]

Following the amendment to the Fabian Basis, the Fabian Women's Group (FWG) was established in 1908. As well as the supporters of the amendment, members in the FWG's early years included Millicent Murby, the actor and theatre producer; Emma Brooke; Letitia Fairfield and Marion Phillips. The Group focussed on three themes: equal citizenship; publicity; and research on women's economic position. It had a separate office, and employed its own secretary. When the money to pay the secretary ran short, Charlotte Shaw would pick up the bill. The FWG's best known research product was the study *Round About a Pound a Week*, by Maud Pember Reeves.

When H G Wells had joined the Fabian Society in 1903, welcomed by the Old Gang, he had seen the Fabians as a promising vehicle for his ideas. By late 1905, the relationship was strained. In January 1906, as the General Election results began to appear, Wells concluded that the time had come for him to strike, and to strike hard.

His attack came in two Fabian lectures. The first, in January, entitled *This misery of boots,* attacked English socialism in general, and Fabianism in particular, with sideswipes at GBS and the Webbs.

Wells scorned permeation:

You will find Socialists about, or at any rate men calling themselves Socialists... who will pretend that some odd little jobbing about municipal gas and water is Socialism, and back-stairs intervention between Conservative and Liberal the way to the Millennium. You might as well call a gas jet in the lobby of a meeting-house, the glory of God in Heaven. [426]

This was the stuff to give the new members. Sharp and Colegate were there:

About half-past seven we went to Clifford's Inn to hear H G Wells read a paper before the Fabian on 'This Misery of Boots'. The meeting was very crowded and quite successful. I spoke for the first time and although I was nervous the result was quite satisfactory. [427]

The second lecture, on 9 February, was entitled *The Faults of the Fabian*. It was a comprehensive indictment: the Society was too small, and needlessly poor – *an extraordinarily inadequate and feeble organization*. Wells argued that the Fabians should be more ambitious. The Society needed to grow; it needed better propaganda, more staff, and more money:

Make Socialists and you will achieve Socialism; there is no other plan.[428]

Both Sharp and Colegate were there. Colegate thought Wells' lecture was excellent:

...condemning the lack of seriousness in the Fabian, its small membership...[429]

After the lecture, the members agreed to establish a Special Committee to examine Wells' proposals.

Wells, remembering Colegate's contribution at the previous meeting, nominated him for the Special Committee. The Committee was appointed by the Fabian Executive, and included Executive members. Both Herbert and Jane Wells were members; Jane was secretary. Sydney Olivier chaired the Committee – an Old Gang member, but sympathetic to change. Maud Pember Reeves was another member. The Committee met through the spring and summer.

The Special Committee having been established, Wells set off for an American lecture tour. Before HG left, the Wellses asked Colegate to dinner.

Colegate was now taken up by the Fabians. In February Hubert Bland invited him to Well Hall. In March, he met GBS.

In May he went to Grosvenor Road for the first time:

In the evening I went to an 'At Home' at 41 Grosvenor Road given by Mr & Mrs Sidney Webb from 8 to 10pm to meet the German delegates of the Trades-unions.[430]

Sidney had attended the February talk by Wells; Beatrice had not. She did not like the reports she heard:

H G Wells has broken out in a quite unexpectedly unpleasant manner...an odd mixture of underhand manoeuvres and insolent bluster... [431]

Wells returned from America in June. In July, the Webbs spent a day with the Wellses; their friendship, wrote Beatrice, was

...undergoing the strain of a certain disillusionment.[432]

Colegate's initiation continued. On 15 June, he went, with Sharp, to a Fabian reception:

...Hyndman, GBS & Mrs Shaw, Mr & Mrs H G Wells, Mrs Reeves etc, were present. I talked...to Mrs Reeves who introduced her daughter a Cambridge undergraduate who thought herself clever... Miss Olivier 'the beautiful one' [433]

The following week, Edith Nesbit (Mrs Bland), invited Colegate to cooperate on a book on socialism.

Sharp was also making his way. He saw Colegate on 30 July, and told him that he was engaged to the Blands' daughter Rosamund.

Clifford and Rosamund married in 1909. In a series of complications, of which first Sharp, then Colegate, then Beatrice, became aware, they learned that Rosamund was not Edith Nesbit's daughter, but the child of Hubert Bland and Alice Hoatson, another Fabian, living in the Bland household. Edith had brought Rosamund up as her own.

When Sharp told Colegate about his engagement, Colegate noted that

...we both have heard & seen & so know, some rather objectionable things about the family – or rather about Hubert. H G Wells knows a good deal about their affairs [434]

What Wells knew about the Blands became clear at a subsequent conversation between Sharp and Colegate: Wells had himself tried to elope with Rosamund. The elopement had only been prevented by Hubert's intervention, at Paddington Station, in the incongruous role of the angry Victorian father. Accounts differ as to whether he had punched Wells or used a horsewhip on him.

The Special Committee reported in October 1906. Accepting much of the Wells critique, the report called for new name (British Socialist Party); a weekly newspaper, brighter premises, a revised Fabian Basis, and a new governance structure. There should be a decisive break with permeation. The new organisation should run parliamentary candidates – though Wells himself was not enthusiastic about this. One writer summarizes the position of Wells and the Special Committee as calling

...for the Fabian Society to turn itself from a study group into a middle-class Socialist Party which would work in co-operation with the ILP and Labour Party. [435]

The report appeared with a response from the Executive, drafted by Shaw. Both reports were debated at a Fabian members' meeting at Essex Hall on Friday

7 December 1906. Shaw was supported by Sidney; Wells by Colegate. After a heated argument the meeting was adjourned to the following Friday.

Wells proposed the Executive Committee should

...make the earliest possible arrangements for the election of a new Executive to give effect to that Report [i.e., of the Special Committee][436]

On 14 December GBS stated that, if this proposal was carried, the Executive would stand down and not seek re-election. They would regard themselves as summarily dismissed.

This changed the debate. The issue had been the merits of the Special Committee report; it became Wells' attacks on the Old Gang and the outgoing executive. Beatrice saw that Wells

...has just now a great glamour for the young folk with his idealism for the future and clever biting criticism of the present...[437]

But at the members' meetings Wells overplayed his hand, enabling GBS to win:

...his accusations were so preposterous – his innuendos so unsavoury and his little fibs so transparent that even his own followers refused to support him and the 80% undecided members swayed round to the old leaders. GBS by a scathing analysis of his whole conduct threw him finally to the ground and trampled on him, somewhat hardly.[438]

Beatrice thought it an *altogether horrid business*. Initially she retained some sympathy for Wells:

Now we shall see whether he will forgive GBS and the Fabian, or become a second 'J R MacDonald' in our little world...[439]

A new Fabian Executive was elected. Both factions contested the election: 11 of the outgoing Executive, and 9 reformers – including both Wellses – were elected. The new Executive continued examining the Special Committee's recommendations – but Wells had lost: he resigned his Fabian membership not long afterwards; Jane Wells left in 1910. Beatrice wrote to her sister Mary Playne in March 1907:

...the Old Gang has beaten back the HG Wells onslaught.[440]

The differences covered both substance and personality. Wells had wanted to transform the Society into something like a political party – with agreed policies for which it campaigned publicly. He had challenged the established Fabian leadership, inviting the membership to abandon the Old Gang – and, at least by implication, replace them with himself.

The Fabians did, however, strengthen their commitment to women's suffrage. According to Edward Pease, the Fabians

...had always been in favour of votes for women. [441]

Before 1906 the principle of equal voting rights did not appear in the Society's policy documents. In November 1906 – at the same time as Beatrice was announcing her personal conversion on the issue – a Fabian General Meeting overwhelmingly carried a resolution, moved by Sydney Olivier, congratulating the Women's Social and Political Union, and

...in particular its members now imprisoned in Holloway... [442]

on the brilliant success of their methods.

The amendment to the Fabian Basis which committed the Society to

...enforcing equal citizenship of men and women. [443]

Two months later, Maud Pember Reeves successfully proposed (and Beatrice seconded) that the members should instruct the Executive Committee should put forward the amendment at the forthcoming February AGM – where it was duly carried.

While London Fabians were absorbed in the Wells affair, Ben Keeling had re-started the Cambridge University Fabian Society (CUFS), which was recognised by the Fabian Executive in February 1906.

Of all the new members, none were quite like the Cambridge Fabians. Beatrice first encountered them in 1907; some came to see the Webbs while they were at the Shaws' house at Ayot St Lawrence:

...mostly clever and enthusiastic and who look upon us as the Patriarchs of the Movement. [444]

A year later, Beatrice was dazzled; they were

...a remarkable set, quite the most remarkable the Fabian Society has yet attracted – fervent and brilliant. [445]

Of the Cambridge Fabians, two made a particular impression on Beatrice. Ben Keeling she thought a *fervent rebel*; Hugh Dalton was

...an accomplished ecclesiastical sort of person, a subtle wily man with a certain peculiar charm for those who are not put off by his mannerism [446]

Writing to her sister Mary, Beatrice described Dalton as astute and thoughtful

...by nature an ecclesiastic – a sort of lay Jesuit – preparing for political life. [447]

For Hugh Dalton it was the golden time:

Hitherto, we thought, we had been too young to think, and soon we might be too busy, and ultimately, we should be too old. The golden time was now.[448]

Youth, beauty, politics, emotion, and aesthetics came together. The Cambridge Fabians overlapped with another network, nicknamed by Virginia Woolf in 1911 the Neo-pagans. This was not a new expression; it came from a fascination with classical paganism, the arts and crafts movement, and the work of Edward Carpenter. Fabians and Neo-pagans shared enthusiasm for outdoor life – walking, camping, and nude bathing. Dalton was a Fabian but not Neo-pagan; Jacques Raverat and Gwen Darwin were Neo-pagans but not Fabians. Rupert Brooke and Ka Cox were both. Alongside their politics and their creativity, the Cambridge Fabians were linked by tangles of fluid, intricate personal relationships.

The Cambridge Fabians, the Neo-pagans, and later Bloomsbury, were greatly influenced by the works of the philosopher G E Moore. Moore had been an undergraduate in the 1890s – a contemporary of Bertrand Russell, (who thought him a genius); he was a little older than Maynard Keynes and Leonard Woolf. In *Principia Ethica* (1903), Moore argued that 'good' was indefinable and did not derive from the knowledge of facts but from the intuition of the goodness inherent in a certain set of values, namely beauty, friendship, pleasure, and knowledge.

Both Keynes and Dalton stressed the personal impact of *Principia Ethica*: Keynes, writing in the 1930s, said that its effect

...on us, and the talk which preceded it and followed it, dominated, and perhaps still dominate, everything else. [449]

The impact on Dalton had been *immense*:

Everything suddenly became clear and, as it seemed to us, incontestable. [450]

Beatrice did not approve; in 1911 she described a *pernicious set,*

...which makes a sort of ideal of anarchic ways in sexual questions...[451]

She *never could see anything* in *Principia Ethica*

...except a metaphysical justification for doing what you like and what other people disapprove of! [452]

In January 1906 Keynes – never a Fabian, then as ever a Liberal – met Ben Keeling to talk politics over breakfast; he described their encounter in a letter to Lytton Strachey:

We began with the labour movement and finished up on Ethics. They seem to know as much about productive cooperation as we know about unproductive copulation.[453]

The Cambridge Fabians grew rapidly. Within a year membership was over 100. They were the first Cambridge student society to admit both men and women. Dorothy Osmaston, a Newnham student, a CUFS Committee member in 1908, described what this meant:

For the first time we regularly met a circle of men as equals, with whom we discussed everything from religious beliefs and social evils to sex in a way that would have been impossible in the more conventional relationships of our homes.
[454].

Keeling first met the Webbs when they spoke at Cambridge Fabian events. Beatrice was struck by his *generous vitality and incontinent intelligence*.[455] Wells, who based a character in the *New Machiavelli* on Keeling, described him after his death as

...a copious, egotistical, rebellious, disorderly, generous and sympathetic young man [456]

Hugh Dalton and Rupert Brooke arrived at King's College Cambridge in October 1906. Dalton called Keeling, who recruited him to the Fabians,

...the acknowledged leader of Cambridge undergraduate socialism...

At the end of his first term, Dalton

...joined the Fabians and declared myself a socialist. I exchanged Joseph Chamberlain for James Keir Hardie – and Sidney Webb. [457]

Dalton had been to Eton; his father was a Canon of Windsor, and tutor to royal princes, including King George V.

Brooke and Dalton met on their first day at King's. Brooke had been at Rugby School, where his father taught. He was 23 days older than Dalton, who wrote many years later that

No Cambridge friendship meant more to me than his, and the radiance of his memory still lights my path. [458]

They set up a society, the Carbonari, named after nineteenth century Italian revolutionaries, to read papers and poetry and to talk. Many of Brooke's early poems were read at Carbonari meetings. After the meetings, Brooke and Dalton would walk round Cambridge:

...sometimes the dawn was in the sky before we got to bed. We walked round the Courts and beside the river for hours, trying to get things clear. For we wanted, half passionately and half humorously, to get everything clear quickly.
[459]

Brooke's conversion to Fabianism took longer than Dalton's. At Easter 1907, he wrote that he was

...terribly Fabian; which in our family is synonymous with 'atheistical' 'Roman Catholic' 'vulgar', 'conceited' and 'unpractical'. [460]

In November he wrote to a friend, saying he would be visiting Oxford with

...an indecorous, atheistical, obscene set of ruffians called the Fabians. [461]

At one stage he told Dalton

I'm not your sort of Socialist; I'm a William Morris sort of Socialist.[462]

Dalton and Brooke were influenced by Wells and Belloc, both of whom came to speak in Cambridge. In March 1908 Brooke heard Wells speak twice:

Wells came and spoke, very well... Wells is a very pleasant little man... He is rather shy.[463]

He wrote to Dalton on 8 April

Under the influence of
(a) Talks with the wee, fantastic Wells.
(b) His books.
(c) Fabian tracts.
(d) Private meditation and prayer.
(e) Arguments on the other side.
(f)–(z) Anything...etc...
I have decided to sign even the present Fabian Basis, and to become a member (if possible) of the central Fabian Society...[464]

Unlike Dalton, Brooke became an Apostle, a member of the selective Cambridge society. Keynes had been a member since 1902; Brooke knew the Keynes family, staying with them when he came for interview in December 1905. Brooke's election as an Apostle took place in January 1908. Up to the 1970s the Apostles were all male. In the Edwardian years, many were also homosexual. G E Moore, who had been elected an Apostle in 1894, played a leading role in the group in the 1900s.

Women Cambridge Fabians included Margery, Sydney Olivier's eldest daughter, who was at Newnham; by autumn 1908, she was the treasurer. Her three younger sisters, Daphne, Brynhild, and Noel, though not yet students, were frequent visitors. Eva Spielman started at Newnham in 1905. Hugh Dalton recruited Leah Manning, a student at Homerton College, after the suspicious college authorities had permitted him, suitably chaperoned, to meet her. Shena Potter (unrelated to Beatrice), from Croydon, began her studies at Newnham in 1904.

Amber Reeves came to Newnham in October 1905; Ka (Katharine) Cox the following year. Amber's parents had offered her a choice between being presented at Court and going to Cambridge. Ka was another second-generation Fabian: her father had been a wealthy Fabian stockbroker; he had asked Ka to choose between a horse and its upkeep, and university. Both Amber and Ka joined the CUFS early in their time at Cambridge, each subsequently becoming treasurer.

Brooke, the Olivier sisters, and Ka Cox were among those who were both Fabians and Neo-pagans. Virginia Stephen (who the following year married Leonard Woolf), wrote in 1911

> *Miss Cox is one of the younger Newnhamites, and it is said she will marry either a Keynes or a Brook.*[465]

Although that forecast was not borne out, Brooke did have a long, unhappy relationship with Ka Cox, as well as a brief involvement with Brynhild Olivier, the second Olivier daughter, and an intense fascination with her sister Noel.

The first secretary of the Cambridge Fabians was John Squire. He invited Keir Hardie, Shaw, and Wells to come and speak. The Hardie meeting was in 1907; rowdy, conservative students made determined, but unsuccessful, attempts to disrupt the meeting. After that the Cambridge Fabians held weekly meetings with national or local speakers. Sidney spoke at one in March 1908; Brooke wrote to his mother:

> *On Thursday, Sidney Webb came and addressed the Fabians on his new scheme for the Unemployed. I thought it was very good and intelligible. I met him at breakfast the next day.* [466]

In May 1908, the Cambridge Fabians held a dinner in Keeling's rooms in Trinity College in honour of Sydney Olivier. Brooke was there, telling his mother it was

> *...a very Socialist dinner of one course and fruit and twenty five persons...* [467]

As well as Sydney and Margaret Olivier, the two youngest Olivier daughters, Daphne, and Noel, were at the dinner.

That evening, Brooke saw Noel Olivier for the first time. Brooke was 20; Noel, 15 years old, still at Bedales School, was in her school clothes. She was shy and broke a coffee cup. Brooke fell for her at once. He did not mention this in his letter to his mother; she disapproved of the Olivier sisters. He did tell her about two other guests

It was great fun. Amber Reeves (your friend!) & Wells were perched up behind on a window sill. They came in too late & couldn't find a seat.[468]

Clifford Allen arrived at Cambridge in autumn 1908. He had previously studied at University College Bristol; he and his parents had intended him to be an Anglican clergyman. At Cambridge, however, Allen became both an agnostic and a Fabian; by 1910 he was Secretary of the CUFS. He later became involved in the task of bringing all the various University Fabian Societies together.

The first Fabian Summer School took place in 1907. The idea had come from two members – Frank Lawson Dodd, a dentist from Tunbridge Wells, and Mabel Atkinson, a suffrage activist who taught economics at Newcastle. Beatrice described the Summer School as

…an odd and interesting institution. [469]

The first schools (1907-1910) were held at Pen-yr-allt, a large house at Llanbedr, on the North Wales coast. Fabian supporters, including the Shaws, put up the money. The Society committed itself to lease the house for an initial four years. The school ran for two months each summer; Fabians could stay for thirty-five shillings a week.

The Webbs did not attend the 1907 Summer School: the reason they were at the Shaws' house in August 1907, when they rehearsed Beveridge's Royal Commission evidence, was that Bernard and Charlotte had gone to Llanbedr for the summer, lending them the house.

GBS worked hard to make the first school succeed

…giving lectures on marriage, education, foreign politics and socialism, reading from his plays, and spending hours in informal talk. [470]

He also led the way in physical activity, on one occasion almost drowning when swimming in the sea.

The school combined learning and exercise – an Edwardian alternative lifestyle. The day began with Swedish gymnastics, led by Mary Hankinson, or 'Hanky'. Hanky's day job was as a games teacher at St Paul's Girl's school in London. (Shaw told her she was a model for his St Joan).

Long walks were organised. Cold baths were included; hot baths cost an extra sixpence. Vegetarian food was always available. Living conditions could be Spartan: Shaw wrote to his friend Harley Granville Barker:

The Fabian School is sleeping five in a room, and apparently enjoying it. [471]

The Cambridge Fabians turned out for the Summer Schools. Ben Keeling went in 1907; so did Blanco White. Keeling and another of the Cambridge group arrived by bicycle; Keeling lectured on economic history and led mountain expeditions. Blanco White also lectured.

Beatrice went for the first time in 1908:

Two or three houses on the mountainous coast of North Wales are filled to overflowing for seven weeks with some hundred Fabians and sympathizers – a dozen or so young university graduates and undergraduates, another stratum of lower middle-class professionals, a stray member of Parliament or professor, a bevy of fair girls, and the remainder – a too large remainder – elderly and old nondescript females who find the place lively and fairly cheap. The young folk live the most unconventional life, giving the Quaker-like Lawson Dodd, who rules the roost, many an unpleasant quarter of an hour – stealing out on moor or sand, in stable or under hayricks, without always the requisite chaperone to make it look as wholly innocent as it really is. Then the 'gym' costume which they all affect is startling the Methodist Wales, and the conversation is most surprisingly open. 'Is dancing sexual?' I found three pretty Cambridge girl graduates discussing with half a dozen men. But mostly they talk economics and political science, in the intervals of breaking off the engagements to marry each other they formed a year ago. [472]

In 1908 more Cambridge Fabians came – as well as Keeling and Blanco White, Hugh Dalton, Dudley Ward, Rupert Brooke, James Strachey, Arthur Schloss, Gerald Shove, Eva Spielman, Amber Reeves and Margery and Daphne Olivier were there. Several of them stayed with Beatrice at a rented farmhouse in Herefordshire for three days on their way to Llanbedr.

Brooke, in a letter to Dalton, listed his essentials for Llanbedr:

I bring a blanket, chocolate, and 19 books, all in a bag. [473]

Beatrice described Brooke as a poetic beauty; many years later she confessed that she was

…poetry blind like some people are colour blind. [474]

Beveridge (though never a Fabian) attended the 1908 Summer School. Newly resigned from the Morning Post, now a civil servant, he signed in as *ex journalist*. Many women participants were also active in the suffrage movement, including Rachel Townshend, who signed herself in as *released prisoner*. Rachel came with her mother, Emily, and her sister, Caroline.

Beveridge and his Oxford friend R H Tawney both spoke at the 1908 school on issues linked to their Royal Commission evidence – Beveridge on labour organisation, Tawney on boy labour. The school logbook records that Beveridge's talk was *thoroughly practical* while Tawney's was *earnest, thoughtful, practical* and led to many questions. [475]

Arthur Colegate arrived at Llanbedr on 15 August. Initially conditions were not to his taste:

> *...wretched night – five in a large room and nearly decided to leave at the end of next week.* [476]

After that, things could only get better. He was bored by Keeling's lectures, and argued with him about republicanism – but went walking with Keeling, the Olivier sisters, Blanco White and others:

> *...marched on in the driving rain. We were wet to the skin but none of us minded. On comparing notes afterwards, it was found out that on the walk home Blanco had outlined a complete theory of marriage to Daphne...and I had rapidly run over the English poets from Chaucer to WB Yeats to Margery, quoting my favourite passages.* [477]

Colegate stayed three weeks, returning to London by train with Eva Spielman on 5 September. He arrived home to another violent argument about socialism with his father.

The golden time was coming to an end; the Cambridge Fabians were graduating and migrating to London.

Keeling asked Sidney's advice:

> *Webb said I might be making £300 a year by writing, if I turn my work into articles, etc, in a few years.*[478]

He wasn't convinced; but in autumn 1908 he went to live at 187b Walworth Road, sharing with Ashley Dukes, another Fabian. He planned to

> *...start stirring up some borough...I think it will be Southwark...*
> *By God! If we could capture a Borough Council or a Board of Guardians we would shift something.*[479]

He became involved in LCC care committees (which organised volunteers in schools to help with meals and health care) and was part of the Fabian network.

One of the Cambridge Fabians who stayed with the Webbs in Herefordshire in 1908 was Amber Reeves. Beatrice described her as

...the brilliant Amber Reeves, the double first Moral Sciences Tripos, an amazingly vital person, but a terrible little pagan – vain, egotistical, and careless of other people's happiness.[480]

That year, her father, Pember Reeves, became the third Director of LSE.; his predecessor, the geographer Halford Mackinder, had resigned to become a Conservative MP. The Webbs, after considering other possibilities, chose *their old friend Pember:*

...a good administrator, with colonial connections, the right opinions.[481]

When Pember had arrived from New Zealand in the 1890s, he had stayed at Toynbee Hall; 500 people turned out to hear him speak at a Fabian meeting in 1896. He was a friend of Shaw – and, later, of Wells. Both Pember and his wife knew Wells; in April 1904 Maud Reeves was there when the Wellses dined at Grosvenor Road to meet Arthur Balfour.

After Amber went to Newnham, Pember would write to Wells with proud updates:

Amber has just made her first speech – to express sympathy with the Russian bomb-throwers and bank-robbers. [482]

Wells became closer to Maud than to Pember. In his account, written and published much later, he gave his own explanation:

She liked me, and she liked very much to talk to me, and she talked very intimately of many things in life that she found perplexing.[483]

Wells found it hard to establish links with Pember: in their biography of Wells, Norman and Jeanne Mackenzie say Pember was

...by nature bitter and self-pitying, caustic with others and supercilious in his manner. [484]

According to Wells, Maud encouraged a *very intimate* friendship between himself and Amber. Early on, Maud wrote to Jane Wells

She adores you both. You are good fairies to all these young people.[485]

For some time, Wells wrote, things remained on the level of a *great and edifying friendship at an austere level*; then,

...one day she broke the thin ice over my suppressions by telling me she was in love, and when I asked 'with whom?' throwing herself into my by no means unwilling arms. [486]

This explained the late arrival of Amber and Wells at the Cambridge Fabian dinner on 10 May 1908: they had been together in Amber's room in Newnham. They then spent the night together in Cambridge, following which

...we contrived a meeting in Soho, when we became lovers in the fullest sense of the word... [487]

They took a room in Southend, and then in London.

The relationship could not remain secret for long; soon Beatrice learned about it. Unaware of the details, Beatrice was censorious from the start. After the 1908 Summer School she wrote about Amber:

A somewhat dangerous friendship is growing up between her and H G Wells. I think they are both too soundly self-interested to do more than cause poor Jane Wells some fearful feelings, but if Amber were my child I should be anxious. [488]

Amber graduated in 1908. She went to live with her parents in Kensington, beginning postgraduate studies at LSE. Alongside her involvement with Wells, she was a member of the Fabian Nursery, the network of younger Fabians; her friends included Jack Squire, Colegate, and Blanco White. Wells wrote

She talked abundantly, and she had a following of animated friends. If she did not flirt with the young men, her contemporaries, she made herself very interesting and companionable to them. [489]

On Christmas Eve 1908, Amber, Blanco White, and Colegate walked along the Thames, from Richmond to Kingston and on to Hampton Court. On Boxing Day, the three of them went to the New Forest, staying overnight,

It was agreed that Amber should pretend to be Blanco's sister. [490]

In the new year, Amber continued to socialize with the Fabian group. On Wednesday 3 March, she went ice skating with Colegate at Olympia, and walked back with him as far as Sloane Street. He wrote

She seems a very good sort on the whole tho' her quick brain tends to make her superficial. [491]

On 17 March Amber chaired an event at which Colegate was the speaker. Ten days later they went to a Fabian party;

She seemed excessively friendly from the first & when we were sitting out our third dance she suddenly flung her arms around my neck and started kissing me passionately! I felt extremely embarrassed. I imagined she wanted me to suggest

an engagement, but I carefully avoided mentioning anything of the sort. In fact, she apparently suggested that she should be my mistress if it were possible.[492]

The circle who knew about Wells and Amber grew. Wells wrote:

…I was keeping our secret tight and close, she gave way to a desire to talk about it and elaborate it. She was intensely proud of what she had done. [493]

At the beginning of April Colegate saw Clifford Sharp, who told him

…the rumour about Amber being Wells' mistress and of her having boasted of it to Mrs Mc Taggart at Cambridge, also of her visit to a doctor, etc. I must confess I partly believe it after the way she behaved last Saturday. [494]

On April 4, Colegate and Amber walked in Richmond Park; he told her

…of the rumour going round about her & Wells & her only reply was that she must get engaged at once.[495]

Amber told Colegate that a man called Coburn had proposed marriage; her choice was between Coburn and Blanco White. She then implied that she would consider him – Colegate – instead; they

…went on to discuss how we (Amber & I) should get on together if we married. We lunched together & about three came back to town. We had a little white wine for lunch & she practically offered to be my mistress. It made her feel acquiescent and incapable of refusing anything etc. She promised not to get engaged to Blanco until after her return from Paris. [496]

Amber's mother was half-aware of what was happening; her father was not. According to Wells, at some point that spring Blanco White went to Pember Reeves, explained that Wells had *ruined* Amber, and offered to marry her. Reeves' reaction was conventional. In Wells' account,

…he became all that an eighteenth-century father should be. He made the whole affair a public scandal; he declared his intention of shooting me, and 'saw red' with zealous thoroughness. [497]

Reeves' biographer wrote that Pember's views on sexual morality were

…rigidly conventional and almost morbidly puritanical. He did indeed act like a stereotype of the outraged father.[498]

Between her father's pressure and Blanco White's persistence, Amber agreed to marry White. On 5 April, the day after his conversation with Amber, Colegate

…was astonished to get a letter from Blanco by the first post announcing his engagement to Amber. [499]

Wells described the behaviour of himself and Amber that spring as *jagged masses of inconsistent impulse.*

After her engagement to Blanco but before the marriage, Amber became pregnant by Wells. According to Wells, this was again on Amber's initiative: in his account they went to their rented London room:

'Give me a child' said Amber, 'whatever happens,' and that seemed heroic to me…and we set about the business there and then. [500]

Wells and Amber then eloped to Le Touquet. The elopement did not last long. In their life of Wells, Norman and Jeanne MacKenzie quote Amber:

…it was not successful. I could not cope, because I was pregnant. HG got more and more restless and kept going back to England. He kept hankering to go back whenever he got invitations from Lady Desborough or anyone. [501]

By early May Amber had returned to England, resolved to marry Blanco White. On 10 May Colegate wrote in his diary

…letter from Amber Blanco White…

I wrote off to Amber & sent it by express to ask whether she had married Blanco.

I rang up Blanco & learned he had married Amber on Friday. I felt awfully sick when he told me this. Later I recd. a reply from Amber confirming it and asking me to meet her for tea in the afternoon…

…she gave me full details. Quite as devilish as ever – poor Blanco! [502]

After the wedding Amber lived in a cottage in Surrey, paid for by Wells, who she continued to see; Blanco White stayed in London until after the birth of Amber's daughter, Anna Jane on 31 December 1909.

Beatrice was censorious:

The blackguardism of Wells is everyday more apparent. He seduced Amber within the very walls of Newnham, having been permitted, as an old friend, to go to her room. [503]

Beatrice was loyal to Maud and Pember; she had some sympathy for Amber, and more for Blanco – but her sympathy was tempered by sharp criticism of Amber:

She is a little liar, she is superlatively vain, and she has little or no pity in her nature – but this triad of bad qualities may be but one of her personalities. [504]

In May 1909, Colegate went to work for Beatrice's Poor Law Campaign. Wells was convinced that a sustained attempt to blacken his name was under way, spreading rumours about himself and Amber. In September 1909 Wells wrote to Beatrice, accusing her and Hubert Bland of running the campaign. He also named

…that unfortunate young man you employ, Colegate…[505]

Perhaps there was something in this. Writing to Beatrice about Wells and Amber at the end of September, GBS wrote

…you have already shut up Colegate as far as you can… [506]

In September Beatrice wrote, bluntly, to Amber

You will have to choose – and that shortly – between a happy marriage and continuing your friendship with HG Wells. That is the one essential fact in the present situation. [507]

She offered to come and talk to Amber, saying

I have the warmest affection for your parents, and real liking for you and a warm respect for Blanco. I have even a quit genuine desire to see HGW saved from a big smash. But I don't want to interfere, if you prefer that I should not. [508]

In October she followed this up with a visit. She advised Blanco White and Pember Reeves to get a good solicitor.

Beatrice held herself partly responsible:

Unwittingly I did HG a bad turn when I introduced him to the Elcho-Balfour-Desborough set. That whetted his social ambition and upset his growing bourgeois morality. [509]

Wells had been

…dining with duchesses and lunching with countesses. I imagine he let himself go, pretty considerably, with women. [510]

She said that Sidney had a *settled aversion* to Wells, thinking him purely selfish, with no redeeming motive.

Slowly, Beatrice's views on sexual morality evolved: twenty-five years earlier, she had recoiled from Eleanor Marx's *evidently peculiar views on love* and *her natural relations with men.* Her early certainty was now replaced by an uneasy agnosticism:

...all this arises because we none of us know what exactly is the sexual code we believe in, approving of many things on paper which we violently object to when they are practised by those we care about. [511]

Life at LSE became difficult for Pember: he and Maud grew distant from many of their Fabian friends. On Boxing Day 1909, just before the baby was due, they dined at Grosvenor Road; Beatrice thought they were

...shrivelled up with the pain of their daughter's past(?) relations to Wells.[512]

According to Beatrice, faced with possible ostracism, Wells had agreed to stay away from Amber for two or three years.

Beatrice also criticized Ben Keeling. Dining at Grosvenor Road on 15 May, Colegate heard

...that Keeling had married Rachel Townshend. [513]

A fortnight later Colegate had dinner with Blanco and Keeling. Keeling told Colegate

...that his wife was in the family way, & this apparently determined them to marry. [514]

In December 1909, Beatrice noted

...Keeling's baby has arrived about six months after marriage – no breach of faith but a breach of continence which will not increase the likelihood of a permanent union. Keeling, however, is working well in harness in the Board of Trade Labour Exchange Department, but apparently living more with his men friends than with his wife. The Fabian Nursery has not distinguished itself this year.[515]

In March 1910 Amber and Blanco lunched with the Webbs. Beatrice concluded *the bad business* was over:

HGW has been frightened off and has definitely broken off the relationship. Amber is settling down with her husband and is absorbed in her baby. [516]

Wells acknowledged that he and Amber had continued to meet up to the birth of Anna Jane, and even occasionally after that.

Wells' trade was writing. He produced two novels which allude to his relationship with Amber: *Ann Veronica* and *The New Machiavelli*. *Ann Veronica* appeared in October 1909. It tells the story of a young woman, growing up in the London suburbs, with a conventional, controlling father. Like Amber Reeves, she takes the initiative in a relationship with an older married man.

Ann Veronica attracted instant hostility. The *Spectator* called it 'poisonous', denouncing

The muddy world of Mr Wells's imaginings...a community of scuffling stoats and ferrets...[517]

Libraries banned the book; sermons were preached against it – all of which probably helped its sales. Beatrice thought that the publication of *Ann Veronica*

...adds a roar of insult to his injury of the Reeves family. [518]

The New Machiavelli appeared in autumn 1910. It contains another portrait of an independent young woman: Isabel Rivers, with whom the rising MP Richard Remington falls in love and runs away to France, abandoning wife and career. Like Amber to Wells, Isabel calls Remington *Master*. Like Amber, she wants children.

This time the targets were Sidney and Beatrice, satirized as Oscar and Altiora Bailey. Leo Amery – himself caricatured in the book – read it soon after publication:

Read [H G Wells's The New] *Machiavelli. In it he gives a bitingly faithful picture of the Sidney Webbs, their ways, their little dinners, not a single trait left out... The rest of the story deals with his own love affair with Reeve's* [sic] *daughter. Altogether one of the nakedest books ever written but very remarkable.* [519]

According to Wells, Altiora was

...a tall commanding figure, splendid but a little untidy in black silk and red beads

Oscar

...a short sturdy figure with a rounding protruding abdomen...
The two supplemented each other to an extraordinary extent...She had discovered very early that the last thing influential people will do is to work. Everything in their lives tends to make them dependent upon a supply of confidently administered detail. [520]

Remington, the hero, discovers that

...rumour and scandal are afoot about me.[521]

Private and confidential letters are circulating; someone *cuts him dead* in the street; similar things happen to Isabel. He couldn't understand where this came from:

Then I got a clue. The centre of diffusion was the Bailey household... They had me now... Bailey, I found, was warning fathers of girls against me as a 'reckless libertine', and Altiora, flushed, roguish and dishevelled, was sitting on her fender kerb after dinner, and pledging little parties of five or six women at a time with infinite gusto not to let the matter go further.[522]

Remington can't think who Altiora's source might be – *she revealed astonishing knowledge* – then he thinks of Curmain, a young man who had worked for him before working for Altiora. As with Wells' letter to Beatrice in September 1909 about Colegate, Remington confronts the Baileys, accusing them of orchestrating the campaign, relying on Curmain for evidence.

They deny this, defending Curmain:

'We're not circulating stories,' she denied. No! And Curmain never told us anything – Curmain is an excellent young man; oh! a quite excellent young man. You misjudged him altogether... [523]

Again, initially Wells struggled to find a publisher for *The New Machiavelli*. Heinemann, turning it down, wrote of the way in which blame is laid on the Bailey/Webbs

It seems to me very unnecessary and, in this case, I think perhaps a little malicious.[524]

There were no libel actions; the book sold steadily from its publication.

'RAGING, TEARING PROPAGANDA'

Sidney and Beatrice had promised themselves a holiday once the Poor Law reports were published. On 6 March 1909, Beatrice wrote to Wells, they were

...taking the boat to Naples... then spending 4 weeks in Rome and the Hill Cities. [525]

In April, Beatrice wrote from Assisi to George McCleary, a London Medical Officer of Health, that she was wondering

...whether ...to start a Society for promoting the propaganda for Breaking up the Poor Law on the lines of the Minority Report. [526]

She invited McCleary to lunch for the Sunday after their return. That day, she wrote that their priorities for the next eighteen months were

...(1) propaganda of the Minority Report, (2) bringing out of books connected with these proposals, and also (3) finishing up our eighteenth-century study of English local government. We are starting a committee for pushing the Minority Report, and we are lecturing considerably: five days next week in the big North Country towns, and odd lectures in London, Oxford, etc. – all before we go for a week to the Fabian school in Wales.[527]

For two years the campaign dominated their lives, attracting large audiences and plenty of volunteers. Beatrice emerged as a formidable public speaker. They were confident of victory; their monthly *Crusade* declared

...of the ultimate success of the campaign there is now no doubt. [528]

By mid-May a campaign organisation had been established:

Enter the National Committee for the Break Up of the Poor Law.

Started on our campaign of forming public opinion. My first attempt at organization. I am trying a new experiment – an executive committee for consultative purposes and a secretariat of young men and women who will initiate policy and carry it out, I acting as chairman and reporting to the executive committee. We start, with very little money and a good deal of zeal, on a crusade against destitution. It is rather funny to start, at my time of life, on the war-path at the head of a contingent of young men and women. What I have got to aim at is to make these young people do the work... [529]

Much of the work was done by volunteers; one early volunteer was Ben Keeling, who wrote

The month of June I spent partly in Missenden and partly in London, where I was mainly occupied with working for Mrs Webb's National Committee to Promote the Break Up of the Poor Law. [530]

The Webbs quickly realised, however, that they also needed paid staff. They turned to the young Fabian activists; Mostyn Lloyd became Secretary.

On 14 May, Arthur Colegate noted that Beatrice had asked him to dinner; on 25 May he was appointed Literature Secretary. Next day, he and Keeling dined at Grosvenor Road – Clifford Sharp and Eva Spielman were there too:

Mrs W buttered Sharp & me a good deal but we were expecting it; she doesn't do it as skilfully as Webb. [531]

As the campaign began, Sharp and Colegate met almost daily:

*Lunched with Sharp at Norwood. We discussed the Poor Law business &
agreed that Mrs Webb seems to under-estimate the task.*[532]

Offices were rented in Clement's Inn, off the Strand; Beatrice explained it was

*...wedged between the Fabian Office close on its right and the London School
of Economics a few yards to its left...* [533]

Later the Campaign moved to larger offices nearby at 37 Norfolk Street.
Colegate obtained print estimates, bought office furniture, attended committee meetings, and undertook research.

More staff were hired: on 17 June they appointed Clement Attlee (who gave
up his Bar practise) Lecture Secretary. Attlee's task was

*...to offer lectures to various societies and then to find suitable lecturers to meet
these engagements.*

He recalled:

*A difficulty was that almost all societies wanted our 'star' lecturers. Sometimes
these broke their engagements and I often had to act as substitute at short
notice.* [534]

On 25 June, Arthur Colegate noted, there was an office summit:

*...Mrs Webb, Keeling, Attlee, Eva Spielman and I met at the Fabian office &
tried to work out a more satisfactory scheme of office work.* [535]

The Committee decided to produce a monthly newspaper, *The Crusade*. Sharp,
who had worked on the *New Age,* was appointed editor. The first edition appeared
in February 1910.

Mary Agnes (Molly) Hamilton, at this time a Liberal, had been at Newnham
before the revival of the Cambridge Fabians. At first Molly supported the
Majority Report; she was converted on hearing Beatrice, who

*...was magnificent in a great hat with ostrich feathers, and of course swept her
audience with her moving picture of the morass of destitution. I thought her
arguments a trifle on the unscrupulous side...* [536]

Molly worked for the campaign. She described the office:

*Young men and young women from the Universities would spend hour after
hour, day after day, in folding and addressing circulars, or acting as stewards
and collectors at meetings, to be amply rewarded by a brilliant if rather vague
smile from the General Secretary when she looked in, in the course of the day.*
[537]

The Crusade lists Attlee as a regular speaker – mostly in London, occasionally further afield. In 1910, he spoke at Bexley Heath, Upper Norwood, Mile End, Kensington, Wandsworth, and Hackney. When he left the job after a year, Beatrice thanked him:

> *What I think you need to make you a* first rate organiser *is rather more of the quality of 'Push' and the habit of a rapid transaction of business. You should always keep before you the attitude of the first rate Chairman of a Committee of pushing forward to 'the next business'…I only mention it by way of a counsel of perfection from an elderly observer of men and affairs* .[538]

By September 1909, the Campaign had 5700 members. In early 1910 there were 20,700; membership peaked in May 1911, at 30,533.

The Webbs led from the front. In June 1909, Beatrice wrote

> *A month's grind at preparing forms, letters, membership cards, leaflets, tracts and other literature for the National Committee. It looks as if Sidney and I will be absorbed in directing the propaganda – probably entirely, for three or four months at any rate, and for most of our time for the next year or so. What I am trying to set on foot is a real comradeship in this crusade – an intensive culture of the membership with a view of enrolling others and getting everyone to give of their best. My band of volunteers are devoted…* [539]

In July she said they were living in a veritable turmoil.

The Cambridge Fabians became enthusiastic campaigners. Brooke was still an undergraduate; one biographer wrote that for two years, the Minority Report

> *…engrossed Brooke's mind, and most of his energies were given to the campaign for the spread of its ideas.*[540]

While the Webbs were in Italy, both Rupert Brooke and the Keynes family were, separately, on holiday in Devon. Rupert Brooke was

> *…in a hut by a waterfall on Dartmoor.* [541]

He wrote beforehand to Noel Olivier

> *I am going to be extremely healthy and laborious in a place called Dartmoor; with one man & the Minority Report on the Poor Law & Euripides (a dirty fellow).* [542]

Maynard took time off from golf with his father and patience with his mother to cross the moors to visit Rupert. Keynes found him

...clad in football shorts, breaking eggs on his knees, and reading the Minority Report of the Poor Law Commission. [543]

Brooke wrote to Dalton in April, wondering whether summer was the right time for Cambridge Minority Report meetings. Minnie Bodkin, the lecturer organising them, was magnificent:

But would her Poor Law meeting draw next term? Or shouldn't it happen the term after? Perhaps that would be too late? [544]

They settled for autumn. Brooke was now President of CUFS, Ka Cox the organiser:

Well, it's now quite definitely fixed like this:

I	*Preliminary and Children*	*Dalton*
II	*Old Age, loonies, sick*	*H Gardner*
III	*Unemployed etc.*	*Toulmin (Geoffrey)*
IV	*Machinery and Majority*	*You*

Won't that do? Because if, as you say, you're reading the Majority, you'd better describe it to us. I think you could manage it. [545]

In letters, Brooke referred to the Webbs as *Sid and Bice*. Planning a meeting for Sidney, he wrote

We will give Webb the time of his life. [546]

In January 1910, Brooke wrote to his cousin Erica Cotterill

I've heard you're all pleased about the Minority Report. I too, in my calm way. I regard it as certain to be taken up, from what I've heard in London.[547]

Dalton had a nickname for the campaign:

...what we all...rather ribaldly called 'the Break-Up' – the Webbs' all-party 'Society for promoting the Break Up of the Poor Law.' [548]

In July 1909 both Webbs attended the Llanbedr Summer School. Beatrice opened proceedings with a *bright, witty and thoroughly thoughtful* [549] talk on 25 July. Cambridge Fabians Brooke, Dalton, Keeling and Margery Olivier went too; Dalton lectured on 'Elements of Socialism'.

Beatrice described the scene to her sister Georgina:

This place is very lovely – we are in lodgings perched up on a hill overlooking Barmouth Bay. The Fabian School is about 2 mins off – with 100 students who change week by week – we gave 7 lectures during the first week – now

we look in once or twice a week and give a talk to the newcomers. They are rather a nice set – almost exclusively professional men and women – medical men and women, teachers, nursing Inspectors, with a sprinkling of Oxford and Cambridge young men.[550]

Beatrice was in training for the autumn:

I practice voice presentation between 6.30 and 8 a.m. every morning on the beach – orating to the Waves. I want to be able to speak without effort, which is really a question of proper tone of the voice. [551]

At the end of the Summer School Beatrice had the idea of running a conference for the campaign as part of the 1910 School.

Both reports had recommended labour exchanges. As the campaign was beginning, Churchill as minister pressed ahead. Beveridge was his main official – at first an advisor, but with executive responsibility after the Labour Exchanges Act received Royal Assent in autumn 1909. The Exchanges were due to open in January 1910. Premises had to be obtained, staff hired, working practises established.

In September 1909 there was another Grosvenor Road dinner:

Winston and his wife dined here the other night to meet a party of young Fabians. He is taking on the look of the mature statesman – bon vivant and orator – somewhat in love with his own phrases...

In the course of the evening he took a fancy to my organising secretary, Colegate, and told him to apply to the Board of Trade. And I have secured a position for Fred Keeling. Winston Churchill said that anyone I really recommended 'on my honour' he would take on. I felt justified in recommending Keeling and Colegate.[552]

Colegate and Keeling were duly hired by the Board of Trade. Keeling started on 29 October; in January he was sent to open the Leeds exchange, Colegate to Leicester. Keeling, newly married, his first child due, certainly needed the job. On 19 August he had written to a friend:

I am full of joie de vivre today. I believe I have a very good chance of getting a Labour Exchange appointment in a few days...I am to meet Winston Churchill – who will have a great deal to do with Labour Exchange appointments – at dinner at the Webbs'.[553]

In January Keeling moved to Leeds:

I live in an attic at the top of the Exchange and am gradually reducing myself to a fruit and nut diet...[554]

The Keeling marriage was not conventional; before the Leeds posting, Ben wrote to Rachel's mother, Emily Townshend

I almost hope for a job in a remote provincial town where I shall have no antecedents– adding

I am puzzled how to work things with R if I am sent a couple of hundred miles away. But I will find a definite solution and then Peace! – and I will pray for a respite from personal incidents in my life till I am, say, thirty.[555]

Mrs Townshend thought his views on marriage came from GBS

...whom he reverenced as the greatest living expert on conduct.[556]

Later, she accused him of forgetting

...his responsibilities as husband and father in a way that was quite incomprehensible...[557]

After some time, Rachel rented a cottage near Leeds, and lived there with their baby, Joan; Ben visited them. But this arrangement did not last; before long, mother and child returned to London. In 1912 they had a son – who they named Bernard Sidney. Keeling wrote to his mother in law

After all, there is no reason why he should not be called after the two greatest men on the earth.[558]

Ben and Rachel divorced in 1914; Keeling continued to exchange regular letters with Rachel's mother.

Keeling's working life was as unorthodox as his personal life. He supported junior staff organizing for better conditions. He wrote in January 1912 that he had

...just been hauled before the General Manager of the Exchange for agitating about our clerks' wages – and accused, absolutely unjustly, of generally 'fomenting discontent'.[559]

By March he was thinking of leaving the civil service.

Colegate's career was altogether more conventional. He was sorry to leave his job with the campaign:

The period so closed began when I definitely abandoned engineering as a profession & joined Mr & Mrs Sidney Webb & I scarcely expected it to be so

short. For many things I am sorry it has been so brief. It has been one of the happiest times of my life. [560]

After six months in Leicester, Colegate was transferred to run the Liverpool exchange. He remained close to the Webbs; before going to Liverpool he went walking in Switzerland with Beatrice, Sidney and Mostyn Lloyd. She wrote:

A vigorous holiday in Switzerland: walking with Colegate or Lloyd or both – perhaps rather too vigorous for an old lady like myself. [she was 52]. *But though it tired my body I believe it really rested my mind.* [561]

She told her sister Mary that their pace was set

…by two young men… Colegate being the best type[?] of 'getting-on' young man, & Lloyd, an inveterate adherent of what does not pay in life. [562]

Beatrice told Betty Balfour that Colegate

…has a delightful sunny nature and is extraordinarily adaptable and able, with a good outlook on life. He is ambitious… [563]

At Christmas 1910, Betty and Gerald Balfour lent the Webbs their Surrey home. Sidney and Beatrice invited Colegate, Mostyn Lloyd, Clifford Sharp and his wife, and Amber Reeves and Blanco White to stay with them – Beatrice noting

Amber seems to have settled down with her husband and apparently made up her mind to play straight. [564]

They passed the time reading, talking, and walking in the Surrey hills. In 1912 Colegate was promoted, and transferred back to London. He also got married. In September 1912 he had a breakdown, attributed to overwork.

In autumn 1909 the Webbs took the campaign on the road. Beatrice wrote in November

We are carrying on a 'raging tearing propaganda' lecturing or speaking five or six times a week. We had ten days in the north of England and in Scotland – in nearly every place crowded and enthusiastic audiences. [565]

Later that month Beatrice was in Yorkshire, Wales, and the Midlands. From Sheffield, she wrote to Sidney

…my meeting was a great success – about 700 persons and a great many guardians and councillors. [566]

Over New Year 1909/10 they stayed at Southsea; Beatrice went walking on the Isle of Wight. They were enjoying themselves:

...organising office work, public speaking and personal persuasion of individuals, work which absorbs all one's time without any severe strain on one's nerves. [567]

Beatrice reflected on their partnership:

Sidney has also been thoroughly happy – partly because our comradeship has never been so complete. Hitherto, we have had only one side of our work together – our research and book-writing. But this last year we have organised together, spoken together, as well as written together. And he has been extraordinarily generous in not resenting, in the very least, my having nominally to take the front place, as the leading Minority Commissioner and ostensible head of the National Committee. Fortunately, in spite of his modesty, everyone knows that he is the backbone of the Webb Firm – even if I do appear, on some occasions, as the Figure Head. [568]

After the January 1910 election, campaigning resumed. In February Beatrice spent an exhausting week in Devon. At the final lecture, in Plymouth

...I was too utterly fagged to keep the verve of the lecturer right to the end. And now and again I felt I might suddenly give way and faint or collapse... [569]

In March Sidney went to Wales – two meetings in Cardiff, one in Swansea. One of the organisers was Cambridge Fabian Bill Hubback, now lecturing in Cardiff, who wrote to Eva Spielman:

...Webb is to be here on Friday on his crusade. The National Committee and the ILP are running a big meeting for him at which I have been labouring... [570]

In the spring Sidney and Beatrice gave six lectures in London, with outsiders – including Gilbert Murray (the classicist and Liberal internationalist), Winston Churchill, Philip Snowden, and GBS – in the chair. Beatrice thought the lectures successful:

Six successive Mondays we have had a full house of good material – majority of men of the governing and professional classes – we have actually cleared a profit of three hundred and fifty pounds! [571]

Local campaign branches were established. Arthur Greenwood, a teacher, was secretary of the Leeds branch; he took on the task of coordinating the branches. Beatrice found the branches hard work: they were

...always getting into debt or relapsing into vacuum. We have not solved the question of branch organisation – even the Scottish branches being insolvent and raising barely enough money to pay postage and stationery. [572]

The Fabian barrister Henry Schloesser drafted a Prevention of Destitution Bill, debated in the House of Commons on Friday 8 April 1910. Burns attacked the Bill: Schloesser wrote that Burns considered it a censure on himself. Burns praised Lord George Hamilton and criticized the Minority proposals. He scattered statistics wildly, blaming poverty and unemployment on drink –

> *Let us never forget it, much of the disorder, the dirt, the disease, the cruelty to children, the assaults on each other, and the improvidence and laziness owe their origin, either directly or indirectly, to drink.*[573]

Burns suggested that he could do whatever was necessary by administrative reform; Asquith praised Burns' administrative record.

Lansbury asked Ramsay MacDonald to back the Bill. He received a blunt answer:

> *My dear Lansbury*
>
> *…the whole affair is a piece of sheer folly, and is a waste of an afternoon. No sane parliamentarian would ever have introduced such a Bill on a day when the sitting is short…*[574]

Arthur Balfour, among others, spoke in support; but the Bill did not make further progress.

Hilaire Belloc, still a Liberal MP until December 1910, launched a vituperative attack in the *New Age*. Belloc was developing the arguments he later published in *The Servile State*[575]. He described the Bill as

> *…a scheme drawn up by Mr Sidney Webb, the statistician, with the aid of his wife, for dealing with the lives of people much poorer than themselves.*[576]

Belloc argued that the Webbs' proposals had nothing to do with socialism, simply increasing the power of the state:

> *It gives the middle class, the politicians and the rest, a fine time of it! It organizes the poor like a flock of sheep.*[577]

In May 1910, the campaign held its first Annual Meeting. At Lansbury's suggestion, the name was changed to National Campaign for the Prevention of Destitution. Lansbury told the meeting they owed an enormous debt to the Webbs, who had shown them for the first time a rational way of dealing with this tremendous problem.[578]

Beatrice asked where it would all end:

> *Having discovered in myself the faculty of the preacher and the teacher, shall I be able to withdraw into the life of research?*[579]

She wondered how to make the movement less dependent on herself and Sidney.

The campaign commissioned a poster, *The disease of destitution,* from Spencer Pryse, a leading poster artist.

Campaign meetings were mostly in towns and cities, but the Committee wanted the message to reach rural areas too:

> *...the propaganda has still to be carried into the villages. Rural England, whatever the townsman may imagine, is still in existence; and has still to be roused.* [580]

Rural campaign ideas included *...propaganda by peripatetic lecturers on walking or bicycling tours,* and open air or 'cottage' meetings. Mostyn Lloyd reported in September 1910; it was not to be expected that

> *...the countryside would be 'set on fire' at once. Harvest-time is, of course, not the best time for propaganda in rural districts, and in one or two cases we thought it wisest to deter speakers from going into agricultural counties in August. Then the persistent wet weather has spoiled a number of open-air meetings.* [581]

Nevertheless, there had been a week's campaign in Devon; solitary activists had gone out around Harrogate, and in North Hampshire and South Berkshire. Two Exeter members ran a three-week campaign across Somerset, the Welsh borders, and Worcestershire:

> *The fame of the Minority Report was carried into districts where it was hitherto unknown; literature was sold and distributed; and a number of new members were obtained... The lecturers did all in their power to make the meetings successful. They carried a banner with them (inscribed with the words 'Crusade against Destitution'); in some places they had their meetings proclaimed by the town-crier.* [582]

Rupert Brooke rallied to the call. In July 1910, with Dudley Ward, another Cambridge Fabian, Brooke toured Dorset and the New Forest in a horse-drawn caravan. Brooke's motives were personal as well as political; Noel Olivier, now aged 17, was still at Bedales School in Hampshire. Brooke continually sought opportunities to meet her – which he succeeded in doing at the end of the tour.

The horse and caravan were borrowed from Cambridge friends. On 3 July he wrote to Ward:

> *Let's send all our things to some station beyond Winchester, some quiet place, and land up there...*

Brooke met Schloesser and another staff member at the NCPD office. They

...advocated <u>open</u> air meetings very much: and proposed that even if we didn't speak in any village we sailed into, we should display the poster, look wise, and scatter pamphlets. They had <u>no</u> special rural information; though they had tried to get some. They <u>may</u> have some by the time we start.

Anyway, Lloyd's writing to you: and sending you the new Lecture Notes, which they've got out for ILP lectures.[583]

A few days later he wrote to Jacques Raverat, another Cambridge friend

Dudley and I are going to – or want to – go to Petersfield before we set off in our cart.[584]

At Petersfield (conveniently close to Bedales), Brooke hoped to stay with the poet Edward Thomas.

Brooke wrote to Dalton

I sit here and prepare stirring harangues for the people of south England on Poor Law. I go there at the end of next week. [585]

They toured for twelve days, speaking in towns and villages. For Poole, there was a special poster:

Poole High Street
Close to the Free Library
Principal Speaker
Mr. BROOKE
Questions invited
In support of proposals for Poor Law Reform
Sponsored by the N.C.P.D.

From Wareham, Brooke wrote to his cousin Erica Cotterill:

I've been fearfully busy; first doing a Prize Essay against time; second getting up a speech on the Minority Report. The last week (and the next) I have been going round delivering it at towns and villages in the New Forest and round here. We travel in a caravan and live like savages. As a public orator I am a great success. As a caravaner less. It rains incessantly.[586]

The horse and caravan were returned to their owners at Winchester; Brooke went on to catch up with other Cambridge friends, among them Bill Hubback and Eva Spielman, who had recently become engaged, and with Noel Olivier, who were all camping at Beaulieu not far away on the Solent.

As planned, the 1910 Fabian Summer School included a campaign conference. In April, *The Crusade* announced that the conference would be at Llanbedr in August:

> *It is expected that at least one hundred of the most active members of the organisation, including many of its lecturers and officers from all parts of Great Britain, will be able to take part in the Conference at one or other of its sessions. Mr and Mrs Sidney Webb have kindly undertaken the direction of the Conference, and will be present throughout its proceedings. Members and sympathisers in different parts of the country will find the Conference an admirable opportunity for combining a holiday in charming country with the intellectual stimulus of discussion on subjects of absorbing interest.* [587]

The Summer School began on 30 July. It was a diverse assembly; Beatrice listed

> *ILP organizers, MOHs, teachers, minor officials of all sorts. 'social workers', literary men, journalists and even such out-of-the-way recruits as auctioneers and 'unregistered dentists'.* [588]

One attendee signed in as a *consulting fruitarian*; another a *humble worker for Brotherhood, Morality, Truth and Justice.* [589]

The campaign conference lasted two weeks; the Summer School itself another four. The campaign fortnight, attended by eighty to a hundred participants at any one time, consisted of intense daily sessions on the Poor Law and the Minority Report. Usually, either Sidney or Beatrice would speak at those sessions, supported by Clifford Sharp or Mostyn Lloyd.

The Cambridge Fabians were well represented; among others, Hugh Dalton, Rupert Brooke, James Strachey, Clifford Allen, and Gerald Shove were there. It was the last time Brooke would attend; he encouraged Ka Cox to come too:

> *You ought to go there once to learn a little about Life, and to teach them — what? Anyhow, it's not so bad as you think.* [590]

Thomas Jones was there, sharing a room with Lewis Namier and R H Tawney. At first TJ had supported the Majority position; by summer 1910 he had come round to the Minority Report:

> *He now appreciated its heartening optimism; in particular, 'the compelling power of a new gospel to thousands of young men and women eager for a constructive organic campaign against squalid poverty in our cities.' He now*

had no hesitation: the nation should opt for the Minority Report which struck at 'the sources and roots of pauperism'.[591]

The Manchester industrialist Ernest Simon was at Llanbedr, leading a discussion on competitive industry. When his father died in 1901, Simon had assumed responsibility for managing the family engineering companies. Now he was looking for wider opportunities; after 1909 he never again put more than half his time into business. In autumn 1909 he gave money to the Poor Law campaign; Sidney and Beatrice stayed with him after a Manchester meeting in December 1909.

Ernest Simon was impressed by the Webbs; they became long term friends. After that Manchester visit, he wrote to his mother that Sidney had

…an exceptionally clear brain with great power of analysis and of seeing, what really is important, great love of work…With all these qualities he has a wife of much the same type which must be a tremendous help. [592]

His mother approved, writing that, whoever he married must be a woman

…who will help you and encourage you in all you care for. I am sure it is true, as you say of the Webbs, that the two together can do more than twice as much as one… [593]

Simon became a member of the NCPD Executive Committee; after attending a January 1911 meeting, he wrote that it was

…was by far the most zealous and effective meeting I was ever at. [594]

That evening he dined with Sidney, Beatrice, George Lansbury, and Winston Churchill – who

…does not see things in their true proportion with anything like Webb's clearness and he is undoubtedly carried away by his own verbosity. [595]

Also at the summer school was a leading eugenicist, Dr Caleb Saleeby. Hitherto, Beatrice had considered eugenicists bitter opponents, who believed

…that all attempts to alter environment are not only futile but positively mischievous as such improvements in environment diminish the struggle for existence and retard the elimination of the unfit. [596]

But at Llanbedr she thought she had persuaded Saleeby that environmental changes were necessary. He signed up to both the Fabian Society and the Poor Law Campaign.

During the conference Arthur Greenwood and Mostyn Lloyd ran a session on branch organisation. Greenwood seized the opportunity to ask Sidney for career advice; he wanted to become an economics lecturer at Huddersfield Technical College. Sidney wrote to him encouragingly

Your long and varied teaching experience ought to count for much: so many economics lecturers have no real power of teaching. [597]

Next day, Sidney, signing himself Chairman of LSE governors, sent Huddersfield a reference

I have great pleasure in testifying to the qualifications of Mr Arthur Greenwood... [598]

The novelist Alfred Ollivant left a vivid picture of the 1910 Summer School in *The Crusade*:

Men in motors, men with knapsacks on their backs and text-books on Economics in their pockets, men with broad speech and men with smooth, the aristocrat and the commercial traveller, the girl from the Hall and the girl from behind the counter, the man from the Carlton Club and the man from the Submerged Tenth, the wife of the Tory Cabinet Minister and the teacher from the slums, soldier, sailor, demagogue and dilettante, Quaker and Clarion Scout, men and women of all creeds, all classes, and all parties... [599]

One session brought together the medical officers of health who had been instrumental in urging the merger of the Poor Law medical service with local government public health functions.

George Lansbury spoke, arguing that

People are poor because they are robbed, and robbed because they are poor. [600]

Many of those at the Summer School were also feminists and suffragettes. On 12 August, some delegates organised a suffrage meeting at the village bridge in Llanbedr. It was chaired by Mary Milton, founder of the Farnham Branch of the Womens' Suffrage Society; speakers included Mabel Atkinson, and TJ (who spoke in Welsh). Ollivant described

...the young lady who stood at the door with Votes for Women underneath her arm and looked reproachful when you passed her by

And

...the three militant young women who went about locked arm in arm and began every conversation with the words – You men. [601]

TJ's Welsh language skills were also needed for a public meeting in the village on the Minority Report. Unfortunately,

...owing to the inclemency of the weather, the attendance was bad. [602]

Like earlier Summer Schools, intellectual and political activity were combined with exercise and entertainment. Ollivant captured the atmosphere:

Between lectures we rambled up stream-haunted valleys amid black cattle and glimmering hills. We bathed in the sea and played basket-ball on the sand. We abolished the Almighty between meals and reinstated Him with quiet complacency over a cigarette before going to bed. We sang songs and danced.[603]

Wednesdays were the main walking day; parties climbed Snowdon and Cader Idris. But Brooke had had enough. He and Gerald Shove established an *anti-athletic league*, whose members swore not to walk more than three miles a day.

Nevertheless, Brooke appreciated Sidney and Beatrice, writing to Ka Cox:

The Webbs, too, are very nice; and even better than they're nice. Apart from all of which, they're fine, and funny.[604]

He said Beatrice was

...the source for you to get the best information about your career.[605]

But for Beatrice the charm of the golden Cambridge generation was fading. Much later Dalton wrote:

For the first year, she rather liked some of us; the second, she screamed with disapproval... we were, I am afraid, cliquish, rude, ribald and irreverent. [606]

Beatrice thought the two-week NCPD conference had been an *unqualified success*, and the main Fabian school *partially a financial success and, I think, a moral success*. For the final fortnight, they had organised an event for University Fabians – and they, wrote Beatrice, tended to leave *more critical and supercilious than they arrived*

... 'They won't come unless they know who they are going to meet' sums up Rupert Brooke. And I gathered that even if they <u>did</u> come they would only talk together and to us. So that it would not be much use. They don't want to learn. They don't think they have anything to learn. They certainly don't want to help others: unless there is something to be got in the way of an opening and a career. They won't come. The egotism of the young University man is colossal. Are they worth bothering about?[607]

The campaign resumed. From September to December 1910 there were several meetings a night, all over the country. Beatrice and Sidney were away from Grosvenor Road for weeks on end.

Most of October was spent in Scotland. On the way north, Beatrice stayed with Haldane. She thought he was ageing:

...terribly stout and pasty, and eats enormously and takes no exercise.[608]

The punishing schedule began to tell. Each worried about the other's health. Beatrice

...felt ill when I left for Hull, and on the day I travelled to Middlesbrough I thought the end had come and that I should find myself in bed with a bad breakdown. But by fasting and prayer (this literally!) I pulled through. [609]

Sidney, left behind in London, was lonely and not sleeping well. No doubt concerned by the idea of Beatrice fasting, he wrote:

...you must not give up eating altogether! (Get some Sanatogen in Edinburgh).

He wrote to the organiser of the Edinburgh meetings, telling him the hotel at which Beatrice would be staying, and that she would

...lie down on arrival; that he was to call *for you* just in time to walk *to the meeting, and not to let you talk too much or too long.* [610]

Beatrice's first Edinburgh lecture was on 12 October; she thought it a failure:

Unfortunately the task of preparing it exhausted my remaining strength, and consequently I did not give the lecture I had prepared but ground out only a mechanical reflection of it. Once or twice I wondered whether I could go on – I kept repeating myself and I was conscious of my best friends in the audience being disappointed and concerned at my evident fatigue. However, I daresay it was not so bad as it seemed to me – some of the value was there...

Shall I pull through – that is the question which frightens me. This cursed sleeplessness – especially when I have not got my boy with me just to tell me it is all right. [611]

Her boy did not join her for another week. On the way to Scotland Sidney did campaign meetings in Birmingham, Manchester, and Nelson. His first engagement in Scotland was in Arbroath; he described it in a letter to Beatrice:

I had quite a good meeting last night – some 500 people. Mostly men, of working class, but with all the local Councillors and School Board, some clergy and teachers and doctors and so on – quite non-party. I gave a good stiff lecture on the Unemployment Scheme, and dealt with the S.D.P. hecklers all right – Harcourt and others of all sides spoke on a vote of thanks. This morning is fine and sunny, but cold; and I go on to Dundee presently.[612]

That week he spoke in Dundee, Edinburgh, Brechin, and Montrose. Next weekend the Webbs rested, spending Sunday 23 October at the home of Sir Alfred Yarrow – an engineer, shipbuilder, and philanthropist, who donated £100 to the campaign.

Sidney also became unwell:

He is suffering a good deal from piles, poor dear, and has been working far too hard during the last few weeks – has had five days continuous lecturing – two a day on two occasions.[613]

For the next fortnight they addressed meetings in Scotland five nights a week. They passed a Sunday with Arthur Balfour – Beatrice and Balfour

…had a long argument as to whether the stately charm of Whittinghame was compatible with either feeling or knowing about the problem of destitution. [614]

Beatrice was pleased with the Scottish campaign:

We have got through the whole programme and the new lectures on Voluntary Agencies, Unemployment and Education which I was rather dreading were the most successful of those which I gave. Indeed. The one drawback was the repetition of the old lectures on the Break-up in different parts of the country. It is very difficult to invent a new way of stating the old thing. [615]

While the Webbs were in Scotland, other speakers – Lansbury, Attlee, Tawney, Greenwood and Mostyn Lloyd – had covered the rest of the country.

Towards Christmas, and the December 1910 election, the Poor Law campaign wound down. On 27 November Sidney spoke to 200 people in Blackburn – but raised doubts:

…I doubt whether that kind of meeting is of much use. The local I.L.P. runs a regular Sunday Evening Meeting all through the year – with songs and choir, just like a Pleasant Sunday Afternoon affair, with the lecture thrown in. The audience comes as to evening service and not to learn! Most of them are I.L.P. members, and many are young people taking it as an alternative to Chapel. [616]

He wrote to Beatrice

Dear One, it is wet and cold and dreary, and I am lonely and dispirited without my companion and partner. I shall go for a little walk presently, just to see the town, and because you say I ought to have a little exercise, and then I shall go on to Liverpool. I think I have had about enough of this provincial lecturing with its perpetual separations. And tomorrow you have to start again, in the cold and wet. Pray be careful of your dear self.[617]

Between them, Sidney and Beatrice had addressed eighty meetings in ten weeks. Beatrice wrote that both were weary and somewhat dispirited:

In spite of all our work the National Committee does not seem to be gaining many new members and our friends are beginning to melt away.

At least they had survived the autumn

But whilst I am depressed on some counts, I am supremely grateful that I have been able to struggle through, with no nervous breakdown, the severe ordeal of this autumn's lecturing. An attack of influenza, or even a bad cold, might have made the Scottish tour a costly fiasco; and it would have been serious not to have been able to fulfil our North Country and Midlands engagements. Sidney, too, has gone on with his lecturing and all his other work – a quite incessant activity – and though strained and weary sometimes, on the whole happy, in the intensity of our comradeship.[618]

ENDGAME:1910-1912

When they launched the Poor Law campaign, Sidney and Beatrice had been confident of victory. They called for legislation to implement the Minority Report. But their confidence was misplaced: there was no legislation before 1914.

In 1910 Sidney stood down as an LCC member; the following summer, Sidney and Beatrice left for a long-planned, sabbatical, twelve-month round-the-world trip.

Ministers became preoccupied with the constitutional crisis: the clash with the House of Lords over the 1909 Budget, the two General Elections of 1910, and the passage of the Parliament Act of 1911. After January 1910, the government depended on Irish and Labour votes. No new social reform legislation could be passed until the conflict with the Lords was resolved.

The Liberal governments from 1905 were reforming governments. But the reforms Ministers enacted were not those the Webbs demanded. Old differences between the advanced Liberals and the Webbs, over education and the Boer War, remained. The Minister responsible for the Poor Law, John Burns, was sympathetic neither to reform in general, nor to the Webbs. Burns remained at the Local Government Board until February 1914, then moving to the Board of Trade until August 1914. The Liberal government's social reforms took place in spite of, rather than because of, Burns's tenure at the LGB. Relations between Burns and the Webbs had never been easy; neither they, nor their allies, nor many of his fellow ministers, considered Burns an effective minister.

Lucy Masterman was married to Charles Masterman, a radical Liberal MP first elected in 1906. She wrote that, although Burns had been a vigorous opponent of the previous Conservative government on unemployment, he

...had perplexed his friends, not merely by not having undertaken any very vigorous measures himself, but by a tone in speeches and replies to questions which seemed to imply no particular eagerness to initiate any, and a marked harshness and want of sympathy with the men out of work.[619]

Robert Ensor believed that Burns,

...the ex-demagogue, sincere and upright, but without administrative experience and lacking either the education or the kind of ability that might have saved him...[620]

was dominated by highly traditional officials.

In June 1907, Lansbury told Beatrice that Burns was completely under the control of Davy, the Poor Law Chief Inspector.[621]

Haldane thought Burns

...vain and ignorant and in the hands of his officials and opposes everything and talks so much that we find it difficult to get to business.[622]

In October 1907 Beatrice wrote that Burns was

...becoming the most hidebound of Departmental chiefs, gulled by an obstructive fact or reactionary argument – taken in by the most naïve commonplaces of middleclass administrative routine.[623]

Nevertheless, Campbell-Bannerman had appointed Burns; Asquith kept him in post. One remedy was appointing new officials; another was surrounding Burns with new junior ministers.

Both were tried. Provis, the LGB Permanent Secretary, had clashed with Beatrice at the beginning of the Commission's work. His retirement was pending. In 1907, Beatrice suggested to Burns that Robert Morant might replace Provis – suggesting that if Burns wanted to make major changes

...you will require a really strong subordinate – a man of the type of Morant (who by the way is a really strong admirer of yours). I do so want your administration to stand out as constructive...[624]

In spring 1908 Asquith appointed Masterman as a junior minister, under Burns, at the Local Government Board. Asquith also told Burns he must consult No 10 before replacing Provis. Beatrice was optimistic:

*...Asquith seems inclined to carry out our ideas: Morant is to succeed Provis,
with a view of bringing in next spring our Poor Law scheme...*[625]

Masterman had been critical of Burns; he accepted the LGB posting only
after Asquith had agreed that the department would be restructured, and that he
would have specific responsibilities. In practice this meant Burns made general
statements, passing details to Masterman.

In May 1908 Beatrice discussed her Poor Law proposals with Burns, who
said the police should be responsible for vagrants and the able-bodied. He raised
Morant's name

*...evidently to see what I should say. I again assured him that Morant was
the only man who could carry out the job and bring order into the LGB. He
is clearly considering the matter and said that, any day, I might hear of great
changes.*[626]

Nothing happened till January 1910. Then Burns promoted an existing LGB
civil servant, Horace Monro, to replace Provis. Beatrice called this a *setback for
the Webb influence*. She wondered if Asquith had agreed.

He had: Burns noted

Jerred called with PM's letter of assent to Munro.[627]

Jerred, Burns's private secretary, was promoted in Munro's place. Beatrice
thought this

*...ruined the Local Government Board as a possible instrument of reform. This
is serious and curiously unexpected.*[628]

Sidney was away; Beatrice wrote to him

JB has done us! But then he was in a position to do so.
Come back darling one.[629]

Beatrice would never see the valedictory letter sent by Provis to Burns:

*It is a pleasure to me now to look back on your success as President in upholding
sound principles...*[630]

After a year with Burns, Masterman was moved to the Home Office, writing
that it would be interesting to experience an efficient and progressive Government
Department.[631] Lucy Masterman thought the Webbs had annoyed Asquith by
'running' Morant for the LGB role – and wrecked Morant's chances.[632]

After the January 1910 election Burns was reappointed, noting

P.M. told me he could not move me. 'L'homme necessaire' at L.G.B. [633]

It had never been likely that Burns would back legislation based on the Minority Report; back in 1906, he had met Beatrice:

Mrs Webb called and gave outline of her views on Poor Law, Destitution, Unemployed, etc. A pleasant chat but a little too doctrinaire. She agrees in the main with my views on Unemployed. [634]

After the reports appeared, he argued legislation was unnecessary: whatever was needed could be done by administrative action, saying, in May 1909,

If the country knew its business it would relegate both reports and the whole of the problem to the President of the Local Government Board for his…practical action whenever he determined that action should be taken. [635]

Burns demonstrated his underlying attitude to the Webbs in a 1910 letter to H G Wells:

The new helotry in the servile state run by the archivists of the School of Economics means a race of paupers in a grovelling community run by uniformed prigs. Rely upon me saving you from this plague. [636]

The government took action on poverty in old age before the Poor Law reports appeared. Asquith's 1908 Budget introduced the first old age pension – non-contributory, five shillings a week for a single person, seven shillings and six pence for a married couple, from the age of seventy. People with a weekly income of ten shillings or more were disqualified. One historian has written that an old person had to be

…very old, very poor, and very respectable… [637]

to qualify. The pension was paid for from general taxation, and came into operation on 1 January 1909.

It had taken twenty five years. Canon Barnett first proposed pensions in 1883:

Pensions of 8s or 10s a week might be given to every citizen who had kept himself until the age of sixty without workhouse aid. If such pensions were the right of all, none would be tempted to lie to get them. [638]

Barnett's support had helped to convert Charles Booth. In the 1890s, Booth found that, in East London, old age was the most frequent cause of pauperism. Some of the evidence came from Sidney. Pensions would remove old people from the scope of the Poor Law.

There had been a Royal Commission and a parliamentary select committee.

The Fabians published three tracts on pensions. New Zealand introduced non-contributory pensions in 1898; Pember Reeves explained the scheme to British audiences.

The Charity Organisation Society and the Local Government Board fought state pensions from the start.

Asquith, while Chancellor, committed the government to pensions; Lloyd George, his successor, took the legislation through. Detailed work was done by Reginald McKenna, Financial Secretary to the Treasury, in 1907 promoted to the Cabinet as Education Minister. Beatrice went to see him in April 1907, to discuss Royal Commission business, and he outlined the government's plans. He was worried by the cost of Beatrice's Poor Law proposals:

> *The worst of all your proposals, Mrs Webb, is that though each one seems excellent, they all mean more expenditure. And where are we to get the money?*
> 639

Introducing pensions had the intended effect: in 1906 there were 168,096 people aged over 70 in England and Wales on outdoor relief; by 1913 there were just 8,563. Outdoor relief for the over 70s had virtually been ended.

Nevertheless, McKenna had been right: the commitment was costly, unquantified, and open-ended. Alfred Watson, later Government Actuary,

> *...was astonished to find that the Act was passed without any actuarial consideration of changes in the age distribution of the population – already becoming evident.*[640]

Lloyd George understood this during the passage of the Bill. He wanted to act on sickness and unemployment, but little scope remained for further advance funded from general taxation.

His attention turned to insurance for any extension of pensions, and for unemployment and sickness. In August 1908 he visited Germany to study social insurance; he returned a supporter of the principle. Over the coming years he led on health insurance, Churchill on unemployment insurance.

In October 1908, the Webbs lunched with Churchill, who had just made an *eloquent* speech on unemployment. Beatrice thought he had

> *...mastered the Webb scheme, though not going the whole length of compulsory Labour Exchanges.*[641]

Lloyd George joined them after lunch, and invited them to breakfast at the Treasury to discuss insurance. Churchill and Haldane attended as well as Sidney, Beatrice and the Chancellor, and Treasury civil servants.

The Webbs were more sceptical about health insurance than about unemployment. The discussion with the Chancellor was heated. Beatrice explained her reservations about insurance:

> ...the State could not enter into competition with the Friendly Societies and Insurance Companies...I tried to impress on them that any grant from the community to the individual beyond what it does for all, ought to be conditional on better conduct, and that any insurance scheme had the fatal defect that the state got nothing for its money – that the persons felt they had a right to the allowance whatever their conduct.[642]

They met again a fortnight later, this time with some Labour MPs (including Arthur Henderson and David Shackleton), discussing Labour Exchanges and possibly Unemployment Insurance.

In November 1908 Shackleton led a TUC delegation on insurance to Germany – less to study the details, more to

> ...ascertain the feeling prevalent among German workers and the attitude adopted by German Trades Unions towards the State systems of insurance.[643]

It was not a government delegation – but British diplomats assisted them. On their return, their favourable report was submitted to the Cabinet without delay.

Thus even before the Poor Law reports appeared, Churchill and Lloyd George were moving towards an insurance-based approach to sickness and unemployment.

Some ministers studied the reports; Masterman saw a pre-publication copy over Christmas 1908:

> I am working away at Mrs Webb's Poor Law Report which is extraordinarily good – an historic document, I should think.[644]

Summaries of both reports, without recommendations, came to Cabinet in February and March 1909. Burns read the report twice, in February and July. In November 1908 Haldane told Beatrice that Asquith had asked him

> ...to get up the whole subject, with a view to drawing up a comprehensive scheme of reform. They would bring in some portions of it next year and the year after (I understand Winston's labour exchanges, and Lloyd George's invalidity pensions) ...[645]

This began to happen: in April 1909, Churchill informed the Cabinet that, while he would legislate for labour exchanges that year

> It will not, of course, be possible to carry a measure of Unemployment Insurance this year...[646]

Lloyd George did not rush to read the Minority Report. William Braithwaite, the Treasury civil servant, who worked on national insurance, wrote

I don't think he had taken any real interest in the Poor Law Report: it was not till the bill was well on its way that so far as I know he started looking at it, and I gathered that he had not read a word of it before.[647]

Lloyd George's inspiration came from elsewhere. He told Frances Stevenson – his secretary, later his second wife – that he thought

…it was Victor Hugo's book Les Miserables *that decided me to do what I could to alleviate the distress and suffering of the poor. That story gives you such a vivid picture of the underside of life, all the wretched & sordid details…*[648]

Lloyd George launched his first budget – the People's Budget – in April 1909. While the Webbs campaigned for the Minority Report, Liberal MPs and ministers became preoccupied with the budget.

The gulf between ministers and the Webbs widened. Beatrice wrote in June

We have been quite strangely 'dropped' by the more distinguished of our acquaintances, and by the Liberal Ministers in particular.[649]

They saw Haldane; they concluded that the Cabinet had become *indifferent if not actually hostile* to the Minority Report. Not that they supported the Majority: there was just

…an inertia and a willingness to accept John Burns's assurance at the Local Government Board that the status quo was the best of all possible worlds. Haldane actually stood up for JB as an efficient Minister…[650]

Then Beatrice met Churchill, walking on the Thames Embankment

'Well, how do you think we are doing, Mrs Webb?'

'You are doing very well, Mr Churchill, but I have my doubts about your Cabinet; I don't think they mean to do anything with the Poor Law'[651]

Churchill told her the government were going to introduce a classified Poor Law. That was enough for Beatrice:

He and Asquith have decided against the break-up of the Poor law. We have a formidable fight before us.[652]

For the next eighteen months ministers were preoccupied with the budget. In November, the Lords refused the Finance Bill a Second Reading. The two General Elections of 1910 followed. After the December election, faced with the threat that, at the request of the government, royal powers would be used to create enough new peers to outvote the existing majority in the House of Lords, the 1911 Parliament Act was passed, enabling the Commons to override the Lords.

Within the government, activity on social reform did not resume until after the December election. Beatrice and Sidney were tired; she wondered

…whether we have not exhausted the interest in the subject and whether our dream of a permanent organization…is possible at present? [653]

Lloyd George, reappointed Chancellor, relaunched work on social insurance. Braithwaite, on leave, playing golf before Christmas, was summoned to the Treasury, and told to go to Germany on Boxing Day for another fact-finding mission. He was to travel between Christmas and New Year, write a report, then meet the Chancellor at Nice.

Braithwaite arrived in Germany on 27 December, leaving again on 1 January 1910; he had four working days and a Sunday to gather information. He wrote later:

I certainly had masses of it; laws, reports, statistics, regulations, books, etc. [654]

As well as government offices, Braithwaite visited the equivalent of a Friendly Society, where

I collected some handbills which later enabled me to answer Mrs Webb's questions. [655]

Braithwaite then caught the train to Nice, arriving on the morning of 3 January.

There he met Lloyd George, Rufus Isaacs (Attorney General), Charles and Lucy Masterman, and civil servants. Braithwaite briefed them for two hours that afternoon, and again before dinner.

Afterwards Lloyd George entertained them all; Braithwaite noted

Dinner party in Casino in the evening given by Chancellor [656]

They stayed at Nice another week, then returning to London.

The government's task now was to evolve a workable insurance scheme. Intense discussion with the Friendly Societies and others about the details ensued. Sidney and Beatrice were unhappy:

…the schemes of insurance are not really helpful to our scheme. Doling out weekly allowances, and with no kind of treatment attached, is a most unscientific state aid, and if it were not for the advantage of proposing to

transfer the millions from the rich to the poor, we should oppose it root and branch. [657]

Lloyd George used breakfast meetings to develop policy: according to Braithwaite,

LG's breakfasts in those days were famous. He did much of his work at them: getting people together and picking their brains.[658]

Sidney and Beatrice were invited for 28 February. Braithwaite describes the breakfast as 'Homeric':

Webb very anxious to assure the Chancellor that he knew nothing about the Government scheme, that he is not in any way opposed to it, etc., etc. Chancellor duly tempted on, begins to unfold a little bit here and there. Before he can speak, Mr and Mrs Webb, singly and in pairs, leap down his throat: 'that's absurd', 'that will never do', 'You should adopt our plan', 'sickness should be prevented, not cured'. 'Friendly Societies are quite incapable of dealing with the question'. 'It's criminal to take poor people's money and use it to insure them; if you take it you should give it to the Public Health Authority to prevent their being ill again'!!

The Chancellor was unable to get a word in and was evidently partly amused and partly annoyed…[659]

Lloyd George was amused. He had just read *The New Machiavelli*. But he told Braithwaite he did not intend to consult Sidney Webb much more – although the Webbs did arrange for him to meet a group of Medical Officers of Health.

The Webbs were leaving for their world tour at the end of May 1911; in preparation, they let Grosvenor Road in February, staying first at Eastbourne, then at Luton Hoo.

The tide was turning against them. In March 1911, Beatrice wrote

It is clear that public opinion has got firmly into its silly head that insurance has some mystical moral quality, which even covers the heinous sin of expenditure from public funds. It is an amazingly foolish delusion.[660]

Before their departure, Beatrice began constructing plans to redirect the proposed expenditure on sickness insurance into a restructuring of public health.

Preparations continued inside government. In April, the Cabinet considered advice from the government actuaries and the draft Health Insurance Bill.

Lloyd George and Burns had both been pro-Boers. But their working relationship in government was not close. As work on insurance progressed Lloyd George needed the cooperation of the LGB and its President. Some LGB officials

– especially Arthur Newsholme, the Chief Medical Officer (an appointment the Webbs had influenced) – had been helpful. But Burns himself had to be brought round to support National Insurance.

Burns spent Sunday 2 April 1911 on the paperwork:

At home all day on Insurance Scheme. [661]

Next day, he noted

A long conference with Chancellor at Treasury. Criticised scheme.[662]

Braithwaite left a fuller account:

John Burns came in and lectured the Chancellor at great length. A most amusing interview. Chancellor very anxious to conciliate him, but almost unable to sit still under the great mass of irrelevancy poured forth. I wondered where it would end. There was always one thing more!

Finally there was one thing more, as JB got close up to the Chancellor and shaking hands with him said, 'You know, this is a bigger thing than either the Majority or Minority Report, and renders them both unnecessary.' When he went out I know we both nearly exploded, and when I looked at the Chancellor I found him watching me with those bright twinkling eyes of his as he said: 'You know it really has been worth while making this special effort to conciliate him.' They are, of course, notoriously on bad terms. [663]

Lloyd George succeeded, where the Webbs had not, in forging an alliance with Burns.

The Bill received its first reading on 4 May. Burns thought Lloyd George's introductory speech was *good, simple and effective*, noting that Labour members were *warm in support.* [664]

After Lloyd George's first reading speech, Charles Masterman said to Lansbury

We have spiked your guns, eh? [665]

Burns said that National Insurance had finally *dished the Webbs.*[666]
Beatrice attributed the Bill's *splendid reception* to Lloyd George's *heroic demagogy:*

He has taken every item that could be popular with anyone, mixed them together and produced a Bill which takes some twenty million [pounds] from the propertied class to be handed over to the wage earners sans phrase to be spent by them, as they think fit, in times of sickness or unemployment. [667]

Beatrice was more dubious than Sidney; he thought that *the big and difficult matter is to get the money voted*; everything else could be sorted out later.

At the end of May, the Webbs organised a national conference on the Prevention of Destitution – opening with a rally in the Royal Albert Hall, continuing at Caxton Hall in Westminster. Balfour, MacDonald, and Sir John Simon spoke; detailed sessions looked at health, education, unemployment, and mental health.

Sidney and Beatrice stayed in the background,

...we were only too glad to be relieved from attendances and responsibility[668]

They then set off round the world, leaving Clifford Sharp in charge:

When we come back next spring we shall have to decide what is to be done – whether we are to close up or to go on, or to divide the work between the National Conference and the Fabian Society. We shall know, too, how this insurance is going to affect us. If it is carried it alters the whole situation and we shall have to begin a new kind of propaganda.[669]

Sharp wrote regularly about the campaign and the wider political situation; Beatrice replied with news of their travels. Beatrice's letters were read out to staff and volunteers at weekly 'At Homes' in the Norfolk Street offices. Some of her letters appeared in *The Crusade*.

The Webbs sailed from Liverpool to Canada in early June; spent June and July crossing Canada; and on 7 August sailed for Japan from the west coast.

In July and early August the government were immersed in the Insurance Bill's Commons Committee stage. In the Lords the struggle over the Parliament Act reached its climax.

And from July to September there was a heatwave; Sharp wrote on 28 July

Practically the whole of the staff adjourned at midday today to the Westminster Swimming Baths [670]

The Webbs had continued to fight for the Minority Report, and against the Insurance Bill until they left England. Lansbury met them on 26 May, to discuss

...the amendment or postponement of Lloyd George's rotten scheme of sickness insurance. The more we examine, the less we like it, both for what it does, and for what it omits to do. [671]

Labour movement opinion – particularly in the Parliamentary Labour Party– was divided. The ILP and the Fabians were against the contributory principle, in favour of the Minority Report. Some trade union opinion had been hostile to state intervention in welfare. In June 1911, however, a special TUC conference voted to accept the contributory principle.

Initially, in the House of Commons, Lansbury, Hardie, and Snowden voted against insurance; MacDonald, and most of the PLP, voted with the government in favour.

The Insurance Bill could not pass without Labour and Irish support. During the July Committee stage, labour flexed its muscles; it appeared the gloating in May, by Burns and Masterman, over the defeat of the Webbs, had been premature.

Burns the minister, and Braithwaite the civil servant could see what was happening. Burns noted on 5 July

Lansbury strongly against Bill [672]

On 19 July he wrote that the bill was *in trouble.*
Braithwaite wrote on 18 July

This a m we breakfasted with the Labour Party again. They are being driven by their extreme men and are turning nasty. [673]

He added next day

Labour Party broke loose on Clause 11 and went on till 5 a m.[674]

The Bill's prospects were uncertain. Sharp wrote to Beatrice on 28 July that he could not confidently forecast the Bill's prospects:

Ten days ago everyone was talking of it as __dead__, that was after the Labour Party had pressed an all-night sitting...[675]

For much of 1911 Lloyd George was in complex negotiations with doctors and friendly societies. But he still needed Labour and Irish votes. In early August, the Parliament Act was passed. The committee stage was adjourned until autumn.

On 28 July Lloyd George met MacDonald and George Barnes, the Labour leaders, telling them

...he must have their terms, and a firm agreement if he found he could grant them.[676]

He was confident of reaching agreement with the Irish Party. Days of negotiation between Labour and ministers followed; Asquith was drawn in, telling MacDonald he was asking too much.

The deal that emerged was about more than Health Insurance. Labour secured some concessions. But the government agreed that, for the first time, MPs would be paid a salary. This mattered to Labour: the Osborne Judgement of 1909 had prevented the payment of trade union MPs from union funds. On 10 August, the Commons voted to approve payment of members.

In late October Sharp informed Beatrice

…the Insurance Bill, I am sorry to report, is as good as law [677]

An announcement by MacDonald

…that on the reassembling of Parliament the Labour Party would officially adopt the Bill and, given one or two (unspecified) amendments, would lend all their influence to getting it through this year. [678]

had *crushed* the continuing opposition of Lansbury and Snowden.

So Lloyd George had achieved agreement with Burns and Macdonald. That with MacDonald might have gone still further: MacDonald's meetings with the Chancellor achieved a more convivial tone than Sidney and Beatrice ever managed:

22ⁿᵈ October. Breakfasted with Chancellor of Exchequer. He sounded me on coalition government: 'not just yet. [679]

By December, the Bill had passed the Commons; it cleared the Lords in just ten days.

Sidney and Beatrice were still travelling. They spent two months in Japan, a week in Korea. In October, they went by train from Korea to China

…a long and tiring two days in the tiny little ramshackle service train, over the mountains and plains of South Manchuria… [680]

They spent a month in China; they reported that

We had not contemplated a 'China in revolution' as part of our holiday experiences. [681]

Their arrival in China coincided with uprisings, leading to the collapse (after 270 years) of the Qing dynasty. Their departure from Beijing was spectacular. The day before they were due to leave, they were told the Imperial Court were leaving that night. Next morning, the Webbs got to the station an hour before their train was due to leave:

Every carriage and truck was crowded with Chinese families – men, women and children were seated on roofs of the carriages – whilst the platform was almost equally crowded with disconsolate ones squatting on their household belongings. [682]

All seemed lost: but the train guard was English – *an enthusiastic member of the ILP and subscriber to the* Labour Leader [683] – and recognized Sidney. Guard and porters together rescued Sidney, Beatrice, and their luggage; they moved on to Shanghai.

Sharp and Beatrice continued to exchange letters. Sharp thought the campaign still had potential – especially with broader objectives, covering, for example, the National Minimum, sweating, and factory conditions. In November 1911, he wrote to Beatrice about MacDonald:

> *With regard to your suggestion that it might be better, in view of JRM's attitude and strength, for you to keep out of Socialist politics, Lloyd and I are both of the view that this would be the worst possible course.* [684]

Sharp argued that Beatrice should play an active part in the socialist movement. He thought Labour had fallen into an attitude of *pathetic and utter reliance on Lloyd George*:

> *I can't believe that it would be very difficult to get most of the Labour Party to look to you instead of Lloyd George for their gospel.*[685]

These exchanges continued into 1912. In February Sharp commented on the idea of a new socialist paper. In March, he told Beatrice that volunteers were still turning up at the campaign office, but that it was difficult to find work for them. He did not want them turning up out of habit rather than enthusiasm. He argued for a new, non-party socialist organisation, committed to the abolition of poverty.

The Insurance Act enacted, attention switched to implementation. In November, Lloyd George made Morant chairman of the Insurance Commission. A separate Welsh Commission was established; Thomas Jones became Secretary. After working for the Royal Commission, TJ had taught economics in Belfast, then worked on tuberculosis policy in Wales – where he met Lloyd George.

Activists from the Poor Law campaign went to work for the government. Sharp wrote to Beatrice in February:

> *An enormous number of appointments are going of course under the Insurance Act and lots of Fabians are getting jobs.*[686]

Several Fabians were hired as 'explainers'. One was the Fabian Executive member Millicent Murby. Another was Clement Attlee, who bought a bicycle and Ordnance Survey maps and spent summer 1912 cycling round Somerset towns and villages explaining the Act.[687]

After Shanghai, the Webbs visited Hong Kong, staying with the Governor, Frederick Lugard, at Government House. Lugard was a colonial office veteran, with long experience in Africa before his posting to Hong Kong. Beatrice thought Lugard the *best type of English administrator*.

...a man of overwhelming conscientiousness, absolute integrity, slow but steady industry – the whole inspired by a broad, sympathetic openminded determination to make the world better. [688]

They then went, via the Malay Peninsula and Burma, to India, staying from January until mid-April. They travelled widely – Calcutta, Allahabad, Bombay, making field trips to villages and country areas. They discussed religion, education, and other subjects.

They made these journeys with British administrators – Collectors. Beatrice was struck by one, John Hope Simpson, with whom they made a tour on 28 January:

...a genuine love of guiding and serving other people...the exact opposite of a bureaucrat...too great an independence of, and indifference to the common rules of law and administration... [689]

They met Indian nationalist leaders, including the Congress, and Gopal Krishna Gokhale.

Leaving India, Beatrice wrote that the longer they had been there

...the graver became our tone, and the more subdued our optimism...

Three months acquaintance has greatly increased our estimate of the Indians, and greatly lessened our admiration for, and our trust in, this Government of officials. [690]

In April they sailed for home; the voyage lasted five weeks.

Sharp kept Beatrice up to date with British politics. He thought the Fabian Society was *played out* – but it would be hard to change it while Pease was there. Ernest Simon was reluctant to sign the Fabian Basis because he disagreed with nationalisation. Sharp argued for a new, non-party socialist organisation, committed to the abolition of poverty.

He thought Beatrice would be elected to the Fabian Executive Committee –

...and, I am afraid, Dr Marion Phillips.[691]

Beatrice sent her final letter, from Bombay, on Sunday 7 April. She had been following the news – she knew that the organisation would have to change –

...but the purpose of the National Committee – the getting of a civilised life for every individual citizen – stands out still as the one imperative necessity if our civilisation is to progress and endure. [692]

Notes to Part Two

Chapter Five

1 Webb, B; *My Apprenticeship*; London, Longmans, 1926; p 414
2 Webb, B; *My Apprenticeship*; London, Longmans, 1926; p 402
3 Gardiner, Alfred George; *Pillars of Society*; London; J M Dent;1916; p192
4 Gardiner, Alfred George; *Pillars of Society*; London; J M Dent;1916; p192
5 Wells, Herbert G; *The New Machiavelli; London*, Penguin, 2005
6 Samuel, Viscount (Herbert Samuel); *Memoirs*; London, the Cresset Press; 1945; p 29
7 Beatrice Webb Diary, 16.08.1892
8 Sidney to Graham Wallas, 29.07.1892, in Webb, B & Webb, S; *The Letters of Sidney and Beatrice Webb;* Vol I; Cambridge; CUP; 1978; p 437
9 Sidney to Edward Pease, 12.08.1892; in Webb, B & Webb, S; *The Letters of Sidney and Beatrice Webb*; Vol II; Cambridge; CUP; 1978; p 1
10 BW to Graham Wallas, September 1892; in Webb, B & Webb, S; *The Letters of Sidney and Beatrice Webb*; Vol II; Cambridge; CUP; 1978 p 3
11 Beatrice Webb Diary, 19.09.1892
12 BW to Graham Wallas, September 1892; in Webb, B & Webb, S; *The Letters of Sidney and Beatrice Webb*; Vol II; Cambridge; CUP; 1978 p 3
13 GBS Diary, 07.10.1892; in Shaw, George Bernard; *Bernard Shaw: The Diaries*; ed Stanley Weintraub; London; Pennsylvania State University Press; 1986; p 859
14 Hamilton, Mary Agnes (Molly); *Sidney and Beatrice Webb;*   London, Sampson Low, 1933; p 72
15 Webb, B; *Our Partnership*; ed. Cole, M & Drake, B; London, Longmans, 1948; p 34
16 Beatrice Webb Diary. 10.1893
17 Beatrice Webb Diary October 1893
18 Kate Courtney to Beatrice, 17.08.1893; bound with typescript diary.
19 GBS Diary, 23.09.1893; in Shaw,

George Bernard; *Bernard Shaw: The Diaries*; ed Stanley Weintraub; London; Pennsylvania State University Press; 1986; p 969
20 Wells, Herbert G; *The New Machiavelli; London*, Penguin, 2005; p164
21 Galton, F W; Investigating with the Webbs; in Cole, M, ed, *The Webbs and their Work*; London, Frederick Muller, 1949, p 32
22 Shaw to Sidney, 12.08.1892; in Michalos, Alex C & Poff, Deborah C; eds; *Bernard Shaw and the Webbs*; Toronto, University of Toronto Press, 2002, p 15
23 GBS Diary, 03.02.1895; in Shaw, George Bernard; *Bernard Shaw: The Diaries*; ed Stanley Weintraub; London; Pennsylvania State University Press; 1986; p 1064
24 Webb, S & B; *The History of Trade Unionism*; London; Longmans Green, 1894; p 233
25 Beatrice Webb Diary 01.12.1892
26 Beatrice Webb Diary 17.01.1893
27 Beatrice Webb Diary 17.01.1893
28 Beatrice Webb Diary 17.01.1893
29 Beatrice Webb Diary 18.10.1895.
30 Beatrice Webb Diary, 25.09.1895
31 Beatrice to Herbert Samuel, quoted in Bowle, J; *Viscount Samuel, a biography*; London, Victor Gollancz, 1957
32 GBS letter to Janet Achurch, 12.04.1895; in Shaw, George Bernard; *Bernard Shaw: The Diaries*; ed Stanley Weintraub; London; Pennsylvania State University Press; 1986; p 1074
33 Beatrice Webb Diary, 25.04.1895
34 Beatrice Webb Diary, 04.08.1895
35 Beatrice Webb Diary, 04.08.1895
36 GBS letter to Janet Achurch, 31.08.1895; in Shaw, George Bernard; *Bernard Shaw: The Diaries*; ed Stanley Weintraub; London; Pennsylvania State University Press; 1986; p 1089
37 GBS letter to Pakenham Beatty, 17.09.1895; in Shaw, George Bernard; *Bernard Shaw: The Diaries*; ed Stanley

Weintraub; London; Pennsylvania State University Press; 1986; p 1091

38 Beatrice Webb Diary, 25.07.1894
39 Beatrice Webb Diary, 25.07.1894
40 Beatrice Webb Diary, 16.09.1896
41 Beatrice Webb Diary, 16.09.1896
42 GBS letter to Ellen Terry, August 1896; in Shaw, George Bernard; *Bernard Shaw: The Diaries*; ed Stanley Weintraub; London; Pennsylvania State University Press; 1986; p 1137
43 Beatrice Webb Diary 01.05.1897
44 GBS to Beatrice, 21.06.1898, in Shaw, George Bernard; *Bernard Shaw and the Webbs; Selected correspondence of Bernard Shaw*; ed Alec C Michalos and Deborah C Poff; Toronto, University of Toronto Press, 2002; p 45
45 Beatrice Webb Diary 21.01.1898
46 Beatrice to Graham Wallas, ? 13.07.1897. In Webb, B & Webb, S; *The Letters of Sidney and Beatrice Webb*; Vol II; Cambridge; CUP; 1978; p 53
47 Beatrice Webb Diary 21.01.1898
48 Beatrice Webb Diary 30.12.1892
49 Beatrice Webb Diary 10.03.1892
50 George Bernard Shaw Diary, 27.08.1893 *Bernard Shaw: The Diaries*; ed Stanley Weintraub; London; Pennsylvania State University Press; 1986; p 964
51 Beatrice Webb Diary 17.09.1893
52 Quoted in Holroyd, M *Bernard Shaw; Volume 1, The Search for Love, 1856 – 1898;* London, Penguin, 1990; p 292
53 John Burns Diary 11.10.1893; British Library Add Ms 46313
54 Beatrice Webb Diary 12.10.1893
55 Beatrice Webb Diary 12.10.1893
56 *Pall Mall Gazette,* 10.01.1891
57 Galton to Burns, 4 April 1894; British Library Add Ms 46287
58 GBS Diary, 25.12.1893; in Shaw, George Bernard; *Bernard Shaw: The Diaries*; ed Stanley Weintraub; London; Pennsylvania State University Press; 1986; p 999
59 Webb, S & B; *The History of Trade Unionism*; London; Longmans Green, 1894; p 1
60 Webb, S & B; *Methods of Social Study*; London, Longmans Green, 1932
61 Beatrice Webb Diary 21.05.1894
62 Beatrice Webb Diary 10.07.1894

63 Beatrice Webb Diary 09.04.1895
64 Beatrice Webb Diary 08.08.1895
65 Beatrice Webb Diary 12.11.1895
66 Beatrice Webb Diary Christmas 1895
67 Beatrice Webb Diary 16.01.1896
68 Beatrice Webb Diary 16.09.1896
69 Beatrice Webb Diary 18.01.1897
70 Beatrice Webb Diary 01.05.1897
71 Beatrice Webb Diary 24.05.1897
72 Harrison, R J; *The Life and Times of Sidney and Beatrice Webb; 1858-1905: the formative years*; London, Macmillan, 2000; p. 236
73 Webb, S & B; *Industrial Democracy*; London, Longmans, Green & Co; 1897; Vol II; p 774
74 Beatrice Webb Diary 11.01.1898
75 Lord Salisbury, November 1894; quoted in Gibbon, G, and Bell, R; *History of the London County Council, 1889 – 1939*; London, Macmillan, 1939
76 Acland, H D; & Llewellyn Smith, H; *Studies in Secondary Education*; London, Percival & Co, 1892; Part III ch.1
77 Acland, HD & Llewellyn Smith, H, (Eds), *Studies in Secondary Education*, 1892; quoted in Saint, A; *Technical Education and the Early LCC*; in Saint, A, Ed; *Politics and the People of London; The London County Council 1889 - 1965*; London, The Hambledon Press, 1986
78 Sidney to Beatrice, 16.03.1892; in Webb, B & Webb, S; *The Letters of Sidney and Beatrice Webb;* Vol I; Cambridge; CUP; 1978; p 394
79 London Metropolitan Archives LMA/ TEB/004 Report of the Special Committee on Technical Education, (H Llewellyn Smith); London, London County Council, 1892
80 *London,* 9 February 1893; quoted in Radice, L; *Beatrice and Sidney Webb, Fabian Socialists*; London, Macmillan, 1984
81 Webb, B; *Our Partnership*; London, Longmans, 1948; p 80
82 Beatrice to Mary Playne, early October 1894; in Webb, B & Webb, S; *The Letters of Sidney and Beatrice Webb;* Vol II; Cambridge; CUP; 1978; pp 26-27
83 Beatrice Webb Diary 06.02.1897

84   Beatrice Webb Diary 15.06.1906
85   LMA/TEB/80/21
86   quoted in Beveridge, W H; *The London School of Economics and the University of London*; in Cole, M, ed; *The Webbs and their Work*; London, Frederick Muller, 1949
87   Account by Graham Wallas in LSE Student Union Handbook, 1925; quoted in Beveridge, *The London School of Economics and the University of London*; in Cole, M, ed; *The Webbs and their Work*; London, Frederick Muller, 1949.
88   Beatrice Webb Diary 21.09.1894
89   SW to Edward Pease, 11.09.94; in Webb, B & Webb, S; *The Letters of Sidney and Beatrice Webb*; Vol II; Cambridge; CUP; 1978; p 23
90   LSE Library; PASSFIELD 10/1
91   LSE Library; PASSFIELD 10/1
92   Beveridge, W H; *The London School of Economics and the University of London;* in Cole, M, ed; *The Webbs and their Work;* London, Frederick Muller, 1949, p 44
93   SW to Pease, 14.09.1894; in Webb, B & Webb, S; *The Letters of Sidney and Beatrice Webb*; Vol II; Cambridge; CUP; 1978; p 23
94   Beatrice Webb Diary 21.09.1894
95   SW to Fabian EC; LSE Library LSE 1/1, 27.11.1894
96   SW to Hutchinson Trustees, 08.02.1895; in Webb, B & Webb, S; *The Letters of Sidney and Beatrice Webb; Vol II*; Cambridge; CUP; 1978; p 29
97   Hutchinson Trust Minutes, March 1895; LSE Library LSE 1/1
98   Beatrice Webb Diary 08.05.1895
99   SW to B Russell, 11.12.1895, in Webb, B & Webb, S; *The Letters of Sidney and Beatrice Webb; Vol II*; Cambridge; CUP; 1978 p 39
100   Beatrice Webb Diary 16.10.1896
101   Beatrice Webb Diary 28.03.1896
102   Beatrice Webb Diary 05.10.1896
103   Beatrice Webb Diary 05.10.1896
104   Jones, T; *Welsh Broth*; London, W Griffiths & Co, 1950; p 12
105   Beatrice Webb Diary 08.05.1927
106   Beatrice Webb Diary 22.02.1917; note added 1918
107   Report of the Hutchinson Trustees on the termination of the Trust, July 1904; LSE Library; LSE 1/1
108   GBS to Beatrice, 01.07.1895; Shaw, George Bernard; *Bernard Shaw and the Webbs; Selected correspondence of Bernard Shaw; ed* Alec C Michalos and Deborah C Poff; Toronto, University of Toronto Press, 2002; p31
109   Beatrice Webb Diary 18.04.1896
110   undated letter, Macdonald to Pease, spring 1896, LSE Library; Fabian Society file A/8/1
111   Macdonald to Pease, 08.04.1896; LSE Library; Fabian Society file A/8/1
112   Beatrice Webb Diary 18.04.1896
113   Pease to Sidney, 27.04.1896; LSE Library; LSE file 1/1
114   Fabian Executive Committee Minutes, LSE Library; 05.06.1896

Chapter Six

115   Sidney to Beatrice, 21.06.1899; LSE Library Passfield 2 3 3 4
116   Beatrice Webb Diary, 01.12.1894
117   Beatrice Webb Diary 21.08.1928s
118   Beatrice Webb Diary 07.10.1900
119   Beatrice Webb Diary 01.01.1901
120   Beatrice Webb Diary 24.04.1901
121   Beatrice Webb Diary 22.05.1900
122   Beatrice Webb Diary 04.07.1900
123   Beatrice Webb Diary 16.11.1900
124   Beatrice Webb Diary 09.12.1901
125   Beatrice Webb Diary 14.04.1927
126   Beatrice Webb Diary 01.10 1901
127   Beatrice Webb Diary 26.03.1902
128   Beatrice Webb Diary 25.04.1902
129   Beatrice Webb Diary 17.01.1904
130   Beatrice Webb Diary 05.10.1903
131   Russell, B; *Autobiography*; London, Unwin, 1978; p 75
132   Russell to Gilbert Murray, 26.09.1903, in Russell, B; *The Selected Letters of Bertrand Russell; Vol I The Private Years, 1884 – 1914;* Edited by Nicholas Griffin. London, Allen Lane, The Penguin Press; 1992; p269.
133   Beatrice Webb Diary 19.12.1903
134   Beatrice Webb Diary 02.06.1905
135   Beatrice Webb Diary 05.10.1905
136   Beatrice Webb Diary 14.10.1905
137   from Wells, H G, *'Essay on the passing of Beatrice Webb'*, quoted in Foot, M; *The History of Mr Wells*; Counterpoint,

Washington DC; 1995

138 quoted in MacKenzie, N & J; *The Life of H G Wells*; London, Hogarth Press, 1987; p 170

139 Beatrice Webb Diary 28.02.1902

140 Beatrice Webb Diary 19.04.1904

141 Beatrice Webb Diary 17.04.1905

142 Beatrice Webb Diary 05.11.1910

143 Mrs Mair was known, at different times, as 'Jessy' and 'Janet'. Here, following Ann Oakley (*Forgotten Wives; How women get written out of history;* Bristol, Polity Press, 2021) she is referred to as Janet throughout.

144 Beveridge, J; *Beveridge and his plan*; London, Hodder and Stoughton, 1954, p 58; quoted in Oakley, Ann *Forgotten Wives; How women get written out of history;* Bristol, Polity Press, 2021

145 Beveridge, W; *Power and Influence*; London; Hodder and Stoughton; 1953 p 35

146 Beatrice Webb Diary 30.07.1905

147 Beatrice Webb Diary 06.05.1887

148 Beatrice Webb Diary 31.12.1890

149 GBS to Sidney, 12.08.1892, in Michalos, Alex C & Poff, Deborah C; eds; *Bernard Shaw and the Webbs*; Toronto, University of Toronto Press, 2002; p 16

150 Beatrice Webb Diary 28.02.1902

151 Beatrice Webb Diary 28.02.1902

152 Webb, B; *Our Partnership*; ed. Cole, M & Drake, B; London, Longmans, 1948; p 96

153 Campbell, John; *Haldane, The forgotten statesman who shaped modern Britain*; London, Hurst, 2020; p 152

154 Beatrice Webb Diary 28.02.1902

155 Beatrice Webb Diary 23.11.1905

156 Abdy, Jane and Gere, Charlotte; *The Souls;* London, Sidgwick & Jackson, 1984; p 13

157 Quoted in Davenport-Hines, Richard; *Ettie; The intimate life and dauntless spirit of Lady Desborough*; London, Weidenfeld and Nicholson, 2008

158 Margot Asquith, *Memoirs*; quoted in Gilmour, David *Curzon*; London, John Murray, 1994; p 101

159 Asquith, Cynthia Mary Evelyn; *Remember and be glad*; London; James Barrie, 1952; pp 42-43; quoted in Renton, Claudia; *Those wild*

Wyndhams; London, William Collins, 2014; p 229

160 Beatrice Webb Diary September 1902

161 Beatrice Webb Diary 19.03.1907

162 Ellenberger, N; *Balfour's World; Aristocracy and Political Culture at the fin de siècle;* Woodbridge, The Boydell Press, 2015

163 Haldane to Beatrice, 05.11.1902; LSE Library; Passfield 2.4.B

164 Beatrice Webb Diary 28.11.1902

165 Beatrice Webb Diary 28.11.1902

166 Beatrice Webb Diary November/December 1902

167 Beatrice Webb Diary November/December 1902

168 Beatrice Webb Diary 25.07.1903

169 Beatrice to Kate Courtney, 25.08.1903; in Webb, B & Webb, S; *The Letters of Sidney and Beatrice Webb* Vol II; Cambridge; CUP; 1978; p191

170 Asquith, Cynthia. *Haply I may remember*. Barrie, 1950. P 14; quoted in Davenport-Hines, Richard; *Ettie; The intimate life and dauntless spirit of Lady Desborough*; London, Weidenfeld and Nicholson, 2008; p 48

171 Beatrice Webb Diary 20.04.1904

172 Beatrice Webb Diary 20.04.1904

173 Beatrice Webb Diary 30.07.1905

174 Beatrice Webb Diary 16.09.1906

175 Beatrice Webb Diary 08.07.1903

176 Beatrice Webb Diary 10.06.1904

177 Beatrice Webb Diary 10.06.1904

178 Beatrice Webb Diary 10.06.1904

179 Frances Chesterton diary, 09.06.1904; quoted in Ward, Maisie; *Gilbert Keith Chesterton*; London, Sheed and Ward, 1944; p 148

180 Tawney, Richard H; *The Webbs in Perspective*; Webb Memorial Lecture 1952; University of London Athlone Press, 1952; p4

181 Hamilton, Mary Agnes (Molly); *Sidney and Beatrice Webb*; London, Sampson Low, 1933; p 80

182 Wells, Herbert G; *The New Machiavelli;* London, Penguin, 2005; p 169

183 Wells, Herbert G; *The New Machiavelli;* London, Penguin, 2005; p 169

184 Tawney, Richard H; *The Webbs and their Work ; Webb Memorial Lecture No*

1; Published for the Webb Memorial Trust by Fabian Publications Ltd, 1945

185 Samuel, Viscount; *Memoirs*; London, The Cresset Press, 1945; p 293

186 Martin, K; *The Webbs in retirement*; in Cole, M, (ed) *The Webbs and their Work*; London, F Muller, 1949; p 286

187 Martin, K; *The Webbs in retirement*; in Cole, M, (ed) *The Webbs and their Work*; London, F Muller, 1949; p 287

188 Webb, B; *Our Partnership*; ed. Cole, M & Drake, B; London, Longmans, 1948; p 149

189 Webb, B; *Our Partnership*; ed. Cole, M & Drake, B; London, Longmans, 1948; p 149

190 Beatrice Webb Diary 28.04.1899

191 Beatrice Webb Diary 09.09.1899

192 Sidney to Beatrice; 16.06.1899; LSE Library; Passfield 2 3 3 4

193 Beatrice Webb Diary 02.04.1901

194 Beatrice Webb Diary 21.07.1902

195 Beatrice Webb Diary 01.10.1901

196 Beatrice Webb Diary 25.04.1902

197 Beatrice Webb Diary 21.07.1902

198 Beatrice Webb Diary 26.06.1905

199 Beatrice Webb Diary 30.07.1905

200 Wells, Herbert G; *Experiments in Autobiography; Vol I*; London, Gollancz; 1934; p 258

201 Marquand, David; *Britain since1918*; London, Weidenfeld & Nicholson; 2008; p 63

202 Hamilton, Mary Agnes (Molly); *Sidney and Beatrice Webb*; London, Sampson Low, 1933; p 182

203 Cole, Margaret; *The story of Fabian Socialism*; London, Heinemann, 1963; p53

204 Webb, Sidney & Beatrice; *English Local Government; Volume 2, From the Revolution to the Municipal Corporations Act: The manor and the borough*, Part One (1908); pp 176-7

205 Fabian Society, Tract No 106, *The Education Muddle and the Way Out*; London, 1901, p 3

206 Beatrice Webb Diary 16.01.1903

207 Beatrice Webb Diary 04.05.1902

208 Beatrice Webb Diary 04.05.1902

209 See Bogdanor, Vernon; *The Strange Survival of Liberal Britain; politics and power before the First World War*; London; Biteback Publishing Ltd,

2022; p 296

210 Beatrice Webb Diary 04.05.1902

211 Ensor, RCK; *Permeation*; in Cole, M, (ed.) *The Webbs and their Work*; London, F Muller, 1949, p 68

212 quoted in Simon, B; *Education and the Labour Movement 1870 –1920*; London, Lawrence and Wishart, 1974 p 223

213 quoted in Allen, B M; *Sir Robert Morant, A great public servant*; London, 1934 p 183

214 LSE Library; Fabian EC Minutes, 17.05.1901; 24.05.1891

215 Webb, B; *Our Partnership*; ed. Cole, M & Drake, B; London, Longmans, 1948 p 253

216 Beatrice Webb Diary, 14.10.1902

217 Webb, B; *Our Partnership*; ed. Cole, M & Drake, B; London, Longmans, 1948; p 252

218 Sidney to Beatrice, 16.07.1902; in Webb, B & Webb, S; *The Letters of Sidney and Beatrice Webb* Vol II; Cambridge; CUP; 1978; p164

219 Beatrice Webb Diary 28.11.1902

220 Beatrice Webb Diary; 12.1902

221 Webb, B; *Our Partnership*; ed. Cole, M & Drake, B; London, Longmans, 1948; p 258

222 Beatrice Webb Diary 25.02.1903

223 Webb, B; *Our Partnership*; ed. Cole, M & Drake, B; London, Longmans, 1948; p 252

224 Beatrice Webb Diary 28.02.1902

225 Beatrice Webb Diary 14.03.1903

226 Beatrice Webb Diary 15.03.1903

227 Beatrice Webb Diary 15.06.1903

228 Beatrice Webb Diary 15.06.1903

229 Beatrice Webb Diary 08.07.1903

230 Beatrice Webb Diary 06.12.1903

231 Martin, Basil Kingsley; *Father Figures*, London, Penguin, 1969; p41

232 Webb, B; *Our Partnership*; ed. Cole, M & Drake, B; London, Longmans, 1948; p 252

233 Ensor, RCK; *Permeation*; in Cole, M, (ed.) *The Webbs and their Work*; London, F Muller, 1949, p 70

234 Webb, B; *Our Partnership*; ed. Cole, M & Drake, B; London, Longmans, 1948; p 253

235 Webb, B; *Our Partnership*; ed. Cole, M & Drake, B; London, Longmans,

1948; p192

236 Ensor, Robert *England 1870-1914*; Oxford, OUP, 1936; p 267

237 Beatrice to Sally Fairchild, January 1900; in Webb, B & Webb, S; *The Letters of Sidney and Beatrice Webb* Vol II; Cambridge; CUP; 1978; p 124

238 Beatrice Webb Diary 10.10.1899

239 Webb, B; *Our Partnership*; ed. Cole, M & Drake, B; London, Longmans, 1948; p194

240 Beatrice Webb Diary 19.07.1900

241 Koss, S; Editor; *The Pro-Boers; The Anatomy of an Anti-war Movement*; Chicago & London, University of Chicago Press, 1973 p.xxiv

242 Burns Diary 18.05.1900; British Library Add Ms 463188

243 Burns Diary 18.05.1900; British Library Add Ms 463188

244 Atkinson, J A; *The war in South Africa: its causes and effects*; London, James Nisbet & Co Ltd; 1900; p189

245 *Justice*, 04.01.1896; 25.04.1896; quoted in Hirshfield, Claire; *The Anglo-Boer War and the issue of Jewish Culpability*; Journal of Contemporary History, Vol 15, No 4 (Oct 1980); p 621

246 Hansard 06.02.1900 Col 796

247 In Hilaire Belloc, *Complete verse*; London, Pimlico, 1991; pp 151-2

248 Quoted in Koss, S ed; *The Pro-Boers; The Anatomy of an Antiwar Movement*; Chicago & London, University of Chicago Press, 1973

249 Beatrice Webb Diary 28.02.1902

250 Beatrice Webb Diary 15.12.1900

251 Quoted in Pakenham, T; *The Boer War*; London; Weidenfeld and Nicholson, 1979

252 Taylor, AJP; *The Trouble Makers*; London, Panther, 1957; p 100

253 Beatrice Webb Diary 09.07.1901

254 Sir Henry Lucy; see Jenkins, Roy *Asquith*; London, Collins, 1964; p136

255 Beatrice Webb Diary 01.03.1904

256 GBS to E R Pease, 10.1899; quoted in Holroyd, M; *Bernard Shaw*; Vol 2, 1898-1918, London, Penguin, 1989, p 36

257 Pease, E R; *The History of the Fabian Society*; London, Fabian Society and Allen and Unwin; 1925; p 128

258 LSE Library; Fabian EC Minutes, 1900

259 Pease, E R, in Cole, M ed. *The Webbs and their Work*; London, Frederick Muller, 1949

260 Shaw, G B, ed; *Fabianism and the Empire, a manifesto for the Fabian Society;* London, Grant Richards, 1900; p 23

261 Sidney to HG Wells, 12.09.1902; in Webb, B & Webb, S; *The Letters of Sidney and Beatrice Webb* Vol II; Cambridge; CUP; 1978; p 170

262 Wells, Herbert G; *Experiments in Autobiography; Vol II*; London, 1934 Gollancz; p761

263 Harrison, R J; *The Life and Times of Sidney and Beatrice Webb; 1858-1905: the formative years;* London, Macmillan, 2000; p 327

264 Wells, H G; *The New Machiavelli*; London, Penguin, 2005 p 269

265 Webb, S; *The Decline in the Birth-rate*; Fabian Tract 131; London, The Fabian Society, 1907; p19

Chapter Seven

266 Report of the Royal Commission on the Poor Laws and the Relief of Distress; Cd 4499 ; 1900; p 12

267 Beatrice to W H Beveridge, 13.12.1908; in Webb, B & Webb, S; *The Letters of Sidney and Beatrice Webb; Vol II*; Cambridge; CUP; 1978; p 319

268 Poor Relief Act, 1601, Sections 1 & 5

269 Thompson, E P; *The Making of the English Working Class*, Penguin, 1968, p 295.

270 Webb, S & B: *English Poor Law Policy*; London, Longmans, 1910, p 1

271 *The Poor Law Report of 1834*; ed SG & EOA Checkland; Penguin, 1973, p 335

272 Quoted in Webb, S & B: *English Poor Law Policy*; London, Longmans, 1910 p 5

273 *Poor Law Report*

274 Webb, S & B: *English Poor Law Policy*; London, Longmans, 1910 p.75

275 Webb, S & B: English Poor Law Policy; London, Longmans, 1910 p 68

276 Webb, S & B: *English Poor Law Policy*; London, Longmans, 1910, pp73-74

277 Cole, M; *Growing Up into Revolution*; London, Longmans; 1949; p 42

278 Snell, H; *Men, Movements, and Myself*; London, J M Dent 1936; p 6

279 Attlee, C.R. *As it happened*; London, Heinemann; 1954; p21

280 Beatrice Webb Diary 29.11.1905

281 Beatrice Webb Diary 29.11.1905

282 Gardiner, A G; *Pillars of Society*; London; J M Dent;1916; p122

283 A G Gardiner to G B Shaw, 24.11.08; quoted in Koss, Stephen; *Fleet Street radical; A G Gardiner and the Daily News*; London, Allen Lane, 1973; p98

284 Webb, B; *Our Partnership*; ed. Cole, M & Drake, B; London, Longmans, 1948; p321

285 Webb, B; *Our Partnership*; ed. Cole, M & Drake, B; London, Longmans, 1948; p321

286 Beatrice Webb Diary 15.12.1905

287 Kent, W; *John Burns: Labour's Lost Leader*; London, Williams and Norgate, 1950, p145

288 Sidney to J Burns, 11 December 1905; in *Webb, B & Webb, S; The Letters of Sidney and Beatrice Webb*; Vol II; Cambridge; CUP; 1978 p 221

289 Beatrice Webb Diary 15.12.1905

290 Ensor, Robert *Permeation*, in Cole, M ed.; *The Webbs and their Work*; London, Frederick Muller, 1949; p 70

291 Braithwaite, W.J; *Lloyd George's Ambulance Wagon;* ed H N Banbury; Bath, 1957

292 Webb, B; *Our Partnership*; ed. Cole, M & Drake, B; London, Longmans, 1948 p. 317

293 Beatrice Webb Diary 02.12.1905

294 Beatrice Webb Diary 29.11.1905

295 Beatrice Webb Diary 02.12.1905

296 Beatrice Webb Diary 02.12.1905

297 Beatrice Webb Diary 15.12.1905

298 Beatrice Webb to Mary Playne, 29.07.1906; in Webb, B & Webb, S; *The Letters of Sidney and Beatrice Webb*; Vol II; Cambridge; CUP; 1978, p 233

299 Beatrice Webb Diary 20.02.1906

300 Beatrice Webb Diary 20.03.1906

301 Beatrice Webb Diary 20.03.1906

302 Beatrice Webb Diary 01.10.1906

303 McBriar, AM; *An Edwardian Mixed Doubles The Bosanquets versus the Webbs; a study in British Social Policy,* 1890 – 1929 Oxford, Clarendon Press; 1987, p180

304 Beatrice Webb Diary 12.02.1906

305 Beatrice Webb Diary 01.03.1906

306 Beatrice Webb Diary 01.10.1906

307 Gardiner, A G; *Pillars of Society*; London; J M Dent;1916; p 194

308 Beatrice Webb Diary 22.05.06

309 Beatrice Webb Diary; 10.04.1907

310 William Smart to Beatrice Webb, 14.02.1906; LSE Library; Webb Local Government Collection Vol 297

311 Majority Report; Para 314; Report of the Royal Commission on the Poor Laws and Relief of Distress; Cd 4499 1909

312 Royal Commission on the Poor Laws and the Relief of Distress; Vol XVII; Final Report by Mr Jones; pp 57,58

313 Beatrice Webb Diary 18.12.1906

314 Beatrice to Pease, 01.07.1907, in Webb, B & Webb, S; *The Letters of Sidney and Beatrice Webb*; Vol II; Cambridge; CUP; 1978, p 244

315 Royal Commission on the Poor Laws and the Relief of Distress; Minutes, Evidence Committee, 11.02.1907; LSE Library; Webb Local Government Collection, vol 286

316 Beatrice Webb Diary 18.02.1907

317 Beatrice Webb Diary 18.02.1907

318 Beatrice to H G Wells, 25.02.1907; in Webb, B & Webb, S; *The Letters of Sidney and   Beatrice Webb*; Vol II; Cambridge; CUP; 1978, p 247

319 Beatrice Webb Diary 17.07.1906

320 Beatrice Webb Diary 28.01.1907

321 Beatrice Webb Diary 10.04.1907

322 Royal Commission on the Poor Laws and the Relief of Distress; Appendix Vol XII; Cd 4983, 1910; Memoranda by individual commissioners; Memorandum by Mrs Sidney Webb; The Medical Services of the Poor Law and the Public Health Departments; pp 305-306

323 Beatrice Webb Diary 08.10.1907

324 Beatrice Webb Diary 29.10.1907

325 Beatrice Webb Diary 29.10.1907

326 'Letters from Medical Officers of Health in reply to a letter from Mrs Webb' - document in LSE Library; Webb Local Government Collection Vol 286

327 LSE Library; Webb Local Government Collection Vol 286

328 Beatrice Webb Diary 12.11.1907

329 Sidney to Beatrice, 13 November 1907, quoted in McBriar, AM; *An Edwardian Mixed Double The Bosanquets versus the Webbs; a study in British Social Policy, 1890 – 1929*; Oxford, Clarendon Press; 1987 p 235

330 Beatrice Webb Diary 12.11.1907

331 LGB Circular 15 March 1886, quoted in Minority Report, Ch.3; Report of the Royal Commission on the Poor Laws and Relief of Distress; Cd 4499 1909

332 Beatrice Webb to Robert Ensor, 0.05.1907; in Webb, B & Webb, S; *The Letters of Sidney and Beatrice Webb*; Vol II; Cambridge; CUP; 1978, p 253

333 John Burns Diary, 1906; British Library Add ms 46325

334 John Burns Diary 13.04.1907; British Library Add ms 46325

335 Beatrice Webb Diary 13.01.1908

336 Beatrice Webb Diary 02.02.1908

337 Beatrice Webb Diary 02.02.1908

338 Beatrice to Mary Playne, 02.02.1908; in *Webb, B & Webb, S; The Letters of Sidney and Beatrice Webb*; Vol II; Cambridge; CUP; 1978; p 280

339 Beveridge, W; *Power and Influence*; London, Hodder and Stoughton, 1953; p 63

340 Beveridge, W; *Power and Influence*; London, Hodder and Stoughton, 1953; p 64

341 Beveridge, W; *Power and Influence*; London, Hodder and Stoughton, 1953; p 64

342 Sidney to Beveridge, 13.02.1908; in Webb, B & Webb, S; *The Letters of Sidney and Beatrice Webb*; Vol II; Cambridge; CUP; 1978, p 282

343 Sidney to Beatrice, 21.02.1908; in Webb, B & Webb, S; *The Letters of Sidney and Beatrice Webb*; Vol II; Cambridge; CUP; 1978, p 284

344 Beatrice to Mary Playne, 22.02.1908; in Webb, B & Webb, S; *The Letters of Sidney and Beatrice Webb*; Vol II; Cambridge; CUP; 1978, p 287

345 Beatrice Webb Diary 11.03.1908

346 Beatrice Webb Diary 11.03.1908

347 W H Beveridge to Annette Beveridge, 12.03.1908; in Beveridge, W; *Power and Influence*; London, Hodder and Stoughton, 1953; p 66

348 The Times; quoted in Jenkins, Roy; *Asquith*; London, Collins, 1964; p 199

349 Quoted in Gilbert, Bentley; *Evolution of National Insurance in Britain*; London, Michael Joseph, 1966; p 248, note 32

350 Asquith to Burns, 08.04.1908, in Burns letters, British Library Add Ms 46282

351 Quoted in Beveridge, W; *Power and Influence*; London, Hodder and Stoughton, 1953; p 68

352 W H Beveridge to Annette Beveridge, 12.03.1908; in Beveridge, W; *Power and Influence*; London, Hodder and Stoughton, 1953; p 68

353 Beatrice Webb Diary 17.07.1906

354 Beatrice Webb Diary 01.10.1906

355 Beatrice Webb Diary 01.10.1906

356 Beatrice Webb Diary 18.01.1907

357 Beatrice Webb Diary 18.01.1907

358 Beatrice Webb Diary 18.04.1907

359 Beatrice Webb Diary 15.05.1907

360 Beatrice Webb Diary 31.07.1907

361 Beatrice Webb Diary 08.10.1907

362 Beatrice Webb Diary 08.10.1907

363 Beatrice Webb Diary 08.10.1907

364 Beatrice Webb Diary 22.10.1907

365 Beatrice Webb Diary 09.12.1907

366 Beatrice Webb Diary 09.12.1907

367 Beatrice Webb Diary 09.12.1907

368 Beatrice Webb Diary 12.12.1907

369 Beatrice Webb Diary 09.12.1907

370 Beatrice Webb Diary 09.12.07

371 Beatrice Webb Diary 13.01.1908

372 Beatrice Webb Diary 30.01.1908

373 Beatrice Webb Diary 18.02.1908

374 Beatrice to Mary Playne, 22.02.1908; in *Webb, B & Webb, S; The Letters of Sidney and Beatrice Webb*; Vol II; Cambridge; CUP; 1978, p 287

375 Circular by Hamilton to Majority Commissioners; 02.06.1908; in McBriar, Alan *An Edwardian Mixed Doubles; The Bosanquets versus the Webbs; a study in British Social Policy, 1890 – 1929*; Oxford, Clarendon Press, 1987

376 Beatrice Webb Diary; 16.10.1908

377 Beatrice Webb Diary 29.10.1908

378 Beatrice Webb Diary 15.12.1908

379 Beatrice Webb Diary 15.12.1908
380 Beatrice Webb Diary 30.01.1908
381 Beatrice Webb Diary 30.01.1908
382 Beatrice Webb Diary 30.01.1908
383 Beatrice Webb Diary 17.02.1908
384 Beatrice Webb Diary 24.03.1908
385 Sidney to Beatrice, 20.04.08; in Webb, B & Webb, S; *The Letters of Sidney and Beatrice Webb*; Vol II; Cambridge; CUP; 1978, p 294
386 Beatrice to Sidney, 02.05.1908; in Webb, B & Webb, S; *The Letters of Sidney and Beatrice Webb*; Vol II; Cambridge; CUP; 1978, p 313
387 Beatrice Webb Diary 15.09.1908
388 Beatrice Webb Diary 15.09.1908
389 Beatrice Webb Diary 02.10.1908
390 Beatrice Webb Diary 02.10.1908
391 Beatrice Webb Diary 15.11.1908
392 Beatrice Webb Diary 15.11.1908
393 Beatrice Webb Diary 17.01.1909
394 Report of the Royal Commission on the Poor Laws and the Relief of Distress; Cd 4499,1909
395 Report of the Royal Commission on the Poor Laws and the Relief of Distress; Cd 4499,1909; Vol II, p 265; (D I 124)
396 Cmd 6527 1944
397 Report of the Royal Commission on the Poor Laws and Relief of Distress; Cd 4499 1909; Minority Report p.686
398 Hamilton to Helen Bosanquet, 03.09.1908; quoted in McBriar, Alan *An Edwardian Mixed Doubles; The Bosanquets versus the Webbs; a study in British Social Policy, 1890 – 1929*; Oxford, Clarendon Press, 1987
399 Report of the Royal Commission on the Poor Laws and the Relief of Distress; Cd 4499,1909; Vol I; Part IV; Ch.10; para 531
400 Report of the Royal Commission on the Poor Laws and the Relief of Distress; Cd 4499,1909; Vol III; Part II; Ch. IV; p 628
401 Report of the Royal Commission on the Poor Laws and the Relief of Distress; Cd 4499,1909; Vol I; Part IV; Ch.8; para 438
402 Jones, Thomas; *Welsh Broth*; London, W Griffiths & Co; 1951; p71
403 Jones, Thomas; *Welsh Broth*; London, W Griffiths & Co; 1951; p72
404 Beatrice Webb Diary, 03.05.1907
405 Ensor, Robert *England 1870-1914*; Oxford, OUP, 1936; p391
406 Cole, M; *Growing up into revolution*; London, Longmans, 1949; p42
407 Beatrice to Mary Playne, 19.03.1907, in Webb, B & Webb, S; *The Letters of Sidney and Beatrice Webb*; Vol II; Cambridge; CUP; 1978; p 250
408 Colegate Diaries 15.01.1906; LSE Library Coll Misc 741/1
409 Colegate Diaries, LSE Library Coll Misc 741/1
410 Beatrice Webb Diary 16.09.1917
411 Colegate Diaries 10.11.1905; LSE Library Coll Misc 741/1
412 Colegate Diaries 24.11.1905; LSE Library Coll Misc 741/1
413 Attlee, C R; *As it Happened*; London, Heinemann, 1954; p 21
414 Attlee, C R; *As it Happened*; London, Heinemann, 1954; p 31-2
415 Attlee, C R; *As it Happened*; London, Heinemann, 1954; p 25
416 LSE Library; Fabian Society Executive Committee Minutes; 22.03.1907
417 Fabian papers; quoted in MacKenzie, Jeanne and MacKenzie, Norman; *The Fabians*; New York, Simon and Schuster, 1977; p 343
418 MacCarthy, Fiona *Eric Gill*; London, Faber and Faber; 1989; p72
419 LSE Library; Fabian Society Executive Committee Minutes 04.01.1907
420 Gill, Eric Letters; London; 1947; quoted in MacKenzie, Jeanne and MacKenzie, Norman; *The Fabians*; New York, Simon and Schuster, 1977; p344
421 LSE Library; Minutes of Fabian meeting, 31.05.1907.
422 LSE Library; Agenda and Minutes for Fabian Society Business Meeting, 11.01.1907
423 Webb, B; *Our Partnership*; ed. Cole, M & Drake, B; London, Longmans, 1948; p 361
424 Sidney to Beatrice, 20.08. 1890; in Webb, B & Webb, S; *The Letters of Sidney and Beatrice Webb*; Vol I; Cambridge; CUP; 1978; ed Mackenzie, N, & Mackenzie, J; p 183
425 Webb, B; *Our Partnership*; ed. Cole, M & Drake, B; London, Longmans,

1948; p 362

426 Wells, Herbert G *This Misery of Boots*; Boston; The Ball Publishing Co; 1908; pp 47,48

427 Colegate Diaries 12.01.1906; LSE Library; Coll Misc 741/1

428 Wells, H G; *The Faults of the Fabian*; London, Fabian Society, 1906; p 10

429 Colegate Diaries 09.02.1906; LSE Library Coll Misc 741/1

430 Colegate Diaries 18.05.1906; LSE Library Coll Misc 741/1

431 Beatrice Webb Diary 01.03.1906

432 Beatrice Webb Diary 15.07.1906

433 Colegate Diaries 15.06.1906; LSE Library Coll Misc 741/1

434 Colegate Diaries 30.07.1906; LSE Library Coll Misc 741/1

435 McBriar, Alan *Fabian Socialism and English Politics, 1884-1918*; Cambridge, Cambridge University Press, 1966; p 322

436 LSE Library; Minutes, Fabian Members Meeting, 07.12.1906

437 Beatrice Webb Diary 15.12.1906

438 Beatrice Webb Diary 15.12.1906

439 Beatrice Webb Diary 15.12.1906

440 Beatrice letter to Mary Playne, 19.03.1907.1907, in Webb, B & Webb, S; *The Letters of Sidney and Beatrice Webb*; Vol II; Cambridge; CUP; 1978; p 250

441 Pease, Edward R; *The History of the Fabian Society*; London, Fabian Society and Allen and Unwin; 1925; p175

442 LSE Library; *Fabian Society, Minutes of meeting. 09.11.1906*

443 Pease, Edward R; *The History of the Fabian Society*; London, Fabian Society and Allen and Unwin; 1925; p176

444 Beatrice letter to Mary Playne, 21.08.1907, in Webb, B & Webb, S; *The Letters of Sidney and Beatrice Webb*; Vol II; Cambridge; CUP; 1978; p 272

445 Beatrice Webb Diary 15.09.1908

446 Beatrice Webb Diary 15.09.1908

447 Beatrice letter to Mary Playne, 09.08, in Webb, B & Webb, S; *The Letters of Sidney and Beatrice Webb*; Vol II; Cambridge; CUP; 1978; p 316

448 Quoted in Brooke, Rupert *The Collected Poems, with a memoir by Edward Marsh;* London, Sidgwick & Jackson, 1918; p. xxx

449 Keynes, John Maynard; *My Early Beliefs,* in Keynes, John Maynard; *Two Memoirs*; London, Rupert Hart-Davis, 1949; p 81

450 Dalton, Hugh; *Call Back Yesterday, Memoirs 1887 – 1931*; London, F Muller, 1953; p52

451 Beatrice letter to Kate Courtney, 18.09.1911, in Webb, B & Webb, S; *The Letters of Sidney and Beatrice Webb*; Vol II; Cambridge; CUP; 1978; p 372

452 Beatrice letter to Kate Courtney, 18.09.1911, in Webb, B & Webb, S; *The Letters of Sidney and Beatrice Webb*; Vol II; Cambridge; CUP; 1978; p 372

453 quoted in Skidelsky, R; John Maynard Keynes: *Hopes Betrayed 1883-1920*; London, Macmillan, 1983

454 Quoted in Hopkinson, D; *Family Inheritance, a life of Eva Hubback*; London, Staples Press, 1954

455 Beatrice Webb Diary 15.09.1908

456 Wells, H G; *Introduction* to *Keeling letters and recollections,* ed ET Townshend; London, Allen and Unwin, 1918, p. ix)

457 Dalton, H; *Call Back Yesterday; Memoirs 1887-1931*; London; F Miller, 1953. p.44

458 Dalton, H; *Call Back Yesterday*; *Memoirs, 1881-1931*; London, F Miller, 1953, p.38

459 Quoted in Brooke, Rupert *The Collected Poems, with a memoir by Edward Marsh;* London, Sidgwick & Jackson, 1918; p. xxx

460 Rupert Brooke to St John Lucas, Good Friday 1907, in Brooke, R; *Letters of Rupert Brooke,* ed Geoffrey Keynes, London, Faber, 1968

461 Rupert Brooke to Francis MacCunn; 11.11.1907; in Brooke, R *Letters of Rupert Brooke,* ed Geoffrey Keynes, London, Faber, 1968

462 Quoted in Brooke, Rupert *The Collected Poems, with a memoir by Edward Marsh;* London, Sidgwick & Jackson, 1918; p. xxix

463 Rupert Brooke to his mother, 03.1908; in Brooke, R; *Letters of Rupert Brooke,* ed; Geoffrey Keynes, London, Faber, 1968

464 Rupert Brooke to Hugh Dalton, 08.04.1908; in Brooke, R *Letters of*

Rupert Brooke, ed Geoffrey Keynes, London, Faber, 1968

465   Virginia Woolf to Clive Bell, 23.01.1911; in *Virginia Woolf, Selected Letters.* Ed JT Banks. London, Vintage, 2008

466   Rupert Brooke to his mother, March 1908; Papers of Rupert Chawner Brooke; Kings College Cambridge; RCB L/6

467   Rupert Brooke to his mother, 12.05.1908; Papers of Rupert Chawner Brooke; Kings College Cambridge; RCB L/6

468   Rupert Brooke to his mother, 12.05.1908; Papers of Rupert Chawner Brooke; Kings College Cambridge; RCB L/6

469   Beatrice Webb Diary 15.09.1908

470   Mackenzie, N & J; *The First Fabians*; London; Quartet Books; 1979; p 347

471   Quoted in Holroyd, M; *Bernard Shaw*; London, Penguin, 1989, Vol II, p 193

472   Beatrice Webb Diary 15.09.1908

473   Rupert Brooke to Hugh Dalton, 24.08.1908; in *Letters of Rupert Brooke*, ed Geoffrey Keynes; London, Faber, 1968, p141

474   Webb, B; *Our Partnership*; London, Longmans, 1948; p 415 n

475   LSE Library Fabian Society G/13

476   Colegate Diary, 15.08.1908; LSE Library; LSE Coll Misc 741/1

477   Colegate Diary, 24.08.1908; LSE Library; LSE Coll Misc 741/1

478   Keeling, Ben *Letters and recollections,* edited by ET; with an introduction by H G Wells; London, George Allen and Unwin, 1918; p 32

479   Keeling, Ben *Letters and recollections,* edited by ET; with an introduction by H G Wells; London, George Allen and Unwin, 1918; p 31

480   Beatrice Webb Diary 15.09.1908

481   Beatrice Webb Diary 19.05.1908

482   MacKenzie, N & J; *The Life of H G Wells*; London, Hogarth Press, 1987; p226

483   Wells, H G; *H G Wells in Love; postscript to an experiment in autobiography*; edited by G P Wells; London; Faber & Faber; 1984; p 71

484   MacKenzie, N & J; *The Life of H G Wells*; London, Hogarth Press, 1987; p

176

485   Quoted in introduction by Margaret Drabble to 2005 Penguin edition of *Ann Veronica*

486   Wells, H G; *H G Wells in Love; postscript to an experiment in autobiography*; edited by G P Wells; London; Faber & Faber; 1984; p 75

487   Wells, H G; *H G Wells in Love; postscript to an experiment in autobiography*; edited by G P Wells; London; Faber & Faber; 1984; p 75

488   Beatrice Webb Diary 15.09.1908

489   Wells, H G; *H G Wells in Love; postscript to an experiment in autobiography*; edited by G P Wells; London; Faber & Faber; 1984; p 78

490   Arthur Colegate Diary; 26.12.1908; LSE Library; Colegate Diaries; LSE Coll Misc 741/1

491   Arthur Colegate Diary; 03.03.1909; LSE Library; Colegate Diaries; LSE Coll Misc 741/1

492   Arthur Colegate Diary; 27.03.1909; LSE Library; Colegate Diaries; LSE Coll Misc 741/1

493   Wells, H G; *H G Wells in Love; postscript to an experiment in autobiography*; edited by G P Wells; London; Faber & Faber; 1984; p 77

494   Arthur Colegate Diary; 01.04.1909; Colegate Diaries; LSE Library LSE Coll Misc 741/1

495   Arthur Colegate Diary; 04.04.1909; Colegate Diaries; LSE Library; LSE Coll Misc 741/1

496   Arthur Colegate Diary; 04.04.1909; Colegate Diaries; LSE Library; LSE Coll Misc 741/1

497   Wells, H G; *H G Wells in Love; postscript to an experiment in autobiography*; edited by G P Wells; London; Faber & Faber; 1984; p 79

498   Sinclair, K; *William Pember Reeves New Zealand Fabian*; Oxford, Clarendon Press, 1965; p317

499   Arthur Colegate Diary; 05.04.1909; Colegate Diaries; LSE Library LSE Coll Misc 741/1

500   Wells, H G; *H G Wells in Love; postscript to an experiment in autobiography*; edited by G P Wells; London; Faber & Faber; 1984; p 80

501   MacKenzie, N & J; *The Life of H G*

Wells; London, Hogarth Press, 1987; p 252

502 Arthur Colegate Diary; 10.05.1909; Colegate Diaries; LSE Library; LSE Coll Misc 741/1

503 Beatrice Webb Diary 27.09.1909

504 Beatrice Webb Diary 22.08.1909

505 HG Wells to Beatrice, 08.09.1909, LSE Library; Passfield 2/4/D

506 Shaw to Beatrice, 30.09.1909; in Michalos, Alex C & Poff, Deborah C; eds; *Bernard Shaw and the Webbs*; Toronto, University of Toronto Press, 2002; p 95

507 Beatrice to Amber Blanco White, 11.09.1909, in Webb, B & Webb, S; *The Letters of Sidney and Beatrice Webb*; Vol II; Cambridge; CUP; 1978; p 335

508 Beatrice to Amber Blanco White, 11.09.1909, in Webb, B & Webb, S; *The Letters of Sidney and Beatrice Web*b; Vol II; Cambridge; CUP; 1978; p 335

509 Beatrice Webb Diary 22.08.1909

510 Beatrice Webb Diary 22.08.1909

511 Beatrice Webb Diary Early August 1909

512 Beatrice Webb Diary 27.12.1909

513 Colegate Diary; 15.05.1909; LSE Library LSE Coll Misc 741/1

514 Colegate Diary; 01.06.1909; LSE Library LSE Coll Misc 741/1

515 Beatrice Webb Diary 27.12.1909

516 Beatrice Webb Diary 20.03.1910

517 Quoted in Wells, Herbert G; *Experiments in Autobiography; Vol II*; London, Gollancz; 1937; p 471

518 Beatrice Webb Diary 04.10.1909

519 Leo Amery Diary; 22.01.1911; Amery, LS; *The Leo Amery Diaries*; Ed Barnes & Nicholson; Vol 1 1896-1929; London, Hutchinson, 1980

520 Wells, Herbert G; *The New Machiavelli; London*, Penguin, 2005; pp167-168

521 Wells, Herbert G; *The New Machiavelli; London*, Penguin, 2005; p 364

522 Wells, Herbert G; *The New Machiavelli; London*, Penguin, 2005 p 366

523 Wells, Herbert G; *The New Machiavelli; London*, Penguin, 2005 p 368

524 MacKenzie, N & J; *The Life of H G*

525 Beatrice to H G Wells, 24.02.1909; in Webb, B & Webb, S; *The Letters of Sidney and Beatrice Webb*; Vol II; Cambridge; CUP; 1978; p 325

526 Beatrice to George McCleary, 06.04.1909; LSE Library COLL MISC 979 Correspondence McCleary

527 Beatrice Webb Diary 25.04.1909

528 *The Crusade*, February 1910, Vol I, No 1

529 Beatrice Webb Diary 15.05.1909

530 Keeling, B; *Letters and Recollections*; edited by ET; introduction by H G Wells; London, Allen and Unwin, 1918; p 49

531 Colegate Diary, 26.05.1909 LSE Library; LSE Coll Misc 741/1

532 Colegate Diary, 28.05.1909; LSE Library; LSE Coll Misc 741/1

533 Beatrice Webb Diary 27.09.1909

534 Attlee, C R; *As it Happened*; London; Heinemann; 1954; p 27

535 Colegate Diary, 25.05.1909; LSE Library; LSE Coll Misc 741/1

536 Hamilton, Mary Agnes (Mollie); *Remembering my good friends*; London, Jonathan Cape, 1944; p 256

537 Hamilton, M A; *Sidney and Beatrice Webb*; London, Sampson, Low, Marston & Co Ltd, 1933; p 200

538 Quoted in Harris, K; *Attlee*; London, Weidenfeld & Nicolson, 1982; p 29

539 Beatrice Webb Diary 18.06.1909

540 Hassall, C; *Rupert Brooke*; London, Faber, 1964; p 193

541 Rupert Brooke to Jacques Raverat, April 1909; in *Letters of Rupert Brooke*, ed Geoffrey Keynes; London, Faber, 1968, p 163

542 Rupert Brooke to Noel Olivier, 26.03.1909; in Harris, Pippa, editor; *Song of Love: The letters of Rupert Brooke and Noel Olivier, 1909-1915*; London, Bloomsbury, 1991; p 4

543 Skidelsky, R; John Maynard Keynes: *Hopes Betrayed 1883-1920*; London, Macmillan, 1983, p.234

544 Rupert Brooke to Hugh Dalton, 16.04.1909; in *Letters of Rupert Brooke*, ed Geoffrey Keynes; London, Faber, 1968, p 167

545 Rupert Brooke to Ka Cox, 04.09.1909;

in *Letters of Rupert Brooke,* ed Geoffrey
Keynes; London, Faber, 1968, p 177

546   Rupert Brooke to Hugh Dalton,
       08.09.1909; in *Letters of Rupert Brooke*,
       ed Geoffrey Keynes; London, Faber,
       1968, p 179

547   Rupert Brooke to Erica Cotterill,
       09.01.1910; in Brooke, R; *Letters of
       Rupert Brooke* ed. Keynes, G; London,
       Faber, 1968; p 206

548   Dalton, H; *Call Back Yesterday,
       Memoirs 1887 – 1931*; London, F
       Muller, 1953, p 72

549   LSE Library; Fabian Summer School
       Log Book 1907-1912; Fabian Society
       /G/13

550   Beatrice to Georgina Meinertzhagen,
       08.08.1909; in Webb, B & Webb, S;
       The Letters of Sidney and Beatrice Webb;
       Vol II; Cambridge; CUP; 1978, p 333

551   Beatrice to Georgina Meinertzhagen,
       08.08.1909; in Webb, B & Webb, S;
       The Letters of Sidney and Beatrice Webb;
       Vol II; Cambridge; CUP; 1978, p 332

552   Beatrice Webb Diary 03.10.1909

553   Keeling to A Y Campbell, 19.08.1909,
       in Keeling, Ben; *Letters and recol-
       lections;* edited by ET; with an
       introduction by H G Wells; London,
       George Allen and Unwin, 1918

554   Letter to EMS (? Eva Spielman?);
       08.03.1910; in Keeling, Ben; *Letters
       and recollections;* edited by ET; with an
       introduction by H G Wells; London,
       George Allen and Unwin, 1918; p 58

555   Letter, Keeling to Mrs Townshend,
       06.09.1909, in Keeling, Ben; *Letters
       and recollections;* edited by ET; with an
       introduction by H G Wells; London,
       George Allen and Unwin, 1918; p 54

556   Keeling, Ben; *Letters and recollections;*
       edited by ET; with an introduction by
       H G Wells; London, George Allen and
       Unwin, 1918; p 57

557   Keeling, Ben; *Letters and recollections;*
       edited by ET; with an introduction by
       H G Wells; London, George Allen and
       Unwin, 1918; p 57

558   Letter, Keeling to Mrs Townshend,
       25.03.1912; in Keeling, Ben; *Letters
       and recollections;* edited by ET; with an
       introduction by H G Wells; London,
       George Allen and Unwin, 1918; p110

559   Letter 04.01.1912 in Keeling, Ben;

Letters and recollections; edited by ET;
with an introduction by H G Wells;
London, George Allen and Unwin,
1918; p 54

560   Colegate diary; note copied in 8 Dec
       1916 from a note written on 11 Jan
       1910; LSE Library; LSE Coll Misc
       741/1

561   Beatrice Webb Diary 08.07.1910

562   Beatrice to Mary Playne, 26.06.1910;
       LSE Library; PASSFIELD/2/4/D

563   Beatrice to Betty Balfour, 08.1910;
       PASSFIELD/2/4/D

564   Beatrice Webb Diary 30.12.1910

565   Beatrice Webb Diary 14.11.1909

566   Letter, Beatrice to Sidney, late
       November 1909; in Webb, B & Webb,
       S; *The Letters of Sidney and Beatrice
       Webb;* Vol II; Cambridge; CUP; 1978,
       p 338

567   Beatrice Webb Diary 31.12.1909

568   Beatrice Webb Diary 31.12.1909

569   Beatrice Webb Diary 25.02.1910

570   Letter, Bill Hubback to Eva Spielman,
       1910, quoted in Hopkinson, D; *Family
       Inheritance, a life of Eva Hubback*;
       London, Staples Press, 1954; p55

571   Beatrice Webb Diary 19.05.1910

572   Beatrice Webb Diary 27.05.1910

573   Hansard, 08.04.1910, Col 846

574   JR MacDonald to Lansbury,
       05.04.1910

575   London, TN Foulis, 1912

576   *New Age*, 14 April 1910

577   *New Age*, 14 April 1910

578   *Crusade,* July 1910, Vol I No 6

579   Beatrice Webb Diary 24.05.1910

580   Crusade, July 1910, Vol I No 6

581   *Crusade*, September 1910, Vol I No 8

582   *Crusade*, October 1910, Vol I no 9

583   Brooke to Dudley Ward 3 July 1910;
       in Brooke, R; *The Letters of Rupert
       Brooke;* ed Keynes, G; London, Faber,
       1968, p 243

584   Rupert Brooke to Jacques Raverat,
       July 1910; in Brooke, R; *The Letters of
       Rupert Brooke;* ed Keynes, G; London,
       Faber, 1968, p 243

585   Brooke to Dalton, 5 July 1910; in
       Brooke, R; *The Letters of Rupert Brooke*;
       ed Keynes, G; London, Faber, 1968; p
       247

586   Rupert Brooke to Erica Cotterill, July
       1910; in Brooke, R; *The Letters of*

Rupert Brooke; ed Keynes, G; London, Faber, 1968, p.252

587 *Crusade*, April 1910, Vol I, No 3

588 Beatrice Webb Diary 19.08.1910

589 LSE Library; Fabian Summer School Visitors Book; Fabian Society/G/9

590 Rupert Brooke to Ka Cox, 05.10.1910; in Brooke, R; *The Letters of Rupert Brooke;* ed Keynes, G; London, Faber, 1968, p.255

591 Ellis, E L; TJ, *A life of Dr Thomas Jones,* C H; Cardiff, 1992; p 135

592 Ernest Simon; letter to his mother, early 1910; in Stocks, Mary *Ernest Simon of Manchester*; Manchester University Press, 1963; p 24

593 Emily Simon to Ernest Simon, quoted in Stocks, Mary *Ernest Simon of Manchester*; Manchester University Press, 1963; p 25

594 Ernest Simon; letter to his mother, January 1911; in Stocks, Mary *Ernest Simon of Manchester*; Manchester University Press, 1963; p 26

595 Ernest Simon; letter to his mother, January 1911; in Stocks, Mary *Ernest Simon of Manchester*; Manchester University Press, 1963; p 27

596 Beatrice Webb Diary 04.09.1910

597 Sidney to Arthur Greenwood, 30.08.1910; ; Greenwood Papers, Bodleian Library, MS ENG C 6248

598 Sidney to Governors, Huddersfield Technical Institute, 31.08.1910, 30.08.1910; ; Greenwood Papers, Bodleian Library, MS ENG C 6248

599 *The Crusade*, September 1910, Vol I No 8

600 *Crusade*, September 1910, Vol I no 8

601 *The Crusade*, September 1910, Vol I No 8

602 LSE Library; Fabian Summer School Log Book, 1907-1912, file G/13

603 *The Crusade*, September 1910, Vol I No 8

604 Rupert Brooke to Ka Cox,05.09.1910, in Keynes, G, ed; The Letters of Rupert Brooke; London, Faber, 1968, p255

605 Rupert Brooke to Ka Cox,05.09.1910, in Keynes, G, ed; *The Letters of Rupert Brooke*; London, Faber, 1968, p255

606 Dalton, H; *Call Back Yesterday; memoirs 1887-1931*; London, F Muller, 1953, pp 248-9

607 Beatrice Webb Diary 04.09.1910

608 Beatrice Webb Diary 09.10.10

609 Beatrice Webb Diary 09.10.1910

610 Sidney to Beatrice 10.10.1910; in Webb, B & Webb, S; *The Letters of Sidney and Beatrice Webb*; Vol II; Cambridge; CUP; 1978; p 349

611 Beatrice Webb Diary October 10/11.10.1910 – but refers to October 12

612 Sidney to Beatrice; 18.10.1910; in Webb, B & Webb, S; *The Letters of Sidney and Beatrice Webb*; Vol II; Cambridge; CUP; 1978; p 352

613 Beatrice Webb Diary 23.10.1910

614 Beatrice Webb Diary 05.11.1910

615 Beatrice Webb Diary 05.11.1910

616 Sidney to Beatrice, 28.11.1910; in Webb, B & Webb, S; *The Letters of Sidney and Beatrice Webb*; Vol II; Cambridge; CUP; 1978; p.361

617 Sidney to Beatrice, 28.11.1910; in Webb, B & Webb, S; *The Letters of Sidney and Beatrice Webb*; Vol II; Cambridge; CUP; 1978; p.361

618 Beatrice Webb Diary 10.12.1910

619 Masterman, Lucy; *C F G Masterman, a biography*; London, Nicholson & Watson; 1939; p 104

620 Ensor, Robert *England 1870-1914*; Oxford, OUP, 1936; p 517

621 Sidney to Beatrice, 06.1907; in Webb, B & Webb, S; *The Letters of Sidney and Beatrice Webb;* Vol II; Cambridge; CUP; 1978; p 259

622 Beatrice Webb Diary 08.10.1907.

623 Beatrice Webb Diary 30.10.1907

624 Beatrice to John Burns, 11.05.1907, in Webb, B & Webb, S; *The Letters of Sidney and Beatrice Webb*; Vol II; Cambridge; CUP; 1978; p 254

625 Beatrice Webb Diary 04.1908

626 Beatrice Webb Diary 19.05.1908

627 John Burns Diary January 1910, Appointments Diary; British Library Add ms 46332

628 Beatrice Webb Diary 08.01.1910

629 Beatrice to Sidney, January 1910; in Webb, B & Webb, S; *The Letters of Sidney and Beatrice Webb;* Vol II; Cambridge; CUP; 1978; p 342

630 Provis to Burns, 22.01.10, in Burns Letters 1909-1911, British Library Add Ms 46301

631 Charles Masterman to Herbert Samuel, 06.07.1909; quoted in Brown, Kenneth D; *John Burns*; London, Royal Historical Society, 1977, p145

632 Masterman, Lucy; *C F G Masterman, a biography*; London, Nicholson & Watson; 1939

633 John Burns Diary 16.02.1910, Appointments Diary; British Library Add ms 46332

634 John Burns Diary, 27.10.1906; British Library Add Ms 46324

635 Burns speech at Carshalton, Times 17.05.1910, quoted in Brown, Kenneth D; *John Burns*; London, Royal Historical Society, 1977, p147

636 Burns to Wells, 16.05.1910, Burns Papers, BL Ms Add 46301

637 Thane, P; *Old Age in English History*; Oxford, OUP, 2000

638 Quoted in Barnett, Henrietta; *Canon Barnett, His life, work and friends*; London, John Murray,1918; p 675

639 Beatrice Webb Diary 27.04.1907

640 Braithwaite, William J; *Lloyd George's Ambulance Wagon*; ed H N Banbury; Bath,1957; p 71

641 Beatrice Webb Diary 16.10.1908

642 Beatrice Webb Diary 16.10.1908

643 Workmen's insurance systems in Germany; Report of Delegation; December 1908; TNA CAB 37/96 no 169

644 Masterman, Lucy; *C F G Masterman, a biography*; London, Nicholson & Watson; 1939; p117

645 Beatrice Webb Diary 15.11.1908

646 National Archives TNA CAB 37/99 no 69, 19.04.1909

647 Braithwaite, William J; *Lloyd George's Ambulance Wagon*; ed H N Banbury;Bath,1957; p 72

648 Frances Stevenson's diary,14 February 1915; in Stevenson, F; Lloyd George: A Diary, edited by A J P Taylor. London, Hutchinson.1971

649 Beatrice Webb Diary 18.06.1909

650 Beatrice Webb Diary 18.06.1909

651 Beatrice Webb Diary 22.06.1909

652 Beatrice Webb Diary 22.06.1909

653 Beatrice Webb Diary 10.12.1910

654 Braithwaite, William J; *Lloyd George's Ambulance Wagon*; ed H N Banbury;Bath,1957; p 83

655 Braithwaite, William J; *Lloyd George's Ambulance Wagon*; ed H N Banbury;Bath,1957; p 83

656 Braithwaite Diary, LSE, 03.01.1910

657 Beatrice Webb Diary January 1911

658 Braithwaite, William J; *Lloyd George's Ambulance Wagon*; ed H N Banbury; Bath,1957; p 92

659 Braithwaite, William J; *Lloyd George's Ambulance Wagon*; ed H N Banbury; Bath,1957; p 116

660 Beatrice Webb Diary 06.03.1911

661 John Burns Diary 02.04.1911 British Library Add ms 46323

662 John Burns Diary 03.04.1911 British Library Add ms 46323

663 Braithwaite, William J; *Lloyd George's Ambulance Wagon*; ed H N Banbury; Bath,1957; p 140

664 John Burns Diary 04.05.1911 British Library Add ms 46323

665 Beatrice Webb Diary 26.05.1911

666 Beatrice Webb Diary 26.05.1911

667 Beatrice Webb Diary 13.05.1911

668 Beatrice Webb Diary 03.06.1911

669 Beatrice Webb Diary 03.06.1911

670 Letter, Clifford Sharp to Beatrice Webb, 28.07.1911; Passfield 2/4/E

671 Beatrice Webb Diary 26.05.1911

672 John Burns Diary 05.07.1911 British Library Add ms 46323

673 Braithwaite, William J; *Lloyd George's Ambulance Wagon*; ed H N Banbury; Bath,1957; p 191

674 Braithwaite, William J; *Lloyd George's Ambulance Wagon*; ed H N Banbury;Bath,1957; p 192

675 Letter, Clifford Sharp to Beatrice Webb, 28.07.1911; LSE Library ;Passfield 2/4/E

676 Braithwaite, William J; *Lloyd George's Ambulance Wagon*; ed H N Banbury; Bath,1957; p 195

677 Letter, Clifford Sharp to Beatrice Webb, 28.10.1911; LSE Library; Passfield 2/4/E

678 Letter, Clifford Sharp to Beatrice Webb, 28.10.1911; LSE Library; Passfield 2/4/E

679 MacDonald Diary, 22.10.1911; quoted in Marquand, David; *Ramsay MacDonald*; London, Richard Cohen Books, 1997; p142

680 Beatrice Webb Diary, 25.10.1911

681   *The Crusade*; March 1912; Vol III no 3;
      p 43

682   Beatrice Webb Diary, November 1911

683   *The Crusade*; March 1912; Vol III no 3;
      p 44

684   Letter, Clifford Sharp to Beatrice
      Webb, 29.11.1911; LSE Library;
      Passfield 2/4/E

685   Letter, Clifford Sharp to Beatrice
      Webb, 29.11.1911; LSE Library;
      Passfield 2/4/E

686   Letter, Clifford Sharp to Beatrice
      Webb, 24.02.1912; LSE Library;
      Passfield 2/4/E

687   Harris, Kenneth; *Attlee*; London,
      Weidenfeld and Nicolson, 1982; p 31

688   Beatrice Webb Diary 26.11.1911

689   Beatrice Webb Diary 28.01.1912

690   Beatrice Webb Diary 16-25.04.1912

691   Letter, Clifford Sharp to Beatrice
      Webb, 10.04.1912; LSE Library;
      Passfield 2/4/E

692   Letter, Beatrice to Clifford Sharp,
      07.04.1912 in Webb, B & Webb, S;
      The Letters of Sidney and Beatrice Webb;
      Vol II; Cambridge; CUP; 1978; p 389

PART THREE:
SOCIAL DEMOCRACY: 'A POOR THING BUT OUR OWN': 1912 - 1931

Chapter Eight: Peace and war 1912-1918

A NEW ENGLAND

Sidney and Beatrice came back to England after their world tour in May 1912. Beatrice, exhausted, wrote nothing in her diary until the autumn. The Fabians organised a 'welcome back' dinner and soirée (with a small orchestra and dancing), for them at the Holborn Restaurant, on 20 May, after the AGM of the National Campaign for the Prevention of Destitution, which was being held nearby that same afternoon. Tickets were six shillings for dinner and soirée, or half a crown for just the soirée. After the dinner the Webbs retreated to Sussex, staying in Madehurst Vicarage, near Arundel, until autumn, only occasionally travelling to London.

They had been away a year. The political landscape had been transformed. The National Insurance Act was law. The struggle between Lords and Commons was over. Balfour had been replaced as Conservative leader by Bonar Law – a Canadian-born Glasgow businessman. The women's suffrage movement, supported by many socialists, was becoming more militant. In April Asquith had introduced the third Irish Home Rule Bill; conflict in Ireland loomed. And there were intractable industrial disputes.

Later, Beatrice looked back on those last years of peace:

Any foreign observers would have reported English society in a state of dissolution, probably they did so. The Suffragettes were burning down churches and mansions, the Trade Unions were threatening our vital public service with paralysis, the Ulsterites were already armed and had actually established a rebel 'Provisional Government', the Nationalists were hurriedly drilling a rival military force.[1]

In a similar vein, a generation later, the American writer George Dangerfield argued that

...fires long smoldering in the English spirit suddenly flared up, so that by the end of 1913 Liberal England was reduced to ashes. From these ashes, a new England seems to have emerged.[2]

Of the three issues, it was the industrial situation which was closest to the Webbs' concerns. Between 1911 and 1914, 70 million working days were lost through strikes. Fourteen major disputes accounted for 51 million working days. One dispute – the Cambrian Combine coal strike in South Wales – lasted from September 1910 to August 1911. The rest – in transport (railways, shipping, docks, carters, and cabdrivers), textiles, coal, and construction – began while the Webbs were away.

One cause of the strike wave was falling real wages; another was the changing climate of ideas. Trade unionists were influenced by ideas of workers' control – French syndicalist ideas, and American concepts of 'one big union' and industrial unionism.

Syndicalism was strongest in the South Wales coalfield. In 1912 the South Wales Miners' Unofficial Reform Committee published *The Miners' Next Step*, written by, among others, Noah Ablett – checkweighman at Maerdy colliery, member of the South Wales Miners' Executive Committee. This argued, not for nationalisation, but that every industry should be

> *...thoroughly organised, in the first place, to fight, to gain control of, and then to administer, that industry.* [3]

To the Unofficial Reform Committee, this was industrial democracy. It was a very different version of industrial democracy from that of the Webbs.

The gulf between mainstream Fabian politics and the weekly *New Age* magazine had widened. The magazine, and its editors Alfred Orage and Arthur Penty, were now associated with the emerging Guild Socialist movement. Like Belloc and G K Chesterton, they were hostile to state-based structures and solutions.

Sidney and Beatrice sensed the changed atmosphere. Speaking that May, Sidney said

> *The country to which I return strikes me, in many ways, as intellectually a new England. The common ideas about the organisation and control of industry have changed.* [4]

While abroad they had reviewed their priorities. The Poor Law campaign had not resulted in legislation. For Sidney and Beatrice, the lesson was clear: the time for permeation of other, non-socialist parties was over. They were not alone in reaching that conclusion.

In 1907 H G Wells, who had wanted the Fabian Society to transform itself into a campaigning, political mass movement, had been defeated by the Old Gang – by GBS and the Webbs. But the Poor Law campaign – a Fabian initiative, if constitutionally separate – was exactly the kind of activity for which Wells had called. He certainly thought so, telling Beatrice in 1909 that the Minority Report was

...quite after my own heart...[5]

Wells endorsed the National Committee.

After Wells' defeat in 1907, and his subsequent resignation from the Fabian Society, the debate within the Fabians over the merits of permeation as a political strategy, and the call for a closer relationship between the Society and other Labour and Socialist groupings had not disappeared. Candidates calling for an end to permeation, and for closer links with Labour, were elected to the Executive Committee. Henry Schloesser was elected in 1910; Clifford Allen, Mostyn Lloyd, Harry Snell and Marion Phillips in 1912. For the first time, Beatrice stood for, and was elected to, the Executive Committee in 1912.

The Webbs now aligned themselves unambiguously with Labour. Between 1912 and 1914 they concentrated on three projects: cooperation between the Fabian Society and the Independent Labour Party (ILP); establishing a new weekly journal for the left; and reorganizing the Fabian Society.

The London School of Economics made few demands on them; in October 1912 Beatrice wrote that it

...rolls on majestically from success to success. Sidney has not even bothered to become chairman again, realizing that the School now has a life of its own. [6]

Sidney did, however, chair the committee which in 1913 appointed Clement Attlee as an LSE lecturer on social services. He was chosen over Hugh Dalton (already a postgraduate at the School).

As well as the Fabian Executive, Beatrice now also joined the Independent Labour Party (ILP). In 1911 the Fabians and the ILP had formed a joint campaign committee; Beatrice became a member in summer 1912. In July she travelled from Sussex for her first meeting; in 1913 she attended every meeting.

Through autumn and winter 1912/13, the joint committee ran a *War on Poverty* campaign, highlighting the Webbs' long-standing call for a National Minimum. This was launched in October at a London conference, followed by an evening demonstration at the Albert Hall. The Woolwich Pioneer Choir sang Edward Carpenter's *England Arise* and specially adapted hymns, including *Onward Friends of Freedom*, based on *Onward Christian Soldiers*. Ramsay MacDonald took the chair; speakers included Lansbury, GBS, and Beatrice. That autumn, *War on Poverty* conferences took place across the country. Both Webbs spoke at them; they were joined by three successive Labour leaders – MacDonald, Lansbury and Attlee.

In December, Beatrice asked the leadership of the Labour MPs to support the *War on Poverty*. She was not impressed:

If we could see into MacDonald's mind I don't believe it differs materially from John Burns's mentality. But the Labour Party exists, and we have to work with it. 'A poor thing but our own.'[7]

She noted *a certain bitter hostility* on the part of Philip Snowden, who she thought *soured.*[8]

Their friendships and holidays continued; they often saw the surviving Potter sisters, and sometimes Graham Wallas, Arthur Balfour and Sidney Olivier. At Christmas 1912 they stayed at Weymouth with Mostyn Lloyd and his wife, walking ten to fifteen miles every day:

Long days in the sea air, even if it be in wind and rain, too tired to think and not too tired to sleep, is the best of recreations.[9]

The following Christmas was spent with GBS:

A fortnight's walking and motoring tour in Cornwall and Devon, with GBS... a delightful and luxurious holiday, with knapsack and mackintosh being transformed by the advent of GBS, into walking over twelve or thirteen miles of picked country with the motor car in attendance to take us, when tired, to the most expensive hotel in the neighbourhood.[10]

Relations with Ministers had not recovered

We have dined twice with Haldane since we returned from India, and Herbert Samuel has dined here once – otherwise we have not even said 'good-day' to a Liberal Minister.[11]

An opportunity occurred in spring 1914. The Webbs went to Covent Garden to see the first London production of *Parsifal*. In the interval they met Lloyd George and Herbert Samuel, with whom they found themselves discussing

...the excessive sickness of married women under the Insurance Act owing to the humorously ignorant omission by the government actuaries of the 'risk' of pregnancy... Lloyd George appealed to us to help him to get out of the financial hole.[12]

This led to another breakfast at 11 Downing Street, (where they were joined by Edwin Montagu, the Financial Secretary, and Christopher Addison – a surgeon, since 1910 a Liberal MP) and then a Grosvenor Road dinner with Lloyd George, enabling him to meet two leading women trade unionists, Margaret Bondfield and Mary Macarthur,

Sidney and Beatrice moved between Grosvenor Road and the Fabian offices and LSE at Aldwych. New organisations – the Fabian Research Department, and the *New Statesman* – established their own offices nearby. This small area of London became the centre of their lives.

A NEW POLITICAL WEEKLY

The idea of starting a weekly political journal had occurred to Sidney and Beatrice during their year away. In March 1912, Sidney had written to Ernest Simon, saying

We have almost made up our minds, when we get home, to try to get going a really good weekly newspaper, with a decent 'tone' so as to provide something better than the NEW AGE, which seems to get more and more odious in spirit. But this will need money as well as work. [13]

At Madehurst, the Webbs planned their new venture:

…there seems to be a clear call to leadership in the labour and socialist movement to which we feel we must respond. For that purpose we are starting a new weekly next spring, and the planning out of this organ is largely devolving on Sidney. [14]

GBS, while agreeing to put up money, thought they were too old:

Unless you can find a team of young lions (coaching them to some extent at a weekly lunch or dinner) and give them their heads, the job cannot be done. Sidney is wonderfully young – hardly in full flower even yet – but he hasn't the smallest idea of making himself fascinating; and nothing short of that will delight the sixpenny public. [15]

Beatrice found her lions, recruiting them from the network she and Sidney had established during the Poor Law campaign. Clifford Sharp, Fabian editor of *The Crusade*, became the founding editor of the *New Statesman*. The NCPD was wound down; the last edition of *The Crusade* appeared in February 1913. Sharp enjoyed considerable editorial independence – though weekly *New Statesman* lunches at Grosvenor Road were started.

Sharp was responsible for editorial appointments. The Literary Editor was Jack Squire: poet and parodist, Squire had been the first secretary of the Cambridge Fabians, and had worked on the *New Age*. Ben Keeling left the civil service, and wrote on industrial affairs, later becoming Assistant Editor.

At the same time as hiring staff, the Webbs had to raise the start-up capital for the paper. After the end of the Poor Law campaign, Bill Hubback – the Cambridge Fabian who had organised Sidney's Cardiff meeting – accepted a job teaching Greek at Manchester University. He and Eva Spielman – who was both a women's suffrage campaigner and a Cambridge Fabian – were married in August 1911. They moved to Didsbury in Manchester. Another Cambridge friend of Eva's was a cousin of Ernest Simon; and so Eva got to know the Simon family.

Shena Potter (no relation to Beatrice) had also been at Newnham with Eva Hubback. After Cambridge Shena went to London, and studied as a postgraduate at LSE. Shena went to spend a weekend with Bill and Eva in Manchester – and was introduced to Ernest Simon at a dinner party. They were married in November 1912. Ernest Simon's biographer, Mary Stocks, wrote that he learned from the Webbs *all they had to teach*

> *...and in the sphere of marital relations they provided him with an inspiring working model.* [16]

In particular, according to Stocks, Ernest Simon observed, then followed, the Webbs' technique of *purposeful entertaining* – inviting to their home guests who would be cross examined about their knowledge and opinions. The catering, however, was better than at Grosvenor Road:

> *Ernest enjoyed good food and was delighted when guests shared his enjoyment. Mrs Webb did not enjoy good food, and took a somewhat dim view of those who did.* [17]

In his letter from India, Sidney had warned Ernest that he would be asked to put up money for the new publication. He became one of four initial main sponsors, each of whom contributed £1000; the others were GBS; Henry Harben (Fabian Executive member; largest shareholder in Prudential Assurance); and Edward Whitley (research chemist; supporter of the Poor Law campaign). A further £1000 in small contributions made up the total launch capital of £5000.

Shaw worried about ownership:

> *You ought to have the power to pay off or to buy out any funders who may become deadheads, or may become party men or the like.*[18]

The next task was marketing: at Christmas 1912, Beatrice noted

> *During the next three months we have to get, by circularization, a large number of postal subscribers...* [19]

Both Webbs worked their contacts, beginning with the membership records of the Fabian Society and the Poor Law campaign, from which they established

...a card catalogue of 20,000 possible subscribers to the paper. To all the most promising of these we send out personal, to the less promising manifolded, letters from me: GBS and Sidney are appealing to the Fabians who are not members of the National Committee.[20]

They needed a 5000-weekly circulation. Their former colleague Arthur Colegate knew the publishers of the Liberal weekly *The Nation*; they had their own estimates of the selling power of GBS, Squire and the Webbs. They thought the *New Statesman* would fail.

The Webbs persisted. Sidney asked GBS

Is there any list of Shaw-worshippers?... You might, at any rate, lend us your own address book, to send an impersonal *circular to.*[21]

By February Sidney had his list of Shaw worshippers:

We shall probably have (after dropping duplicates) several thousands (possibly 5000 or more) of people interested in the drama, and largely in Shaw.

Now it is rather a pity, with such a list, which will cost £25 to circularise, not to do it as effectively as possible. It seems a shame to send them merely a letter signed by Sidney Webb. [22]

The first issue was planned for 12 April 1913. Gradually, the marketing effort succeeded. By mid-February, there were more than 600 advance subscriptions; by the end of February, 850. Beatrice wrote to GBS

Your circular is bringing in a rich yield from the Fabians and my invitations to three afternoon parties have turned out excellently – I had 17 new subscribers this morning – and from first rate people. [23]

Just before the launch Beatrice wrote that they had finished promoting; and

...we start with 2,300 postal subscribers, a notable result.[24]

The paper quickly established a reputation. Keeling's 'Blue Book' supplements summarized government publications; in autumn 1913 he visited the Balkans and sent back a series of articles.

Squire published poems by Rupert Brooke, Belloc, Edward Thomas, and W B Yeats. He also published his own parodies; sometimes readers could not tell which was original poem, which parody. Sidney reassured Ernest Simon that the paper was not becoming too literary. Dr Saleeby the eugenicist covered science, signing himself 'Lens'.

Relations between GBS and Sharp were uneasy. Sharp wanted the new paper to have a consistent tone, and therefore insisted that all articles would be unsigned.

But readers had subscribed on the basis that Shaw would write regularly. Matters came to a head in July 1913; Beatrice wrote

Sharp has now decided that if Shaw insists on these terms we are better without him. Meanwhile, persons who subscribed for their weekly portion of Shaw are angry and say they were got to subscribe on false pretences. The New Statesman is in fact the one weekly in which Shaw's name never appears, and it is Shaw's name which draws, not his mind.[25]

Beatrice worried whether the initial subscribers would renew after twelve months. Enough did: by the end of April 1914 1,800 had paid up; the four sponsors agreed to put in more funds.

FABIANS AND GUILD SOCIALISTS

Edward Pease, Fabian secretary and historian, wrote that, once Beatrice had joined the Fabian Executive Committee, she became

...on the whole the dominant personality in the Society. [26]

Backed by the Webbs, in June 1912 the Executive established two Committees of Enquiry – one on land and rural development, the other on the control of industry. The land enquiry, led by Henry Harben, was uncontentious, producing a substantial report in 1913.

Beatrice chaired the industry committee. She wrote to Pease:

I think we should try to make a big thing of this Report on the Control of Industry – something the whole Society might feel proud of. [27]

The industry enquiry was where the Webbs challenged syndicalism and Guild Socialist ideas. They wrote a critique of syndicalism, referencing *The Miners' Next Step*, and French syndicalist publications, which they published in the August 1912 edition of *The Crusade*.

Sidney and Beatrice argued that syndicalism would replace independent trade unions, be administratively complicated, and could not achieve its aim of abolishing the wage system. They wanted the Control of Industry Committee to denounce syndicalism outright.

Guild socialism, described by Pease as

...a variant on Syndicalism, of a more reasoned and less revolutionary character... [28]

emerged in the years before 1914. Guild Socialist objectives, codified by the

National Guilds League (established 1915), included

...abolition of the Wage-system, and the establishment of Self-Government in Industry through a system of National Guilds working in conjunction with the State.[29]

A Guild was defined as

...a self-governing brotherhood of producers having a complete monopoly of the labour-power of their industry.[30]

According to Molly Hamilton, the Webbs thought these ideas threatened

...all that they cared for and had worked for. [31]

Margaret Cole thought the Webbs – especially Sidney – regarded Syndicalism as

...pernicious anarchistic nonsense. [32]

The Industry Committee developed a life of its own. By September 1912 it had 55 members and an office – a room in the NCPD offices. In October, a clerk was appointed – Julius West, a young man of Russian origins, already working for the Fabians – at a salary of £2.00 per week. They also took on William Mellor, formerly of the Oxford University Fabians. Initially Mellor was unpaid – he had had to leave Oxford

...for drinking beer in a place and at an hour which was prohibited by University discipline...

The head of his college sent Beatrice £50, and

...begged us to accept it as payment to Mellor for some work in connection with the new Research Department... [33]

In December they expanded to two rooms. West left to join the embryonic *New Statesman*; Mellor became the salaried clerk. By May 1913, Fabian Committee minutes referred to the Research Department and the Research Committee.

The 1913 Fabian Annual Report stated:

The new departure of the year under review has been the constitution of a Research Department.[34]

In 1913, Mellor was joined on the Committee by another Oxford Fabian, GDH (Douglas) Cole. Cole went to Balliol College Oxford in 1908, soon becoming a Fabian. Cole had campaigned for the Minority Report. Both Mellor and Cole advocated syndicalism and Guild Socialism, and were critical of the Webb influence on the labour movement.

Cole wrote in 1913 that the recent labour unrest was

...the sign that Labour has at last used up the inspiration of the early Fabians and is turning elsewhere for light – to what is vaguely called Syndicalism from what Mr Punch has named 'Sidney Webbicalism.' [35]

Cole, Mellor, and their allies became the Webbs' main opponents within the Fabians. In May 1913, at a members meeting, they proposed the Society should disaffiliate from the Labour Party. This was defeated by ninety two votes to forty eight. A year later another resolution from Cole, calling on members to recognize that the Fabians' primary function was research and propaganda, was nearly carried, over the Webbs' opposition. In 1914 Cole was elected to the Fabian Executive Committee.

The Industry Committee's output was prolific. The 1913 Annual Report said its report

...will probably constitute a book, rather than a pamphlet. [36]

The 1914 Report said

It now appears that it will be a library rather than a book. [37]

In spring 1914, to Beatrice's relief, Mellor left to help Lansbury launch the *Daily Herald.*

Beatrice worried about the future of the Fabians and the Research Department

We do not seem to be securing competent successors to take over the leadership. [38]

She thought the LSE was self-sufficient; she hoped the *New Statesman* would go the same way.

The same is true of Sidney's work on the LCC – in every case he created something that superseded him. But hitherto we have failed with the Fabian Society. The successive groups of individuals, who have aimed at taking over the leadership, have not had the combined conduct, brains, and faith to enable them to do it...

Cole is the ablest newcomer since HG Wells. But he is intolerant, impatient and not, at present, very practical. I am not certain whether the present rebel mood is in good faith or whether it is just experimental, seeing how it will go down. [39]

Summer Schools continued; the 1911 school was in Switzerland; the next three were at Barrow House in the Lake District – described by Beatrice as a

...large, ugly, bare and somewhat dirty house... [40]

The Webbs played a growing role in the programme. In 1913 and 1914, some time was used to discuss the Society's joint work with the ILP. In 1913, a week was allocated to the Industry Committee, with about 70 participants, drawn from the cooperative movement, local government, the civil service, and trade unions – including the syndicalist Noah Ablett.

Beatrice thought the 1913 School *extraordinarily successful*:

For six days, for five hours a day, sat I in the chair, directing the various discussions on the material gathered together by the department. [41]

At the 1914 school, in late July, the Research Department were allocated two weeks: one on Control of Industry, one on insurance (the next planned topic). The Guild Socialist/Oxford contingent turned out in force, refusing to obey the house rules or to go to bed. The domestic staff were mutinous, threatening to walk out.

Beatrice

...found the admirable 'Hanky' [Mary Hankinson] in a state of exasperation, and the Oxford men in an attitude of heroic defiance.

She became the peace maker:

I cut the gordian knot of rebellion by quietly informing the rebels that I should sit up with them every night, for as many hours as they had the heart to keep an old woman out of her bed.

She was only partly successful:

...the atmosphere remained hostile to the management, and the eight Oxford boys, with Cole and Mellor, sat at a separate table, drank copiously and defiantly of the beer they ordered in, hoisted the Red Flag in front of the house and brought the police inspector to remonstrate with us for singing revolutionary songs at the station and in the market place, at the exact time when the great Keswick Evangelical Convention was arriving for the week of religious experiences. At our daily discussions they sat in a corner of the room, a solid Guild Socialist phalanx, and walked out of the room when any of their number were called to order... [42]

Suddenly it was all irrelevant. Beatrice wrote that Sidney had refused to believe in the possibility of war among the great European powers: *It would be too insane.* But within days they were back in London.

A hideous business. Ulsterites, Suffragettes, Guild Socialists and rebels of all sorts and degrees may be swept out of mind and sight in national defence and national subsistence. [43]

THE COMING OF WAR 1914-1916

Britain was at war. At the Summer School, recalled Beatrice

...there had been the rumblings of the approaching earthquake without our awakening to the meaning of it. [44]

When Britain's ultimatum to Germany expired at midnight on Tuesday 4 August, John Burns had already resigned from the government, writing to Asquith on 2 August:

Dear Mr Asquith
The decision of the Cabinet to intervene in an European War is an act with which I profoundly disagree.
I therefore place in your hands my resignation as President of Board of Trade. [45]

John Morley, the Lord President, was the only other cabinet minister to resign; that other former pro-Boer, David Lloyd George, did not. Irish Home Rule was suspended. Burns remained an MP till 1918. He never gave any further explanation of his resignation. In 1918 he did not stand for re-election.

On 5 August Parliament voted for war credits. The Labour MPs voted in favour. MacDonald, against the war, resigned as leader. His replacement was Arthur Henderson, secretary of the Labour Party, an MP since 1903. Henderson was a Methodist, a teetotaller, and a craft trade unionist. He started his apprenticeship as an iron moulder aged 12. He began in politics as a Liberal, becoming an election agent, and Mayor of Darlington. He became known as 'Uncle Arthur'.

The Webbs had not worked with Henderson before 1914. The Fabian representative on the Labour Executive Committee was Stephen Sanders. Sanders had a low opinion of most Labour MPs – but, according to Beatrice, he made

...an exception for Arthur Henderson, who feels that the Labour members ought to take a more distinctive line. [46]

In May 1915, Asquith formed a coalition with the Conservatives and one Labour minister – Henderson. Haldane, after a virulent campaign accusing him of pro German sympathies, was dropped from the Cabinet. In December 1916, Asquith, criticized for insufficiently vigorous conduct of the war, was replaced by Lloyd George leading a small War Cabinet.

In 1915 and 1916, two issues dominated British politics: the supply of munitions, and the supply of troops. To address the first, Lloyd George gave up the role of Chancellor, becoming Minister of Munitions. His success in that role eased his path to supplant Asquith.

The second prompted a long argument about conscription – resolved in spring 1916 in favour of universal military service for men aged up to 41. In 1914 young men of military age faced a choice: to volunteer or not to volunteer? Conscription made that choice sharper: to accept conscription? To appeal? Or to resist? Some could secure exemption from military service on grounds of health or conscience; others because their civilian occupations (including munitions work) were important to the war effort.

Both Webbs were called upon to endorse, or condemn, the war. They declined. Beatrice wrote to Gilbert Murray:

> *We have both of us a rooted disinclination to sign statements on questions about which we have no special information or enlightenment. It was largely this feeling that made us refrain from taking sides in the South African war – much to the disgust of many of our fellow Socialists.* [47]

And to Russell

> *My dear Bertie*
>
> *…We are disinclined to sign anything about the war…* [48]

Sidney and Beatrice reacted differently to the war. Sidney absorbed himself in addressing the practical consequences for working people, first through the War Emergency Workers National Committee, later through the Labour Party itself, becoming close to the Party's emerging future leadership.

Beatrice, shocked by the destruction and human waste of the war, sank into a long depression. Casualties mounted in her family and in the network of young activists she had encouraged. Her gloom was intensified by the illness, and death in November 1914, of another Potter sister, Georgina. Georgie had seemed a *vigorous elderly woman* – but now she slowly died of liver cancer, accentuated by an operation for gall stones.

In November 1914 Beatrice felt idle and distracted, suffering from mental and physical depression:

> *The great war will raise issues which I no longer have the strength and elasticity to understand. The root of my trouble is, of course, a bad conscience: I am neither doing my share of emergency work nor yet carrying forward, with sufficient steadfastness, my own work.* [49]

By April 1915, she could not bear seeing the

...fresh young faces in each week's 'Roll of Honour'.[50]

She could not sleep

...the horror and terror of war eats into one's vitality, and I exist in a state of chronic weakness brought about by continuous sleeplessness. [51]

In summer 1916 Beatrice became convinced that she was physically ill, had an internal growth, needed an operation, and was about to die. A specialist reassured her. Then Beatrice concluded that she was suffering from neurasthenia, or nervous exhaustion:

This illness was the opening phase of a breakdown, which lasted in an acute form for six months and from which I did not recover for over two years. Partly war neurosis, partly too persistent work to keep myself from brooding over the horrors of the war, partly I think general discouragement arising out of our unpopularity with all sections of the political and official world. [52]

Things were bad at the Summer School that September; Beatrice

...suffered from perpetual head trouble; throbbing and dizziness during the night destroying sleep and dizziness and pain during the day – a nervous breakdown as disheartening as it has been disagreeable. Clearly I am in a rotten state... [53]

A month later she stayed with her sister Mary in the country, trying to recover her strength, still suffering from sleeplessness and dizziness. She spent November in Margate, Sidney visiting when he could.

In late 1916 her condition improved; in December she noted that the neurasthenia had cleared away. In January 1917

I have recovered my health except that I am no longer able to walk long distances. [54]

THE WEBB NETWORK AND THE WAR

Like many families, the Potters were divided by the war. Kate's husband, Leonard (now Lord) Courtney, campaigned for a negotiated peace up to his death in May 1918.

Margaret Potter's son, Stephen Hobhouse, was a conscientious objector. Margaret and Kate both supported him; Leonard testified at his Court Martial. Sidney kept Beatrice informed:

Stephen is to be court-martialled today, and both the Courtneys have gone down to Warminster to be present... [55]

Stephen's sentence was six months' hard labour. In March 1917 Margaret and Kate visited him in prison:

We went into a pen like a horse box, and there he stood about a yard off, but with two thicknesses of fine wire gauze between us so that I could only see his outline and his smile. [56]

Stephen's brother, Paul, was killed in the war; so was Rosie's son Noel Williams. The husband of one of Beatrice's nieces was also killed.

The toll of the war for our family is three killed and four others wounded, two seriously injured, out of a total of seventeen nephews and nephews-in-law in khaki... Every day one meets saddened women, with haggard faces and lethargic movements, and one dare not ask after husband or son. [57]

The Attlees were also split: Clement volunteered, and fought at Gallipoli; one brother, Tom, was a conscientious objector; another a soldier; another a military chaplain.

The Cambridge Fabians were divided. After his energetic campaigning for the Minority Report, Rupert Brooke had become distant from the Fabian Society. His emotional life was complicated. After meeting Noel Olivier in May 1908 he pursued her, intermittently but at times intensely, for several years. They met only occasionally; the distance between them was as much emotional as physical. In September 1910 they became secretly engaged, although Brooke neither sought nor received Sydney Olivier's consent. The distance between them continued. In 1911 Brooke began to fall in love with Ka Cox. That relationship was also complicated; Ka was also attracted to Henry Lamb, an artist.

Then, in early 1912, Brooke had a nervous breakdown. Bitter, disturbed, he wrote angry, chauvinistic letters to Ka. Influenced by Belloc and by Jacques Raverat, there had long been an element of antisemitism in Brooke's outlook; to some extent this reflected attitudes common in Edwardian Britain. But his casual antisemitism now became more explicit in his letters.

Brooke never formally resigned his Fabian membership, but he ceased to be active. He travelled, in Europe, North America, and then Tahiti, finally returning to England in the summer of 1914. Rumours of the impending war reached him; on 31 July he wrote to the artist Stanley Spencer

...this damned war business...If fighting starts, I shall have to enlist, or go as a correspondent. I don't know. It will be Hell to be in it, and Hell to be out of it.
[58]

318

The next day Brooke wrote to Jacques Raverat:

Everything's just the wrong way round. I want Germany to smash Russia to fragments, and then France to break Germany. Instead of which I'm afraid Germany will badly smash France, and then be wiped out by Russia.[59]

Brooke volunteered in August 1914; he died, in 1915, of sepsis, while on the way to Gallipoli. Brooke's friend Hugh Dalton spent the war as an officer, mostly on the Italian front.

In 1912 Bill Hubback had taken a London-based civil service job, working for the Board of Education. He and Eva moved back to London. In July 1915 he volunteered, becoming a Second Lieutenant; he served on the Western Front. Bill Hubback died of wounds received in action in February 1917 near the Butte de Warlencourt on the Somme, aged 32.

Gerald Shove, (instigator, with Brooke, of the anti-athletic league), was a conscientious objector. At first he worked at Toynbee Hall. But, Noel Olivier wrote to Rupert Brooke,

Gerald doesn't like Toynbee hall, so he came hurrying back to Bloomsbury last night to a party of Vanessa's, to refresh himself with the company of all his evil old friends.[60]

Shove spent the rest of the war rather ineffectively looking after Ottoline Morrell's chickens at Garsington before returning to Bloomsbury and Cambridge.

Ben Keeling had been the acknowledged leader of the Cambridge Fabians. By 1914, although Keeling remained personally close to the Webbs, his politics were turning Liberal. He enlisted in August 1914, as a private – unlike Brooke, turning down a commission as an officer. Keeling became a serjeant major; he was sent to the Western Front in spring 1915.

Keeling wrote anonymous *New Statesman* articles, and pencil letters to Sidney:

I am jolly glad I didn't take a commission.

I do despise the officers for living a standard of luxury out of all relation to the privates' life.[61]

Keeling kept in touch with Arthur Greenwood, to whom he had been introduced by the Webbs while he was in Leeds.

In July 1915 Keeling was wounded. He wrote, from a field hospital, to Greenwood, John Squire, Robert Ensor, and Eva Hubback. Keeling was sent back to the Somme, where he was killed in August 1916. A week before his death he wrote to his mother-in-law

I may be knocked out in the next few days. If so, this is just a last line to you, dear. I don't anticipate death, but it is all bloody chance out here.

If there is any sort of survival of consciousness, death can hardly fail to be interesting, and if there is anything doing on the other side, I will stir something up.

Nirvana be damned! Love from Ben. [62]

Beatrice did not comment in her diary on the deaths of individual soldiers she had known outside the family. In July 1916, when the Somme offensive began, during Beatrice's long depressive illness, she and Sidney were staying at Wyndham Croft in Sussex. They could hear the guns in France:

We hear from overseas the dull noiseless thud beating on the drum of the ear, hour after hour, day after day, telling of the cancelling out of whole populations on the vast battlefield. One sometimes wonders how one can go on, eating and drinking, walking and sleeping, reading and dictating, apparently unmoved by the world's misery. [63]

It remained on her mind; in 1917 she wrote:

The sustained horror of it is depressing. Friends lose husbands and sons; promising men, on whose career one had counted, are swept away. One realizes that an indescribable torrent of misery and bestiality has overwhelmed millions of men on the battlefields and desolated cities and countrysides in the occupied districts. [64]

In September 1909 Rupert Brooke, Bill Hubback, Dudley Ward and Margery and Bryn Olivier had gone walking in Somerset. They talked about their fear of growing old. They agreed that on 1 May 1933 they would meet at Basle railway station, turn their backs on England, and disappear.

They tried to recruit others. In November, Brooke wrote to Jacques Raverat, another Neo-pagan:

Will you join us? Will you, in twenty years, fling away your dingy wrappers of stale existence, and plunge into the unknown to taste Life anew? There'll be many, I hope – not too many, though! [65]

Ben Keeling turned the invitation down. For Brooke, it was *a damn serious and splendid offer.* He called it *an organised chance of living again:*

...RB will be fishing for tunnies off Sicily or exploring Constantinople or roaring with laughter in some Spanish Inn or fitting up a farmhouse or two with some friends, in America, or rushing wild-haired through Tokio pursuing

butterflies, or very sick on an Atlantic tramp. What does it matter? Only – we'll be living. [66]

But most of them were not living: there was no reunion. Brooke, Hubback, and Keeling died in the war. Long before 1933 Raverat was dead of a debilitating disease. Margery suffered from long term mental illness.

Beatrice always insisted that she was blind to Brooke's poetry. But Hubback and Keeling were surely two of the promising men on whose careers she had counted.

Clifford Sharp did not enlist, staying at the *New Statesman*. His relationship with GBS deteriorated; Shaw wrote less, and in October 1916 resigned from the board:

My dear Webbs

As I have got on poor Sharp's nerves… it is mere cruelty to animals remaining on the Statesman Board…My resignation will be a great relief to everybody, probably… [67]

Sharp had already been seeking exemption from conscription; a few days later, Shaw wrote to Beatrice again:

…this conscription business is exceedingly trying to the nerves…the suspense of playing for exemption is far worse than actual service. [68]

Sharp's editorial line had become independent of the Webbs; he loathed Lloyd George, preferring Asquith. When Lloyd George became Prime Minister in December 1916, Sharp wrote a scathing editorial, accusing Lloyd George of lacking *high moral purpose*. The printers refused to set the copy; the *New Statesman* appeared with blank pages. Beatrice kept the full text, noting

I doubt whether Sharp will get his exemption extended… [69]

She was right; Sharp was summoned to a further hearing in January 1917; although Sidney gave evidence for him, he did not gain another exemption. But Sharp's time as an ordinary army officer was brief:

… he was, within a few weeks, withdrawn from his training as an artillery officer and sent by the War Office to Stockholm – nominally as an independent journalist but really as the agent of the Ministry of Intelligence to fathom Swedish opinion and to pick up opinion from foreign socialists. [70]

When Sharp left, Squire (exempt from military service on eyesight grounds) became acting editor.

The Fabians were divided. Sanders, (Secretary from 1914), worked to support army recruitment. In November 1915 he took leave to become an officer himself; Pease returned from retirement until the war ended.

Mostyn Lloyd, formerly Poor Law campaign secretary, now on the Fabian Executive Committee, also became an officer. By 1918 he was a captain. Lloyd kept in touch with the Webbs, visiting Beatrice at Grosvenor Road early in 1916

C M Lloyd is back on leave; he is very pessimistic. He does not believe that there is much chance of the British breaking through. He is disgusted with the drinking habits, slackness and want of intelligence of the British officer [71]

Lloyd was friendly with R H Tawney, who gave up his up his job as Director of the Ratan Tata Foundation at LSE, enlisting, like Keeling, as a private soldier. Both Lloyd and Tawney were wounded on 1 July 1916, the first day of the Somme offensive. Lloyd wrote to Sidney from the 4th London General Hospital:

I was knocked out on the first day of the 'Show.' [72]

Lloyd's injury was relatively minor; but Tawney

...could only just hobble on sticks, and would not be well for months. He was shot through the liver. [73]

In February 1916, Keeling, Sanders, Tawney, and Lloyd were summoned to headquarters in St Omer, to meet Jimmy Mallon (formerly of Toynbee Hall, and the Anti-Sweating League; now working as the government Commissioner on Industrial Unrest). According to Beatrice, who later described Mallon as

...the secret agent of the War Office.

Mallon wanted them to produce a

...soldier's manifesto to the Clyde workers who were threatening a strike. [74]

A draft was produced; but no more was heard of it.

Mallon was one of several people from the Webb network who spent the war in the civil service. Another was Beveridge. Having established Labour Exchanges, Beveridge moved to the new Ministry of Munitions when it was established in summer 1915, as assistant secretary responsible for labour organisation. A month after Beveridge arrived, Janet Mair, wife of Beveridge's cousin David, started work at the ministry as an administrative assistant. She was the only woman administrator; at first no office was found for her and she worked from a tent, pitched on a balcony. She soon became Beveridge's private secretary.

When Lloyd George became Prime Minister in December 1916, Whitehall was reorganised again; new Ministries – of Labour, and of Food – were created. Beveridge went to the Food Ministry. Janet Mair also joined the Ministry of

Food; by the end of the war she was Director of Bacon and Allied Fats. She was rewarded with an OBE.

The Cambridge Fabian Dudley Ward spent the war in the Treasury with Keynes, joining the Peace Conference delegation in 1919. In 1914 Arthur Greenwood moved from Leeds to London; in 1916 he became a civil servant. By 1917 he was an Assistant Secretary in the Ministry of Reconstruction.

Beatrice thought Thomas Jones, as Secretary of the Wales National Insurance Commission, had

...won Lloyd George's liking. [75]

In December 1916 Lloyd George brought TJ to London as Assistant Secretary to the Cabinet.

Arthur Colegate, who worked on Labour Exchanges from 1910, was promoted to a London based role in 1912, and remained in the civil service during the war. Dining with the Webbs in summer 1916, he was angry that the *New Statesman* criticized government policy. Colegate became liaison officer between the Board of Trade and the Foreign Office, and later Private Secretary to Christopher Addison, Minister for Reconstruction. Sharp wrote from Stockholm:

And I see Colegate has become Addison's Private Secretary... That's a big step I imagine... What does Colegate think of him, I wonder? [76]

Politically, Colegate moved to the right, downgrading his Fabian membership to associate status in 1918. Beatrice was not impressed:

Colegate's 'career,' regarded as a whole excites slight contempt – a contempt that effectually destroys friendship as distinguished from friendliness. He has steadily pursued his own advantage and his social creed has reflected his advancement in social status. He has deliberately 'chosen inequality' first in his private life and secondly in his political and economic creed. The ultimate purpose of his life is a common one. He is lowering the values of human society. [77]

Much later Colegate became a Conservative MP.

THE MOVEMENT

In autumn 1914 the Fabian Society moved offices. The new premises, in Tothill Street, Westminster, were shared, uneasily, between the society and the Fabian Research Department. The caretaker suspected the researchers were *eating Mr Pease's jam.* Older members who just wanted to sit in the new Common Room found

...something between a revolution and a romp going on. [78]

The researchers opposed the war. There was intense pressure on munitions manufacturers to increase supply. This became pressure on munitions workers and their trade unions to increase productivity. In response, the Research Department began collecting information for unions – on labour conditions, wages, profits, and strikes – across many industries. They collated all wage agreements in munitions industries. They read trade union journals, published a monthly bulletin, and provided an information service for unions.

This information mattered to the government as well as the unions. GDH Cole objected to the war – but was exempted from military service because he was undertaking work of national importance for the Engineers' Union

...in connection with the Dilution of Labour and Munition Act. [79]

Beatrice watched, with amusement, the

...three young men, who are the kernel of the Fabian Research Department, struggling to escape the net of conscription. Cole, Mellor and Arnot [Robin Page Arnot, the Research Department secretary] *are pleading 'conscientious objection', also work of national importance.* [80]

Beatrice was amused; the security services were not. From 1916 until the 1950s they kept an eye on Cole. Notes about him passed between Vernon Kell, the head of MI5, and Basil Thomson of Scotland Yard.

An anonymous Oxford informant wrote

...I thoroughly and openly detest him...

and that he had made the Military Tribunal which had heard his appeal

...look like a pack of fools. [81]

In August 1916, an MI5 document called Cole

...the most dangerous of the Oxford cranks. [82]

Security twice tried to revoke Cole's exemption. In April 1916 this was considered by Beveridge as an official, and Addison as Minister.
Beveridge minuted

If the Tribunal have really exempted Mr Cole on the ground that he was assisting the supply of munitions, they have been bamboozled. [83]

Both in April, and again in January 1917, Cole's exemption remained in force. Cole, on the Fabian Executive from spring 1914, continued trying to change the Fabians. In 1914 he tried to amend the Fabian Basis; in 1915 he tried to limit the Society to research and propaganda. This proposal was supported by Herbert Morrison – a young veteran of the SDF and the ILP, recently appointed secretary of the London Labour Party – and Ellen Wilkinson, trade union organiser, previously Secretary of the Manchester University Fabian Society.

Cole's resolution came to the May 1915 AGM; it was opposed by Sanders, Sidney and GBS, and was heavily defeated. One member complained

...I've been a member of the Fabian Society for forty years, and now these young men make me come all the way from Streatham *to vote against them.*[84]

Beatrice thought Cole *disgraced himself and ruined his cause.* A show of hands went against him; someone suggested there was no need to count:

'Let us know how many fools there are in the world' he spat out. When called to order, he sprang to his feet: 'I withdraw the word fools, I say "bloody fools"' Then, white with rage, he sprang from the platform and marched dramatically out of the hall. [85]

Cole then resigned from the Fabians. Beatrice assumed most Oxford Fabians would follow him – as indeed they did.

So there ends my amicable attempts to work peacefully with the rebels. [86]

The Guild Socialists were defeated in the Fabian Society. But, as Margaret Postgate wrote, they had

...captured and manned the Research Department... [87]

The Department became their main focus.

Margaret had studied classics at Cambridge, leaving in summer 1914. Her first job was teaching at St Paul's Girls School in London. Another St Paul's teacher was a Fabian, Ethel Moor, who shared a weekend cottage with Mary Hankinson – Hanky – the manager and gym instructor at Fabian Summer Schools. They told her about

...a wickedly subversive young man who was doing his best to ruin the Fabian Society and thwart and hamper the great Webbs; his name, they said, was G D H Cole. [88]

She taught for two years. In autumn 1916, her brother Raymond, a student, was called up. He refused to go, and was briefly imprisoned as a conscientious objector. He told Margaret that she should keep the flag flying. So she became a volunteer in the Research Department, meeting Cole, Mellor, and Page Arnot.

Margaret called the world she had joined 'the Movement'; it became, she wrote

…my second University, taking up the major part of my time and thought, sleeping and waking, for the next few years… [89]

Soon there was a vacancy for a paid worker. There were two candidates; Sidney wrote to Beatrice to describe

…Miss Postgate, daughter of the professor, who is a first-class Classic, now an assistant mistress at St Paul's School for Girls at £160, but wants to leave teaching: and has been a volunteer in the office two days a week, and will not be free until Xmas. Cole is away, so I said he must be consulted…Arnot evidently thinks Miss Postgate the better worker… [90]

Margaret got the job.

Beatrice still chaired the Research Department; Margaret did not meet Beatrice until she came to the office, one day in summer 1917. Margaret described Beatrice as

…a tall lady, wearing a large and very ugly hat, with a beaked nose, a very thin pale face, a harsh high voice, and a bright commanding eye…I thought she looked infinitely old and frail and would probably disintegrate if I sneezed or shouted suddenly. [91]

Margaret and another researcher had been playing tennis with two fly whisks and a ginger biscuit:

Nothing was said; but the atmospheric tension made it quite clear that this was not the sort of behaviour which the eminent lady expected from those who were privileged to work in the Socialist cause. [92]

Later Margaret heard about the judgement Beatrice had formed that day:

…she had sized me up as a possibly attractive young female, and had warned the Honorary Secretary – Cole – not to allow me to entangle the young men in the office. [93]

The researchers were not sympathetic towards the Webbs. Margaret wrote later

I had been well-conditioned to regard them as reactionaries before I ever set eyes on either of them. I knew that they were wilfully wicked opponents of the legitimate aspirations of the working class, supporters of the Government in an imperialist war… [94]

The researchers were not well paid; this gave a practical edge to the antipathy. Parodying GK Chesterton, they wrote

In the perfect Fabian State, Sidney Webb

Do they pay the Standard Rate, Webb oh Webb? [95]

Douglas Cole and Margaret Postgate married in August 1918. Even this late in the war, their Sussex honeymoon had to be interrupted for Douglas to appear before another Military Service Tribunal. In November, the Webbs called on the Coles in Chelsea. Beatrice wrote approvingly of *this promising union of two devoted fellow workers:*

> *These two are now friendly with us, convinced that, however we may differ from their vision of the future, we mean to help, not to hinder, their career in the Labour movement.* [96]

Of Margaret, Beatrice wrote

> *...though her manners have been disorderly, her ways have been straight: she has wit and reasoning power of an unusual quality, and she is fundamentally sweet-tempered and kind.*

Douglas, she said, was

> *...from the intricate convolutions of his subtle brain to the tips of his long fingers, an intellectual and an aristocrat.* [97]

Since Douglas had stormed out of the Fabian Society a hesitant, uncertain coexistence had developed. Membership of the Research Department was no longer restricted to Fabians – anyone in a coop, a trade union or a socialist society could join. Beatrice tried to promote a 'Labour Research Society' – a sort of federation of the Fabians, the Guildsmen, and the Trades Unions. She noted that

> *...Cole and Mellor stuck to the Research Department in spite of their break with the Fabian Society. These young men were, it was clear, real enthusiasts, inspired by the ideal of Industrial Democracy, and intent on getting it translated into fact by persistent work.* [98]

Beatrice thought Guild Socialism was neither feasible nor desirable. Neither did she think it likely to happen:

> *The Political State is getting far too much power and this power is far too much in the hands of the capitalist brainworker...* [99]

She wrote:

> *...our points of view are slowly converging. We let them make every possible use of the FRD, and they cease to attack us.* [100]

The following year, the department became the Labour, rather than the Fabian,

Research Department.

THE WEBBS AND THE WOOLFS

In spring 1914, after meeting European socialist leaders, Beatrice concluded that the British left needed an international policy. The obvious people to develop one were the Research Department:

But who is to do the heavy and highly skilled brainwork involved? The young men talk but they do not get through much work...[101]

In 1913 the Webbs had seen an article by Leonard Woolf on the cooperative movement. Woolf (a Cambridge classicist, and an Apostle) was making his way as a freelance writer, having left the Ceylon Civil Service. He had recently married Virginia Stephen.

The Webbs, sitting at the centre of their Fabian spider-web, always kept an eager eye for some promising young man who might be ensnared by them...the result was an invitation to lunch, and on July 12 I ate my first of many plates of mutton in Grosvenor Road. [102]

Leonard was soon ensnared, joining the Fabians, and attending Summer Schools (in 1914 Virginia came too). In November 1914 Beatrice asked him to write a report on the legal profession in Britain, Europe, and America.
More followed. In December, Virginia wrote

The Sidney Webbs ask us to dinner about once a week, and Leonard has got to go tomorrow, though it sounds too dismal. They've clawed him for a huge job...
[103]

The Quaker philanthropist Seebohm Rowntree gave the Fabians £100 to study

...the whole arrangements of international control over Foreign Policy, Armaments and methods of warfare. [104]

In January Beatrice reported to the Fabian Executive

We have thought over possible people; and we suggest the name of LS Woolf, a practised writer, ex-Civil Servant in Ceylon; a member of the Fabian Society and of the Research Department ...[105]

The committee agreed, and thanked Rowntree.
The following week the Woolfs went to a Fabian meeting on the war:

The Fabians were well worth hearing; still more worth seeing. The interest was watching Mrs Webb seated like an industrious spider at a table, spinning her webs (a pun!) incessantly. The hall was full of earnest drab women and of broad nosed, sallow, shock headed young men, in brown tweed suits. They all looked unhealthy and singular and impotent. It was all very dull and sensible and the idea that these frail webspinners can affect the destiny of nations seems to me fantastic. [106]

Leonard worked assiduously, reading official documents:

You could not become an authority on international government in 1915 by reading books, because the books did not exist. [107]

A draft was ready in May; the Webbs convened another Barrow House conference to discuss it. Woolf proposed establishing an international authority to prevent war.

Beatrice thought the conference was successful. Woolf's draft would be developed into

…a big work on International Relations, past, present and future. The absence of a clique bent on hostilities, like the Cole-Mellor group at the last conference, added much to the efficiency and amenity of the gathering. [108]

A revised version appeared in July; Sidney and Leonard then drafted a treaty, outlining steps towards establishing the international authority.

Leonard worked with both Webbs, meeting them frequently. Shortly after the January meeting described by Virginia, she noted

…Leonard off to lunch again with the Webbs [109]

Virginia had already experienced one long bout of mental illness, including a suicide attempt. Another began in February 1915; relations had become close enough for Beatrice to write sympathetically to Leonard:

My dear Mr Woolf
I am so grieved to hear of your trouble: I hope your anxiety will not be too long drawn out… I cannot believe that it will be good for you to give up thinking about outside things however anxious and saddened you may be by your wife's illness. In that sort of trouble I have always found it restful and comforting to work on some impersonal problem. [110]

So began a strange friendship between the Webbs and the Woolfs, which endured for the rest of their lives. Sidney was not a foreign policy specialist; the Webbs had acknowledged this in commissioning Leonard. Sidney's interest was more in structure and process than in the substantive issues of nationhood and peace; this irritated Leonard.

The Woolfs became regular guests at Grosvenor Road. In June 1916, when Beatrice herself was depressed, the Woolfs spent a weekend with the Webbs in Sussex, at Wyndham Croft. Ka Cox, the former Cambridge Fabian, had cared for Virginia during her 1913 illness; now Virginia wrote to Ka to describe the experience:

…last weekend we spent with the Sidney Webbs, in Sussex (next door to Dalingridge) and there were the Bernard Shaws, and they all talked incessantly. I liked it better than I expected. At any rate one can say what one likes, which is unusual with the middle aged; indeed, I felt much more of a mature woman with a passionate past than Mrs Webb… [111]

To her sister Vanessa Bell she wrote

Mrs Webb pounces on one, rather like a moulting eagle, with a bald neck, and a bloodstained beak. [112]

In September 1918 Sidney and Beatrice spent a wet weekend together at the Woolfs' Sussex home. Leonard recalled how they

…boldly, if not recklessly, asked Beatrice and Sidney to come to us for a weekend at Asham and we were rather astonished and a little dismayed when they accepted. [113]

Virginia wrote to Vanessa:

God! What a weekend we had! Incessant talk for 46 hours and the Webbs up at 5.30 chattering in their rooms… [114]

They walked on the downs; by Southease church, Beatrice detached Virginia, and they talked alone. Virginia outlined the plot of her current novel. Beatrice

…proceeded to warn me against the dissipation of energy in emotional friendship. One should only have one great personal relationship in one's life, she said; or at most two — marriage and parenthood. Marriage was necessary as a waste pipe for emotion, as security in old age when personal attractiveness fails, and as a help to work. We were entangled at the gate of the level crossing when she remarked, 'Yes, I dare say an old family servant would do as well.' [115]

Leonard tells the same story; in his version marriage is called the wastepaper basket of the emotions.

WAR EMERGENCY WORKERS NATIONAL COMMITTEE

Labour movement organisations called a conference for 5 August 1914 to set up a Peace Emergency Committee to halt the drift to war. But by 5 August that objective had been overtaken by events. What emerged was the War Emergency Workers National Committee (WEWNC) – chaired by Arthur Henderson (Party Secretary and Chairman of the Parliamentary Labour Party), with Jim Middleton, Labour Party Assistant Secretary, as secretary. It brought together an unprecedented range of organisations – trade union, cooperative, and political, including the Fabian Society, the British Socialist Party (BSP{; the former SDF had become the BSP in 1911), and the Independent Labour Party.

The Committee consisted of nine delegates from the founding organisations, and six members elected by the conference on 5 August. The Miners Union President, Robert Smillie, topped the poll; Sidney Webb and Marion Phillips tied for second place. The committee also co-opted other members. When Henderson joined the Cabinet in 1915, Smillie succeeded him in the chair.

The Committee's brief was the impact of the war on workers' lives – food prices, rents, separation allowances and compensation for disability. Before the end of August 1914, Sidney had produced a 32-page pamphlet, *The War and the Workers* – subtitled *Handbook of some Immediate Measures to Prevent Unemployment and Relieve Distress*. This argued the importance of maintaining employment, without compromise on trade union wage rates, or Fair Wages clauses. It emphasised women's employment, under the heading *Remember the Women*. The committee relied for its work on continuous contact with the national network of trade union branches and local trades councils.

The Committee brought Sidney closer to Labour's leadership. Stephen Sanders had been the Fabian representative on Labour's National Executive (NEC). When he joined the forces in 1915, Sidney replaced him on the NEC. Pease – reinstated as Fabian Secretary for the duration – called at Grosvenor Road to persuade Sidney to take on the role. Later Pease wrote that this was his second-best day's work – his best being when he

> ...*invited the future Fabians to meet at my rooms.* [116]

By autumn 1915 Beatrice thought Labour had never been more united. The committee had

> ... *laid down the policy for the Labour and Socialist Movement during the war. Sidney, representing the Fabian Society, has been able to make himself useful by drafting the resolutions, the pamphlets and leaflets that the Committee*

has issued... One result of its existence is that we have never been more intimate with all sections of the Labour Movement. [117]

During the war Sidney, Jim Middleton and Arthur Henderson shaped the policy, constitution, and organisation of the Labour Party for the interwar period and even beyond. First the Emergency Committee, then the Labour Party, produced a series of policy reports. These were substantially Sidney's work. Pease wrote:

... whenever Webb is on a committee, it may be assumed in default of positive evidence to the contrary that its report is his work. [118]

The Committee continued working on living standards. But, throughout, Sidney thought it should look to the longer term, aiming to prevent post war unemployment. In June 1915 he asked

What is to be the organisation for getting the soldiers back to work, disabled or fit? Unless something decided is said to the Govt., we shall find it has committed to some dreadful scheme. [119]

In spring 1916, Beatrice noted Sidney's opinion that the

... trade union MPs are doing their worst to prevent the War Emergency Committee getting to work on an After the War programme, largely from jealousy but also because they don't want to be compelled to think... [120]

In November, Sidney wrote to Beatrice that the union leaders were hopeless

Yesterday I spent two hours (on Labour after the War) struggling with their complacent stupidity and apathy, and with the real desire of some of them to prevent anything being published that would 'arouse expectation', and lead to anything beyond what the Government is conceding. [121]

Once conscription of labour had happened, the War Emergency Committee in summer 1917 demanded conscription of riches. Hyndman of the British Socialist Party proposed that

Since practically the whole adult male population of Great Britain is liable to conscription for active service in the field, thus being compelled to risk life and limb for the defence of a country which they do not own... the entire riches of this island be conscripted and placed at the disposal of the Community at large. [122]

Hyndman defined 'riches' as bonds, shares, debentures, bank accounts, insurance companies and land.

Two days later Sidney wrote to Middleton

As regards Hyndman & the War Emergency Committee, I will try to prepare a draft resolution for the Cttee, avoiding his impossibilities. [123]

Sidney suggested the tax system should be the instrument. He argued that, in war, government already controlled many industries. They could take over what they were already running. But he did not think the government should take over all 300,000 farms – or local councils manage 500,000 shops. Sidney proposed a tax on capital – like Death Duties (Inheritance Tax) – combined with increased income tax rates and 'sequestration' – confiscation – of 'unearned income' – rents, dividends, and annuities – except on Savings Bank and Cooperative Society accounts.

Sidney's approach was accepted. The Committee declared

...that for all the future money required to carry on the War, the Government ought, in common fairness, to accompany the conscription of Men by the Conscription of Wealth; that a suitable measure would be the immediate imposition, in lieu of any further loans, of a Graduated Levy on all Capital Wealth on the basis of the existing Death Duties.[124]

Hyndman described his tacit collaboration with Sidney:

When anything important comes up, I bring out a root-and-branch revolutionary proposal, and set it well before them. That puts them in a fright; and then Webb comes in with his proposal only a few degrees milder than mine; and they are so relieved that they pass Webb's motion unanimously. [125]

In the later stages of the war, Sidney's focus shifted away from the WEWNC towards the Labour Party itself.

IMPACT OF THE RUSSIAN REVOLUTION

The war changed British politics; the Russian revolutions of 1917 accelerated the transformation. The left welcomed the end of the autocracy; the old parties were apprehensive. The February revolution came at the same time as the decision by the United States to enter the war; Beatrice wrote:

The Russian revolution and the entry of the USA into the war completely alter the situation. The Entente does now represent democracy at war with autocracy.
[126]

On 31 March George Lansbury chaired an Albert Hall rally supporting the revolution. Clara Butt sang; Robert Smillie spoke; the meeting congratulated to the democrats of Russia. They sang William Morris's *March of the Workers* and Edward Carpenter's *England Arise*. Kate Courtney noted the hall was *nearly wild with excitement*; they cheered the conscientious objectors for a full five minutes.[127]

In April, the Socialist International decided to hold a conference on war aims, in neutral Stockholm. The French Socialists were reluctant to meet the German and Austrian parties in wartime. The Labour Party, swayed by Henderson, agreed with the French – but proposed a London conference for just the Allied socialist parties. Henderson agreed to go to Russia to try and persuade Kerensky's provisional government to support the conference.

Lloyd George asked Henderson to visit Russia for the British government, to assess the situation – and possibly to stay on as ambassador.

Henderson arrived in Petrograd on 1 June 1917, meeting Kerensky and others, and addressing the Petrograd soviet. He returned to London convinced Russia would only remain in the war if a broad Stockholm conference proceeded.

The ILP and the BSP convened a conference in Leeds on 3 June to hail the revolution. Chaired by Robert Smillie, it was attended by over 1100 delegates. They passed a resolution supporting Russia's provisional government's peace aims, and called for the establishment of workers and soldiers councils across Britain. Speakers included MacDonald, Philip Snowden, Bertrand Russell, and WC Anderson. Leonard Woolf, Marion Phillips, and Noah Ablett were all there.

So were the security services, reporting that the delegates were

...well-known rebels and pro-Germans. [128]

They were convinced the organisers wanted it to lead

...if possible, to a revolution in this country. [129]

The Webbs did not attend. Beatrice thought the delegates incapable of coherent thinking. The speakers did not impress her:

...one would think they shared the thoughts and feelings of the Petrograd extremists. But who can imagine MacDonald or the Andersons or the Snowdens leading a revolution of the Russian type – even if there existed the material for such a revolution in the British working class. [130]

Henderson returned from Russia in late July. Now committed to participating in the Stockholm Conference on the lines discussed in Petrograd, he persuaded the Labour Party to call a conference for 10 August to consider changing its position. He went to Paris with MacDonald and Russian delegates to talk to the French socialists. His two roles – Minister, and Labour Party Secretary – were becoming incompatible. Other ministers criticized Henderson.

Henderson came back from Paris on 1 August. He was summoned to a cabinet meeting, but kept waiting while other Ministers discussed his conduct. This became known as the 'doormat' incident. He then met Lloyd George privately on 7 August, before the Labour conference on 10 August.

Beatrice thought Labour surprised itself

...by deciding by a three to one majority in favour of going to Stockholm. [131]

Lloyd George was surprised too: he had thought that either Henderson would recommend against going, or the conference would decide not to send anyone.

On the evening of the conference Henderson met TJ in the street. He had just seen Lloyd George, and thought his time in government was nearly over:

They want to sack me. I won't resign. If they ask me to resign I'll take my resignation to the Labour Party. [132]

Sack him they did, next day. Beatrice noted

Henderson has been dismissed by the PM – not only dismissed but dismissed with a public charge of having deceived the War Cabinet and misled his own party. [133]

Beatrice thought Henderson was in a strong position – at least for the present. She worried that the labour movement might not hold together.

The significance of Henderson's dismissal only gradually became clear. The following year Beatrice wrote

We none of us realised the enormous importance of Henderson's ejection from the Cabinet...He came out of the Cabinet with a veritable hatred of Lloyd George...From that day Henderson determined to create an Independent political party, capable of becoming HM Government – and he turned to Sidney to help him. [134]

Their first task was to prepare a statement of Labour's war aims. Sidney had already started on this, drawing on Leonard Woolf's work, when drafting proposals for the 10 August Labour Conference.

Those proposals formed the basis of the *Memorandum of War Aims* – approved by a British Labour conference in December 1917, then, in February 1918, by a London conference of socialist representatives from the Allied countries. It was written by Sidney, Henderson, and MacDonald, in cooperation with Camille Huysmans, the Belgian secretary of the Socialist International, who spent the war years in London. According to Jim Middleton, while Sidney was not the sole author of the War Aims document, he made a major contribution.

The *Memorandum* was ambitious and idealistic. It went beyond the oppositional positions of the Stop the War Committee of the Boer War, and the No Conscription Fellowship of the First World War to lay down positive, radical principles for relations between peoples and states. It underpinned the foreign policy of the left until at least the 1930s.

Its core commitment was that the world should be made safe for democracy. This required a League of Nations and an International High Court. All disputes should be submitted to arbitration. In Middleton's words:

> *Thus was the British Labour Movement committed to the popular doctrine of Collective Security which inspired all phases of its Foreign Policy thereafter.* [135]

Force was to be eliminated as a means of settling international disputes. Private manufacture of armaments was to be prohibited. If weapons were required, they were to be made by governments

> *...so as entirely to abolish profit-making armament firms, whose interest lies always in the war scares and progressive competition in the preparation for war.* [136]

The document also made proposals on disputed areas – including Belgium, Alsace Lorraine, and Poland. It proposed that Palestine, *freed from the harsh and oppressive government of the Turk*, should become a Free State under international guarantee

> *...to which such of the Jewish people as desire to do so may return and may work out their own salvation free from interference by those of alien race or religion.* [137]

Before the *Memorandum* was finalised, the Bolsheviks had displaced Kerensky's Provisional Government in Russia. Some on the British left welcomed the new regime; the Webbs did not.

> *The folly of the ILP in acclaiming the Russian Soviet government of 'Workmen and Soldiers' representatives' as the 'new model' is becoming every day more obvious.* [138]

By January 1918 Maxim Litvinov, (later Russian Foreign Minister), had arrived in London as the new regime's first official representative. On 9 January Litvinov lunched at Grosvenor Road. He was pessimistic, telling the Webbs that unless capitalism was overthrown in other countries the revolution would not survive.

If European militarism does not destroy it, economic pressure will. When we asked him what was the alternative to the success of the Bolshevik revolution, he replied: 'We shall become a colony of the German empire.'[139]

Later that month, Litvinov addressed the Labour Party Conference. Before the March 1918 Brest-Litovsk peace treaty between Russia and Germany, Litvinov and other Russian representatives also met representatives of the British peace movement; the Webbs arranged a meeting with Leonard and Kate Courtney.

Litvinov's speech to the Labour Conference in January was balanced by an address by Kerensky to the June conference, Kerensky embarrassing Henderson by kissing him on the cheek at the end of his speech.

Other Russian visitors came to Grosvenor Road: on Sunday 28 July, the editor of Pravda called – a *sallow faced, dark haired, unhealthy Russian* – with an introduction from Litvinov. He issued their first invitation to visit:

'Will you not return with me to Russia and see for yourself what is happening?' 'no thank you' I replied with a pleasant laugh 'we remember that there are such things as hostages and their usual fate in revolutions.' [140]

REMAKING LABOUR

Before the *Memorandum of War Aims* was finalised, Sidney began drafting an overall Labour policy statement. *Labour and the New Social Order*, published on 1 January 1918, was agreed by the June 1918 Labour conference. For Beatrice, the endorsement of the *Webb programme* was one of the conference successes: delegates were satisfied that

...they had a programme, more complete than that of either of the two great parties and that the Labour movement was sweeping forward to national leadership. No doubt there is a great deal of nasty suspicion abroad; a certain growling of the revolutionary elements on being headed off rebellion into a network of detailed and measured reform. [141]

This was Labour's first national programme; a Labour government seemed a real possibility. The programme built on the Webbs' work of the previous twenty years: the National Minimum, the Minority Report; the War Emergency Committee; and the *Memorandum of War Aims* (whose proposals it incorporated). *Labour and the New Social Order* was based on four 'Pillars':

- Universal enforcement of a National Minimum

- Democratic control of industry

- Revolution in national finance

- Surplus wealth for the common good

It proposed nationalisation of railways, mines, and electricity. In the Emergency Committee, Sidney had seen how the taxation system could be used as an instrument of redistribution. The Capital Levy now became a central feature of Labour policy:

> ...chargeable like the Death Duties on all property, but (in order to ensure approximate equality of sacrifice) with exemption of the smallest savings, and for the rest at rates very steeply graduated, so as to take only a small contribution from the little people and a very much larger percentage from the millionaires. [142]

The American magazine *The New Republic* printed the whole document, calling it

> ...the most mature and carefully formulated programme ever put forth by a responsible political party. [143]

Henry Pelling thought that *Labour and the New Social Order*

> ...formed the basis of Labour Party policy for over thirty years – in fact until the general election of 1950. [144]

At the same time Sidney and Arthur Henderson rewrote Labour's constitution. Before 1918 Labour was a federation of trade unions and socialist societies, without individual members. The new constitution, agreed at a conference in February 1918, established individual membership; created local Labour Parties; made the whole annual conference responsible for electing the Party Executive Committee; and, in its Clause IV, for the first time committed the party to a socialist objective:

> ...to secure for the producers by hand or brain the full fruits of their industry... [145]

Beatrice thought Henderson wanted the best of two worlds:

> By the new constitution he aims at combining the mass vote and financial support of the big battalions incorporated in the national unions with the initiative and enthusiasm of the brainworking individual members of the local Labour Parties. [146]

Even before approval of the rules, local Labour Parties began to form. In December 1917, Sidney wrote to Middleton, to affiliate the Westminster Local Labour Party, enclosing the 15 shilling minimum fee. Next month Rose

Rosenberg, Secretary of the City of London ILP, wrote to say that

The draft Constitution and Mr Webb's explanatory leaflet were enthusiastically welcomed at last night's City ILP Branch Meeting. [147]

With a constitution and a new programme, Labour needed more, and different, staff. Key appointments came from the Webb network. William Gillies, an ILP member, was secretary of the Glasgow Fabians before the war. He attended the 1910 Fabian Summer School and was involved in the Poor Law campaign in Scotland. He joined the staff as intelligence officer. Beatrice described him as *the little, dwarf-like Gillies*:

…an honest, over sensitive but well-informed little Glasgow Fabian. [148]

Gillies worked as Labour's International Officer until 1944.

Beatrice took a close interest in Gillies' welfare. In 1917 she sent an anonymous donation to Middleton:

I shall be grateful if you will use the enclosed sum to ease the arrangements for Mr Gillies' holiday. You can say it is sent by an admirer who wants to see him well enough to serve the Democratic movement in one or other of its phases, and who appreciates his gifts. He is an honest and loyal little soul and he must not be left to sink into chronic neurasthenia. [149]

The Party's Chief Women's Officer was Marion Phillips – the LSE economics PhD, who had worked with Beatrice at the Poor Law Commission and was a regular speaker during the Poor Law campaign. Beatrice's attitude to Phillips was ambivalent; she wrote in 1917 that she was

…shrewd and capable but contentious and she tries to oppose anything I propose, out of some vague desire not to be considered a Webb disciple. [150]

When Phillips went to work for the Labour Party, however, Beatrice admitted that

On the whole I rather like her, her keen rationalist intellect is refreshing… [151]

A network of advisory committees also developed, described by Middleton as *one of the most useful and fruitful of Webb's schemes.* Beatrice referred to the

…circle of rebellious spirits and idealist intellectuals who have gathered around GDH Cole and ourselves – Tawney, JJ Mallon, Delisle Burns, Arthur Greenwood, Arnold Toynbee and H J Gillespie. [152]

Sidney chaired the International and Imperial Committee, which met weekly; Leonard Woolf was secretary for more than twenty years. Cole was secretary of the committee on trade and finance; Jimmy Mallon, of the committee on industrial policy. A committee on the machinery of government was chaired by MacDonald; Beatrice was Secretary. The advisory committees were coordinated by a secretary – initially GDH Cole, later Arthur Greenwood, who subsequently became head of research.

In July 1918 the Labour Research Department moved to the party offices, on contract to work for the party. Beatrice commented:

> *Henderson has shown a certain breadth of vision in risking having turbulent elements inside the party office and Cole has sacrificed some of his rebellious morals and manners to the opportunity for influence. The Fabians, in permitting the transfer, and the old Fabians – GBS and the Webbs – in actually promoting it, have acted with wise magnanimity.* [153]

Labour's changed role demanded better premises. In March 1918 Beatrice had noted that

> *The Labour Party is the most ramshackle institution in its topmost storey. Henderson sits alone in the untidy office at 1 Victoria Street…the fair-minded and gentle-natured Middleton, the assistant secretary, sits in another tiny room.* [154]

Middleton wrote to his parents each week with the news. In June, he told them that Labour was moving to 33 Eccleston Square, close to Victoria Station. The building had been Winston Churchill's London home. In 1909 Churchill had had the first floor equipped as a library: now Churchill's library became Henderson's office, partitioned with folding doors that could be opened for Executive meetings. There were offices for Marion Phillips and William Gillies – and at the top of the building a room that could be used for committee meetings:

> *…we have set up eight or nine advisory committees that will be very much alive shortly.* [155]

RECONSTRUCTION

By the end of 1916 Beatrice's long bout of depression was over. She bought a typewriter, and started work on her first autobiographical book, published in 1926 as *My Apprenticeship:*

> *…I am using up some of my spare hours in the afternoon in copying out and editing my manuscript diaries so as to make a book of my life.* [156]

It did not last. In February 1917, Beatrice joined a government committee

1. The Potter family 1865. Left to right: Georgina, Mary, Lawrencina Potter, Margaret, Beatrice, Richard Potter, Teresa, Blanche © LSE Library Passfield 3 8 11

2. Charles Webb, Sidney's father, in his Westminster Rifle Volunteer uniform © LSE Library Passfield 14 20

3. Elizabeth Webb, Sidney's mother © LSE Library Passfield 14 20

4. Beatrice in the late 1870s
© National Portrait Gallery, London

5. Beatrice in ball gown, 1885
© LSE Library Passfield 3 8 1 58

WORKING MEN'S COLLEGE,
45, GREAT ORMOND STREET, W.C.

Session 1883-4.

POLITICAL ECONOMY.

MR. SIDNEY WEBB
(2nd Whewell Scholar in International Law and Moral
Philosophy, Cambridge, 1883.)

WILL GIVE

A SERIES OF EIGHT LECTURES

BEGINNING ON

TUESDAY, OCTOBER 9, 1883,

AT 7.45 P.M.

SUMMARY.

Scope and method of Political Economy—Wealth—
The Production of Wealth—Land—Labour—Capital—
Law of Diminishing Return from Land—Growth of
Population—Increase of Capital—Methods of Production
—Industrial Organisation—Division of Labour—Co-oper-
ation—Communism—Socialism—Systems of Land Tenure
—Peasant Proprietorship—Nationalisation of the Land.

Text books recommended : Marshall's "Economics of Industry" (Macmillan, 2/6); or Mrs. Fawcett's "Political Economy for Beginners"
(Macmillan, 2/6).

FEE (for Members of the College) 1s.
Non-Members will also pay an Entrance of 1s. 6d.

6. Leaflet for a course of lectures
by Sidney, 1883
© LSE Library Passfield 6 8

7. Sidney 1885
© LSE Library Passfield 3 8 1 3

8. The British Museum Reading Room in the 1880s

9. 1889 Dock Strike – one of the daily demonstrations led by John Burns

10. Katherine Buildings, Cartwright Street, Aldgate, East London. Beatrice and Ella Pycroft worked here as housing managers in 1885-86

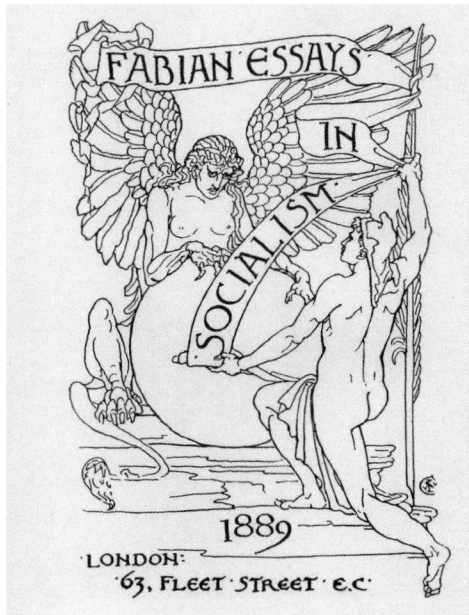

11. *Fabian Essays* -1889 first edition cover design by Walter Crane

12. Sidney & Beatrice, 1890s/1900s © LSE Library, Passfield 3 8 1 59

13. Sidney & Beatrice, 1903-4 – picture by HG Wells © LSE Library BW
Manuscript diary Vol 24 Reproduced with the permission of H G Wells estate

14. 41 Grosvenor Road SW, the Webbs home from 1892 until the 1920s
© LMA London Picture Archive 139761

15. Beatrice 1908 © LSE Library Passfield 3 8 1 60

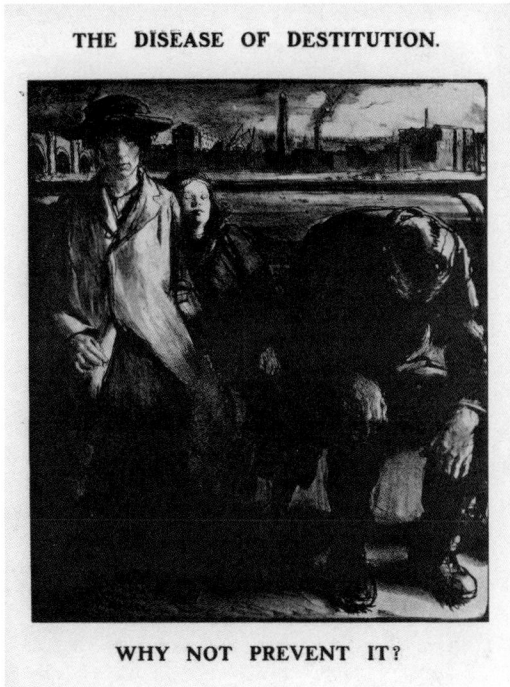

16. *Disease of Destitution* poster designed by Gerald Spencer Pryse for the
National Campaign for the Prevention of Destitution © From The Crusade,
September 1910. Reproduced by permission of the estate of Gerald Spencer Pryse

17. Beatrice – chalk drawing attributed to Jessie Holliday. Circa 1909
© National Portrait Gallery, London

18. Sidney – chalk drawing attributed to Jessie Holliday. Circa 1909
© National Portrait Gallery, London

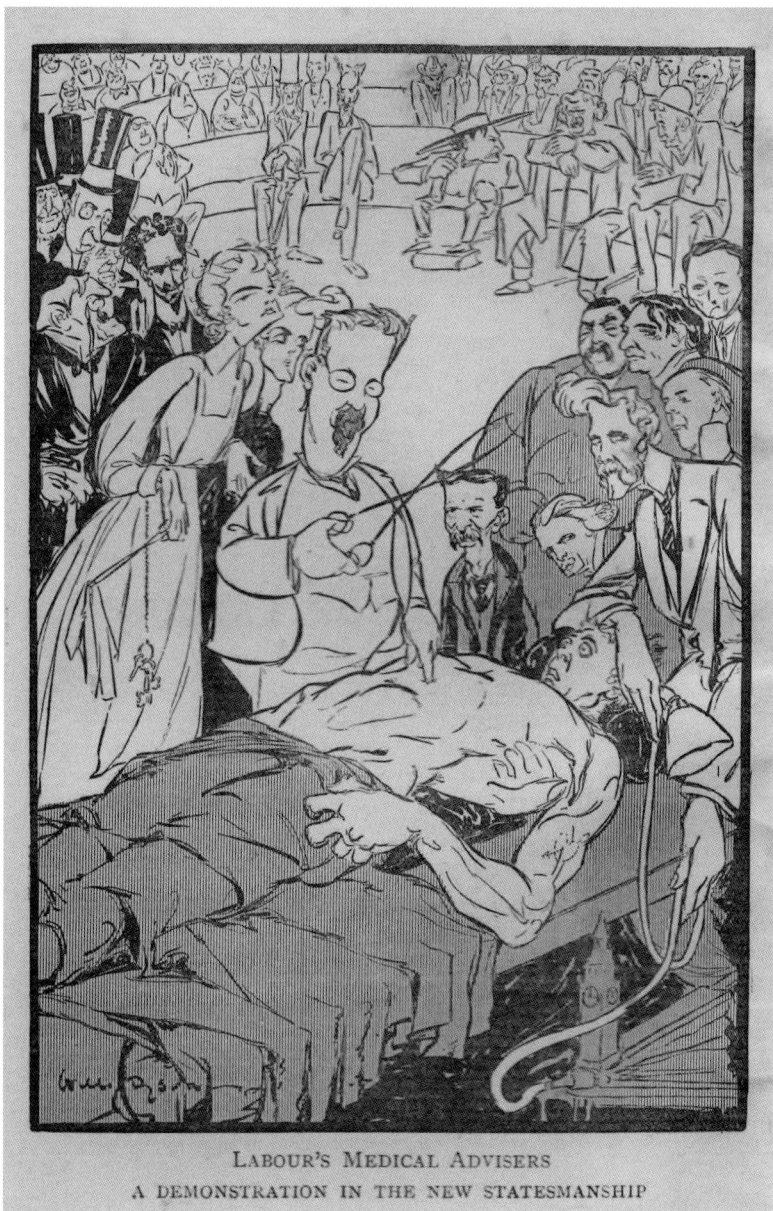

LABOUR'S MEDICAL ADVISERS
A DEMONSTRATION IN THE NEW STATESMANSHIP

19. Labour's Medical Advisers cartoon by Will Dyson. Frontispiece to *The World of Labour* by GDH Cole (1913); one of very few cartoons showing both Sidney and Beatrice. The Labour Giant, on the couch, is being anaesthetised with hot air from the House of Commons, pumped by Ramsay MacDonald. Sidney stands over the patient with a surgical instrument; Beatrice stands next to him.n Also in the picture: GBS; Belloc; Chesterton; Lloyd George; Hubert Bland.

20. The Sankey Commission on the Coal Industry, 1919, in session at the
House of Lords. Sidney and R H Tawney on the right. Beatrice compared
it to a 'revolutionary tribunal'.

THE WEBB OF DESTINY.

Mr. Sidney Webb. "I AM WAVING THIS RED FLAG, NOT PROVOCATIVELY, BUT TO SIGNALISE WHAT I HAVE SO HAPPILY CALLED THE 'INEVITABILITY OF GRADUALNESS' WHICH MARKS OUR ROLLER'S ADVANCE."

21. *The Webb of Destiny*: Punch cartoon published the week after Sidney's Labour on the Threshold speech, 1923

22. Sidney, 1932, takes a day return to London to talk at LSE. Beatrice wrote:
We have shared the glory and the income of Cabinet office, but he takes
the title and I travel first class! A concession so I tell myself to old age!

23. Sidney and Beatrice at Passfield Corner, with Maynard Keynes, September
1926 © Keynes papers. Reproduced by permission of Kings College Cambridge Ref:
JMK/PP/94/287

24. Beatrice & Sidney, 1926
© LSE Library Passfield 3 8 1 57

STATION: LIPHOOK 2 MILES.
TELEGRAMS: PASSFIELD.
TELEPHONE NO.: PASSFIELD 6.

PASSFIELD CORNER,
LIPHOOK,
HANTS.

ON THE THRESHOLD OF THEIR NINTH DECADE ;

SIDNEY AND BEATRICE WEBB

AT HOME

SATURDAY, 12TH JUNE, 1937.   3 TO 7 P.M.

TO ALL THE DESCENDANTS OF RICHARD AND LAURENCINA POTTER,
TO THE THIRD AND FOURTH GENERATIONS, AND THEIR SPOUSES.

———————

CARS COMING SOUTHWARD BY THE PORTSMOUTH ROAD, TURN SHARP RIGHT AT LIPHOOK
VILLAGE, BEFORE REACHING THE ANCHOR HOTEL; TAKING ROAD B.3004 FOR 2 MILES TO
PASSFIELD OAK HOTEL, WHERE TURN RIGHT, DOWN WINDING LANE FOR 200 YARDS, TO
FIRST GATE ON RIGHT.

25. 1937 party invitation: Beatrice and Sidney *on the threshold of their ninth decade* © LSE Library, In Beatrice Webb Manuscript Diary Vol 51 p1a8

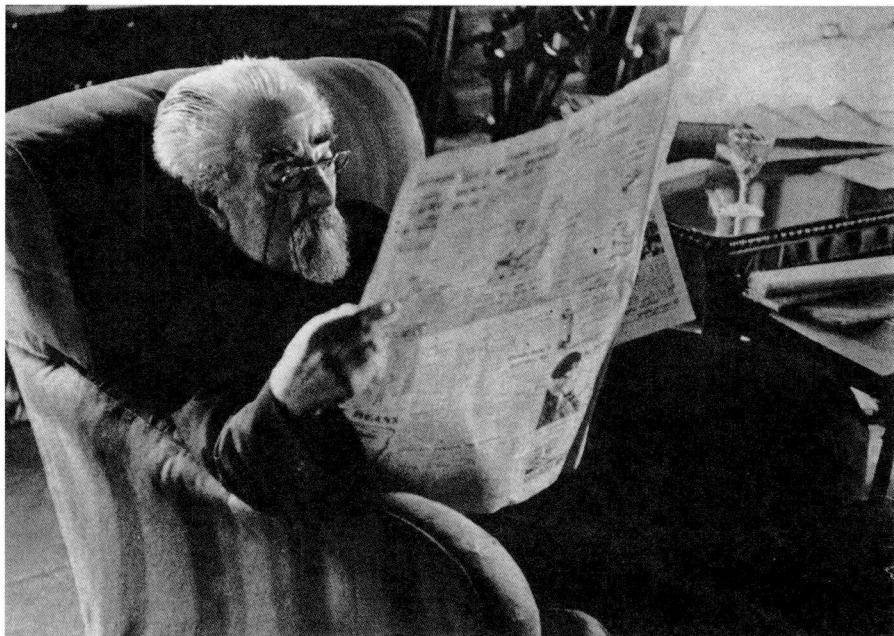

26. Sidney, at Passfield Corner, August 1941 © Picture Post, 13 September 1941

27. Beatrice, at Passfield Corner, August 1941 © Picture Post, 13 September 1941

28. Interment of ashes, December 1947; Two vergers at Westminster Abbey carry the ashes of Beatrice and Sidney to their resting place.. As the caskets were being committed, Rosy, last of the Potter sisters, was heard to whisper: *Which is Sidney and which is Beatrice?* © Life Magazine Jan 1948

on post war reconstruction; the diaries went back to the bank.

When he became Prime Minister in December 1916, Lloyd George wanted to shake up post-war planning. Under Asquith there had been a ministerial committee; Lloyd George chaired the new Reconstruction Committee himself. Edwin Montagu (a minister under Asquith) was deputy chair. But Lloyd George wanted a wider group. He told the cabinet secretariat to

Bring me a list of persons with ideas, [157]

TJ told Beatrice what happened next. The list was provided; Lloyd George

…spent a spare ten minutes in considering it. He struck out some names – H G Wells and GBS, for instance – and added some others, among them Jack Hills and Seebohm Rowntree. Then he proceeded to pick out fourteen. He came to the Webbs and pondered: 'Yes, we will have one of the Webbs… Mrs Webb I think… Webb will be angry, Mrs Webb won't.' [158]

Beatrice was optimistic: the committee meant the sort of work

…that Sidney and I are skilled in – if only I have the strength…

It would not be a standard government committee:

…of retired officials, retired admirals and generals with a couple of countesses and a few philanthropists thrown in, but of young and vigorous persons… Out of the fifteen persons there are three Fabians, as well as two Labour men, and one of the two assistant secretaries is a Fabian. [159]

TJ was on the committee himself; Beatrice called him the keeper of Lloyd George's *democratic conscience*:

In spite of our hostility to his chief, he has remained markedly friendly to us and it is to him that I owed my seat on the R C. [160]

On 25 February TJ lunched at Grosvenor Road with both Webbs and Tawney:

I always enjoy a talk at No 41, each takes up the idea of the other before the other has quite finished with it – 'two in one' combination…

Mrs Webb is full of interest in Reconstruction and eager to begin devouring reports… [161]

A few days later, Lloyd George met a Labour delegation, whose membership included Marion Phillips. TJ was there:

At the end PM asked me would not Dr M.P. do for Reconstruction Committee. I said Yes, ran after her and brought her back, and she was 'appointed' then and there. [162]

Beatrice wrote to say she approved of the appointment.

The Fabian Assistant Secretary was Arthur Greenwood – an old Webb protégé. Beatrice now saw him as a *lost disciple*, with a *certain hostility to us or our ideas* – one of a *little group of idealists*, who

…hover between the Guild Socialists and the young men of the Round Table. [163]

She was not impressed. Greenwood

…was incurably slack in getting through any work in which he was not personally interested, he was, in fact, an unconscientious official. [164]

The Committee disappointed Beatrice. By June she was exhausted

…suffering again from dizziness and general incapacity, especially for physical exercise… The Committee is not a satisfactory creation and I think it is bound to be superseded. [165]

Lloyd George and TJ were preoccupied with the war; the Prime Minister

…intervenes suddenly when matters become critical, peremptorily reorganises some department or starts a new one in a few hours, and leaves the new one to find its own level in a hostile world of old-established government offices. [166]

She thought Montagu

…a dead failure…; …wholly inexperienced in committee work…

The secretary, Vaughan Nash, was

…woolly-headed, easily frightened off any decisive step, and like most weak men in responsible positions, suspicious and secretive.

The other staff were

…dreamy, cultivated amateurs, preachers of ideals rather than practical administrators…

They seemed to Beatrice

…to spend most of a very short working day talking together, over cigarettes or tea – or listening to committees talking. No one seems to read the papers… [167]

Dining with Montagu in May, Beatrice told him his staff were inefficient.

She learned from Montagu that storms were brewing in Whitehall over reconstruction and munitions.

The main Reconstruction Committee met for the last time on 18 July;
Montagu became Secretary of State for India; Christopher Addison became
Minister for Reconstruction. But Beatrice had become a member of two sub
committees – on Machinery of Government, and on local government – which
continued after the closure of the main committee; she thought she would have
enough to do.

Haldane chaired the Machinery of Government Committee; Morant was
secretary. Beatrice described her task as

> *...discovering the land of Whitehall for the future Labour Cabinet.* [168]

That autumn they met twice weekly, over tea and muffins in Haldane's Queen
Anne's Gate home.

The Webbs knew both Haldane and Morant well; Beatrice thought Morant

> *...the only man of genius in the civil service: but he excites violent dislike in
> some men, and much suspicion in many men.* [169]

Morant had helped the Webbs on the Poor Law; their relationship was less
close after he went to run National Insurance. On the Machinery of Government
Committee

> *Our relations though friendly have not been quite those of working
> comradeship. Robert Morant and the Webbs have different ends and they
> suspect each other' methods...He is a strange mortal, not altogether sane...* [170]

Haldane, Morant and the other members knew more about the workings of
government than Beatrice. Sidney helped with drafts; Beatrice turned to old
contacts – Beveridge, and Herbert Samuel, who had been Home Secretary at
the end of the Asquith government – for advice. She wrote to Samuel

> *We have put too little thought into the structure of government departments
> and we have hardly become aware of certain typical diseases which affect the
> bureaucrat.* [171]

She looked for ways of combining bureaucratic efficiency with democratic
control. She spent an afternoon trying to explain the concept of an *efficiency
audit* to a puzzled senior civil servant.

Beatrice prepared a plan for 14 ministries and a secretariat, and discussed it
with Permanent Secretaries. Over afternoon tea, she outlined the proposals to TJ

*As she said, if you ask these Permanent Secretaries to put forward schemes on
their own, to a Committee, they are very slow and cautious, but if you put
before them a well thought out scheme, they are most helpful in improving
it...* [172]

In February 1918, the Webbs dined with Haldane and Lloyd George – ostensibly to talk about Beatrice's recommendations. But

*It is needless to say that there was no such discussion, neither the PM nor the
host showing any inclination for it.* [173]

They had not met Lloyd George for several years; what he really wanted
to discuss was cooperation between Labour and his wing of the Liberals. He
approached the Webbs, rather than Henderson, because he thought that Sidney
was responsible for Labour's recent progress:

*'I know Henderson,' he laughingly remarked. 'It is not Henderson who has
made the* réclame *– all the distinction comes from'... and he waved his hand
towards Sidney.* [174]

Sidney and Beatrice remained impervious to Lloyd George's charms:

*He is a blatant intriguer, and every word he says is of the nature of an offer 'to
do a deal'! He neither likes nor dislikes you: you are a mere instrument, one
among many, sometimes of value, sometimes not worth picking up. He bears no
malice for past opposition, he has no gratitude for past services.* [175]

The Machinery of Government Committee met throughout 1918. On
Mondays and Fridays Beatrice sat with Haldane, Morant and senior civil servants.
On Thursdays, with Ramsay MacDonald, she met junior civil servants, as secretary of the Labour Advisory Committee on the same subject. She found *great
unrest* in the civil service.
Permanent Secretaries were

*...sore about the intrusion of the 'business' man and scornfully sarcastic of his
ignorance of the larger responsibilities of government and of his casual and
disorderly habits of work.* [176]

They had contempt for parliamentary criticism; perpetual sniping in parliament and press produced the wrong sort of official – critical rather than
constructive:

*The man who was prized in a department was he who kept his Minister out of
trouble and had a smart answer to an awkward question.* [177]

Younger civil servants, many in trades unions, were not worried by external criticism – which they often thought justified. They were more concerned by their lack of prospects – for adequate salaries, interesting or responsible work, and political participation.

The Local Government Committee's task was Poor Law reform, or:

...the better coordination of Public Assistance in England and Wales [178]

The Committee was chaired by Donald Maclean, an Asquithian Liberal MP and Deputy Speaker; as well as Beatrice, members included Morant and the railway trade unionist and MP, J H Thomas.

Beatrice seized her moment:

With Montagu's permission I set out to get agreement between the representatives of the Majority and the Minority of the Poor Law Commission and the LGB. [179]

This demanded cooperation with old antagonists. She had worked with Samuel Provis on a government pensions committee; now she convinced him that the LGB was being *throttled*:

No government dared give any function to a Poor Law authority – central or local. [180]

Apprehensively, she then met Lord George Hamilton – but

He walked all the way to Hyde Park corner with me...
'You want me to serve on this Committee Mrs Webb? Very well, I will.' were his parting words. [181]

Hamilton wrote to Lancelot Phelps, who had signed the Majority Report, saying that Beatrice was in 'a very attractive and repentant mood':

She admitted she had made a mistake in trying to break up the family and in persistently objecting to our proposal to make for the future the Home Assistance Committee the foundation of Poor Law Relief and Poor Law Assistance. She told me she was on a reconstruction Committee which seemed to me of a somewhat ambitious character... [182]

The outcome, wrote Beatrice, was a *unanimous report embodying all the conclusions of the Minority Report.* She regarded this as her masterpiece. Hamilton said Beatrice made concessions. Nevertheless, he acknowledged that she

...showed great ability and was absolutely straight. She stuck to her bargain, and enjoyed herself by sitting upon certain members of the Committee whom

she demolished with her tongue; but we saw the best and bright side of her...
183

Beatrice had won. The report of the Maclean Committee, published in January 1918 (Cd 8917 1918), recommended the abolition of Guardians and the transfer of their functions to the relevant local authority committees. Provision for the sick and infirm would be under public health powers; provision for children through the local education authority; mental health care through the Lunacy and Mental Deficiency Acts. It was the Minority Report scheme.

When the Woolfs came to lunch Beatrice could speak of little else:

Mrs W began to talk almost at once about the Reconstruction Committee which she is on. She talked incessantly and every tenth word was Committee... but the scheme for the Cosmos is not complete because she has so far failed to invent a committee for the able-bodied and the unemployed. However, she still has hopes... Immediately after luncheon we fled. 184

Beatrice attributed her success to Hamilton's help – and to her years of campaigning. She reflected

I have learnt committee manners – an art in itself. 185

But – still there was no legislation. Almost the only recommendation that was implemented was establishing a Ministry of Health, with Addison as Minister, and Morant as Permanent Secretary. The new Health Ministry took over the Poor Law (for now unchanged) from the LGB.

During the war unemployment had virtually disappeared. The numbers on outdoor relief had fallen dramatically. When in 1920 the initial post war boom collapsed, unemployment insurance could not cope. In urban areas, and traditional industrial communities, thousands were driven back on to poor relief. Not until 1929 were the Guardians abolished.

In autumn 1918, Beatrice was appointed to another committee on post war policy – this time on women in industry. The committee's membership comprised four men, Beatrice, and one other woman. As with the Poor Law Commission, Beatrice submitted a Minority Report, which concluded that

That the popular formula of 'Equal Pay for Equal Work', or, more elaborately 'Equal Pay for work of Equal Value in Quantity and Quality', whilst aiming at the expression of the right ideal, is so ambiguous and so easily evaded as not to constitute any principle by which the relation between men's and women's wages can be safely determined. 186

In December 1917 Beatrice wrote

Sidney has become the intellectual leader of the Labour Party and he is happy and contented with his work. [187]

The Webbs had won Henderson's trust, and – for the time being at least – had rebuilt a cooperative relationship with MacDonald. Sidney had played a leading role in drafting both the domestic and the international policy of the Party; these been acclaimed well beyond the ranks of Labour. With Henderson, he had written the Party's constitution. Key roles on the Party's staff and advisory committees were filled by people from the Webbs' extensive network. With her government committees, Beatrice had discovered the land of Whitehall, and negotiated a compromise solution for Poor Law reform.

Confident that Labour would be in a stronger parliamentary position after the war, Sidney and Beatrice began to discuss future tactics. Labour was courted by both Liberal factions; as well as the approach from Lloyd George, Beatrice had been contacted by Margot Asquith on her husband's behalf. But they were now clear:

The policy of permeation is played out and Labour and socialism must either be in control or in whole-hearted opposition... [188]

In April 1918, the Webbs hosted a dinner for Labour leaders – Henderson, William Anderson, Mary Macarthur, JH Thomas, and George Lansbury: what should Labour do if the Lloyd George coalition collapsed and Asquith was asked to form a government? Anderson was a Labour MP with a strong ILP and trade union background, married to Mary Macarthur, a leading trade unionist for working women.

In June, Beatrice noted that every week they were inviting Labour people to come and meet Henderson

We had all the chairmen of the Advisory Committees – MacDonald, Anderson, Jowett, Tawney and J A Hobson to meet Henderson, and all the secretaries came in afterwards. [189]

Early in 1918 Labour hoped for an electoral breakthrough; by the autumn those hopes had faded:

...most of the glamour around the Labour Party during the spring due to its international and national programme has faded away, personal jealousies and internecine strife having dissipated it from below, whilst the near prospect of a brilliant peace has dissolved it from above. [190]

The December 1918 General Election became known as the 'Coupon' election: candidates who supported the Lloyd George coalition received a letter of approval, signed by Lloyd George and by Bonar Law, the Conservative leader. Labour withdrew from the coalition and fought the election as an independent party. Sidney contested the election, unsuccessfully, as Labour candidate for London University.

Sinn Fein did not take their seats; only 30 Asquith Liberals were elected. The 57 Labour members became the official opposition – against a government majority of 382 Conservatives and 127 Lloyd George Liberals. The main Labour leaders – MacDonald, Henderson, and Snowden – were all defeated.

Before the election Beatrice wrote:

We are not personally depressed because we have the patience of lifelong propagandists who have watched their ideas taking root in the minds of former opponents. But we are contemplating retirement from active political life after the elections, to finish our books and watch the young folk work for the success of social democracy at some future election. [191]

Chapter Nine: Inevitable gradualness 1919-1924

THE COAL CRISIS AND THE SANKEY COMMISSION

Beatrice was already sixty when the war ended; Sidney was fifty nine. They dreamed of retirement to the country. They urgently needed to complete old pieces of work, otherwise

...disease or death or some emergency task may prevent us from completing these excellent but unfinished products. The Poor Law Commission broke into our researches and we have never been free to resume our old life as learned publicists. It is now or never. [192]

The dream was postponed: an emergency task arrived.

The war had expanded Government's role in the economy; coal was a key sector. The government controlled the mines, so, in effect, employed the miners. In January 1919, the Miners Federation (MFGB) demanded a 30% wage increase, a cut in working hours from eight to six, and nationalization of the mines with an element of workers control.

The Cabinet monitored the industrial situation, with weekly reports on disputes, and on revolutionary activity. In February, ministers responded to the miners' claim. They called for delay, but offered a small wage increase – and an inquiry. The MFGB then balloted:

In favour of strike action:	615,164
Against	105,082
Majority for strike	510,082

On 15 February, before the ballot result was known, Haldane passed on a message from Lloyd George to Sidney and Beatrice: he wanted another dinner with them. The Webbs didn't want to go to Downing Street, so the meal was at Haldane's home on Queen Anne's Gate

Lloyd George's life was hectic, commuting between industrial disputes in London and peace negotiations in Paris. He regaled Sidney and Beatrice with tales about Clemenceau and Woodrow Wilson.

He wanted the Webbs' advice on membership of the Coal Inquiry Commission.

He forgot to bring his list of names; he asked Haldane's butler to telephone No 10. Noone answered. So Lloyd George said

'Tom Jones – you know Tom Jones – he has the matter in hand. See Tom Jones about it. Tell him I told you to see him.' 'I will telephone him tomorrow to come to lunch,' I agreed.[193]

Sidney suggested a Commission with four groups: trade unionists, employers, and two groups of outsiders, *holding the rival assumptions of the parties concerned.* Next day, TJ lunched at Grosvenor Road:

He let the cat out of the bag, and a very ugly cat it was. The persons in the list of names which could not be got from Downing Street were all hostile to nationalization .[194]

Afterwards Sidney and Beatrice agreed

That little game of appointing a committee to report against nationalization must be stopped... [195]

Sidney alerted Robert Smillie, MFGB President. On Saturday 22 February, Sidney briefed Smillie and Frank Hodges (MFGB Secretary). Lloyd George was pressing the miners to accept the inquiry; Sidney feared the Commission would be stacked against them. He recommended to the miners that they should accept the Commission – provided they could nominate half the members.

The MFGB wanted a fight; Smillie was not sure they would accept Sidney's suggestion. But they did: Beatrice saw an angry Lloyd George at a conference:

The miners had told the PM their terms: the conference had decided that morning to postpone the strike until the 22ⁿᵈ [March] and to accept service on the commission provided they nominated half the commission, and they had on the spot nominated Chiozza Money [Sir Leo, a radical Liberal former MP], Tawney, and Sidney as their outsiders. They had given the PM ten minutes to decide whether he would accept their terms or have a strike. 'The delegates must catch the five o'clock train' Smillie said. The PM had felt he had to accept the terms and this explains his anger.[196]

So the government established the Coal Commission; it was chaired by a judge, Mr Justice Sankey, and empowered to summon witnesses and take evidence on oath. The membership followed Sidney's formula: Smillie, Hodges, and another MFGB representative; three coalowners; the three experts sympathetic to the miners' cause; and three business representatives – including Allan Smith, of the Engineering Employers (described by Beatrice as *the star among the professional representatives of capitalism* [197]); and Sir Arthur Duckham, a leading gas engineer.

With the strike postponed, it was decided that the Commission would produce an interim report on wages and hours by 20 March. A second report would cover nationalization.

The first meeting was on 3 March at the House of Lords. A few days later Beatrice went to watch; the hearings were more like

> ...*a revolutionary tribunal sitting in judgement on the capitalist owners and organizers of the nation's industries*
>
> ...*owing to the superior skills of the miners' representatives it has become a state trial of the coal-owners and royalty owners conducted on behalf of the producers and consumers of the product.*[198]

The trade unionists and their allies cross-examined witnesses relentlessly. After ten days, Beatrice thought public opinion was *indignant with the coal owners' profits at the consumers' expense.* Sidney spent long days at the commission hearings; Beatrice wrote that he was enjoying himself:

> *I have never seen him so keen on any task since the halcyon days of the LCC.* [199]

Three Interim Reports appeared on 20 March; the Cabinet was scheduled to discuss them that day.

Sidney drafted the report from the miners and their allies, which backed the wage claim:

> *We find that the miners' claim to an advance in their standard of life is justified; and that the percentage of rise of wages asked for, namely 30 per cent (on earnings apart from war wage) is not excessive).*[200]

They backed the reduction in hours, and – in principle – nationalization.

The three coalowners backed wage increases of 1s 6d a day for miners over 16, and 9d a day for under-16s. Daily working hours should be reduced to seven. They made no recommendation on nationalization.

Sankey himself, and the three business nominees, recommended increases of 2 shillings a day for over-16s, and 1 shilling for under-16s, and a reduction in working hours to seven. Sankey's report did not reach a conclusion on nationalization – but contained a strong statement:

> IX
>
> *Even upon the evidence already given, the present system of ownership and working in the coal industry stands condemned, and some other system must be substituted for it, either nationalization or a method of unification by national purchase and/or by joint control.* [201]

351

Lloyd George was in Paris at the Peace Conference. Two days before the reports appeared, he was visited by J H, Jimmy, Thomas, the General Secretary of the National Union of Railwaymen – who, according to Frances Stevenson, was *playing our game at the moment.* The railway workers had promised to support the miners. Thomas told Lloyd George that the trouble with the miners was that they were

...trying to get the grievances of a century righted in five minutes... [202]

With Lloyd George away, the Conservative Bonar Law was in charge.

The Webbs were drinking tea with Tawney at Grosvenor Road when an excited Tom Jones arrived:

He had seen the three reports. The W.C. was meeting at six o'clock to consider what they would do. They were determined not to be bullied into conceding the miners' demands – especially nationalization. [203]

TJ thought some ministers – including Churchill (War Minister) and Curzon (Foreign Secretary) wanted confrontation with the miners, using troops if necessary. They would do anything to prevent nationalization. He told the Webbs

The Exchequer could subsidise the bad mines so that the price of coal should not be raised – the Cabinet would be willing to do that. They would do anything from shooting the miners or starving their wives and children to subsidising profits or wages out of taxes to avoid nationalization. [204]

The Cabinet, chaired by Bonar Law, met at 6.00 pm; Lloyd George dialled in from Paris. He sent a message in the middle of the meeting: he had just read the *remarkable* Section IX:

All the members of the Commission, except the coal-owners, condemn the present system of ownership and working in the coal industry, and I understand, privately, that the coal-owners agree with this view. [205]

He said it was essential that Sankey should now report on alternatives. Meanwhile, the Cabinet accepted Sankey's proposals on wages and hours.

That evening, Bonar Law reported the decision to the House of Commons; he said that, if the miners rejected the offer, and reverted to strike action, it would be a strike against the community. If that happened, the government would

...use all the resources of the State without the smallest hesitation... [206]

Bonar Law wrote to the MFGB, saying that the government were prepared to carry out Sankey's recommendations

...in the spirit and in the letter...

In a fresh ballot, the miners accepted the Sankey terms with 693,084 in favour, 76, 992 against.

Commission meetings restarted. The coalowners and the business representatives were close to walking out: Sankey told Sidney that the leading business representative, Allan Smith

...intended to break up the Commission, and that it was for the Commission not to give the Mineowners an excuse for withdrawing.[207]

If the coalowners withdrew, the strike would be back on. A truce was brokered; the hearings resumed. The Commission started with evidence from economists and technical experts, moved on to testimony from the coalowners, and then heard from owners of coal royalties.

Two Commission members, Sidney and Chiozza Money, appeared as witnesses. Sidney's statement, on which other Commission members questioned him, was based on *How to pay for the war.*

Smillie asked that the leading peers among the coalowners (or their representatives) – the Duke of Hamilton's agent, the Duke of Northumberland, Lord Durham, Lord Dynevor, Lord Tredegar, Lord Dunraven, the Marquis of Bute, and Captain Wemyss – should be called as witnesses.

This made for tremendous political theatre; they were cross-examined by the miners' representatives as to how they (or their ancestors) came by their estates, and about the living and working conditions of miners in their areas.

The three interim reports were followed, on 20 June, by four final reports. The Chairman recommended:

...on the evidence before me that the principle of state ownership of the coal mines be accepted[208]

Details were to follow; but there should be immediate action to acquire the coal royalties, paying *fair and just* compensation to the existing owners.

Sidney and the other labour representatives broadly agreed with the chairman – except the MFGB members, who would not support any compensation for the coalowners. Seven of the thirteen Commission members therefore supported nationalization in principle.

The three coalowners, and two of the business representatives, opposed the principle:

Neither past experience of State enterprise nor any evidence submitted to the Commission gives any reasonable ground for belief that the coal industry could

or would be as efficiently conducted by the State in the future as by private enterprise in the past.[209]

They were, however, prepared to accept state ownership, not of the mines, but of the coal itself, provided proper compensation was paid.

The fourth report came from the other business member, Arthur Duckham. He proposed that government should acquire all mineral rights, and that these should be supervised by a Ministry of Mines. Collieries would be unified; there would be a system of District Boards.

Beatrice thought the miners' tactics had been counter-productive:

Smillie's melodramatic cross-examination of the Dukes and his fanatical and unintelligent obstinacy about 'no compensation' to the royalty owners injured the miners' case in the country.[210]

The government now had to decide. According to the Webbs, when Sankey supported nationalization, he believed Lloyd George wanted this: there would be a general election; Lloyd George would break with his more reactionary supporters; his manifesto would include nationalization.

It did not happen. After 1918 the Coalition was overwhelmingly Conservative. On 12 July, 274 MPs (mostly Conservatives) signed a round robin letter opposing nationalization. On 30 July, the Federation of British Industries published a report on nationalization, starting from the proposition that

...centralised management by a Government Department is fatal to commercial efficiency and enterprise. [211]

In mid-July Lloyd George held a conference of ministers and advisers at his Welsh home, in Criccieth. TJ lists Auckland Geddes, (Board of Trade), and Robert Horne, (Minister of Labour), as being there, as well as Llewellyn Smith, Permanent Secretary at the Board of Trade. Beatrice heard about another participant:

...the sinister reactionary Winston Churchill had been down to Criccieth, colloguing with his chief, and he tells everyone that he is going to 'root out Bolshevism' at home and abroad.[212]

The Criccieth meeting decided against nationalization, but in favour of nationalizing coal royalties. It also supported some social improvements and some local combining of pits.

The decision in principle having been taken, it remained to process it formally, and to create a supporting political narrative. On 23 July, Beatrice wrote

The Cabinet seems bent on provoking a big strike so as to avoid the issue of nationalization and clear up on the relations between Capital and Labour. [213]

The government's opportunity came in Yorkshire. Owners and miners had agreed a local wage increase. The government, having first agreed that it was a matter for local negotiation, then forbad it. A strike followed: by 21 July, the Yorkshire coalfield was shut, including staff who operated the pumps to stop the mines flooding. The government sent naval stokers to operate the pumps. Other coalfields were poised to join the strike.

On 23 July, the Cabinet discussed the strike. Lloyd George said that it

...was practical, and not theoretical, Bolshevism, and must be dealt with with a firm hand. He was rather inclined to agree that the mine-owners were right, and that a fight had got to come... The whole of the future of the country might be at stake, and if the Government were beaten and the miners won, it would result in Soviet government. [214]

With sailors working the pumps in the Yorkshire pits, police protecting the sailors, and soldiers standing by to protect the police, the Cabinet were ready to resume their discussion of nationalization.

This was pure theatre: the real decision had been taken at Criccieth before the strike started; the Coalition, even if it had wanted to, had no majority to nationalize the industry. Conservative and Liberal Ministers agreed: the votes were not there. Lloyd George told the Cabinet that

...it was impossible to carry out nationalization in the present Parliament. [215]

Formal discussion began on 7 August. Lloyd George and Bonar Law spent some time explaining away their March statements of support for the spirit and the letter of the first Sankey report.

All *he* had ever said, explained the Prime Minister, was that:

...it was a valuable document which would be carefully considered by H M Government.[216]

Another Minister said that

...according to his recollection, all Mr Bonar Law had done was to speak in favourable terms of that part of the Report which contained a sweeping condemnation of the present system.[217]

Miners, mining communities, even some ministers, believed there had been a commitment. The Cabinet, however, turned to Duckham's minority report as a possible way forward. This left Montagu, former Reconstruction Minister, now Secretary of State for India, uneasy. He circulated a paper saying that he thought there had been

...an implied undertaking that the policy of the Government would embody the results of the Commission's deliberations, that is to say, the report of the majority of the Commission...

Now he was perplexed:

For the Government, after discarding the proposals of the majority, is apparently to accept the proposals of the smallest minority, a minority of one...[218]

The Cabinet met twice on 7 August, again next day, and on 14 August. Montagu's reservations were overridden. After much argument, the final decision was:

1. State purchase of the mineral rights;

2. A central fund to improve living conditions;

3. Rejection of nationalization, on the grounds both that the case had not been made out, and that it could not be afforded;

4. A commitment to improve housing conditions and amenities;

5. Encouragement of district amalgamations of collieries;

6. Measures to protect consumers and strengthen the export trade.

The decision was presented to the House of Commons by the Prime Minister on 18 August, just before the summer adjournment. Lloyd George and Bonar Law again denied that they had ever committed themselves to nationalization ahead of the Sankey reports.

Lloyd George then took aim at two targets. The first was Sidney, together with Chiozza Money – the two Commission members who had appeared as witnesses:

Two of its members left the seat of judgment to go into the witness box. It is difficult to treat with respect Commissioners who take that view of their functions. They were there to deliberate on very vital matters. They were supposed to reserve judgment, whatever were their preconceived opinions, until they had heard the whole of the evidence. What happens? They go into the witness box and express an opinion. It was a most regrettable incident.[219]

Then there were the Yorkshire miners. Most had now returned to work. This did not inhibit Lloyd George:

What is the theory of those who say that nationalisation will promote harmony? It is the theory that, while they would ask the worker to strike against the employer who is making profit, he will not strike against the State, which has only the common interest of all to look after. But there was the Yorkshire strike. The Yorkshire strike was a direct strike against the Government. [220]

Labour MPs, like the miners' leaders, believed that, in the spring, the government, under pressure, had committed itself to nationalization. Vernon Hartshorn, MP for Ogmore, a leading member of the South Wales Miners Federation who had given evidence to Sankey, told the Commons the miners had been deceived:

...we did not ask for a Commission. We accepted it. We gave evidence before it. Why was the Commission set up? Was it a huge game of bluff? Was it never intended that if the Reports favoured nationalization we were to get it? Why was the question sent at all to the Commission? That is the kind of question the miners of the country will, ask, and they will say, 'We have been deceived, betrayed, duped.' [221]

Most of the government deal was never delivered. It was referred to, contemptuously, as *Duckham and water*, and rejected by the MFGB. Promised legislation to nationalise mining royalties never materialised.

There was a legacy of anger and bitterness; Sidney described the failure to implement even the uncontentious welfare reforms proposed by Sankey in stark terms:

The breach of faith was thus gross, naked, and unashamed. [222]

The Fife miner William Adamson was Labour Leader, and Leader of the Opposition. In that August 1919 debate Adamson warned that nationalisation of the mines and the railways would be an issue at the next election and

...at every succeeding election until the principle has been secured and is made part and parcel of our national policy. [223]

This prediction of Adamson's was fulfilled by Labour almost to the letter, starting with the 1922 election:

Our industrial policy involves the prompt Nationalisation of Mines, as recommended by the Sankey Commission... [224]

And continuing to 1945, after which it was finally implemented:

For a quarter of a century the coal industry, producing Britain's most precious national raw material, has been floundering chaotically under the ownership of many hundreds of independent companies. Amalgamation under public

ownership will bring great economies in operation and make it possible to modernise production methods and to raise safety standards in every colliery in the country.[225]

SIDNEY, LABOUR, AND SEAHAM

After the war, and Sidney's work in 1919 on the Sankey Commission, his standing with Labour in general, and the MFGB in particular, was high. At the June 1919 Labour Conference, supported by the miners, he topped the poll for Labour's National Executive Committee.

In August 1919, Sidney began to receive invitations from miners' lodges and Independent Labour Party branches in Seaham, Durham, to stand as their parliamentary candidate. At first, the Durham Miners Association opposed this, insisting their candidate should be a miner. So in February 1920 Sidney withdrew.

But the approaches continued. In June Sidney and Beatrice spent two weeks in Seaham. Beatrice thought there was little doubt that Sidney would be chosen. She thought their support came from *bookish miners* – with shelves of

...well-known poets and classics, a little philosophy and more economics. [226]

Sidney was selected, and after the summer he and Beatrice focussed on winning the election. Although Seaham was a mining seat, a Coalition Liberal had been elected in 1918.

They left nothing to chance: Sidney wrote a history of the Durham miners; they card-indexed local groups – clubs, institutes, churches and chapels, friendly societies – and then wrote, offering *innocuous sounding lectures* – on the history of mining, the social services, and other topics.

In a long stay in the autumn they delivered over forty lectures in pit villages. The miner Jack Lawson, the MP for nearby Chester le Street, thought Beatrice made the greater impact:

...Mrs Webb gripped the women much more than he ever did. There was the real stuff of the north when she addressed meetings... [227]

They found it tiring; they were pleased to get back to Grosvenor Road for Christmas. As they were packing up to leave, an already exhausted Beatrice heard that another sister – Margaret Hobhouse – had been diagnosed with terminal cancer.

Andrew Bonar Law had replaced Arthur Balfour as Conservative leader in 1911; he took his party into Asquith's 1915 coalition. From 1916 he was Lloyd

George's Deputy Prime Minister. In March 1921, exhausted and unwell, he resigned from the government and as leader of the Conservative Party. His successor as leader was Austen Chamberlain. A long stay on the French Riviera appeared to partly restore Bonar Law's health.

In October 1922, against Chamberlain's view, Conservative MPs voted to leave the Lloyd George coalition. Chamberlain resigned the leadership; Bonar Law was chosen in his place, and became Prime Minister. The Conservative backbench 1922 Committee took its name from these events.

Parliament was dissolved and the Conservatives won the November 1922 election, with 344 seats to Labour's 142. Sidney was elected MP for Seaham.

MacDonald, who had been defeated in 1918, returned as MP for Aberavon, in South Wales. MacDonald was quickly reinstated as Leader – the position from which he had resigned in August 1914. Arthur Henderson, also defeated in 1918 but re-elected at a 1919 byelection, lost his seat.

Parliament met in February 1923; Beatrice thought Sidney was

...like a boy going for his first term to a public school! [228]

At MacDonald's request, Sidney joined the front bench. He did not take easily to the Commons chamber. Rowdy elements on the government benches sensed that this small, mild man of 63 might be easy prey. In March 1923, speaking on unemployment, he was barracked and jeered by Conservatives. According to Beatrice, this

...threw him off his subject; he repeated himself and failed to make all his points, and sat down without making his last words intelligible... [229]

Disruption continued. Some Conservatives resented Sidney, a newcomer, sitting on the front bench. Beatrice described how they would arrive, well oiled, in the evening:

...the crowded Tory benches, hilarious from dinner, amuse themselves and vent their spite by talking loudly, and then when they have made the speaker inaudible, crying out 'Speak up'. [230]

In April Beatrice watched Sidney reply to a debate. Hansard records repeated shouts of *Speak up*. The Speaker interjected:

The hon Member is speaking quite loud enough if hon Members would only listen. [231]

Later that evening Sidney intervened to correct a ministerial statement. A Conservative shouted, *Sit down, Nanny*. David Kirkwood, a Clydeside ILP member, objected. He said that Sidney, a *revered* member of the party, had been insulted. The session was quickly brought to a halt.

The Webbs had known MacDonald for longer than most Labour MPs. They viewed him with a guarded, wry detachment. On his election, Beatrice wrote

If he is not the best man for the post, he is at any rate the worst and most dangerous man out of it.[232]

By June 1923 she admitted MacDonald was

…proving a far better leader than I should have expected…[233]

Sidney

…does not seem in the least to resent JRM's leadership, always treats him as his leader, with no reserves, and with no desire to 'manipulate'.[234]

This was despite her noting, in March, that

JRM of course does not like him, though he has behaved very well and even generously since he has been the Leader of the Party.[235]

Beatrice listened to MacDonald in November 1923; she thought he was clever, sometimes eloquent

…not the oration of a great *leader of men, but certainly of an accomplished leader of the Labour Party…the speech lacked intellectual and emotional grip and utter sincerity.*[236]

Beatrice supported Sidney becoming an MP. His instinct had been to refuse the approaches; she begged him to pause. After his selection, she wrote

…on the whole we are content to proceed with this adventure…[237]

Once he was elected, she saw supporting him as her first responsibility. She wrote regularly to women Labour members in Seaham. In her first letter, in December 1922, she described their home – *a little house on the Westminster Embankment* – and their routine:

Every morning at eight o'clock punctually we have each one cup of coffee and bread and butter on a tray in our workroom; we read our letters and skim through the Times *and the* Herald *newspapers, and then we get to work, and work steadily until our midday meal at one o'clock.*[238]

Mostly she wrote about current politics. In July 1924 she wrote about the Communist party request for affiliation to Labour

I do not think that you have many Communists in the Seaham Division? The miners are a hard-headed lot... [239]

In August 1920 Sidney and Beatrice attended a Socialist International conference in Geneva with Frank Hodges of the MFGB and his wife Henrietta. Henrietta told Beatrice how lonely her life was in London, away from friends and family. She knew no one. Her husband was often away; she worried about drink.

Beatrice thought the answer could be to help Labour women to meet socially. The male leadership were sceptical; Egerton Wake, Labour's National Agent told her:

Not even your genius for organising, Mrs Webb, will make the wives of Labour men come out of their homes and hob-nob with the women organisers and the well-to-do women. [240]

Nevertheless, Beatrice persisted. The outcome was the Half Circle Club: part social, part educational, meeting sometimes at 41 Grosvenor Road, sometimes elsewhere. By July 1921 Beatrice thought she had overcome the antipathy:

Only J R MacDonald remains actively hostile. George Lansbury is suspicious, and some others jeer. [241]

When the Webbs went to Durham at Easter 1921, Beatrice left early to get back for a Half Circle Club event:

Over a hundred persons turned up and we had a rollicking evening [242]

Even the prospect of a rollicking evening, however, was not enough to eliminate the suspicion of condescension; Molly Hamilton records that a dissident group started an 'Anti Beatrice Society.'

In 1922-1923, Sidney chaired the Labour Party National Executive Committee. He used his Chairman's Address at the Labour conference in June 1923 to give a comprehensive statement of his political position. The speech was published by the Fabians, with the title *The Labour Party on the Threshold* – the threshold of power. Sidney forecast that, on current trends, the party could win a clear majority of votes by about 1926.

It was a visionary speech, building on Sidney's work on international and domestic policy during the war. He called for international cooperation, and denounced the Versailles settlement:

Europe could no more be rebuilt upon the passion of hate, the passion of greed, and the passion of fear, than upon anger and violence. [243]

He raised the possibility of an international currency, a European Customs

Union, and the *undisturbed and untaxed* passage of goods and passengers. He also called for common, cross-European education in schools and universities,

...in substitution for the ludicrously false history and economics still inserted, in the supposed interests of patriotism, in the school books of the world.[244]

In the best-known passage Sidney spoke about the *inevitable gradualness* of Labour's plans:

...why, because we are idealists, should we be supposed to be idiots? For the Labour Party, it must be plain, socialism is rooted in political Democracy; which necessarily compels us to recognize that every step towards our goal is dependent on gaining the assent and support of at least a numerical majority of the whole people.[245]

Labour was a non-violent party:

Violence persuades no one, convinces no one, satisfies no one...that is to say violence may destroy, but it can never construct.[246]

He concluded by reminding the conference that the founder of British socialism was not Marx, but Robert Owen, and by invoking the spirit of William Morris:

...fellowship is life, and lack of fellowship is death, and the deeds that ye do upon the earth, it is for fellowship's sake that ye do them...[247]

Beatrice thought things had gone well:

Sidney is presiding over the Labour Party conference for five days this week and doing it very successfully. His opening address, 'Labour on the Threshold' has been well received and considerably reported.[248]

THE LSE AND THE NEW STATESMAN AFTER THE WAR

Sidney and Beatrice sometimes referred to the LSE and the *New Statesman* as their children.

Pember Reeves had been Director of LSE since 1908. By 1919, some staff were unhappy with his leadership. In a painful meeting in April 1919, Sidney persuaded Reeves to resign.

For the next Director, Sidney first thought of Maynard Keynes. The Webbs knew of Keynes; they did not yet know him well. The chair of the governors,

Arthur Steel-Maitland (now a Conservative MP, previously an investigator for the Poor Law Commission) had reservations.

Other candidates were considered; Sidney then turned to William Beveridge. Beveridge's future in the civil service was uncertain. He was 39; he had been a Permanent Secretary; he was Sir William; but he was not in favour with Lloyd George. The approach was made; by mid-May Sidney was pressing Beveridge for an answer:

> I don't want to hurry you, or to imply anything either way. But you ought to be reminded that time is running on...[249]

Beveridge negotiated the conditions of his employment in correspondence with Sidney, who agreed that:

> the tenure of the post would not exclude my becoming a candidate or member of Parliament, subject, of course, to any necessary readjustment of duties and salary to enable the work of the School to be efficiently carried on. [250]

By the end of June everything was settled. Beatrice, with some reservations, approved:

> ...he is not the sweetest-tempered of men and has a certain narrowness of outlook. But he is a good administrator, an initiator of both ideas and plans...[251]

Both Webbs considered Beveridge's appointment a success. In 1921 Beatrice recorded that:

> The London School of Economics (Sidney's favourite child) is brilliantly developing under the able direction of Beveridge, whom Sidney selected. [252]

Beveridge and Sidney worked well together. In November 1919, Beatrice noted that Sidney was acting as if he was chairman; Beveridge himself wrote much later that

> ...it remained true of the Governors, as of many other gatherings, that wherever Sidney Webb happened to sit, there was the Chair – the source of ideas and practical expedients and reconciling compromises.[253]

In January 1921 Beatrice was researching in Manchester; Sidney wrote to her from Grosvenor Road:

> I lunched with Beveridge, who is in great form and good spirits.[254]

In April, Beveridge missed an evening at Grosvenor Road – probably the *rollicking* Half Circle Club party. Beatrice wrote

...we were very sorry not to see you here last night. We had a very jolly party here. [255]

Janet Mair, who had worked alongside Beveridge in the wartime civil service, soon joined him at LSE. According to Beveridge's biographer, when Sidney appointed Beveridge, he acknowledged that Mrs Mair was *the price he would have to pay.*[256] She arrived at the School as Administrative Secretary in 1919. The following year she took on the additional role of Dean of Admissions. She stayed until Beveridge left in 1937. Staff, students, and even Beatrice, speculated, sometimes over-excitedly and sometimes pruriently, about the relationship between Beveridge and Mrs Mair.

Mrs Mair carried a heavy administrative workload at LSE. Her predecessor, Miss Mactaggart, had joined LSE in its early days (she had originally been hired as the Shaws' housekeeper, when they were living over the shop at Albion Terrace); she had been responsible for almost everything. Janet used her civil service experience to create a more systematic administration.

Deservedly or otherwise, Janet Mair quickly became unpopular with the academic staff. And Beatrice listened to her critics. In 1922 LSE had use of Dunford, a country house in Sussex, formerly the home of the Cobden family. The Webbs spent weekends there with staff members, including Harold Laski, Graham Wallas, RH Tawney, and Mostyn Lloyd. Barbara Wootton had given up a Cambridge post to work first for LRD, subsequently for the TUC. She spent a weekend at Dunford, with the Webbs and others, in February 1922.

At Dunford, Beatrice was struck by *the hatred of Mrs Mair*, who she thought had an *ambitious and domineering temperament.*[257] The Webbs did not waver in their support for Beveridge; their attitude to Janet Mair was more ambivalent. Beatrice was told that Mrs Mair was *ruining Beveridge's influence* and that she *comes between the Director and his staff.* The issue would not go away.

The *New Statesman* survived the war, though costs were high and viability uncertain. Clifford Sharp returned as editor in 1919.

Jack Squire, the Literary Editor, and wartime acting editor, left to start a literary monthly, the *London Mercury*, which appeared in November 1919. The *Mercury* relied on the talent pool Squire had developed at the *New Statesman*. He published new poetry – by Belloc, Siegfried Sassoon, Walter de la Mare, and others, including, in the first edition, a previously unpublished poem by Rupert Brooke. Reviews, at first, were strictly anonymous; the magazine reviewed Virginia Woolf's *Night and Day* favourably, and also reviewed Maynard Keynes' *Economic Consequences of the Peace.*

Sidney still chaired the *New Statesman* board. Two issues were dominant: the political relationship between chairman and editor; and the commercial viability of the paper.

'Permeation' was over: the Webbs were firmly aligned with the Labour Party. Although Sharp had joined the Fabians in 1905, his sympathies were with the Liberals – and with Asquith, rather than Lloyd George. Beatrice wrote that, in 1921, Sharp told her

> ...*he was not and had never been a member of the Labour Party which, seeing that he is a member of the Fabian Society, is hardly correct.*[258]

Beatrice was scathing about the Asquith influence on Sharp:

> ...*the same political temperament as Asquith; the same coarse-grained character and strong commonplace intelligence; the same conventionality of culture and outlook; the same contempt for enthusiasm and idealism; the same liking for heavy drinking, smoking and card playing, the same taste for ornamental and parasitic women.*[259]

When the *New Statesman* began, GBS had recommended weekly lunches. These continued after the war, on Tuesdays at Grosvenor Road – though, according to Sharp, Sidney

> ...*was always careful to avoid even the appearance of seeking to direct general policy.*[260]

Desmond MacCarthy, Literary Editor from 1920, sometimes went; Sharp attended only occasionally:

> ...*he no longer regards us as colleagues either in the direction of the* New Statesman *or in the world of politics. There is no break but there is no longer any intellectual intimacy.*[261]

One day in February 1922, Sharp did turn up; his appearance worried Beatrice:

> *Clifford Sharp, alas, looks as if the rumour that he is a heavy drinker was correct: he has the unmistakable lines about the mouth which one recognises as a result of alcoholic self-indulgence.*[262]

Sidney resigned as board chair in November 1922, after becoming an MP; Beatrice noted

> *Our relations with Clifford Sharp and the NS practically tho' not ostensibly severed.*[263]

The gulf between Sharp and the Webbs widened; while the paper remained left of centre, there was too much criticism of Labour to ignore. Meanwhile, two other people from the Webb network became regular contributors.

Mostyn Lloyd, like Sharp, had worked on the Poor Law campaign. Close to the Webbs, he started writing leading articles for the New Statesman after leaving the army. He was not full-time; his day job was as head of Social Science at LSE. Lloyd impressed Beatrice:

He is gloomy and disgruntled, but he is a success as a journalist and lecturer and an exemplary husband and father.[264]

A story was told in Lloyd's family that, in 1919 or 1920, Sidney told Lloyd and Attlee that one or other must stand for parliament. Both refused, so a coin was tossed, and Lloyd stayed where he was.[265]

The other new regular contributor – again a part time leader writer – was GDH Cole, who gave the paper a radical cutting edge. Closer to the Labour Party than previously, Cole was still emotionally a Guild Socialist. Lloyd had served in the war; Cole had opposed it.

Beatrice worried about their future under Sharp – who, she thought,

…lacks all the finer loyalties of life. How long he will employ CM Lloyd and GDH Cole as leader writers is an interesting question.[266]

Sales of the paper slowly increased. It still lost money – but on a modest scale. It survived because it had long-term backers – two of the original, 1913 investors, Ernest Simon, and Edward Whitley; Arnold Bennett; and Glynne Williams. GBS and the Webbs remained shareholders, but on a smaller scale.

In 1916, the *New Statesman* sold 6000 copies a week; between 1919 and 1925 sales fluctuated between 7000 and 10,000. In 1919-1920, it lost £4,000, rising to £6,500 in 1920-1921. Sharp and John Roberts, the business manager, worked to reduce this; by 1923, they were budgeting for a deficit below £1,000. And anyhow, according to the *New Statesman's* first historian:

…apart from the very long established Spectator, *and* Punch, *no sixpenny weekly review had ever come within £1,000 a year of paying its way…*[267]

As Beatrice observed in 1921:

The New Statesman, though still losing money, is not losing our money (!)[268]

In winter 1922-1923 there was a possibility of resolving both issues – politics and viability. The *New Statesman* was a – more or less – Labour-supporting weekly with a Liberal-sympathizing editor; the *Nation* was a Liberal weekly with a Labour-sympathizing editor (Henry Massingham). Both were commercially precarious.

The *Nation*, backed by Rowntree money, had been launched following the 1906 Liberal landslide. By 1922, Rowntrees had had enough. A fresh consortium of Liberal supporters – backed by Keynes and Ernest Simon (still at this point a Liberal) – was formed to take over the *Nation*.

According to Beatrice, it occurred to the new consortium that

> ...*the* New Statesman *with C Sharp as Editor represented their views; that both papers were losing money, that the two together had a combined circulation of near 20,000 and that even if some of this double circulation were lost on amalgamation there would be sufficient left to make the amalgamated paper a handsome commercial proposition.* [269]

Sharp, at first, was keen. But he asked the prospective proprietors for

> ...*virtual security of tenure and complete freedom of control and the political independence of the paper.*[270]

He was not sure they would agree. He also wanted Sidney's agreement. Sidney was prepared to be bought out – but only if the other collectivist shareholders – Whitley and Glynne Williams – took the same view.

They did not. They objected, and were prepared to underwrite further losses. Meanwhile, the prospective owners made it clear that, if they succeeded, the new amalgamated paper would be distinctively Liberal, not collectivist. Glynne Williams became the new Chairman of the *New Statesman*.

Sharp told Beatrice that he was more than satisfied. She agreed:

> ...*the Liberal Group would not have left him as free of control as we have and I very much doubt whether he would have got any kind of security of tenure.*[271]

The *Nation* enjoyed another eight years of independence, with Keynes as chairman, and fellow Cambridge economist Hubert Henderson as editor, before it was absorbed by the *New Statesman*.

People in the Webb network moved easily between its different branches. Attlee and Mostyn Lloyd both taught at LSE; in March 1919 the Fabian Finance and General Purposes Committee encouraged both to stand for the Fabian Executive – to which both were duly elected.

THE FIRST LABOUR GOVERNMENT

Bonar Law's term of office as Prime Minister was brief. In spring 1923 his voice began to fail; in May, he was diagnosed with inoperable throat cancer; and on 20 May he resigned, dying in October. His successor was Stanley Baldwin: a midlands steelmaker, and an MP since 1908.

Twenty years after Joseph Chamberlain had first raised the issue, tariff reform still divided the Conservatives. In 1922, Law promised that Conservatives would not introduce tariffs in the new parliament. Baldwin was pro-tariff; in October 1923, as Prime Minister, he re-opened the subject, saying unemployment could only be fought by protection. Law's promise a year earlier meant that there must be another election. Parliament was dissolved on 16 November; polling day was 6 December.

The Webbs were at Seaham when the election was announced. Beatrice thought it meant *reaction with a vengeance*:

> *...the capture of the PM by the Tory Machine and the younger members of the cabinet. Apparently a full-blooded Protectionist policy is to be put before the country in the near future and a verdict taken.* [272]

Beatrice predicted that the Conservatives would also try to restrict trade union funding for Labour, although in fact this did not happen until later in the decade. Baldwin did not win a new mandate, but lost his majority. The result was:

Conservative	258
Labour	191
Liberal	158

In Seaham, Sidney was re-elected. Before polling day, Beatrice wrote

> *...we are on velvet in this ideal constituency... The miners have become genuinely attached to their member. They are proud of him, they are attached to him, they trust him and they feel he is 'their man'...the best member Seaham has ever had for local purposes.* [273]

In the chair at the June 1923 Labour Conference, Sidney had forecast that Labour would achieve a majority by about 1926. The Webbs had worked towards this outcome since 1912. Sidney's wartime reports, the Labour Party 1918 constitution, and Beatrice's mission to *discover the land of Whitehall* were all part of the process.

But the reality now was not a Labour majority, but the possibility of a minority government. Labour would not be free to implement the programme contained in *Labour and the New Social Order*. They would hold office on sufferance.

In December 1923 Labour faced three tasks: celebrating the gains that had been made; debating whether, and on what terms, to accept office; and, once the decision to form a minority government had been taken, deciding the composition of the government. Sidney and Beatrice were central to all three.

TJ spent election night at 10 Downing Street. His sympathies were hardly secret. He described how one Conservative lady

...was almost beside herself with panic for the fate of a country so blind to its best interests as to vote against the one policy which could save it. I watched the growing tale of Labour victories with undisguised joy amid cries of 'You Bolshevist! [274]

Baldwin returned to London on Friday 7 December. He decided not to resign at once, but to face the House of Commons in January.

Next day the Webbs came home. Beatrice called what came next

...the hectic days of victory tempered by the cold feet of the leaders at the consequences of victory. [275]

Grosvenor Road was the setting for frenetic political and social activity.

On Saturday evening, Massingham (Labour-inclined editor of the Liberal-inclined *Nation*) called round. He argued against any deal with the Liberals.

Henderson came to lunch on Sunday. Once again, he had lost his own seat. Henderson thought Labour should form a government – but with a moderate programme, courting Liberal support. Sidney disagreed:

...agreed to taking office but demurred to 'moderateness' – if it was moderateness in order to get Liberal support and not a moderateness synonymous with administrative practicability. [276]

Clifford Sharp (Liberal-inclined editor of the broadly Labour-supporting *New Statesman*) arrived, with an article supporting a Liberal-Labour coalition. By the time of the *New Statesman* lunch on Tuesday he had changed his mind

...as even the Liberals were against it. We laughed at him... [277]

Monday evening's guests were the Labour leadership

... a dinner here of leaders: JRM, Henderson, Clynes, Thomas and Snowden – to discuss taking office and what exactly they would do if they did. [278]

Sidney thought the most cautious about the prospect of power were MacDonald and Snowden; Henderson was the only one who was not hesitant.

Snowden...is chicken-hearted and will try to cut down expenditure – he even demurred to a programme of public works for the unemployed... [279]

In his own diary MacDonald wrote

Met Clynes, Thomas, Henderson, Snowden and Webb at Webb's. All agreed that we shd take office...Discussed Foreign Policy, Unemployment and Budget. Unanimous that moderation and honesty were our safety. [280]

That consensus was endorsed by Labour's National Executive, who agreed that

...should the necessity for forming a Labour Government arise, the Parliamentary Party should at once accept full responsibility for the Government of the country without compromising itself with any form of coalition.[281]

The victory party on Wednesday was hosted by Sidney and Beatrice:

Our little house was crowded with over 200 chattering men and women – some 20 or 30 MPs; another 20 defeated candidates – all in a state of emotional strain and physical and mental fatigue – easy to congratulate and console...It was a funny thought, this first gathering of the victorious Labour party – at the house of Altiora and Oscar Bailey – HGW should have been here to describe it!
[282]

Hugh Dalton had been defeated in Cardiff. He returned to London that Wednesday:

'Squash at the Webbs'. Candidates victorious and vanquished. Short speeches by MacDonald, Webb, who tells us all to be discreet and not ask for jobs, Uncle [Arthur Henderson] and Wake. [Egerton Wake, Labour's National Agent].[283]

MacDonald then went home to Lossiemouth, his highland birthplace. A Labour Government was now probable; if it happened, MacDonald would be Prime Minister, and Sidney a minister.

Sidney had known MacDonald since the 1880s: Beatrice had known him almost as long. The relationship had endured through battles in the Fabian Society, the LCC, and over the Boer War. MacDonald and the Webbs had taken different views over the First World War.

But for now, hostilities were suspended:

Funniest of all is the cordial relationship between JRM and ourselves – all the more cordial because there is no pretence of personal intimacy or friendship. We have learnt not only to accept each other but to respect and value our respective qualities. JRM is apparently not capable of personal intimacies – he never had 'loves' among his colleagues...[284]

...when one recollects the record of the Parliamentary Labour Party 1910-14 one begins to doubt the leadership of JRM. However, you cannot get better bread than there is wheat...[285]

From Lossiemouth, MacDonald wrote asking Sidney to take charge of unemployment policy as Minister of Labour, supported by Margaret Bondfield:

As little legislation as you can do with, please, though you will need some. Think over your staff and get everything ready to put into operation at once.[286]

Sidney accepted by telegram; he was amused:

If anyone had prophesied ten years ago that JRM would be Prime Minister and would invite me to be in his Cabinet, I should have thought the first extremely unlikely, but the two combined a sheer impossibility.[287]

While Sidney began to plan, MacDonald tried to give his government a broader base. He needed ministers with experience, and ministers in the Lords. He turned to Haldane, who wrote to Sidney on 12 December

Ramsay MacDonald telephoned urgently for a meeting. In the evening he offered me anything I chose if I would help him: the leadership of the House of Lords, the Chancellorship, Defence, Education...[288]

On Christmas Eve MacDonald asked Haldane to be education minister. Haldane replied by inviting MacDonald to Cloan. MacDonald stopped there, on his way back from Lossiemouth – with the outcome that Haldane agreed to become Lord Chancellor. Before MacDonald arrived, Haldane alerted Sidney:

I have been in communication with Ramsay MacDonald who comes here for a night on Thursday, on his way South (This had better be private).[289]

After Christmas, London politics resumed. On 12 January, the Webbs dined with Haldane

...one of those little confabs we have had for over thirty years with this fellow conspirator...we talked to him freely about all the possible persons for all the possible posts; and he was to pass these suggestions on as his own to JRM...[290]

Haldane was a Liberal who rallied to MacDonald. Beatrice's brother-in-law, Alfred Cripps, now Lord Parmoor, had been a Conservative. Always deeply religious, he had supported peace initiatives during the war. In January he joined the cabinet as Lord President, speaking on foreign affairs in the Lords, (MacDonald was Foreign Secretary as well as Prime Minister). Beatrice commented

So there will be two 'RP' husbands in the Labour Government: the Tory and the Socialist![291]

Parliament was due to meet on Tuesday 15 January. The evening before, it was preceded by a

...secret dinner at Haldane's last night, to which Sidney and others had been invited by JRM to discuss the King's Speech and procedure.[292]

The Baldwin government was defeated on the King's Speech; on Tuesday 22 January MacDonald was called to the Palace and appointed Prime Minister. The King wrote in his diary:

Today 23 years ago dear Grandmama died. I wonder what she would have thought of a Labour Government! [293]

On his way home TJ saw the evening newspaper placards:

Lenin dead (official) Ramsay MacDonald Premier [294]

MacDonald gave his list of Ministers to the King on Tuesday. Sidney had been upgraded from the Ministry of Labour to the more ancient (and senior) office of President of the Board of Trade. Snowden was Chancellor; Henderson – not yet an MP, soon to be elected at a byelection – Home Secretary.

They met as Ministers for the first time that afternoon. Haldane coached them on procedure, with anecdotes about past cabinets. Next morning, after rehearsing, they were sworn in at the palace. Afterwards several came back to Grosvenor Road for lunch:

Uncle Arthur was bursting with childish joy over his HO seals in the red leather box which he handed round the company; Sidney was chuckling over a hitch in the solemn ceremony in which he had been right and Hankey wrong; they were all laughing over Wheatley [John Wheatley, Clydesider, ILP, Minister of Health] – the revolutionary – going down on both knees and actually kissing the King's hand... [295]

The Webb network was strongly represented. As well as Haldane the fellow-conspirator and Parmoor the brother-in-law, Sydney Olivier – the founding Fabian who had worked with Sidney in the Colonial Office, and since been a colonial governor – became Lord Olivier, Secretary of State for India. The First Lord of the Admiralty, in charge of the Navy, was Lord Chelmsford; twenty years earlier, as Frederic Thesiger, he had been one of the LCC Conservatives with whom Sidney cooperated on education.

Outside the Cabinet, Henry Slesser became Solicitor General. As Henry Schloesser, he had drafted the Prevention of Destitution Bill; in 1912 he had been appointed Standing Counsel to the Labour Party. When war broke out, faced with anti-German hysteria, he had anglicized his name to Slesser. During the war he had advised the War Emergency Workers National Committee and the Labour Party. He was not yet an MP, but was urgently summoned to London and made King's Counsel.

Among civil servants, as well as Tom Jones, Hubert Llewellyn Smith – author of the 1892 technical education report and now Chief Economic Adviser – called at Grosvenor Road. Beatrice thought he had *fought shy of the Webbs all these years*. But when he arrived, she

> ... *welcomed him so affectionately as my lost son that he unbent and became quite sentimentally reminiscent of our rambles together on The Argoed hill together before my marriage.*[296]

Beatrice wrote to the Seaham women, caricaturing the press hysteria at Labour's success:

> ...*the horrible spectre of Ramsay MacDonald seated cross-legged and in his shirt sleeves, with the red cap of Liberty on his head, in the Cabinet Room at 10 Downing Street – Henderson, Clynes, Thomas and Snowden – those grim ogres of democracy crouching by his side, with the wily Webb somewhere in the shadows.*[297]

MacDonald's Government had little freedom of action. It had no majority; other parties could defeat it at any time. There was no chance of it implementing Labour's ambitious programme. The most successful domestic minister was John Wheatley, the ILP Clydesider appointed Minister of Health, who led a significant housing programme, and at least initiated new studies on how to end the Poor Law.

Snowden, as Chancellor, brought Gladstonian rigour to controlling public spending. Winston Churchill, Snowden's successor as Chancellor, later wrote

> *The Treasury mind and the Snowden mind embraced each other with the fervour of two long-separated kindred lizards...*[298]

Sidney played three roles: as departmental minister at the Board of Trade; chairing the cabinet committee on unemployment; and as a member of the inner leadership.

At the Board of Trade Sidney followed the department's agenda. The Board regulated business and shipping; on 1 February Sidney brought to Cabinet a list of proposed legislation, concerned with contracts, shipping, and the coastguard service. The most pressing item was to validate, retrospectively, charges that had been levied by government during the war; Sidney successfully took through the necessary legislation. He initiated some new work – studies on monopoly and competition policy, a proposal to give local councils the power to sell domestic coal, and an inquiry into the long-term prospects for British trade and industry. None of this bore fruit before the government fell.

In March, Beatrice noted that the Labour ministers were liked by civil servants:

...hard working and unpretentious in manner, they bring with them an atmosphere of comradeship in public service.[299]

That month Sidney and Beatrice gave a reception for two hundred staff

All the Heads of Department turned up and representatives of all the various grades and sports associations, right down to girl typists. 'We have never yet seen a President of the Board of Trade – leave alone his wife' said one delighted guest to the Head of his Department.[300]

In July Beatrice and Haldane discussed which ministers were effective. He rated Snowden, Wheatley, and Lord Arnold (ex-Liberal – Colonial Office junior minister) – and Sidney:

Sidney is self-effacing; but he always knows his subject and has control of his officials.[301]

Unemployment had been central to Labour's 1923 General Election campaign:

After a year of barren effort, the Conservative Government has admitted its inability to cope with the problem of Unemployment, and is seeking to cover up its failure by putting the nation to the trouble and expense of an election on the Tariff issue.[302]

The manifesto asserted that tariffs would not solve unemployment. Labour's remedy would be national schemes of productive work, with adequate maintenance for those who cannot obtain employment. Examples of productive work included electrification, transport investment, afforestation, and housebuilding.

A Cabinet Committee, chaired by Sidney and advised by Llewellyn Smith, was established to implement this programme. The manifesto commitment and the programme had two origins. There was the long tradition of government relief works – usually seasonal – to mitigate the worst effects of unemployment; and there was the aspiration to manage the national demand for labour so as to eliminate unemployment altogether, as advocated in the Minority Report.

During the war, unemployment had virtually disappeared. For the first eighteen months of peace, the economy boomed; then, in mid-1920, unemployment reappeared. The role of the state had grown in the war years; as peace returned, the Coalition began cutting spending. Soon unemployment insurance could not cope with the numbers. Unemployed people exhausted their entitlement to benefit; after some short term extensions, they could be driven back onto outdoor relief.

By 1924 it was clear that traditional industrial communities would bear the brunt of rising unemployment, although talk of regional problems and regional policy did not appear until the 1930s. A February report to Sidney's committee [303] mentions shipbuilding and marine engineering, engineering, iron and steel, ceramics, and textiles. Areas particularly affected included the North East coast, Cumberland, Barrow, Merseyside, Sheffield, and the metal industries of the West Midlands.

Sidney's Committee had to meet conflicting expectations: it was supposed to make a long-term difference, but had also to make an immediate impact on the unemployment figures. Reconciling these pressures was impossible within the term of a government lasting only from January to October.

In February, reporting to Cabinet, the Committee set out their prospectus:

> ...the policy of the present Government will, from the start, aim at the augmentation of the total volume of employment and the consequent absorption of the unemployed in their own trades and industries, and that the Government will regard the _ad hoc_ schemes for the temporary relief of the unemployed as of secondary importance and as being merely supplementary expedients...[304]

Schemes would go on all year round, not limited to winter. The priority was economic development by restoring trade, rather than just relief of unemployment.

This was a tough message to communicate, even to sympathetic ears: on 1 February TJ met Sidney:

> We then talked of Unemployment, and it was rather disappointing to find Sidney Webb, the author of pamphlets innumerable on the cure of unemployment regardless of cost, now, as Chairman of the Unemployment Committee, reduced to prescribing a revival of trade as the one remedy left to us.[305]

The committee met regularly, with sub committees for unemployment and for housing. It endorsed major road schemes. Three of these – the East Lancs Road, linking Liverpool and Manchester; the Chertsey Road, in outer South West London; and the London North Orbital Road – were in the pipeline before the government took office. All were – eventually – partly constructed, although work on site did not begin in the lifetime of the 1924 Government. The Committee encouraged Wheatley's housing programme; this lasted until 1933, leading to the building of over 500,000 council homes.

Research was commissioned on the future supply and distribution of electricity. Nothing changed while the 1924 MacDonald government was in office – but it was part of the process of establishing a national framework for the sector. The Committee examined the case for a Severn barrage. They put resources into export credits.

It was uphill stuff, with no easy results. Labour Ministers were vulnerable to criticism that they were not cutting the unemployment figures here and now. On holiday in May, Beatrice wrote

Unemployment is certainly the crux – and up to today the Labour Party has not succeeded in putting forward a practicable policy – probably because such a policy could only be developed slowly through a long course of years and with great deliberation and continuity of action. Where I think the Labour leaders have been at fault – and we among them – is in implying, if not asserting, that the prevention of unemployment was an easy and rapid task instead of being a difficult and slow business involving many complicated transactions and far more control of capitalist enterprise than anyone has yet worked out.[306]

The real failure was not Ministers' inability to solve unemployment between January and October 1924. It was that, in opposition for the next five years, the party did not generate new thinking before returning to government in 1929.

After Easter an inner group emerged: MacDonald convened Monday lunchtime meetings, with Sidney, Henderson, Clynes, (Leader of the House of Commons), Snowden, Jimmy Thomas (Colonial Secretary), and Ben Spoor, the Chief Whip, to discuss the week's business. Beatrice thought it a curious grouping – more a party caucus than the leadership of the cabinet. If the government had lasted into the autumn wider meetings were planned, to plan future strategy.

Those meetings never happened: the government fell in October, over the issue of the *Workers' Weekly*, a Communist newspaper.

On 25 July, the paper published, anonymously, an article by Harry Pollitt (already a Communist Party organiser; later its General Secretary) calling on service personnel not to turn their guns on workers:

Refuse to shoot down your fellow-workers!
Refuse to fight for profits!
Turn your weapons on your oppressors![307]

On 30 July the paper's acting editor, John Ross Campbell, was arrested and charged that he

...feloniously, maliciously and advisedly endeavoured to seduce divers persons unknown, then serving in His Majesty's Navy, Army and Airforce, from their allegiance to His Majesty...[308]

Campbell was bailed; on 5 August, police raided the paper's offices and took away 2000 copies and other documents.

Next day, three ILP MPs – the Poplar MP John Scurr, and two Clydesiders,

Jimmy Maxton and George Buchanan – raised Campbell's arrest at Question Time. Maxton went to see Patrick Hastings, the Attorney General, and told him that Campbell was the acting, and not the permanent editor, that he had fought throughout the war, and that he had been seriously wounded.

That day the Cabinet discussed the arrest. The prosecution had been initiated by the Director of Public Prosecutions but authorised by Hastings, who told the Cabinet that:

> ...he took full responsibility for the case, which disclosed a bad criminal offence, but inasmuch as it transpired that the person charged was only acting temporarily as editor, and was prepared to write a letter to that effect, steps could be taken not to press the prosecution...[309]

Jimmy Thomas moved that

> ...it be an instruction that no prosecution of a political character shall take place without prior sanction of Cabinet.[310]

Cabinet agreed the proposals of Hastings and Thomas: no political prosecutions without Cabinet approval, and acceptance of a letter from John Ross Campbell. To the outside world it looked like political overruling of the law officers – which was the allegation opposition parties made.

Parliament would not normally have returned before the end of October. But, reluctantly, the parties had decided in July that they would come back on 30 September, to discuss the Irish border.

Liberals and Conservatives took advantage of the fact that Parliament was sitting to question MacDonald about the decision to stop the prosecution.

MacDonald, under pressure, gave misleading answers; the opposition parties, scenting blood, put down critical motions. The Conservatives called for a vote of censure; the Liberals for an inquiry. The debate was on Wednesday 8 October. The Cabinet decided that, if either motion passed, it would constitute a vote of no confidence in the government.

The Liberal motion was carried; Labour called for the dissolution of parliament and a general election. MacDonald saw the King at 10.00 the next morning, 9 October; the dissolution was agreed; the election would be on 29 October. Back at Downing Street, there was a meeting of the Cabinet at 11.00. They agreed

> That the President of the Board of Trade, in consultation with such Departmental officials as he might think desirable, should immediately prepare a draft for a King's Speech, to be read on the prorogation of Parliament the same afternoon.[311]

According to Beatrice, MacDonald looked round the Cabinet table:

*The King's Speech must be written and ready for him to see at one o'clock.
Webb, you had better go and do it.*[312]

Tom Jones describes what happened next:

*…about 11.30 am Sidney Webb suddenly entered my room and announced
that Parliament would be dissolved at 6 o'clock today and that he wanted a
draft of the King's Speech in 20 minutes to take back to the Cabinet or failing
that to the Prime Minister. This was a bit startling but of course the attempt
had to be made.*[313]

They did make the attempt, and it was successful:

*So Sidney and Tom Jones summoned the heads of the different departments,
and a dozen men sat down at tables and drafted paragraphs, while Sidney
strung them together and polished up the whole.*[314]

Neither MacDonald nor the King amended the draft. The speech was agreed
by the Privy Council at 3.00 and read to both Houses of Parliament by Lord
Chancellor Haldane on behalf of the King later that afternoon.

When that week's *New Statesman* appeared, it carried an article by Clifford
Sharp that was highly critical of MacDonald, from a pro-Asquith standpoint.
Sharp praised MacDonald's record as Foreign Secretary, but damned him as
Prime Minister:

*As Foreign Secretary he has been an immense success; as Prime Minister he has
been an utter failure. He has never recognised the inevitable limitations of a
minority Government. He has never poured oil on the troubled waters…he
has missed no opportunity of insulting and deriding those who placed him in
power.*[315]

The situation at the magazine had remained unresolved since the merger with
the *Nation* had fallen through in 1922. Sidney remained a director – no longer
chairman – despite his expressed intention to resign, and his ministerial post.
Sharp remained editor, despite the growing political distance between himself
and his board and shareholders.

In 1922, Beatrice had remarked on Sharp's drinking, (a habit she linked with
Asquith). Now she commented acidly:

*Clifford Sharp burnt his boats in writing a furiously malignant attack on
MacDonald in the interests of Asquith. 'If I did not know that Clifford Sharp
was a strictly sober man,' say I, 'I should have said he was drunk when he wrote
that article'. So ends our relationship.*[316]

Many readers disapproved of the article: the next edition contained a selection of critical letters. One wrote from Kingston on Thames:

Sir

My wife and I quite recently decided to take in THE NEW STATESMAN. Your uncalled-for, mad, vicious, and malicious attack on the Prime Minister has caused us to withdraw our support...

Another, signing themselves 'LIB-LAB', asked

Is it too late to rename your journal 'The New Dustman'? [317]

By the end of the 1920s Sharp's alcoholism was such that he could no longer act as editor. In 1924, however, he could rely on Mostyn Lloyd and GDH Cole, who frequently covered for him. Lloyd came close to the truth writing to Beatrice afterwards:

The New Statesman article was indeed a deplorable affair. I will tell you in confidence the main points of it. Sharp wrote it in the small hours of the Thursday morning when he was no doubt tired and nervous & ought not to have written at all. [318]

With parliament dissolved, Sidney stayed in London another day to draft the manifesto. He then went to Seaham, where he worked on the minutiae of campaign organisation.

Following Sharp's article, Sidney resigned from the *New Statesman* board – but wrote to Beatrice

Do not be troubled about Sharp's article: it will soon blow over and be forgotten. [319]

The Board met on Friday 24 October – less than a week before polling day. Sharp wrote to Sidney:

The Board met this afternoon and demanded my instant resignation. [320]

That evening, Sharp went to Shaw's home at Ayot St Lawrence, where he told a slightly different story:

Clifford Sharp turned up...and told me he had been sacked, but had been asked at the same time to carry on for a fortnight. [321]

GBS wrote to Sidney to say that sacking Sharp was a mistake: it would make the *New Statesman*

...a tied Labor-Party-Right-or-Wrong party journal. It will also have the effect of making the Party responsible for what is to be said in the paper in the future (and even in the past, though that does not matter).[322]

In his letter to Sidney, Sharp had offered to buy out the shareholders:

I can of course do that very easily <u>ten</u> times over. I could get a cheque tomorrow morning.[323]

GBS could see exactly what that meant:

Sharp will be forced to sell out to Beaverbrook; and he will give value in respect of having his knife into all of us for having taken from him his paper – for he regards the paper, rightly enough, as his creation.[324]

Sidney, no longer a director, remained a shareholder. Shaw suggested that the two of them, and a majority of shareholders – he named Arnold Bennett and Ernest Simon – ought to ensure that Sharp's notice period was prolonged indefinitely.

Sharp lasted as editor, in name at least, until 1929, when the board, their patience finally exhausted, awarded him a year's sabbatical from which, it was understood, he would not return.

In 1928 he was partly reconciled to the Webbs, telling them he would like to meet again. Beatrice wrote that she wanted to *close the episode of unfriendliness:*

He has not changed except that he looked more physically shattered by drink; but he was sane, cynically able, and frank...I should not be surprised if CS ended by deliberately drinking himself past recovery; he seems to have lost hope either for himself or for the world.[325]

The 1924 election began with the Campbell case and ended with the Zinoviev letter: a document, supposedly from Moscow, inciting revolution in Britain, complete with instructions to the cadres. The letter complemented the notorious July edition of Workers Weekly:

The military section of the British Communist party, so far as we are aware, further suffers from a lack of specialists, the future directors of the British Red army.

It is time you thought of forming such a group...[326]

Was the letter a forgery? It scarcely mattered: MacDonald was on a road tour of the country, speaking to large and enthusiastic crowds, in only intermittent contact with the Foreign Office.

Whether through malice or misunderstanding, the Foreign Office released the letter to the press on Friday 24 October (with polling due on 29 October). The official report to the incoming government states that MacDonald was 'genuinely dumbfounded' on learning that the newspapers had copies, both of the letter and of the Foreign Office note protesting about it to the Russian government. But then, apparently, the *Daily Mail* already had a copy. Press reports appeared on the Saturday; on Sunday, Mostyn Lloyd wrote to Beatrice

What an abominable nuisance this Zinovieff letter is.[327]

She herself, in Seaham, noted on polling day:

...in the country at large, the Labour Party has had a bombshell thrown into its ranks in the Zinoviev letter, whether authentic or forged, and the inept Foreign Office reply – all due to MacDonald's shifty and bungling management...[328]

Sidney's election was not in doubt, though his majority was reduced. Nationally, the Conservatives won 412 seats; Labour 151, losing 40; Labour's popular vote increased by one million.

The Liberals were the big losers. By joining forces with the Conservatives to defeat the government they had helped to precipitate the election; but their strength fell from 158 seats to 40. Their leader, Asquith, lost his seat to Labour. Beatrice commented

The big joke of the General Election is that the grave of anti-communism, which the Liberal leaders dug so energetically, swallowed them up instead...[329]

She described Asquith as the *dupe* of Lloyd George – who, still an MP, now inherited the Liberal leadership. She wrote (and then crossed through) that Asquith was *senile and alcoholic*; earlier in the year, TJ, gossiping to Baldwin, had said that Asquith was

...too far gone even to be Master of Balliol.[330]

Sidney thought that the experience of minority government would be good for the education of the Labour Party – and that it was

...a good joke which like most good jokes ought not to be repeated.[331]

Chapter Ten: Passfield Corner 1924-1929

'THE HOME OF THE AGED WEBBS'

The years 1919 to 1924 had been intense. Sidney and Beatrice were no longer young; Beatrice's old melancholy was now combined with a recognition of her own impending mortality:

> *Our personal life flows smoothly to its end with a settled conviction, on my part, that for me the end is not far off. Every night when I embrace my boy and give him my blessing before I retire to my room there is sadness in my heart at the thought that some day – and a day that cannot be far off – it will be our last embrace and that one or other of us will have to live for days, months, possibly a decade of years, alone, bereft of our comrade in work, thought and happiness…In some ways Sidney and I have never been so happy in our personal lives* [332]

In fact they had 20 working years ahead of them. Nevertheless, every ailment was recorded. On holiday in 1921, Sidney had a breakdown, Beatrice had colitis

> *…living the life of invalids, anxious about each other and unpleasantly doubtful about the future of 'the Webbs'* [333]

A year later, Sidney was fine, but, Beatrice wrote

> *I suffer from a chronic bowel trouble, and I find my life distracted, distressingly distracted…* [334]

Two more Potter sisters had died; Margaret in March 1921, aged 67, of breast cancer. Beatrice spent time with Margaret in her illness. She was the second sister to die from cancer:

> *In my young days it was tuberculosis that was the fearsome thought: now it is cancer. All elderly folk live in terror of it…* [335]

Mary was 74 when she died of lung cancer in September 1923; in her final months she lost her memory. Beatrice stayed with her in August.

Now only Kate, Beatrice and Rosie remained.

Sidney and Beatrice continued to socialize and entertain; their network flourished. Their guests included old friends – such as Bertrand Russell, GBS, Alice

Green, Beveridge, Tawney, TJ, Henry Harben, Haldane, Arthur Greenwood, and George Lansbury – as well as the Labour leadership, and younger MPs. They also kept up with the group around the Coles, Page Arnot, and the Labour Research Department.

They had long hoped to retire to the countryside; while LSE had access to the Cobden country house in Sussex, the Webbs planned to build a cottage in the grounds. Beatrice talked to Beveridge and to Janet Mair about the idea: they would have the use of the house in their lifetime, after which it would revert to LSE. Beatrice thought it was

> ...now or never! If Sidney gets into Parliament we can't go on working through every week end...[336]

The plan came to nothing. LSE gave up Dunford; the terms of the Cobden bequest proved onerous. The Webbs had to look elsewhere.

In July 1923 they advertised in the *New Statesman*:

> Mr and Mrs Sidney Webb require a building site of an acre or more within a radius of 50 (or 75) miles of London in any direction (south preferred); preferably with a habitable cottage which could be developed. It must be relatively high with a pretty view; and above all completely isolated from houses harbouring cocks or dogs. Anyone knowing of such a site is begged to inform Mr Webb, 41 Grosvenor Road, Westminster.[337]

Other papers picked up the story. Sidney wrote to Beatrice, saying he had received two dozen letters, offering houses and land from Hereford and Norfolk to Dover. In August, while Beatrice was caring for Mary, she and Sidney reviewed the properties, and later went to see some possibilities.

They chose Waterside Copse, an 8½ acre site between Hindhead and Liphook, on the Surrey/Hampshire border. The freehold cost £1750. They renamed the house Passfield Corner. There was a view, and woodland, a hayfield, and a garden. The house needed work – *a third sitting room and three more bedrooms* – but it would be

> ...a home we can retire to in case one or other of us breaks down. [338]

The timing of the 1923 election meant that Beatrice moved in on 21 November, without Sidney, accompanied only by her servant Jessie:

> Entered with furniture and Jessie yesterday according to plans made before general election; stay here five nights; lock cottage up and go to Seaham. Impression of our new home not altogether favourable in this dank weather. [339]

Passfield was as quiet as they had hoped – no dogs, cocks; not even cars. It was comfortable; the countryside was beautiful for walking. But that November Beatrice found it cold. The water supply was from a pump.

At first Beatrice wondered whether they could live there all year round, or whether it could only be a weekend or holiday cottage. But by the time she set off for Seaham, the following week, she was praising the rest and silence at Passfield:

I think I shall get very fond of this place: it is sympathetic to me even in these days of dank darkness – pierced now and again by feeble gleams of moonlight or sunlight – silence, stillness and mysterious indistinctness in form and colour. [340]

In December, while MacDonald went to Lossiemouth and Haldane to Cloan, they retreated to Passfield Corner

…Sidney and I have had a peaceful Xmas in our dear little cottage…[341]

MacDonald's letter offering Sidney a ministerial post came to Passfield. Until then, they had preserved some sort of normality – Beatrice had managed to work.

But for these last four days I have been companionising him, discussing his plans for the Cabinet and for his own office, and settling with the architect and the builder for the additions to the cottage. [342]

They had bought Passfield for peace, quiet and solitude. To Beatrice's dismay, over Christmas,

…thirteen separate persons have come here to see us.

Never mind, said Sidney

We should have had thirty in London [343]

Next summer building work started. Beatrice was pleased they had moved – but worried about the longer term:

The cottage with its comfortable study and delightful loggia, its woods and views and walks, is almost too good to be true! To make a new home when one is nearing seventy seems, in some moods, a melancholy task: one is haunted by a vision of the funeral procession wending its way down the new drive, a few years hence, perhaps a few months hence…[344]

In August she called Passfield *the Home of the Aged Webbs.*

Gradually, they emptied Grosvenor Road, bringing books and furniture to Passfield. After the 1924 election, part of no. 41 was let to their friend Susan Lawrence, a freshly elected Labour MP; they kept the rest of the house as a London base.

In January 1928, the Thames flooded; the Millbank area was one of the worst affected. Six people sleeping in basements on Grosvenor Road were drowned. The basement at no 41 could no longer be used, and the Webbs gave up more of the house to Susan Lawrence; *we shall seldom go to Grosvenor Road*, Beatrice predicted. [345]

In September 1929 Susan took over completely. Beatrice wrote

Goodbye little house on the Thames. I doubt whether you will outlive the Webbs! [346]

It did not. Grosvenor Road was badly damaged in the blitz. In 1963 the Millbank Tower (originally the Vickers Tower) was built on the site.

The Webbs kept a London flat in Artillery Mansions, Victoria Street.

'AN AUTOBIOGRAPHY WITH THE LOVE AFFAIRS LEFT OUT'

One reason for Beatrice moving out of London was to concentrate on her writing; one stalled project was the book on her own early life she had started in wartime. In late 1916 she had begun transcribing her diaries; they were put away again as she became absorbed in reconstruction in 1917.

My Apprenticeship was eventually published in 1926. In it, Beatrice creates a narrative for her life before her marriage. It is a complex book – literary, factual, personal, psychological, and spiritual, it by turns conceals and reveals a portrait of the artist as a young woman.

After putting the project aside in 1917, the next time Beatrice worked on the book was on holiday in Wales in May 1918. From time to time other opportunities occurred; at Christmas 1921 she wrote

I have started on a task which I delight in – this little book on my experiences and investigations in which I mean to give my philosophy of life. [347]

The following spring, they went to Wales again with Kate Courtney:

After an interval of five months I am back again at my little book with the summer before me…I mean to finish this book before taking up any other work and I mean to write it according to my conscience and not shamefacedly in fear of scoffing remarks. [348]

In October, she called it

…a little book of my own, which is a big book in its high endeavour really to explain my craft and my creed. [349]

In February 1923 they spent a week at Lyme Regis, walking six or seven miles a day, and reading (Sidney brought twenty books, *even too many for him to get through*). Beatrice reflected

> *There is a certain morbid tendency in writing this book – it is practically an autobiography with the love affairs left out – the constantly recurring decision of what degree of self revelation is permissible and desirable.* [350]

And there was the issue of Sidney's feelings to be considered.

It was not just that love affairs were left out: the love affair was left out. By the time *My Apprenticeship* was published, Joseph Chamberlain was twelve years dead. But in the book Beatrice does not describe the intensity of her feeling for him, nor does she refer to the possibility that they might have married. There is plenty about Chamberlain: long accounts of her visits to Birmingham, taken directly from the diary. Her fascination with Chamberlain is transparent; but her personal attraction to him, and the visits to the Chamberlain household, are omitted.

Molly Hamilton, writing in 1933, began to suggest the real nature of the relationship. But not until Margaret Cole's posthumous biography appeared in 1945 could readers learn that

> *…there was a definite chance that she would become his [Chamberlain's] third wife…* [351]

As the manuscript approached completion, Beatrice showed sections to others. Mary Booth loved the references to Charles Booth. The Shaws had helped edit Webb publications for thirty years. In March 1925, at Charlotte's request, Beatrice sent them four chapters; she was worried GBS himself wouldn't find the time to read it all.

> *I await with some anxiety the opinion of the Shaws; they are sufficiently true friends to give an honest one.* [352]

In fact, Shaw sent extensive comments:

> *The Victorian reserve about your love affairs is funny in these shameless psycho-analytic days. It even suggests they were affairs rather than states of mind, and destroys confidence between you and the reader…*
>
> *If you decide to say nothing, say nothing: dont say that you will say nothing. Dont kick the sleeping dog if you mean to let him lie.* [353]

Graham and Audrey Wallas also read the draft, pronouncing it a *work of art*:

Of course, it describes the state of things they remember and therefore they are interested – but there are not many readers who are over 65. [354]

Their reaction heartened Sidney; he was away at Labour Party conference, and wrote

…what strikes them will strike other people. It will *be a great book: my only doubt is as to how* quickly *it will sell…* [355]

My Apprenticeship was the first book Beatrice had written on her own since her marriage. It is unlike the works she and Sidney wrote together. Their histories are dry and empirical; *My Apprenticeship* is creative, thoughtful, and personal. The language, like that of the diary, can be sharp, barbed, even mischievous. Beatrice describes her *choice of a craft* – the process by which she became a social investigator; and her *search for a creed* – the stages by which she became a socialist.

My Apprenticeship was mostly well reviewed; Beatrice was pleased. Haldane's review for the *Observer* had a slightly critical note; Beatrice wondered if she had failed to write enough about Haldane's early friendship with herself and Sidney:

The Webbs are very able, whether as writers or organizers; they are honest and public-spirited; they are remarkably hard-working and purposeful. But alike in intellectual gifts, personal culture and social standing, they are restricted in range – they are in fact 'little people' who have accomplished a useful but not outstanding important book. [356]

A different kind of book appealed to a different audience. Beatrice wanted Maynard Keynes to review *My Apprenticeship*; Keynes came to lunch at Grosvenor Road with GBS on 19 March and she gave him a copy. No review appeared; but Keynes took the book on holiday with him to Andalucía in April, following which Duncan Grant wrote to Vanessa Bell

Maynard almost became a socialist owing to his reading Mrs Webb on the train in Spain. [357]

Vanessa's sister Virginia Woolf already had a copy:

I am reading Mrs Sidney Webb's autobiography and find it enthralling [358]

Ella Pycroft, Beatrice's colleague from Katherine Buildings, read it and wrote

If you hadn't married, you would have been abbess of a sisterhood. [359]

A week later, as the general strike was beginning, Ramsay MacDonald himself wrote:

My Dear Mrs Webb

I have finished your book & find it most interesting & further than that I <u>like</u> it. [360]

COAL AND THE GENERAL STRIKE: 1924-1926

Lacking a majority, the 1924 Labour government had not been able to resolve the problems of the coal industry. Baldwin's Conservative government had neither the mandate nor the desire to act.

Instead, by returning to the Gold Standard, they made things worse. In April 1925 the Chancellor, Winston Churchill, (a Conservative again) restored sterling to its 1914 exchange rate with the US Dollar: £1= $4.86. In July, Leonard Woolf published Maynard Keynes' *Economic Consequences of Mr Churchill.* Keynes demonstrated that, if British collieries tried to compete with American and European coal, they would have to cut their price by one shilling and ninepence a ton. This would reduce the miners' standard of living. As Keynes wrote

> *…the miners are to be offered a choice between starvation and submission, the fruits of their submission to accrue to the benefit of other classes.* [361]

The coal owners gave notice that the national wage agreement would end in July 1925; they proposed wage cuts and longer hours. The Miners Federation (MFGB) rejected this.

The Government then agreed to subsidise wages for six months, and appointed another Royal Commission, with four members – two of them well-known to the Webbs: the Chairman, former Liberal Home Secretary Herbert Samuel, and Beveridge. Two businessmen completed the membership. The miners' slogan was *Not a minute on the day. Not a penny off the pay.*

Samuel's Commission reported in March 1926. It recommended reducing wages – perhaps by 10% – but leaving hours unchanged. Beveridge hoped wage cuts would be easier to reverse than increased hours. He also supported family allowances.

Beatrice, unimpressed, dismissed Samuel and Beveridge as *typical Liberals.* She said the recommendations were

> *…typical of Samuel's state of mind – sound but ineffectual – sound in doctrine but ineffectual in practice.* [362]

The Webbs spent a gloomy Easter at Seaham.

> *…with the dark prospect of an embittered strike hanging over our little meetings of miners and their wives.* [363]

Fruitless talks continued over the report. When the owners threatened a national lockout, other unions agreed to support the miners, and placed the dispute in the hands of the TUC General Council. When negotiations finally collapsed, a general strike began on the night of Sunday 2 May.

Beatrice opposed the General Strike, thinking it would prove ineffective in the conditions of 1926. It seemed a last, desperate flourish for syndicalism and Guild Socialism, which they had fought against since 1912 – *the death-gasp of the workers' control daydream.* Beatrice noted on 3 May

The General Strike will fail... We have always been against a General Strike. But the problem of the collapse of capitalism in the coal industry will remain – and woe to the governing class that refuses to solve it by taking control, in one form or another, of the organization of the industry. [364]

She feared the strike would lead to disillusionment and victimization.

The Webbs observed the strike; they did not participate. On the first morning Sidney was in London; he saw:

A dense block of every kind of motor car packed with people, a few loaded charabancs, heaps of pedal and motor-cycles covered with people: and crowds walking. [365]

They passed the nine days of the strike between Passfield and London. Parliament was sitting; Sidney had to be there. He also spent some time researching the Poor Law in the Public Record Office.

On 7 May Sidney came home from London with their neighbour, Earl Russell, Bertie's brother. Russell stopped to talk at Passfield; Beatrice noted

...they were both of them, particularly Russell, far more apprehensive of a long strike and of bloodshed in the streets before it ended than I had been. [366]

The following Thursday, Beatrice went to London with Susan Lawrence. They attended a mass meeting of railway workers in Ilford, then went on to the local Councils of Action in East Ham and Poplar. In these meetings, wrote Beatrice,

...the men seemed determined but depressed, and I gathered from Susan's manner that she also was disappointed... [367]

Herbert Samuel, who had been in Italy, was concerned negotiations had broken down. He said the government had misrepresented his report. He arrived back in London on 7 May, and started operating as an unofficial intermediary – in Sidney's words

...not at the Government's request and even, I believe, against their advice(!) [368]

Samuel worked diligently in an impossible situation. The MFGB would not compromise on *not a minute on the day, not a penny off the pay.* The coalowners would not compromise on wage cuts. Government was split, between hardliners around Churchill, and a more conciliatory group around Baldwin and Birkenhead (the former FE Smith). The peacemakers were sustained by TJ, backed up by discreet support from the Palace.

The government demanded unconditional surrender: the strike must be called off, without preconditions, before negotiations. Samuel agreed a detailed text with the TUC – the Samuel Memorandum. This called for new coal industry negotiations; a National Wages Board for coal; no changes to wage rates until plans to reorganise the industry were agreed; arrangements to transfer, and retrain miners, and building new housing – much of what the Samuel Commission had recommended.

Sidney thought the Samuel Memorandum clarified the recommendations of the Commission, and that it represented

> ...*all that is practicable under this Government. Of course, this has not happened without secret consultations, and* implicitly *the Government is committed to it – with the result that Churchill in the Cabinet, and the Tory MPs generally, are said to be raging furiously.* [369]

The General Council called off the strike, believing, or hoping, like Sidney, that the Government, while they had not endorsed the Samuel Memorandum, had some sort of implicit commitment to it.

But the miners would not settle. Slowly, inexorably, by the end of 1926, district by district, as Keynes had foreseen, poverty and hunger drove them back to work. Beatrice, watching it happen, felt powerless:

> *The million miners are obdurate and no one can take their place... There are only two ways of breaking them: sheer starvation, or a sufficient importation of coal to make them feel that the struggle was is useless. But dare the government let them and their wives and children starve?* [370]
>
> *The agony of the miners' resistance to the owners' terms has begun* [371]
>
> ...*this needless misery, the burden of debt in the miners' homes...* [372]

She wondered how long the miners could hold out. Tawney had been working for the MFGB; he thought perhaps to the end of the year. In October, in a final effort, the miners withdrew safety cover from the pits. This led to further retaliation by the owners and the government. Finally, the Federation accepted the government's terms – but left everything to the districts, which then rejected them.

Writing to the Seaham women in December Beatrice gave her verdict: the general strike had been

…like sending a squadron of cavalry against a wall of machine guns. [373]

'THE OLD WEBBS CHUCKLING OVER THEIR CHICKENS': POLITICS 1926 – 1929

After the 1924 election, Sidney decided not to stand again. He told Arthur Henderson when Henderson spent an August weekend at Passfield in 1925. He suggested to R J Herron, the Labour agent in Seaham, that he could stand.

Nothing came of this. At Whitsun 1928, the Hendersons stayed at Passfield once more. Webbs and Hendersons discussed the possibility of another Labour Government. Henderson assumed Sidney would accept a peerage; Beatrice heard his response

'I shall obey orders,' Sidney remarked, 'but quite sincerely I should prefer not.' To which I added 'Amen…' [374]

There was a new plan for Seaham: since 1922, MacDonald had represented Aberavon. MacDonald felt Aberavon, and its Labour Party, demanded too much of his time and money; so

…Henderson and Sidney are conspiring to hand over the safe and cheap seat of Seaham Harbour to 'our Leader'… [375]

The deal was done; Beatrice wrote to congratulate the Seaham women:

It will be an honour as well as an advantage to Seaham to have as its Member the Leader of the Labour Party… [376]

MacDonald's wife had died in 1911; he was supported in Seaham by his daughter, Ishbel. Beatrice took her there for a first visit in October 1928. Beatrice found her

…an upright good-looking girl, plain-speaking, puritan and public spirited… proud of, but not intimate with her father… We did not interest each other, but we made pleasant conversation… [377]

Sidney remained active in Parliament up to the 1929 election; in 1927 he played a part in opposing the Trade Disputes Act introduced by Baldwin's government after the general strike.

Neville Chamberlain – an MP since 1918; son of Joseph and his second wife, Florence – was Minister of Health in that government. In November 1928

Chamberlain introduced a Local Government Bill. The Bill covered more than the Poor Law – but it did abolish the Guardians, transferring their functions to County Councils, as both the Minority Report and the Maclean Committee had proposed. It did not end the Poor Law: ten years later there were still a million paupers. Outright abolition did not come till 1948.

Sidney spoke for Labour. He said Chamberlain was not sweeping the Poor Law away; he was abolishing the Guardians,

> ...but not the Poor Law. He has transferred the work of the boards of guardians with their powers and liabilities to the county councils and the county borough councils. That is a step and I thank the right hon. Gentleman for that step. It is said that the time-lag in England is 19 years, and the 19 years is up this year. 378

Beatrice watched. Sidney had never been at home in the Commons, but

> ...the speech was a great success; delighted his own party and was attentively listened to by the opposite benches. ...
>
> He is one of the 'characters' of the House and is always being caricatured as the enigmatic learned person at once absurd and impressive...379

The Bill became law in 1929.

They spent the New Year at Passfield, finishing their *History of the English Poor Law*. Beatrice reflected that, 20 years earlier, they had been completing the Minority Report. With the Chamberlain Bill going through, she felt *a certain exhilaration and self-complacency*. They had not won everything. But

> ...to be able to make *history as well as to write it* – or to be modest, to have foreseen, twenty years ago, the exact stream of tendencies which would bring your proposal to fruition, is a pleasurable thought! So the old Webbs are chuckling over their chickens! 380

A general election was due in 1929; another Labour government seemed possible. Labour had agreed its programme – *Labour and the Nation*, based on *Labour and the New Social Order* – at its 1928 conference. Sidney was one of a small group (the others were Snowden, Willie Graham and Tom Shaw) tasked with preparing a list of *administrative reforms and legislative measures* for the first parliamentary session.

It was a short document. They recommended repealing the 1927 Trade Disputes Act, and Conservative legislation on miners' working hours. They proposed raising the school leaving age (from 14 to 15); they called, optimistically but vaguely, for an action plan on unemployment, and more resources for road building and slum clearance. Although nationalizing the mines figured prominently in *Labour and the Nation*, the group recommended that there should be no attempt to pass the legislation in that initial session.

'WHO IS COMING FORWARD AMONG THE YOUNG MEN?' THE NEXT GENERATION

As they grew older, the Webbs realised that socialism might not come in their lifetime.

They remained ambivalent towards MacDonald. In 1926, Beatrice dismissed him as

> ...*a magnificent substitute for a leader. He has the ideal appearance...but he is shoddy in character and intellect. Our great one is yet to come. Shall I live to see him? Or will it be* she *who must be obeyed?* [381]

But she did not anticipate the early arrival of a woman leader (though Margaret Thatcher was born in 1925).

She remained fascinated by the nature of political leadership; she still frequently referred to the *vocation of leadership*. She continued to believe in the need for a disinterested governing elite. She hoped such an elite would emerge. H G Wells' Samurai were one model that appealed to her; she and Sidney continued to think that they had influenced Wells. Other models were the Jesuits and the Salvation Army. Later, the leadership of the Bolsheviks became an important element in her study of the Soviet Union

Margaret Cole described Beatrice's interest in the emerging generation of Labour leaders:

> 'Who is coming forward among the young men?' was the question which visitors to Passfield were continually called upon to answer – she was never much interested in the young women...[382]

One runner was Oswald Mosley. In June 1923, Sidney met Mosley in the House of Commons, and brought him back to Grosvenor Road for dinner. Beatrice thought him

> ...*the most brilliant man in the House of Commons... 'Here is the perfect politician who is also a perfect gentleman,' said I to myself.* [383]

Even then she had some doubts:

> *So much perfection argues rottenness somewhere.* [384]

When the Webbs first met Mosley, he was the independent MP for Harrow. Elected as a Conservative in 1918, he resigned the whip in 1920. In 1922 and 1923 he was re-elected as an independent, joining Labour in 1924.

By 1928, Mosley was a Labour MP; he and his wife stayed at Passfield in December that year. Already Beatrice thought him a possible successor to MacDonald:

> *…with his money, his personal charm and political gifts, his good-looking and agreeable wife, he is dead certain of Cabinet office, and probably has a chance of eventual premiership.* [385]

Others already had reservations. Six months later, newly appointed Chancellor of the Duchy of Lancaster in MacDonald's second government, Mosley was on the threshold of the Cabinet. Tom Jones spent a weekend with Baldwin, outgoing Conservative Prime Minister, who told him:

> *Tom Mosley is a cad and a wrong 'un, and they will find it out.*[386]

Hugh Dalton had returned to LSE to teach economics after the war, becoming a Labour MP in 1924. Before long, Beatrice mentioned him as a potential leader. In April 1927 she declared him *probably the ablest of the younger men.* In June she agreed with Henderson that, if there was another Labour government in the next ten years, Dalton would be in the Cabinet.

> *I neither like the man nor do I dislike him: but as stuff for the Front Bench he is far above the average of his fellows.* [387]

In looks he was no match for the louche Mosley:

> *When we first knew him in 1907 he was a tall slim graceful Cambridge undergraduate…* [388]

But by 1927 he was

> *…practically bald and somewhat pasty-faced.* [389]

In 1928 Beatrice ranked Dalton with Mosley and CP Trevelyan as one of MacDonald's likeliest successors.

In 1924 Beatrice wrote about Arthur Greenwood as part of the new generation of Labour MPs – along with Mosley, Emmanuel Shinwell, and others. He had worked on the Poor Law campaign, come to London, and become a wartime civil servant, before taking charge of Labour Party research. He was elected a Labour MP in 1922. By 1924 he was a junior minister. Beatrice described him as

> *…one of the more attractive and useful of the younger Ministers… his creed is not far removed from ours in substance, but more romantic in expression.*[390]

In 1929 Greenwood became Minister of Health.

But Beatrice had a cold eye for the weakness that limited Greenwood's later career. As early as 1925 she and Sidney went to a party given by MacDonald

...Ben Spoor [Chief Whip] was there, smelling of whisky; Arthur Greenwood looked as if he were going the same way. [391]

In 1939 she reported a conversation in which Susan Lawrence said that Greenwood was a *confirmed drunkard*.[392]

As Margaret Cole pointed out, most of the potential leaders vetted and cultivated by Beatrice were men. One exception was Ellen Wilkinson. Beatrice met Ellen before the war, at the end of the Minority Report campaign. Ellen was a student in Manchester, a suffragist, a Fabian, and an activist in the Universities Socialist Federation. Subsequently she became a trade union organiser, and in 1923 was elected MP for Middlesbrough. Beatrice thought she was a *real good sort*; she stayed at Passfield more than once.

In 1927 Beatrice wrote that Ellen's opinions did not

...strike old people like ourselves as wise or particularly relevant; she is a left-winger who has altered her views to suit the fashion of the hour; she was in 1913, syndicalist, in 1917, communist and now 'agin MacDonald' and enthusiastic for 'Socialism in our day'. 'Ellen Wilkinson, regarded as a practical politician, is a fool', says Sidney. [393]

She thought parliament was taming Ellen's spirit:

...she is becoming, unknown to herself, moulded for the Front Bench and eventually for office – I should imagine she would make a good departmental minister. [394]

The Webbs had known Clement Attlee longer than they had known most Labour MPs, yet Beatrice never identified him as a potential Labour leader. His name does not occur on guest lists at Dunford or Passfield. If he lunched at 41 Grosvenor Road after the war (and most Labour MPs did), his presence passed without comment.

Attlee had been demobilized in January 1919. He returned to live in east London and to teach at LSE. In November 1919 he became Mayor of Stepney, and at the 1922 general election was elected MP for Limehouse. When MacDonald resumed the Labour leadership, Attlee, an ILP member, became one of his two Parliamentary Private Secretaries.

During his early months in parliament Attlee continued teaching at LSE; he left before the formation of the first Labour government, in which he was a War Office junior minister. He did not become a minister when MacDonald formed his second government in June 1929; he had been out of the country for much of the previous year, on a committee of inquiry into the government of India.

Sidney and Beatrice had both helped Attlee early in his career. Even before he became an MP, however, he had begun to establish a distinctive position of his own. In 1918, while he was still a soldier, he wrote to his brother Tom to say that, while his outlook had not changed since before the war, he thought he had then taken too narrow a view:

> *We were too Webby – I'm sure I was, having a fatal love of statistics and a neat structure of society.* [395]

LIFE AT PASSFIELD CORNER

The timing of the snap 1923 election meant that the move to Passfield was rushed. In summer 1924 Beatrice supervised building work; only after the government had fallen could the Webbs really settle in. By December 1924 they were landscaping the grounds:

> *Surrounded at present with wage-slaves digging, planting, building and path-making, some dozen of them in all. Shocking sight, the aged Webbs adding acre to acre (the original eight has now grown to near twelve!), laying out these acres in park-like avenues, cutting down trees to make vistas...* [396]

Engineers dug a new artesian well, with an electric pump, to provide a continuous water supply.

By 1929 they were well established. Beatrice wrote

> *I love this little house in sunshine and rain: the absolute quietude during the night, the distant sounds now and again in the day, the long rambles in Woolmer Forest and Ludshott Common, honeymooning with my beloved or brooding alone with Sandy [her dog] as my companion.* [397]

They began to appreciate music more. As a young woman. Beatrice had sometimes attended the Three Choirs Festival: in 1883, when the festival was at Gloucester Cathedral, the Potters had a house party at their Gloucestershire home for festival goers. In London, she had continued to enjoy choral works, often walking along the Thames from Westminster to Evensong at St Paul's.

The move to Passfield came at just as the newly established BBC was beginning to broadcast music. In 1925, Beatrice wrote that

> *With the wireless I am gradually being taught to listen to music* [398]

At Christmas 1925 she wrote that radio was a source of delight

...I have attended as many concerts these last six months as I have in the last twenty years! Music has become my main recreation... [399]

There was also a vigorous local musical culture in the area around Passfield. The Haslemere Musical Society, just over the border in Surrey, began in 1923; by 1925 it was running regular concerts. Beatrice wrote that she was

...beginning to go to concerts at Haslemere and London. [400]

In 1928 she was still going to *more concerts than ever before* [401]. She thought of buying Groves Dictionary of Music *so as to educate myself in musical lore*, or of spending a winter in Leipzig or Munich. On holiday in Germany in May 1929, *by far the most enjoyable experience* in three days in Munich was

...a really fine concert by the Berlin Philharmonic Orchestra... [402]

Throughout her life Beatrice relied on domestic servants. At Standish, there had been a regiment of indoor and outdoor staff. After her mother's death, when Richard Potter kept three homes and Beatrice managed them, there were twenty-three staff. When Beatrice visited Bacup, her guide and accomplice had been her nurse Martha Jackson, 'Dada', her mother's confidante and distant relative. At Katherine Buildings one escape from poverty for young women had been to place them as servants.

In the 1920s, the economic position of domestic service was changing. In wartime hundreds of thousands of women had moved out of service into occupations previously reserved for men. While some were forced back, for many – and for later generations – the change was permanent. There was a tension between those wider changes and Beatrice's own expectations.

By the late 1930s Beatrice had concluded that

...the old fashioned upper and middle class home is no longer practicable... there will be no ladies who can't cook or wait on themselves... [403]

When they moved to Passfield, the Webbs brought Jessie Norris, one of two live-in servants who had been with them since before 1914. The other, Emily Wordley, stayed in London, looking after Susan Lawrence, and the Webbs when they were there. Both Webbs thought highly of Jessie.

Two years later, Beatrice noticed that bottles of whisky were disappearing:

'Look for the man.' In poor Jessie's case a dissolute married man...the son of our builder and has frequently worked here...ended in the infatuated Jessie outrunning all discretion by letting him sleep with her in the scullery... Here is the explanation of all the rest of her misbehaviour – pilfering whiskey

and perhaps other things, underhand dealings of all sorts, and general untrustfulness. [404]

To her shock, 'Poor Jessie' was dismissed. Poor Beatrice felt so guilty she fixed her up with another job – with Alys Russell, former wife of Bertrand, who took her on knowing the whole story.

They also employed a gardener – surname Oliver; Mrs Oliver now helped in the house while Beatrice searched for permanent staff. She advertised in the *Daily Herald* – which produced a better response than the *Morning Post* or the *Church Times*.

Beatrice chose two respondents to the *Herald*:

…an ex-Wesleyan Deaconess and her friend who had exchanged their faith for ardent Labour views, middle aged and highly respectable in appearance and character each asking £50 a year. [405]

It was not a success: the two complained that the work was too continuous, there was too much cooking, and there was not enough labour-saving machinery. They told Beatrice that *the old kind of servant was extinct* and that she had *the mistress's ideology.*

They were more direct with Oliver the gardener, telling him, *Mrs Webb is a rank Tory.* They left after ten days, saying that otherwise they would break down.

Beatrice reflected

Clearly there are some disadvantages in 'comrades'. Highly respectable and well spoken; but neurasthenic, incompetent and workshy – would be the character I should give these two specimens.[406]

In July 1926, the Webbs organized a garden party at Passfield for 2000 Labour supporters from Surrey, Sussex, and Hampshire. The star attractions were MacDonald and Margaret Bondfield. Planning began the previous autumn; in December 1925 Sidney wrote to Beatrice:

I spoke to MacDonald about a weekend in the early summer, for a garden party of the two constituencies. He was very approving, and practically agreed to come (by car, for the Saturday afternoon) …[407]

In May (just as the General Strike was starting) Sidney met Egerton Wake, Labour's National Agent. Wake was worried that the event would create too much work for Beatrice, and that too many people would come. Sidney and Wake went into detail on the practical arrangements: tickets, stewards, should there be a band? If there was a band, could they escape Entertainment Tax?

Beatrice worried that preparations were taking all her time; she was making no progress on the Poor Law book.

> *But I felt I must do something for the local Labour people; they are down-*
> *hearted, living as they do in a hostile environment. We shall pay for it out of the*
> *parliamentary salary.* [408]

In the days before the party Beatrice occupied herself with the marquee, the flowers – and the cakes. The Liphook baker returned her order for 2000 cakes, saying he had another large order for the flower show. But Beatrice learned that

> *…he is a strong Conservative and that his customers did not approve – more*
> *likely that we don't deal with him but with A.N. [Army and Navy Stores] for*
> *groceries.* [409]

Beatrice worried about overspending, telling Sidney

> *…you will be rather short until our November cheque from Longmans.*
> *However this gathering will not occur again and it is more useful than sending*
> *it to the Miners' fund – which I believe is simple waste in their present mood.*
> [410]

Beatrice thought it went off brilliantly. The weather held; eighty charabancs brought the guests:

> *We did what we intended to do: we showed headquarters how to wake up these*
> *tracts of commons and residential parks, of small towns and seaside resorts…*[411]

Her ambivalence towards MacDonald remained. He was *in his best form.* But

> *Directly you turn the conversation off trivial personalities on to subjects,*
> *whether it be general questions or the domestic problems of the Labour Party,*
> *JRM dries up and looks bored.* [412]

The pattern of the Webbs' hospitality changed. The Grosvenor Road salon was replaced by the Passfield Corner weekend house party. The Passfield weekends developed through the 1920s and 1930s; Sidney and Beatrice entertained fewer people; but there was more time to talk to them.

Kingsley Martin (at this point a politics lecturer at LSE; from 1931 Editor of the *New Statesman*) spent his first weekend there in February 1927:

> *We talked incessantly all our waking hours from 4.30 on Saturday afternoon,*
> *when the Kingsley Martins arrived, to nine o'clock on Monday morning…*[413]

Martin became a regular guest; Martin, Margaret Cole, and TJ left accounts of the Passfield weekend. Beatrice would send instructions about the trains from Waterloo; then there was the arrival, as described by Martin:

The Webbs had been working intensively all the week, and their immense fund of argument and conversation was bottled up inside them. You arrived for tea on Saturday. Mrs Webb met one very graciously at the door. Sidney gave you a rather perfunctory handshake. [414]

You would be shown to your room; then there was tea, probably with other guests.

Serious talk began at once. The condition of the world, and of the Labour and Socialist movements in particular, and immediate topics of the day, were systematically dealt with. One could almost hear Mrs Webb putting a mental tick after each item. [415]

Dinner, according to Margaret Cole, would be early, and eaten quickly; the Webbs – not the guests – would go to bed at 10.30. Before that

The long, meaty conversation would continue at night by the fire. [416]

No one who was a frequent guest at Passfield Corner during the 'thirties can fail to retain a vivid recollection of Beatrice sitting on a low stool in front of the fire, her skirt pulled back and her stockings as like as not in wrinkles about her ankles, seeking information about current politics and current relationships and proffering in return incisive recollections of Asquith, Haldane, Balfour, and other figures of her prime... The tone of voice in which Beatrice could refer to some well-known figure as 'an odious woman' or 'a very common sort of person' will probably never be heard again in our lifetime. [417]

In her own autobiography, Margaret Cole added that Beatrice

...loved a good gossip, of her own kind, as much as any other woman. [418]

After Dalton stayed in 1932, he noted that Beatrice was

...full of gossip, much of it feline. [419]

When the guests came down to breakfast at 8.30 or 9.00 am, Beatrice – as ever, sleeping badly – would have been up and working for some hours. According to TJ they would have breakfasted at 7.30 on a cup of tea and an apple. She would question or lecture the guests, sitting on the dining room window seat as they breakfasted. Later in the morning would come the walk – up to six miles, through woods and over heaths – with Sidney, Beatrice, and Sandy the dog.

Their network grew. As well as potential Labour leaders, their guests included friends from the 1880s and 1890s; people from the Edwardian generation; current political colleagues; and newer acquaintances, from LSE, the *New Statesman*, or Bloomsbury.

By now, Richard Haldane was in his last years. Little older than Sidney and Beatrice, Haldane's decades of high living had taken their toll. His only visit to Passfield was for an afternoon, in summer 1925. Beatrice said that he

…wanted to see his old friends in their last home. [420]

She found him

…a delightful old heathen and the best of friends. [421]

When, that autumn, Beatrice lunched with him in London, she noticed his decline; she wondered if it would be their last lunch together.

The hand of death seemed to be moulding his features. To me it was inexpressibly sad watching him eating, drinking and smoking away his life, though he looks so far gone that what he does matters little. [422]

In January 1927, *old and ill*, he was still working on judgments. Eighteen months later they had a *melancholy* dinner with *dear old Haldane* and his sister; Haldane

…looking desperately ill and feeling miserable; if I had not seen him looking almost equally bad before, I should imagine he was near his end. [423]

A month later he was dead; Beatrice said he was their *oldest and most constant friend.*

GBS and Charlotte became regular guests. They came in June 1925; Beatrice noted that Charlotte appreciated the *comfort and attraction of our new home.* They stayed again in November

Charlotte has taken a fancy to this cottage; or rather, she now dislikes Ayot and is glad to get away for visits. [424]

GBS was enjoying success. *Saint Joan* played to packed houses. He won the Nobel Prize for literature. In *The Apple Cart,* he lampooned the MacDonald governments. The Webbs saw the play in October 1929 – Beatrice called it *that amusing and annoying satire on democracy.* [425]

In 1928 Beatrice noted

The Shaws and the Webbs love each other and flatter each other. Today he and we have not enough in common to argue or discuss. Bertrand Russell came to lunch and he and Bernard Shaw scintillated… [426]

When the Shaws stayed at Passfield Corner in December 1929, Beatrice wrote that she would miss GBS more than anyone else

...he is the one most closely associated with our long married life, most continuously our friend. [427]

Of the other early Fabians, contact with the Oliviers and the Peases was occasional: Sydney Olivier served in the first MacDonald government, but not in the second. He stayed at Passfield in 1929 and 1935. Pease remained a member of the Fabian Executive Committee, but spent more time gardening than on politics.

Graham Wallas, no longer a Fabian, still taught at LSE. He and Audrey stayed at Passfield several times: the Wallases and the Webbs would read and comment on drafts of each other's books:

He is a dear old friend and I find him interesting to listen to...Sidney, who does not appreciate unnecessary communications even from me, is apt to be bored or impatient. [428]

Graham's final visit was in February 1932; he died that year:

...he had lived the life he liked to live and had done the work he wanted to do. Which can also be said of his four comrades of the 80s and 90s – Pease, Olivier, Shaw and Webb. [429]

In March 1927 Beatrice wrote to Thomas Jones

...when are you coming to visit the old Webbs in their last home? We should delight in a talk with you about old times and the future of this queer world. [430]

TJ came in May. They talked about current politics: the Webbs thought Baldwin had not understood the impact of the trade union bill his government was pushing through following the general strike:

From his account [Baldwin] is stupider and weaker than we thought – he lives an isolated life, never reads, or talks with experts, and has a horror of clever brains 'like Keynes or the Webbs.' [431]

TJ thought ministers became absorbed in routine and ceremonial; Balfour and Haldane were the only ones

...who really care for the advancement of science and learning. [432]

Lloyd George's great quality had been his readiness to seek out knowledge and the people who could give it to him; Churchill had some of the same eagerness to learn.

Jones came to Passfield again in September 1929. He went walking with the Webbs; Beatrice asked TJ what Baldwin thought of them:

He was afraid of you: too intellectual for him. But I think he would enjoy walking through these woods with you. [433]

TJ left the civil service in 1930, becoming Secretary of the Pilgrim Trust. He and his wife stayed at Passfield again in February 1933.

As well as old friends, the Webbs invited current political colleagues to Passfield.

Some lived locally:

...we are making ourselves a neighbourhood round our home. There are a few members of the Labour Party within easy motoring distance – the Snowdens, Ponsonby and Lord Russell... [434]

Philip and Ethel Snowden bought a Victorian villa nearby; TJ thought their house had *nothing of the charm of Passfield Corner.* The Webbs and the Snowdens continued to meet socially up to August 1931. Beatrice had long held reservations about Ethel; when the 1924 Labour government took office, she dismissed her as

...a 'climber' of the worst description, refusing to associate with the rank-and-file and plebeian elements in the Labour Party. [435]

The gulf widened. In December 1924 they lunched together; the Snowdens were

Bitter about MacDonald and would have been more bitter if Sidney had encouraged it even to the extent that I did, out of a woman's curiosity! They are obsessed with the danger of communism... [436]

In summer 1925 the Snowdens visited Passfield

...neither are socialists and they are far more intolerant of revolutionary socialists than we are. [437]

In September 1929, the Webbs, with TJ, called on the Snowdens. The Labour Chancellor talked of little but his meeting with the King at Sandringham:

This romancing about the royal family is, I fear, only a minor symptom of the softening of the brain of socialists, enervated by affluence, social prestige and political power. [438]

Arthur Ponsonby, a Liberal, then a Labour MP, later a peer, was the son of Queen Victoria's private secretary. A junior minister in both MacDonald governments, he lived nearby at fourteenth-century Shulbrede Priory. Beatrice disliked Ponsonby:

...a sentimentalist and without horse-sense, an amateur and a dilettante in politics;

his wife:

...sickly, critical, and somewhat rude

And their home:

...deadly dank and dark to live in. [439]

The Webbs remained close to the Hendersons, who stayed at Passfield in 1927; 'Uncle Arthur' thought MacDonald's influence was waning, because

...he was constantly in the company of the great who emphatically don't belong to the Labour Party. [440]

Henderson thought the Clydesiders and the ILP were ready to turn MacDonald out, and that they would back Snowden.

The Hendersons returned in spring 1927; Beatrice's comment was mixed:

Was there ever a more sterling character than his? Conduct more uniformly guided by public spirit and personal devotion and good comradeship? He is thickheaded – intellectually he is a clumsy instrument – but there is shrewdness in his judgment. [441]

The Webbs and the Coles had begun as antagonists; Sidney and Beatrice detested syndicalism and Guild Socialism, as preached by Douglas. They thought the Coles wanted to destroy the Fabian Society.

Over thirty years the relationship mellowed, to the point where Margaret Cole became a trustee of Beatrice's will. By then, Beatrice thought the Coles

...practically share our views as to the future organisation of society, national and international... [442]

This transformation took time: Margaret Cole could not remember the stages by which Beatrice changed from '*Bogie-woman*'

...first to a human creature and then to a friend and a woman I admired and was very proud to have known, but it was a gradual process. [443]

Despite differences, the Webbs remained in contact with the Coles. A first visit by the Webbs to the Coles was followed by others:

...a visit from Mr and Mrs Sidney Webb, bearing a codfish of moderate size. Mrs Webb explained that when invited to the houses of some of her more aristocratic friends or relatives they were expected to bring a salmon with them. Salmon, however, were nowadays costly – 'but I have brought you a fish.' [444]

Leonard and Virginia Woolf met Douglas and Margaret in 1919:

Sharp, positive, hard minds, in tense, taut bodies, in Cole's case the mouth seems fixed in a kind of snarl at the world. [445]

A year later the Woolfs dined with the Coles. Virginia concluded

...the Coles are Webbs in embryo... [446]

It was not a compliment.

During the 1924 MacDonald government, Coles and Webbs lunched together. Beatrice thought Douglas was lost: working at LRD, teaching for the WEA, writing for the *New Statesman* – but without a settled political home

He still trots out his 'workers control' – but in a disheartened fashion, without conviction that anyone cares about it. The waste of so brilliant an intelligence is pitiful. It is he who is strangled by stale doctrines... [447]

Beatrice thought that Cole's best escape would be

...to retire into an academic career, at any rate for a time. [448]

Perhaps following this advice, in 1925 Cole became Reader in Economics at Oxford, with a fellowship at University College.

In 1926 the Coles stayed at Passfield, before going, with the Webbs, to the post-General Strike TUC. Beatrice thought them *saner and more charitable in their outlook*:

He is still a fanatic but he is a fanatic who has lost his peculiar faith; he is disillusioned about workers' control... I doubt whether today his vision of the future development of society seriously differs from ours. [449]

Slowly Margaret and Beatrice learned that each was capable of human warmth. After that 1926 visit, Beatrice thought Margaret was

...more human and more capable of affection and intimacy, but not so tenaciously clever or coldly incisive. [450]

Later, Margaret wrote about Beatrice

...she was not merely the greatest woman I have ever known, but a kind person, with human affections and human friendliness, perennially interested in the individuals who were coming after her... [451]

It remained a strange relationship, Margaret described how, even after they had become regular guests,

...I felt that Douglas was in her eyes the important person and I a kind of umbrella which he had to be allowed to bring with him. [452]

The friendship that developed between the Webbs and Maynard Keynes and his wife Lydia Lopokova, after Keynes read *My Apprenticeship* in 1926, was political as well as social; it also gave the Webbs a window on Bloomsbury.

It began with an article by Keynes in the *Nation*. After the failed attempt to merge the *New Statesman* and the *Nation*, Keynes chaired the *Nation's* board. Keynes wanted to give the Liberal Party a new philosophy for government. His 20 February 1926 article, published under the headline *Liberalism and Labour*, began:

I do not wish to live under a Conservative Government for the next twenty years. [453]

Keynes argued that sensible Liberals should talk to sensible socialists; the function of the Liberal Party might be to supply Conservative Governments with Cabinets and Labour Governments with ideas.

Beatrice noticed the article and wrote to Keynes saying that, while they had only met once, and that long ago, the article interested her and Sidney. She thought that

…the new inventiveness must necessarily concern itself with the control of capitalist enterprise and landlordism at the top in its highest activities.

It would be an immense service

…if you and your friends could discover how national finance and international trade could be controlled in the interests of the whole community. [454]

Permeation was over. The Webbs were committed to Labour. Nevertheless, Beatrice wrote to Keynes, saying that, for a long time, she had felt that the Webb-inspired Fabian policy of the National Minimum had reached the end of the road.

She worried that the labour movement had no young people

…at once sufficiently detached from party politics and sufficiently able and experienced to discover ways and means. [455]

The Webbs knew not to expect radical economics from Snowden. They worked with Mosley, and with ILP members.

In March 1926 Maynard and Lydia lunched with GBS and the Webbs; in August they stayed at Passfield. Beatrice noted:

There must be a shortage of politically constructive minds if J M Keynes seems such a treasure!

...when I look around I see no other man who might discover how to control the wealth of nations in the public interest. He is not merely brilliant in expression and provocative in thought; he is a realist: he faces facts and he has persistency and courage in thought and action... [456]

And the Webbs impressed Maynard and Lydia. In September Virginia Woolf wrote to her friend Margaret Llewellyn Davies:

The Keynes, Lydia and Maynard, are both completely under the sway of the Webbs. Beatrice and Lydia exchange headdresses; (I know you'll like to hear this). How charming she is, says Lydia: Maynard is deeply impressed by her book. [457]

After leaving Passfield, Keynes spoke at the ILP Summer School on *The Future Balance of British Industry*. Beatrice wrote to him again in October, enclosing an ILP report on economic policy, which she described as

...far more hopeful than the old slogan of the Labour Party – the nationalisation of the means of production, distribution and control. [458]

The ILP document argued for control of capitalist business from the standpoint of public advantage.

The following week the Webbs attended the Labour Party conference. Beatrice was not impressed:

The predominant tone is chaotic. No one knows what to be at... There is today no reason why Keynes, E D Simon, and Herbert Samuel should not be among the leaders of the Labour Party – they are certainly more advanced than MacDonald and Thomas in their constructive proposals... MacDonald would rejoice in having these Liberal intellectuals as possible Cabinet members. [459]

While Keynes continued to speak to Labour audiences, however, for the next two years his political energies were focussed on the Liberal Industrial Inquiry. This was led by Lloyd George and supported by Herbert Samuel and Ernest Simon – both long-standing Webb contacts, both occasional guests at Passfield Corner.

A first version of the Liberal industrial report appeared in January 1928. Keynes invited TJ to a private meeting to discuss it. A few days later Beatrice wrote to Jones:

I wonder what you think of the Liberal Industrial Report: the reviews read as if it were a Fabian document tempered by a desire not to appear socialistic. [460]

Unlike many other Liberals at this period (but like Beveridge), Keynes never joined, and would not join either the Labour Party or the Fabians: in Labour, he argued

>...*too much will always be decided by those who do not know* at all *what they are talking about.* [461]

The Webbs' other link with Bloomsbury was through Leonard and Virginia Woolf. From 1918, Leonard, at Sidney's request, chaired Labour's international and imperial committee. In January 1927, the Woolfs spent a weekend at Passfield; Beatrice wrote

>...*we had lost sight of them and were glad to renew relations with this exceptionally gifted pair.* [462]

Virginia was dreading the visit; she wrote to a friend

>*Oh what a ghastly weekend I'm just off to – the Sidney Webbs.* [463]

Beatrice described Virginia as a

>...*spare, self-contained ascetic-looking creature, startlingly like her father, Leslie Stephen...*

Her verdict on Bloomsbury was

>...*belonging to a rather decadent set (Clive Bell is her brother-in-law) but themselves puritanical...* [464]

The weekend concluded with a raging argument about religion and religious education.

In a letter to Vita Sackville-West, Virginia described a classic Passfield weekend:

>...*I was launched on a 6 mile walk on a cold common on a rainy morning with Sidney Webb. All my sentences leapt into the middle of the pond without a moment's reflection.* [465]

In February 1929 Beatrice, at Passfield, heard that Kate Courtney, now 81, was dangerously ill with influenza. When Beatrice arrived, Kate was near to death, and Beatrice stayed with her for the final 24 hours. Leonard Courtney had died in 1918; after that, Beatrice had seen more of Kate – but did not think the two of them had been really close.

'THE BEVERIDGE-MAIR DICTATORSHIP': LSE 1924-1929

When Beveridge joined LSE, in 1919, he had intended to write books. In fact he became an administrator – leading building projects, establishing a new commerce degree, increasing the academic staff. LSE flourished under Beveridge's leadership, becoming the largest centre in Britain for social sciences. Its budget increased sevenfold; its premises increased threefold.[466]

Beveridge was central to the building of Senate House, London University's new headquarters in Bloomsbury. Initially he worked through the University Senate; then, from 1926 to 1928, he was Vice Chancellor. Beveridge steered the plans through the university's own governing bodies, negotiating with Chancellor of the Exchequer and the Rockefeller Foundation for funding. The Chancellor was Winston Churchill; Beveridge called him *my old chief*. Ramsay MacDonald, however, was not impressed. He

...burst out about the wickedness of London University securing the Bloomsbury site... [467]

Sidney saw this as

...a flaring up of his old opposition to the University on the LCC a quarter of a century ago, then *largely motivated by hostility to me!*[468]

Beatrice was seventy in January 1928, Sidney in July 1929. Beveridge decided to mark the birthdays by commissioning a joint portrait. Herbert Samuel circulated a fundraising appeal to their friends and contacts; contributors included Winston Churchill and GBS; Beatrice suspected that Shaw had privately agreed to underwrite the costs in case contributions were insufficient.

The commission went to William Nicholson, a leading portrait painter. He painted the Webbs by the fireplace at Passfield Corner; Beatrice wrote to Beveridge in March that Nicholson:

...has made a very good study of us and is coming down with his big canvas next week end. [469]

Nicholson spent ten days at Passfield; Beatrice thought it

...a pleasant waste of Sidney's time and my strength and other people's money. [470]

Beatrice thought the result *a clever picture*; Shaw added

...especially of the brickwork... [471]

The picture was ready by the end of 1928. In January 1929, there was a reception at LSE when it was placed in the Founders' Room. Beatrice thought it a *really lovely picture*; she said that Beveridge made a gracious little speech:

...far too impressive about us – he is a very faithful admirer. [472]

Beveridge and Janet Mair continued to run LSE together. When Beveridge was absent – as he was during the work of the 1925/6 Coal Commission, and between 1926 and 1928, when he was Vice Chancellor of London University – Mrs Mair would deputize for him.

Beatrice thought their dual roles inappropriate; if they had been married,

...Mrs Mair would not have been appointed secretary of the school – it is not the position the wife of the Director ought to occupy... [473]

And she worried about the morality; she understood that social mores had changed, but lamented what she termed

...complete anarchy in opinion about sex relations. [474]

In relation to Beveridge and Mrs Mair,

Whether they are or have been technically 'lovers' I really don't know. But they are inseparable and have all the appearance of being more than friends. [475]

In 1928 Beveridge visited the United States. Mrs Mair asked Beatrice if she might go too – *at any rate travel there in the same steamer.* Better not, replied Beatrice:

It is, I am pretty certain, a platonic relationship – but in spite of their mature age it is far too romantic for the institution over which they preside, as Director and Secretary, or agreeable to her husband and children. [476]

Many academic staff resented Mrs Mair's influence over Beveridge. Sidney and Beatrice could not avoid being drawn into the resulting tension; later they had to resolve the situation. Their personal friendship with Beveridge, however, survived throughout.

When Kingsley Martin spent a weekend at Passfield in February 1927, he was working as an assistant lecturer at LSE, alongside R H Tawney and Harold Laski. He was at odds with Beveridge; Beatrice wrote that Martin was

...in revolt against the Beveridge-Mair dictatorship and in the black books of these high and mighty personages because of his booklet on the General Strike. [477]

Later that year he left, moving to Manchester to work as a leader writer on the *Manchester Guardian*. He returned in 1930, replacing Sharp as editor of the *New Statesman*.

In 1928 Graham Wallas complained to Sidney about Mrs Mair's allegedly extravagant spending. Sidney replied to Wallas

It is always useful to have gossip brought to notice, though it is seldom accurate and always exaggerated.[478]

Chapter Eleven: The second Labour Government: 1929-1931

EAST AFRICA

Like the 1923 General election, the 1929 election resulted in a hung parliament. Unlike 1923, Labour became the largest single party, leading to a second minority Labour government.

Polling day was Thursday 30 May. The Webbs were away for much of the campaign; leaving in early April, they went by sleeper to Venice, then by boat to Athens. There they saw John Hope Simpson, now working with refugees for the League of Nations, who they had first met in India in 1912. They continued to Turkey, (where they met the exiled Leon Trotsky), Austria and Germany.

Sidney had helped the Labour leadership plan for the election result; in March Henderson told him

You will be wanted in a Labour Government. [479]

The Webbs didn't believe it: didn't believe there would be a Labour majority, or that there would be a basis for a deal with Lloyd George and the Liberals. Beatrice thought another Labour minority government was just conceivable, but that, if it happened, it wouldn't last long:

…it might be long enough to send Sidney to the Lords…If he is wanted in the Lords he will go and do his best, and on the whole, he will be glad to go… [480]

They returned to London in late May, staying at Kate Courtney's old home on Cheyne Walk. The Friday before the election, Sidney lunched with Thomas Jones, who wrote to his daughter that no one knew how the election would go, but that everyone agreed that there would be a big increase in Labour's vote.

On Sunday, when TJ and his wife had dinner with both Webbs, each tried to predict the result. They all overestimated Liberal strength; only Beatrice predicted that Labour would be the largest party.

TJ again spent election night in Downing Street, as he had in 1924. He gave the Webbs a vivid account: Baldwin, his family, Churchill, the Downing Street and Conservative Party staff were all there, watching Conservative losses mount. No one was prepared for the result; TJ told the Webbs:

The Baldwins were cast down by the news – the wife indignant. WC [Winston Churchill] got wildly excited and would not listen to the tape – thought it was being tampered with, drank whisky continuously and was left scowling at the tape at 3 o'clock. [481]

The Webbs sat up late with the Laskis

...listening to the flowing tide of Labour victories – almost hysterical at the prospect of Labour being in a majority in the House. [482]

That did not happen; the result was:

Labour	287
Conservative	260
Liberal	59
Independent	8

Unlike 1924, Baldwin resigned quickly, on Tuesday 4 June. Over the weekend the Labour leadership had agreed they would accept office. On Wednesday 5 June, at Windsor, King George appointed MacDonald Prime Minister.

MacDonald again made Snowden Chancellor. After that, the key appointments were the Foreign Office, and lead responsibility for unemployment. Henderson became Foreign Secretary; his appointment was a conspicuous success, culminating in the award of the Nobel Peace Prize in 1933.

Jimmy Thomas was put in charge of unemployment policy, as Lord Privy Seal, with three other ministers to help him: George Lansbury (First Commissioner of Work), in the Cabinet; and Oswald Mosley (Chancellor of the Duchy of Lancaster) and Tom Johnston (Under Secretary for Scotland), both outside the Cabinet.

Parmoor, Beatrice's brother-in-law, again became Lord President and Leader of the Lords. Parmoor had asked MacDonald what he would offer Sidney: the answer was a peerage but not a ministerial post. Parmoor called on Sidney and Beatrice to pass on this news. Neither was interested

...we could afford neither the income nor the energy, for attendance merely to speak and vote, on occasions, and ... we should very much object to being 'enobled'. [483]

However, Beatrice noted

...I think Sidney and I were a wee bit disconcerted by Parmoor's news that JRM did not intend to include him in his Cabinet. Such is the weakness of human nature! [484]

At midnight, they were woken by the doorbell. Beatrice thought it was Maud, the maid, locked out – but met her coming downstairs to answer the door:

'Must be a telegram'
She said – I followed on – opened the telegram –
'Phone me tonight: MacDonald'
I woke Sidney who came near swearing, trying to discover – still dazed with sleep – JRM's phone number. He is to be up at Hampstead by nine.
'Wants to persuade you to accept a peerage without office',
Said I.
'I shall not do it'
Said he, and returned to his bed. [485]

Next morning, MacDonald offered Sidney a peerage, combined with the roles of Colonial Secretary and Dominions Secretary. Hurrying to complete the Cabinet, MacDonald had overlooked the requirement for two Secretaries of State in the Lords.

Sidney was delighted with the CO: it is his old office as a civil servant, one about which he knows a good deal more than about some others. [486]

Sidney took the title 'Lord Passfield'.
Beatrice thought it ironic that Sidney had now held two of the same Cabinet offices as Joseph Chamberlain:

An odd parallel between two careers in which I have been specially interested. [487]

Until the election, Joseph's son Austen had been Foreign Secretary. That summer, Sidney met Austen at a dinner. Chamberlain asked whether Beatrice remembered him

...coming with my father to stay with Mr Potter when she was acting as hostess? I was a boy at Cambridge... [488]

She did; she remembered how Austen might have become her stepson; she had described him as

...a big fair-haired youth of handsome feature and open countenance and sunny sympathetic temperament. [489]

Beatrice accepted Sidney becoming Lord Passfield; she refused to become Lady Passfield. She had changed her name for him once; she would not change it again:

I am an old woman and I am not going to change [490]

Instructed by Sidney, Colonial Office invitations to receptions, complete with the royal arms, were sent in the name of *Lord Passfield and Mrs Sidney Webb*. The Palace was outraged and complained to MacDonald – who tried to bring Sidney into line

My dear Passfield
You are getting me into hot water…
They object most strongly to this and have referred the matter to me. It is
rather awkward as without consultation it does set a precedent which needs the
consent of the King who is the boss of the Peerage… the King wants to know
your reply.
With kindest regards to you both
Yours
JRM [491]

After that, invitations went out in Sidney's name only.

For the first year Sidney answered for both departments; then, in the June 1930 reshuffle, Thomas became Dominions Secretary – responsible for relations with Australia, Canada, New Zealand and South Africa.

Sidney was responsible for the Colonial Office throughout the life of the government. The workload was substantial. As well as British colonies, the Department was responsible for the League of Nations mandates – administering former territories of defeated countries.

Therefore, just before his seventieth birthday, Sidney took on the heaviest executive political role of his life. The Labour government, without a majority, had to rely on support from other parties. The Colonial Office agenda in 1929 included problems which would haunt British governments for the next hundred years: the practical implications of Balfour's 1917 commitment to the creation of a national home for the Jewish people; the creation of the post-1919 state of Iraq; and the position of the African majority, the white settlers, and the Asian communities in East Africa.

The Victorian scramble for Africa had left Britain as the colonial power in Kenya and Uganda; after the war, Britain had been awarded the League of Nations mandate for the German colony of Tanganyika.

The outgoing Conservative Colonial Secretary was Leo Amery. The Webbs knew Amery well. His first job had been working for Leonard Courtney;

Beatrice had introduced him as *a brilliant Oxford Fabian*.[492] Later he had been a Coefficient. Amery was the imperialist's imperialist, a disciple of Joseph Chamberlain, and a tariff reformer. He took a close interest in East Africa.

Once Sidney's appointment was known, Amery briefed him. Amery had already briefed J H Thomas, who had been Colonial Secretary in 1924, thinking Thomas would be reappointed. In 1924, Thomas was said to have told his officials

I'm here to see that there is no mucking about with the British Empire. [493]

Since 1900 Britain had encouraged white settlement in Kenya. The acknowledged leader of the Kenya settlers was Lord Delamere, who had moved permanently to Kenya in 1899. In 1903 Delamere acquired a 99-year lease on 100,000 acres of grazing land for an annual rent of 1/2d per acre. The same year, he set up the Farmers and Planters Association to promote settler interests. In 1905 he was appointed to the government's Land Commission. Subsequently he became a member of every official body in the colony.

Delamere was a flamboyant character: a lion hunter, and a heavy drinker

He participated in many a drunken brawl, and once shot out the newly installed street lights of Nairobi. [494]

Behind the coarse behaviour lay an unmistakeable political purpose:

All his energy was directed at making the highlands and, if possible, all Kenya and East Africa a white man's country. [495]

The British government gave the settlement movement a boost after the war, with a scheme to help former military officers move there on favourable terms. Many did so, in particular to the 'White Highlands' area. AJP Taylor wrote that, in general, the British colonies in tropical Africa were disappointing – liabilities, not assets. But

Kenya was perhaps an exception, when it was discovered that white men could live in the highlands. Englishmen escaped democracy and high taxation by establishing themselves in Kenya as territorial aristocrats on the old model. [496]

After Britain was allocated the League of Nations Mandate for Tanganyika, British settlement there was also encouraged; George Schuster, visiting in 1928, was not impressed by the results:

…a very truculent lot. Men of no stability, little capital or education, and Croydon stockbrokers' politics. [497]

Winston Churchill, Colonial Secretary at the end of the Lloyd George coalition, sympathized with the settlers. In 1922 and 1923 there were settler deputations to London; in January 1922, Churchill told an 'East Africa and Uganda' dinner attended by Delamere

> *We do not contemplate any settlement or system which will prevent Kenya becoming a characteristically and distinctly British Colony, looking forward in the full fruition of time to responsible self-government.* [498]

That is, a government dominated by the settlers.

By contrast, Churchill's successor in the 1922-24 Conservative governments, the Duke of Devonshire, was less sympathetic to settler aspirations. In a White Paper in June 1923,[499] Devonshire set out the doctrine of *native paramountcy*:

- The interests of the native African population were paramount;

- The British government held Kenya in trust for the Africans;

- That trust would be fulfilled by the British government.

Although paramountcy remained formal government policy, between 1924 and 1929, Amery made no attempt to advance it. His objective, working with the settlers, was Closer Union – bringing together Kenya, Uganda, and Tanganyika – and possibly later Nyasaland (Malawi) and Northern Rhodesia (Zambia). For some, at least, the goal was the establishment of another autonomous dominion in East Africa, like that in South Africa – with power in the hands of the settlers. Closer Union was to be the first step.

In 1925, Amery appointed Sir Edward Grigg, a supporter of Closer Union, Governor of Kenya. Grigg had worked with Amery at the *Times* before 1914. He served in the Guards in the war, became first, Military Secretary to the Prince of Wales, and then Lloyd George's Private Secretary. In 1922 he became a Liberal MP. Having appointed Grigg, Amery noted in his diary

> *The king is very pleased about Grigg.* [500]

While Delamere led the Kenya settlers, he did not speak for all the white population. Norman Leys, a doctor who had studied at Glasgow with Thomas Jones, worked in Kenya as a government medical officer from 1905 to 1913. Jones wrote later that Leys

> *…protested against the planting of the tribesmen on the poorer lands and was defeated…I disappointed him because I could not make Prime Ministers read his books or squarely face the problem of Kenya.*[501]

Leys was a Christian socialist, close to protestant missionaries in Kenya. He saw the missionaries as inheritors of the Puritan tradition; that tradition was

...notoriously unpopular among those classes of English people from which the settlers in Kenya are chiefly drawn. It stigmatises many of their pleasures, such as horse racing and the use of alcohol. [502]

In 1913, Leys had to leave Kenya, having supported the Masai people facing forced eviction from their lands. He then worked in Nyasaland [Malawi] before returning to Britain. From 1918 he worked closely with Joseph Oldham of the International Missionary Council. In 1924 the first edition of his book, *Kenya*, was published by Leonard and Virginia Woolf.

Another opponent of Closer Union, and of Delamere, was McGregor Ross, a civil engineer who had worked on the Uganda Railway. From 1905 to 1923 he was Director of Works for the East Africa Protectorate – until forced out by Delamere. He returned to Britain, and campaigned for paramountcy.

Back in Britain in the 1920s, both Ross and Leys published highly critical books about their experience in Kenya; Sidney had his own copy of Leys' book. Both joined Labour's Imperial Advisory Committee, of which Leonard Woolf was secretary. In 1926 the Committee published a policy statement – *The Empire in Africa: Labour's Policy* – highlighting the different approaches Britain had pursued in West and East Africa. In West Africa, African land rights were protected; in East Africa, they were being eroded. During the years of Conservative government, Labour MPs, and peers – including Sydney Arnold, Sydney Olivier, and Haldane – raised the issues in debate.

In November 1927 Amery appointed a commission on Closer Union, to consider

...whether, either by federation or some other form of closer union, more effective co-operation between the different Governments in Central and Eastern Africa may be secured... [503]

Amery chose Hilton Young to chair the Commission. Young, a fringe Neo-pagan and Bloomsbury figure, had been a friend of Keynes at Eton and of Rupert Brooke at Cambridge. Now a Conservative MP, Young had been Chief Whip of the Lloyd George Liberals from 1922; he left the Liberals in 1925.

Young chose the other Commission members: Joseph Oldham, secretary of the International Missionary Council; Sir George Schuster, the Colonial Office Economic and Financial Advisor; and Sir Reginald Mant. Mant was nominated by the government of India, who were concerned about both Grigg and the Commission – anxious that it should not set constitutional precedents for India and concerned about the treatment of the Indian minority in East Africa.

The Commission left London on 22 December 1927, arriving in Uganda three weeks later. They spent 10 days visiting hospitals, colleges, and missions, before going on to Kenya, where they saw African reserves, farms, and railway workshops. Wherever they went they collected oral and written evidence. They spent another 10 days in Tanganyika, and then travelled overland to Nyasaland and Northern and Southern Rhodesia. From South Africa, they sailed back to Southampton, arriving on 7 May 1928.

But the Commission's work did not go as Amery had intended. Once Young was back in London, he went to see the minister:

> *Gave lunch at the Carlton Annexe to Hilton Young just back from East Africa. He tells me that it will not be easy to shepherd his team into any report. They are all very anti-Kenya and got at cross purposes with Grigg.* [504]

Young and Grigg – the two ex-Coalition Liberal MPs – had worked well together; the other commission members had quickly taken a dislike to Grigg. Schuster noted that

> *Hilton Young throughout had been working alone, seeking no exchange of views with us...* [505]

Drafting a report took the rest of 1928; even then, Young, the Chairman, submitted a minority report.

In November, Oldham saw Thomas Jones, who recorded that Oldham and Schuster were

> *...at loggerheads with Hilton Young on the Kenya Commission Report and especially on the effective protection of natives in the Kenya Parliament.* [506]

The main report endorsed only a limited version of Closer Union. The Commission reaffirmed the principle of native paramountcy. They recommended improved arrangements for coordinating transport and communications across East Africa. Young wanted to go much further than the others in entrenching the political power of the settlers.

What was at stake was the 'common roll': should Europeans, Indians and Africans vote on the same electoral register? Or on separate ones? Status quo was separate rolls, with reserved seats for Europeans and Indians. The majority African population was represented by members nominated by the colonial administration.

The majority of the Commission thought that in the long run this should change:

> *Our view is that, inasmuch as the progress of the territory must depend on co-operation between the races, the ideal to be aimed at is a common roll on an equal franchise with no discrimination between the races.* [507]

They acknowledged that this could only happen by consent; but a footnote adds that *the Chairman dissents* from this sentence. The absence of a common roll was particularly disliked by the Indian population.

Amery read the report over Christmas 1928. It was published in January 1929, and immediately denounced by the settlers.

The government then had to decide what action to take. Amery's solution, endorsed by the Cabinet in March, was that the Colonial Office Permanent Secretary, Sir Samuel Wilson, should go to Kenya, talk to people there, and try to secure agreement on the best way forward. Amery also negotiated the wording of a parliamentary question-and-answer with the ever-obliging Jimmy Thomas, so that the opposition was kept informed.

The only real scrutiny came from the Lords, where Sydney Olivier and Frederick Lugard – the, now retired, colonial administrator, who had been made a peer in 1928 – raised the issue, with a debate on the Hilton Young report on 13 March 1929. In the debate Olivier suggested a joint select committee of both houses of parliament to consider Closer Union.

Appointed Secretary of State in June 1929, Sidney did not start from a position of strength. The Labour Government lacked the majority to implement a distinctive new policy. On East Africa, Sidney faced a belligerent, sometimes lawless, sometimes brutal, settler community, supported by Conservative interests in Britain. Within the Labour Party there was growing sympathy for the political aspirations of the African majority. No government could satisfy both.

Immediately after the 1929 election, Amery wrote in his diary about his plan for Closer Union in East Africa

I only hope the new Government won't wreck it.

Years later, he added a note:

They did. [508]

By 1931 the dream of a new white dominion in East Africa was finished, largely as a result of Sidney's work at the Colonial Office.

Samuel Wilson, the Colonial Office Permanent Secretary, was in East Africa during the 1929 election campaign and the change of government. He left London on 9 April; travelling via Marseilles, he reached Mombasa on 29 April. He spent a month in Kenya, Tanganyika, and Uganda before meeting the three governors in Nairobi. He arrived back in London on 1 July.

Next day, Wilson reported to Sidney: nobody on the ground had any time for any of the subtleties or variants of the Hilton Young report:

I had not been in East Africa for long before I realised that no little doubt and anxiety had been caused in the minds of most sections of the community by the Report of the Hilton Young Committee. [509]

The settler members of the Kenya Legislative Council regarded the Report

...as implying the condemnation of the whole policy of white settlement in East Africa. [510]

The Kenya settlers were highly sceptical about any change that might dilute their political position.

In July the Cabinet deferred a decision on Wilson's report, for Sidney to consult interested parties. Before the election, after the Lords debate in March, Lugard, the Archbishop of Canterbury and others had established a committee to pursue the issue – including the idea of a Select Committee. Sidney spent the next three months discussing East Africa with Lugard's committee and others.

The Webbs had stayed with Lugard in 1911, when he was Governor of Hong Kong; they had been impressed by his conscientiousness and integrity. [511]

Lugard, working with Joseph Oldham, lobbied ministers, and civil servants, about Kenya; Amery denounced them for mischievous lobbying. Two weeks after the Cabinet meeting, Beatrice and Sidney stayed overnight with Lugard – he lived not far from them, in the Surrey hills – for the first of many meetings. Beatrice noted that Lugard was

...pressing Sidney to do something to curb the naively barbaric capitalism of the white settlers in Kenya or elsewhere. The policy these settlers are carrying out is to deprive the natives of land ownership and subject them to taxation in order that they should be at their mercy as wage earners. [512]

Lugard introduced Sidney to Oldham – but Oldham was not impressed, preferring to work directly with MacDonald. Sidney and Lugard established a closer working relationship; Lugard's biographer tells how Lugard came to Passfield Corner in September, and the two men stayed up talking past midnight, Sidney taking notes.

Beatrice thought that the mistake had been made

...when the White Settlers were given self-government and freed from the control of Whitehall. [513]

But it was not feasible simply to take back that autonomy once it had been granted. Sidney had no illusions about how long the Labour government might last:

'You won't have a Labour Government in power for long,' says Sidney – 'get the most you can now – before the SA dominion joins up with a reactionary British government. [514]

The Webbs saw three options: the status quo – which was condemned by all parties; the Hilton Young Report – which was contradictory; and the Wilson Report, which, according to Beatrice

…does not pretend to be more than a statement of what the White Settlers would accept as satisfactory.

And

…is denounced by everyone in the Labour Party who is interested in the native question. [515]

As well as talking to Lugard and his committee, Sidney invited Leonard Woolf, Charles Roden Buxton MP, (chair of the Labour Committee on Imperial Affairs), and other ILP members, to meet him on 23 October 1929 (the Woolfs had dinner with the Webbs the night before).

Buxton, a Quaker, had been a Liberal MP between the two 1910 elections. A founder member of the Union for Democratic Control, he had supported the peace movement during the war, working with the Courtneys. In 1917 he left the Liberals, joining the Independent Labour Party. He had met Beatrice in 1920, after going to Russia as secretary of a Labour Party delegation; she referred to him as *the admirable C R Buxton*[516]. He was a Labour MP from 1922-23, and again from 1929-31.

Before the meeting, Buxton wrote to Sidney

…we are at the parting of the ways on Imperial policy…it is absolutely necessary to take a firm line now, if what may be roughly called the 'South African' view of native policy are not to spread Northwards. [517]

The lobbying persisted: Sidney received letters about Kenya from all sources. Beatrice sent a warning:

'Tell Oldham,' said I to Tawney, 'it is useless to wire-pull an old-hand wire-puller; it arouses derision.'[518]

The storm continued, with a meeting of the Labour Party committee, and a lobbying letter to MacDonald from A D Lindsay, Master of Balliol College Oxford.

Sidney reported to Cabinet on 5 November: no subject had concerned him more than East Africa

*...Kenya has been in my thoughts every single day since we took office...
whatever we do, we shall be faced with a minor hurricane of criticism and
denunciation; and if we decide to do nothing, we shall have no less of a storm,
together with the real discredit of shirking the issues.* [519]

He took up the suggestion, from Olivier and Lugard, of a joint committee of
both houses of parliament to consider the future of East Africa; a new statement
of native policy; a limited form of Closer Union, with a High Commissioner
responsible for shared economic services; and changes to the Kenya Legislative
Council. The Cabinet deferred the report during November, finally deciding to
refer the papers to the joint committee of both houses without making recommendations, except that the new native policy would be non-negotiable. The
issue of the franchise for the Indian community made the relationship with the
India Office, and the Secretary of State for India, Wedgwood Benn, sensitive. A
Cabinet Committee was appointed to take things forward.

Beatrice wrote that

*...the Left Wing is in revolt – determined to have the blood of the settlers – to
make them feel they are beaten.* [520]

Hesitantly, cautiously, Sidney's position moved closer to that of the Labour
Party than the settlers. In early 1930 the Colonial Office prepared two reports,
which were ready for Cabinet Committee in April. TJ noted anxiously

*What is to be done about Kenya?... Should the scheme for Closer Union of the
three territories be pushed forward?...Can Labour Government hold up rights
of natives 'with our professions of democracy'? Jim Thomas thinks you can carry
that doctrine too far...Passfield thinks democracy is the ideal for Kenya, say a
hundred years hence.* [521]

The first report was the *Memorandum on Native Policy* (Cmd 5373 1930). This
reaffirmed the 1923 commitment to paramountcy, adding a new emphasis on
the political, social and economic development of the African population; the
second, a statement on Closer Union (Cmd 3574), endorsed the proposal that
there should be a new High Commissioner for East Africa, with responsibility
for transport, communications and other central services. But it rejected the plan
– versions of which had been in the Hilton Young and Samuel Wilson reports
(and partly supported by Sidney) – for greater political power to be given to the
representatives of the Kenya white settlers.

As for the common electoral roll, there was a general commitment:

...His Majesty's Government are of the opinion that the establishment of a common roll is the object to be aimed at and attained, with an equal franchise of a civilisation or education character open to all races. [522]

But this was an objective for the future; the High Commissioner, once in post, should launch a study on how it might be achieved.

On 30 April 1930 Cabinet agreed both reports – subject to Sidney consulting

...certain Members of Parliament who have made a special study of this subject. [523]

He explained to Beatrice what this meant:

The Cabinet agreed today to my Kenya proposals, but still subject to my seeing C R Buxton and Snell privately, so as to persuade the malcontents on that side! [524]

Harry Snell, now a Labour MP, and Chairman of the Parliamentary Labour Party, had known the Webbs since the 1890s; he was a member of Labour's Imperial Affairs committee, and a dogged questioner of ministers on Kenyan issues. He wrote to Sidney on 3 May:

...I have read the draft with a feeling of relief and with some satisfaction. The terms of the draft are such that a great deal of what people like myself have been asking for may be covered... [525]

Buxton wrote articles supporting the policy for journals such as the *Friend* and the *Social Democrat*.

The pressure on Sidney from the party committee, and from the ILP Africa specialists, had paid off. The price was the growing hostility of the Governor and the settlers.

Sidney's junior minister, Drummond Shiels, wrote later

Our stalwarts were fairly well satisfied, though they would have liked more constructive proposals, but the Kenya settlers were somewhat uneasy... [526]

Grigg – understandably – interpreted the two Command papers as undercutting the basis of his appointment. Before the native policy statement appeared, Sidney wrote to Grigg:

...the change of Government which came about a year ago makes a very real difference, and it is reflected at once in the closer supervision which we give to native affairs... it is my duty as Secretary of State to ensure that native policy in East Africa is in accordance with the views of the Government which is in power. [527]

This provoked an extraordinary response from Governor to Minister

Your party is by its very nature a party of zealous and militant reformers; and many of them have had to learn from responsibility that there is a very wide and difficult debateable land between the enunciation of political principles and the practical application of those principles to the circumstances of the time.
528

Sidney minuted his Permanent Secretary

Sir S Wilson
I fear I must ask you to read this remarkable letter. 529

Leonard Woolf was worried that Grigg was misleading Sidney; he wrote

There is every possibility that Lord Passfield is being lied to. 530

In fact their private exchanges were forthright and direct. Sidney replied to Grigg in July; responding to the charge of excessive zeal, he pointed out that

There are a good many of us who have had a long training in administration of one kind or another, and are not likely to underrate its practical difficulties or to allow theory to get in front of the daily task. 531

Once the Cabinet had agreed the reports, the joint committee could be established. Pressure on parliamentary time meant that this did not happen till November 1930; before this, however, there were two House of Lords debates. At the first, in July, Sidney was criticized by Conservatives, but supported by Lugard and the Bishop of Salisbury. Lord Cranworth thought the government should just have implemented the Samuel Wilson report.

When Olivier and Lugard first suggested a joint committee, in March 1929, their aim had been consensus; speakers in the subsequent Lords debates spoke of taking the future of East Africa out of party politics. In the November debate, Cosmo Gordon Lang, Archbishop of Canterbury, supporting the case for the joint committee, quoted General Smuts of South Africa, who had stated that:

…the question of white and black on the Continent of Africa was going to be the most interesting and enthralling problem of the twentieth century. 532

Thirty years before, Lang (then Bishop of Stepney) had worked with Sidney on education policy, and had been a frequent guest at Grosvenor Road.

The reality of a joint committee under a minority government was that Labour would only have 8 of the 20 places. Two places went to Sidney and to Drummond Shiels. A further three seats went to internationalist ILP MPs with a close interest in East Africa – Charles Roden Buxton, Wilfred Wellock, and James Hindle Hudson. Both Hudson and Wellock had been imprisoned as wartime conscientious objectors. Hudson knew the Webbs of old: before the war he had been a teacher in Salford, Secretary of the Manchester and Salford ILP, and active in the Poor Law campaign, attending the 1910 Summer School. Wellock was a Lancashire nonconformist who had been sympathetic to Guild Socialism.

On the Conservative side, both Amery and Ormsby-Gore, who had been his Under Secretary, became members, as did Lord Cranworth, who had criticized the establishment of the Committee. Lugard was also appointed.

The initial chairman was Lord Stanley of Alderley, a Liberal – described by Shiels as

...a man of progressive and tolerant outlook... [533]

Amery took care to brief Stanley:

Had a good long talk with Eddie Stanley who had been put on the E African Select Committee to give him the right point of view. [534]

The *East African Standard*, a settler newspaper, was not impressed by the Committee membership:

Most of the peers are too old for the work entailed, while among the House of Commons selections are two or three members who have strong anti-Empire views.
[535]

The paper condemned Sidney as knowing nothing about East Africa, Amery as knowing little, while Lugard

...knows nothing about modern life and conditions.

Wellock, they considered

...an ultra Socialist pacifist to whom a uniform is anathema,

Buxton and Hudson were dismissed as *Negrophiles.*[536]

Before the formal establishment of the joint committee in October 1930, a group of Labour MPs, including Buxton, James Hindle Hudson, and Wilfred Wellock, asked Sidney to ensure that African witnesses would be able to give evidence to the Committee, and that the Government would meet the costs.[537]

This was contentious; it had never happened before. After the Committee's first meeting on 4 December 1930, Amery noted in his diary that he had shocked some of the other members by suggesting that

...half a dozen unhappy niggers in front of a committee in the House of Lords would not really give us much guidance. I think the whole thing is likely to prove a sad waste of time.[538]

Travel costs had to be met; this had to be agreed by the House of Lords Offices Committee; at first, in December, they rejected the estimate of £2,625. Sidney had to appear before the committee and plead for the decision to be reversed – which it was, reluctantly, in February.

Nine African witnesses, three from each territory, came to London. They were not independent; they were nominated by the colonial administration, from Chiefs and members of local Native Councils.

On the ground, more independent structures were emerging. In particular, in Kenya, younger Kikuyu men had formed the Kikuyu Central Association. Grigg, in a confidential letter to Sidney in March 1930, quoted a description of the Kikuyu Central Association by a District Officer:

An organized and conscious attempt to rob the present Chiefs and Elders of real authority, and to ensure that the power shall rest with a native political organization, which will dictate the policy to such chiefs as are allowed to remain. [539]

From 1928 Johnstone (Jomo) Kenyatta was general secretary of the Kikuyu Central Association. Kenyatta made a first visit to London in 1929/30; from his arrival he was watched by the security services. Sidney agreed that Drummond Shiels, his junior minister, should see Kenyatta. McGregor Ross brought him to meet Shiels in January 1930, Kenyatta

...impressed [Shiels] more favourably than I had expected. [540]

Shiels tackled Kenyatta on the question of female genital mutilation; missionaries, and colonial staff, had tried to discourage the practice; the Kikuyu Central Association had defended it as traditional. An elderly female missionary had been killed over the issue. Shiels – a medical doctor – explained some of the consequences of FGM; Kenyatta responded that imposing changes of this sort by government circulars and pulpit denunciations was counterproductive – but that the Association

...would not object to but would welcome Government Doctors coming into the territory and speaking to the people on the physical dangers of circumcision. [541]

Kenyatta returned to Britain in 1931, but was not permitted to give evidence to the joint select committee. Apart from a year in the Soviet Union (1932-3), he stayed in Britain until 1946. He studied for a diploma in Social Anthropology at LSE.

In early 1931, once the principle of hearing the African witnesses, and covering their costs, had been agreed, the Colonial Office started practical preparations. In the London of 1931, it was virtually impossible to find a hotel prepared to accommodate nine black African visitors. Sidney approached Hilton Young, who had become a Director of the Southern Railway, about the problem.

Eventually, the witnesses were accommodated at Hitherwood, a Holiday Fellowship hostel in Sydenham, South London, at a cost of £57 10s a week for the whole party. Hitherwood was described by the civil servants as

...an international hostel where all sorts and kinds of queer people go...

The Colonial Office staff noted that

There are of course a good many white women about...

Fortunately,

The Manageress was very much alive to the various difficulties and dangers.[542]

Sidney thanked the staff who had made the arrangements

This has involved much trouble and ingenuity, for which thanks are well deserved. [543]

After the visit, Sidney's office wrote thanking the manageress of the hostel.

The first witnesses arrived on 22 April; all left on 14 May. The Colonial Office organized a full programme for them. They saw the FA Cup Final; they went to the Tower of London, Westminster Abbey, and the Mint. They lunched at Lyons Corner Houses. They visited the Army at Aldershot, and the Navy at Portsmouth. They were taken to Eton, and to Oxford University; the Ugandan visitors were taken to Manchester to see the cotton industry.

On 27 April they were received by Sidney in his office; he told them it was a historic occasion

Never before have representatives of the native population in East Africa been gathered together in this room. [544]

The joint committee's first meeting was in December 1930. They took evidence from February 1931 until the end of June. They finalised their report at the end of September – after the fall of the Labour government, but before the October dissolution of parliament. There were forty seven meetings; Sidney attended almost all, playing an active part in the questioning of witnesses.

The committee approached their task systematically, hearing fifty one witnesses and receiving written evidence from more. The first was Samuel Wilson; he was followed by Hilton Young and Edward Grigg. They then heard from other colonial administrators (current and retired); business representatives; clergy; the Indian community, the settlers, and the nine African witnesses.

James Hindle Hudson questioned Hilton Young on the issue of the Common Roll; Young's responses revealed his underlying assumptions:

It is really impossible to contemplate the East African tribal native ever discharging the functions of a democratic voter as long as the tribal system is still the basis of his civilization.[545]

Shiels (who sometimes thought his Secretary of State unduly cautious) wrote later that establishing the joint committee was a *wise and big thing* for Sidney to have done.

The African witnesses gave their evidence in late April and early May. None of them supported even the limited version of Closer Union in the Hilton Young report.

The Kenyans came before the Committee on 28 April. In answer to a question from James Hudson, Chief Koinange, the leader of the delegation said that, if there was a High Commissioner, they were afraid that all that would happen would be

...that people like Lord Delamere would get the ear of the High Commissioner, and that they would not be able to do so.[546]

A week later the Tanganyika witnesses gave evidence, saying that Closer Union would involve great difficulties for them:

Both in Kenya and Uganda there are restrictions upon the extent to which the native inhabitants are permitted to make use of the land, and when they desire to extend their cultivation there are regulations imposed on them.[547]

One of the Uganda witnesses, representing the Kabaka of Buganda (hereditary ruler of part of Uganda), told the Committee

...no good can be derived by the Kingdom of Buganda from this Federation.[548]

By the spring both Stanley and Sidney had concluded that even the government's limited version of Closer Union was unlikely to survive the Committee's scrutiny.

On 28 April Stanley circulated a note beginning:

The Committee cannot recommend Political Closer Union.[549]

His reasons were that the economies of the three territories were depressed; the costs could not be justified; and he believed that a link to Kenya and Uganda could not be shown to be in the interests of Tanganyika. He also concluded that almost any change in Tanganyika would breach the League of Nations Mandate.

Sidney had arrived at similar conclusions in a handwritten note a few days earlier. In his formal report to Cabinet in May he added a further argument:

> ...the striking unanimity with which the native witnesses now oppose any form of Closer Union. Those from Uganda and Tanganyika shudder at the idea of coming under the influence of Kenya, whilst all alike distrust the possible interference of a new dignitary...[550]

Stanley drafted the report. He died in August, before the report was finalised, though after it was substantially completed. As expected, it did not endorse any form of Closer Union.

The report recommended abolishing the remaining forms of forced labour, and increasing the power of the Native Councils, and the Chief Native Commissioner. Shiels commented

> These two proposals are excellent and should make stronger the position of the Africans vis-à-vis the European community.[551]

The Labour MPs on the Committee submitted detailed proposals, based on the principle that

> ...the Native has the same right to political development as the white man.[552]

While these were not agreed they did influence the final report.

Leonard Woolf was eternally disappointed in Sidney as Colonial Secretary:

> ...where the British Empire was concerned, he was a common or garden imperialist conservative.[553]

Woolf thought Sidney was slow to act on proposals from the Labour Committee on Imperial Affairs; he had higher hopes of Shiels, who attended the Joint Committee regularly. He believed Shiels

> ...was dismayed by Sidney's conservatism and his masterly inactivity...[554]

To some extent this was true; Shiels quotes a letter from Sidney, in April 1930, to a critic in Kenya:

> We cannot get improvements in these places faster than our officials can be persuaded to go! Theirs are the hands that must carry out the reforms...[555]

But Shiels also thought – rightly, as things turned out – that the Joint Committee had disposed for good of the idea of Closer Union. Writing in 1949, he concluded that this was one of Sidney's best achievements. [556]

Sidney's positive contribution was acknowledged in Margery Perham's 1960 biography of Lugard. Herself a witness before the 1930-1931 Joint Committee, she wrote that the policy of Closer Union had failed because of

...a combination of political events and personal efforts. Chief among the events were the advent of Labour to power with the appointment of Passfield as Colonial Secretary. His tenure was brief and he had his shortcomings. But, as he told Grigg in rather rebuking letters, he approached the question not as a Labour doctrinaire, but as a trained administrator who had to see both sides of any case, in this case the native as well as the settler side. [557]

PALESTINE

The Colonial Office, alongside its responsibility for British colonies, was the lead department for Britain's League of Nations mandates. The former German colony of Tanganyika was one such; the former Ottoman territory of Palestine another.

The League was established by the Versailles Treaty; the Mandates were defined in the Treaty as *a sacred trust of civilization*; the Mandatory Power was responsible for the *well-being and development* of the people of the territory.

Two factors led to Britain's involvement in the Middle East: international pressure to establish a national home for the Jewish people; and military campaigns in the region during the war.

In 1917 Arthur Balfour – Foreign Secretary in Lloyd George's government – issued the Balfour Declaration:

His Majesty's Government view with favour the establishment in Palestine of a national home for the Jewish people and will use their best endeavours to facilitate the achievement of this object, it being clearly understood that nothing shall be done which may prejudice the civil and religious rights of existing non-Jewish communities in Palestine. [558]

The Statement of War Aims, drafted by Sidney for the allied socialist parties, contained a similar pledge.

Balfour's statement came after years of campaigning by supporters of a national home. Chaim Weizmann, originally from what is now Belarus, moved to Britain in 1904 to teach chemistry at Manchester University, acquiring British citizenship in 1910. During the war he directed the Admiralty's research laboratories, while working for the creation of a national home. Beatrice first met Weizmann in 1919:

...a disinterested idealist, a clever administrator, an accomplished intellectual, all rolled into one. But he is a champion manipulator...[559]

Both Britain and France fought in the Middle East during the war. In 1916 they agreed future spheres of influence: France would take care of Syria; Britain would take responsibility for Palestine. In 1917 and 1918 forces from both countries occupied areas of territory – the British, with TE Lawrence, fighting alongside Arab rebels in support of growing Arab nationalism. Both encouraged the expectation that Ottoman rule would be replaced by autonomous Arab governments. In December 1917 British troops entered Jerusalem.

Britain's military presence on the ground, and the Balfour commitment, came together in the form of the Mandate. Confirmed in August 1922, this provided for the establishment of a Jewish national home

...and also for safeguarding the civil and religious rights of all the inhabitants of Palestine, irrespective of race or religion. [560]

The Mandate also provided that an *appropriate Jewish agency* was to be recognised to cooperate with economic and social administration; the body chosen was the Zionist Organization.

Britain, the mandatory power, was therefore committed to two potentially incompatible positions: local self-government for the existing populations; and the establishment of a Jewish national home in Palestine.

From 1918 to 1920 Palestine was under British military rule. In 1920, before the Mandate came into force, Britain established a civilian regime, under a High Commissioner: Herbert Samuel, former Liberal Home Secretary, well known to the Webbs. He had lost his Commons seat in the 1918 Coupon election. Jewish by ethnicity, but atheist in practice, Samuel had been an early supporter of the concept of a Jewish national home. He remained High Commissioner until 1925, subsequently returning to British domestic politics.

Samuel worked through traditional structures. The Ottomans had exercised the right to appoint the Mufti of Jerusalem, the leader of the Moslem community. In 1921 Samuel asserted this right, overturning an election for the post, and appointing a candidate from a different leading family – Hajj Amin al-Husseini. Al-Husseini was an uncompromising nationalist, committed to frustrating moves towards a Jewish national home, and determined to keep a Moslem majority in Palestine. Later he turned towards Nazi Germany in pursuit of his aims, and appeared alongside Hitler.

The beginning of the Mandate was relatively calm. Samuel reduced the British military presence; in 1920 the garrison was 25,000; by 1921 it was 7000. Later the territory was policed with a Palestinian gendarmerie of Arabs and Jews, with

British officers, and a British gendarmerie, staffed with former Black-and-Tans redeployed from Ireland.

Samuel's successor was Lord Plumer, a First World War general. Plumer did not address political issues; he was

...not troubled by any emotional or spiritual ties to either race in Palestine. He had no intellectual interest in or knowledge of Zionism and he opposed all constitutional initiatives. [561]

The Lloyd George Coalition Cabinet considered Britain's commitment to Palestine, publishing a White Paper in 1922, when Churchill was Colonial Secretary (Cmd1700 1922). This rejected the idea that the purpose was

...to create a wholly Jewish Palestine. [562]

It defined the National Home as

...not the imposition of a Jewish nationality upon the inhabitants of Palestine as a whole, but the further development of the existing Jewish community... [563]

Contradictions remained: one was between the commitment to local self-government and the creation of a Jewish national home; a second was whether a Jewish national home necessarily implied the creation of a Jewish state. The issue of Jewish immigration made both contradictions harder to resolve.

In 1918, 8% of the population of Palestine were Jewish. When British civilian government began in 1920, immigration of up to 16,500 people a year was permitted, provided the Zionist Organization took responsibility for their support for the first year. Samuel found, however, that the British government had underestimated the degree of Arab resentment this would provoke. In 1921, therefore, he issued revised regulations, restricting the numbers of migrants. This angered the Jewish community – internationally as well as locally. The 1922 Churchill White Paper also established the policy that immigration should be linked to the country's capacity to absorb new arrivals. The regulations were revised again in 1924, 1925, and 1927. In 1927 there was no Jewish immigration; in 1928 net immigration was only ten people.

Migration had an impact on land ownership, and land ownership on employment and the wider economy. New arrivals would go to settlements for which land had been bought; that land would then be retained by the Jewish community. Many settlements had a policy of reserving jobs for Jewish people. Often Arab owners were ready to sell to buyers. The overall outcome was a shift in the balance of economic activity.

Plumer retired in 1928. His replacement was Sir John Chancellor – an experienced colonial governor, but without previous knowledge of Palestine or the

Middle East. Chancellor's relationships with Whitehall and local officials were poor. He believed the Balfour Declaration had been a mistake, and unfair to the Arab population. During Chancellor's term the situation began to deteriorate.

The Wailing Wall in Jerusalem is sacred to both Muslims and Jews; as Haram as-Sharif, it is the third-holiest place in Islam; it is a surviving remnant of the second Jewish temple. Both communities expected to be able to worship there. Under the Mandate, the Palestine government tried to regulate access and conditions of worship by protecting the *status quo*: whatever had been the practice in Ottoman days was permitted; no departure would be tolerated.

After earlier incidents, there was trouble at the Wall on the Day of Atonement in 1928, leading to complaints; in November, Amery presented a White Paper (Cmd 3229 1928) on the disturbances to parliament. Tension continued. Sidney was briefed when he took office:

The Secretary of State should perhaps see this draft…It is typical of the country and its sectarian strife…

The problem could only be solved

…by direct agreement between the Jews and Muhammedans. The Government can use its good offices to bring the two parties together; but it is not in a position to dictate to either… [564]

Further disturbances occurred in August 1929. On Saturday 17, a brawl left one young Jewish man dead and many injured. In riots across Palestine on Friday 23 August and the following days, 133 Jews and 116 Arabs were killed, and 198 Jews and 232 Arabs injured. In Safed and Hebron, members of the Jewish communities were massacred. In other places Jewish populations were evacuated under police protection. The week's events revealed the inadequacy of British security. Both Sir John Chancellor, the High Commissioner, and the Zionist leadership, were on leave at the time.

The British Government's first responsibility was to restore peace. They therefore strengthened the military presence, sending five warships from the Mediterranean fleet and three battalions of infantry, backed up by aircraft and armoured cars.

After the first incident, Weizmann wrote to Sidney, raising future policy and immigration as well as the immediate consequences of the violence. The Mufti wrote to the London *Times*, denouncing Jewish *aggression* at the Wailing Wall [565], and quoting the Koran. Correspondents from the Zionist Association responded.

Events in Palestine preoccupied both Webbs. Beatrice wrote to Elizabeth Haldane, saying that Sidney thought

... There must have been some very bad staff work in the Palestinian government not to have been aware of what seems to have been an organized movement. [566]

She noted that Sidney was coming under pressure from the Jewish community, but that

...no representative of the Arabs – not even a casual admirer of the Arabs – has appeared on the scene. [567]

Beatrice could see that the Government had to restore order and stop killing and looting. But she was not convinced by the Zionists:

I admire Jews and dislike Arabs. But the Zionist movement seems to me a gross violation of the right of the native to remain where he was born and his father and grandfather were born – if there is such a right. To talk about the right of the Jew to return to the land of his inheritance after an absence of two thousand years seems to me sheer nonsense, and hypocritical nonsense. [568]

She found it ironic that some Labour MPs – like Josiah Wedgwood – who were critical of the Kenya settlers, were nevertheless supporters of the Jewish settlers in Palestine.

On 9 September the cabinet agreed to hold an inquiry into the causes of the dispute, and to keep two infantry battalions in place until after the Day of Atonement in October. The military authorities thought the other reinforcements could soon be withdrawn.

The chair of the Inquiry Commission went to Sir Walter Shaw, a colonial judge. The other three members of the Commission were MPs; the Labour representative was Harry Snell. The Commission was given the power to take evidence on oath. The Commissioners arrived in Jerusalem on 24 October. They spent two months travelling the country, hearing from witnesses, including representatives of the British and Palestine governments, the military, the police, and both Arab and Jewish communities.

While the Commission was taking evidence, the situation in Palestine remained volatile. Sidney reported to the Cabinet on 28 November that the position was *not without some danger*. Telegrams from Chancellor, the High Commissioner, in October referred to *bitter* Arab feelings against the Jews, and to a *state of desperation*.[569]

The Cabinet asked the Chiefs of Staff for their advice. This arrived just before Christmas: the Chiefs recommended better policing and better intelligence, but concluded that

Incidents between Jews and Arabs are bound to continue. [570]

By December, the British garrison in Palestine amounted to 1450 troops, twelve planes, and seven armoured cars, dispersed across the country. The Chiefs thought this was probably adequate, as reinforcements were available in an emergency. In February, the Cabinet agreed with the Chiefs of Staff.

After the Commission had finished taking evidence, but before their report had been written, Chancellor, the High Commissioner, sent Sidney a despatch giving his own views. While recommending that the Balfour Declaration should be reaffirmed, Chancellor proposed asking the League of Nations to amend the Mandate to remove

> ...those provisions which give or appear to give the Jews a privileged position in Palestine over the indigenous population. [571]

Chancellor asserted that all the land in Palestine that could be cultivated was already occupied; and that

> ...no cultivable land now in possession of the indigenous population can be sold to Jews without creating a class of landless Arab cultivators. [572]

He argued that Jewish immigration should be limited to the numbers necessary to cultivate the land already in Jewish hands. Chancellor's recommendations were neither accepted by the Cabinet nor made public before the Shaw Commission reported at the end of March.

Walter Shaw's Commission found that the main cause of the August 1929 riots had been

> ...the Arab feeling of animosity and hostility towards the Jews consequent upon the disappointment of their political and national aspirations and fear for their national future. [573]

The Commission aimed to produce a balanced report, rejecting criticism of the actions of the Mufti and of the British and Palestine governments. They warned, however, that immigration and the land problem were together leading to a crisis:

> There is no alternative land to which persons evicted can remove. In consequence a landless and discontented class is being created. Such a class is a potential danger to the country. Unless some solution can be found to deal with this situation, the question will remain a constant source of present discontent and a potential cause of future disturbance. [574]

They called for a clear government statement on future policy towards Palestine – giving the government's interpretation of the commitments in the Mandate to safeguarding the rights of the non-Jewish population, and laying down future policy on land and immigration.

While all Commission members signed the report, Snell also submitted a note of reservation. Where his colleagues exonerated the Mufti and other Arab leaders, Snell was more critical. He accused them of a

> ...*studied desire to provoke and wound the religious susceptibilities of the Jewish people.* [575]

Policy towards Palestine presented complex problems of political management for the government. While the Colonial Office was the lead department, it was a minority government, so the attitudes of other parties mattered; Labour also had to carry its own supporters. Because of the Mandate, the Foreign Office were involved. There were varying degrees of support for the Zionist and Arab positions within all the parties.

Revised proofs of the Shaw report were due at the Colonial Office on Saturday 22 March. The Prime Minister was promised a copy; MacDonald had already arranged to meet representatives of the Jewish community (Weizmann, Lord Reading, and Lord Melchett) on 28 March, to give them the report, and outline future government policy.

When MacDonald saw the report, according to Beatrice, he was *much perturbed*; it was

> ...*far too pro-Arab for the PM's taste.* [576]

The Colonial Office, meanwhile, were concerned that if MacDonald saw Jewish representatives, he should also see Arabs; a delegation was arriving in London at the same time, and, an internal minute to the Permanent Secretary on 20 March stated,

> *The Jewish visit to Downing Street can hardly be kept secret from them, or from anyone else. We must be careful not to make them think that matters of high policy have been settled in consultation with the Jews alone and behind their own backs. I submit that if the Prime Minister carries out his programme in regard to the Jews, it is very desirable that, before any public pronouncement is made, he should also accord an interview to the Arab delegation.* [577]

Sidney wrote on this recommendation '*Done on 31/3/30*'.

After meeting Jewish representatives MacDonald saw the other party leaders – Baldwin, Lloyd George, and Herbert Samuel. The outcome was a proposal that General Smuts, former South African Prime Minister, should be asked to review the Mandate, supported by Sir John Campbell, economic adviser to the Colonial Office. This had reached the point of a telegram to Smuts before MacDonald had second thoughts; Smuts had Zionist sympathies. The government then reverted to a more limited enquiry, focussed on immigration, land settlement, and development.

For this review, Sidney picked Sir John Hope Simpson. The Webbs had met, and been impressed by, Hope-Simpson in India in 1912; more recently, they had seen him in Athens, where he was working on refugee issues for the League of Nations. Since then Hope Simpson had visited Passfield Corner, and had dined with Sidney in London.

Hope Simpson arrived in London to start work at the end of April; Sidney wrote

He is full of life and eagerness for his Palestine job, for which I am sure we are lucky to get him. [578]

Others were less convinced. On 7 May, Weizmann and Lewis Namier called on Thomas Jones. Namier had known TJ for twenty years; they had shared a room at the Fabian Summer School in 1910. They came to complain about Hope Simpson's appointment, and about Sidney: they dismissed Hope Simpson as a civil servant – *not the big man we expected.* [579]

Weizmann complained to TJ, demanding an immediate meeting with the Prime Minister

I want to tell you, Mr Jones, that I can bear the burden no longer. My patience is broken...I can hold up no longer; I shall be crucified by my own people, that is inevitable, the Jews have a habit of crucifying their leaders. [580]

Hope Simpson went to Palestine in May; he worked on his report in May and June. Meanwhile, the immigration issue returned to centre stage. In 1929, the government of Palestine had reduced the maximum annual number of immigration certificates to 2,300; Charles Roden Buxton had written to Drummond Shiels in December, within days of Shiels' appointment as Under Secretary, questioning this.

Now, in spring 1930, the government suspended the issue of further certificates. 950 of the totals for the year had already been issued; the rest were to be delayed. Weizmann lobbied MacDonald, both directly and via MacDonald's son Malcolm; on 2 July, Sidney saw a delegation from the Board of Deputies of British Jews.

Sidney gave the delegation an emphatic clarification of government policy:

There had been no change in the policy of the Government and no change in the execution of the Mandate, but the Mandate did not envisage the establishment of a Jewish State, only of a Jewish National Home in Palestine consistently with the maintenance of the position and rights of the Arab

population. There must be a limit to Jewish immigration determined by the absorptive capacity of the country. [581]

Hope Simpson submitted his draft report on 22 August. He had worked closely with Sir John Chancellor, and the report reflected the analysis developed by Chancellor and in the Shaw Report. His conclusion on the availability of land for settlement was that

...there is at the present time and with the present methods of Arab cultivation no margin of land available for agricultural settlement by new immigrants, with the exception of such undeveloped land as the various Jewish Agencies hold in reserve. [582]

Hope Simpson proposed an active agricultural development policy

...having as its object close settlement on the land and intense cultivation by both Arabs and Jews. [583]

To implement this policy there should be a Development Commission, with three members – one Arab, one Jewish, and a British chair. Hope Simpson went into detail in a letter to Sidney: any area of land to be developed by the Commission should be allocated simultaneously to Arab and to Jewish people; and should be let on long leases, rather than sold. He argued that there was no other way of implementing the commitment in the Mandate to facilitate Jewish immigration while not prejudicing the rights of the existing population. He acknowledged that this would cost the British Government money:

This expenditure cannot be avoided. The Palestine Budget cannot bear it. And it is right that the expense should fall on the British people, for it was their Government which accepted this remarkable Mandate. [584]

In the letter Hope Simpson also commented on the leadership of both communities, saying of Colonel Kisch, the Chairman of the Jewish Agency in Palestine, that

He is not a man who inspires confidence, and personally, I do not feel that I could trust him. [585]

He was even more dismissive of the Mufti:

He is a man of small attainments, and, had he not been appointed Grand Mufti by Sir Herbert Samuel, nothing would ever have been heard of him.

Hope Simpson had tried, unofficially and unsuccessfully, to persuade the Mufti to reach agreement on the Wailing Wall

The impression which he made on me was that of a man who had no conception of the method in which such a subject should be handled. He has a petty mind, and his whole attention is directed to manoeuvres which will fortify his personal position. [586]

He was more forthright still in a private letter to Sir John Campbell:

You may remember the Mufti. A first class scoundrel, I think, who only maintains his position because of the religious difference with the Jews. He is not going to allow the question [of the Wailing Wall] *to be settled.* [587]

He told Campbell that he thought that, when it appeared, his report would be

…torn letter from letter. That cannot be helped.

And he warned that

Things here might boil up at any minute partly due to bigotry on the part of the Arabs, and partly due to unwisdom on the part of the Jew. [588]

Once Hope Simpson's report was finished, the government had to publish it, and to clarify and confirm its own policy.

At the end of July, the Cabinet appointed a committee, chaired by Snowden, to draw together policy on Palestine, and to respond to issues about the Mandate that had been raised by the League of Nations. Sidney was on the committee; Henderson, the Foreign Secretary, was not.

The statement they produced became the Passfield White Paper of October 1930 (Cmd 3692). It was largely an exercise in consolidation, intended to remove

…misunderstanding about the past actions and future intentions of His Majesty's Government [589]

The White Paper:

- Reaffirmed the Government's commitment to the Palestine Mandate, but stressed that this involved obligations to both Jews and non-Jews;

- Stated that Government would work to promote the interests of all the inhabitants of Palestine;

- Referred back to the Churchill White Paper of 1922;

- Restated the 1922 definition of the Jewish National Home;

- Confirmed that immigration numbers should be based on the capacity to absorb;

- Defined the role of the Jewish Agency.

The Government also outlined plans to strengthen the police force. Earlier proposals to establish a Legislative Council had failed through lack of Arab support; another attempt would be made. And they intended to implement the Hope Simpson proposals for economic development.

The principles were agreed by the Cabinet and its committees; on 10 September, Sidney wrote to Beatrice

I got my great draft declaration of policy on Palestine through the Cabinet Committee today easily enough. Snowden, Thomson and Thomas expressed admiration for it. It is really the work of the office... [590]

Agreeing the principles was straightforward; agreeing the money for Hope Simpson's economic development plan, which aimed to be fair to both Jews and Arabs, was more difficult. The Cabinet asked experts to examine the details; at Cabinet on 19 September, Snowden reported that he had heard that the Expert Committee

...had brought to light certain facts that he thought had not been in the minds of the Cabinet Committee when they reported. [591]

Apparently, the Hope Simpson scheme would cost £6 million, *the interest on which would have to be guaranteed by the Exchequer.*

It was deferred again; the next week, the Cabinet Committee reported

...that in present circumstances a proposal to spend many millions on land settlement of Jews and Arabs in Palestine would meet with serious opposition in parliament and the country. [592]

The Cabinet discussed the issue again on 24 September. It was becoming increasingly difficult to balance the two sets of obligations inherent in the Balfour Declaration and the mandate.

The Cabinet had approved the Hope Simpson report in principle; they had not approved the necessary resources. They accepted some moral responsibility to provide for dispossessed Arab tenants but considered that further development of the land reserved for the Jewish settlements should be paid for by the Jewish organisations.

Sidney had to communicate the decision. The minute read:

That the Secretary of State for the Colonies should be authorised to communicate verbally to Dr Weizman, [sic] in confidence, the purport of Sir John Hope Simpson's Report and of the draft statement of policy... The Secretary

of State was asked to consider the advisability of mentioning to Dr Weizman the need for limiting the immigration of Jewish urban workers. [593]

They also suggested that he might see Lord Reading: (Rufus Isaacs) first. That evening, Sidney wrote to Beatrice, telling her the proposals had been agreed

…and I am to have the troublesome task of imparting them confidentially to Lord Reading (at once), and to Dr Weizmann when he returns next week. Whether we can avoid a shriek of anguish from all Jewry I don't know! [594]

He also wrote to Weizmann, meeting him and on 17 October sending him, in confidence, an advance copy of the White Paper.

Publication was set for Tuesday 21 October; Weizmann called a press conference on 20 October, and announced his resignation as President of the Zionist Organization and the Jewish Agency. This was followed by Melchett's resignation as Chairman of the Jewish Agency Council, and by the resignation of the American banker Felix Warburg from his position on the Jewish Agency Executive. There were demonstrations against the White Paper in London, Palestine, New York, South Africa, and Warsaw.

On Wednesday Sidney sent Beatrice news of Warburg's resignation

The Jewish hurricane continues… They seem to go wild with excitement and rage, on mere partisan telegraphic summaries and interpretations of a lengthy document. [595]

He emphasized, however, that

…we do negative the idea of a Jewish State, which the British Government has consistently done – and this (rather than a National Home in Palestine) is what so many of them want. [596]

Sidney was sure it was a misunderstanding; on Saturday, he wrote to Weizmann expressing his regret that he should have resigned after so many years *devoted toil* for the Zionist cause; he felt

…your action can only be based on an imperfect appreciation of the Government's attitude and intentions. [597]

Beatrice, ferociously loyal to Sidney, thought it would blow over. She wrote at the end of the month

The hurricane is unpleasant for you and for the P.M. but I think the worst is over and reaction will set in. [598]

In late October Beatrice wrote two long, angry diary entries. She noted that Sidney remained unperturbed and that he had *done his best to hold an even balance*. She had no such inhibitions; privately, she had become pro-Arab:

> *At the time of the Balfour declaration, the one and only consideration was the relative power (to help us win the war) of the international Jewish financiers on the one hand and on the other the Arabs in revolt against the Turkish empire. The man on the spot gave promises to the Arabs; the British Cabinet gave promises to the Jews – always qualifying the promise of a Jewish Home by the perfunctory condition of the well-being of the Arab inhabitants.* [599]

> *…the fatuous promise of a Palestine Jewish Home which, if it meant anything worth having for the Jews, meant a Jewish Palestine from which the Arabs would be gradually extruded by economic pressure.* [600]

And she asked

> *Why is it that everyone who has dealings with Jewry ends by being prejudiced against the Jews?* [601]

But the worst was not over; the storm had not passed.

The new parliamentary session opened on 28 October; Lloyd George and Baldwin raised the White Paper in response to the King's Speech, accusing the government of changing policy towards Palestine. The following week, a letter was published in the *Times* from two lawyers, the Conservative Lord Hailsham and the Liberal Sir John Simon, alleging that the White Paper broke the terms of the Mandate, and urging the government to get the League of Nations to obtain an opinion from the Court at The Hague before implementing crucial policies. [602]

Sidney replied, explaining that

> *…the inferences drawn by Lord Hailsham and Sir John Simon are unfounded and are based on a misconception of the declared intention of His Majesty's Government.* [603]

But the damage had been done; the issue now came to the attention of the Foreign Office. Henderson, the Foreign Secretary, had neither been on the Committee which considered the draft White Paper, nor attended the Cabinet on 24 September which had approved it. But he was the Government's representative on the Council of the League of Nations, and so closely involved in discussions about the Mandate. Henderson raised the issue at Cabinet on 6 November: the Foreign Secretary should be consulted before any statements about Palestine. A new Cabinet Committee – including the Foreign Secretary – was necessary to consider Palestine.

Hugh Dalton, Henderson's junior minister, noted

Uncle raised Palestine urgently. The Jews all over the world, and in Whitechapel particularly, where a byelection is pending, are off their heads with indignation.
604

The new committee started work at once. It began by seeking a meeting with Weizmann and other Zionist leaders. Before the committee could make progress, however, it emerged that Sidney had given an interview to a New York Jewish paper. Sidney had thought he was off the record. But he had been quoted extensively. Now the Zionists were refusing to meet the committee.

Henderson, as Foreign Secretary and chair of the new Committee, now took the lead on Palestine. Sidney was an active member of the committee – but,

...the whole conduct of the proceedings was taken out of my hands. Some Ministers would have resigned rather than take what I have had to stand since last October. But my resignation would have aggravated the Government's troubles; and I don't do that sort of thing. So I have put up with everything...[605]

On 12 November, Dalton wrote

10.30 I find Uncle closeted with Weizmann and Namier. He has taken charge of the Cabinet Committee on Palestine and is negotiating with the Jews, who won't meet Webb or Colonial Office officials. [606]

This was followed by moments of pure comedy. Henderson's Private Secretary reported that Sidney wanted to see the Foreign Secretary:

'Lord Passfield is here.' Consternation! The Jews are still in the waiting room, but may emerge at any minute. Passfield is put in Selby's room down the side passage, to wait till they have gone. French farce scene! In the end no collision occurs. [607]

Negotiations on the White Paper now started between Henderson's committee and Weizmann. Slowly, the parties arrived at a form of words that would enable them to talk: the government accepted that doubts had been expressed about the compatibility of the Mandate and the White Paper.

Weizmann asked if Malcolm MacDonald MP – Ramsay's son – could join the discussions. He wrote to MacDonald on 12 November:

...it would be most highly appreciated by us if you saw your way to associating your son, Mr Malcolm, in some official capacity with the forthcoming conference. He has our complete confidence, and, if you will allow me to say so, our most sincere affection and respect. [608]

Weizmann's attitude to Sidney was different. It was not that he did not know the subject; unlike Henderson and the other committee members, to whom the detail was new, Sidney was on top of his brief. Weizmann wrote to Warburg in December:

> *Passfield does know the thing, but he is so artful and shifty that you never know when you have got him to agree something.* [609]

A similar attitude was taken by the *Jewish Times*, which warned:
LORD PASSFIELD CANNOT CONDUCT NEGOTIATIONS

> *...we must emphasise that the Jewish people has not the slightest faith in Lord Passfield and cannot have the slightest faith in any negotiations in which he will play the chief part.* [610]

Leonard Stein – a barrister, and Liberal activist, who was honorary legal adviser to the Jewish Agency, previously Political Secretary of the World Zionist Organization – prepared a critique of the White Paper. The Colonial and Foreign Offices responded with a lengthy refutation of Stein's paper.

On 17 November, the House of Commons debated the White Paper. Lloyd George was highly critical. He suggested that MacDonald had not been fully consulted; he called it one-sided and biased:

> *Its whole drift is hostile to the spirit of the mandate. It breathes distrust and even antagonism of the Jewish activities. If it had been written by an anti-Semitic official, I could understand it.* [611]

MacDonald was enthusiastic about Jewish settlement in Palestine. After the war, while out of Parliament, he had visited Palestine; following the visit, he wrote a pamphlet, *A Socialist in Palestine*, which was published by the Jewish Socialist Labour Confederation Poale-Zion in 1922. He described his visit in his speech on 17 November, and praised the achievements of Jewish settlers.

In his contribution, Drummond Shiels went into detail about the proposed development scheme.

In parliament, in the Committee, and in negotiations with Weizmann, Ministers defended the White Paper, saying it had been misunderstood or misinterpreted. The plan was for Henderson to write to Weizmann, responding to the disputed points – rather than issuing a new White Paper. Drafts of the letter passed back and forth between the Foreign Office and the Jewish Agency; discussions dragged on through November and December to the frustration of both sides.

Sidney returned to Passfield, depressed, for the weekend 13/14 December; Beatrice recorded his mood:

'*People will say,*' he sadly observed, '*that your husband has not been a success as a Minister.*' *The PM is cross about Palestine…*[612]

He would have liked to retire; but

…it would be taken as a victory for the Jews over the Arabs and might lead to trouble in Palestine. [613]

After Christmas events moved to a conclusion. On 26 December, Sidney wrote to Henderson; he was concerned that the Jewish Agency was trying to widen the scope of the negotiations, aiming to cut out both the High Commissioner, and any consultation with the Arab population. Within the Colonial Office, work on the development scheme, on land policy, and other issues had stopped. Weizmann, Sidney argued, was trying to get the decisions on all these issues taken in London, in meetings between Ministers and the Jewish Agency, rather than by the government of Palestine.

Henderson replied that, while he agreed with much of Sidney's argument

Though our proceedings are being extended, they have prevented in some measure a continuation of the agitation that began with the publication of the White Paper. It may well be that that is the only gain secured, but that admitted I think it has been on the whole advantageous. [614]

In other words, keeping talking was the price of peace. But now

I shall have to expedite matters as much as I can as Chairman as I leave for Geneva on the 14th. [615]

Two points in the draft had separated the sides before Christmas: immigration and land purchase. These issues were central to the analysis developed by Chancellor, Shaw, and Hope Simpson, and endorsed by Sidney and the Cabinet in the September White Paper.

Now, on each point, the government conceded enough to satisfy Weizmann: On immigration, the final text stated

His Majesty's Government did not prescribe and do not contemplate any stoppage or prohibition of Jewish immigration in any of its categories.[616]

And on land:

…the statement of policy of his Majesty's Government did not imply a prohibition of acquisition of additional lands by Jews. It contains no such prohibition, nor is any such intended. [617]

The letter was agreed by Cabinet on 4 February; they also decided that

MacDonald should sign it. A suggestion that the Cabinet Committee's life should be extended, with responsibility for wider areas of policy towards Palestine (as Weizmann had suggested) was rejected. So was a proposal that responsibility for Palestine should pass to the Foreign Office.

In effect, MacDonald's February 1931 letter accepted the main criticisms that Weizmann and others had made of the September White Paper. It marked a significant shift in British policy towards Palestine. Sidney had attempted to follow an even-handed approach; the effect of the MacDonald letter was to shift the balance towards the Jewish settlers.

The verdict of Drummond Shiels, Sidney's junior minister, writing long afterwards, was that

> *...one more effort to bring about better relations in Palestine had failed; and the belief of the Arabs in the good faith of the United Kingdom Government was shaken.* [618]

Why, having continued through the autumn of 1930 to maintain the position that the criticisms were all down to a misunderstanding, did the government give way in the New Year?

Weizmann certainly thought that the explanation lay in his effective campaign against the White Paper. A more recent writer, Carly Beckerman-Boys, has argued that a more plausible explanation is the difficulties and pressures of party management in the circumstances of a minority government:

> *It appears that the weight of holding the Labour Party together on an issue made more divisive by the arguments of Conservative and Liberal politicians, who were partially motivated by preserving their own leadership positions, was simply too tiresome.* [619]

THE ECONOMY, UNEMPLOYMENT, AND THE FALL OF THE LABOUR GOVERNMENT

With Sidney absorbed in his department, Beatrice anxiously watched the government's overall performance, entertaining ministers and MPs in London and at Passfield.

The government's main priorities were foreign policy and unemployment. Henderson was Foreign Secretary; Dalton was his deputy. J H Thomas, assisted by Lansbury, Mosley, and Tom Johnston, was responsible for measures to address unemployment. Thomas's relationships with his assistants, and with Snowden the Chancellor, were poor.

TJ went to Thomas's first meeting and talked to him afterwards:

I said there were two views about him – that he was a fool to take on the task, and that it was a sporting and courageous thing to do. [620]

The 1924 Labour Government had lacked a strategy to overcome unemployment; none was developed before Labour's return to office in 1929. Snowden remained a champion of Treasury and Bank of England orthodoxy. Within Labour, there had been some new thinking, mostly by Mosley and the ILP – but it had not become party policy.

At the 1929 election the most radical proposals had come from the Liberals, led by Lloyd George, advised (among others) by Maynard Keynes. Keynes told a Liberal meeting in March 1928

Let us be up and doing, using our idle resources to increase our wealth. With men and plant unemployed, it is ridiculous to say we cannot afford new developments. [621]

Their ideas had been opposed by Snowden (and the Treasury) and defeated. Plenty of critics opposed the Treasury view. But there was no consensus about an alternative; in the words of AJP Taylor,

In 1929 the new ideas were still too new. [622]

Labour made few explicit election promises. The old 'work or maintenance' formula was there:

The Labour party's plan for dealing with Unemployment is to provide work; but pending the absorption of the unemployed in regular occupations it will take steps to relieve the present distress. [623]

The Manifesto also proposed reducing labour market *congestion*. This meant reducing labour supply – raising the school leaving age (from 14 to 15); and enabling older workers to retire by improving pensions.

There was a short term breathing space. Unemployment among insured workers never fell below one million between 1921 and 1939. But in mid-1929 it was lower than it had been in 1928. In June 1929 there were 1,164,000 insured workers unemployed; in November, 1,326,000 as compared with 1,453,000 a year earlier.

Other indicators were less encouraging. The Bank of England's gold reserves were running down, funding a stock market boom in the United States: by the end of July, the Bank had lost $100 million of its $800 million reserves. Losses continued in August.

On 20 September, Clarence Hatry, a flamboyant London company promoter, turned himself in to the authorities, admitting large scale fraud, and leaving liabilities of £21 million. In January Hatry was sentenced to 14 years imprisonment; more immediately, on 26 September, the Governor of the Bank, Montagu Norman, increased Bank Rate from 5 ½ % to 6 ½ %. The stock market fell 17 points.

The following weekend the Webbs went to Labour's annual conference. Beatrice found ministers

...self-possessed and self-confident and just at present purring over the popularity of their government... [624]

She saw trouble ahead, between Snowden's Treasury and

... Thomas egged on by Mosley and supported by Henderson, representing a forward policy on Unemployment. [625]

Also the Hatry fraudulent collapse and the rise of the Bank Rate have brought about a demand for a public and expert enquiry into currency and credit which can hardly be resisted. [626]

In response the government established an enquiry into finance and industry, chaired by Hugh Macmillan, a Labour-sympathizing Scottish lawyer. Enquiry members included three critics of the gold standard – Keynes, Ernest Bevin, and the former Liberal Chancellor Reginald McKenna.

On 29 October, Black Tuesday, just before the Macmillan Committee was appointed, the American stock market crashed. $16 million was wiped off the value of 240 stocks in one week.

The London *Financial News* charted the crash in its front-page headlines that week:

Wild day in Wall Street
Black Day on Wall Street
New Wall Street Debacle
New Big Break on Wall Street

In the short term the crash halted the outflow of Britain's reserves. Soon, however, international demand for British goods fell. British exports fell from £839 million in 1929 to £666 million in 1930 and £461 million in 1931.

Beatrice was concerned:

...dark, thunderous clouds are arising among our own people – coal and unemployment... [627]

She worried that

All the more courageous and gifted men in the Cabinet are absorbed in foreign affairs and government of the British Empire. [628]

She was contemptuous of Thomas:

…nothing wrong with the poor man except that there is nothing in him!

As for his lieutenants:

Lansbury and Mosley – an aged agitator ci-devant small master and a young aristocratic rentier without training except that of a popular orator. [629]

The Labour leaders, she wrote

…have neither knowledge nor experience of Capitalist enterprise. [630]

Beatrice thought there was an *intellectual hollowness* in Labour's position. They called for nationalisation: but she worried that the *trade union pull* was the only thing that really mattered to them:

Their cry is higher and higher wages, shorter and shorter hours, supplemented by more doles, as the only means of equalising incomes or even of securing a bare subsistence to every citizen. [631]

Economic policy was securely back with the Treasury and the Bank. Snowden worked closely with Montagu Norman, the Bank Governor, who often called on the Chancellor on his way to and from the Bank. In 1926 Snowden had written about Norman

…He is a friend – I know nothing at all about his politics. I do not know if he has any. [632]

Both Snowden and Norman were equally committed to the defence of the Gold Standard and to tight control of public spending.

There were two other potential centres of economic policy making within government; neither succeeded in challenging the orthodox hegemony.

Since 1918 there had been sporadic suggestions (from Beveridge among others) that there should be an Economic General Staff. In 1924 MacDonald had commissioned a paper on the subject; in 1929 he returned to the idea, asking TJ to organise Downing Street lunch meetings for economists and business people. Maurice Hankey, the Cabinet Secretary, TJ's superior, was sceptical

It looks like a feckless duplication of work already done quite efficiently by departments. I hope that the Cabinet Office will be able to keep clear of it. [633]

The economists included Keynes, GDH Cole, and Henry Clay, (adviser to

Montagu Norman). As well as business representatives, Walter Citrine, the TUC Secretary, attended.

TJ was asked to prepare a proposal; he recommended an Economic Advisory Council with a small staff:

> ...*rather more than the Treasury would welcome but less than Keynes and Cole would like to see.* [634]

This was approved by the Cabinet in January 1930. TJ noted

> *Passfield all in favour and had talked it over with Beveridge.* [635]

In February they settled the membership: Cole and Keynes as economists, and the business representatives who had attended the lunches. Ernest Bevin was the main trade unionist; TJ was secretary.

The other potential source for economic policy making was Jimmy Thomas and his advisory ministers. They seldom met as a committee; it is not clear whether they were intended to.

In July 1929 Thomas asked Lansbury, Mosley, and Johnston, to report on how the manifesto pledge to improve pensions, taking a tranche of older workers out of the labour market, could be implemented.

They produced a three-part report in November: a description of five possible early retirement schemes; a paper by the three ministers recommending one of them; and a paper signed by seven civil servants recommending against all of them. TJ called this an *unusual* Cabinet paper. He highlighted the last paragraph of the civil servants' report: under the recommended scheme, by 1980, every five males aged between sixteen and sixty

> ...*would be required not only to earn their own living and provide for their wives and children, but also to support between them three old persons in addition to meeting their share of every other public burden.* [636]

In December the Cabinet appointed a Sub Committee to review the report. The Sub Committee met Lansbury, Mosley, and Johnston, and concluded that the scheme would be expensive and potentially unfair. By two votes to one, they recommended against the proposals; this was endorsed by the Cabinet in January 1930.

Thomas had inherited responsibility for the previous government's limited public works programme; in autumn 1929 he had some success in easing the grant conditions. Frustrated with the slowness of the road programme, Mosley argued that some of it should be taken away from local government. This brought him into conflict with Herbert Morrison, the transport minister.

Beatrice watched things deteriorate. In July 1929, the Labour peer Lord

Arnold told her he was discontented with Thomas's

> *...incapacity as organizer of unemployment. Oswald Mosley and Lansbury report that Thomas does not see them...*

Arnold told Beatrice that Thomas was in the hands of reactionary officials (among them Horace Wilson, with whom Beatrice had clashed in the past). Beatrice called Wilson *that arch-reactionary*; Arnold told her that Thomas obeyed Wilson; that he would not read his papers, and therefore could not defend them in Parliament.

> *Then he gets 'rattled', and when not under the influence of drink or flattery is in an abject state of panic about his job.* [637]

Henderson came to Passfield in December. He enjoyed being Foreign Secretary, and was still running Labour's head office. Apart from his own duties, he was

> *...most concerned about the collapse of Thomas – who is completely rattled and is such a state of panic, that he is bordering on lunacy...* [638]

Henderson thought that Thomas was too neurotic to take advice; he said that MacDonald feared Jimmy might be suicidal. Henderson also told Beatrice that Jimmy was drinking heavily and should be sent away for a rest.

Just before Christmas the City of London gave a grand lunch for MacDonald and Snowden. Beatrice talked to Thomas there:

> *The poor man was almost hysterical in his outburst of self-pity: everyone had been against him and the 'damns' flowed on indiscriminately...the d--- windbags of the Clyde were responsible for not fulfilling the d--- pledge, which he had never made, to stop this d--- unemployment* [639]

She noted that he

> *...took no counsel not even with Mosley and Lansbury who had been appointed to help him...* [640]

Then came what was for Beatrice the ultimate condemnation:

> *In reactionary views, in his helplessness in the hands of an accomplished and hostile civil service, he is another John Burns.* [641]

But Thomas lacked the dignity and sobriety of Burns:

> *Jimmy is a boozer, his language is foul, he is a stock exchange gambler; he is also a social climber.* [642]

Thomas's position began to unravel. The previous week Mosley saw the Prime

Minister to complain. MacDonald noted:

> *Visit from Mosley on behalf of Lansbury & Johnston & himself, saying impossible to work with Thomas, & threatening resignation. Probably impossible to work with them, but I fear that T. has handled them badly.* [643]

Over Christmas, Mosley wrote a forty page paper on unemployment and the economy, which became known as the 'Mosley Memorandum'.[644] He sent it to MacDonald on 23 January 1930.

Mosley argued for a restructuring of government, with the Prime Minister leading on unemployment, supported by an executive organization and economic research capacity. A distinction was needed between long term planning for permanent economic recovery, and short-term schemes for the relief of unemployment.

Mosley argued that Thomas's department could not create jobs; it had to rely on others. Examples included:

- Housing and Slum Clearance – Ministry of Health

- Land Drainage – Ministry of Agriculture

- Unemployment Grants Committee Grants – Ministry of Labour

- Road, rail, canal construction and improvement, and electrification – Ministry of Transport.

Mosley proposed the *maximum possible programme of road construction and reconstruction*– financed by borrowing, without regard to cost, or the impact on the rail network. The Memorandum was written before the Cabinet's rejection of the pensions proposals, which Mosley continued to advocate.

Mosley argued for better planning of public spending. Under the existing system, Departments were like

> *...a crowd of bookmakers jostling through a turnstile on the racecourse. The man who can push hardest and make the most noise gets through first and takes the money. Unemployment Ministers, without any Department, can never by the nature of their case at present be in the fortunate position of getting through first.* [645]

Lansbury and Johnston agreed with Mosley. Lansbury wrote (while assuring Thomas that their differences were not personal) that he was *in substantial agreement* with the memorandum. [646]

Tom Johnston was more blunt:

...I fully endorse the Chancellor of the Duchy's critical examination of the present method of dealing with relief work schemes.

The honorary advisory committee of Ministers – as the Chancellor of the Duchy describes the three of us – Lansbury, Mosley and myself – have only been summoned to a meeting, I think, on two occasions during the past six months. The belief that such a Committee sits regularly with either deliberative or executive powers is liable to give rise to misunderstanding among the members of the Government, the Party, and the Public, and it is likely to place the three Ministers in undeserved difficulties in the future, as they may be held partly responsible for decisions which are not theirs and about which they were never, in fact, consulted. [647]

When the Cabinet discussed the Memorandum, on 3 February, TJ summed up their attitude towards Thomas as

Don't shoot him, he's doing his best. [648]

There was no consensus, so they set up another committee, under Snowden, to consider unemployment, and the papers from Mosley and the other Ministers, and report back.

This took three months. On 1 May they reported, dismissing Mosley's proposals out of hand. The Prime Minister could not take charge of unemployment:

We do not see how the Prime Minister, who in virtue of his great position is unavoidably encompassed with problems and responsibilities of the most varied kinds, could add to his burden so great and intricate a responsibility. [649]

Nor could other departmental ministers spare the time to help him. As for Mosley's distinction between long-term economic restructuring and short-term relief, this

...indicates, we submit, a confusion of mind...

This policy involves the acceptance of non-remunerative and wasteful schemes...

On borrowing, the report states that Mosley appeared

...to have swallowed, without properly digesting it, the Keynes-Lloyd George programme of internal development loans.

The report conjures up stern warnings of a collapse of political and economic confidence, declaring that

...we must not be rushed into shovelling out public money merely for the purpose of taking what must be a comparatively small number of people off the unemployed register...[650]

The report reiterated the case against the policy of early retirement through improved pensions, already rejected by the Cabinet in January.

When Lansbury (the only one of the three 'unemployment ministers' who was a Cabinet member) saw Snowden's report he denounced it:

Our Party, and certainly not Mosley, Johnston and myself, do not cry for the moon nor expect our whole policy to be carried through in a year or even twenty years, but it is the apparently contemptuous rejection of policies adopted by the Party, and on which we obtained votes, which I object to, and that a policy of loan raising and spending up to, I think, 200 million pounds, advocated by Lord Passfield in the House of Commons, is now spoken of in terms of something like ridicule. It makes me ask whether, if the Cabinet does anything at all, we should not tell the nation without reservation that the statements in 'Labour and the Nation' and in our Election Manifesto concerning unemployment, were ill-thought out and not worth the paper they were written on. [651]

When the Cabinet discussed Snowden's report, on Thursday 8 May, it was referred to yet another committee – this time under MacDonald. Relations between Thomas and his team had deteriorated; the report was leaked to the *Daily Herald*; Thomas suggested the three ministers might be responsible. Lansbury lost his temper.

MacDonald's committee met twice, inconclusively, on 13 and 19 May. Money voted by government for relief works was not being spent. Road building was a complicated matter; Transport Minister Herbert Morrison was called in and held to account:

He said it was always so. When money voted no plans in being. Take Shooters Hill by-pass. It was found there was a railway in the way: houses on the route; tramway being built. There are always physical difficulties. [652]

Before the meeting on Monday 19 May, Mosley saw MacDonald:

...had to see me urgently: informed me he was to resign. I reasoned with him & got him to hold his decision over till we had further conversations. [653]

The night before the resignation, the Mosleys stayed at Passfield Corner

Oswald and Cynthia Mosley here for the night, at a critical stage of his career. After the turning down by Cabinet etc under Snowden's influence of his plan for coping with unemployment, is he or is he not going to resign? [654]

Mosley shared Beatrice's contempt for Thomas, but retained some respect for Snowden and MacDonald. Beatrice thought Mosley sincere. Mosley thought the government should hire Keynes (and Arthur Salter, the head of the Economic Section of the League of Nations) and give them a free hand to work on unemployment – *we are inclined to agree to this suggestion*, wrote Beatrice.

If he resigned, Mosley told Beatrice, he would lead a critical group in Parliament that would vote to keep Labour in power, and organize propaganda outside.

Sidney and Beatrice wondered about Mosley's future:

Whether Mosley has sufficient judgment and knowledge to lead the Labour party in home affairs I have no means of judging – Sidney thinks not. [655]

At lunchtime on Tuesday 20 May, Mosley resigned. MacDonald tried to keep him, but, according to Tom Jones,

It was a case of Snowden v. Mosley and plainly Mosley must go. [656]

Mosley then took his case to the Parliamentary Labour Party. At a meeting on Wednesday 21, he was persuaded to delay a motion censuring the party leadership on unemployment until Thursday 22. On the Thursday he misjudged his tactics, forcing a vote rather than responding to an appeal from Arthur Henderson. He lost by 29 votes to 210.

The following week there was a Commons debate on Mosley's resignation, on a Conservative motion to cut Thomas's salary. Mosley's speech was a parliamentary set piece, described by Beatrice as

…wholly admirable in manner and style. [657]

MacDonald, Baldwin, Lloyd George, and Winston Churchill all spoke.

The government survived, but its difficulties persisted. MacDonald had now promised to give *personal and complete attention* to unemployment, chairing the Cabinet Committee. As his biographer points out, at most he had bought time:

…he had staked his reputation on his ability to succeed where Thomas had failed; and, in doing so, he had used up the Government's chief alibi. [658]

After the debate Beatrice still saw Mosley as a leader:

Has MacDonald found his superseder in Oswald Mosley?… Hitherto he has had no competitor in personal charm and good looks, delightful voice and the

gift of oratory. But Mosley has all these with the élan of youth, wealth and social position added to them. [659]

She could also see a downside. Mosley knew nothing of trade unionism or cooperation; she doubted if he could work well with working or lower middle-class people. Could he build effective working relationships with people like Arthur Henderson, Ernest Bevin, Herbert Morrison, or Walter Citrine?

He is, in fact, an intruder, a foreign substance in the labour movement, not easily assimilated. [660]

Sixty Labour MPs now signed a petition demanding that Thomas should be sacked. Sidney and Beatrice were about to go to Jersey on holiday. Before they left, Sidney went to see MacDonald.

According to Beatrice, Sidney offered to give up either, or both, of his two offices – Colonies and Dominions. MacDonald told him he couldn't retire altogether – the Government still needed two Secretaries of State in the Lords. Sidney therefore told the Department to prepare for the two roles to be split *and came off for our fortnight's holiday in excellent spirits.* MacDonald's personal loyalty to Thomas was such that he would not let him go altogether

…sooner than accept Thomas's resignation he, MacDonald, would resign himself. One up for Jimmy. [661]

So, while the Webbs were away, Thomas was appointed Dominions Secretary, while Sidney retained the Colonies. The new Lord Privy Seal was Vernon Hartshorn, the Welsh miner and Primitive Methodist, who had been in the 1924 Government. Hartshorn had not been available for appointment in 1929, as he had been one of the two Labour representatives on the Simon Commission, reviewing the government of India.

The other Labour member of the Simon Commission, also not given Government office a year earlier, had been Clement Attlee. MacDonald now appointed Attlee Chancellor of the Duchy of Lancaster. It would be difficult to imagine a greater contrast with the louche, flamboyant Mosley. MacDonald asked Attlee to work closely with the Economic Advisory Council; TJ (who, aged 60, was about to retire from the civil service), wrote to one of the business members of the EAC:

There has been a new development this week. The Prime Minister has asked Major Attlee, MP, the Chancellor of the Duchy of Lancaster, to concentrate on the study of the state of trade, remedies etc, to come into residence here and have the use of the staff. [662]

Attlee did not stay long in this role: in spring 1931 he became Postmaster General. At the end of July, however, he circulated to the Cabinet a remarkable paper on the problems of British industry (CAB/24/214) which foreshadowed much future Labour economic policy. He was dismissive of laissez-faire policies, protectionism, and Empire Free Trade, but called for a Ministry of Industry *with a staff including experts on labour, industrial management, finance, transport and power, housing and town planning.*

Attlee's paper was never even discussed by the Cabinet. It appeared on the agenda on 19 September, and again on 19 November; it was going to be considered along with a major report by the economist members of the Economic Advisory Council; but the Cabinet was always too busy, its agendas too crowded. In November 1930, a copy reached Hugh Dalton; he thought it *not a very distinguished production* – but at least

> *...it recommended that a Ministry of Industry should be set up to rationalise on socially sound lines – armed with considerable powers. The only result has been that Horace Wilson (of all people) has been set up as Industrial Adviser, to rationalise, with no powers!* [663]

Mosley was out of office; he remained in the Labour Party. In October he took his fight to the Labour conference in Llandudno.

The conference met under a shadow: on Sunday 5 October, the day before it started, Lord Thomson, Secretary of State for Air, was killed when the airship R101 crashed in France. Thomson was probably MacDonald's closest friend in politics. He was also close to the Webbs; just a week earlier he had stayed at Passfield. Beatrice felt his loss:

> *The inner circle has lost one of its very few charmers – indeed, barring the PM, is there any other charmer in Government circles? The forty odd Ministers are a drab company!* [664]

MacDonald spoke on the Tuesday morning. Starting with a tribute to Thomson, then making an uncompromising defence of the government's record, he stressed the international causes of the slump, and promised further action, ending on a rousing note:

> *So, my friends, we are not on trial; it is the system under which we live...I appeal to you to go back to your socialist faith.* [665]

He received a tremendous reception and then hurried back to London to receive the bodies of the crash victims at Victoria Station.

A motion censuring the government, moved by Jimmy Maxton of the Clydeside ILP, was defeated. But a resolution calling on the National Executive

Committee to examine all the proposals in the Mosley memorandum and to report back received over a million votes and came close to being carried. Mosley was elected to the Executive; Thomas was defeated.

Beatrice thought MacDonald had triumphed at the conference. She still thought Mosley could succeed him; Mosley had established himself as

...an arrival to the front rank of Labour leaders – all the more impressive because he stood alone – of Oswald Mosley. If he keeps his head and minds his personal conduct Mosley will win through and beat MacDonald, at any rate on the platform. [666]

Unemployment continued to rise: in July 1930 it reached two million; in November two and a half million.

Despite Mosley's conference success, and Beatrice's view of his prospects, the distance between him and Labour widened. On 1 December he issued the Mosley Manifesto, calling for protection, Empire Free Trade, and loan-financed public works, supervised by a Cabinet of five 'overlords.' He was supported by 17 Labour MPs (including Aneurin Bevan) and the miners' leader A J Cook. Dalton (who never had much time for Mosley) labelled it *a move towards Toryism*.

Sidney, writing to Beatrice a week later, thought

...the Mosley document is going to prove a very damp squib. It is rather a revelation of Mosley's failure in leadership. ...It paints no picture of a remedy against Unemployment. [667]

The New Year came. On 22 January 1931 Beatrice was seventy five. The Mosleys sent a telegram; the Soviet Embassy sent flowers. She reflected

The trend of my reputation is clearly to the left and not to the right. [668]

For many years, from when it had seemed a remote dream, Beatrice and Sidney had worked for a Labour government. They had lived with reservations about MacDonald; he had appeared the only possible leader. Now they developed wider doubts.

In late January, the Government scraped through a major vote in the House of Commons on trade union legislation. Next morning, Sidney told Beatrice

I should not like to say it to anyone else, but I wish we had been defeated last night. [669]

This was partly because he was tired; it was also because of Labour's lack of a plan to deal with unemployment. Sidney thought that Snowden and MacDonald were contemplating benefit cuts – and that, if benefits were cut, it would destroy the Labour Party.

In home affairs, wrote Beatrice, Labour

…has no policy – it has completely lost its bearings…What I am beginning to doubt is the 'inevitability of gradualness', or even the practicability of gradualness in the transition from a Capitalist to an equalitarian civilisation. [670]

The Webbs saw the policy vacuum and the coming crisis for the country and the party. They could not see a way forward:

And no one is doing the thinking? So we shall just drift on into some sort of disaster as we did into the great war. I turn to writing Our Partnership because I feel totally unable to think a way out of the problem before the country. Sidney says, 'All I know is that I don't know how to do it.' [671]

Their sympathies did not lie with the existing Labour leadership. Beatrice thought that, if social revolution came to Britain,

Snowden and MacDonald, one or both of them, will be in the House of Lords, defending the existing order. If we were twenty years younger we should be drawing up a constitution for the rebels. [672]

They began to watch what was happening in the Soviet Union.

Also in January 1931, Beatrice's nephew Stafford Cripps became an MP. He was the son of Beatrice's sister Theresa (who had died in 1893) and Alfred Cripps – now, as Lord Parmoor, Leader of the House of Lords. Stafford had had a successful career as a barrister. He had joined Labour in 1929, encouraged by Herbert Morrison. In October 1930, the Solicitor General had died in office and Cripps was appointed in his place. To Beatrice's delight, he then succeeded at a byelection:

And now Stafford Cripps enters the political arena as Solicitor-General and the winner, by a huge majority, of the Bristol seat…tall, good-looking, pleasant voice, an essentially modest and well-mannered man; but a first-rate advocate, in receipt of a large income. He is the only one of the 155 nephews and nieces who might become a big figure in public life. [673]

Cripps soon joined Beatrice's list of potential Labour leaders. For now, they still had hopes of Mosley. They were less optimistic about the ILP and the trade union leadership.

By the Labour Conference in autumn 1931 Beatrice was talking up Stafford's prospects:

*The most notable newcomer – one who is already acclaimed the future leader –
is Stafford Cripps. He moved among the younger men with ease and modesty…*
674

In January, Mosley was still in the Labour Party, pressing unsuccessfully in
the PLP and the NEC for an urgent conference on unemployment policy. That
changed in February 1931: Mosley and four followers walked out, to found the
New Party. Beatrice described the move as *an amazing act of arrogance*:

*I regret the loss of Mosley – he was the only orator in the Labour Movement,
except MacDonald. But I am afraid he has slammed the door behind him and
not even Uncle Arthur will be able to let him in again, not even as a prodigal
son!* 675

On 10 March Labour expelled Mosley.

The slump and the costs of unemployment were now imposing severe pressures
on the budget. On 11 February the Conservatives moved a censure motion on
the Government *for its policy of continuous additions to the public expenditure*. In
response Snowden said

*It is no secret that I shall have a heavy deficit at the end of this year. No Budget
in the world could stand such an excessive strain as that which has been placed
upon it by the increase of unemployment during the last 12 months.* 676

Beatrice listened from the gallery. She noted that this statement

*…was cheered by the Tories and received in deadly silence by the Labour back
benchers… The likelihood of the government being turned out by their own
followers, supported by the Tories, is growing greater every day.* 677

Sidney thought the Government would soon fall. The outcome of the censure
debate was that the Government accepted a Liberal amendment calling for a
committee to review spending. This was established in March, chaired by Sir
George May, of the Prudential Assurance Company. Its brief was to make recommendations for *all possible reductions in National Expenditure*.

The storm continued to gather. Unemployment, having reached 2.5 million
at the end of 1930, remained over 2.6 million in January, February, and March.
It fell slightly in April and May, then reached 2,707,000 in June and rose again
in July.

The slump meant that the tax take was falling; the cost to the exchequer of
unemployment benefit was rising. The government response had been to meet
the shortfall by borrowing, but to appoint a Royal Commission (the Holman
Gregory Commission) to investigate *abuses* and to look at ways of making the

Insurance Fund *self-supporting*.

The international economic situation worsened. On 11 May 1931, the Credit Anstalt, Austria's largest bank, failed. The Bank of England contributed £ 4.3 million to a rescue package – but at the cost of alienating the French.

Since 1929 the government had referred three major issues to enquiry committees: finance to Macmillan, unemployment to Holman Gregory, and public spending to May. All were now due to report.

On 4 June, interim reports from the Holman Gregory Commission appeared: a majority report, and a minority report from the two Labour members. The majority report recommended benefit cuts, increased contribution rates, and tougher eligibility criteria – but accepted that for now the fund could not become self-supporting. It recommended an increase in the Insurance Fund's borrowing powers.

On 10 June, the Cabinet agreed to the borrowing powers, but deferred the main recommendations. The legislation on borrowing was linked to action on what were termed 'anomalies' or abuses; in an all-night sitting in the House of Commons, this was fought all the way by the ILP members, who called 33 divisions against the Labour Government.

The Macmillan report on finance and industry appeared on 13 July. Its tone was reassuring; but it revealed that the City's short-term liabilities exceeded £ 20 million, and it confirmed Britain's diminished standing in the world. The report argued against devaluation, and in favour of world reflation. But it came too late and was never properly discussed by the Cabinet.

The international position deteriorated further. The problems in Austria spread to Germany, and then to Rumania and Hungary. The pound fell against the dollar; Britain was again losing its gold reserves. The net outflow of gold from London between 15 July and 20 September was £33 million.

Against this background, May's report on public expenditure appeared on Tuesday 4 August. This stated that

> ...*in order to produce a properly balanced budget in 1932...a deficiency of £120,000,000 had to be made good by new taxation or by economies.* [678]

More than half was to be raised by a 20% cut in unemployment benefit; pay in the armed services was to be cut back to 1925 levels; police pay was to be cut by 12½%; teachers' pay by 20%. Road building and public works to relieve unemployment were to be cut; May proposed cutting both work and maintenance.

The report concluded

> ...*only by the strictest regard to economy and efficiency over a long period can the trade of the country be restored to its pre-war prosperity and any substantial number of the unemployed be re-absorbed into industry.* [679]

462

Keynes thought the May Report

...the most foolish document I have ever had the misfortune to read. [680]

The Cabinet saw the report on Thursday 30 July, their last meeting before the summer recess. As usual when faced with a difficult report, they set up a committee to consider the report of the previous committee. This time the members were MacDonald, Snowden, Henderson, Jimmy Thomas and Willie Graham, the President of the Board of Trade. Departments were asked to comment by 18 August, so that the Committee could meet on 25 August and subsequent days.

August 1931 was a crisis for the country and for the Labour Party; it was also a crisis for the Webbs.

Sidney told Beatrice that Cabinet on 30 July had been *jolly and cordial*, dominated by reports from MacDonald and Henderson about their international work. Beatrice thought that the Cabinet was *in a very tight place*; and that the May report – *the product of five clever hard-faced representatives of Capitalism and two dull Trade Unionists* – was

...a sensational demand for economy in public expenditure – not merely cutting down what they consider 'doles'; but also Health and Education services. Luxury hotels and luxury flats, Bond Street shopping, racing and high living in all its forms is to go unchecked; but the babies are not to have milk, and the very poor are not to have homes. The private luxury of the rich is apparently not <u>wasteful expenditure</u>. [681]

She concluded the best outcome for the Labour Government would be for it to be defeated for refusing to implement the report

But Snowden is responsible for appointing the Committee. And he is really in agreement with the Report! So is MacDonald except that he is too indifferent to Home affairs to have an opinion of his own about it. [682]

She condemned the new Cabinet Sub Committee as having

...neither the enthusiasm nor the knowledge to cope with the economic crisis on socialist principles...[683]

Sidney was tired; for months he had been trying to retire from the government. Now he had the additional reason that

...he does not like to accept responsibility for a reactionary policy. [684]

On 31 July Parliament went into recess. MacDonald left for Lossiemouth. He wrote to Keynes asking his view of the May report. Keynes replied that they were not fit for publication, or even for circulation to the Economic Advisory

Council. Privately he advised MacDonald that

> …*it is now nearly* certain *that we shall go off the existing gold parity at no distant date.* [685]

Keynes recommended a 25% devaluation and an international currency union. Without that, cuts on the scale recommended by May would be inevitable.

Snowden, the Treasury, and the Bank of England, on the other hand, believed that the only way to restore international confidence was to make the cuts and balance the budget.

While MacDonald was in the Highlands, Snowden remained in London. On Friday 7 August, Ernest Barker, Deputy Governor of the Bank (Montagu Norman had collapsed from overwork on 29 July), informed Snowden that, over the previous month, the Bank had lost more than £60 million in gold and foreign exchange, and that

> *If the flood does not abate we cannot maintain ourselves long.* [686]

Snowden forwarded the letter to MacDonald, saying that he did not think they could wait until Tuesday 25 August, the date when the Cabinet Committee would consider the May recommendations

> *The collapse is almost certain to come before then if we delay… Three millions of unemployed is certain in the near future and four millions next year is not out of the question.* [687]

Snowden asked Macdonald to bring the meeting forward.

Snowden, the Treasury, and the Bank prevailed over Keynes: MacDonald chose orthodoxy. He returned to London on Monday 10 August, chairing the first meeting of the committee on Wednesday. It met again on Thursday, broke for the weekend, and resumed on Monday 17. By the time of the first meeting the estimated size of the deficit had risen from £120 million to £170 million.

That weekend Philip and Ethel Snowden came to lunch at Passfield Corner. Beatrice thought it would be useful for the two ministers to talk. But

> …*the Chancellor of the Exchequer did not welcome the suggestion. He did not take the opportunity of telling Sidney anything whatever about his own proposals, he did not ask for SW's views of the situation…we gather there has been no direct consultation by the big five with any other member of the Cabinet; whilst they have been talking with the leaders of the opposition.* [688]

Beatrice wondered if other ministers would protest. *And if they protest, would they have any clear idea of an alternative policy?*

Over lunch they argued about the monarchy, and about the Soviet Union

...they denouncing it as a cruel slave state and we upholding it as a beneficent experiment in organising production and consumption for the common good. [689]

The Cabinet discussed the report on Wednesday 19. After that, Cabinet met daily until Monday 24. Beatrice stayed at Passfield Corner; mostly, Sidney travelled up for the meetings, coming home at night.

The Sub Committee recommended that half the revised deficit of £170 million should be met by spending cuts, half by tax increases. Their main departure from the May proposals was a refusal to cut the basic rate of unemployment benefit: instead of a £67 million reduction in spending on unemployment benefit, they now proposed £48.5 million. Henderson insisted that, as a member of the Sub Committee, he had reserved his position on the overall package.

One proposed saving was to transfer 500,000 recipients of 'transitional benefit' to the Poor Law

Sidney stopped that by a vigorous protest. [690]

Ministers worked their way through the list of proposed cuts. Meanwhile, MacDonald met opposition leaders; Snowden met the Bank of England; the Cabinet as a whole met the Labour Party National Executive and the TUC General Council.

Conservatives and Liberals demanded the full May package; the TUC wanted no cuts at all. Exasperated, Sidney reported to Beatrice

The General Council are pigs... they won't agree to any cuts of U.I. benefits or salaries or wages. They are referring their conclusions to TUC meeting Sept 7ᵗʰ.
[691]

The crisis deepened. The choice facing the Cabinet changed. It began as: what would the members of the Cabinet accept? What would the Labour Party NEC and the TUC General Council accept? It became, what was the price of the support of the opposition parties? By the evening of Sunday 23 August, it had become: what level of spending cuts would be required in order to assure the support of British and American bankers?

On Saturday morning, 22 August, MacDonald warned that the Conservatives and Liberals would not accept the current Labour package:

...the proposals were wholly unsatisfactory, and that none of them would give any support. [692]

The other parties wanted to deal with the deficit with a mixture of 75% cuts (mostly to the dole) and 25% tax increases.

MacDonald and Snowden asked the Cabinet to agree another £20 million of cuts – £12.25 million from a 10% cut in unemployment benefit, £7.75 million from other sources.

> *The Cabinet were not prepared to authorise the Prime Minister to make this offer.*
>
> *The Chancellor of the Exchequer and the Secretary of State for Dominion Affairs asked that their dissent from this conclusion should be recorded.* [693]

Sidney thought it was all over: MacDonald would resign; Labour would go into opposition; the Conservatives as the next largest party would form a government. But MacDonald raised the possibility of a coalition:

> *The impression left on SW's mind was that JRM, Snowden and Jimmy might consider it. 'A good riddance for the Labour Party' I said.* [694]

At the end of the meeting Ministers reluctantly agreed that the further £20 million cut might be tested on the opposition leaders

> *…it being distinctly understood, however, that, in making this inquiry, they were merely seeking information, and that the Government were in no way committed to the proposal.* [695]

MacDonald and Snowden were meeting the other party leaders over the lunch break; the Cabinet would meet again at 2.30 p.m.; the Cabinet were told that the King was on his way back to London immediately.

The party leaders answered that it was not a question for them, but for the financial authorities responsible for raising the contemplated loan in New York and Paris. Neville Chamberlain, for the Conservatives, added that, if he accepted the proposal, he nevertheless would reserve the right to press for bigger cuts in Unemployment Insurance.

The afternoon Cabinet then gave MacDonald and Snowden authority to talk to the Bank of England, and gave the Bank's representatives authority to talk to the Federal Reserve.

There matters rested on Saturday, with the Cabinet due to meet again on Sunday evening.

At Passfield Corner, on Sunday, before the outcome was settled, Beatrice puzzled over what had happened:

> *The problem is how to prevent the subtle disease of mental enfeeblement in the next Labour Cabinet? Can we grow a socialist faith, entailing rules of conduct for the faithful without developing a group of self righteous and self-centred cranks like the ILP, reiterating shibboleths and refusing to face facts?* [696]

At 7.00 p.m., when the Cabinet met, the answer from the American bankers had not arrived. Ministers talked inconclusively for 45 minutes, then adjourned. At 9.10 MacDonald called them together again: the reply, though positive, was inconclusive. MacDonald also told the Cabinet that the Bank and *certain important and influential financial interests in the City of London* were prepared to support the package.

MacDonald and Snowden then asked each minister to express their view on the 10% benefit cut:

> *He then pointed out that, if on this question there were any important resignations, the Government as a whole must resign.* [697]

Twelve, including Sidney, voted to accept the cut; eight against. Several of the eight said that they would resign.

MacDonald left the meeting and went straight to the Palace. He told the King

> *...that, while the Government had agreed that the Budget should be balanced, they had been unable to reach agreement on proposals to deal effectively with the existing financial emergency, and accordingly that it was impossible for them to continue in office as a united Cabinet.* [698]

It was agreed that the King would meet MacDonald and the other party leaders at 10.00 on Monday morning, following which there would be another Cabinet meeting at midday.

Sidney stayed in London. On Sunday night he telephoned Beatrice, then wrote in the morning

> *Dear One*
>
> *I did not get away until 11pm last night; and after consideration, I thought it best to telephone you, though at the risk of waking you up...*
>
> *We meet again at 12 noon today, when I assume all will be settled; and we may hand in our seals this afternoon! Or at latest tomorrow.* [699]

He passed a busy morning at the Colonial Office:

> *I am clearing out my office drawers and tables, directing the Cabinet papers etc to be moved to Artillery Mansions in locked tin boxes!* [700]

The files Sidney removed that morning probably included his personal files on East Africa, now preserved in the LSE archive as the Webb East Africa Collection (Coll Misc 156), including his frank correspondence with Grigg.

MacDonald opened the Cabinet meeting by announcing

...as a result of the failure to reach agreement the previous day, the financial position had greatly deteriorated, and the situation was now one of the gravest possible character. [701]

And so, Sidney wrote to Beatrice, MacDonald told his colleagues

...he had been asked, and had agreed, to head a non-party Emergency Government of about a dozen ministers, personally selected from all parties, for duration of crisis only... [702]

Beatrice first heard the news on the radio

Just heard over wireless what I wished to hear, that the Cabinet as a whole has resigned, JRM accepting office as Prime Minister in order to form a National Emergency Government including Tories and Liberals. [703]

Only three Cabinet ministers went with Macdonald: Snowden, Thomas, and Sankey, the Lord Chancellor. Beatrice regretted Sankey's departure, but

...I am glad the other three will disappear from the Labour world – they were rotten stuff... [704]

Sidney stayed in London till Wednesday morning, to go to Buckingham Palace and formally surrender his seals of office as Secretary of State. His pocket diary laconically records

BP Seals 10.30
Fab s sch party [705]

The Fabian Summer School was taking place near Passfield Corner; Beatrice reported in greater detail:

SW came back early in the afternoon of our second Fabian garden Party. He was exhausted and rather upset by the queer end of the Labour Cabinet – but delighted to be out of it all. [706]

The House of Commons met on 8 September and, by 311 votes to 251, gave the new government a vote of confidence. Two days later, Snowden, still Chancellor, presented a budget, based on the package discussed in August, now including the further cut in unemployment benefit.

Once the National Government had been formed, the international loans to support sterling had materialised. But on 14 September came news of a threatened mutiny on navy ships stationed at Invergordon, in Scotland; the Admiralty were proposing to implement the cuts in service pay in a way which hit the lower ranks hardest.

The prospect of a naval mutiny made the outflow of funds worse: on Wednesday 16, £5 million of gold was withdrawn; on Thursday, £10 million; on Friday, £18 million. The new credits raised in August were virtually exhausted. On Saturday 19 September, the Bank of England advised the Government formally advised the Government to suspend the Bank's obligation, under the 1925 Gold Standard Act, to sell gold at a fixed price.

Henderson, now Labour Leader, came to Passfield for the weekend. He had already asked Sidney and Beatrice to

...draft a programme for the Labour Party so that he might have it in his pocket for the Labour Party Conference – which we have promised to do. [707]

While he was out, the phone rang: first the editor of the Daily Herald, then Downing Street. An urgent letter from MacDonald was on its way.

When she learned the purpose of the call, Beatrice was scathing:

At the meeting with the TUC Thomas and Mac had slobbered over the agony of 'going off gold' – had vividly described the sudden and simultaneous disappearance of all luxuries and most necessities from the homes of the workers.

And now having dismissed the Labour Government and exacted the 'Economy' budget and thrown the Unemployed back on the Poor Law, the Bankers advise the Government to repudiate gold and go back to the prosperous pre-parity days of 1918-26. [708]

Sidney's subsequent response was short, sad and to the point:

No one ever told us we could do that. [709]

Except, of course, that Keynes had told MacDonald, in early August, that it was nearly certain that

...we shall go off the existing gold parity at no distant date. [710]

MacDonald had neither shared nor acted upon the advice.

After the fall of the Labour government Keynes had invited the Webbs to stay overnight with Lydia and himself at Tilton, their house on the South Downs; the date had been set for Monday 21 September. When they met before dinner that evening, Beatrice found Maynard

...in a great state of inward satisfaction at the fulfilment of his policy of a measure of inflation. Apparently he either knew or suspected the outcome of the crisis; for he said he assumed the announcement of going off the Gold Standard would come over <u>Sunday</u> wireless. [711]

Keynes had lunched that day with Churchill, who told him he had never really favoured returning to the Gold Standard: he had been talked into it by the Bank and the Treasury.

In August, the plan had been that the National Government would not last long; when the emergency period ended

...the political Parties would resume their respective positions. [712]

At the subsequent general election, when it came.

...there would be no 'coupons' pacts or other party arrangements [713]

After the Gold Standard decision, Conservative pressure for an early election became overwhelming; clear lines were drawn between supporters and opponents of the National Government. Parliament was dissolved on Wednesday 7 October, and voting took place on Tuesday 27.

Seaham Labour Party disowned MacDonald. The former agent, William Coxon, stood for Labour. Beatrice sent a last letter to the Seaham women, exhorting them to vote for Coxon.

It was not enough; the election took place in an atmosphere of fear, stirred up by Snowden, who denounced the Labour programme as *Bolshevism*. Beatrice referred to his rhetoric as *acid malignity*.

Winston Churchill later described how Snowden

...found himself compelled by public duty to turn the whole of his vitriolic eloquence and propagandism against his own creation... [714]

Even TJ did not vote Labour in 1931.

The Conservatives won 472 seats; MacDonald's National Labour 13 seats; two Liberal factions won 33 and 35 seats each – and Labour, 52 seats – of which six were held by the increasingly semi-detached ILP, shortly to disaffiliate. Henderson lost his own seat at Burnley. Few Labour ministers survived. Beatrice wrote

On the Front Opposition Bench there will be only one ex-Cabinet Minister – George Lansbury, and only two ex-Ministers of rank – Stafford Cripps and Attlee... [715]

Lansbury became leader; Attlee his deputy.

If the history of the collapse of the Labour government was not written by the victors, it was certainly written by the Webbs. In 1927 Beatrice had lunched with a group of associates – including RH Tawney, Kingsley Martin, W A Robson, Mostyn Lloyd and Leonard Woolf – to talk about the possibility of a new quarterly political magazine. At the time, she had been discouraging; but the project eventually emerged as the *Political Quarterly*, with Woolf as editor.

Early in September 1931 – barely a fortnight after the formation of the National Government – Robson wrote to Beatrice asking for an article on the crisis. For the time being she turned him down:

S. is too busy and I am too perplexed to write on the political crisis so soon after the event. It is a far-reaching declaration of war by the financiers of the USA and Great Britain on the standard of life of the workers, and how it ought to be countered is a question to answer, and what I do not yet know. [716]

In the event Sidney, not Beatrice, wrote the article that appeared in *Political Quarterly* in 1932. It was republished by the Fabians entitled *'What happened in 1931: a Record'*. Sidney makes two main charges against MacDonald: that the move to the National Government had been a long time in the planning, and that MacDonald had gradually drifted away from the Labour Party.

Sidney describes the crisis as

...sixty-three days of a single drama, in all its development foreseen in advance, it is safe to say, only by the statesman who was at once its author, its producer and its principal actor... [717]

He pointed out that, although Labour had lost four fifths of its MPs, it had only lost one million of the eight million votes it had polled in 1929:

...the Labour Party, more than ever Socialist in policy, is not 'smashed', but rather consolidated and purified. [718]

He thought the shock would do Labour good.

August 1931 was a cathartic moment for Sidney and Beatrice. Their relationship with Macdonald had been complex and troubled for 40 years. They had known him, worked with him, endured him, longer than other colleagues – through the Fabian Society, the Hutchinson Trust, the LSE, the LCC, and the years of the Poor Law campaign. They had accepted him as the leader by default, the best available substitute for a leader. They had sustained him; they had not undermined him. Had he betrayed them? They certainly thought he had let them down.

Every ancient battle, every old wound, was remembered.

Behind the *Political Quarterly* article lies a file in the Passfield Papers at the LSE archive *Memoranda and Papers on the crisis of 1931 and the October 1931 General Election*, (Passfield 4/26) which includes Sidney's pencil notes, in his clear, inimitable handwriting, for the article – some of them written on the back of a draft typescript about Closer Union in East Africa.

In those notes he records his raw emotions in September 1931:

...from the very beginning of the Labour Government (June 1929) the Prime Minister became more and more out of sympathy with every section of the Party.

...his inveterate lack of candour amounting to virtual insincerity...

MacDonald was jealous of Henderson as Foreign Secretary.

But the Labour Party, as a Party, is much more keenly interested in Home Affairs, and especially in industrial legislation and the social services than in Foreign, Dominion and Indian issues. Unfortunately Macdonald is not interested in all this range of subjects. He positively hates thinking and talking about them. He dislikes and distrusts the practical measures suggested. It is quite characteristic of him that he actually opposed, when in opposition, the Provision of Meals for School Children (1907), the Legal Minimum Wage to be fixed by Wages Boards (1908) and the Minority Report of the Poor Law Commission (1909). He shrinks back when his Utopian Socialism is embodied in any practical proposal that could be actually put into practice. He avoids all discussion of such 'ugly' questions; and consequently, the people who insist on talking about them. He prefers those who will share his interest in literature, pictures, old furniture, and the like.

Though my personal relations with him have been of unbroken cordiality, I have never once, in the whole nine years that I have been in Parliament, had a quiet talk with Macdonald on any economic or political subject – indeed, hardly any leisurely talk at all. [719]

MacDonald disliked the *rough manners and shabby surroundings* of Labour people; he was equally out of sympathy with the political convictions of the Labour intelligentsia and with his old allies among the pacifists and the utopians. Sidney thought he *patently despised* the party rank and file.

Unsurprisingly, Cabinet Ministers had suffered a *loss of all respect for the character of the Prime Minister*.

For those who, in 1931, repudiated MacDonald and remained with Labour, Sidney's views, as expressed in the *Political Quarterly* article, became, and remained, the Authorised Version of what happened in 1931.

Notes to Part Three

Chapter Eight

1   Beatrice Webb Diary 13.10.1915
2   Dangerfield, George; *The strange death of Liberal England, 1910-1914*; New York, Capricorn Books, 1961; p viii
3   Ablett, Noah, and others; *The Miners' Next Step*; in Coates, Ken, Editor; *Democracy in the Mines*; Nottingham, Spokesman Books, 1974; p 30
4   *The Crusade*, Vol III, No 7, p114
5   Undated letter in Wells archive; quoted in MacKenzie, Jeanne and MacKenzie, Norman; *The Fabians*; New York, Simon and Schuster, 1977
6   Beatrice Webb Diary 11.10.1912
7   Beatrice Webb Diary Christmas 1912
8   Beatrice Webb Diary Christmas 1912
9   Beatrice Webb Diary Christmas 1912
10   Beatrice Webb Diary 02.01.1914
11   Beatrice Webb Diary 13.07.1913
12   Beatrice Webb Diary 23.04.1914
13   Sidney Webb to Ernest Simon, quoted in Stocks, Mary *Ernest Simon of Manchester*; Manchester University Press, 1963; p 29
14   Beatrice Webb Diary 11.10.1912
15   GBS to Beatrice, 10.07.1912, quoted in Michalos, AC & Poff, DC; editors; *Bernard Shaw and the Webbs*; Toronto, University of Toronto Press, 2002, p 117
16   Stocks, Mary *Ernest Simon of Manchester*; Manchester University Press, 1963; p 29
17   Stocks, Mary *Ernest Simon of Manchester*; Manchester University Press, 1963; p 27
18   GBS to Sidney, 22.07.1912, quoted in Michalos, AC & Poff, DC; editors; *Bernard Shaw and the Webbs*; Toronto, University of Toronto Press, 2002, p120
19   Beatrice Webb Diary Christmas 1912
20   Beatrice Webb Diary 01.1913
21   Sidney to GBS, 05.01.1913, quoted in Michalos, AC & Poff, DC; editors; *Bernard Shaw and the Webbs*; Toronto, University of Toronto Press, 2002, p121

22   Sidney to GBS, 04.02.1913; in Webb, B & Webb, S; *The Letters of Sidney and Beatrice Webb*; Vol III; Cambridge; CUP; 1978; p 13
23   Beatrice to GBS, 19.02.1913, quoted in Michalos, AC & Poff, DC; editors; *Bernard Shaw and the Webbs*; Toronto, University of Toronto Press, 2002, p123
24   Beatrice Webb Diary 03.04.1913
25   Beatrice Webb Diary 05.07.1913
26   Pease, E R; *The History of the Fabian Society*; London, Fabian Society and Allen and Unwin; 1925; p 220
27   Beatrice to Pease, 02.09.1912; in Webb, B & Webb, S; *The Letters of Sidney and Beatrice Webb*; Vol III; Cambridge; CUP; 1978; p 7
28   Pease, E R; *The History of the Fabian Society*; London, Fabian Society and Allen and Unwin; 1925; p 230
29   National Guilds League, Rules and Constitution; Tawney papers; LSE COLL MISC 302 1
30   National Guilds League, *A Catechism of National Guilds*; Tawney papers; LSE COLL MISC 302 1
31   Hamilton, M A; *Sidney and Beatrice Webb*; London, Sampson Low, 1933 p.211
32   Cole, M; *Labour Research*, in Cole, M ed.; *The Webbs and their Work* London, Frederick Muller, 1949; p.155
33   Beatrice Webb Diary; supplementary note, 1918
34   Fabian Society Annual Report, 1913
35   Cole, G D H; *The World of Labour*; London, G Bell and Sons, 1913; p 3
36   Fabian Society, Annual Report, 1913
37   Fabian Society, Annual Report, 1914
38   Beatrice Webb Diary 03.05.1914
39   Beatrice Webb Diary 03.05.1914
40   Beatrice Webb Diary 28.09.1913
41   Beatrice Webb Diary 28.09.1913
42   Beatrice Webb Diary 31.07.1914
43   Beatrice Webb Diary 31.07.1914
44   Beatrice Webb Diary; note added in 1918
45   Burns to Asquith, 02.08.1914; British

Library Burns letters Add Ms 46282

46   Beatrice Webb Diary 18.02.1914
47   Beatrice to Gilbert Murray, October
      1914, with Diary for 14.10.1914
48   Beatrice to Russell, 14.10.1914; in
      Webb, B & Webb, S; *The Letters of
      Sidney and Beatrice Webb*; Vol III;
      Cambridge; CUP; 1978; p 43
49   Beatrice Webb Diary 03.11.1914
50   Beatrice Webb Diary 18.04.1915
51   Beatrice Webb Diary October 1915
52   Beatrice Webb Diary 24.06.1916
53   Beatrice Webb Diary 13.09.1916
54   Beatrice Webb Diary 03.01.1917
55   Sidney to Beatrice, 15.11.1916; in
      Webb, B & Webb, S; *The Letters of
      Sidney and Beatrice Webb*; Vol III;
      Cambridge; CUP; 1978; p75
56   Courtney, K; *Extracts from a diary
      during the war*; Printed for private
      circulation, December 1927; p 112
57   Beatrice Webb Diary 17.11.1918
58   Rupert Brooke to Stanley Spencer,
      31,07.1914; in Brooke, Rupert; *The
      Letters of Rupert Brooke*, ed Geoffrey
      Keynes, London, Faber, 1968; p 601
59   Rupert Brooke to Jacques Raverat,
      01.08.1914; in Brooke, Rupert; *The
      Letters of Rupert Brooke*, ed Geoffrey
      Keynes, London, Faber, 1968; p 603
60   Noel Olivier to Rupert Brooke,
      07.01.1915, in Harris, Pippa, editor
      *Song of Love: The letters of Rupert Brooke
      and Noel Olivier, 1909-1915*; London,
      Bloomsbury, 1991; p277
61   Corporal F H Keeling to Sidney,
      PASSFIELD 2/4/G letters 1915-23
62   Keeling, B; *Letters and recollections*,
      edited by ET; London, George Allen
      and Unwin, 1918; p.311
63   Beatrice Webb Diary 02.07.1916
64   Beatrice Webb Diary 05.10.1917
65   Rupert Brooke to Jacques Raverat,
      03.11.1909; in Brooke, R; *Letters of
      Rupert Brooke*, ed. Geoffrey Keynes,
      London, Faber, 1968
66   Rupert Brooke to Jacques Raverat,
      03.11.1909; in Brooke, R; *Letters of
      Rupert Brooke*, ed. Geoffrey Keynes,
      London, Faber, 1968
67   GBS to Sidney and Beatrice,
      05.10.1916, in Michalos, AC & Poff,
      DC; editors; *Bernard Shaw and the
      Webbs*; Toronto, University of Toronto

Press, 2002; p 157
68   GBS to Beatrice, 13.10.1916, in
      Michalos, AC & Poff, DC; editors;
      Bernard Shaw and the Webbs; Toronto,
      University of Toronto Press, 2002; p
      163
69   Beatrice Webb Diary 09.12.1916
70   Beatrice Webb Diary 15.05.1917
71   Beatrice Webb Diary 22.02.1916
72   C M Lloyd to Sidney, 11.07.1916;
      Passfield 2/4/G
73   Sidney to Beatrice, 31.10.1916; in
      Webb, B & Webb, S; *The Letters of
      Sidney and Beatrice Webb*; Vol III;
      Cambridge; CUP; 1978; p 69
74   Beatrice Webb Diary 03.06.1916;
      22.02.1916
75   Beatrice Webb Diary May 1918
76   Letter from Clifford Sharp.
      04.12.1917; PASSFIELD 2/4/G
77   Beatrice Webb Diary 22.09.1917
78   Cole, M; *Growing up into revolution*;
      London, Longmans, 1949; p 65
79   TNA KV – 2 – 1756 _ 095. Cole's
      Security Services file
80   Beatrice Webb Diary 22.02.1916
81   TNA KV – 2 – 1756 _ 095
82   TNA KV – 2 – 1756 _089;
      04.08.1916
83   TNA KV – 2 – 1756 _086
84   Cole, M; *Labour Research*; in Cole, M,
      ed. *The Webbs and their Work*; London,
      F Muller, 1949, p158
85   Beatrice Webb Diary 15.05.1915
86   Beatrice Webb Diary 15.05.1915
87   Cole, M; *Growing up into revolution*;
      London, Longmans, 1949; p 64
88   Cole, M; *Growing up into revolution*;
      London, Longmans, 1949; p 57
89   Cole, M; *Growing up into revolution*;
      London, Longmans, 1949; p 61
90   Sidney to Beatrice, 08.11.16; in Webb,
      B & Webb, S; *The Letters of Sidney and
      Beatrice Webb*; Vol III; Cambridge;
      CUP; 1978; p 74
91   Cole, M; *Growing up into revolution*;
      London, Longmans, 1949; p.65
92   Cole, M; Beatrice Webb; London,
      Longmans, 1945; p 122
93   Cole, M; *Growing up into revolution*;
      London, Longmans, 1949; p.65
94   Cole, M; (ed) *The Webbs and their
      Work*; London, F Muller, 1949; p158
95   quoted in Morgan, K; *Labour Legends*

and Russian Gold; Bolshevism and the British Left Part 1; London, Lawrence and Wishart, 2006

96   Beatrice Webb Diary 07.11.1918
97   Beatrice Webb Diary 07.11.1918
98   Beatrice Webb Diary 01.06.1916
99   Beatrice Webb Diary 01.06.1916
100   Beatrice Webb Diary 01.06.1916
101   Beatrice Webb Diary, 08.03.1914
102   Woolf, L; Beginning Again; An autobiography of the years 1911-1918; London, Hogarth Press, 1964; p114
103   V Woolf to M Llewellyn Davies, 09.12.1914; in Woolf, V; Letters, 1912-1922; London, Chatto & Windus, 1980
104   Beatrice to Leonard Woolf, 16.12.1914; in Webb, B & Webb, S; The Letters of Sidney and Beatrice Webb; Vol III; Cambridge; CUP; 1978; p 45
105   Memorandum with minutes of Fabian FGP Committee, 14.01.1915; Fabian C12
106   V Woolf diary; 23.01.1915; in Woolf, V; Selected Diaries; abridged and edited by Anne Olivier Bell; London, Vintage, 2008
107   Woolf, L: Beginning Again; An autobiography of the years 1911-1918; London, Hogarth Press; 1964, p187
108   Beatrice Webb Diary 05.06.1915
109   V Woolf diary; 28.01.1915; in Woolf, V; Selected Diaries; abridged and edited by Anne Olivier Bell; London, Vintage, 2008
110   Beatrice to Leonard Woolf, 16.03.1915; in Webb, B & Webb, S; The Letters of Sidney and Beatrice Webb; Vol III; Cambridge; CUP; 1978; p 53
111   Virginia Woolf to Ka Cox, 25.06.16; Woolf, V; Letters; The Question of things happening; Letters, 1912-1922; London, Chatto and Windus, 1980
112   Virginia Woolf to Vanessa Bell, 28.06.1916; Woolf, V; Letters; The Question of things happening; Letters, 1912-1922; London, Chatto and Windus, 1980
113   Woolf, L: Beginning Again; An autobiography of the years 1911-1918; London, Hogarth Press; 1964, p116
114   Virginia Woolf to Vanessa Bell, 16.09.1918; in Woolf, V; Letters; The Question of things happening; Letters,

1912-1922; London, Chatto and Windus, 1980
115   Woolf, V; Selected Diaries; abridged and edited by Anne Olivier Bell; London, Vintage, 2008; p 55
116   See Harrison, Royden; The war emergency workers' national committee; in Briggs, Asa and Savile, John; editors; Essays in Labour History 1886-1923; London; Macmillan; 1971; p 244
117   Beatrice Webb Diary 09.09.1915
118   quoted in Middleton, J, Webb and the Labour Party; in Cole, M; The Webbs and their Work; London, Frederick Muller, 1949, p 171
119   Sidney to Jim Middleton, 16.06.1915, People's History Museum, File WNC 14/5
120   Beatrice Webb Diary 04.04.1916
121   Beatrice Webb Diary 02.11.16
122   Hyndman memorandum, 22.07.1917; People's History Museum, File WNC 5/3/1
123   Sidney to Jim Middleton, 19.07.1917; People's History Museum, File WNC 5/3/1
124   War Emergency Workers National Committee Leaflet: THE CONSCRIPTION OF RICHES: WAR TAXES AND WAR LOANS; with WEWNC Minutes, LSE COLL Misc 956
125   quoted in Tsuzuki, C; H M Hyndman and British Socialism; Oxford. OUP, 1961 p 223
126   Beatrice Webb Diary 18.03.1917
127   Courtney, Katherine; Extracts from a diary during the war; Printed for private circulation, December 1927; p 117
128   TNA CAB 24/16/49
129   TNA CAB 24/16/49
130   Beatrice Webb Diary 07.06.1917
131   Beatrice Webb Diary 12.08.1917
132   Jones, T; Whitehall Diary; Volume I 1916-1925; ed. K Middlemas; Oxford, OUP, 1969; p 35
133   Beatrice Webb Diary 12.08.1917
134   Beatrice Webb Diary 05.1918 (note added afterwards by BW to entry for 22.08.1917)
135   Middleton, J, Webb and the Labour Party; in Cole, M; The Webbs and their Work; London, Frederick Muller, 1949,

p 173

136 Memorandum on War Aims, in PASSFIELD 4/10

137 Memorandum on War Aims, in PASSFIELD 4/10

138 Beatrice Webb Diary 05.10.1917

139 Beatrice Webb Diary 10.01.1918

140 Beatrice Webb Diary 29.07.1918

141 Beatrice Webb Diary 30.06.1918

142 Labour Party, *Labour and the New Social Order*, London, 1918, p 9

143 *New Republic*, 16.02.1918

144 Pelling, H; *A short history of the Labour Party*; London; Macmillan, 1961; p 44

145 Labour Party, 1918 Constitution, Clause IV

146 Beatrice Webb Diary 21.01.1918

147 Ruth Rosenberg to Jim Middleton, 18.01.1918; People's History Museum; MID 14; General Correspondence 1917-1918

148 Beatrice Webb Diary 20.03.1918

149 Beatrice to Jim Middleton, nd, 1917, PHM MID 14

150 Beatrice Webb Diary 03.06.1917

151 Beatrice Webb Diary May 1918

152 Beatrice Webb Diary 20.03.1918

153 Beatrice Webb Diary 01.07.1918

154 Beatrice Webb Diary 20.03.1918

155 J S Middleton; letter to his parents, 23.06.1918; J S Middleton General Correspondence 1917-18, PHM MID 14

156 Beatrice Webb Diary 03.01.1917

157 Beatrice Webb Diary 22.02.1917

158 Beatrice Webb Diary 22.02.1917

159 Beatrice Webb Diary 19.02.1917

160 Beatrice Webb Diary; note added to diary, May 1918

161 Jones, T; *Whitehall Diary; Volume I 1916-1925*; ed. K Middlemas; Oxford, OUP, 1969; 25.11.1917; p 24

162 Jones, T; *Whitehall Diary; Volume I 1916-1925*; ed. K Middlemas; Oxford, OUP, 1969; 06.03.1917; p 25

163 Beatrice Webb Diary; 22.02.1917; note added to diary, May 1918

164 Beatrice Webb Diary; 2.02.1917;note added to diary, May 1918

165 Beatrice Webb Diary 03.06.1917

166 Beatrice Webb Diary 15.05.1917

167 Beatrice Webb Diary 03.06.1917

168 Beatrice Webb Diary 14.11.1917

169 Beatrice Webb Diary; note added to 1917 diary, 1918

170 Beatrice Webb Diary; note added to 1917 diary, 1918

171 Beatrice to Herbert Samuel, 27.10.1917; in Webb, B & Webb, S; *The Letters of Sidney and Beatrice Webb*; Vol III; Cambridge; CUP; 1978; Vol III, p 93

172 Jones, T; *Whitehall Diary; Volume I 1916-1925*; ed. K Middlemas; Oxford, OUP, 1969; p 45

173 Beatrice Webb Diary 01.03.1918

174 Beatrice Webb Diary 01.03.1918

175 Beatrice Webb Diary 01.03.1918

176 Beatrice Webb Diary 13.07.1918

177 Beatrice Webb Diary 13.07.1918

178 Report on the Transfer of Functions of Poor Law Authorities in England and Wales, Cd 8917, 1918

179 Beatrice Webb Diary; 1918 note to 1917 Diary

180 Beatrice Webb Diary; 1918 note to 1917 Diary

181 Beatrice Webb Diary; 1918 note to 1917 Diary

182 Lord George Hamilton to Phelps, 17.01.1918; quoted in McBriar, A M; *An Edwardian Mixed Doubles; The Bosanquets versus the Webbs; a study in British Social Policy, 1890 – 1929*; Oxford, Clarendon Press, 1987; p 355

183 Lord George Hamilton to Phelps, 17.01.1918; quoted in McBriar, A M; *An Edwardian Mixed Doubles; The Bosanquets versus the Webbs; a study in British Social Policy, 1890 – 1929*; Oxford, Clarendon Press, 1987; p 355

184 Woolf, V; *Selected Diaries*; abridged and edited by Anne Olivier Bell; London, Vintage, 2008; Vol 1 p 75 CHECK

185 Beatrice Webb Diary; 11.12.1917

186 WOMEN IN INDUSTRY; REPORT OF THE WAR CABINET COMMITTEE; Cmd 135 1919; p254

187 Beatrice Webb Diary; 11.12.1917

188 Beatrice Webb Diary; 31.01.1918

189 Beatrice Webb Diary; 16.06.1918

190 Beatrice Webb Diary; 04.11.1918

191 Beatrice Webb Diary; 04.11.1918

Chapter Nine

192 Beatrice Webb Diary 11.02.1919

193 Beatrice Webb Diary 22.02.1919

194 Beatrice Webb Diary 22.02.1919
195 Beatrice Webb Diary 22.02.1919
196 Beatrice Webb Diary 28.02.1919
197 Beatrice Webb Diary 23.06.1919
198 Beatrice Webb Diary 12.03.1919
199 Beatrice Webb Diary 12.03.1919
200 Cmd 85 1919
201 Cmd 84 1919
202 Taylor, AJP ; editor *Lloyd George: A diary by Frances Stevenson;* London; Hutchinson; 1971; p 173
203 Beatrice Webb Diary 20.03.1919
204 Beatrice Webb Diary 20.03.1919
205 TNA War Cabinet Minutes, 20.03.1919; CAB/23/9/35
206 Hansard, HC Deb 20 March 1919 vol 113 cc 2341-8
207 Sidney to Beatrice, 22.04.1919
208 COAL INDUSTRY COMMISSION ACT, 1919; SECOND STAGE; REPORTS; Cmd 210 1919
209 COAL INDUSTRY COMMISSION ACT, 1919; SECOND STAGE; REPORTS; Cmd 210 1919
210 Beatrice Webb Diary 23.06.1919
211 Federation of British Industries, The Control of Industry; CAB/24/86
212 Beatrice Webb Diary 15.07.1919
213 Beatrice Webb Diary 23.07.1919
214 War Cabinet Minutes, 21.07.1919; CAB/23/15
215 War Cabinet Minutes, 07.08.1919; CAB/23/15
216 War Cabinet Minutes, 07.08.1919; CAB/23/15
217 War Cabinet Minutes, 07.08.1919; CAB/23/15
218 memorandum by Secretary of State for India, 02.08.1919. CAB/24/85
219 Hansard, House of Commons Debates, 18 August 1919 vol 119 col 2001
220 Hansard, House of Commons Debates, 18 August 1919 vol 119 col 2004
221 Hansard, House of Commons Debates, 18 August 1919 vol 119 col 2096
222 Webb, S; *The Story of the Durham Miners, 1662-1921,* London, Fabian Society, 1921, p107
223 Hansard, House of Commons Debates, 18 August 1919 vol 119 col 2031
224 *Labour's Call to the People,* 1922
225 *Let us face the future,* 1945
226 Sidney to Beatrice, 25.06.1919; in Webb, B & Webb, S; *The Letters of Sidney and Beatrice Webb;* Vol III; Cambridge; CUP; 1978; p124
227 Lawson, J; *The Discovery of Sidney Webb;* in Cole, M ed. *The Webbs and their Work;* London, Frederick Muller, 1949; p 197
228 Beatrice Webb Diary 13.02.1923
229 Beatrice Webb Diary 06.03.1923
230 Beatrice Webb Diary 11.05.1923
231 Hansard, 25.04.1923
232 Beatrice Webb Diary 23.11.1922
233 Beatrice to Elie Halevy, 01.06.1923; in Webb, B & Webb, S; *The Letters of Sidney and Beatrice Webb;* Vol III; Cambridge; CUP; 1978; p 173
234 Beatrice Webb Diary 08.06.1923
235 Beatrice Webb Diary 06.03.1923
236 Beatrice Webb Diary 05.11.1923
237 Beatrice Webb Diary 08.06.1920
238 Beatrice to Seaham Women Labour members, December 1922; LSE Library Passfield Papers 4/15; Letters Vol III p 159
239 Beatrice to Seaham Women Labour members, 23.07.1923; Passfield Papers 4/15; Letters Vol III p 176
240 Beatrice Webb Diary 16.07.1921
241 Beatrice Webb Diary 16.07.1921
242 Beatrice Webb Diary 27.04.1921
243 Webb, S; *The Labour Party on the Threshold,* Fabian Tract no 207; London, Fabian Society, June 1923; p 6
244 Webb, S; *The Labour Party on the Threshold,* Fabian Tract no 207; London, Fabian Society, June 1923; p 7
245 Webb, S; *The Labour Party on the Threshold,* Fabian Tract no 207; London, Fabian Society, June 1923; p 11
246 Webb, S; *The Labour Party on the Threshold,* Fabian Tract no 207; London, Fabian Society, June 1923; p 12
247 Webb, S; *The Labour Party on the Threshold,* Fabian Tract no 207; London, Fabian Society, June 1923; p 15
248 Beatrice Webb Diary 28.06.1923
249 Sidney to WH Beveridge, 17.05.1919, Beveridge 2/B/67, in *Letters,* Vol III, p118
250 Beveridge to Sidney, 06.06.1919; LSE Library, BEVERIDGE 2/B/67
251 Beatrice Webb Diary 23.06.1919

252 Beatrice Webb Diary 16.07.1921
253 Beveridge, WH; *The London School of Economics;* in Cole, M ed. *The Webbs and their Work*; London, Frederick Muller, 1949; p 52
254 Sidney to Beatrice, 13.01.1921; in Webb, B & Webb, S; *The Letters of Sidney and Beatrice Webb*; Vol III; Cambridge; CUP; 1978 p 147
255 Beatrice to Beveridge, 23.04.1921, LSE BLibrary, EVERIDGE 2/B/67
256 See Harris, Jose; *William Beveridge, a biography;* Oxford, OUP, 1977; p 278
257 Beatrice Webb Diary 14.05.1922
258 Beatrice Webb Diary 10.10.1921
259 Beatrice Webb Diary 10.12.1922
260 quoted in Hyams, E; *The New Statesman; the history of the first fifty years*; London, Longmans, 1963; p. 22
261 Beatrice Webb Diary 10.10.1921
262 Beatrice Webb Diary 20.02.1922
263 Beatrice Webb Diary 10.12.1922
264 Beatrice Webb Diary 10.07.1922
265 See *Lloyd, Antony Charles, 1916-1994* in Proceedings of The British Academy – the British Academy appreciation of Antony Lloyd, son of Mostyn Lloyd.
266 Beatrice Webb Diary 10.12.1922
267 Hyams, E; *The New Statesman; the history of the first fifty years*; London, Longmans, 1963; p. 83
268 Beatrice Webb Diary 16.07.1921
269 Beatrice Webb Diary 11.01.1923
270 Beatrice Webb Diary 10.07.1922
271 Beatrice Webb Diary 10.07.1922
272 Beatrice Webb Diary 27.10.1923
273 Beatrice Webb Diary 03.12.1923
274 Jones, T; *Whitehall Diary; Volume I 1916-1925*; ed. K Middlemas; Oxford, OUP, 1969; p 258
275 Beatrice Webb Diary 12.12.1923
276 Beatrice Webb Diary 12.12.1923
277 Beatrice Webb Diary 12.12.1923
278 Beatrice Webb Diary 12.12.1923
279 Beatrice Webb Diary 12.12.1923
280 quoted in Marquand, D; *Ramsay MacDonald*; London, Richard Cohen Books, 1997; p 298
281 quoted in Marquand, D; *Ramsay MacDonald*; London, Richard Cohen Books, 1997; P298)
282 Beatrice Webb Diary 12.12.1923
283 Dalton, H; *The Political Diary of Hugh Dalton, 1918-40;1945-60*; ed Pimlott, B; London, Jonathan Cape, 1986; p 36
284 Beatrice Webb Diary 12.12.1923
285 Beatrice Webb Diary 18.12.1923
286 undated copy letter, interleaved with BW typescript diary, Dec 1923
287 Beatrice Webb Diary 03.01.1924
288 Letter, R B Haldane to his mother, 12.12.1923, quoted in Sommer, D; *Haldane of Cloan*; London, Allen and Unwin; 1960; pp 390-391
289 Haldane to Sidney, 29.12.1923, interleaved with BW typescript diary, Dec 1923
290 Beatrice Webb Diary 15.01.1924
291 Beatrice Webb Diary 15.01.1924
292 Beatrice Webb Diary 15.01.1924
293 Quoted in Sommer, D; *Haldane of Cloan*; London, Allen and Unwin; 1960; p397
294 Jones, T; *Whitehall Diary; Volume I 1916-1925*; ed. K Middlemas; Oxford, OUP, 1969;   p 266
295 Beatrice Webb Diary 15.01.1924
296 Beatrice Webb Diary ?28.01.1924
297 Beatrice to Friends of Seaham, 22.01.1924; in Webb, B & Webb, S; *The Letters of Sidney and Beatrice Webb*; Vol III; Cambridge; CUP; 1978 p193
298 Churchill, W S; Great Contemporaries; London, Leo Cooper;1990; p187
299 Beatrice Webb Diary 31.03.1924
300 Beatrice Webb Diary 31.03.1924
301 Beatrice Webb Diary 21.07.1924
302 *Labour's Appeal to the Nation, Labour Manifesto 1923*, in Craig, FWS, Ed; British General Election Manifestos1900-1974; London, Macmillan, 1975; p 47
303 TNA; CP (83)24 – Unemployment Committee – Interim Report to Cabinet 07/02/1924 CAB/24/164
304 TNA; CP (83)24 – Unemployment Committee – Interim Report to Cabinet 07/02/1924 CAB/24/164
305 Thomas Jones' diary; 01.02.1924; in Jones, T; *Whitehall Diary; Volume I 1916-1925*; ed. K Middlemas; Oxford, OUP, 1969; p269
306 Beatrice Webb Diary 25.05.1924
307 Workers' Weekly No 77, 25.07.1924; quoted in Klugmann, J *History of the Communist Party of Great Britain; Vol I; Formation and Early Years 1919-1924*; London; Lawrence & Wishart, 1968;

p367

Chapter Ten

308 Quoted in Klugmann, J; *History of the Communist Party of Great Britain; Vol I; Formation and Early Years 1919-1924*; London; & Wishart, 1968; p343

309 TNA; Cabinet Minutes, 06.08.1924; CAB 23/48/23

310 Jones, T; *Whitehall Diary; Volume I 1916-1925*; ed. K Middlemas; Oxford, OUP, 1969; p289

311 TNA; Cabinet Minutes 09.10.1924; CAB/23/48

312 Beatrice Webb Diary 10.10.1924)

313 Jones, T; *Whitehall Diary; Volume I 1916-1925*; ed. K Middlemas; Oxford, OUP, 1969; pp 294-5

314 Beatrice Webb Diary 10.10.1924

315 *New Statesman* 11.10.1924

316 Beatrice Webb Diary 10.10.1924

317 *New Statesman*, 18.10.1924

318 C M Lloyd to Beatrice, 20.10.1924; Passfield 11)

319 Sidney to Beatrice; 12.10.1924; in Webb, B & Webb, S; *The Letters of Sidney and Beatrice Webb*; Vol III; Cambridge; CUP; 1978 p 218

320 Clifford Sharp to Sidney, 24.10.1924; LSE Library; Passfield 11

321 GBS to Sidney; 26.10.1924; LSE Library; Passfield

322 GBS to Sidney; 26.10.1924; LSE Library; Passfield 11

323 Clifford Sharp to Sidney, 24.10.1924; LSE Library; Passfield 11

324 GBS to Sidney; 26.10.1924; Passfield 11

325 Beatrice Webb Diary 12.08.1928)

326 TNA; History of the Zinoviev Incident; CAB/24/168

327 C M Lloyd to Beatrice, 26.10.1924; LSE Library; Passfield 11

328 Beatrice Webb Diary 29.10.1924

329 Beatrice Webb Diary; note on The Fall of the Labour Government, after diary entry for 29.10.1924

330 Jones, T; *Whitehall Diary; Volume I 1916-1925*; ed. K Middlemas; Oxford, OUP, 1969; p 276

331 Beatrice Webb Diary; note on The Fall of the Labour Government, after diary entry for 29.10.1924

332 Beatrice Webb Diary 16.07.1921

333 Beatrice Webb Diary 09.08.1922

334 Beatrice Webb Diary 09.03.1923

335 Beatrice Webb Diary 16.03.1921

336 Beatrice Webb Diary 24.10.1922

337 quoted in Webb, B & Webb, S; *The Letters of Sidney and Beatrice Webb*; Vol III; Cambridge; CUP; 1978, p180)

338 Beatrice Webb Diary 31.08.1923

339 Beatrice Webb Diary 22.11.1923

340 Beatrice Webb Diary 25.11.1923

341 Beatrice Webb Diary 03.01.1924

342 Beatrice Webb Diary 03.01.1924

343 Beatrice Webb Diary 03.01.1924

344 Beatrice Webb Diary 28.06.1924

345 Beatrice Webb Diary 07.02.1928

346 Beatrice Webb Diary 29.09.1929

347 Beatrice Webb Diary Xmas Eve 1921

348 Beatrice Webb Diary 25.05.1922

349 Beatrice Webb Diary 28.10.1922

350 Beatrice Webb Diary 09.02.1923

351 Cole, M; *Beatrice Webb*; London, Longmans, 1945; p 24

352 Beatrice Webb Diary 31.03.1925

353 GBS to Beatrice, 14.04.1925; in Michalos, AC & Poff, DC; editors; *Bernard Shaw and the Webbs;* Toronto, University of Toronto Press, 2002; p 203

354 Beatrice Webb Diary 27.09.1925

355 Sidney to Beatrice, 28.09.1925; in Webb, B & Webb, S; *The Letters of Sidney and Beatrice Webb*; Vol III; Cambridge; CUP; 1978, p 246

356 Haldane review of *My Apprenticeship* in *The Observer*. March 1926; quoted in Diary, 30.03.1926

357 Duncan Grant to Vanessa Bell, 18.04.1926, quoted in Skidelsky, R *John Maynard Keynes: The economist as saviour: 1920-1937*; London, Macmillan, 1992, p247

358 Virginia Woolf to Clive Bell, 09.04.1926; in *Letters*, Volumes I – VI; London, Chatto & Windus, 1980

359 Ella Pycroft to Beatrice, 28.04.1926. LSE Library; Passfield 2/4/H

360 JRM to Beatrice, 04.05.1926. LSE Library; Passfield 2/4/H

361 Keynes, J M; *The Economic Consequences of Mr Churchill*; London, The Hogarth Press, 1925; p 23

362 Beatrice Webb Diary 28.06.26
363 Beatrice Webb Diary 14.04.1926
364 Beatrice Webb Diary 03.05.1926
365 Sidney to Beatrice, 04.05.1926; in Webb, B & Webb, S; *The Letters of Sidney and Beatrice Webb*; Vol III; Cambridge; CUP; 1978; p 262
366 Beatrice Webb Diary 07.05.1926
367 Beatrice Webb Diary 14.05.1926
368 Sidney to GBS, 13.05.1926; in Webb, B & Webb, S; *The Letters of Sidney and Beatrice Webb*; Vol III; Cambridge; CUP; 1978; p265
369 Sidney to GBS, 13.05.1926; in Webb, B & Webb, S; *The Letters of Sidney and Beatrice Webb*; Vol III; Cambridge; CUP; 1978; p265
370 Beatrice Webb Diary 31.05.1926
371 Beatrice Webb Diary 21.08.1926
372 Beatrice Webb Diary 21.08.1926
373 Beatrice to Seaham Women, 09.12.1926; LSE Library; Passfield 4/15
374 Beatrice Webb Diary 28.05.1928
375 Beatrice Webb Diary 28.05.1928
376 BW to Seaham women, 25.08.1928; in Webb, B & Webb, S; *The Letters of Sidney and Beatrice Webb*; Vol III; Cambridge; CUP; 1978; p 304
377 Beatrice Webb Diary 26.10.1928
378 Hansard; 28.11.1928; Col 457
379 Beatrice Webb Diary 29.11.1928
380 Beatrice Webb Diary 04.01.1929
381 Beatrice Webb Diary 02.08.1926
382 Cole, M; *Beatrice Webb*; London, Longmans, 1945; p181
383 Beatrice Webb Diary 08.06.1923
384 Beatrice Webb Diary 08.06.1923
385 Beatrice Webb Diary 24.12.1928
386 Jones, T; *Whitehall Diary; Volume II 1926-1930*; ed. K Middlemas; Oxford, OUP, 1969; p 195
387 Beatrice Webb Diary 20.06.1927
388 Beatrice Webb Diary 20.06.1927
389 Beatrice Webb Diary 20.06.1927
390 Beatrice Webb Diary 24.03.1924
391 Beatrice Webb Diary 19.09.1925
392 Beatrice Webb Diary 20.03.1939
393 Beatrice Webb Diary 07.02.1927
394 Beatrice Webb Diary 07.02.1927
395 C R Attlee to T Attlee, 29.03.1918, quoted in Bew, J; *Citizen Clem; A biography of Attlee*; London, Riverrun, 2017; p 104
396 Beatrice Webb Diary 02.12.1924
397 Beatrice Webb Diary 04.08.1929
398 Beatrice Webb Diary 05.12.1925
399 Beatrice Webb Diary 23.12.1925
400 Beatrice Webb Diary 05.12.1925
401 Beatrice Webb Diary 21.01.1928
402 Beatrice Webb Diary 19.05.1929
403 Beatrice Webb Diary 01.11.1938
404 Beatrice Webb Diary 05.08.1926
405 Beatrice Webb Diary 29.11.1926
406 Beatrice Webb Diary 29.11.1926
407 Sidney to Beatrice, 10.12.1925; in Webb, B & Webb, S; *The Letters of Sidney and Beatrice Webb*; Vol III; Cambridge; CUP; 1978; p255
408 Beatrice Webb Diary 18.07.1926
409 Beatrice to Sidney, end July 1926; in Webb, B & Webb, S; *The Letters of Sidney and Beatrice Webb*; Vol III; Cambridge; CUP; 1978; p 269
410 Beatrice to Sidney, end July 1926; in Webb, B & Webb, S; *The Letters of Sidney and Beatrice Webb*; Vol III; Cambridge; CUP; 1978; p 269
411 Beatrice Webb Diary 02.08.1926
412 Beatrice Webb Diary 02.08.1926
413 Beatrice Webb Diary 07.02.1927
414 Martin, K.; Editor; London, Penguin, 1968; p 89
415 Martin, K.; Editor; London, Penguin, 1968; p 89
416 Martin, K.; Editor; London, Penguin, 1968; p 89
417 Cole, M; *Beatrice Webb*; London, Longmans, 1945
418 Cole, M; *Growing up into revolution*; London, Longmans, 1949; p135
419- Dalton Diary, 23-25.01.1932; in Dalton, H; *The Political Diary of Hugh Dalton, 1918-40*;1945-60; ed Pimlott, B; London, Jonathan Cape, 1986
420 Beatrice Webb Diary 21.07.1925
421 Beatrice Webb Diary 21.07.1925
422 Beatrice Webb Diary 19.11.1925
423 Beatrice Webb Diary 19.07.1928
424 Beatrice Webb Diary 22.11.1925
425 Beatrice Webb Diary 02.10.1929
426 Beatrice Webb Diary 20.06.1928
427 Beatrice Webb Diary 10.12.1929
428 Beatrice Webb Diary 27.11.1925
429 Beatrice Webb Diary 09.08.1932
430 Beatrice to TJ, 01.03.1927; in Jones, T; *Whitehall Diary; Volume II 1926-1930*; ed. K Middlemas; Oxford, OUP, 1969;

p 97

431 Beatrice Webb Diary 08.05.1927
432 Beatrice Webb Diary 08.05.1927
433 TJ Diary, 08.09.1929; in Jones, T; Whitehall Diary; Volume II 1926-1930; ed. K Middlemas; Oxford, OUP, 1969; p 209
434 Beatrice Webb Diary 23.12.1925
435 Beatrice Webb Diary 28.01.1924
436 Beatrice Webb Diary 19.12.1924
437 Beatrice Webb Diary 22.08.1925
438 Beatrice Webb Diary 09.09.1929
439 Beatrice Webb Diary 09.06.1929
440 Beatrice Webb Diary 08.08.1925
441 Beatrice Webb Diary 05.04.1927
442 Beatrice Webb Diary 25.09.1942
443 Cole, M; *Growing up into revolution*; London, Longmans, 1949; p 135
444 Cole, Margaret; *The life of G D H Cole*; London, Macmillan, 1971; p 98
445 Virginia Woolf Diary; 24.04.1919; Woolf, Virginia; *Selected Diaries*; abridged and edited by Anne Olivier Bell; London, Vintage, 2008
446 Virginia Woolf Diary; 24.04.1919; Woolf, Virginia; *Selected Diaries*; abridged and edited by Anne Olivier Bell; London, Vintage, 2008
447 Beatrice Webb Diary 17.05.1924
448 Beatrice Webb Diary 17.05.1924
449 Beatrice Webb Diary 05.09.1926
450 Beatrice Webb Diary 17.05.1924
451 Cole, M; *Growing up into revolution*; London, Longmans, 1949; p 135
452 Cole, M; Growing up into revolution; London, Longmans, 1949; p 135
453 *The Nation*, 20.02.1926; quoted in Skidelsky, R; John Maynard Keynes: *The economist as saviour: 1920-1937*; London, Macmillan, 1992; p 245
454 Beatrice to Maynard Keynes, 22.02.1926, in Webb, B & Webb, S; *The Letters of Sidney and Beatrice Webb*; Vol III; Cambridge; CUP; 1978; p 256
455 BW to Maynard Keynes, 22.02.1926; in Webb, B & Webb, S; *The Letters of Sidney and Beatrice Webb*; Vol III; Cambridge; CUP; 1978; p 256
456 Beatrice Webb Diary 09.08.1926
457 Virginia Woolf to Margaret Llewellyn-Davies, 02.09.1926; in Woolf, V; *Letters, Volumes I – VI*; London, Chatto & Windus, 1980
458 Beatrice to Maynard Keynes,

03.10.1926; in Webb, B & Webb, S; *The Letters of Sidney and Beatrice Webb*; Vol III; Cambridge; CUP; 1978; p 271
459 Beatrice Webb Diary 12.10.1926
460 Beatrice to TJ, 06.02.1928; in Jones, T; *Whitehall Diary; Volume II 1926-1930*; ed. K Middlemas; Oxford, OUP, 1969; p129
461 quoted in Skidelsky, R; *John Maynard Keynes: The economist as saviour: 1920-1937*; London, Macmillan, 1992; p 234
462 Beatrice Webb Diary 06.02.1927
463 V Woolf to Ethel Sands, 29.01.1927, in Woolf, V; *Letters, Volumes I – VI*; London, Chatto & Windus, 1980
464 Beatrice Webb Diary 06.02.1927
465 V Woolf to V Sackville-West, 31.01.1927, in Woolf, V; *Letters, Volumes I – VI*; London, Chatto & Windus, 1980
466 See Harris, Jose; *William Beveridge, a biography; Oxford*, OUP, 1977; p 263
467 Letter, Sidney to Beatrice, 27.07.1927; in Webb, B & Webb, S; *The Letters of Sidney and Beatrice Webb*; Vol III; Cambridge; CUP; 1978; p 291
468 Letter, Sidney to Beatrice, 27.07.1927; in Webb, B & Webb, S; *The Letters of Sidney and Beatrice Webb*; Vol III; Cambridge; CUP; 1978; p 291
469 Letter, Beatrice to Beveridge; 19.03.1928; in Webb, B & Webb, S; *The Letters of Sidney and Beatrice Webb*; Vol III; Cambridge; CUP; 1978; p 297
470 Beatrice Webb Diary, 05.05.1928
471 Beatrice Webb Diary, 05.05.1928
472 Beatrice Webb Diary 16.01.1929
473 Beatrice Webb Diary 30.08.1928
474 Beatrice Webb Diary 20.08.1925
475 Beatrice Webb Diary 20.08.1925
476 Beatrice Webb Diary 30.08.1928
477 Beatrice Webb Diary 07.02.1927
478 quoted in Harris, J; *William Beveridge, a biography*; Oxford, OUP, 1977; p 282

Chapter Eleven

479 Beatrice Webb Diary 28.03.1929
480 Beatrice Webb Diary 28.03.1929
481 Beatrice Webb Diary 09.09.1929
482 Beatrice Webb Diary 01.06.1929
483 Beatrice Webb Diary 05.06.1929

484 Beatrice Webb Diary 05.06.1929

485 Beatrice Webb Diary 05.06.1929

486 Beatrice Webb Diary 06.06.1929

487 Beatrice Webb Diary 06.07.1929

488 Beatrice Webb Diary 06.07.1929

489 Beatrice Webb Diary 16.03.1884

490 Hamilton, MA; *Sidney and Beatrice Webb*; London, Sampson Low, 1933; p275

491 letter dated 31.07.1929; copy with BW Diary for 04.08.1929

492 Beatrice Webb Diary 05.10.1896

493 Quoted in Harris, Kenneth ; *Attlee*; London, Weidenfeld and Nicolson, 1982; p63

494 Gregory, R G; *Sidney Webb and East Africa; Labour's Experiment with the doctrine of native paramountcy*; University of California Press, Berkeley and Los Angeles, 1962, p19

495 Gregory, R G; *Sidney Webb and East Africa; Labour's Experiment with the doctrine of native paramountcy*; University of California Press, Berkeley and Los Angeles, 1962, p19

496 Taylor, AJP; *English History 1914 – 1945* Oxford, OUP, 1965; p151

497 Schuster, G; P*rivate Work and Public Causes;* Cowbridge, D Brown, 1979; p 74

498 Times, 28.01.1922, quoted in Ross, W McGregor; *Kenya from Within; a short political history;* London, Frank Cass, 1968 (reprint of 1927 edition)

499 Cmd 1922, 1923

500 Leo Amery Diary, 26.05.1925; Amery, LS; *The Leo Amery Diaries; Vol1* 1896-1929; London, Hutchinson, 1980; p 412

501 Jones, T; *Welsh Broth*; London, W Griffiths & Co;1950; p 47

502 Leys, Norman *Kenya*; London, Hogarth Press, 1926; p226

503 Cmd 3234 1929 Ch.1.Introduction

504 Leo Amery Diary, 11.05.1928; Amery, LS; *The Leo Amery Diaries; Vol 1 1896-1929*; London, Hutchinson, 1980; p 544

505 Schuster, G; Private Work and Public Causes; Cowbridge, D Brown, 1979; p76

506 Thomas Jones Diary,15.11.1928; Jones, T; *Whitehall Diary; Volume II 1926-1930*; ed. K Middlemas; Oxford, OUP, 1969; p158

507 Report of the Commission on Closer Union of the Dependencies in Eastern and Central Africa (Hilton Young Report); Cmd 3234 1929; p210

508 Amery, LS; *The Leo Amery Diaries; Vol 1 1896-1929*; London, Hutchinson, 1980; p 598

509 CAB/24/205/2 Report by Sir Samuel Wilson on his recent visit to East Africa, 2 July 1929

510 CAB/24/205/2 Report by Sir Samuel Wilson on his recent visit to East Africa, 2 July 1929

511 Beatrice Webb Diary 26.11.1911

512 Beatrice Webb Diary 13.08.1929

513 Beatrice Webb Diary 13.08.1929

514 Beatrice Webb Diary 13.08.1929

515 Beatrice Webb Diary 20.10.1929

516 Beatrice Webb Diary 20.08.1920

517 C R Buxton to Sidney Webb, 08.10.1929, LSE Library; Webb East Africa Collection, Coll Misc 156

518 Beatrice Webb Diary 20.10.1929

519 CAB/24/206 05.11.1929

520 Beatrice Webb Diary 28.11.1929

521 Thomas Jones Diary, 09.04.1930; Jones, T; *Whitehall Diary; Volume II 1926-1930*; ed. K Middlemas; Oxford, OUP, 1969; p 251

522 Cmd 3574 1930; para 9

523 Cabinet Minutes 30.04.1930; CAB 23 64 1

524 Sidney to Beatrice, 30.04.1930; in Webb, B & Webb, S; *The Letters of Sidney and Beatrice Webb*; Vol III; Cambridge; CUP; 1978 p 325

525 H Snell to Sidney, 03.05.1930, Webb East Africa Collection, LSE Library, Coll Misc 156

526 Shiels, D; Sidney Webb as a Minister; in Cole, M (ed) The Webbs and their Work; London, F Muller, 1949; p 210

527 Sidney Webb to Edward Grigg, 01.05.1930; LSE Library, Passfield 4/22

528 Edward Grigg to Sidney Webb, 23.06.1930; LSE Library, Passfield 4/22

529 LSE Library, Passfield 4/22

530 Quoted in Gregory, R G; *Sidney Webb and East Africa; Labour's Experiment with the doctrine of native paramountcy*; University of California Press, Berkeley

531 Sidney to Edward Grigg, 29.07.1930; Passfield 4/22

532 Hansard; 12.11.1930; Col 87

533 Shiels, Drummond; *The East Africa Report*; In *The Political Quarterly, Vol III*, no 1, Jan-Mar 1932; p.71

534 Leo Amery Diary, 19.11.30; in Amery, L S; *The Empire at Bay; The Leo Amery Diaries 1929 -1945*; Ed John Barnes & David Nicholson; London, Hutchinson, 1988 p 136

535 *East African Standard*, 18.12.1930

536 *East African Standard*, 18.12.1930

537 Letter, Buxton et and others to SW; 09.10.30; LSE Library, LSE Coll Misc 156

538 Leo Amery Diary, 04.12.1930; in Amery, Leopold S; *The Leo Amery Diaries; Vol 2 1929 – 1945*; Ed John Barnes & David Nicholson; London, Hutchinson, 1980

539 Grigg to Sidney, 21.03.1930, in TNA CO 533/384/9

540 Note by Shiels, January 1930, in TNA CO 533/384/9

541 Note by Shiels, January 1930, in TNA CO 533/384/9

542 TNA COL 822/33/1

543 Minute by Sidney, 19.03.31; TNA COL 832/33/1

544 TNA COL822/33/4

545 Closer Union in East Africa, Joint Committee on; Vol II, Minutes of evidence; Cmd 156, 1931; evidence of Hilton Young; p37 Q 229

546 Closer Union in East Africa, Joint Committee on; Vol II, Minutes of evidence; Cmd 156, 1931; p 415; Question 4095

547 Closer Union in East Africa, Joint Committee on; Vol II, Minutes of evidence; Cmd 156, 1931;p 479; Question 4808

548 Closer Union in East Africa, Joint Committee on; Vol II, Minutes of evidence; Cmd 156, 1931; p 549; Question5617

549 Note by Lord Stanley of Alderley, 28.04.1931; TNA Webb East Africa, Coll Misc 156

550 CAB/24/221; 15.05.1931

551 Shiels, Drummond; *The East Africa Report*; in *The Political Quarterly, Vol III*, no 1, Jan-Mar 1932; p 85

552 Memorandum by C R Buxton, J H Hudson, J A Parkinson and W Wellock, 01.07.1931, in LSE Library, Webb East Africa, Coll Misc 156

553 Woolf, L; *Downhill all the way, an autobiography of the years 1919-1939*; London, Hogarth Press, 1967; p 237

554 Woolf, L; *Downhill all the way, an autobiography of the years 1919-1939*; London, Hogarth Press, 1967; p 237

555 Shiels, D; *Sidney Webb as a Minister*; in Cole, M ed *The Webbs and their Work*; London, F Muller, 1949; p. 207

556 Shiels, D; *Sidney Webb as a Minister*; in Cole, M ed *The Webbs and their Work*; London, F Muller, 1949

557 Perham, M; *Lugard, The Years of Authority, 1898 – 1945*; London, Collins,1960; p p 690-691

558 Letter, Arthur Balfour to Lord Rothschild, 02.11.1917

559 Beatrice Webb Diary 30.10.1930

560 League of Nations, Mandate for Palestine, 12.02.1922, Article 2

561 Cohen, M J; *Britain's Moment in Palestine; Retrospect and Perspectives*, 1917-1948 London, Routledge, 2014; p 213

562 Cmd 1700, 1922

563 Cmd 1700, 1922

564 CO 733/163/4

565 Times, 27.08.1929

566 Beatrice to Elizabeth Haldane, 30.08.1929, in Webb, B & Webb, S; *The Letters of Sidney and Beatrice Webb*; ed MacKenzie, N & J; Vol III; Cambridge, CUP, 1978; p.318

567 Beatrice Webb Diary 02.09.1929

568 Beatrice Webb Diary 02.09.1929

569 TNA CAB/24/207

570 TNA CAB/24/209

571 Chancellor to Passfield, 17.01.1930; TNA CAB/24/211

572 Chancellor to Passfield, 17.01.1930; TNA CAB/24/211

573 Report of the Commission on the Palestine Disturbances of August 1929. (Shaw Report) Cmd. 3530 1930; Ch. XIV para 44

574 Report of the Commission on the Palestine Disturbances of August 1929. (Shaw Report) Cmd. 3530 1930; Ch. XIV para 35

575 Report of the Commission on the Palestine Disturbances of August 1929. (Shaw Report) Cmd. 3530 1930; Note of Reservation by Mr Snell; p 173

576 Beatrice Webb Diary 30.03.1930

577 TNA CO 733/183/1

578 Sidney to Beatrice, 30 April 1930; in Webb, B & Webb, S; *The Letters of Sidney and Beatrice Webb*; Vol III; Cambridge; CUP;1978; p 325

579 Jones, T; *Whitehall Diary; Volume II 1926-1930*; ed. K Middlemas; Oxford, OUP, 1969; p 255

580 Jones, T; *Whitehall Diary; Volume II 1926-1930*; ed. K Middlemas; Oxford, OUP, 1969; p 255

581 TNA CO 733/193/4

582 Palestine; Report by Sir John Hope Simpson, CIE; Cmd 3686, 1930; Ch. XI

583 Palestine; Report by Sir John Hope Simpson, CIE; Cmd 3686, 1930; Ch.XI

584 TNA CAB /24/215

585 TNA CAB /24/215

586 TNA CAB /24/215

587 Hope Simpson to Campbell, 22.7.1930; TNA CO 733/193/1

588 Hope Simpson to Campbell, 22.7.1930; TNA, CO 733/193/1

589 Cmd 3692, 1930

590 Sidney to Beatrice, 10.09.1930; in Webb, B & Webb, S; *The Letters of Sidney and Beatrice Webb*; Vol III; Cambridge; CUP; 1978; p 330

591 TNA Cabinet Minutes 19.09.1930

592 TNA; CAB/24/215

593 TNA Cabinet Minutes 24.09.1930

594 Sidney to Beatrice, 24.09.1930; in Webb, B & Webb, S; *The Letters of Sidney and Beatrice Webb*; Vol III; Cambridge; CUP; 1978; p 332

595 Sidney to Beatrice, 22.10.1930; in Webb, B & Webb, S; *The Letters of Sidney and Beatrice Webb*; Vol III; Cambridge; CUP; 1978; p 334

596 Sidney to Beatrice, 22.10.1930; in Webb, B & Webb, S; *The Letters of Sidney and Beatrice Webb*; Vol III; Cambridge; CUP; 1978; p 334

597 Sidney to Weizmann, 25.10.1930; in Webb, B & Webb, S; *The Letters of Sidney and Beatrice Webb*; Vol III; Cambridge; CUP; 1978; p 336

598 Beatrice to Sidney, end October 1930; in Webb, B & Webb, S; *The Letters of Sidney and Beatrice Webb*; Vol III; Cambridge; CUP; 1978; p 335

599 Beatrice Webb Diary 26.10.1930

600 Beatrice Webb Diary 26.10.1930

601 Beatrice Webb Diary 30.10.1930

602 Times 04.11.1930

603 Times 06.11.1930

604 Dalton Diary, 06.11.1930; Dalton, H; *The Political Diary of Hugh Dalton,1918-40;1945-60*; ed Pimlott, B; London, Jonathan Cape, 1986; p 126

605 Sidney to Lord Amulree; 10.02.1931; in Webb, B & Webb, S; *The Letters of Sidney and Beatrice Webb*; Vol III; Cambridge; CUP; 1978; p 345

606 Dalton Diary, 12.11.1930; Dalton, H; *The Political Diary of Hugh Dalton,1918-40*;1945-60; ed Pimlott, B; London, Jonathan Cape, 1986; p 128

607 Dalton Diary, 12.11.1930; Dalton, H; *The Political Diary of Hugh Dalton,1918-40*;1945-60; ed Pimlott, B; London, Jonathan Cape, 1986; p 128

608 Weizmann to MacDonald, 12.11.1930; copy at TNA FO 800 282

609 Weizmann to Felix Warburg, 11.12.1930; quoted in Beckerman-Boys, Carly (2016). *The Reversal of the Passfield White Paper, 1930-31: A Reassessment. Journal of Contemporary History* 51(2): 213-233

610 *Jewish Times* English Section, London Wednesday Nov 19[th]1930

611 Hansard, 17.11.1930

612 Beatrice Webb Diary 14.12.1930

613 Beatrice Webb Diary 14.12.1930

614 Henderson to Sidney, 01.01.1931; TNA, FO 800 283

615 Henderson to Sidney, 01.01.1931; TNA, FO 800 283

616 MacDonald letter, 13.02.1931

617 MacDonald letter, 13.02.1931

618 Shiels, D; *Sidney Webb as a Minister*; in Cole, M ed; *The Webbs and their Work*; London, F Muller, 1949; p 215

619 Beckerman-Boys, C; *The Reversal of the Passfield White Paper, 1930-31: A Reassessment. Journal of Contemporary History* 51(2) (2016)

620 Jones; *Whitehall Diary; Volume II 1926-1930*; ed. K Middlemas; Oxford, OUP, 1969; p 188

621 J M Keynes addressing National Liberal Federation, 27 March 1928; quoted in Skidelsky, R; *John Maynard Keynes: The economist as saviour: 1920-1937;* London, Macmillan, 1992

622 Taylor, *AJP English History 1914 – 1945* Oxford, OUP, 1965; p 268

623 Labour's Appeal to the Nation; Labour Election Manifesto 1929

624 Beatrice Webb Diary 02.10.1929

625 Beatrice Webb Diary 02.10.1929

626 Beatrice Webb Diary 02.10.1929

627 Beatrice Webb Diary 02.11.1929

628 Beatrice Webb Diary 09.11.1929

629 Beatrice Webb Diary 09.11.1929

630 Beatrice Webb Diary 09.11.1929

631 Beatrice Webb Diary 09.11.1929

632 Philip Snowden, article in The Banker, 1926, quoted in Kynaston, D; *The City of London; Vol III Illusions of Gold 1914 – 1945*; London, Pimlico, 2000; p 174

633 Hankey to Jones, 28.11.1929; Jones, T; *Whitehall Diary; Volume II 1926-1930;* ed. K Middlemas; Oxford, OUP, 1969; p 219

634 Jones, T; *Whitehall Diary; Volume II 1926-1930*; ed. K Middlemas; Oxford, OUP, 1969; p 223-4

635 Jones, T; *Whitehall Diary; Volume II 1926-1930*; ed. K Middlemas; Oxford, OUP, 1969; p 236

636 TNA CAB/24/207

637 Beatrice Webb Diary 28.07.1929

638 Beatrice Webb Diary 02.12.1929

639 Beatrice Webb Diary 21.12.1929

640 Beatrice Webb Diary 21.12.1929

641 Beatrice Webb Diary 21.12.1929

642 Beatrice Webb Diary 21.12.1929

643 MacDonald Diary, 12.12.1929; quoted in Marquand, D; Ramsay MacDonald; London, Richard Cohen Books, 1997; p534

644 TNA CAB/24/209/30

645 TNA CAB/24/209/30

646 TNA CAB/24/209

647 Johnston to MacDonald, 24.01.1930; TNA CAB/24/209/32

648 Jones, T; Whitehall Diary; Volume II 1926-1930; ed. K Middlemas; Oxford, OUP, 1969; p241

649 Snowden Report, TNA CAB/24/211/33

650 Snowden Report, TNA CAB/24/211/33

651 TNA CAB/24/211/44

652 Thomas Jones diary, 19.05.1929; Jones, T; Whitehall Diary; Volume II 1926-1930; ed. K Middlemas; Oxford, OUP, 1969; p257

653 MacDonald Diary, 19.05.1930; quoted in Marquand, D; *Ramsay MacDonald*; London, Richard Cohen Books, 1997; p539

654 Beatrice Webb Diary 19.05.1929

655 Beatrice Webb Diary 19.05.1929

656 Thomas Jones Diary, 20.05.1930; Jones, T; *Whitehall Diary; Volume II 1926-1930*; ed. K Middlemas; Oxford, OUP, 1969

657 Beatrice Webb Diary 29.05.1929

658 Marquand, D; *Ramsay MacDonald*; London, Richard Cohen Books, 1997; p 543

659 Beatrice Webb Diary 29.05.1929

660 Beatrice Webb Diary 29.05.1929

661 Beatrice Webb Diary 31.05.1930

662 TJ to Sir Alfred Lewis, General Manager, National Provincial Bank; Jones, T; *Whitehall Diary; Volume II 1926-1930*; ed. K Middlemas; Oxford, OUP, 1969; p 271

663 Dalton, H; *The Political Diary of Hugh Dalton, 1918-40*;1945-60; ed Pimlott, B; London, Jonathan Cape, 1986; p 129

664 Beatrice Webb Diary 06.10.1930

665 Labour Party Conference Report 1930, quoted in Marquand, D; *Ramsay MacDonald*; London, Richard Cohen Books, 1997; p569

666 Beatrice Webb Diary 14.10.1930

667 Sidney to Beatrice, 08.12.1930; in Webb, B & Webb, S; *The Letters of Sidney and Beatrice Webb*; Vol III; Cambridge; CUP; 1978; p 340

668 Beatrice Webb Diary 22.01.1931

669 Beatrice Webb Diary 04.02.1931

670 Beatrice Webb Diary 04.02.1931

671 Beatrice Webb Diary 04.02.1931

672 Beatrice Webb Diary 12.02.1931

673 Beatrice Webb Diary 19.01.1931

674 Beatrice Webb Diary 10.10.1931

675 Beatrice Webb Diary 01.03.1931

676 Hansard, 11.02.1931, Col 448

677 Beatrice Webb Diary 12.02.1931

678 May Report, TNA CAB 24/222/44

679 May Report, TNA CAB 24/222/44, para 565

680 *Daily Herald*, 17.09.1931; quoted in Harrod, R; *The Life of John Maynard Keynes*, London, Macmillan, 1951; p 438

681 Beatrice Webb Diary 04.08.1931

682 Beatrice Webb Diary 04.08.1931

683 Beatrice Webb Diary 04.08.1931

684 Beatrice Webb Diary 04.08.1931

685 Keynes to MacDonald, MacDonald papers, quoted in Marquand, D; *Ramsay MacDonald*; London, Richard Cohen Books, 1997, p 610

686 MacDonald papers, quoted in Marquand, D; *Ramsay MacDonald*; London, Richard Cohen Books, 1997, p 612

687 Snowden to MacDonald, 07.08.1931; MacDonald papers, quoted in Marquand, D; *Ramsay MacDonald*; London, Richard Cohen Books, 1997, p 613

688 Beatrice Webb Diary 18.08.1931

689 Beatrice Webb Diary 18.08.1931

690 Beatrice Webb Diary 22.08.1931

691 Beatrice Webb Diary 22.08.1931

692 Cabinet Minutes 22.08.1931; TNA CAB/23/67

693 Cabinet Minutes 22.08.1931; TNA CAB/23/67

694 Beatrice Webb Diary 23.08.1931

695 Cabinet Minutes 22.08.1931; TNA CAB/23/67

696 Beatrice Webb Diary 23.08.1931

697 Cabinet Minutes 23.08.1931; TNA CAB/23/67

698 Cabinet Minutes 23.08.1931; TNA CAB/23/67

699 Sidney to Beatrice, 24.08.1931, in Webb, B & Webb, S; *The Letters of Sidney and Beatrice Webb*; Vol III; Cambridge; CUP, 1978

700 Sidney to Beatrice, 24.08.1931, in Webb, B & Webb, S; *The Letters of Sidney and Beatrice Webb*; Vol III; Cambridge; CUP, 1978

701 Cabinet Minutes 24.08.1931; CAB/23/67

702 Sidney to Beatrice, 24.08.1931, in Webb, B & Webb, S; *The Letters of Sidney and Beatrice Webb*; Vol III; Cambridge; CUP, 1978

703 Beatrice Webb Diary 24.08.1931

704 Beatrice Webb Diary 24.08.1931

705 LSE Library, Passfield 3.1

706 Beatrice Webb Diary 25 (26?).08.1931

707 Beatrice Webb Diary 20.09.1931

708 Beatrice Webb Diary 23.09.1931

709 Dalton, Hugh; *Call Back Yesterday, Memoirs 1887 – 1931*; London, F Muller, 1953; p 298

710 Keynes to MacDonald, MacDonald papers, quoted in Marquand, D; *Ramsay MacDonald*; London, Richard Cohen Books, 1997, p 610

711 Beatrice Webb Diary 23.09.1931

712 Cabinet Minutes, 24.08.1931; TNA CAB/23/67

713 Cabinet Minutes, 24.08.1931; TNA CAB/23/67

714 Churchill, W S; *Great Contemporaries*; London; Leo Cooper; 1990; p188

715 Beatrice Webb Diary 28.10.1931

716 Beatrice to W A Robson; 11.09.1931; in Webb, B & Webb, S; *The Letters of Sidney and Beatrice Webb*; Vol III; Cambridge; CUP; p 365

717 Webb, S; *What happened in 1931: a Record*; Fabian Tract No 237; London, 1932; p 3

718 Webb, S; *What happened in 1931: a Record.*; Fabian Tract No 237; London, 1932; p 12

719 LSE Library, Passfield 4/26

PART FOUR:
A NEW CIVILIZATION? 1931 - 1947

Chapter Twelve: Soviet Communism

'WITHOUT DOUBT, WE ARE ON THE SIDE OF RUSSIA'

On 2 April 1932, this announcement appeared in London's *Evening Standard*:

A Russian Adventure

Lord Passfield and Mrs Sidney Webb are going to Russia this summer to study the co-operative movement there. They leave England on May 14 and will be away at least eight weeks.

As the combined age of the Webbs is one hundred and forty-seven, it will be a courageous as well as an instructive adventure. Incidentally, Lenin acquired his first knowledge of English by translating a book of Sidney Webb's during his Siberian exile. [1].

After the collapse of the second Labour government, the Webbs turned towards the Soviet Union. This new direction did not appear from nowhere.

Their antipathy towards MacDonald, Snowden, and Thomas, forcibly expressed in Sidney's *Political Quarterly* article, was widely shared. Beatrice attended the Labour Conference in Scarborough in October 1931; she refers to a *silent contempt* for the ministers who had joined the National Government, calling them *apostates*:

No one wants to think about them. If JRM, Jimmy and Snowden were suddenly to appear in our midst they would be ignored – passed by without a word or smile of greeting – shown the door with cold politeness and perfunctory expression of regret for unintentional discourtesy. [2]

This was about more than personalities. Beatrice had sensed for some years that the political ground was shifting. Kevin Morgan writes that

...the couple were extraordinarily receptive to the changing intellectual currents that repeatedly threatened to pass them by. [3]

In 1926, Beatrice had written to Keynes

For a long time I have felt that the particular line of research which we in the Fabian Society started in the nineties – the working out of a national

minimum of civilised life, so far as regulation and public services can secure it – is now exhausted as a discovery though not yet applied, and that the new inventiveness must necessarily concern itself with the control of capitalist enterprise and landlordism at the top in its highest levels. [4]

She wrote again in October 1926, enclosing a copy of the ILP *Living Wage* document:

...I think the lines on which it proceeds are far more hopeful than the old slogan of the Labour Party – the nationalisation of the means of production, distribution and control...Personally, I feel that this control of capitalism will want a far more expert treatment than is open to anyone in the Labour Party... [5]

When these letters were sent Keynes had been advising Lloyd George and the Liberals; under the Labour government he joined the Economic Advisory Council, where his advice, regularly offered, was rarely taken.

In the last months of the Labour government, Sidney and Beatrice worried that they – and Labour – had no answer to the economic problems. In February 1931, Beatrice wrote that it was absurd that Labour should be in power: it had no policy; it had lost its bearings.

For the future, Beatrice thought Britain had to choose between the USA and the USSR:

In the course of a decade we shall know whether American Capitalism or Russian Communism yields the better life for the bulk of the people. [6]

By September 1931 her own answer was already clear:

...without doubt we are on the side of Russia. [7]

They developed a broader analysis: the first Labour government had been *hatched prematurely*: called upon to assume power before it was ready or fit to do so. With MacDonald gone, the new leadership had

...a dour determination never again to undertake the government of the country as the caretaker of the existing order of society. [8]

But did Labour have the people to take control and achieve real change? Ironically, this had been one of MacDonald's concerns:

We have not the material in our party that we ought to have. [9]

Beatrice feared that Labour lacked the will and the capacity to run a revolution – peaceful or tempestuous:

We have got rid of the rotten stuff from the movement but we have not yet sufficient Will Power and Knowledge to take control of the big formless business of Capitalist production distributive and exchange...[10]

Beatrice had long been preoccupied by the *vocation of leadership*: where could Labour find the equivalent of Wells' Samurai? Or Jesuits or Salvation Army officers? Now, she asked

Have we the material in the British labour movement from which can be evolved something of the nature of a religious order, a congregation of the faithful who will also be skilful technicians in social reconstruction? ...You cannot engineer an equalitarian state if you yourself are enjoying the pomp and circumstance of the city of the rich surrounded by the city of the poor.
[11]

The policies developed by the Fabian Society in the 1890s, by the Poor Law campaign before the First World War, and in *Labour and the New Social Order* were inadequate when faced with the structural economic change and mass unemployment of the post-war years. Even if they had been adequate, Snowden's subservience to Treasury orthodoxy meant that the necessary cash would not be found.

The longer-term alternative – demand management, full employment policy, regional development, economic planning – had yet to emerge. There were glimpses of it in Keynes' papers to the Macmillan Committee and the Economic Advisory Council, and in Attlee's 1930 paper on the *Problems of Industry*. Perhaps Mosley had been searching for something on these lines. In the Minority Report, when they wrote about the organisation of the labour market, the Webbs had begun to see what could be done – begun to foreshadow the 1944 Employment White Paper.

And then there was the Soviet Union. Since 1917 Sidney and Beatrice, like many on the left, had viewed Russia with a mixture of fascination and hostility, but followed developments there attentively. They turned down early opportunities to visit; others did make the journey – including, in 1919, H G Wells and Bertrand Russell. George Lansbury, out of parliament but from November 1919 mayor of Poplar, went in the spring of 1920, and published a book about his experiences. Lansbury was impressed by Lenin, suggesting to him that

...he should ask Sidney and Beatrice Webb to go out and teach his friends how to organize administration. [12]

Lenin smiled.
Lansbury also met Peter Kropotkin, who he had known in London. Kropotkin,

ever an anarchist, was *scornful and condemnatory* of the Soviet government.

In September 1920, the Fabians allocated a week of their Summer School at Godalming for visits by foreign socialist delegates. Many withdrew at a late stage; others were refused passports by their own governments. But representatives from France, Belgium, Holland, Denmark, and Germany came, and the discussions went well enough. Then Beatrice had the idea of inviting *our Russian comrades:*

> *...the crowning success was the lightning visit of Kamenev and Krassin on the Thursday afternoon.* [13]

Like Litvinov, Kamenev and Krassin were overseas representatives of the Bolshevik government, not yet officially recognized as diplomats. Their duties were part commercial, part propaganda. Their movements were watched assiduously by the British security services. [14] Some Fabians were shocked:

> *...to invite the official representatives of Lenin who had expressly denounced all Fabians as traitors, and the Webbs as particularly pernicious ones, was really carrying the principle of tolerance too far!* [15]

But the event seems to have gone off well; Beatrice wrote afterwards to HG Wells, offering to fix up a dinner for him with Krassin and Kamenev at Grosvenor Road. But she described Soviet industrial organisation as

> *...the most rigid form of state socialism...applied without any regard for personal freedom or group autonomy.* [16]

In a 1924 letter to Charles Sarolea, Professor of French at Edinburgh, who had published a book on Russia, Beatrice protested that she and Sidney had never been state socialists.

> *My husband and I have always been against the Soviet System, and have regarded it as a repetition of Russian autocracy based on a creed – a very Eastern conception.* [17]

Relations with the Soviet Union played a major part in the fall of the first MacDonald government. Nevertheless, through the 1920s the Webbs' interest in Russia grew; they began to think of visiting. In February 1928 Beatrice wrote

> *Now and again Sidney and I prospect a trip to Russia by aeroplane; probably it won't come off, for there are limits, and rather narrow limits, to my physical endurance...* [18]

In April 1928 Sidney talked to Susan Lawrence, their tenant at Grosvenor Road, about the right time of year for the journey:

...no one can travel in Russia in March or April. No Russian does so. I thought this was the case. We may have either (1) to go elsewhere, or (2) put off our trip until May, so as to get to Odessa in June. [19]

The visit was postponed when Sidney became a minister again in June 1929.

Just before the May 1929 general election, on holiday in Turkey, they had met Leon Trotsky, who was living in exile on the island of Prinkipo, off Istanbul. Beatrice thought him charming and accomplished:

...more like an intellectual musician than an organiser of war and revolution. [20]

Trotsky did not want to talk in any detail about either Britain or Russia, but about the inevitability of world revolution: he thought Soviet Communism could not survive if capitalism found a new equilibrium in the USA. He was also interested in coming to Britain if there was a Labour government. In fact, the Labour cabinet that took office a couple of months later spent a lot of time considering, and ultimately rejecting, applications from Trotsky to come to Britain.

Although for two years Sidney was absorbed in his ministerial work, he and Beatrice continued to take a close interest in Russia. In February 1930, Grigory Sokolnikov, the Russian Ambassador, and his wife, came to dinner. Beatrice thought he was more like an adult education tutor than a diplomat; the Sokolnikovs spent most of their spare time in the British Museum Reading Room. In the autumn they stayed overnight at Passfield Corner, and had lunch with Philip Snowden.

Trotsky sent Beatrice a copy of his autobiography (which, as a fellow autobiographer, she found *badly planned and badly written*). She read it in April.

...it is fascinating not only as a description of that great and tragic drama, the Russian revolution, but also as a study of religious fanaticism of a high order. And yet Trotsky probably believes he is a free thinker! [21]

Beatrice was now reading whatever she could find on Russia – published and unpublished.

One of the advantages of being a Cabinet Minister's wife is that S shows me interesting despatches – the private reports of foreign Ambassadors. [22]

The British Ambassador to Moscow was Sir Edmund Ovey. She summarised one of his reports in June; Ovey believed

...the Communist Party will succeed in destroying the Capitalist system within its territories and will bring into practice a way of life based on common property, equality of income and the supremacy of the working interests. [23]

She read more reports in September. There was hardship and scarcity; physical conditions were tough; but the reports spoke of the *restrained and dignified bearing of the crowds*.

In November they lunched at the Soviet embassy. Unlike other diplomatic missions, it was hard to tell the difference between the Ambassador and the staff serving the meal. Sidney was the only Labour minister who was socialising with the Sokolnikovs. They encouraged the Webbs to visit Russia. They

> *...altogether denied that we should find it expensive, if we arranged the trip through their Tourist Agency.* [24]

A week later, Beatrice reflected

> *How I should revel, (if I were thirty years younger) in a year spent in the USA and also in Russia, just to see what is actually happening in those two stupendous social experiments; in uncontrolled capitalism on the one hand, and on the other despotically controlled Communism.* [25]

As the economic situation, and the prospects of the MacDonald government, worsened in the winter of 1930-31, so Beatrice's attention turned more and more to the Soviet Union:

> *Only Russia is hopeful. But even here the hopefulness seems hysterical, and based on a fanatical faith in a coming salvation. The present state of things in Russia is at best purgatory – some would say Hell.* [26]

In July 1931 GBS went to Russia, in a group which included Jimmy Mallon of Toynbee Hall and the Conservative MP Nancy Astor. He received an enthusiastic welcome (including, on some accounts, shouts of *Hail Shaw!* on his arrival in Moscow), and met Stalin. His praise for Soviet achievements was fulsome. Beatrice was sceptical about his approval of what he had seen; she remembered his *equally demonstrative admiration for Italian Fascism* three years earlier.

Shaw came to stay at Passfield a few days after his return, and spoke to the Fabian Summer School:

> *It <u>must</u> be right! The paradox of the speech: Russian revolution was pure Fabianism – Lenin and Stalin had recognised the 'Inevitability of gradualness'! Also they had given up 'workers' control' for the Webbs' conception of the threefold state – citizens, consumers, and producers organization. What is not Webbism or Western is the welding together of all three by a <u>Creed</u> oligarchy...* [27]

The Labour Government fell. Sidney was out of office. Beatrice went with the Shaws to the annual theatre festival at Malvern; GBS said he was the festival's *patron saint* [28]. Beatrice went, partly because she enjoyed the company of the Shaws, and because she wanted to go on to the Three Choirs Festival, held in Gloucester that year

…to renew my memories of fifty years ago. [29]

Her main reason for going to Gloucester, however, was to hear the music direct. She was not disappointed; her taste, as ever, was for big choral works. One day she heard Handel's *Messiah*; on another, she was *carried away* by the premiere of Gustav Holst's *Choral Fantasia*. She was flattered to be told by GBS that Edward Elgar wanted to be introduced to her

…as he has a great admiration for Mrs Webb… [30]

But the introduction did not happen, and at times it was hard to concentrate on the music: Beatrice's

…brain whizzed and I was preoccupied with the catastrophic politics of today and tomorrow… [31]

Beatrice compared the choice between capitalism and communism to the mediaeval struggle between Christianity and Islam:

There was no third creed open to the civilized world of those days: they had to follow Christ or Mahomet. [32]

She asked herself

Am I strong enough to go to Russia so as to give vividness to any line we take? [33]

The next week Susan Lawrence visited Passfield; Beatrice wrote that they were

…planning a trip to Russia, more or less together, in the late summer! [34]

In the end Susan Lawrence did not travel with Sidney and Beatrice. But in the autumn and winter of 1931/32 the project slowly became more definite. In December Douglas and Margaret Cole spent a weekend at Passfield; earlier in 1931 they had been involved in setting up the New Fabian Research Bureau (NFRB), which was now planning its own commission of enquiry into Soviet Communism. That weekend in December, they *endlessly discussed* Russia with the Webbs. It would be ironic, thought Beatrice, *if the highly respectable Fabian Society*

…becomes the protagonist of…Soviet Communism in Great Britain. [35]

In her retrospective diary entry for 1931, Beatrice wrote that she hoped her next book would be about *What we can learn from Russia.*

In January she wrote of a

...pilgrimage to the Mecca of the equalitarian state led by a few Fabians, all well over seventy years of age...

What attracts us is Soviet Russia, and it is useless to deny that we are prejudiced in its favour.[36]

They thought the Russian constitution matched their blueprint for Britain, with political democracy, vocational organisation, and consumer cooperatives – and

There is no damned nonsense about Guild Socialism! [37]

Beatrice saw the Communist Party as a spiritual power:

The spot light of intriguing difference between the live creation of Soviet Russia, and the dead body of the Webb constitution, is the presence, as the dominant and decisive force, of a religious order: the Communist Party, with its strict discipline, its vows of obedience and poverty...It is the invention of the religious order...which is the magnet that attracts me to Russia. [38]

She compared the Communist Party to the Catholic Church or a religious order:

...it has its Holy Writ, its prophets and its canonised saints; it has its Pope, yesterday Lenin and today Stalin; it has its code of conduct and its discipline; it has its creed and its inquisition. [39]

By early 1932, Beatrice was not just prejudiced in favour of the Soviet Union; she had decided in advance what she was going to discover – including a real exemplar of the vocation of leadership.

Approvingly, she noted

Communists are expected to be puritan in their personal conduct, not to waste energy, time or health on sex, food or drink. The exact opposite of ...D H Lawrence's cult of sex which I happen to detest. [40]

In spring 1932, Sidney and Beatrice continued their preparations: a meeting with the NFRB Commission members at LSE in February, an overnight visit by the Sokolnikovs to Passfield in March. They worried about their physical fitness for the trip. They met people who had visited, lived, and worked in Russia, and they read widely: official reports, novels, and memoirs. Beatrice veered between commitment and neutrality:

All I know is that I <u>wish</u> Russian Communism to succeed – a wish which tends to distort one's judgment. When one becomes aware of this distortion, one has

'cold feet'. To be for or against Soviet Communism is, today, a big gamble of the intellect. [41]

The Webbs met critics of the Soviet regime as well as supporters. R H Tawney introduced them to Rhea Clyman, a Canadian journalist who later played a major role in exposing the famine in Ukraine. Clyman stayed overnight at Passfield on Friday 8 April; the Webbs did not like her; but she told them that collective farms were a failure, and that famine was coming. Beatrice paraphrased Rhea's verdict:

What's the good of all this effort and sacrifice? Nothing will come of it; it is all wasted. Noone will be the better for it. Meanwhile everyone is wretched except the party fanatics and officials who delight in bossing the show. [42]

Another visitor stressed the restrictions on freedom of opinion. Beatrice acknowledged that the big drawback about the Soviet Union *lies in the activities of the GPU*. (09.04.1932)

Beatrice knew that there would be defects and shortcomings

...in what will necessarily be a managed *tour – managed by the Soviet Government owing to our old age, socialist prestige and ignorance of the language.* [43]

Molly Hamilton had just started writing her life of the Webbs; she stayed with Sidney and Beatrice at Passfield Corner shortly before they set off

...I found them literally knee deep in books, pamphlets, papers of every sort, about Russia. [44]

'A NEW KIND OF ROYALTY'

In summer 1932 the Webbs spent eight weeks in Russia and Ukraine. Over the following two years they wrote their book, *Soviet Communism, A new civilisation?* published in November 1935. Sidney made a follow-up visit in 1934. A second edition of the book, without the question mark, appeared in 1937.

They were drawn to the Soviet Union by their disillusionment with the record of the second MacDonald government; they had begun to doubt whether gradualness was inevitable after all. They were aware of the criticisms of Russia – indeed, earlier, they had expressed those same criticisms.

While they were working on the book, press coverage in Britain drew attention to contemporary evidence of famine, and the lack of personal liberty, in Russia. Privately Sidney and Beatrice worried about these issues. In their writing, however, they varied between ignoring or dismissing the evidence, and defending the perpetrators.

They sailed for Leningrad on Saturday 21 May 1932. On the voyage they attended a meeting of the ship's soviet – which welcomed them, as authors of a book translated by Lenin himself, and as having

...all their lives been supporters of the proletariat. [45]

In 1932, the Soviet Union was in the middle of a centrally led social and economic upheaval. In *Soviet Communism*, the Webbs took at face value the intricate party and constitutional structures which existed. But by 1932 these simply obscured the personal and autocratic power of Stalin. As Nikita Khrushchev pointed out in his secret speech to the 1956 congress of the Communist Party:

...Stalin had so elevated himself above the party and above the nation that he ceased to consider either the Central Committee or the party. [46]

Trotsky's exile – at the start of which Sidney and Beatrice had met him in 1929 – had come after a long struggle with Stalin; Trotsky believed that without international, permanent revolution, socialism was doomed.

Stalin believed in building socialism in one country. The Five Year Plan, launched in 1928, consisted of rapid, forced collectivization of agriculture, and the development of heavy industry.

The Webbs were shown the showpieces of change. As the western economies endured depression, it appeared to them, and to many others in the west, that the Russian people were taking control of their economic destiny. At least something was happening.

There were undoubted achievements; there were also grave problems. Famine had begun in the Ukraine and the Northern Caucasus.

Beatrice's niece Kitty Dobbs, Rosie's daughter, had married Malcolm Muggeridge in 1927. In autumn 1932 the Muggeridges moved to Moscow, planning to live there, with Malcolm reporting for the *Manchester Guardian*.

The Webbs were welcomed to Leningrad by representatives of the city soviet, the Foreign Ministry, the trade unions, and the cooperative movement, and given a hotel suite for the day, before travelling to Moscow by overnight sleeper. Beatrice said of their welcome that

We seem to be a new kind of royalty. [47]

In Moscow they stayed in the Foreign Ministry guest house – a villa, formerly home to a millionaire, next to the ministry, equipped with the cutlery and linen of the imperial household – but

…a universal absence of chamber pots and other domestic requirements, and the plumbing of the lavatories and bathrooms is indescribably bad. [48]

At least the food was good.

It was, as Beatrice had anticipated, a managed tour. Their itinerary was planned for them. They went where their hosts wanted them to go; they saw what their hosts wanted them to see. The plan was to spend the first part of the visit in Moscow, then travelling to the Caucasus and Ukraine before returning to Moscow and Leningrad.

In Moscow they went to the theatre, and met representatives of the Komsomol youth movement. They also met the British ambassador Edmund Ovey, whose despatches had interested Beatrice. Visiting a school, Beatrice noted that

The girls wanted to be either engineers or medicals – they all resented becoming nurses except as a social task in the event of an epidemic. [49]

She told the students they

…must make the Russian Socialist State a success so that we might imitate them, whereupon they all cheered enthusiastically. [50]

On leaving Moscow they went by sleeper to Nizhniy Novgorod, then by steamer down the Volga for four days to Stalingrad. The boat journey had its charm; but their cabin was

…too hot and noisy to get sleep in the afternoons or during the nights. I am fearing that I may have to drop out of some of the programme. [51]

Sidney, too, was very tired. They visited a car factory at Nizhniy Novgorod (*a failure*) and a tractor plant at Stalingrad (*a success*). Wherever they went, they interviewed extensively.

After Stalingrad, they moved on to Rostov for a hectic programme of farm visits

…those three long days of travelling, either in the rail car of the President of the Grain Trust of the North Caucasus, or by motor over mud roads and the two nights in the farm lodging houses with their noise and rather coarse meals was my undoing. When I reached Rostov again I had an attack of what the Russian doctor called stomach fever. [52]

Beatrice was prescribed castor oil, two days without food, and a stay in a spa in the Caucasus, meeting up with Sidney again in Moscow.

Beatrice's illness meant that Sidney was on his own for the Ukraine part of the visit. He wrote to Beatrice on Monday 20 June from Kharkov; the Donetz river basin, through which he had travelled the previous day, reminded him of England's Black Country: ...*mines, cement works, chemical factories and so on.*

The Webbs' itinerary was based on showing them successes. In Ukraine, construction of the Dnieper hydroelectric dam, started in 1927, was approaching completion. It was intended to boost industry in the region. Meanwhile reports of famine in Ukraine were appearing in the British press.

Sidney and Beatrice were reunited back in Moscow. There, Beatrice met the feminist revolutionary Alexandra Kollontai, now the Russian ambassador to Sweden. Kollontai reminded Beatrice that, as a student, she had come to Grosvenor Road in 1899 – and said that Beatrice had been very kind to her.

They returned to England at the end of July, laden with documents. Autumn 1932 and winter 1933 passed in planning the book and assembling the material. In February 1933 Thomas Jones and his wife spent a weekend at Passfield. He described it afterwards to his daughter Eirene:

They plunged you into the Russian Revolution between the taxi and the front door and kept it up throughout our visit, so wrapped up are they in the great experiment. [53]

Later that month, Sidney and Beatrice took a holiday in France and Italy before starting writing.

Neither Sidney nor Beatrice ever learned Russian; they relied on S P Turin, a Russian emigre economics lecturer at LSE (his wife Lucia was Beveridge's secretary). The Turins performed a range of tasks for Sidney and Beatrice: translators, researchers, and critical friends. They stayed at Passfield regularly. Sometimes they challenged the Webbs' credulity; in November 1933, Beatrice noted

Turin says we have <u>invented</u> a constitution for the USSR. 'Are you now going to <u>invent</u> the meaning of their activities?' with a stress on the word invent. 'Telling the truth about things, which you cannot tell until you have discovered it, is always invention,' I retorted. [54]

A couple of weeks later, Sidney sent the Turins a draft of the chapter entitled *The Liquidation of the Landlord and the Capitalist*, with the apologetic note

Our idea has been to put all the 'horrors' together, and get over them at once. [55]

By spring 1933, Malcolm Muggeridge was established in Moscow. His disillusion with the Soviet Union had been rapid. He visited the areas the Webbs had visited, describing what he had seen in private letters to Beatrice, and in anonymous articles for the *Manchester Guardian*. Beatrice called them his *curiously hysterical denunciations* of the USSR: a

...vivid and arrogantly expressed picture of the starvation and oppression of the North Caucasus and the Ukraine. [56]

Muggeridge had no doubt that there was famine, and that the famine was the direct result of government policy. Before the Webbs went to Russia, Rhea Clyman had warned them this would happen.

In the privacy of her diary, Beatrice admitted that there was some fire

...behind this smoke of Malcolm's queerly malicious but sincerely felt denunciation ... [57]

Muggeridge stated that Russian peasants were starving. But

What makes me uncomfortable is that we have no evidence to the contrary. [58]

In *Soviet Communism: A New Civilisation*, their book on the Soviet Union, the Webbs devote several pages to the question *Was there a Famine in the USSR in 1931-1932?*

They warn the reader that

Those who think this is a simple question to answer will probably already have made up their minds. [59]

They acknowledged that there had been food shortages. But they blamed the victims: *recalcitrant peasants*. What the soviet government faced was not a famine

...but a widespread general strike of the peasantry, in resistance to the policy of collectivisation, fomented and encouraged by the disloyal elements of the population... [60]

Beatrice's lingering illness meant that more of the writing fell to Sidney:

Sidney begins the book today and I shall strain and stumble after him... [61]

The book took two years; it soon became clear that a follow-up research visit would be necessary.

In autumn 1932, Sokolnikov, the Russian Ambassador, was recalled. His successor Ivan Maisky was a former Menshevik, who had lived in exile in London from 1912 to 1917. Maisky was quick to contact the Webbs; he became a close friend. He and his wife Agniya spent the first of many weekends at Passfield in April 1933, returning in August.

In summer 1933 the Webbs worked steadily on the draft of Part I of *Soviet Communism*, covering the constitution, and trade unions, and finishing in the autumn. Beatrice admitted

...the section on collective farms is very imperfect as we have not got the material...[62]

Sidney was doing most of the writing. Beatrice noted on 24 November that she had *spurts of capacity* on the book, but that

...I do little or nothing in its actual execution. Fortunately Sidney is thoroughly absorbed in it... [63]

Beatrice's illness recurred in autumn 1933. While attending the Labour Conference at Hastings in October, she was admitted to hospital for bladder surgery. This did not resolve the problem. In December she began haemorrhaging; after Christmas she went into a London nursing home for tests, followed by an operation to remove one of her kidneys on 12 January. She stayed five weeks in the nursing home, returning to Passfield in February.

Meanwhile Sidney carried on writing. On Boxing Day 1933, Beatrice noted

...Sidney goes marching on – with his Planned for Consumption chapter... [64]

While in the nursing home she worried about the prospect of Sidney having to complete the book by himself:

...if only Sidney could be spared this time of anxiety. But he has to finish the book, with me or without me. And finish it he will – and keep his health in order to do it. [65]

By mid-February, in a *feeble way*, Beatrice was back at work. In April the Maiskys came to stay again; Sidney and Beatrice both had long talks with the Ambassador, trying out their ideas.

They worked through summer 1934. In September Sidney returned to Russia for the further visit; Beatrice was not well enough to travel. He was accompanied instead by Beatrice's niece Barbara Drake and great nephew John Cripps (son of Stafford Cripps). They visited farms and the Ministry of Agriculture. Sidney returned

...completely reassured as to the eventual success of the new social order.[66]

When Sidney was in Moscow in September 1934, officials

...laughed at the idea of 6 million deaths from famine and minimised the extent of failure of crops. [67]

Beatrice noted, however, that there was a *dark spot*

...the lack of free expression among those intellectuals who are against the Communist creed and the practice thereof, and would like to be an acknowledged opposition. [68]

Proofs of Volume I began to arrive in November and December, and were complete by January 1935. In January, *fed up with the book*, they went off to Ventnor for a long weekend.

Sidney continued to be responsible for a lot of the writing:

I am a wash-out except for flashes lighting up a dark corner of our big canvas... This heavy load of thought and expression – too heavy for my bent shoulders – Sidney's little figure goes bounding on – but even he is breathless. [69]

In March 1935 the Maiskys came for a weekend. It was an important moment in the development of their friendship. Ivan Maisky told Sidney and Beatrice that he had read their *History of Trade Unionism* (Lenin's translation), as a student in St Petersburg in the early years of the century, before he knew their names, before going into exile.

They said Maisky was complimentary about the book. He wrote:

In spite of their age (he is 75 and she is 77), they are working hard on their political testament, Soviet Communism. Two volumes of about 1,000 pages. Nine-tenths of it is ready. We spoke about the book at length and I made a series of critical comments and corrections. The authors listened, sometimes objecting but mostly agreeing. [70]

Beatrice thought Maisky trustworthy, hardworking, shrewd, and lively; Maisky described the Webbs as *the cream of the world intelligentsia*. But they were showing the proofs of their book to the Russian ambassador, and amending what they had written in the light of his comments.

The first edition of *Soviet Communism: A new Civilisation?* appeared on November 25, 1935. The Webbs involved themselves in the details of the publication process: advance copies for friends, press copies, a cheap edition for students. Beatrice wondered if labour movement activists would read it:

These two long volumes – 1200 pages – will they be read or shelved? That to us is the most interesting question... [71]

A month after publication, 450 copies of the main print run had been sold, and the book was *selling steadily*:

The sale of the 6000 5/- edition has probably lost us some potential buyers: but it has yielded a profit over and above the extra cost ...All the same we could not have done the job without an independent income: (one up to the capitalist system) …[72]

In December they celebrated with a lunch at the LSE for everyone who had helped by reading and correcting proofs – including Shaws, Maiskys, Beveridge, Laski, Turin, and Mostyn Lloyd. The lunch was followed by a Russian embassy dinner; Maisky, proposing their health, explained how reading the Webbs' books had made him a revolutionary. Other speakers included GBS and Herbert Morrison.

In its first year, *Soviet Communism* sold 20,000 copies in Britain, 5000 in the USA, and some elsewhere. According to Maisky, translation into Russian was *proceeding*. Mrs Tobinson, who had acted as Beatrice's guide/interpreter, told Shena Simon, who visited Russia later, that some passages in the book would *require explanation* and might be omitted from the Russian version. By autumn 1937 a second edition was in prospect; 15,000 had been sold to Gollancz in advance for the Left Book Club. It was the best seller of all the Webb canon.

When *Soviet Communism* was first published, Beatrice noted in her diary that it had received a good press; the review in the *New Statesman* was favourable, while Walter Citrine in the *Daily Herald* and J A Spender in the *Observer* were more critical. The longer-term verdict, however, has been uniformly negative: AJP Taylor wrote that *Soviet Communism* was

…despite serious competition, the most preposterous book ever written about Soviet Russia. [73]

Kenneth Morgan describes the book as *'absurdly uncritical'.*[74]

When writing *Soviet Communism*, the Webbs were aware of the issues of hunger and food shortages. They were also aware of, and concerned about, restrictions on individual liberty. Beatrice noted, after their return home in July 1932, that

Some features of Soviet Russia will be and remain repulsive to more developed races. For instance its crude metaphysics, the fanatical repression of heresy, its 'behind the scenes' killings of unwanted persons belong to the middle ages and devastate its reputation in the modern world. [75]

Later, she referred to *ruthless heresy hunts* – comparing life in Russia to the Inquisition – the *suppression of free thought and free speech* could not continue indefinitely.

The purges and show trials began after the Webbs' 1932 visit, but before completion of the first edition of *Soviet Communism*. On 1 December 1934 Sergei Kirov, the head of the party organisation in Leningrad, was assassinated.

His death was the occasion for the launch of a campaign of repression. Beatrice wrote in January 1935

> *Some of the leading men in the Leningrad GPU have been arrested and are awaiting trial.* [76]

This continued through 1936, 1937 and 1938.

The Webbs reacted to the renewed terror in the Soviet Union in two ways: private distress was combined with public attempts at justification. In August 1936 Beatrice wrote that

> *...for defenders of Soviet Communism the sensational trial in Moscow denounced by Trotsky as a monstrous lie, is a nasty shock...repugnant to the British conception of jurisprudence.*
>
> *For the defendants to plead guilty, to refuse the aid of counsel, to vie with each other in abject confession of their crime and in accusation of other persons in the case of Zinoviev and Kamenev a revolting exhibition of treachery ...lends a suspicion of torture ...capped by the immediate execution – the whole 16 of them – after the verdict.* [77]

She argued that British legal practice in Ireland and in India had also been disreputable.

In the second edition of *Soviet Communism*, published in 1937, the Webbs compared the situation in the Soviet Union in the 1930s with the position in Britain after the Civil War or France after the revolution:

> *Has there ever been a great and successful revolution without attempts at a counter-revolution?* [78]

THE WEBBS AND LABOUR AFTER MACDONALD

After the collapse of the second MacDonald government in August 1931, the Webbs concentrated their energies and hopes on the Soviet Union. They wanted to believe that the new society emerging in Russia could fulfil their dreams. They knew about the failures: the famine, the brutality, the loss of liberty, and then the purges, trials, and executions. They could not avoid knowing: among the victims were people they knew. But any anguish was private: publicly they were apologists for the regime.

They remained committed to the Labour Party. They participated in its affairs, attending its annual conference up to 1937. They took a lively interest in its policy and future leadership, and in the Fabian Society.

They had little time for the Communist Party of Great Britain; in 1932 Beatrice noted

...the British Communist Party is a ludicrous caricature of a revolutionary movement. [79]

She thought British Communists should belong to the Labour Party

...they ought not to belong to an organisation ostensibly and actually controlled by the governing class of another country. [80]

Labour was traumatized by MacDonald's departure and the subsequent election defeat. The party, with the Webbs, questioned whether gradualness was still inevitable: could socialism come by peaceful or parliamentary means? How could radical economic change be achieved?

Later in the decade, as the international situation darkened, Labour became more focussed on the need to confront the fascist threat in Europe.

Sidney and Beatrice shaped the bitter reaction of the Labour Party to the collapse of the second MacDonald Labour government: the departed leaders had been rotten; [81] *the new leadership* were determined never to allow themselves to become caretakers for the old order. [82]

That mood was slow to lift; in autumn 1932 Beatrice noted

A deep depression settled over the Labour Party... [83]

Viewed by an aged observer, the Labour Party of today is depressing and dreary... [84]

While Labour mourned, there were signs of a renewal of socialist ideas. New policy organisations were established; the initiative came from people close to the Webbs, who followed their work. Leadership came from Douglas Cole; resources from Stafford Cripps. The first new groups began in the closing months of the Labour government.

The Fabian Society was at a low ebb. Frank Galton (who had started work for the Webbs in 1892) was secretary. Margaret Cole said Galton's *amiability was matched by his obstinacy*, suggesting that he issued the same newsletter, word for word, every month.

Sidney and Beatrice both attended the launch of the New Fabian Research Bureau (NFRB) in March 1931. Douglas Cole was organizer and secretary. Beatrice called it an attempt to restart the Fabian Research Department. Cole attracted a broad spread of attendees – Stafford Cripps; Ernest Bevin, of the Transport and General Workers Union (TGWU); and Robson, Laski, and Mostyn Lloyd from LSE. Attlee was appointed Chairman, Hugh Gaitskell assistant secretary. Cole called the Bureau the *loyal Grousers*. Beatrice thought it was

...a very pleasant family party – and may lead to something. [85]

The NFRB sent their own delegation to the Soviet Union – including Margaret Cole and Hugh Dalton. They published a report in 1933.

In June 1931, the Coles launched the Society for Socialist Inquiry and Propaganda (SSIP), known as ZIP, at a meeting chaired by Bevin. Its membership overlapped with the NFRB, and also included some former Guild Socialists, such as William Mellor. The purpose was to make propaganda for ideas generated by the Research Bureau. SSIP's first publication, on the economic situation, by Cole and Bevin, appeared in 1931.

In 1932 the Independent Labour Party disaffiliated from the Labour Party. Not all ILP members wanted a complete break. Those who wanted to stay with Labour chose the SSIP as their vehicle; the Socialist League was created as a merger between the SSIP and those ILP members who wanted to stay with Labour.

The League, over Cole's opposition, then chose Frank Wise of the ILP rather than Ernest Bevin of the TGWU as its chairman. This experience, wrote Margaret Cole, convinced Bevin that

...intellectuals of the left were people who stabbed you in the back. [86]

Douglas Cole invited Bevin to be a vice chairman of the NFRB; Bevin's response was

I have decided to take no office at all outside of those I already hold and those within the Union. I think it better I should stick to my last. [87]

The first meeting of the League was at the October 1932 Labour conference; the Webbs attended. Beatrice did not think it got off to a good start.

During the conference itself, however, members of the Socialist League succeeded in defeating the Labour leadership on key votes, including the nationalization of the clearing banks.

In 1933 Stafford Cripps became chair of the Socialist League., Speaking to Labour students in January 1934, he argued that when Labour came to power, as well as facing resistance from the City and the House of Lords

...we shall have to deal with opposition from Buckingham Palace and other places as well. [88]

Such interventions were no better received by the leadership of the TUC or the Labour Party than they were by the King. A few spoke up for Cripps; one was Attlee, who said Cripps was being attacked because he

...is one of the ablest critics of the capitalist system and is directing his attacks just where they feel it – at the financial system. [89]

Beatrice thought the Socialist League could be a successor to the ever more *respectable and seedy* Fabian Society. It was

...not a promising faction within the Labour Party, but at any rate a party of young people... [90]

From 1933, the security services watched Cripps. They filed cuttings of his speeches, opened his letters, and recorded his phone calls. The police sent reports of his meetings to Special Branch.

Beatrice and Sidney continued to take a close – almost proprietorial – interest in Labour's future leadership. Most of the likely candidates they had known for over twenty years; they invited them to Passfield. Beatrice had a keen eye for their limitations.

She approved of Henderson, leader immediately after MacDonald's departure. He stayed at Passfield in 1931,1932 and 1933: affectionately, she referred to him as *Dear old Henderson,* [91] *Dear Uncle Arthur.*[92] But it was clear that Henderson could not be the longer-term leader. He lost his own seat in 1931. He did get back into parliament, but he was already a sick man. In August 1932 Beatrice found him

Shrunken in frame, and drawn in feature, inert and depressed, he is manifestly incapable of any general leadership of the Labour Party and very worried about its future. [93]

In 1932 he was succeeded by Lansbury – older than Henderson, the same age as Sidney. Clement Attlee was Deputy Leader; Dalton quoted an unnamed colleague on Attlee's role – *a purely accidental position.* [94]

In January 1932, before Sidney and Beatrice went to Russia, two leadership contenders spent weekends at Passfield. Herbert Morrison and family stayed on 16 and 17 January. The Webbs had known Morrison since before 1914. Beatrice remembered him as a *cocky and self-assertive* young London clerk with an *unpleasing personality* who *did not look promising.*[95] Then she had known him during the war – Secretary of the London Labour Party – ascetic, vegetarian, teetotal

...very Fabian in opinion – a Webbian, in fact. [96]

Now his habits had changed:

...now a heavy smoker and moderate whiskey drinker and meat eater – and he takes no exercise. [97]

As Transport Minister from 1929 to 1931, Morrison had been successful

...a remarkably shrewd administrator and parliamentarian...

But

What he lacks and lacks completely is any kind of personal magnetism or charm. [98]

In 1934 Morrison led Labour to victory in the London County Council elections. Beatrice approved; Morrison

...is a Fabian of Fabians; a direct disciple of Sidney Webb's: his method and purpose are almost identical with that of the Sidney Webb of 1892. [99]

Beatrice saw the Labour LCC as a test bed for future Labour politics: could gradualness work?

Or will it end in another disillusionment about the worthwhileness of reformist tactics. That is the question. Incidentally the answer to that question, through the events of the next three years, will decide the minor question of the leadership of the National Labour Party; whether it is to be vested in the right wing or the left wing, in Herbert Morrison or Stafford Cripps? [100]

The Webb network was well represented on the Morrison LCC: Ivy Bolton, who had been Beatrice's secretary, was an LCC Councillor. So was Rachel Keeling, Ben Keeling's widow. Beatrice's niece Barbara Drake became an LCC Alderman. Harry Snell (now Lord Snell) was elected Chairman of the Council.

A week after the Morrisons' weekend at Passfield, Hugh and Ruth Dalton came to stay for the first time in five years. Beatrice found Dalton *much improved*:

...he has lost that ingratiating manner which he displayed to aged and important folk and the queer artificial cynicism... [101]

Dalton found the Webbs *more human than of old* [102]
Beatrice thought Dalton

...feels obliged to look more Left than he feels in order to counter suspicion. He is certainly one of the soundest intellectuals and strongest characters of the Labour Party and is certain of Cabinet rank when Labour comes back to office. [103]

They talked about Russia; Beatrice thought Dalton's attitude was like their own

...he has his eyes fixed on Russia... [104]

Dalton, on the other hand, wrote that Sidney and Beatrice were much interested in Russia

> *…and hope for the success of this Socialist exemplar.* [105]

By autumn 1932 both the Webbs and Dalton had visited Russia. Dalton had become more cautious: he was dubious on grounds of gross inefficiency in detail

> *…but on balance thinks it will pull through.* [106]

Arthur Greenwood was not invited to Passfield. He lost his seat in the 1931 election, returning to parliament in a 1932 byelection, and remaining Labour's head of research. He had not changed; the same issue always came up. In 1932, Harold Laski had a long conversation with Beatrice about the shortcomings of head office, in which he referred to Greenwood as *sodden with drink.*[107]

A year later, the young writer and Labour candidate A L Rowse spent a weekend at Passfield Corner; he spoke to the Webbs about his

> *…low opinion of the Labour party staff at Transport House: regards the 'drinking' of Greenwood and some of the staff as deplorable.* [108]

None of the Labour leadership front runners appealed to Beatrice. Before 1935 she barely acknowledged Attlee as a possibility. But after her nephew Stafford Cripps became an MP and Solicitor General in 1931, she had her candidate.

The Webbs had not known Stafford well before he entered politics. Beatrice was his godmother, as well as his aunt, but he recalled

> *…I never came close to her as a child – she was rather a terrifying person…It was not until I really grew up that I came into close contact with her.* [109]

Stafford and his wife Isobel visited Passfield for the first time in March 1932. Beatrice sized him up for the prospective vacancy:

> *In manners and morals, in tastes and preferences, Stafford would make an ideal leader for the Labour Party.* [110]

She thought he could get on with trade unionists, coop managers and socialist intellectuals. He was charismatic – *tall, good looking, with a good voice and pleasant gestures.* In short, he was cast in the Joseph Chamberlain/Oswald Mosley mould.

The trouble was that Stafford

> *…does not <u>know</u> his own limitations.* [111]

She found him *oddly immature* in intellect and unbalanced in judgment.

Other leadership candidates were sceptical about Cripps. Beatrice discussed him with Morrison. Morrison had encouraged Stafford into Labour politics; now he thought Cripps might be *spoilt* by too quick a rise:

...it must be rather trying to see this rich young lawyer rise to leadership after little more than a year's membership of the Labour Party. [112]

Dalton came to Passfield again in October 1932. He told Beatrice that he saw Cripps as a strong personality and a *likeable fellow* – but prone to take up *silly ideas*. He said that Cripps was *too hard worked at the bar*.[113]

Stafford and Isobel Cripps had a country house in the Cotswolds; the Webbs stayed there in autumn 1933. Isobel had been well off; Stafford was earning a good income. Stafford himself lived austerely, but Beatrice thought both were trapped

...in a standard of expenditure too high for the leader of a revolution. [114]

She thought Stafford had now become one of the most impressive speakers in the Labour movement.

Stafford is certainly one of the ablest and most upright and devoted of the leaders today. He has our warmest wishes. [115]

In May 1934, Sidney and Beatrice saw Cripps again, over a *first rate* dinner at Barbara Drake's home; Maisky was among the other guests. After others had gone, the Webbs stayed late talking to Stafford. Beatrice thought he was not yet

...a matured statesman – has he got it in him to become so?...he is still an amateur – and a clumsy one – at the political game; and I doubt his judgment of men and policies. But, at present, he has no rival as leader of the left wing. [116]

Cripps said Transport House was trying to stop him speaking in the regions, but that wherever he went he drew huge crowds. By autumn 1934 Beatrice believed that Stafford was the confirmed leader of the left. Personally, he became more austere, becoming teetotal in protest against the alcoholism of the Parliamentary Labour Party.

LABOUR'S INTERNATIONAL POLICY 1931-1937

Labour's international policy after 1918 was derived from the work the Webbs had commissioned from Leonard Woolf on creating international institutions, and from Labour's Statement of War Aims. Labour was committed to the League of Nations, arbitration, and disarmament.

In 1924 MacDonald had been Foreign Secretary as well as Prime Minister. From 1929 to 1931, Henderson was Foreign Secretary; after leaving office he chaired the international Disarmament Conference in Geneva. In 1934 he was awarded the Nobel Peace Prize.

In the 1920s Labour had successfully brought together ex-servicemen and those – like MacDonald and Snowden – who had opposed the war. Many on the left believed that the war had been a terrible waste, and that there should never be another one. In Britain, there was strong opposition to rearmament; on the left and beyond, there was a sustained pacifist mood, and a desperate faith in collective security and the League of Nations as the means of avoiding armed conflict.

Neither Sidney nor Beatrice had ever been pacifists; in both the Boer War and the First World War, Sidney had taken the view that, if the country was at war, it should not be defeated. The Potter family had been divided between supporters and opponents of the war.

After Hitler came to power in Germany in January 1933, the left's faith in the League of Nations and collective security began to crumble. In March 1933, Beatrice referred to Hitler's

> …*ferocious persecution of the Jews – financiers and scientists, teachers and doctors, as well as money-lenders, multiple shop-keepers and Communists…* [117]

A month after Hitler became Chancellor the Reichstag parliamentary building in Berlin was burned down. Four Communist leaders were arrested and charged with involvement in the destruction. Cripps joined an international legal commission to conduct an alternative investigation into the fire.

Hitler's coming to power marked the first stage in a shift in the focus of the left: away from the lessons of 1931, to the worsening international situation; away from outright opposition to war, towards an acceptance of rearmament. Between 1933 and 1937 Labour moved from a pacifist position to one based on armed deterrence. Labour's retreat from its pro-League of Nations, pro collective security position was anguished, complex and protracted.

For Margaret Cole,

> …*the process of conversion began in February 1934, with the crushing of the Austrian Socialists.* [118]

In February 1934, the Austrian government defeated a rising by the Social Democratic Party. Artillery was deployed against municipal flats in Vienna; 1500 people were killed. The party was declared illegal.

In 1929, Sidney and Beatrice had spent a week in Vienna. Beatrice wrote of

> …*our intense admiration for the little group of Viennese socialists who had made Vienna, with its admirable housing and other social services, the mecca of evolutionary socialism.* [119]

Now the Vienna socialists were being *ruthlessly slaughtered.*

The next critical moment was the Italian invasion of Abyssinia in the autumn of 1935. Lansbury, still party leader, a passionate defender of the League, was opposed to military sanctions. So were Stafford Cripps and Ponsonby, Labour leader in the Lords – a First World War peace campaigner and a founder member of the Union for Democratic Control.

At the beginning of September, the TUC voted overwhelmingly in favour of League of Nations military sanctions against Italy. Shortly afterwards, Lansbury made it clear that he did not support the decision. Cripps went further, resigning from Labour's National Executive. Ponsonby also resigned; his replacement was Harry Snell.

In October, the Labour Conference supported military sanctions; that decision marked the end of George Lansbury's leadership. Supporting sanctions, Ernest Bevin denounced Lansbury for

> *...taking his conscience round from body to body, to be told what you ought to do with it.* [120]

The Webbs were at the conference. But Beatrice's diary entry is focussed on Stafford Cripps (also strongly attacked by Bevin) and his prospects. It does not discuss the confrontation between Bevin and Lansbury.

Lansbury resigned as leader on 8 October. A General Election was imminent; Attlee, Lansbury's deputy, became acting leader. He had previously acted as leader when Lansbury had been unwell in 1934. Attlee's role was seen as temporary; the real choice would come after the General Election, with a stronger field of candidates, including Morrison, who had been out of parliament since 1931.

Before the conference Beatrice discussed the leadership with visitors to Passfield. In early September Susan Lawrence warned her that

> *...the inconspicuous and irreproachable Attlee might well become the chairman of the parliamentary labour party, as a compromise man.* [121]

At the end of the month Cripps spent a day with the Webbs. Beatrice and Stafford dismissed Attlee:

> *...who, though gifted with intellect and character, and also with good will, has alas! no personality! He is neither feared, disliked nor admired...* [122]

Stanley Baldwin, who had taken over from MacDonald as Prime Minister in June, announced the dissolution of parliament on 23 October; polling was on 14 November. Beatrice found it comic that Labour went into the election

...with Attlee and Snell as parliamentary leaders – both alike the very embodiment of bourgeois respectability and good manners – and the very antithesis to the professional revolutionary. [123]

Labour made gains at the General Election – but the National Government retained a majority of over 250. In a fresh leadership election Attlee was elected, defeating Morrison and Greenwood. Greenwood became Deputy Leader.

Stafford Cripps' view on sanctions differed from that of Lansbury and Ponsonby. Just before the 1935 Labour Conference Cripps resigned from the NEC rather than support sanctions. His father, Lord Parmoor, a Foreihn Office minister in both 1920s Labour governments, championed collective security and the League of Nations. Stafford supported the principle of the League, but not the fact that its policy was directed by the capitalist governments of Britain and France. For Stafford, according to a recent biographer

It was not war that was the issue, but war waged by Imperialist Governments. If, and only if, the Governments of the League countries were Socialist, could a real war against Fascism be conjectured. [124]

Parmoor was disappointed by Stafford's resignation from the NEC, and wrote to say so; Stafford replied

...it has become more and more obvious every year that the League is being run by France and England for purely imperialist purposes... [125]

The next stage in the transformation of Labour's attitude came with the outbreak of the Spanish civil war. The military uprising, led by General Franco, against the government of the Spanish republic took place on 18 July 1936; Franco was soon supported by troops from Italy and Germany. The official position of Britain and France was non-intervention. For Margaret Cole,

It was the war in Spain which completed my conversion and that of many others. [126]

Beatrice saw the implications; on 6 August, she noted the attempts by the British and the French governments to insist on neutrality. In November, she asked rhetorically

...on what side will Great Britain range herself? Or will her present governing class succeed in isolating her? That is clearly what they desire to do and no wonder. They will have the aid of the pacifists, whether saints or cowards. [127]

At the start of the new year she effectively answered her own question:

...in the tragic Spanish war, the government of Great Britain and France are for practical purposes on the side of the Fascist Franco... [128]

After the 1935 conference the Socialist League became as much concerned with international as with domestic policy. Cripps chaired the League until the summer of 1936, continuing after that to act as its leading campaigner. At the beginning of 1937 two further organisations were added: the Unity Campaign or United Front – dedicated to uniting the forces of the left against fascism – and Tribune newspaper (with William Mellor as its first editor, and the young Michael Foot and Barbara Betts (later Castle) as its reporters). Cripps was the main funder of all; in 1936 he contributed between £800 and £1000 to the League[129], leading to the charge by Hugh Dalton that it was *little more than a rich man's toy* [130]

Cripps wrote to Parmoor early in 1936, saying that the Labour leadership – Attlee and Greenwood – was *extremely unsatisfactory*:

I am busy doing meetings in the country, but I am not taking any particular part in the House of Commons... [131]

For the next three years, Stafford Cripps spoke all over the country – supporting the Spanish Republic and the United Front, and sometimes on Indian and colonial issues as well.

In February 1936 Morrison again stayed at Passfield. He said Cripps was keeping quiet; Beatrice thought

...Stafford is in the wilderness preparing an assault on the capitalist stronghold with his scratch body of followers. 'A senseless adventure', Morrison thinks'. [132]

That month, Cripps spoke in Liverpool on colonial freedom and addressed the Socialist League in Hammersmith Town Hall. On 23 February he told an audience in Battersea

Whatever happened, the workers must refuse to have any part or lot in imperialist or capitalist war. [133]

The following Wednesday, he spoke at a London reception for Nehru, the Indian Congress leader.

From July, Cripps' speeches began to cover Spain as well. In November 1936 he spoke at an Albert Hall rally of 8000 people, supporting the Spanish Medical Aid Committee; in December he sent a donation to the funds of the International Brigade.

Cripps spoke at the launch of the United Front in Manchester in January 1937. Also on the platform were Mellor, James Maxton of the ILP, and Harry

Pollitt, Secretary of the Communist Party. The United Front demanded joint action against fascism, from Labour, the ILP and the Communist Party.

The launch was followed by large United Front meetings across the country – and official disapproval from the Labour Party. In January, Labour disaffiliated the League. In March, Labour's NEC ruled that, from June, individual members of the Socialist League would no longer be eligible for Labour Party membership.

This alarmed the Webbs. Sidney wrote to Parmoor

We are perturbed about Stafford's recent action in getting the Socialist League to enter into alliance with the ILP and the Communist party in flat defiance of the Labour Party ruling. We have had no opportunity of talking it over with Stafford...I am more bewildered than ever as to what Stafford's line is... [134]

In April Sidney and Beatrice caught up with Cripps

Sidney had a long discussion with him about dissolving the Socialist League, and he agrees; but insists on the unity campaign. It remains to be seen whether the Labour Party executive accepts that compromise. If they wish to get rid of Stafford, which I think the leaders do, they will refuse it. [135]

Two days later Ivan Maisky came to Passfield Corner. Maisky cross-examined Beatrice

...as to Stafford's staying power if he were confronted with a revolutionary situation – would he not break down? [136]

Beatrice mused about Stafford's *queer immaturity of conduct and the company he keeps*:

...he has a subconscious contempt for his proletarian colleagues... [137]

Soon afterwards the leadership of the Socialist League decided to compromise, recommending that the organisation should dissolve itself. Labour's NEC then warned Labour members that anyone appearing on a platform with Communist Party members would be expelled. Cripps agreed to dissolve the National Unity Campaign Committee as well.[138] One of the speakers at the League conference in support of the decision to dissolve was Barbara Betts, who argued:

This is not a funeral, but a conscious political tactic. [139]

This kept Cripps within the Labour Party until January 1939.

'A REAL GOOD SORT': BEVERIDGE LEAVES LSE

The friendship between Sidney and Beatrice, and William Beveridge, lasted from the early 1900s until the death of both Webbs in the 1940s. This was despite disagreements; Beveridge never agreed with the Webbs about the Soviet Union.

Sidney and Beatrice saw less of Beveridge while Sidney was a minister in the second MacDonald government, although in July 1931 they stayed overnight at his Wiltshire bungalow. Beatrice did not approve of the domestic arrangements:

...Beveridge has in fact annexed the Mair family, minus the husband and father; what has happened to this unhappy man no one cares or knows. [140]

The issues at LSE remained unresolved.

In 1932 and 1933 the Webbs were preoccupied with their work on the Soviet Union. They depended on the support of Mr and Mrs Turin, who often stayed at Passfield Corner. Mr Turin – no Bolshevik – was not afraid to challenge the conclusions Sidney and Beatrice drew about the Soviet Union, while his wife talked to Beatrice about the difficulties she encountered as Beveridge's secretary. In August 1933 Lucia Turin confided in Beatrice:

She gives a deplorable account of Mrs Mair's passionate jealousy, first of one woman, then of another; treating the private secretary, from whom she asks information about Beveridge's whereabouts, sometimes as a rival, at other times as a confidant. [141]

Beatrice tried to calm her down

Treat Mrs Mair kindly and considerately, as a mentally afflicted person, over whom you have no control and for whom you are not responsible; just as something to be borne with like bad weather, or noise in the street... [142]

Beatrice worried about her own position:

...ought one, or ought one not, to condone this or that sexual irregularity in one's associates?...

Moral: – avoid gossip, as SW instinctively does, about sex relationships. [143]

When Beatrice was in a London nursing home in January 1934, Beveridge visited her. She found him *delightfully affectionate and intimate*. He appreciated all their help:

The London School of Economics opened another career and a bigger one... it was to us that he owed this new start in life as he had done his first appointment by Winston Churchill. [144]

In February Beatrice returned to Passfield, still an invalid. One evening in March Beveridge turned up

...as we were listening to the 6 o'clock news and stayed to supper. [145]

He was troubled by Marxist students and left-wing lecturers – including Harold Laski. His hostility towards Soviet communism was implacable.
But Beveridge and the Webbs remained friends:

Beveridge, in spite of his antagonism to the old Webbs' studies, is genuinely fond of us, and has promised to turn up again – we are equally attached to him – he is a real good sort, notwithstanding his ambiguous relations to Mrs Mair! [146]

Laski wrote to Beatrice about LSE: Sidney must understand that Beveridge and Mrs Mair bore a serious responsibility:

To run a place like the School on a policy of favouritism and benevolent autocracy always must result in an explosion somewhere. [147]

The situation worsened. In May 1934 Beatrice wrote

...the Beveridge-Mair entanglement has become a hot-bed of intrigue and scandal at the School. [148]

Mrs Mair's husband David moved abroad. Lucia Turin asked Beatrice for advice: Mrs Mair was asking her to spy on her boss, wanting to see his private correspondence and his bank book. Beatrice responded

Be strictly professional in your behaviour, give her nothing she has no right to, but be polite and never mention the one lover to the other. [149]

Beatrice thought the situation was unsustainable:

The plight of our old and loyal friend worries me – I don't see a way out for him – the woman has become a fury and is in control of his home and his work-place. For his own and the students' sake, Beveridge would do well to move off to other work. But no one is in a position to suggest it to him. [150]

LSE was becoming unmanageable. Beveridge was in despair about the world economy. He thought the USA was losing faith in free market capitalism; he bracketed Roosevelt with Hjalmar Schacht, Hitler's economy minister. He had little time for Keynes. At LSE he preferred the mainstream economics of Lionel Robbins to Harold Laski's socialism.

Nevertheless, despite their differences over Russia, the friendship with the Webbs endured. After a visit in September, Beatrice noted

We parted friends, each of us believing that the other will see light through the events of the next decade or two. [151]

At the beginning of January 1935, the Turins stayed at Passfield again. They brought the Webbs up to date with LSE. Beatrice thought Mrs Mair was

...rapidly developing into a veritable virago of jealousy about Beveridge. [152]

Beatrice concluded the only safe way out for Beveridge was

...for him to retire from the directorship of the School, and take Mrs Mair, whom he could not and should not desert, with him. [153]

In 1934 Beveridge had been appointed to a government role (chairing the Unemployment Insurance Statutory Committee, newly established to review the insurance system) which would give him both an excuse for leaving, and some income.

In January 1935, the Webbs had tea with Beveridge. They found him in high spirits,

...absorbed in his new job of re-moulding the insurance scheme... [154]

In the spring they disagreed publicly over Russia. Beatrice wrote a hostile review of a book critical of the Soviet Union; Beveridge responded:

B rapped an old lady on the knuckles and she retorts with a slap in the face – more in amusement than in anger. Poor Beveridge... [155]

She thought he was in a *somewhat hysterical frame of mind.*

One outcome of the tension at LSE was reform of the School's governance. The process began in 1934 with a committee to review the structure. In September 1935 Beveridge came to Passfield to discuss his own ideas. In 1936 the discussions concluded with a transfer of power from the Director to the senior teaching staff.

By then Beveridge had few allies among the staff. He tried to restrict Harold Laski's political activities – but was compromised by his own acceptance of government work. Internal change was not enough to overcome the divisions.

Harold Laski and Eileen Power (LSE Professor of Economic History) were persistent critics of Janet Mair and her role. Power stayed at Passfield in February 1936; Beatrice always found her charming. She was unhappy about LSE; she warned Beatrice that Beveridge's health was giving way,

...and his influence over the staff – largely owing to the Mair entanglement – is nil. <u>Mrs Mair must go</u> is the solution of the difficulty. (The poor lady is nearing 60) and the Governors must refuse all extensions of her term. [156]

Perhaps because of the news about Beveridge's health, Sidney and Beatrice invited him to come on holiday with them to Majorca, where Rosie Dobbs was living. The trip started badly: they went by sea, and endured a storm in the Bay of Biscay.

After Beveridge had joined them things improved. Beatrice wrote that he was *very good company* and that his presence *added to the pleasure and interest.*[157] Beveridge brought work with him: he was reading Keynes' *General Theory*, and reviewing *Soviet Communism* for the *Political Quarterly*.

Beatrice described Beveridge's attitude to Keynes' book as *somewhat contemptuous*. He was dismissive of *Soviet Communism*:

He complains there are no statistics in our book: (if there were he would say they were faked!) [158]

She criticized his approach, saying he had contempt for other experts, and lacked substance. Nevertheless, they liked him:

Beveridge is kindly, amusing, and very clever. To those whom he likes personally and even to those he meets casually he is a charming companion. But to those he directs, but who regard themselves as colleagues and not as subordinates, he is tactless. [159]

But friendship was no longer enough to keep Beveridge in post. In summer 1936, as Janet Mair approached the retirement age of 60, she requested an extension of her contract. Staff on left and right united in opposition. She wrote to Beveridge

My heart is nearly broken by the thought of the intrigue against me. [160]

The LSE governors were now chaired by Josiah Stamp, former LSE student and businessman. In July Stamp stayed with the Webbs. He told them there was a violent upheaval among the academic staff

against the Beveridge-Mair directorship or, as they style it, dictatorship. [161]

Stamp told the Webbs that government inspectors, and American donors, objected to the continued involvement of Mrs Mair.
Sidney and Beatrice agreed that

…the crisis must be ended, and Mrs Mair must go…So we encouraged Stamp to refuse to extend Mrs Mair's term of office. [162]

A few days later, Beatrice saw Mrs Mair

...she seemed to me ill and rather mad, talked hysterically about Beveridge's greatness... [163]

Stamp's visit to Passfield did not resolve matters. Late in 1936, Beveridge asked a subgroup of the LSE governors, to extend Mrs Mair's contract for five years. Backed by Sidney, the governors refused.

On New Year's Eve, Beveridge turned up at Passfield:

He and Sidney had a long interview during which Sidney spoke of the 'impossible situation' at the School. Beveridge said he had never heard of the 'scandal'!!! But he looked tragic after the interview... [164]

Sidney said Beveridge should persuade Mrs Mair to resign, with an agreed period of absence. This formed the basis for a solution in the New Year: Mrs Mair was retained for a year, followed by a year's paid leave.

This was eased by Beveridge's election as Master of University College Oxford; Beveridge was first approached in February 1937, and resigned from LSE in May. The College economics fellow was GDH Cole. Beveridge and Cole had not previously been close. Beatrice thought that Beveridge had turned Cole down for a lectureship at LSE, and they had been antagonists when Beveridge was at the Ministry of Munitions during the war. Now, however, Beatrice believed

...it was Cole as Fellow of the College, who got Beveridge made master of University College. [165]

The new Director of LSE was Alexander Carr-Saunders, another Toynbee Hall alumnus. In May 1937, while Sidney was busy with the appointment, Beatrice lunched with Beveridge, who

...was in splendid spirits about his new life as head of University College and had not the remotest resentment at our intervention at Christmas... [166]

By the time Beveridge left LSE, according to Sidney, he sat alone in the staff restaurant at lunchtimes, boycotted by other staff.

Beatrice worried about how Beveridge (and Mrs Mair) would be received in Oxford. Mrs Mair's reputation preceded her; it was rumoured that the Fellows of University College had stipulated that the new Master should not bring her to Oxford. [167]

Poor Beveridge: he has always been so kind to the old Webbs, and he is so able and disinterested, if only he had better manners. [168]

Chapter Thirteen The last years 1937-1947

AGEING

Beatrice was eighty in January 1938, Sidney in July 1939. Anticipating these dates, the Webbs gave a party at Passfield for over a hundred family members and others on Saturday 12 June 1937. The invitation stated that the Webbs were *on the threshold of their ninth decade*. The party was for descendants of Richard and Laurencina Potter and their spouses ...*to the third and fourth generations*.

A few non family guests were invited. One was Beveridge, who later recalled Beatrice's

> ...*pride and interest in her nephews and nieces and great nephews and nieces.*
> 169

GBS and Charlotte were there; so were two of Sidney's fellow Labour peers, Arthur Ponsonby, and Harry Snell. Sidney and Beatrice had known Snell since the 1890s; he had lectured for the Hutchinson Trust, and had been the first administrator at the LSE. Beatrice found him

> ...*too much of the saint and too little of the self-assertive intellectual, too dull, self-absorbed and unassuming.* 170

She thought Harry – a non-smoking, celibate, total abstainer – would have been a holy monk in earlier times.

The weather was perfect; they served tea and cakes and sherry (and cigarettes). The work was done by Beatrice's two maids, Jean and Annie; Jessie, her former servant from Grosvenor Road (forgiven, presumably, after her departure in disgrace); and her secretary, Gabrielle Irwin. Beatrice doubted whether they would ever run another party on such a scale – and they did not. But she was pleased and proud to have done it.

During the day, greeting messages arrived from Richard Potter's old firm, Price Potter & Co of Gloucester, and from the Soviet Embassy:

> ...*a very old association and a very new one, curiously representative of the old and new civilization, British capitalism and Soviet Communism.* 171

Now only Beatrice and Rosie remained of the Potter sisters. Beatrice's main interest was the lives of the children:

...it pleased me to think how the seven sisters would have loved to be there and watch their descendants eagerly talking and laughing together. Dear old father, how delighted he would have been at the thought of the successful careers of many of his descendants and their spouses. Three peers, four privy councillors, two cabinet ministers, two baronets and two FRS – a typical XIXth and XXth upper middle class family, rising in the government of the country. [172]

In the months before the party, Sidney worked on the introduction to the new edition of *Soviet Communism*; Beatrice's main preoccupation in 1937 was her second autobiographical volume, *Our Partnership*.

But that spring she did no work on the book. Their library was in chaos:

...the books had overflown onto tables and chairs so that those I sought were hopelessly out of sight – whilst those we did not want, were piling up in front. [173]

Beatrice worked with Gabrielle Irwin, weeding out duplicates and unwanted items; some went to LSE; some were pressed on party guests on 12 June.

On Beatrice's actual 80th birthday, 22 January 1938, there was an article by GBS in the *Spectator*, one by H G Wells in the *New Statesman*, and pieces in other papers. Flowers arrived at the house; in the afternoon the Ponsonbys organised a concert at Shulbrede Priory. Beatrice was content:

What strikes the Webbs about their own career is that we have had a precious good time of it. [174]

Before Christmas 1937 there had been warning signs about Sidney's health. He could not walk far without severe pain in his leg. But a new doctor, Dr Gray, had said that all would be well with treatment, and when the warmer weather came.

The problems continued into the new year. Beatrice had to walk on her own while Sidney rested. The Monday after Beatrice's birthday, Sidney was fit enough to walk two miles. The following morning, however

...when I knocked at his door at 6.30, his voice sounded queerly grim...after he had gulped down his tea there was silence, with a twitching of the hand. He insisted on getting up for his breakfast downstairs, but when I joined him he was again silent and when he tried to answer me his answers were difficult to understand. [175]

Dr Gray came: it was a stroke: a clot in the arteries on one side of the brain. Sidney tried to speak – occasionally he could manage a 'yes' or a 'no', but mostly just silence and frustration.

I have been here before thought Beatrice: her mind went back to the long months of waiting and caring, after Richard Potter's stroke in November 1885. She thought it was the end of the Webb partnership.

Beatrice told GBS what had happened. He wrote back:

> ...*Sidney has given us rather a fright. We are the only members of the old gang left; and we shouldn't do such things...*
> *The alarm is over: if Sidney can talk he is all right. I sleep a lot now in the daytime: make him do the same.* [176]

On 11 February, she noted Dr Gray's cautious advice:

> ...*unless he gets worse, he will undoubtedly get better and might even return to normality, but on a low level of achievement.* [177]

Next day Beatrice recorded that Sidney's speech was coming back. But she feared it would be a long time before he could manage without constant care. They would have to employ another person – could they find someone suitable? What skills would be needed?

Sidney's recovery was partial. His memory and concentration were limited; he did not attempt to work again. He read a lot; he subscribed to the Times Book Club, and had parcels of books sent from the London Library. Sometimes Beatrice would read to him, or they would listen to music on the radio together. After a month she tried her first day trip to London, to see the Shaws.

In spring 1938 they went to Eastbourne for a month. They walked; friends visited them. Sidney enjoyed the change. While they were there Beatrice recruited a new *nurse attendant*: Mrs Grant, a *stalwart scotch woman...*with a *breezy personality* – Beatrice wondered how she would fit in with the existing household.

By the summer Sidney was able to join in when visitors came – though he was often exhausted. When Beveridge visited in August, Sidney

> ...*listened, but was depressed with his own tiredness and inability to argue. He and Beveridge found little to talk about.* [178]

On Sunday 30 October, the Maiskys spent five hours at Passfield Corner; Beatrice and Ivan talked *incessantly*, with interventions from Agniya and Sidney. Maisky noted in his diary the extent to which Sidney had recovered from his stroke.

In November there was a crisis over Sidney's care: Annie, one of the two maids, exploded at Mrs Grant. Beatrice worried that Jean and Annie

> ...*were not suited to a household with a permanent invalid and a third servant to look after him... British women are no longer suited to domestic service in private houses, especially in the country.* [179]

She feared the old fashioned upper middle-class home was no longer viable.

In December 1938 Beatrice reviewed the year. Their partnership, though less active, survived. Sidney was not in pain. He was reading widely – novels, history, and biographies. In January he explained to Edward Pease

A year ago I was attacked by what was called a seizure. This has destroyed all my capacity for inventing anything, and also my power of writing. My life is now a happy contentment in reading books of every kind, and in remembering other things, but without any capacity for using either invention or discovery in any new enterprise. [180]

In May 1939 they went to Cornwall. Beatrice climbed in and out of little coves and rocks, while Mrs Grant took Sidney for walks on the beach.

That July Sidney celebrated his eightieth birthday; Beatrice reported that he was

…happy and peaceful, pleased with his past life of successful adventure in public administration and the writing of books… [181]

When Beatrice went for a walk, Sidney would go for a shorter one, Mrs Grant carrying a stool for him to rest.

'ONE MAN DISGUISED AS A COMMITTEE': BEVERIDGE AFTER 1937

Although Sidney and Beatrice had helped to ease Beveridge out of LSE, their friendship continued. In August 1938 Beveridge stayed at Passfield again:

Beveridge here, thoroughly enjoying his new life as Master of University College, Oxford; an easy job, within a cultured and well-mannered group; dignity and prestige, without any particular responsibility or hard work. [182]

At LSE Beveridge had always intended to get back to research; at Oxford he succeeded in doing so, aiming to write a sequel to his pre-war publication *Unemployment – a Problem of Industry*. To help him he recruited a *first-rate research student* [183] – Harold Wilson, who had graduated that summer with an outstanding first.

Wilson found Beveridge difficult, later referring to his

…arrogance and rudeness to those appointed to work with him and his total inability to delegate. [184]

Beveridge reminded Beatrice that it was 31 years since she and Sidney had coached him before his evidence to the Poor Law Commission;

Ever since that time we have been loyal friends to each other; and certainly, his attitude to the old Webbs has been extraordinarily kind and appreciative; ideal good manners which in other relationships he has lacked. [185]

That weekend, eighty year old Beatrice went on two three mile walks with Beveridge, discussing unemployment; he, as ever, argued for lower wages. Sidney, after his stroke, could only listen as Beveridge and Beatrice argued.

While the Webbs never converted Beveridge to their views on the Soviet Union, he did believe in a strong, executive state; he was at least influenced by their work on economic planning.

As the threat of war grew, Beveridge urged government to make plans. He wanted a job organising the home front; he was considered, but rejected, for some Whitehall opportunities. In Autumn 1938, he became ill with a viral infection, which lasted for months. Beatrice sent good wishes in November, inviting him back to Passfield –

…ever since I have known you, you have had bouts of serious illness, and always returned to the scene with increased health, and a capacity for work. [186]

Janet Mair's daughter had been living in the Master's Lodgings, acting as housekeeper; then, when Beveridge fell ill, Mrs Mair moved in. She then broke her leg and stayed.

When war came Beveridge was even more determined to return to government service. From September 1939 he joined Keynes and others of their generation who had worked in Whitehall during the First World War and hoped to do so again. They met once a week at Keynes' Bloomsbury home, calling themselves the Old Dogs. It was the beginning of a rapprochement between Beveridge and Keynes.

At first, government was slow to accept help from the Old Dogs; it was only after Churchill replaced Chamberlain as Prime Minister in May 1940 that they began to be reabsorbed.

Beveridge wrote to Churchill, and to the Labour Ministers, offering his services. It still took time; but by the end of June Beveridge was back in Whitehall as Commissioner responsible for a manpower survey, reporting to Ernest Bevin, now Minister of Labour. Friends saw the appointment as significant; Beveridge was more cautious

I knew that it was nothing of the sort. But it kept me in the field where I wanted to be. [187]

The survey was carried out quickly, using volunteers. One of them was Douglas

Cole, who in turn involved Margaret. She ran the London end of the survey from the Fabian offices. In her report, she

...seized on everything that had gone wrong – all the waste, all the muddle, and all the stark foolishness, of which there was a great deal to be found. [188]

Another researcher recruited by the Coles was GBS, now aged eighty two. On 18 July he wrote to Beatrice

We are extremely busy here helping Douglas with his Man Power Survey... The state of things disclosed so far even you would think hardly credible. [189]

In August Beveridge came to lunch at Passfield. Beatrice had been warned in advance that he was sad and depressed. His role was purely advisory, not administrative. He had no paid staff and no authority. He had contempt for Bevin. Beatrice wrote

Poor Beveridge was in a state of collapse. I have never seen him so despondent about public affairs, so depressed about his own part in bettering them. [190]

Beveridge stayed at the Ministry of Labour until June 1941; from December 1940 he was a full-time civil servant. His relationships with Bevin, and with civil servants, were poor. Bevin associated Beveridge with policies of industrial compulsion.

In May 1941 Kingsley Martin spent a day with the Webbs. He told Beatrice that Beveridge, who was still depressed, thought Bevin was

...entirely in the hands of the reactionary civil servants. [191]

Beveridge had hoped to be made Director General of Manpower in the Ministry of Labour – but in June 1941 Bevin appointed another candidate.

Another opportunity appeared. On 10 June, Arthur Greenwood announced that Beveridge would chair a committee to undertake a comprehensive survey of social insurance and allied services. According to Beveridge's biographer:

Ernest Bevin, however, was by now determined to remove Beveridge from the Ministry of Labour... The social insurance inquiry had originally been opposed by Ernest Bevin, but he changed his mind when he saw that it was a chance of ridding himself of Beveridge. [192]

Beveridge was in tears. He was sure that he had been kicked upstairs.

Greenwood, the former Leeds organiser for the campaign against the Poor Law, was now Minister without Portfolio, responsible for reconstruction. Molly Hamilton – another veteran of the Poor Law campaign, and the Webbs' first biographer – had been a Labour MP, and was now a civil servant, reporting to

Greenwood. Beatrice's opinion of Greenwood had gone steadily down. Earlier in 1941 William Robson, visiting the Webbs, had told them

Greenwood, with Mary Hamilton as his assistant, is a hopeless failure as Minister for reconstruction… [193]

Elsewhere in the same diary entry Beatrice dismisses him as *drunken Greenwood.*

Ostensibly, Beveridge's role was to chair a committee of civil servants. Hamilton was a member of that Committee; she had known Beveridge since before 1914. Beveridge's biographer wrote that committee members found that

…in order to persuade Beveridge to listen to their views it was useful to get them put forward by Mrs Hamilton. [194]

In February 1942, the role of the civil servants on the Committee was redefined: they became advisers, rather than full members (and therefore signatories). This change was approved by Greenwood just before leaving his post. In his autobiography, Beveridge described the approach as *one man disguised as a committee.*[195]

The Committee took evidence between summer 1941 and November 1942. Beveridge – determined not to take a narrow view of his task – also wrote substantial papers.

In autumn 1942 rumours circulated about the contents of Beveridge's report. Stafford Cripps, by now Leader of the House of Commons, lunched at Passfield on 26 October. He told the Webbs that he believed in the projects of Keynes and Beveridge, and said the Beveridge report was *a great work.* Cripps told them publication of the report

…has been postponed…as some of the cabinet object to it as revolutionary. [196]

The report was finally published on 6 December. In it, Beveridge wrote:

A revolutionary moment in the world's history is a time for revolutions, not for patching. [197]

The Beveridge Report identifies five giants on the road to reconstruction: want; disease; ignorance; squalor; and ignorance.

The Report received a warm reception from the public – and even, after some hesitation, from the government. Beatrice was less enthusiastic. Certainly, the Report was

…a bomb thrown into the political arena; which will hit the Tories and Liberals who want to go back to the status quo of capitalist civilization. [198]

She acknowledged, too, that it was

...a striking testimony to Beveridge's outstanding capacity for invention and argument. [199]

But she expressed two deep policy disagreements.

The first was her old objection to National Insurance. After the report of the Poor Law Commission, Beatrice had opposed the unconditional nature of insurance benefits:

The better you treat the unemployed in the way of income, without service, the worse the evil becomes; because it is pleasanter to do nothing, than to work on low wages and in bad conditions... [200]

The second disagreement was fundamental: in the 1920s and 1930s, Beatrice had come to believe that unemployment could not be cured under capitalism. In the last months of her life she expressed that conclusion forcefully, in letters to friends, in *Cooperative News* and in her diary:

Beveridge himself calls it a revolution – though a peaceful one. But it is based on what seems to me a radically false hypothesis: the <u>continued existence of the capitalist and landlord as the ruling class</u>. [201]

Few agreed with Beatrice. Beveridge, aged 63, not previously a public figure, became an overnight celebrity. Two days after the Report's publication there was a public meeting in support in Oxford. Beatrice noted that

...the extraordinary applause of the audience of some 2000 and of crowds outside has added to his reputation... [202]

The following week Beveridge finally married Janet Mair, whose estranged husband had died that summer. The civil wedding, at Caxton Hall, Westminster, was followed by a blessing by William Temple – Beveridge's Oxford contemporary and friend, now Archbishop of Canterbury.

Maisky was there; Beatrice was invited but couldn't go. She wrote to Tawney, Beveridge's brother in law

I see that Mrs Tawney signed the register of Beveridge's marriage to that remarkable woman – his life-long companion for twenty years. I had the most friendly letter from him inviting me to the wedding – and I replied with sincere congratulations – it is good that that episode is closed. [203]

In Oxford Mrs Mair had rapidly become as unpopular with academic and domestic staff as she had been at LSE. On the evening of the wedding, the Beveridges returned to Oxford. As they stood on a balcony overlooking the

Master's Garden, students serenaded them with a chorus of

The old grey mare, she ain't what she used to be

Ain't what she used to be

According to the College archivist

It appears that the happy couple either could not or would not hear the words,
and merely waved benignly at the performers. [204]

Beatrice reflected on what had happened: Beveridge had had a great personal triumph:

It is a queer result of this strange and horrible war that Beveridge, whose career
as a civil servant and as Director of the School of Economics was more or less a
failure, should have risen suddenly into the limelight, as an accepted designer of
a New World Order. I wonder whether he will see my criticism of the Report. If
so whether we shall see the Beveridges again. I doubt it! [205]

They did not meet again before Beatrice's death in April. Early in the new year the Maiskys were back at Passfield; they had dined with the Beveridges and brought greetings.

Learning from the experience of the Minority Report, Beveridge and Cole quickly established a campaigning organisation, the Social Security League, to press for the Report's full, early implementation. As well as the Coles, the League's Council included Eva Hubback, a veteran of the Poor Law campaign, now Principal of Morley College. Other members included William Robson, and the new Lady Beveridge. Barbara Wootton chaired the Council; in autumn 1943 Beveridge became President. In 1943 and 1944, Beveridge barnstormed the country in support in support of the Report.[206]

Riding a wave of popularity, in October 1944 Beveridge was elected Liberal MP for Berwick on Tweed. The following year he was defeated at the general election. But his short period in parliament lasted long enough for the Fellows of University College to declare that service as an MP was incompatible with his role as Master, and to force his resignation.

When Beveridge joined LSE in 1919, Sidney had agreed that

...the tenure of the post would not exclude my becoming a candidate or
Member of Parliament... [207]

No similar assurance had been given by University College; his sponsor, Cole, whose home had been bombed, was away; so his fate was sealed.

He became Lord Beveridge; for five years he chaired the board of Newton

Aycliffe New Town; and he chaired an enquiry into broadcasting. But he played no part in implementing his Report. Lady Beveridge died in 1959, so they had over fifteen years of married life. Beveridge himself lived on until 1963.

Beveridge always acknowledged his long friendship with Sidney and Beatrice. He compared them to Samuel and Henrietta Barnett:

Each was a childless pair; in each pair the wife often appeared dominant but the spade work was done by the husband; in each pair the wife possessed means, giving both leisure from earning a living and easy access to the wielders of power... [208]

In a paper marking the Webbs' centenary, Beveridge wrote

To my mind they are among the dozen most important people of the past hundred years. I say this although I did not share their political opinions at any time. [209]

He thought the establishment of the LSE was their *greatest single contribution made to humanity.*[210]

Beveridge's report, as implemented by the 1945 Labour government, established the framework for the post war welfare state. Some historians see this as a belated victory for the Webbs. In 1965 AJP Taylor wrote that the Beveridge Report

...fulfilled at last the Fabian plans laid down by the Webbs before the first World war. [211]

Peter Hennessy has written that the 1946 National Insurance Act was

...the embodiment of the idea of a 'national minimum standard' so cherished by the Webbs... [212]

Some aspects of the post 1945 settlement can be traced directly to the Minority Report. It rejected the idea of separate services for poor people, and proposed a National Health Service (an enduring element of the settlement) for the first time. The 1948 National Assistance Act, in its first clause, finally completed the work of the Royal Commission:

The existing poor law shall cease to have effect... [213]

But Beveridge's conclusions do not flow directly from the Minority Report, and in important respects contradict it. The insurance principle, which the Webbs opposed between 1910 and 1912, was at the heart of Beveridge's scheme; in 1942 and 1943 Beatrice continued to oppose insurance.

Sidney and Beatrice's real achievement was two-fold. First, they identified, supported, and encouraged a network of people who would research, campaign for, and ultimately implement anti-poverty policies. In effect, they mentored William Beveridge for 35 years – coaching him before his Royal Commission evidence, publicizing his ideas, introducing him to Churchill, appointing him to LSE, and supporting him while he was there. Beveridge and the Webbs disagreed on many things – but their friendship endured.

They did the same for others, drawn from the Fabian Society, the settlement movement and elsewhere – employing them, writing references, advising them, and listening to them.

Second, the Minority Report prepared the ground for future public debate. The support the Webbs mobilised in the years before the First World War moved the issues of poverty, public health, and social policy to the heart of the political agenda.

THE WEBBS AND THE SHAWS

The Shaws stayed at Passfield before the June 1937 party. They were older, and more fragile, than Sidney and Beatrice. In fact, GBS outlived both Webbs; but that week Beatrice thought him

...visibly frail and in decline...[214]

Sidney had known Shaw nearly sixty years; the couples had been friends since the 1890s. In 1935, Beatrice had noted that they were

...each other's oldest friends, and we all dread the death of any one of the quartet and would feel responsible for the remaining partner. [215]

Up to the mid-1930s they visited each other's homes regularly; this became difficult after Sidney's stroke. They met less often, exchanging letters and postcards instead.

After staying at Ayot St Lawrence in October 1936, Beatrice wondered if they would meet again:

Staying in friends' houses does not suit my infirmities and I feel a wreck after four days talking, and eating or not eating unsuitable food. However better wear out than rust out! [216]

They did meet again, in October 1937; Charlotte's health was alright, but she was becoming deaf; GBS was

...looking frail, with uncertainty in his glance and gait...[217]

Then came Sidney's stroke; now, only Beatrice could get away to visit friends.

In June 1938 she saw the Shaws in London; GBS had been persuaded to have insulin injections to deal with pernicious anaemia. Despite his health, Shaw,

> ...was full of wit and delighted to see his old friend. [218]

For the first time in their acquaintance Beatrice kissed him.

In November Beatrice lunched with the Shaws during a visit to London; afterwards, Charlotte wrote it had been

> ...the most interesting time we have had for many months. It was grand to find you so strong and brilliant. [219]

Seeing the Shaws again in the new year, Beatrice wondered

> How long shall we four old friends linger on the stage? [220]

Beatrice's visits continued in the spring and summer of 1939; after the outbreak of war in September they do not seem to have met for the rest of the year, simply exchanging letters.

After his stroke Sidney rarely left Passfield. By 1940 he was missing Shaw, so they met in May:

> ...we drove up to lunch with the Shaws at Whitehall Court. Sidney insisted on doing so: he had not seen them for two and a half years and wanted badly to see them 'once again'... They were delightfully affectionate. [221]

Afterwards GBS wrote to Beatrice; he took a light view of the harm done by Sidney's stroke:

> We were delighted to find that Sidney's mind is still in full blast, in spite of some negligible damage which will probably vanish by absorption. [222]

That was the last time they met in person: afterwards, they only communicated by post. Although London suffered the worst of the blitz, the war in the air did touch Passfield and Ayot. Beatrice went to London only occasionally; Sidney did not go at all. Over the winter of 1940/41 neither did GBS or Charlotte.

Before the war, the Shaws had spent part of each week at Ayot, part in London; they kept to this pattern for the first year of the war. In September 1940, at Ayot, Charlotte had a bad fall; she was bedridden for several months. In February 1941 GBS wrote to Beatrice

> Up to the middle of November we had a searchlight here and were consequently under fire. After a grand bombardment in which we had 8 High Explosive Bombs in the village (one in the next garden) and incendiaries ad lib, the

searchlight was taken away; we ceased to be a military objective; and now we see and hear the raids on London... [223]

At the end of April Shaw and his secretary, Blanche Patch, spent a day in London. Afterwards Blanche wrote to Beatrice; Charlotte was still in a bad way

I don't tell them, but I have my doubts as to whether Mrs S is likely to get much better. Her whole body is very bent and altered with this arthritis... [224]

As for GBS, however, he was

...really pretty well, but I think misses seeing people and some days lives in a kind of dream. [225]

Letters continued in 1941 – GBS commented on drafts by Beatrice; they wrote about the progress of the war. And there was news of Sidney

...happy and content and reads incessantly – and enjoys seeing the stream of nephews and nieces and old friends who come to tea here every day or two. [226]

In February 1942 Sidney and Beatrice saw the new film of Shaw's *Major Barbara* – they had seen the play, with Arthur Balfour, in November 1905. Beatrice found the film topical. The final scene was

...extraordinarily expressive of the brutal power of mass murder in modern war. [227]

They wanted to meet; in March, Beatrice wrote that

...with the petrol ration and the unpleasant weather it is difficult for us to get to London...I suppose it would be impossible for you to come for a night, (we have a small bedroom) and see Sidney once again as he would love to see you. [228]

It was impossible; Charlotte had another six weeks in bed; in late May she was just able to take a brief turn in the garden.
Blanche told Beatrice that

...Charlotte becomes more and more fractious. 'All doctors are fools' she asserts. To which the answer is 'You can't cure old age.' [229]

Talk of visiting ceased; the number of letters reduced. Beatrice thought she and Sidney had better conditions than the Shaws:

...poor Charlotte Shaw has to endure the absence of adequate help and a rationing of food which she declares is a conspiracy of the shopkeepers to starve her to death. [230]

When Beatrice died at the end of April 1943, Shaw did not tell Charlotte; he feared it would just add to her anxieties. Charlotte herself died in November 1943.

After Beatrice's death, Shaw was approached to write an obituary. He declined. As he explained to Sidney:

...I could not write funereally about her; for, as we were all young together and never thought of ourselves as great people, I felt that those of a later generation would see her in her true perspective... [231]

IVAN AND AGNIYA MAISKY

The Webbs' friendship with the Maiskys continued after the publication of *Soviet Communism*. He was the Soviet Union's London ambassador from 1932 to 1943; his predecessor, Sokolnikov, had been recalled after three years. The only other Soviet ambassador to last as long was Alexandra Kollontai, the veteran Bolshevik feminist, ambassador to Stockholm.

Maisky kept a detailed diary at a time when most Soviet diplomats were afraid to express their thoughts in writing. Such fears were well founded: in 1937 Sokolnikov was convicted of conspiring to overthrow the Soviet government. He escaped the death penalty, and was sentenced to ten years imprisonment. Beatrice wrote that in the USSR this meant

...useful work with adequate detention in some district where they cannot escape. [232]

In fact, Sokolnikov was killed in prison in 1939, probably by the NKVD.

Sokolnikov had encouraged the Webbs to visit Russia. Before hearing of his death, Beatrice wrote that she and Sidney

...had a friendly feeling for Sokolnikov and his wife, who had stayed here more than once; it was a horrible thought that he might be shot at dawn. [233]

Maisky told Beatrice he had known Sokolnikov slightly, and that he had been

...a recalcitrant objector to Stalin's policy of socialism in one country ... [234]

Sokolnikov was not the only victim of the purges known to the Webbs: Rose Cohen had worked in the Fabian Research Department, later joining the Communist Party. She married a Russian and went to live in Russia. Rose and her husband were arrested; she was shot in November 1937.

When Maisky stayed at Passfield in December 1937, Beatrice raised Rose's case:

Of course he is reserved about the arrests and rumours of arrests; justifies some, denies the fact of others. Rose Cohen, who is said to have been arrested is now in London... [235]

But she wasn't in London. She had been dead for a fortnight. In a note added to the diary in April 1938, Beatrice said that Maisky *must have been mistaken* as Rose Cohen's arrest and detention were now acknowledged by Moscow.

And in August 1938, when the Maiskys were at Passfield again,

He knew nothing about Rose Cohen and quite clearly had refused to enquire. [236]

Maisky's own revolutionary past had been as a Menshevik; but he had made his peace with Stalin. He was not going to expose himself to the same risks as Sokolnikov. Beatrice, in working with Maisky, was working with Stalin's man in London. She could, and did, worry about the trials and the purges: her anguish remained private.

As London ambassador, Maisky developed a new way of working. The Webbs had never seen anything like it. He was the first ambassador who

...deliberately and incessantly cultivated the representatives of the people – journalists, Trade Union and Cooperative officials, Labour MPs and any intellectuals who are left wing and willing to know him. [237]

Maisky's contacts were not restricted to the left. In his own diary, Maisky left an account of working with parliament, the civil service, and the press:

...you must meet the person more or less regularly, invite him to breakfast or dinner, take him to the theatre from time to time, go when necessary to the wedding of his son or daughter, wish him many happy returns on his birthday, sympathize with him when he is ill. [238]

The Webbs, however, were not just 'embassy contacts'. Beatrice thought she and Sidney were

'the most trusted of friends' of the USSR in Great Britain. [239]

They were more than that; they became personal friends as well. The Webbs and the Maiskys met frequently in London or at Passfield. Maisky described Passfield as a

...serene but thoughtful spot. A simple but comfortable and cosy country house. Fields, hills and small groves all around. Close by is a small village hotel, once a shady inn which served for centuries as a smugglers' den. There is nothing luxurious, nothing redundant in the house itself, but there are plenty of books, files, manuscripts... [240]

In April 1937 they stayed at Passfield for a weekend. Maisky asked Beatrice for advice: should the embassy organize an Albert Hall rally to support the 20th anniversary of the Bolshevik revolution. She advised against:

Do you think the British public would tolerate an Albert Hall meeting to commemorate the advent to power of Hitler – or even of Mussolini? To some of our countrymen Lenin and Stalin are just as hateful as Hitler, Mussolini and the others. [241]

In July 1937, the Maiskys spent a day at Passfield; Beatrice recorded her impressions

He is an honest able and hard working little man, but strikingly unattractive in body, voice and manner...Maisky and his wife are, I think, genuine Marxists: he an intellectual who accepts Marxism as the gospel of science; she a fanatic who regards the Marxian theory, in all its details, as an article of faith separating the righteous from the damned. [242]

After another visit in autumn 1938, Maisky noted

Beatrice carries herself wonderfully for her 80 years – fresh and hale and hearty. Incidentally they both complain about 'getting old' and tiring. 'Pull the other one! What I'd do to be like them at 80!' [243]

APPEASEMENT AND THE NAZI-SOVIET PACT 1937-1939

The 1935 Labour Conference had voted for League of Nations sanctions to be imposed on Italy, following the Italian invasion of Abyssinia; the vote ended Lansbury's leadership. But the British, French, and other governments in the League did not deliver the sanctions, revealing the League as toothless and ineffective.

The League was a Labour, and a Fabian, policy. Its origins could, in part, be traced back to the work on international government and the prevention of war that the Webbs had commissioned from Leonard Woolf in 1914, and to Labour's *Statement of War Aims*. Up to 1935 Woolf believed that Labour, and British, international policy should be based on support for the League. By 1935 he had become convinced that the British and French governments

...had finally destroyed the League as an instrument for deterring aggression and preventing war...the League was to all intents and purposes dead and it was fatal to go on using it as a mumbled incantation against war. [244]

Woolf – who still chaired Labour's International and Imperial Advisory Committee – argued that the new situation required a new policy. Hitler could only be deterred, and war prevented, if Britain and France united with other governments,

> ...*including the USSR if possible, who would be prepared to guarantee the small powers against attack by Hitler.* [245]

Such a new policy would require serious rearmament.

Sidney and Beatrice were no longer involved in day-to-day Westminster politics. But they retained a wide range of contacts, and were particularly close to Maisky and Cripps.

Their approach to international affairs in the late 1930s was shaped by three factors.

They wanted soviet communism to succeed. They were aware of its weaknesses: the denial of liberty, the trials; nevertheless, they believed that a new civilisation was being created.

In Britain, they continued to back the Labour Party. They had no time for the Communist Party of Great Britain – in part, at least, because of its subservience to the Third International.

And they were opposed to Nazi Germany; opposed both to Hitler's internal policies, and to the appeasement of Germany by the British government. Sidney and Beatrice understood the nature of the Hitler regime from the start; shortly after Hitler came to power in March 1933, Beatrice noted the ferocious persecution of the Jews.

The Webbs were increasingly out of sympathy with the residual pacifist strand in the Labour Party: Lansbury, no longer Labour leader, travelled widely, pleading for peace. In April 1937 he met and talked to Hitler. Sidney and Beatrice knew Lord (Sydney) Arnold, a former Liberal who had served as a minister in both MacDonald's Labour governments and had for a time rented the bungalow at Passfield Corner. In 1937 Beatrice described him as

> ...*a violent isolationist ...a liberal pacifist, pure and simple.* [246]

The following year, she thought him

> ...*anti-interventionalist, almost Germanophil, and very contemptuous of the Labour Party.* [247]

Ponsonby, the former Labour Leader in the Lords, remained a pacifist: in May 1939 Beatrice wrote that Ponsonby

...would like to keep out of all commitments which might end in war, by giving way rather than fighting. [248]

Beatrice saw the division in the Labour Party as between:

...pacifist isolationists versus pro-soviet-antagonism to German aggression. [249]

But not all opponents of German aggression were pro Soviet.

Before the 1935 general election, MacDonald had been replaced as Prime Minister by the Conservative Stanley Baldwin. In May 1937, Baldwin in turn retired; his successor was Neville Chamberlain, younger son of Joseph. In December 1935 Anthony Eden, aged 38, became Foreign Secretary in Baldwin's government, remaining in post when Chamberlain took over. Chamberlain's background was in domestic politics; he mistrusted the Foreign Office. As his main adviser, Chamberlain retained Horace Wilson, formerly of the Ministry of Labour, for whom Beatrice had a deep dislike. In 1930 Wilson had been right hand man to J H Thomas in the search for a policy on unemployment; Beatrice called Wilson

...one of the most reactionary of officials... [250]

Chamberlain, by contrast, thought Wilson

...the most remarkable man in England. I couldn't live a day without him. [251]

Britain did rearm under Chamberlain,. But the core of Chamberlain's foreign policy was appeasement: avoiding war by negotiating with, and making concessions to, Italy and Germany. Churchill summed up Chamberlain's position in his memoirs:

The Prime Minister wished to get on good terms with the two European Dictators, and believed that conciliation and the avoidance of anything likely to offend them was the best method. [252]

Like Leonard Woolf, the Webbs thought that Britain and France should cooperate with the Soviet Union in order to confront Hitler's Germany. Maisky's instructions, until August 1939, were to pursue that objective.

The rise of the dictators, and the politics of appeasement, produced different reactions within the Webb network. Shortly after Hitler came to power, William Beveridge and others at LSE launched the Academic Assistance Council, to support refugee scientists and scholars.

Thomas Jones, on the other hand, became close to the appeasers. In 1934 he wrote to a friend in the United States

...rightly or wrongly, all sorts of people who have met Hitler are convinced he is a factor for peace. [253]

TJ had retired from the civil service in 1930; he still saw Baldwin, but was also on friendly terms with the Webbs. When Jones had stayed at Passfield in February 1933, just before Hitler came to power, Beatrice had noted his connections to various political networks – among them the 'Astor-Lothian set'. This grouping, around the Conservative MP Nancy Astor and Philip Kerr, Marquess of Lothian, became one of the main centres of support for appeasement. It was also known as the 'Cliveden Set', after the Astors' Thameside country home. Other members included James Louis Garvin, editor of the *Observer* (owned by Nancy Astor's husband Waldorf) and Geoffrey Dawson, editor of the Times, (part-owned by Waldorf Astor's brother). Dawson was one of several leading appeasers to be fellows of All Souls College, Oxford.

TJ facilitated their activities; he got to know Ribbentrop, from 1936 German ambassador in London. In May 1936 TJ spent a weekend with Ribbentrop in Germany. Ribbentrop asked him

...to go to and fro between him and Mr Baldwin in confidence... [254]

Jones and Ribbentrop then had an hour and a half's conversation with Hitler, who

...urged the importance of an alliance with England, and his great desire to meet Mr Baldwin. [255]

He tried to arrange for Baldwin to meet Hitler. This never happened, but in September 1936 TJ went with Lloyd George for tea with Hitler at Berchtesgaden.

AL Rowse encountered TJ at All Souls, where he was a frequent visitor, describing him as

...a great busybody and contacts man. [256]

Rowse thought TJ was doing Ribbentrop's dirty work.

TJ enthusiastically recounted Lloyd George's meeting with Hitler to Charlotte Shaw; when Charlotte saw the Webbs, she was *glowing* over TJ's *brilliant description* of the visit. This marked the end of the Webbs' long relationship with TJ: Beatrice concluded that Lloyd George and his *little Welsh admirer* were *past numbers on the political scene*. Jones, she wrote, was

...a melancholy instance of a good man with considerable intelligence being gradually but surely transformed into a nonentity... [257]

After Munich, however, TJ was less of an advocate for appeasement.

Between 1936 and 1939, Germany took a series of initiatives against the 1919 peace settlement and in favour of German expansion; Britain and France did not respond effectively to the German moves. That cumulative failure made war more likely.

In March 1936 Hitler sent troops to reoccupy the Rhineland (demilitarized by the post war Locarno Treaty); Beatrice commented

Germany breaks her bonds and rearms; all three aggressive powers [Germany, Italy, Japan] openly glorify war as an instrument – as the instrument to settle the relation of one state to another. [258]

The civil war in Spain began in July 1936; Britain and France supported a policy of non-intervention. Franco's nationalists asked Italy and Germany for help. Before the end of July Germany had responded, sending planes, anti-aircraft guns and other supplies. This was followed, in September, by the first supplies to the republican government from the Soviet Union.

At the end of July, Sidney and Beatrice saw Parmoor, who had handled the relationship with the League in the MacDonald governments. Despairing of the League, he was relapsing into isolationism. In foreign policy, thought Beatrice, much would depend on which side won in Spain.

In February 1938, Eden, the Foreign Secretary, resigned after disagreements with Chamberlain over appeasement. Chamberlain then appointed Lord Halifax Foreign Secretary.

In March Hitler sent German troops into Austria, incorporating the country into Germany. Beatrice, at home at Passfield six weeks after Sidney's stroke, listened on the radio to news of

…the triumphant march of Hitler's Third Reich to a German domination of central Europe – the very disaster that the great war was waged to prevent! [259]

Czechoslovakia was next after Austria, in 1939. The issue was the position of the Sudeten German minority – ethnic Germans, living within the Czechoslovak boundaries, in a mountainous region important for Czechoslovak defence. The Sudeten territory was bargained away at meetings between Chamberlain, the French premier Daladier, and Hitler, culminating in Munich on 29 and 30 September. The Czech government were not present.

As the crisis unfolded through September, the Webbs followed developments, listening to English and French radio news:

Wednesday, September 20th, 1938
4.00am
…the horror and humiliation of the situation…

Czecho-Slovakia, the darling child, the creation of the British and French governments at Versailles 1919...now handed over, in the course of three days...to Hitler with his pack of German hun wolves.

...it is the British premier who has sold the pass.

Thursday, September 21ˢᵗ, 1938

3 a.m.

A sleepless night after listening to the 9.40 news. The bitterly expressed acceptance by the Czech government of the British-French plan... We shall be at war or at an agreed peace in a few days or perhaps hours, according to the prejudice, temper and tactics of a tiny group of mediocre men – a shameful peace or a world war.

Tuesday September 27ᵗʰ, 1938

3 a.m.

Like the rest of this mad generation of the human race, we listened to the maddest of speeches by the maddest of men broadcast to the world. [260]

Beatrice's immediate reaction to the Munich agreement was one of relief rather than disgust. Nevertheless, she recognized that it meant

...the dominance of Germany in Europe through the threat of brute force...it kills the League of Nations with its strivings for a reign of new international affairs. [261]

Parliament was recalled at the end of September; Stafford Cripps spoke for the Labour opposition on the final day of the Munich debate, arguing that the government had never had any constructive policy for peace:

At best they have tried to prevent war when the danger of war has been imminent, but on every occasion they have succeeded in that objective only by giving way unqualifiedly to the demands of the aggressor. [262]

On 17 November Beatrice wrote to Beveridge (who had been unwell at the time of Munich), seeking confirmation of his view:

I gather...that you are, on the whole, dead against the Munich friendship with Germany. The last move of the Nazi government, its outrageous persecution of the Jews, seems to have brought a reaction, especially in the USA... [263]

The same day she referred in her diary to

The Nazi persecution, one might almost say, annihilation, of the German Jew... [264]

At Christmas she noted in her diary that *Chamberlain's policy of appeasement* was a tragic absurdity:

...the aggressor states, far from being satisfied, are every day more outrageous in their demands, and war seems inevitable. [265]

Stafford Cripps continued to argue for broad cooperation – against fascism abroad, against appeasement at home. His position had moved from support for a United Front – bringing the left together – to a Popular Front, including Liberals as well. He believed the Chamberlain government must be replaced, and that Labour could not be sure of a majority on its own. There would be a general election in 1939 or 1940.

On 9 January 1939 he sent what became known as the Cripps Memorandum to Jim Middleton, Labour's General Secretary. This invited all genuine anti-Government parties or groups to cooperate around a programme to include:

- Protection of democratic rights against internal and external attack

- Peace by collective action

- Social reform

On 13 January, Labour's National Executive (NEC) voted down the Cripps Memorandum. The same evening, Cripps circulated the Memorandum to all local Labour Parties. This attracted Beatrice's attention:

The home news today is Stafford Cripps' sensational defiance of the executive of the national Labour Party (of which he is a member) by issuing, the very night that he had been defeated on this question, a detailed and ably reasoned appeal for a united front with all opponents of the present government. [266]

Beatrice knew the policy advocated by Cripps was that of Communist parties internationally – a united front against fascism;

Fortunately we have not been asked to express any opinion; and intend not to do so. My own impression is that the <u>more done and the less said</u> about a United Front, the better the result. [267]

Stafford, she thought, was a brilliant advocate and an attractive personality – but he was autocratic and aloof. *Like all the Cripps he is an egotist.*[268]

That week, R H Tawney visited Passfield. He thought Cripps was being inconsistent in switching from the United Front to the Popular Front:

It is difficult to welcome a heretic into your command who is always changing his creed.[269]

The Labour NEC met again on 25 January. They received a lengthy report on Cripps, and expelled him from membership. He responded by launching a petition in favour of peace and democracy, establishing a new campaign organisation, and undertaking another round of national mass meetings. The night of his expulsion, Cripps addressed a London rally organised by the Left Book Club and the Spanish Emergency Committee. Keynes wrote to him on 9 February, saying

> *I am in full sympathy with what you are doing. It seems to me very important not to split existing parties, but to capture them...*[270]

Attlee, who had not previously criticised Cripps personally, attacked him for inconsistency, in a *Daily Herald* article. Beatrice attributed Stafford's faults to the fact that he was a Cripps: Attlee thought they were there because he was a Potter; the day after his *Herald* piece, Attlee wrote:

> *It is a great pity about Stafford, but like all the Potter family he is so absolutely convinced that the policy he puts forward for the time being is absolutely right that he will listen to no arguments.* [271]

Two Potters – Beatrice and her niece Barbara Drake – met at Passfield to see what they could do to help Stafford –

> *...short of signing his manifesto...a policy which neither of us support...*[272]

They decided to try and get an influential signed appeal against his expulsion

> *...and the <u>threatened</u> expulsion of all his followers and the still more absurd ousting of all members of the Left Book Club.* [273]

Beatrice said that Morrison and Dalton had *gone crazy* about Cripps *and other heretics.* She was worried that it would end in their *gifted but egotistical* nephew being ousted from the Labour Party.

Beatrice then wrote to Morrison, assuring him that, although Cripps was her nephew, *I am well aware of his defects*, and that she and Sidney were not in favour of a united front with the Liberals, or anyone else outside Labour. What she was opposed to was expelling people on the grounds of disagreements on tactics or policy. Her objection was based not on moral principle, but on expediency and experience:

> *Surely it would be better for the National Executive to quietly reject policies which it does not approve of, and merely ignore the promoters of those policies.*
> 274

Beatrice's appeal was turned down; the NEC agreed to delay a decision to Labour's Whitsun annual conference; two other MPs – Aneurin Bevan and G R Strauss – had also been expelled.

The situation in Europe deteriorated further. On 15 March 1939, German troops occupied Prague; Hitler slept in the city that night. Beatrice's fears were confirmed:

The news last night of Hitler's crash into Czecho Slovakia and the Halifax-Chamberlain shamefaced admission of it, in Lords and Commons, roused in me horror at the cruelty to Czecho Slovakia, and a sort of grin – a contemptuous grin – at the imbecility a bare six months ago of the Munich episode. [275]

It was clear that Poland would be Hitler's next target.

And the Spanish republic collapsed. After long resistance, Franco entered Madrid on 5 March; Britain immediately recognised the new government.

The popular front campaign continued. On 24 April Cripps spoke at a Left Book Club rally at Earls Court, in London. Between 9000 and 1000 people attended; others on the platform included Paul Robeson, Harry Pollitt, and Lloyd George. Cripps charged Chamberlain with deliberately

…manoeuvring to avoid any cooperation with the USSR…it was undoubtedly the aim of the present Government to allow Italy and Germany to wax stronger and stronger. [276]

Maisky had reached similar conclusions. In spring 1939, contact between Maisky and the Webbs increased. The Maiskys visited Passfield on 13 February; they were, noted Beatrice

…in good spirits about the USSR. The Ambassador convinced that Great Britain will be faced, in the next few months, with war if they refuse to surrender territory to Germany and Italy. [277]

In late March Beatrice saw them at the embassy. Maisky was due to meet Halifax, the Foreign Secretary; every day the meeting was postponed. Maisky was worried that the British and French would do a private deal over Poland, without Russia. Just as Beatrice and Maisky sat down to coffee, he was summoned to the Foreign Office; the meeting was back on.

The next week the Maiskys returned to Passfield. Maisky asked Beatrice why the British put up with Chamberlain? why did the Conservative Party continue to trust him? He implied that Moscow did not trust Chamberlain and would be unlikely to join a pact while Chamberlain remained Prime Minister.

After Hitler seized Prague in March 1939, Beatrice thought that an alliance between Britain and the Soviet Union was inevitable. It was certainly Maisky's objective; Britain – and France – continued to talk.

But Russian policy became more volatile. Maisky was summoned back to Moscow; on 21 April he met Stalin, with Litvinov, the Foreign Minister, Molotov, and other Politburo members. The negotiations with France and Britain could continue, but it was clear that Stalin had reservations.

Beatrice watched from Passfield

...Maisky is at Moscow with other diplomats – summoned by Stalin for consultation. We will hear about that interview on Maisky's next visit and perhaps (?) some indication of Maisky's reaction to the spiritual dictator of the USSR. [278]

Shortly after Maisky's return to London, Litvinov was replaced by Molotov as Foreign Minister. Like Maisky, Litvinov had lived in exile in London; Maisky had been a protegee of Litvinov. Molotov, unlike Litvinov, was in favour of talking to Germany. Maisky was still in post; his position became increasingly vulnerable; his brief remained to seek agreement between Britain, France, and the Soviet Union.

On 11 June the Maiskys spent four hours at Passfield. Beatrice reported that the Ambassador, *in his queer, voluble and rather ugly English, let himself go* as he described his meeting with Stalin, and the talks at Geneva. When she asked him about Stalin,

From his sullen expression and monosyllable reply, I gather he has no particular liking for the idolised leader of the masses. [279]

Maisky again said that he distrusted Chamberlain's real intentions; by contrast, he told Beatrice that he had a high opinion of Churchill and was on friendly terms with him.

That day, Maisky and Beatrice separately recorded their opinions of each other: Maisky wrote that Passfield Corner was

...a hotbed of thought and intellectual inquiry. This wonderful old couple – the best representatives of the nineteenth-century bourgeois intelligentsia – are in their eighties, but they refuse to give in. They read, follow world events, think and write. Beatrice has a particularly bright mind... [280]

Beatrice's summary of Maisky was that

I like the man; he is honest and self-devoted in character, acute, broad-minded in intelligence – a good husband, friend and citizen. [281]

The appeal by Cripps against expulsion from the Labour Party came before the Conference in late May. Both the appeal, and a pro-Popular Front resolution, were defeated overwhelmingly. The three expelled MPs – Cripps, Strauss, and Bevan – immediately reapplied for membership; the party agreed to consider their cases in the autumn. No longer subject to the Labour whip, Cripps now began to operate as an independent MP. He campaigned for a broadly-based government, without Chamberlain; and for a pact with the Soviet Union. He met anyone who might be interested – including, on 22 June, Winston Churchill. According to an early biographer of Cripps, Churchill was extremely critical of Chamberlain; he told Cripps that he and Anthony Eden

> *...had been ready to join the Cabinet ever since Hitler had entered Prague. But Chamberlain would not have them because their entrance into the government would have put an end to his policy of appeasement.* [282]

Harold Nicolson was a former diplomat, now (after a brief encounter with Mosley's New Party) a National Labour – MacDonaldite – MP. A few days before Cripps met Churchill, Nicholson had lunch with Beatrice and Maisky:

> *He detests Chamberlain, despises the Labour opposition; would like a newly constituted government, with Halifax as PM and Winston Churchill as Leader of the House of Commons. Stafford, he said, was supreme as a debater – the Labour Front Bench was like a 'company of village fiddlers, with a star professional violinist occasionally intervening to make the village fiddling sound an absurd disharmony of low-grade amateurs.'* [283]

By mid-summer, Chamberlain was at last – hesitantly – pursuing a pact with the Soviet Union. But as AJP Taylor wrote

> *No alliance has been pursued less enthusiastically. The government behaved as if they had all the time in the world.* [284]

Frustrated at the delay, Cripps now approached Ministers directly, offering to go to Moscow himself, lead the negotiations, and conclude the agreement. On 3 July, his offer was declined by Halifax, the Foreign Secretary.

The following Saturday Stafford and Isobel Cripps spent two hours at Passfield en route to Glyndebourne. It was a hectic day, starting with Cripps addressing a London conference on colonial freedom. Cripps was depressed, telling the Webbs that Labour was losing ground:

> *...no one was interested in their worn-out programme; if there was a general election they would lose seats... The time was past for a mere reiteration of socialist principles. We were faced with national disaster, owing to Chamberlain's still-held policy of appeasement with the Fascist powers.* [285]

He thought Chamberlain

> *...still hankers after Hitler's friendship and no Soviet alliance.* [286]

He told Beatrice that there were Conservatives, including ministers, who distrusted Chamberlain, and wanted to see Halifax as Prime Minister, and Churchill and Eden in the Cabinet.

Beatrice wondered what Cripps was up to:

Where exactly Stafford is standing or moving, in the political world, I could not make out. Why is he consulting with conservative leaders? [287]

They were not hopeful; they thought it would be hard for him to return to a leading role in Labour

Indeed, from one or two observations he let drop, I am not sure that he is not looking forward to the leadership of another party on the left, which will rival if not supersede the Labour Party. [288]

Or possibly, she thought, the front bench of a National Government. A fortnight later, at the Durham Miners Gala, Cripps

…appealed for unity against Chamberlain at home and against the Fascist States abroad. [289]

In late July, the Cripps family set off for a Mediterranean holiday. Meanwhile negotiations between Britain, France and the Soviet Union proceeded slowly. In early August, a military mission left London for Moscow by ship. Maisky noted

…the English and French military missions are travelling to Moscow by freight steamer! It must be a freighter, to judge by its speed! And this comes at a time in Europe when the ground is beginning to burn beneath our feet! Incredible! Does the British Government really want an agreement? [290]

Maisky visited Passfield again the following weekend

…chuckling over Chamberlain's covert hostility to the USSR. [291]

The slow freighter was one example. There were others: when they arrived, the military delegates had no satisfactory credentials. While credentials were being obtained, talks between Russia and Germany started.

Even as the negotiations between Britain and France and Russia collapsed on 21 August, a commercial treaty between Russia and Germany was announced; Pravda observed that this might lead to an improvement in German/Soviet political relations.

Two days later the British press announced that Germany and the USSR had negotiated an anti-aggression pact. Ribbentrop, now German foreign minister was flying to Moscow to sign it. For Beatrice it was a *day of holy horror:*

...it looks like a complete reversal of the foreign policy of the USSR – all the more discreditable because of its secrecy and obvious inconsistency with the anti-aggression protestations of the Soviet government at Geneva and elsewhere on behalf of Spain, Czecho-Slovakia and China. [292]

The pact shocked Beatrice. Everything she had said and written for years was thrown into doubt. On August 25 she wrote that the pact

...seems a great disaster to all that the Webbs have stood for. Even Sidney is dazed, and I am, for a time at least, knocked almost senseless! ...a terrible collapse of good faith and integrity...evil behaviour on the part of the USSR government... So far as our faith in Soviet Communism is concerned, the last few days have been tragic. [293]

Many others were left in the same position. The Nazi-Soviet pact had a profound impact on British support for the Soviet Union. Harry Pollitt opposed the pact. He was removed as Secretary of the Communist Party of Great Britain, only returning after Germany turned on Russia in 1941. In September, Maisky wrote in his diary

The events of the past weeks have wreaked havoc with people's minds. Gollancz is in despair: in his view, the Soviet-German pact killed off communism. [John] Strachey, in connection with the same pact, came to Harry [Pollitt] with tears in his eyes. [294]

PHONEY WAR 1939-1940

The signing of the Nazi-Soviet pact meant war was imminent. On 29 August, the household at Passfield were warned by an Air Raid Warden that blackout regulations would soon come into force. Beatrice, with the two maids Jean and Annie, and Mrs Grant, Sidney's carer/nurse/valet, set to work to deal with windows and lamps.

Two days' work completed the blackout, leaving Beatrice even more exhausted. The next warning came the following Monday:

A banging at the door and a grim voice calling 'Air Raid.' I had just come from my bath and looked out of my window. There stood a man with a bicycle, his gas mask slung over his shoulder, who explained that a warning had been given from Portsmouth that German aeroplanes were in the neighbourhood. A few minutes later I went into Sidney's room and saw him sitting up with his gas mask on! I suggested that he should take it off which he promptly did. Mrs Grant had been in and was angry. 'You have no right to tell Mr Webb to take his off' she said in a menacing voice. 'Pardon me' I laughed – 'I am his wife and the mistress of this house. Keep yours on if you like. It is damned nonsense putting on gas masks out in the countryside. The Germans won't waste their gas on us...[295]

The pact left Germany free to attack Poland. On 1 September German troops crossed into Poland; German aircraft bombed Warsaw. At 9.00 on Thursday 3 September, the British government issued an ultimatum; this expired at 11.00.

Beatrice listened to the broadcast of Chamberlain's declaration of war. Her reaction was idiosyncratic:

His voice, amplified by the wireless, was strikingly like his father's. [296]

After the pact, Beatrice questioned whether the Soviet Union was

...intending to take part in the conquest and division of Poland? The German official news, hints at this outcome of the non-aggression pact. [297]

She worried about

...the problem of the internment of the Polish defeated armies: how will the Soviet government meet that emergency? If they are wise they will be benevolent and proselytise their unwelcome guests. [298]

They were neither wise nor benevolent: Beatrice never knew, but they shot most of their unwelcome guests in spring 1940. The week that Beatrice died in 1943, Maisky, on Stalin's instructions, was denying to Churchill that the massacres had happened.

On 17 September Russian troops moved into Eastern Poland: Beatrice's disillusionment was complete

Satan has won hands down: Stalin and Molotov have become the villains of the piece. Molotov's broadcast to the peoples of the USSR justifying the march of the Red Army into Poland is a monument of international immorality – cloaked in cynical sophistry. [299]

Churchill gave a radio talk in October on the first month of the war; Beatrice thought:

If only our old acquaintance were Prime Minister in the place of the reactionary and mechanical-minded Chamberlain...[300]

She thought Churchill was emerging as the leader of progressive forces; she added that Maisky suggested Churchill would be trusted by Moscow. Two weeks later the Maiskys spent three hours at Passfield. They told Beatrice that Cripps was working hard behind the scenes, briefing ministers.

In October the request by Cripps, Strauss, and Bevan for readmission to the Labour Party was considered. Strauss and Bevan gave the assurances demanded; Cripps did not. He was asked to express regret for his past conduct; not to campaign against party policy, and to accept Labour's policy and programme. He refused, saying not just that his action was justified,

> ...*but was the only action that I could have taken consistently with my duty to my constituents and the best interests of the workers of this country.* [301]

He remained an independent MP until 1945; Beatrice thought Stafford, *with his wayward brilliancy and independent means* had the best of the argument.

Cripps took advantage of his independent position to pursue initiatives with ministers and more widely. In September, he wrote to Halifax proposing an all-party delegation to Moscow

> ...*in order to try to influence Russian opinion in our direction.* [302]

The same day, the Special Branch log of his phone calls relates that Cripps:

> *"16.9.39 Rang POLLITT to ask if he could come and see him – very urgently. POLLITT said he could not come until later. CRIPPS said he might have to go to the Foreign Office and see Halifax and he wanted to see POLLITT first. POLLITT said then he would come now."* [303]

He kept talking to Halifax, Pollitt and Maisky. Halifax was happy for him to visit Moscow – but as a private citizen, not officially. Beatrice heard about the plan to go to Russia from Maisky; she thought it *frivolous and futile*.

Cripps, nevertheless, carried on developing his idea. He decided to make an unofficial visit to India and China, with a brief trip to Russia at the end, without formal support from government, aiming to explore options for post war policy in India. He left his law chambers on 29 November, wrote to his Bristol constituents explaining that he would be out of the country until spring, and left at once. Beatrice approved:

> ...*as a British politician, he is well out of home politics. The Labour Party, dominated by Citrine, through the trade union movement, is the handmaid of the Chamberlain government. The only unity there is in the country is the unity of muddleheadedness.* [304]

The Webbs received intermittent news about Stafford's journey. In February, Beatrice met Isobel Cripps in London, and heard about Stafford's enthusiasm for Chiang Kai Shek. In March, Maisky brought the Chinese ambassador – who had made Stafford's arrangements in China – to Passfield.

In February 1940 Cripps flew from China to Moscow and met Molotov for 1 ¾ hours.

Over the winter 1939-40, the Maiskys regularly visited the Webbs. Like Beatrice and Stafford, Maisky was frustrated by the inertia of the 'phoney war', the continued presence of Chamberlain in the government, and British official reluctance to work with Russia.

Relations between Britain and Russia worsened when Russia invaded Finland in late November 1939; normal diplomatic contact virtually ceased.

The Maiskys visited Passfield twice over Christmas; on the second visit, they also saw Lloyd George, another persistent government critic, who lived nearby at Churt. Maisky asked Beatrice if Labour would continue to be subservient to Chamberlain. He told the Webbs how much he appreciated them, saying

If I happen not to visit your home again, please remember that I spent the best hours of my stay in England here. [305]

He added in his diary entry

This is true. For the Webbs, despite everything, are the most interesting, the most pleasant, and the dearest (in so far as the word is appropriate in this case) of all the people I have met in my ambassadorship in Great Britain... [306]

In March Beatrice spent two days in London, and heard Attlee speak on war aims. She was not impressed:

His hour's lecture was pitiable: he looked and spoke like an insignificant elderly clerk... a string of vague assertions about an international authority, peace not dictated but agreed to by a new Germany without Hitler or his party... Altogether a hopeless failure. [307]

That winter, Beatrice, Maisky and Cripps worried that the passivity of the Chamberlain government, and underlying British and French hostility to the Soviet Union, could lead to an early, negotiated, peace with Hitler. Both Britain and France came close to breaking off relations with Russia.

In January, Maisky told the Webbs that he thought

...there was a growing feeling in British governing circles in favour of a break with the USSR and any day it might occur. [308]

Many on the left were also anti-Soviet; in October, Maisky complained to Beatrice about Greenwood

...who fancies himself as 'a future Prime Minister of a national government to fight the Red Menace.' He has lost his head. [309]

In January, she noted that Citrine, General Secretary of the TUC, was in Finland, gathering evidence against the Soviet Union.

Maisky told Beatrice in February that he believed that the Conservative government did not want war with Russia

...but might find it difficult to resist pressure from the Labour Party in that direction. [310]

In March, Sidney and Beatrice signed a letter to the press, drafted by Charles Trevelyan, and signed by GBS, Richard Acland and others, objecting to any war with Russia.

Russia and Finland agreed peace terms on 13 March. Beatrice was relieved: the threat of British involvement was ended.

By spring 1940, the phoney war was coming to an end. On 9 April, German troops invaded Denmark and Norway. Denmark was occupied at once; Norway resisted. A doomed, hopeless, British and French force attempted to support the Norwegians. Beatrice was shocked at the speed and efficiency of the German attack:

In six hours, with no loss of life, Germany has annexed the whole of Denmark and is in control of the capital and Southern ports of Norway. A sinister warning for Moscow; and a dramatic challenge to the allies' blockade and their confidence in ultimate victory. [311]

She concluded:

Even I admit that Hitler's Germany must be conquered if life is to be bearable for the rest of Europe. [312]

The Maiskys visited Passfield on 12 April. They told Beatrice and Sidney that Labour now wanted to talk to the embassy again. She said Maisky was still contemptuous of Labour.

Maisky saw Attlee and Greenwood the following Monday. He

...got the impression that Attlee's attitude was more favourable than Greenwood's. Greenwood drank a lot, as is his wont, while Attlee merely sipped his cherry brandy.

And so, diplomatic relations are restored! [313]

Cripps arrived back on 23 April and saw Maisky the next day; Maisky told him that he had not seen Halifax for over three months.

By the beginning of May it was clear that the British expedition to Norway had been a disaster. The troops were unprepared; there was confusion about objectives between the War Cabinet and the chiefs of staff. *Everything went wrong*, wrote AJP Taylor. [314] On Thursday 2 May Chamberlain made a grim statement to the House of Commons on the losses sustained.

Beatrice listened to radio reports of Chamberlain's speech with her niece, Barbara Drake

> *The worst of the present situation is that there is no leader, still less any group, that seems more worthy of confidence than Chamberlain's & Co. Churchill is the one man who attracts most support but he has accepted Chamberlain as Premier. Assuredly the front opposition bench – backed by Citrine and Bevin, would be a step downward in capacity and trustworthyness.* [315]

The Commons debated the Norway rout on 7 and 8 May. At the start of the second day came news of the death of George Lansbury, aged 81. Chamberlain and Attlee paid tribute to him; Attlee reminded MPs that Lansbury had signed the Minority Report.

The debate was not on a formal confidence motion – it was simply a vote on the adjournment. Attlee, Morrison, and Greenwood led for the Labour opposition. Dissident Conservatives – including Leo Amery – called for Chamberlain's resignation. Several of the Conservatives who spoke against the Prime Minister were servicemen in uniform who had been in Norway and could give first hand testimony of the chaos. On the second day, Cripps made a powerful intervention, referring to what he had heard while abroad. Lloyd George also called on Chamberlain to resign.

The government majority fell from 213 to 81. The collapse in support for Chamberlain made change inevitable. Next day, 9 May, Chamberlain and the whips tried to persuade the Conservative rebels and the Labour leadership to join the government. Both refused to do so without a change in Prime Minister; with the bitter memory of 1931 still fresh, Labour would only accept ministerial office with the agreement of the party.

That night Hitler invaded Holland and Belgium. Maisky wrote:

> *This fact had a tremendous effect in England. The temperature immediately shot up. Events developed at breakneck speed… It was clear to all that the reconstruction of the Government should be carried out immediately and in a far more radical way than conceived before.* [316]

Labour's National Executive met on 10 May, and decided that Labour would refuse to serve under Chamberlain – but would join a new government under a new Prime Minister.

That evening the King asked Churchill to form a government. Churchill agreed. He did, however, retain Chamberlain (who remained Leader of the Conservative Party until his death in October 1940) and Halifax as Ministers.

Beatrice had known Churchill almost 40 years – sometimes working closely together, at other times distant and mistrustful. In the appeasement years their positions had gradually converged. Now, on Saturday 11 May, she wrote

At long last we are actively at war… Finally Chamberlain is no longer Premier; Churchill is our Champion and the Labour Party have accepted office. [317]

Several of the Labour ministers who joined Churchill's government in May 1940 had started in socialist politics before the First World War, with the Webbs' campaign against the Poor Law. They went on to play leading roles in the majority Labour government of 1945. Sidney and Beatrice could be tough critics, ready to point out the limitations and frailties of their protegees; but they were proud of their achievement.

Attlee became Lord Privy Seal – in effect, Deputy Prime Minister. Beatrice had appointed him meetings officer of the Poor Law campaign; later Sidney had appointed him to teach social work at LSE, and encouraged him to stand for the Fabian Executive Committee.

Greenwood, the Leeds teacher who had led the Leeds branch of the Poor Law campaign, met the Webbs at the 1910 Summer School. Sidney acted as referee for him when he became an economics lecturer, and later helped him become Labour's head of research. He joined the War Cabinet as Minister without Portfolio; in that capacity he commissioned the Beveridge Report.

Hugh Dalton had been one of the original Cambridge Fabians. He had campaigned for the Minority Report, and later taught at LSE. Dalton now became Minister of Economic Warfare.

Ellen Wilkinson, who became a junior minister in May 1940, first met Beatrice as a student campaigner in Manchester before the First World War; later she had become a regular visitor to Passfield Corner.

The new war cabinet met frequently – often more than once a day. The news from Holland, Belgium and France was grim. The Cabinet received detailed reports about the imminent threat of an invasion of England.

Ambassador Maisky was concerned about whether Britain had the will or the capacity to resist such an invasion. On Saturday 18 May he set out to test opinion.

First Maisky saw Anthony Eden, now Secretary of State for War. Eden told him

...if there were a misfortune, and France really did not hold out, Britain would all the same continue the war alone. We cannot accept peace with Hitler. [318]

Maisky was relieved but not completely reassured.

From Eden, Maisky next went to see David Lloyd George at his Surrey home. If France falls, he asked, what will England do?

I had hardly finished the phrase when the old man cried 'Fight, fight, and go on fighting... The English aren't easily frightened. I am a Welshman you know,' said the old man with a smile, 'and I can judge the English objectively.' [319]

Having spoken to Lloyd George he decided

...to make one last test. Straight from Lloyd George I went to see the Webbs... [320]

In his memoirs, Maisky describes how

...when I had to ascertain how the British Government would conduct itself in any particular circumstances, I often sought a resolution of my doubts from the Webbs. [321]

Beatrice, 82 years old, was

...sitting on the fireguard with her back to the fire. Her slender hands were clasped about her knees and she listened closely... [322]

Maisky put his questions provocatively: how could Britain continue the war? Her army was only coming into being. How could Britain carry on fighting? Sidney and Beatrice picked up his pessimistic note:

Man for man, plane for plane, the British air force were superior to the German; but we were outnumbered three to 1. What folly to leave rearmament so long and even during the last year to be so slow about it. [323]

Maisky asked what would Britain do if France was taken out of the game?

They answered without hesitation: 'Then England would have to fight alone.'

They then produced a precedent (the English cannot manage without their precedents!): the era of the Napoleonic wars. The same response was found then. Very significant! [324]

Beatrice said

It was only the sixth Coalition that put an end to Napoleon: but it did put an end to him... That's the pattern we shall follow today as well. [325]

For Sidney, the initial alliance with France represented the first coalition: if

France was defeated

Well, we'll go back to our islands, defend them, and wait for the day when a new coalition will become possible. That time will come. [326]

The cumulative impact of Maisky's meetings with Eden, Lloyd George and the Webbs was such that, that evening, Maisky sent a despatch to Moscow to reassure the Russian government that, in the event of France being defeated, Britain would remain at war with Germany.

In the early days of Churchill's government, as ministers came to terms with the imminent fall of France and the threat of invasion, the issue of improving relations with Russia moved up the agenda.

An early War Cabinet meeting decided to send a new representative to Spain

…some outstanding figure in public life…in order to maintain our prestige. [327]

They sent Samuel Hoare, a veteran appeaser. His (relatively successful) role was to try and ensure Franco's Spain stayed neutral.

Attlee suggested that the same approach

…might not with advantage also be adopted in regard to Russia. [328]

British trade with Russia had not recovered from the shock of the Nazi-Soviet pact. Trade talks were stalled. Maisky blamed the fact that Chamberlain and Halifax remained ministers even under Churchill, telling Beatrice,

So long as Halifax, backed by Chamberlain, decides the foreign policy, there will be no understanding with the USSR. [329]

This left Beatrice depressed:

I had hoped that the Churchill Cabinet might offer to send some 'Plenipotentiary Envoy' to settle finally with Molotov – Stafford for instance. There was no sign of that taking place. [330]

While the government had turned down Cripps' offer to go to Russia in autumn 1939, Cripps and Halifax had remained in contact. Therefore, when Attlee suggested sending a special envoy to Russia, Halifax thought of Cripps.

There were obstacles: some of the Labour ministers had spent the past year expelling Cripps from Labour. On 17 May, Dalton, wrote

Halifax wants to send Cripps to Moscow. I throw some doubts on his suitability. I say that I have had an uncomfortable experience of him, and that it fell to me, when the Labour party finally despaired of training him to the House, to put him outside. [331]

Cripps was given narrow terms of reference, and a 'minder' from Dalton's ministry. The minder chosen was Michael ('Mouna') Postan, the Cambridge historian, then on secondment to the civil service. In the event Postan was refused a visa for Russia.

There was an argument about whether Cripps would be a special envoy, or (as the Russians preferred) the replacement, regular ambassador. In the end he was confirmed as the regular ambassador. While this was happening, Cripps was briefed by both Maisky and the Foreign Office. Maisky summarized the story in his diary:

The Foreign Office Mandarins are furious at Cripps appointment. First, because he is not one of theirs, and secondly because he is Cripps. Hence all the sabotage. [332]

Cripps told Harry Pollitt about his appointment; on 21 May, the Special Branch tap on the phones at the Communist Party's King Street headquarters picked up this message

CRIPPS wanted Harry Pollitt urgently. He rang up twice during the morning but would leave no message and said he would ring again. CRIPPS' message finally left for POLLITT was that 'he is going on the journey he mentioned to POLLITT on Thursday or Friday and wants urgently to see POLLITT before he goes. [333]

News of Cripps' appointment appeared in the press on 25 May. Beatrice was delighted.

BEATRICE AND SIDNEY, 1941-1947

The Webbs were still in contact with Leonard and Virginia Woolf. Early in the war, the Woolfs said they would like to meet again; Beatrice saw them in London in October 1939. Virginia described Beatrice

...wearing a white spotted headdress,...as alive as a leaf on an autumn bonfire: burning, skeletonised. [334]

Although Beatrice thought Leonard looked unwell, he was *as gently wise as ever.* Virginia

... seemed troubled by an absence of any creed as to what was right and what was wrong. [335]

According to Beatrice, *this gifted and charming lady*

...with her classic features, subtle observation and symphonic style badly needs a living philosophy. [336]

Beatrice thought Leonard and Virginia saw liberty as the absence of restraint – but opportunity was also necessary.

In June 1940 Beatrice spoke at the Fabian AGM. She praised Fabian research, mentioning Leonard's work on international policy alongside the Coles and Laski.

In April 1941 came news of Virginia's death – *presumed drowned in the River Ouse.* Beatrice was haunted by the memory of

...that tall talented woman... [337]

and of Virginia's father, Leslie Stephen, who Beatrice had known in the 1880s. Beatrice looked back on their friendship with the Woolfs: the couples had stayed with each other, but never became sympathetic friends:

I think we liked them better than they liked us. In a way which I never understood, I offended Virginia. I had none of her sensitiveness... [338]

Beatrice was pursued by the thought of

...that beautiful and brilliant Virginia, yielding to the passion for death, rather than endure the misery of continued life. [339]

Why? What led to the tragedy? Beatrice linked Virginia's death to that conversation eighteen months earlier, and the lack of a *living philosophy.* She called Virginia's suicide a *voluntary withdrawal from life.*

This was no casual phrase. She had known other suicides – the young poet Amy Levy, who she had known at the British Museum in the 1880s; her own sister Blanche, who hanged herself in 1905. Her eldest sister Lallie had died in 1906 after a long period of cocaine addiction, which Beatrice referred to as *self-poisoning.*

Beatrice had long argued that old people who were tired of life should

...be allowed to leave it in a painless and dignified way. [340]

In 1930 she wrote

If Sidney were to go I doubt whether I should stay out Nature's time... [341]

She wondered whether

...voluntary withdrawal from life, after the years of physical ease and mental activity are past, may become the rule and not the exception? [342]

She proposed the establishment of

...Temples of Death, where in an environment of peaceful charm and beauty of sight and sound, any human being who is weary of life, could fade out of existence without pain or distressing circumstances, and without discredit to surviving relatives. [343]

In her last years Beatrice returned to this theme. In March 1942 she was

...desperately tired, and can no longer enjoy the process of living...[344]

But she hesitated about herself withdrawing from life;

...it would pain my still living life companion... [345]

The Battle of Britain began in summer 1940. Mrs Grant, Sidney's nurse/valet, was the most terrified member of the household. On the morning of 13 August, when Beatrice was in the bath, planes roared over Passfield, followed by machinegun fire and explosions, shaking the building.

Mrs Grant, white and trembling, was downstairs and stationed herself in the back kitchen with white face and her hands folded. [346]

On 20 August there was a night of bomb explosions. Beatrice and Sidney could not sleep

...poor Mrs Grant is crouching in the back of the kitchen, comforted by Annie, whilst Sidney and I keep to our beds. [347]

Beatrice tried to keep writing *Our Partnership*. She walked each day in the countryside. Sidney kept on reading. By mid-September Beatrice could report that the main focus of the Blitz had moved to London, and that Mrs Grant had got over her panic.

Beatrice had to keep the peace between the two maids – Jean and Annie – and Mrs Grant. There were rows about food for Mrs Grant's dog.

In February 1942 both maids had flu, while

...Mrs Grant maintains her egotistic aloofness... [348]

Beatrice had to admit that she was ignorant about household tasks (and probably unsafe as well).

If only I had been brought up to know how to cook and to clean. [349]

Her health deteriorated. Her bladder was irritable. She attributed this to cystitis. She consulted her doctor, trying various remedies. In November 1941 she complained about the *persistent and tiring pain of cystitis.*[350]

The following September she felt desperately ill. She

...discovered blood in my urine – which is, I think, the sign of my remaining kidney going rotten, with death round the corner... What haunted me during the night was not the prospect of death but the presence of pain. [351]

She saw the doctor again – it was a bladder inflammation. She should keep warm, stay in bed, drink china tea and water, and she should get better. She could have had another operation but turned it down when it could not be performed locally.

A few days later Beatrice's niece Barbara Drake stayed overnight. Sidney, Beatrice, and Barbara talked about their property and estate. They amended their wills, removing two trustees – Mostyn Lloyd, because he was himself dying of cancer; and Herbert Morrison – who Beatrice thought had become

...reactionary and anti-Soviet. [352]

The new trustees were John Parker MP, Fabian General Secretary, and Margaret Cole – representing herself and GDH Cole. Beatrice said the Coles

...practically share our views, as to the future organisation of society, national and international. [353]

This appointment confirmed the Coles' thirty year evolution, from critics of the Webbs to bearers of the Webb flame.

Passfield Corner, with its grounds and contents, was left to the LSE. Beatrice thought the Director might want to live there; or that the School might use Passfield

...to have parties of professors and students for discussion, or for cricket in the field that surrounds it. [354]

In fact, after Sidney's death, LSE sold the house and contents, including the library. In the austere conditions of 1948, the 15,000 books only raised £200. They included sets of the complete works of Herbert Spencer, VI Lenin, and HG Wells.[355]

Having decided against another operation, Beatrice agreed with her doctor, Dr Hodgkinson, in September 1942 that he would not come again unless she sent for him. He advised her to eat more, and to live as normal a life as possible. There is no cure for old age, she told herself.

But it was hard. A week later, she collapsed while out walking. She could barely carry on her ordinary life, suffering from intestinal trouble and sleeplessness. She asked herself

Ought I, or ought I not, to walk, eat, take narcotics to give me a few hours sleep, talk and write to friends? To collapse into inactivity, in body and mind, would be unendurable and would not be consistent with looking after Sidney and giving him a happy, healthy and interested life...So courage old lady! Carry on as a wife, and an active citizen so far as strength admits! [356]

After all, she and Sidney were leading a relatively comfortable life compared to men and women working to win the war against a return to barbarism and slavery. So she carried on.

They followed the progress of the war closely, relying on radio news bulletins, backed up by visits from Cripps and Maisky. When Cripps was away, his wife Isobel forwarded his letters.

In 1939 the Webbs had been deeply shocked by the Nazi-Soviet non-aggression pact. When Germany attacked the Soviet Union in June 1941, they welcomed the fact that this made Britain and Russia allies. Beatrice wrote that it saved

...Great Britain from a defeat or a stalemate peace. [357]

Beatrice came under media pressure: photographers and journalists wanted pictures and interviews. On 15 August she noted that three photo agencies had come to take pictures of her – American and Canadian agencies, and one from the British weekly paper *Picture Post*. She wrote that requests for interviews were

...extremely tiresome to the aged Mrs Webb, and I shall be glad when this temporary notoriety, useful for the sale of the book, is over... [358]

GBS wrote the article in *Picture Post*, headlined *Two Friends of the Soviet Union*, and accompanied by seven pictures.

Although Beatrice died before the war ended, she lived to see the Allies advance, first in North Africa, then on the Eastern Front. In October 1942 Beatrice heard Churchill's speech from Edinburgh, when he was made a Freeman of the City. Accompanied by Cripps, Churchill was cheered when he praised the *heroic Russians*.

News of the Allied victory at El Alamein came in November. In the east, Russia first halted the German advance, then forced a retreat. At Christmas 1942, Beatrice wrote

Over wireless comes, day after day, the cheering news of continuous victories on the Soviet Front of 1000 miles; the collapse of the German armies; the taking of huge quantities of munitions and above all the surrender of thousands of German soldiers to the Red Army. As this coincides with the retreat of the Germans in North Africa and the air supremacy of the Americans and the air supremacy of the Americans and the British in the Mediterranean, it looks as if victory were bound to come. [359]

The trend continued – in January 1943 she noted

The Germans are on the run in Russia and in North Africa – that was the news triumphantly announced to me by the BBC: it looks like total defeat for Germany – within the next six months. [360]

'Carrying on' meant still welcoming visitors – even if it was exhausting. On 15 October 1942, the Maiskys came, anxious for the opening of a second front in Europe. Ten days later Cripps – soon to become Minister of Aircraft Production – came. There was talk (not least by Cripps himself) of him as an alternative to Churchill – especially if the war went badly.

The Webbs were depressed by his visit

He seemed too self-centred and self confident – and did not share our own outlook and hopes for the future. Perhaps I am too tired mentally and physically... [361]

A stream of other visitors came in the last weeks of 1942: grandnephews in the forces; academics and researchers; old political colleagues. Sidney was frustrated he could not sustain his end of the conversation.

William Robson, LSE professor and co-founder of the *Political Quarterly,* visited often. Beatrice found him

...well informed, enlightened but dull minded, with an unattractive personality. [362]

Robson was married to the cellist Juliette Alvin; they had three children, who were also welcome visitors to Passfield. Beatrice found Juliette charming; in her last year, Juliette played for her.

In September 1942 Beatrice had resolved not to trouble the doctor; but in the New Year her health worsened. 4 January 1943 was *the worst night of unremitting abdominal pain*[363] She was sick in the night; Annie, one of the two maids, stayed up, sleeping on the sofa. Beatrice called out Dr Hodgkinson again; he told her there was a lot of gastric dysentery around; everyone in his house (except himself) had it. She was comforted; but

The pain of living, with rotten intestines, swollen feet, and a tired and sleepless brain, is qualified by the fear for Sidney if I am not there to look after his daily life and not be his daily companion of fifty years standing. [364]

People wanted to meet her and Sidney; there were letters to answer. On 22

January she was eighty-five. At nights she was restless; during the day, comatose.

Hodgkinson orders me to take drugs so as to make life bearable – but the doses of narcotics add to the depression of mind and discomfort of the body by day and by night. I carry on in our comfortable little home so that my beloved may remain well and happy, reading, reading, reading, by day and by night. He likes to see visitors if I will talk to them, and has no wish to disappear from this puzzling and cruel world. [365]

In late February she was sleeping four or five hours a night. She was better able to work, and to walk, in daytime. The bleeding recurred in March – Beatrice saw her doctor again; he reassured her that the problem was her bladder, not her kidney. Neither the pain nor the bleeding was as bad as the previous autumn.

In April she summarised her condition: physical discomfort, but mental satisfaction. Living was painful:

Severe cystitis and a paralysed colon mean physical pain by day and by night. But it is clear that as long as Sidney is alive I could not leave him. [366]

They continued to follow the war on the radio, listening to the speeches of Churchill and Roosevelt. By April 1943, Beatrice believed that the war in Europe would be over by the end of 1943, and that Japan would be defeated by the end of 1944.

Visitors still came to Passfield – Margaret Cole; John Parker; the faithful Maiskys; and Rosie Dobbs.

In February, Kingsley Martin, *New Statesman* editor, came with Raymond Mortimer, literary editor. Martin described Beatrice that winter afternoon, in her last weeks:

Wearing a lace cap, emaciated but with an aquiline beauty, she looked, as Raymond said, like a most venerable and formidable abbess. The love of power, which she had never openly exercised was unmistakeable. [367]

Martin told Beatrice that Sidney seemed *much more alive and able to talk* than on an earlier visit. [368]

Herbert Samuel came in March; they had known him fifty years. Like Martin, Samuel commented on Sidney's recovery:

...he looks solidly well, and reads an average of a book a day. [369]

Herbert Samuel, too, described Beatrice as he found her in the spring of 1943

...wearing a gay-coloured blouse and a dark skirt, with a lace scarf over her hair. Her complexion was that of a very old woman, but her welcoming smile,

her charming voice and her keen alert mind were the same as when I first knew her, just fifty years ago. [370]

Afterwards Samuel was sure he would not see Beatrice again.

Her diary entry on 19 April, in which she had written of a combination of physical discomfort and mental satisfaction, was almost the last entry after seventy years. That night she wrote one, final, visionary, apocalyptic entry:

…we shall all disappear…The garden will disappear and all our furniture, the earth and the sun and the moon…Even Churchill and Roosevelt, Stalin and Kingdoms would disappear… [371]

After that she did not regain consciousness. She died at 5.00 am on Friday 30 April.

Beatrice was cremated at Brookwood, near Woking, a few days later. Sixty people, mostly family, were there; almost the only outsiders present were Ivan and Agniya Maisky.

In June, the Maiskys returned to Passfield. But this time

…we were not met, as in the past, by a tall, beautiful old woman with lively eyes and a profoundly spiritual face… [372]

Sidney told them that he felt very lonely. He showed them the urn containing Beatrice's ashes:

'I've found a spot in the woods,' said Webb, slowly, 'which is just right for this urn, but it takes so long for orders to be processed at the moment and I am still waiting for the bronze slab with the inscription…'

Then, after a period of silence, the old man added: 'That's where I will end up too.' [373]

Next month Maisky was recalled to Moscow; he and Sidney never met again Maisky interpreted for Stalin at the Yalta and Potsdam conferences in 1945; apart from that, he never held another senior diplomatic post. He narrowly avoided the fate of his predecessor Sokolnikov; in the 1950s he was accused of having been a British spy. Before Stalin's death in 1953 Maisky was interrogated thirty-six times. One Russian historian considers that, if Stalin had lived a month or two longer, nothing would have saved Maisky.[374]

But he was imprisoned from 1953 to 1955, and only fully rehabilitated in 1960. He died, aged 91, in 1975. In the 1960s Maisky published several volumes of memoirs. His diaries – with detail on the relationship with Sidney and Beatrice – were published in English translation in 2015 and 2017.

Shortly before his death, Maisky wrote to the then Russian ambassador to London: his nostalgia for his time in London – in exile before 1917, then the eleven years as ambassador – remained undimmed:

> *We keep remembering the relationships we forged with the Webbs and Bernard Shaw.* [375]

Before his recall, Maisky had been announced as a speaker at a meeting on 14 July 1943 at the House of Commons, to discuss the formation of a Beatrice Webb Memorial Trust Fund. He left a message of support; the fund was launched by Herbert Morrison, Margaret Cole, Harold Laski, and A V Alexander. There were plenty of suggestions for its use – the two main activities in the early years of the trust were the creation of a residential conference centre, and the holding of an annual lecture.

The appeal was successful; the centre – Beatrice Webb House, on the slopes of Leith Hill, in Surrey – was opened by Clement Attlee as Prime Minister on Saturday 13 September 1947. In his speech he said that the country was full of useless and ugly memorials, but here was one that was both beautiful and useful, designed to help others carry on the work done by Beatrice Webb.[376] One of the last letters Sidney wrote, in September 1947, was to apologise for being unable to manage the short journey from Passfield Corner to the opening.

Sidney stayed on at Passfield, still cared for by Mrs Grant. Shaw kept in touch by post. Shortly after Beatrice's death, GBS wrote to Sidney

> *I used to take it as a matter of course that if Beatrice died you would come and live with us; for I never counted on our living to this ridiculous age and being incapable of taking care of ourselves or anyone else.* [377]

But, as had been the case since the start of the war, they could not meet:

> *I wish we – you and I – did not live so far apart. I am forbidden to take the car farther than ten miles and am allowed petrol enough for that distance only. And as I am older (88) physically than mentally anything like a long drive fatigues me overmuch.* [378]

In 1944 the government awarded Sidney the Order of Merit for *eminent services to social and political science*; when people wrote to congratulate him (and many did), his reply was that he was sorry Beatrice was not there to share the honour.

Sidney died on 15 October 1947 at Passfield Corner, a month after the opening of Beatrice Webb House. An austere, correct, secular, socialist, memorial meeting was held at London's Kingsway Hall – scene of many Fabian lectures, and appropriately a few minutes' walk one way from his birthplace in Cranborne Street, and in another direction, a few minutes from LSE. The programme was illustrated with an elegant pencil profile sketch of Sidney by Eric Gill, winner of one of those London County Council art prizes fifty years earlier.

Participants sang Edward Carpenter's socialist anthem *England Arise* – just as it had been sung at the joint Fabian ILP *War on Poverty* rallies in 1912. Clement Attlee gave a eulogy; other speakers included two other veterans of the campaign against the Poor Law – Hugh Dalton, now Chancellor of the Exchequer, and Margaret Bondfield.

But the Kingsway Hall meeting was not the end of the matter. After Beatrice's death, GBS had proposed a memorial to her in either Westminster Abbey or St Paul's. That did not happen. In 1944 he wrote to Sidney with another idea: if the memorial appeal was successful:

> *...a couple of thousand of it should be spent in a statue of Sidney and Beatrice on the same pedestal, to be sculpted by Lady Kennet of the Dene (Scott's widow) and placed on the embankment by the LCC.* [379]

Shaw was 91 when Sidney died. A letter from him appeared in the *Times* the morning after Sidney's death, proposing that the ashes of both Beatrice and Sidney should be placed in the Abbey:

> *It is to the Abbey that their ashes are due; for it owes its secular sanctity not to its stones but to the mighty dead enshrined. The time has come to open its doors to greet world-betterers and to famous women as widely as to kings and captains, novelists and actors.* [380]

The following day, careful minutes, drafted with cautious precision, began to flow inside 10 Downing Street:

MR BEVIR

Bernard Shaw has written to the Minister for Economic Affairs [Stafford Cripps] suggesting that Lord Passfield should be buried in Westminster Abbey. You will remember that he wrote to 'The Times' in this sense yesterday. Sir Stafford Cripps has commended the suggestion to the Prime Minister.
The Prime Minister feels I think that this is not primarily the concern of No10. But he suggested that it might be possible for you to take informal soundings which might show the reaction of the Abbey authorities.
Apart from other considerations there may, I think, be a doubt about Lord Passfield's orthodoxy.
LMH
[Laurence Helsby] [381]

It was a complicated issue for church and state; both the high church Cripps and the Fabian John Parker were persistent lobbyists. Anthony Bevir, the No 10 civil servant who dealt with Church of England matters, told Attlee that

Mr Parker, however, had no intention of taking my advice, which would have cleared the air, and also not put the onus on you or the Government...[382]

Bevir, who had previously worked at No 10 for Churchill, is described by Anthony King in his study of Prime Ministers as

...a figure from Trollope, who left a trail of snuff and a whiff of claret behind him.[383]

Bevir advised Attlee:

It is not perhaps easy to ask the Abbey to give Abbey burial to those who are believed to have been Free Thinkers, but they have a place in our history, and they were of complete integrity of a type which is, I think, only born in Christian civilisation.[384]

While it might have been reasonable to describe Sidney as a free thinker, it scarcely did justice to Beatrice's lifelong interest in religion – of which Bevir appears to have been unaware. He was also concerned that Shaw might be making a pre-emptive claim for himself for a spot in the Abbey: he proposed to see the Dean

...purely personally and make this point in case he has missed it.[385]

On 29 October Attlee signed a letter, drafted by Bevir, asking the Dean to agree that Sidney and Beatrice could be buried in the Abbey:

...they led lives of devotion to their work which lay in improving the social circumstances and conditions of their fellow beings. They were never satisfied in their search for truth, and their integrity and probity no-one could question.[386]

The Dean first asked for time to think it over

...you will appreciate how onerous is the responsibility that rests upon the Dean of Westminster in a matter of this kind.[387]

On 4 November, the Dean wrote again: after *the most careful consideration*, he had concluded that he would be justified in agreeing to the burial of the ashes in the Abbey. The urns could be placed beneath the floor of the north aisle and covered with a stone with the words *Sidney and Beatrice Webb*. The reinterment could take place at Evensong one Friday afternoon before Christmas; 12 December was agreed. Attlee was asked to speak; he replied that he would be proud to do so.

The chosen spot was near the tomb of the eighteenth-century statesman

Charles James Fox, and not far from the bust of Joseph Chamberlain. On the day, almost all the Cabinet were there – Harold Wilson pleaded a prior engagement in the north of England.

There had been one major change in the Cabinet since October: following a budget leak in November, Hugh Dalton had been replaced as Chancellor by Stafford Cripps. One of the last people to arrive at the service was 82-year-old Rosie Dobbs, last of the Potter sisters.

There were lessons – *Let us now praise famous men* – and hymns – one of them Chesterton's *O God of earth and altar*. In his address, Attlee said

> *By their work, Sidney and Beatrice Webb, more widely than any others of their generation, changed for the better the condition of the masses of the people. In field after field of social endeavour we are today reaping the fruits of the seed which they sowed in the minds and hearts of men and women. They declared an unceasing war on poverty.* [388]

Attlee and the Webbs had not always seen eye-to-eye. But the government he led was now, patiently and systematically, legislating to turn their hopes and dreams into reality. The 1946 National Insurance Act established a universal social insurance scheme; the scheme was more Beveridge than Webb, but it did embody the aim of a national minimum. The National Health Service Act had been passed; the detailed negotiations to make it work were under way.

Then, at last, the week after Sidney died, the government announced the abolition of the Poor Law. The King's Speech was on 21 October. George VI told parliament that they would be asked to

> …*approve legislation to abolish the poor law and to provide a comprehensive system of assistance for all in need. …* [389]

That afternoon, in the debate on the King's Speech, Attlee said

> *I wish that Lord Passfield had lived long enough to see the last vestige of the old Poor Law swept away, but he saw sufficient to realise that that work of his had not been in vain.*[390]

The National Assistance Bill – *An Act to terminate the existing poor law* – had its second reading in late November. Its first clause stated bluntly

> *The existing poor law shall cease to have effect.*

Key ministers implementing the changes came from the Webb network. The Prime Minister's first job in politics had been as the meetings organiser of the National Campaign for the Prevention of Destitution. Dalton, Chancellor of the Exchequer until November 1947, was one of the 'brilliant' Cambridge Fabians, campaigning with Rupert Brooke and Ben Keeling. Greenwood, once secretary of the Leeds branch of the campaign, was now Lord Privy Seal. Ellen Wilkinson, now Education Minister, had been a student in Manchester before the First World War when she first met Beatrice.

The legacy of the Webbs is wider than social policy – but they inspired the main reforms of the 1945 Labour government.

That December afternoon in Westminster Abbey, when Attlee had finished speaking, the two small urns were carried in procession to the grave site. As the Dean was putting them in place, the silence was broken by an audible whisper from the last of the Potter sisters:

Which is Sidney and which is Beatrice?

After the final blessing Rosie had the last word:

They should have left them where they were.[391]

Notes to Part Four

1   *Evening Standard* 02.04.1932
2   Beatrice Webb Diary 10.10 1931
3   Morgan, K; *The Webbs and Soviet Communism; Bolshevism and the British Left Part 2*; London, Lawrence and Wishart, 2006; p 17
4   Beatrice to J M Keynes; 22.02.1926; in Webb, B & Webb, S; *The Letters of Sidney and Beatrice Webb; Vol III*; Cambridge; CUP; p 256
5   Beatrice to J M Keynes; 03.10.1926; in Webb, B & Webb, S; *The Letters of Sidney and Beatrice Webb; Vol III*; Cambridge; CUP; p 271
6   Beatrice Webb Diary 10.09.1931
7   Beatrice Webb Diary 10.09.1931
8   Beatrice Webb Diary 10.10.1931
9   MacDonald to Sidney, 14.07.1931, in Beatrice Webb Diary, 27.08.1931
10 Beatrice Webb Diary 10.10.1931
11 Beatrice Webb Diary 28.10.1931
12 Lansbury, G; *My Life*; London, Constable & Co, 1928; p 243
13 Beatrice Webb Diary 04.09.1920
14 See, for example, TNA, KV-2-573; KV-2-574
15 Beatrice Webb Diary 04.09.1920
16 Beatrice to H G Wells, 08.09.1920, in Webb, B & Webb, S; *The Letters of Sidney and Beatrice Webb; Vol III*; Cambridge; CUP; 1978; p 141
17 Beatrice to Charles Sarolea, 16.06.1924, in Webb, B & Webb, S; *The Letters of Sidney and Beatrice Webb; Vol III*; Cambridge; CUP; 1978; p 207
18 Beatrice Webb Diary 07.02.1928
19 Sidney to Beatrice, 25.04.1928, in Webb, B & Webb, S; *The Letters of Sidney and Beatrice Webb*; Vol III; Cambridge; CUP; 1978; p 298
20 note with Beatrice Webb diary for April 1929
21 Beatrice Webb Diary 16.04.1930
22 Beatrice Webb Diary 13.09.1930
23 Beatrice Webb Diary 30.06.1930
24 Beatrice Webb Diary 12.11.1930
25 Beatrice Webb Diary 19.11.1930
26 Beatrice Webb Diary 12.02.1931
27 Beatrice Webb Diary 08.08.1931
28 see Holroyd, M; *Bernard Shaw; Volume 3, The Lure of Fantasy*, London, Chatto and Windus, 1991 pp148-149
29 Beatrice Webb Diary 10.09.1931
30 Beatrice to Sidney, September 1931, in Webb, B & Webb, S; *The Letters of Sidney and Beatrice Webb; Vol III*; Cambridge; CUP; 1978; p 364, 365
31 Beatrice Webb Diary 19.09.1931
32 Beatrice Webb Diary 19.09.1931
33 Beatrice Webb Diary 19.09.1931
34 Beatrice Webb Diary 16.09.1931
35 Beatrice Webb Diary 10.12.1931
36 Beatrice Webb Diary 04.01.1932
37 Beatrice Webb Diary 04.01.1932
38 Beatrice Webb Diary 04.01.1932
39 Beatrice Webb Diary 14.05.1932
40 Beatrice Webb Diary 04.01.1932
41 Beatrice Webb Diary 05.04.1932
42 Beatrice Webb Diary 09.04.1932
43 Beatrice Webb Diary 09.04.1932
44 Hamilton, M A; *Remembering my good friends*; London, Jonathan Cape, 1944; p 257
45 Beatrice Webb Diary 24.05.1932
46 Khrushchev, N; *The dethronement of Stalin*; full text of the Khrushchev speech; Manchester Guardian, June 1956
47 Beatrice Webb Diary 25.05.1932
48 Beatrice Webb Diary 25.05.1932
49 Beatrice Webb Diary 25.05.1932
50 Beatrice Webb Diary 25.05.1932
51 Beatrice Webb Diary 06.1932
52 Beatrice Webb Diary 06.1932
53 Jones, T; A *Diary with Letters, 1931-1950*; Oxford, OUP, 1954; p 99
54 Beatrice Webb Diary 29.11.1933
55 Sidney to S P Turin, 16 December 1933; LSE Library, Passfield 16/1/Turin
56 Beatrice Webb Diary 29.03.1933
57 Beatrice Webb Diary 29.03.1933
58 Beatrice Webb Diary 29.03.1933
59 Webb, S & B; *Soviet Communism: A New Civilisation*; London, Longmans, 1935, 1937, 1941; p 258
60 Webb, S & B; *Soviet Communism: A*

New Civilisation; London, Longmans, 1935, 1937, 1941; p 265

61 Beatrice Webb Diary 27.03.1933
62 Beatrice Webb Diary 21.09.1933
63 Beatrice Webb Diary 24.11.1933
64 Beatrice Webb Diary 26.12.1933
65 Beatrice Webb Diary 06.01.1934
66 Beatrice Webb Diary 10.10.1934
67 Sidney to Beatrice, 12.09.1934; in Webb, B & Webb, S; *The Letters of Sidney and Beatrice Webb; Vol III*; Cambridge; CUP; 1978; p 398
68 Beatrice Webb Diary 10.10.1934
69 Beatrice Webb Diary 05.03.1935
70 Maisky, I; *The Complete Maisky Diaries*; Edited by Gabriel Gorodetsky; New Haven & London, Yale University Press, 2017; Vol I, p 105
71 Beatrice Webb Diary 15.11.1935
72 Beatrice Webb Diary 15.12.1935
73 Taylor, AJP; *English History 1914 – 1945*; Oxford, OUP, 1965; p348
74 Morgan, K O; *Labour People*; Oxford, OUP,1992; p 60
75 Beatrice Webb Diary 28.07.1932
76 Beatrice Webb Diary 15.01.1935
77 Beatrice Webb Diary 28.08.1936
78 Webb, S & B; *Soviet Communism: A New Civilization*; London, Longmans, 2nd edition, 1941; p1160
79 Beatrice Webb Diary 03.10.1932
80 Beatrice Webb Diary 15.09.1936
81 Beatrice Webb Diary 10.10.1931
82 Beatrice Webb Diary 10.10.1931
83 Beatrice Webb Diary 03.10.1932
84 Beatrice Webb Diary 03.10.1932
85 Beatrice Webb Diary 08.03.1931
86 Cole, Margaret; *Growing up into revolution*; London, Longmans, 1949; p 150
87 Bevin to GDH Cole, 29.09.1932; quoted in Bullock, Alan *The Life and Times of Ernest Bevin; I Trade Union Leader 1881 – 1940*; London, Heinemann; 1960; p 516
88 Cripps speech, 06.01.1934; Quoted in Pimlott, Ben; *Labour and the Left in the 1930s*; Cambridge; CUP; 1977; p 52; also on Cripps Special Branch File TNA KV2/668
89 *Daily Herald* 19.01.1934; quoted in TNA KV2/668
90 Beatrice Webb Diary 24.08.1933
91 Beatrice Webb Diary 04.08.1932
92 Beatrice Webb Diary 05.08.1933
93 Beatrice Webb Diary 04.08.1932
94 Hugh Dalton Diary 08.10.1932; in Dalton, Hugh; *The Political Diary of Hugh Dalton, 1918-40;1945-60*; ed Pimlott, B; London, Jonathan Cape, 1986
95 Beatrice Webb Diary 17.01.1932
96 Beatrice Webb Diary 17.01.1932
97 Beatrice Webb Diary 17.01.1932
98 Beatrice Webb Diary 17.01.1932
99 Beatrice Webb Diary 14.03.1934
100 Beatrice Webb Diary 14.03.1934
101 Beatrice Webb Diary 27.01.1932
102 Hugh Dalton Diary, 23 – 25.06.1932; in Dalton, Hugh; *The Political Diary of Hugh Dalton, 1918-40;1945-60*; ed Pimlott, B; London, Jonathan Cape, 1986; p 166
103 Beatrice Webb Diary 27.01.1932
104 Beatrice Webb Diary 27.01.1932
105 Hugh Dalton Diary, 23 – 25.06.1932; in Dalton, Hugh; *The Political Diary of Hugh Dalton, 1918-40;1945-60*; ed Pimlott, B; London, Jonathan Cape, 1986; p 166
106 Beatrice Webb Diary 30.10.1932
107 Beatrice Webb Diary 19.03.32
108 Beatrice Webb Diary 02.02.1933
109 Estorick, Eric; *Stafford Cripps, a biography*; London, William Heinemann Ltd, 1949; p 32
110 Beatrice Webb Diary 07.03.1933
111 Beatrice Webb Diary 07.03.1933
112 Beatrice Webb Diary 07.03.1933
113 Beatrice Webb Diary 30.10.1932
114 Beatrice Webb Diary 28.09.1933
115 Beatrice Webb Diary 28.09.1933
116 Beatrice Webb Diary 03.05.1934
117 Beatrice Webb Diary, 30.03.1933
118 Cole, Margaret; *Growing up into revolution*; London, Longmans, 1949; p171
119 Beatrice Webb Diary, 14.02.1934
120 Ernest Bevin speech, Labour Party Conference, 1.10.1935. Quoted in Bullock, Alan *The Life and Times of Ernest Bevin; I Trade Union Leader 1881 – 1940*; London, Heinemann; 1960; p 568
121 Beatrice Webb Diary 02.09.1935
122 Beatrice Webb Diary 28.09.1935
123 Beatrice Webb Diary 23.10.1935
124 Bryant, Chris *Stafford Cripps, The first*

modern Chancellor; London, Hodder and Stoughton, 1997

125 Cripps to Parmoor, 20.09.1935; in Estorick, Eric; *Stafford Cripps, a biography;* London, William Heinemann Ltd, 1949; p141

126 Cole, Margaret; *Growing up into revolution*; London, Longmans, 1949; p173

127 Beatrice Webb Diary 15.11.1936

128 Beatrice Webb Diary 07.01.1937

129 Pimlott, Ben; *Labour and the Left in the 1930s*; Cambridge; CUP; 1977; p226 n.40

130 Pimlott, Ben; *Hugh Dalton*; London; Jonathan Cape, 1985; p241

131 Cripps to Parmoor, early 1936; in Estorick, Eric; *Stafford Cripps, a biography*; London, William Heinemann Ltd, 1949; p149

132 Beatrice Webb Diary 02.02.1936

133 National Archives KV 2/668

134 Sidney to Parmoor, early1937, in Estorick, Eric; *Stafford Cripps, a biography*; London, William Heinemann Ltd, 1949 pp155-6

135 Beatrice Webb Diary 16.04.1937

136 Beatrice Webb Diary 18.04.1937

137 Beatrice Webb Diary 18.04.1937

138 See Pimlott, Ben; *Labour and the Left in the 1930s*; Cambridge; CUP; 1977; p105

139 Castle, Barbara *Fighting all the way*; London; Macmillan; 1993; p 86

140 Beatrice Webb Diary 01.07 1933

141 Beatrice Webb Diary 18.08.1933

142 Beatrice Webb Diary 18.08.1933

143 Beatrice Webb Diary 18.08.1933

144 Beatrice Webb Diary 05.01.1934

145 Beatrice Webb Diary 12.03.1934

146 Beatrice Webb Diary 12.03.1934

147 Harold Laski to Beatrice Webb, 13.03.1934, in Beatrice Webb Diary

148 Beatrice Webb Diary 25.05.1934

149 Beatrice Webb Diary 25.05.1934

150 Beatrice Webb Diary 25.05.1934

151 Beatrice Webb Diary 23.09.1934

152 Beatrice Webb Diary 05.01.1935

153 Beatrice Webb Diary 05.01.1935

154 Beatrice Webb Diary 12.01.1935

155 Beatrice Webb Diary 24.03.1935

156 Beatrice Webb Diary 15.02.1936

157 Beatrice Webb Diary 10.03.1936; 17.03.1936

158 Beatrice Webb Diary 17.03.1936

159 Beatrice Webb Diary 17.03.1936

160 Mrs Mair to Beveridge, 30.05 (?) 1936; quoted in Harris, J; *William Beveridge, a biography*; Oxford, OUP; 1977; p 308

161 Beatrice Webb Diary 12.07.1936

162 Beatrice Webb Diary 12.07.1936

163 Beatrice Webb Diary 17.07.1936

164 Beatrice Webb Diary 31.12.1936

165 Beatrice Webb Diary 11.08.1940

166 Beatrice Webb Diary 01.05.1937

167 Information from Robin Darwall-Smith, Archivist, University College Oxford

168 Beatrice Webb Diary 27.08.1937

169 LSE Library Beveridge Papers 7/97

170 Beatrice Webb Diary 23.10.1935

171 Beatrice Webb Diary 13.06.1937

172 Beatrice Webb Diary 13.06.1937

173 Beatrice Webb Diary 05.05.1937

174 Beatrice Webb Diary, 23.01.1938

175 Beatrice Webb Diary, 25.01.1938

176 GBS to Beatrice, 06.02.1938; in Michalos, Alex C & Poff, Deborah C; eds; *Bernard Shaw and the Webbs*; Toronto, University of Toronto Press, 2002; p 232

177 Beatrice Webb Diary, 11.02.1938

178 Beatrice Webb Diary, 10.08.1938

179 Beatrice Webb Diary 01.11.1938

180 Sidney to Pease, 12.01.1939, in Webb, B & Webb, S; *The Letters of Sidney and Beatrice Webb; Vol III;* Cambridge; CUP; 1978; p 426

181 Beatrice Webb Diary 13.07.1939

182 Beatrice Webb Diary 10.08.1938

183 Beveridge, W; *Power and Influence*; London; Hodder and Stoughton, 1953; p 259

184 Quoted in Pimlott, B; *Harold Wilson*; London; Harper Collins; 1992; p 62

185 Beatrice Webb Diary 10.08.1938

186 Beatrice to William Beveridge, 17.11.1938; in Webb, B & Webb, S; *The Letters of Sidney and Beatrice Webb; Vol III;* Cambridge; CUP; 1978; p 424

187 Beveridge, W; *Power and Influence*; London, Hodder and Stoughton, 1953; p 274

188 Cole, Margaret; *Growing up into revolution*; London, Longmans, 1949; p 204

189 GBS to Beatrice, 18.07.1940, in

Michalos, Alex C & Poff, Deborah C; eds; *Bernard Shaw and the Webbs*; Toronto, University of Toronto Press, 2002; p 252

190   Beatrice Webb Diary 11.08.1940
191   Beatrice Webb Diary 31.05.1941
192   Harris, J; *William Beveridge, a biography*; Oxford, OUP; 1977; p 376
193   Beatrice Webb Diary 24.02.1941
194   Harris, J; *William Beveridge, a biography*; Oxford, OUP; 1977; p 384
195   Beveridge, W; *Power and Influence*; London, Hodder and Stoughton, 1953; p 317
196   Beatrice Webb Diary 26.10.1942
197   Social Insurance and Allied Services; Report by Sir William Beveridge; Cmd 6404 1942; para 7
198   Beatrice Webb Diary 30.11.1942
199   Beatrice Webb Diary 06.12.1942
200   Beatrice to Reginald Pott, 14.12.1942, in Webb, B & Webb, S; *The Letters of Sidney and Beatrice Webb; Vol III*; Cambridge; CUP; 1978; pp 460-461
201   Beatrice Webb Diary 06.12.1942
202   Beatrice Webb Diary 09.12.1942
203   Beatrice to R H Tawney, 14.12.1942; in Webb, B & Webb, S; *The Letters of Sidney and Beatrice Webb; Vol III*; Cambridge; CUP; 1978; p 461
204   Darwall-Smith, R; *Can a great man be a good master? William Beveridge as Master of Univ*; unpublished paper, 2015
205   Beatrice Webb Diary 19.12.1942
206   LSE Library Beveridge 8/52
207   Beveridge to Sidney, 06.06.1919; in LSE Library Beveridge 2/B/67
208   LSE Library Beveridge/9B/43/3
209   LSE Library Beveridge 9A/51/1
210   LSE Library Beveridge 9A/51/1
211   Taylor, AJP *English History 1914 – 1945* Oxford, OUP, 1965; p 567
212   Hennessy, Peter *Never Again*; Britain 1945-51; London, Jonathan Cape, 1992 ; p 130
213   National Assistance Act 1948; clause 1
214   Beatrice Webb Diary 05.06.1937
215   Beatrice Webb Diary 12.01.1935
216   Beatrice Webb Diary 29.09.1936
217   Beatrice Webb Diary 27.10.1937
218   Beatrice Webb Diary 30.06.1938
219   Charlotte Shaw to Beatrice, 07.11.1938; in Beatrice Webb Diary

220   Beatrice Webb Diary 11.01.1939
221   Beatrice Webb Diary 24.05.1940
222   GBS to Beatrice, 13.06.1940, in Michalos, Alex C & Poff, Deborah C; eds; *Bernard Shaw and the Webbs*; Toronto, University of Toronto Press, 2002; p 244-5
223   GBS to Beatrice, 17.02.1941, in Michalos, Alex C & Poff, Deborah C; eds; *Bernard Shaw and the Webbs*; Toronto, University of Toronto Press, 2002; p 253
224   Blanche Patch to Beatrice, 29.04.1941, in Michalos, Alex C & Poff, Deborah C; eds; *Bernard Shaw and the Webbs*; Toronto, University of Toronto Press, 2002; p 256
225   Blanche Patch to Beatrice, 29.04.1941, in Michalos, Alex C & Poff, Deborah C; eds; *Bernard Shaw and the Webbs*; Toronto, University of Toronto Press, 2002; p 257
226   Beatrice to GBS, 02.08.1941; in Webb, B & Webb, S; *The Letters of Sidney and Beatrice Webb; Vol III*; Cambridge; CUP; 1978; p 451
227   Beatrice Webb Diary 28.02.1942
228   Beatrice to GBS, 19.03.1942, in Michalos, Alex C & Poff, Deborah C; eds; *Bernard Shaw and the Webbs*; Toronto, University of Toronto Press, 2002; p 266
229   Beatrice Webb Diary 17.08.1942
230   Beatrice Webb Diary 09.12.1942
231   GBS to Sidney, 24.05.1943; in Michalos, Alex C & Poff, Deborah C; eds; *Bernard Shaw and the Webbs*; Toronto, University of Toronto Press, 2002; p 271
232   Beatrice Webb Diary 01.02.1937
233   Beatrice Webb Diary 01.02.1937
234   Beatrice Webb Diary 27.02.1937
235   Beatrice Webb Diary 13.12.1937
236   Beatrice Webb Diary 07.08.1938
237   Beatrice Webb Diary 23.01.1938
238   Maisky, Ivan; *The Maisky Diaries*; ed Gorodetsky, G; London, Yale UP, 2015; p 269
239   Beatrice Webb Diary 07.08.1938
240   Maisky Diary, 12.06.1939; Maisky, Ivan; *The Complete Maisky Diaries*; ed Gorodetsky, G; New Haven & London, Yale University Press, 2017; p 258

241   Beatrice Webb Diary 18.04.1937
242   Beatrice Webb Diary 25.07.1937
243   Maisky Diary, 30.10.1938; Maisky, Ivan; *The Complete Maisky Diaries*; ed Gorodetsky, G; New Haven & London, Yale University Press, 2017;
244   Woolf, Leonard; *Downhill all the way, an autobiography of the years 1919-1939*; London, Hogarth Press, 1967; p 243
245   Woolf, Leonard; *Downhill all the way, an autobiography of the years 1919-1939*; London, Hogarth Press, 1967; p 243
246   Beatrice Webb Diary 25.05.1937
247   Beatrice Webb Diary 29.08.1938
248   Beatrice Webb Diary 26.05.1939
249   Beatrice Webb Diary 17.07.1936
250   Beatrice Webb Diary 23.01.1930
251   Clark, Kenneth; *Another part of the wood;* London, 1974; p 271; quoted in Bouverie, Tim; Appeasing Hitler; London, Vintage, 2020.
252   Churchill, Winston; *The Gathering Storm*; Vol 1 of The Second World War; London, Cassell; 1948; p188
253   Jones, Thomas; *A Diary with Letters, 1931-1950*; Oxford, OUP, 1954; p125
254   Jones, Thomas; *A Diary with Letters, 1931-1950*; Oxford, OUP, 1954; p 197
255   Jones, Thomas; *A Diary with Letters, 1931-1950*; Oxford, OUP, 1954; p 201
256   Rowse, Alfred Leslie; *All Souls and Appeasement*; London; Macmillan; 1961; p 35
257   Beatrice Webb Diary 15.11.1936
258   Beatrice Webb Diary 10.04.1936
259   Beatrice Webb Diary 12.03.1937
260   Beatrice Webb Diary, September 1938
261   Beatrice Webb Diary 01.10.1938
262   Hansard, 05.10.1938, Col 412
263   Beatrice to William Beveridge, 17.11.1938; in Webb, B & Webb, S; *The Letters of Sidney and Beatrice Webb; Vol III*; Cambridge; CUP; 1978; p 424
264   Beatrice Webb Diary 17.11.1938
265   Beatrice Webb Diary 31.12.1938
266   Beatrice Webb Diary 21.01.1939
267   Beatrice Webb Diary 21.01.1939
268   Beatrice Webb Diary 21.01.1939
269   Beatrice Webb Diary 21.01.1939
270   J M Keynes to Stafford Cripps, 09.02.1939; in Estorick, Eric; *Stafford Cripps, a biography*; London, William Heinemann Ltd, 1949; p166
271   Clement Attlee to Tom Attlee, 23.02,1939, in Harris, Kenneth; *Attlee*; London, Weidenfeld and Nicolson, 1982; p 159
272   Beatrice Webb Diary 27.02.1939
273   Beatrice Webb Diary 27.02.1939
274   Beatrice to Herbert Morrison, 03.03.1939; in Webb, B & Webb, S; *The Letters of Sidney and Beatrice Webb; Vol III*; Cambridge; CUP; 1978; p 428
275   Beatrice Webb Diary 16.03.1939
276   Police report of Cripps speech, 24.04.1939, in TNA KV 2/668
277   Beatrice Webb Diary 13.02.1939
278   Beatrice Webb Diary 22.04.1939
279   Beatrice Webb Diary 12.06.1939
280   Maisky Diary, 12.06.1939; Maisky, Ivan; *The Complete Maisky Diaries*; ed Gorodetsky, G; New Haven & London, Yale University Press, 2017
281   Beatrice Webb Diary 12.06.1939
282   Estorick, Eric; *Stafford Cripps, a biography*; London, William Heinemann Ltd, 1949; p 174
283   Beatrice Webb Diary 18.06.1939
284   Taylor, AJP *English History 1914 – 1945* Oxford, OUP, 1965; p 448
285   Beatrice Webb Diary 09.07.1939
286   Beatrice Webb Diary 09.07.1939
287   Beatrice Webb Diary 09.07.1939
288   Beatrice Webb Diary 09.07.1939
289   *Daily Worker* 24.07.1939 in TNA KV 2/668
290   Maisky Diary, 04.08.1939; in Maisky, Ivan; *The Maisky Diaries*; ed Gorodetsky, G; London, Yale UP, 2015; p 212
291   Beatrice Webb Diary 07.08.1939
292   Beatrice Webb Diary 23.08.1939
293   Beatrice Webb Diary 25.08.1939
294   Maisky Diary, 19.09.1939; in Maisky, Ivan; *The Maisky Diaries*; ed Gorodetsky, G; London, Yale UP, 2015; p 226
295   Beatrice Webb Diary 07.09.1939
296   Beatrice Webb Diary 03.09.1939
297   Beatrice Webb Diary 31.08.1939
298   Beatrice Webb Diary 14.09.1939
299   Beatrice Webb Diary 18.09.1939
300   Beatrice Webb Diary 02.10.1939
301   *Daily Worker* 05.10.1939; Tribune

06.10.1939 in TNA KV 2/668

302 Cripps to Halifax, 16.09.1939; in Estorick, Eric; *Stafford Cripps, a biography*; London, William Heinemann Ltd, 1949; p 181

303 TNA KV 2 /786

304 Beatrice Webb Diary 18.01.1940

305 Maisky Diary, 24.12.1939; Maisky, Ivan; *The Complete Maisky Diaries*; ed Gorodetsky, G; New Haven & London, Yale University Press, 2017; p 706

306 Maisky Diary, 24.12.1939; Maisky, Ivan; *The Complete Maisky Diaries*; ed Gorodetsky, G; New Haven & London, Yale University Press, 2017; p 706

307 Beatrice Webb Diary 29.02.1940

308 Beatrice Webb Diary 29.01.1940

309 Beatrice Webb Diary 15.10.1939

310 Beatrice Webb Diary 29.02.1940

311 Beatrice Webb Diary 10.04.1940

312 Beatrice Webb Diary 10.04.1940

313 Maisky Diary, 15.04.1940; in Maisky, Ivan; *The Maisky Diaries*; ed Gorodetsky, G; London, Yale UP, 2015; p 271

314 Taylor, AJP *English History 1914 – 1945* Oxford, OUP, 1965; p 470

315 Beatrice Webb Diary 04.05.1940

316 Maisky Diary, 13.05.1940; in Maisky, Ivan; *The Maisky Diaries*; ed Gorodetsky, G; London, Yale UP, 2015; p 276

317 Beatrice Webb Diary 11.05.1940

318 Maisky, Ivan Memoirs *of a Soviet Ambassador; The War 1939 – 43*; London; Hutchinson; 1967;p 79

319 Maisky, Ivan; *Memoirs of a Soviet Ambassador; The War 1939 – 43*; London; Hutchinson; 1967; p 80

320 Maisky, Ivan; *Memoirs of a Soviet Ambassador; The War 1939 – 43*; London; Hutchinson; 1967; p 81

321 Maisky, Ivan; *Memoirs of a Soviet Ambassador; The War 1939 – 43*; London; Hutchinson; 1967; p 81

322 Maisky, Ivan; *Memoirs of a Soviet Ambassador; The War 1939 – 43*; London; Hutchinson; 1967; p 81

323 Beatrice Webb Diary 20.05.1940

324 Maisky Diary, 18.05.1940; Maisky, Ivan; *The Complete Maisky Diaries*; ed Gorodetsky, G; New Haven &

London, Yale University Press, 2017; p 813

325 Maisky, Ivan; *Memoirs of a Soviet Ambassador; The War 1939 – 43*; London; Hutchinson; 1967; p 82

326 Maisky, Ivan; *Memoirs of a Soviet Ambassador; The War 1939 – 43*; London; Hutchinson; 1967; p 82

327 War Cabinet, 15.05.1940; TNA CAB 65/7/27

328 TNA War Cabinet Minutes 15.05.1940

329 Beatrice Webb Diary 20.05.1940

330 Beatrice Webb Diary 20.05.1940

331 Hugh Dalton Diary, 17.05.1940; Dalton, Hugh; *The Second World War Diary of Hugh Dalton 1940 – 1945*; edited by Ben Pimlott; London, Jonathan Cape, in association with the London School of Economics and Political Science, 1986; p 10

332 Maisky Diary, 05.06.1940; Maisky, Ivan; *The Complete Maisky Diaries*; ed Gorodetsky, G; New Haven & London, Yale University Press, 2017; p 828

333 TNA KV 2 /668

334 Woolf, Virginia; Diary 22 October 1939; in *Selected Diaries*; abridged and edited by Anne Olivier Bell; London, Vintage, 2008; p 462

335 Beatrice Webb Diary 27.10.1939

336 Beatrice Webb Diary 27.10.1939

337 Beatrice Webb Diary 07.04.1941

338 Beatrice Webb Diary 07.04.1941

339 Beatrice Webb Diary 07.04.1941

340 Beatrice Webb Diary 18.09.1926

341 Beatrice Webb Diary 18.04.1930

342 Beatrice Webb Diary 18.04.1930

343 Beatrice Webb Diary 29.04.1936

344 Beatrice Webb Diary 05.03.1942

345 Beatrice Webb Diary 11.03.1942

346 Beatrice Webb Diary 14.08.1940

347 Beatrice Webb Diary 20.08.1940

348 Beatrice Webb Diary 24.02.1942

349 Beatrice Webb Diary 24.02.1942

350 Beatrice Webb Diary 27.11.1941.

351 Beatrice Webb Diary 13.09.1942

352 Beatrice Webb Diary 25.09.1942

353 Beatrice Webb Diary 25.09.1942

354 Beatrice Webb Diary 11.11.1942

355 Malcom Muggeridge Diary, 25.04.1948; in Muggeridge, Malcolm; *Like it Was; The Diaries of Malcolm*

Muggeridge; Selected and Edited by
John Bright-Holmes; London, Collins,
1981

356 Beatrice Webb Diary 25.09.1942
357 Beatrice Webb Diary 23.06.1941
358 Beatrice Webb Diary 15.08.1941
359 Beatrice Webb Diary 25.12.1942
360 Beatrice Webb Diary 18.01.1943
361 Beatrice Webb Diary 26.10.1942
362 Beatrice Webb Diary 29.07.1941
363 Beatrice Webb Diary 04.01.1943
364 Beatrice Webb Diary 04.01.1943
365 Beatrice Webb Diary 05.02.1943
366 Beatrice Webb Diary 19.04.1943
367 Martin, Basil Kingsley; *Editor*;
London, Penguin, 1968; p 95
368 Beatrice Webb Diary 12.02.1943
369 Samuel, Viscount (Herbert Samuel);
Memoirs; London, the Cresset Press;
1945; p 293
370 Samuel, Viscount (Herbert Samuel);
Memoirs; London, the Cresset Press;
1945; p293
371 Beatrice Webb Diary 19.04.1943
372 Maisky, Ivan; *The Maisky Diaries*; ed
Gorodetsky, G; London, Yale UP,
2015; p 524
373 Maisky, Ivan; *The Maisky Diaries*; ed
Gorodetsky, G; London, Yale UP,
2015; p 524
374 For this period in Maisky's career,
see Maisky, Ivan; *The Maisky Diaries*;
ed Gorodetsky, G; London, Yale UP,
2015; pp546-561
375 Maisky, Ivan; *The Maisky Diaries*; ed
Gorodetsky, G; London, Yale UP,
2015; p 560
376 Webb Memorial Trust Papers, in LSE
Library, Passfield Papers,
377 GBS to Sidney, 24.05.1943; in
Michalos, Alex C & Poff, Deborah
C; eds; *Bernard Shaw and the Webbs*;
Toronto, University of Toronto Press,
2002; p 271
378 GBS to Sidney, 02.04.1944; in
Michalos, Alex C & Poff, Deborah
C; eds; *Bernard Shaw and the Webbs*;
Toronto, University of Toronto Press,
2002; p 275
379 GBS to Sidney, 02.04.1944; in
Michalos, Alex C & Poff, Deborah
C; eds; *Bernard Shaw and the Webbs*;
Toronto, University of Toronto Press,
2002; p 275

380 Letter, GBS to The Times, 16.10.1947
381 Laurence Helsby to Anthony Bevir,
17.10.1947 TNA PREM 8/462
382 Anthony Bevir to Attlee, 28.10.1947;
TNA PREM 8/462
383 Jones, G W; *The Prime Minister's Aides*;
in King, Anthony, editor; *The British
Prime Minister*; London, Macmillan,
1985; p 85
384 Anthony Bevir to Prime Minister,
28.10.1947; TNA PREM 8/462
385 Anthony Bevir to Laurence Helsby,
18.10.1947; TNA PREM 8/462
386 Attlee to Dean of Westminster.
29.10.1947; TNA PREM 8/462
387 Dean of Westminster to Prime
Minister, 30.10.1947; TNA PREM
8/462
388 *Daily Herald*, 13.12.1947
389 Hansard 21.10.1947
390 Hansard 21.10.1947
391 These details from Muggeridge, K &
Adam, R; *Beatrice Webb: A life 1858-
1943* London, Secker & Warburg,
1967; p 258

ANNEXES

1. Acknowledgments and thanks

2. Biographical Index

3. Bibliography

4. The Potter sisters

5. Abbreviations and acronyms

Annexe One: Acknowledgements and Thanks

This book has been a long time in the making, and along the way many people and institutions have helped me. I am very grateful to all of them for their support, and their patience; needless to say, any errors of fact or judgment are mine and not theirs.

Through the Smith Institute (John, not Adam), and its Director Paul Hackett, I was invited by the trustees of the Webb Memorial Trust to write a booklet commemorating the centenary of the 1909 Minority Report of the Poor Law Commission, (*Beatrice Webb: her quest for a fairer society*, 2011). Subsequently the Webb Memorial Trust generously supported me in taking on this project. They have waited patiently for the result.

The Trust also funded the digitisation by LSE of Beatrice Webb's manuscript and typewritten diary, which made my task much easier than for previous writers on the Webbs. All the extracts from the diary come from the online version and appear here by permission of LSE.

I have been inspired by three gifted historians. At school in Wimbledon, I was taught by Richard Milward, who was a prolific local historian as well as a dedicated teacher. Early in my time at Oxford, I met Raphael Samuel, from whom I learned a great deal; Raphael remained a friend up to his untimely death in 1996. And in 1978, at Birkbeck, I was taught by Eric Hobsbawm. All three had their differences with the Webbs. But I am sorry that none of the three are still here to argue about the book.

At Birkbeck, I was also taught by Susanne MacGregor; Susanne is now an Honorary Professor of Social Policy at the Centre for History in Public Health, at the London School of Hygiene and Tropical Medicine. She introduced me to the Centre, where I became a Visiting Research Fellow. As well as facilitating my access to academic libraries, this fellowship provided access to a supportive academic community. Susanne also read and commented on a number of chapters in draft. I would also like to thank Professor Virginia Berridge, Director of the Centre when I took up the Fellowship; Ingrid James, the Centre administrator; and the other academic and support staff.

When I began working on this book, I was able to discuss it with Robin Murray. Robin's early death in 2017 meant that I could no longer talk to him as the book took shape.

Professors Chris Wrigley, of Nottingham, and Jerry White, of Birkbeck, took time to discuss my original outline for the project. Professor Pat Thane of Kings

College London read both this book, and my 2011 pamphlet, in draft, and on both occasions gave me sound advice. I have appreciated the assistance of old friends. Penelope Corfield read sections in draft, and recommended me to an anonymous academic reviewer, who gave me useful independent advice. Sean Creighton helped with sources, and stoutly defended the good name of John Burns against Beatrice's negative views.

After a long period I got back in contact with Jane Winter, who has been writing about Ka Cox, Rupert Brooke, and other Neo-pagans; we have continuously exchanged information about sources and references. Anne Seex read the whole text – but ended up disliking Beatrice. Mark Jones and Reg Race helped with advice about publishers.

I am very grateful for all the help I have had from archivists in the course of this study. The LSE archives hold, not only the extensive records left by the Webbs themselves (the well-known Passfield Papers, and other collections, covering local government, trade unions, and East Africa), but also the records of the Fabian Society; the papers of Charles Booth, William Beveridge and R H Tawney; and the diary of Arthur Colegate. My regular contact at the LSE Archive was with Anna Towlson, who has been most helpful throughout.

I went to the archive at the People's History Museum in Manchester to research Labour Party papers; Darren Treadwell also drew the extensive War Emergency Workers National Committee Archive to my attention.

At the Bodleian Library in Oxford I read Arthur Greenwood's papers; at the London Metropolitan Archives I read material on the early London County Council, and its Technical Education Board. I went to the Kings College Archive Centre in Cambridge to look at papers in the Rupert Brooke and Maynard Keynes collections. At the National Archives I read Colonial Office and Cabinet papers; I also found Sidney's Civil Service personnel file including his first letter of application, written at the age of 19. At the other end of the story, I found the PREM file containing Mr Attlee's correspondence, with Westminster Abbey and others, about the burial of the ashes of both Webbs in the Abbey.

I read John Burns' diary, and some of his correspondence, at the British Library, where I also read many of the secondary sources referenced in the book.

The online version of the Oxford Dictionary of National Biography (courtesy of West Sussex Public Libraries) has been an invaluable resource.

I have sought to obtain the appropriate permissions from copyright holders for every image and every substantial quotation, but accept responsibility for any inadvertent errors or omissions.

The illustrations in the book come from a range of sources; each image is acknowledged. Many of the small pictures of individuals in the Biographical Index are from the National Portrait Gallery, under an academic licence. Many other pictures are from the LSE archive.

Charles Foster, with whom I worked in the 1980s, when he was responsible for most of the publications of the Industry and Employment Branch of the Greater London Council, designed the map endpapers, showing the Webbs' London.

In 2015 University College Oxford held an event about Beveridge; I spoke about Beveridge and the Webbs; Robin Darwall Smith, the College archivist, and Professor Ben Jackson, also spoke. I am grateful to Robin Darwall Smith for permission to refer to some of the material he used.

The Literary Consultancy arranged for someone to read and advise on an earlier draft. Old colleagues Hilary Wainwright and Sheila Rowbotham were always ready to discuss on the phone how the book was going.

Sheila also introduced me to Hugo Radice, who is a grandson of Ben Keeling, one of the Cambridge Fabians who was killed in the First World War. We exchanged information about his grandfather and other family members. Very late in the process, I was amazed to meet members of the Aked family - Beatrice's Bacup cousins – living a few streets away from me in Arundel.

Camilla Lambert, another Arundel resident, was one of the organisers of the inaugural Arundel Literary Day in March 2023, at which I gave a talk about the Webbs. I learned later that Camilla is a grand daughter of two other Cambridge Fabians – Bill and Eva Hubback.

Thank you also to Nic Nicholas for her thoroughness and efficiency in preparing the index.

The book is being published by the Conrad Press. I would like to thank James Essinger for agreeing to take this project on, and Charlotte Mouncey of Bookstyle for her indefatigable work on typesetting and design, and her endless patience.

One day in spring 2019, I turned up (unannounced) at Passfield Corner, the Webbs' former home on the Surrey/Hampshire border, the former owner, Mrs Valerie Herdwick kindly took the time to show me round. More recently I have met the current owners, Toby and Kate MacLachlan, who enabled me to take copies of some photographs kept at the house.

My family have had to put up with Sidney and Beatrice for a long time. This they have usually done with great forbearance, and I would like to thank them.

My partner Hilary Knight has read a lot of the book in draft; our children Rosie and James have also read sections. Hilary already knew about the Webbs: when, as an undergraduate student in the 1970s, she switched from Economics to Social and Political Sciences, her LSE-educated, businessman/economist father gave her Beatrice's *My Apprenticeship* to read.

Annexe Two: Biographical Index

Ablett, Noah
1883-1935
Miners' leader and adult educator;
Syndicalist ILP member
1907 Ruskin
Plebs League
South Wales Miners Unofficial
Reform Cttee
Involved in founding College as an
alternative to Ruskin
1917 attended Leeds Convention

Acland, Arthur (Sir)
1847-1926
Educational reformer and
administrator
Curate to Mandell Creighton
Mentor to Llewellyn Smith, Michael
Sadler, and others
Liberal MP for Rotherham, 1885
1892 Vice President of Council for
Education (I.e. education minister)
Worked with Llewellyn Smith on
Technical Education

Acland, Richard (Sir)
1906-1990
Politician and educationalist
Grandson of Sir Arthur Acland
Founded WW2 Common Wealth
Party
Later Labour MP

Adamson, William
1863-1936
Politician and trade unionist
1908 General Secretary, Fife and
Kinross Miners' Association
1910 (December) Labour MP
1917-1921 Chair, PLP
1924; 1929-1931 Secretary of State
for Scotland

Addison, Christopher
1869-1951
Doctor and politician
1910-22 Liberal, MP
1916 Min Munitions
1919 1st Minister of Health
1923 Joins Labour
1929-31 and 1934-35 Labour MP
Agriculture minister in 1929 Labour
government
1937 peer
Minister in Attlee government

Allen, Clifford; later Lord Allen of
Hurtwood
1889-1939
Politician and peace campaigner
Cambridge Fabian; WW1
Conscientious Objector; imprisoned
1931 supported Macdonald decision
to form National Government
1932 peerage from Macdonald

Amery, Leopold
1873-1955

© National Portrait Gallery, London
Politician and journalist
Fabian at Oxford in 1890s
Worked for Leonard Courtney
1900-1909 wrote *Times History of
South African war*

Conservative MP 1911-45
Coefficient; Imperialist
1924-9 Precedes Sidney as Colonial
Secretary,
Secretary of State for India in 1931
National Government

Anderson, William Crawford
1877-1919 Politician
ILP member
Worked for Shop Assistants' Union
1910-1913 Chair, ILP
1911 married Mary MacArthur
1914-1918 MP, Sheffield Attercliffe
Opposed war; UDC member
Member, War Emergency Workers
National Committee
1917 spoke at Leeds convention

Argyle, Jesse
1859-1924
Social investigator and statistician
Employee of Charles Booth from early
1880s
Helps Beatrice in 1886
Continued to work with Booth to
1904

Arnold, Sydney; 1st Baron Arnold
1878-1945
Politician
1912-1921 Liberal MP
1922 joined Labour Party
1924 Under Secretary, Colonial Office
1929-1921 Paymaster General
An appeaser in late 1930s
1938 left Labour Party

Arnot, Robin Page
1890-1986
Political activist and historian
1914 Secretary, Fabian Research
Department. Guild Socialist
WW1 Conscientious Objector;
imprisoned
Largely responsible for Miners
evidence to Sankey Commission
Foundation member Communist
Party of Great Britain

Asquith, Herbert Henry; later Earl of
Oxford & Asquith
1852-1958

© National Portrait Gallery, London
Prime Minister 1908-1916
Barrister; Liberal MP
Liberal Imperialist ('Limp')

Asquith, Margot (née Tennant)
(Emma Margaret)
1864-1945
Political hostess and diarist
Soul
Second wife of H H Asquith (married
1894)

Atkinson, Mabel
1876-1958
Feminist and socialist
Studied at Glasgow
1897 Fabian member
1904 lecturer at Armstrong College
Durham
1908 moved to London to work for
WEA
A founder of Fabian Society Women's
Group
1909-1919 Fabian Executive
Committee
1 of originators of Fabian Summer
Schools
1914 married Andrew Palmer,
Australian
1921 moved to S Africa; academic
jobs; strong campaigning efforts

Attlee, Clement Richard (later Earl Attlee)
1883-1967

© National Portrait Gallery, London

1907 Joins Fabian Society
Attends Fabian Summer School
1909-10 works for Poor Law Campaign
Then for Toynbee Hall
1912-14 Lecturer, LSE; returns after war
1922 Labour MP
1930 Chancellor of the Duchy of Lancaster;
1931 Postmaster General
1931 Deputy Leader Labour Party
1935 Leader
1940 Deputy Prime Minister
1945-51 Prime Minister

Baldwin, Stanley
1867-1947
Businessman and Prime Minister
1908   Conservative MP for Bewdley (inheriting seat and business appts from his father)
1916   PPS to Bonar Law
1917   Financial Sec Treasury
1921   Pres Board of Trade
1922   supported ending of Coalition; Chancellor of Exchequer
1923   Prime Minister
Again PM 1924-1929; 1935-37
Widely blamed for the failure to rearm in the 1930s, and for appeasement

Balfour, Arthur (later Earl Balfour)
1848-1930

© National Portrait Gallery, London

1902-05 Conservative Prime Minister; Soul
Beatrice meets for 1st time in 1884
1887-1891 Chief Secretary, Ireland; 'Bloody Balfour'
1905 Appoints Beatrice to Poor Law Commission
1916-1919 Foreign Secretary; responsible for Balfour Declaration

Balfour, Betty (Elizabeth)
1867-1942
Wife of Gerald Balfour; hostess; friend of Beatrice; frequent correspondent Soul
From 1910 a supporter of the suffrage movement
Countess of Balfour after Arthur Balfour's death in 1930

Balfour, Gerald William
1853-1945
Politician
Brother of Arthur Balfour; Soul
1895-1900 Chief Sec Ireland
1900-5 President Board of Trade
1905 President Local Gov Board
Beatrice called him a *medieval and saintly knight*

Barker, Harley Granville Granville-
1877-1946
Theatre director and playwright
Fabian; member of Stage Society
Acted in, and directed, Shaw plays

Barnes, George Nicoll
1859-1940
Trade unionist and politician;
1896-1908 General Secretary,
Engineering Union
1900 Delegate to the founding
conference of the Labour
Representation Committee
1906-1922 MP
Minister in wartime coalition;
1917 succeeds Henderson in War
Cabinet
Resigns from Labour party; does not
stand again in 1922

Barnett, Henrietta, Dame (*née*
Rowlands)
1851-1936
Spouse, collaborator, and biographer
of Samuel Barnett

Barnett, Samuel, Canon
1844-1913

(Samuel & Henrietta Barnet, © National
Portrait Gallery, London)
Church of England clergyman and
social reformer
Rector of St Jude's Whitechapel
1884-1906 Founder & Warden
Toynbee Hall 1884-1906 - a 'settlement' - a residential colony of
graduates.
Beatrice credited Samuel and
Henrietta Barnett with shaping
the 'rediscovery' of poverty in the
1880s, and with breaking with the
narrow orthodoxy of the Charity
Organisation Society

Belloc, Hilaire
1870-1953

© National Portrait Gallery, London
Poet, politician, contrarian
Pro Boer. Catholic apologist and
propagandist
1906-10 Liberal MP for South
Salford
1912 Author of *The Servile State*
Critic both of the Minority Report,
and of National Insurance
Frequently debated with GBS on ILP
platforms. Shaw dubbed Belloc and
his drinking partner, Chesterton, *the
Chesterbelloc*
His poetry was admired by, among
others, Rupert Brooke and Hugh
Dalton
Some of his writings are anti-Semitic

Besant, Annie
1847-1933

© National Portrait Gallery, London
Secularist
Joined socialist movement 1884
Editor of magazine *Our Corner*
01.1885-meets GBS

Early Fabian
1886-90 Fabian Executive Committee
1889 contributor to Fabian Essays
Became involved with the Social
Democratic Federation and the Law
and Liberty League; led one of the
processions to Trafalgar Square on
Bloody Sunday in 1887. Helped the
women workers at the Bryant and
May match factory in East London
form a trade union.
Subsequently became involved in the
theosophist movement and moved to
India.

Betts, Barbara (Castle)
1910-2002
Labour politician
1935-6 Worked with Stafford Cripps
and William Mellor on Socialist
League and Tribune Cabinet Minister
in Wilson governments in 1960s and
1970s.

Beveridge, William; (later Lord Beveridge)
1879-1963

© National Portrait Gallery, London
Social reformer and economist
1903 Sub Warden, Toynbee Hall;
meets Webbs
1907 gives evidence to Poor Law
Commission
1908 appointed Director of Labour
Exchanges, Board of Trade,
1919-37 Director of LSE
1926-28 Vice Chancellor, London
University

1937-1945 Master, University College
Oxford
1941-42 Chair, Beveridge Committee;
leading to Beveridge Report
1944-45 Liberal MP
1946 Peerage

Bevin, Ernest
1881-1951
Trade unionist and politician
Nonconformist
Van driver
After 1902 began to attend SDF and
ILP meetings
1911 official, dock workers' union
1916 Executive Committee, National
Transport Workers' Federation
1920 Assistant General Secretary,
Dockers Union
1922 General Secretary, Transport and
General Workers' Union (TGWU)
1929 member, Macmillan Committee
1940 Minister of Labour; Labour MP
1945 Foreign Secretary

Black, Clementina Maria
1853-1922
Political activist, suffragist, and writer
Fabian
Regular researcher at British Museum
Reading Room
Involved in Women's Trade Union
Association (WTUA), and later the
Women's Industrial Council (WIC)

Bland, Hubert
1856-1914

© LSE Library Coll Misc 705 4 1

Journalist and politician
Founder member of Fabian Society;
Treasurer 1884-1911
Contributor to Fabian Essays.
1880 married Edith Nesbit
Unconventional relationship

Bondfield, Margaret
1873-1953

© National Portrait Gallery, London

Trade unionist; feminist; politician
Pupil teacher, then shop assistant Active in TU organizations,
1890s-1920s
1923-4; 1926-31 Labour MP
1929-31 Minister of labour; 1st
woman cabinet minister
1947 Spoke at Sidney's memorial
meeting, October

Booth, Charles
1840-1914

© National Portrait Gallery, London

Liverpool shipowner and merchant
Originator of survey of *Life and
Labour of the people of London.*

Disapproved of Beatrice marrying
Sidney
Member of Poor Law Commission;
signatory of Majority Report

Booth, Mary (*née* Macaulay)
1847-1939
Cousin of Beatrice
1871 married Charles Booth
Worked with Booth on *Life and Labour*

Bosanquet, Bernard
1848-1923
Philosopher and social theorist
Strong Charity Organisation Society
supporter

Bosanquet, Helen (*née* Dendy)
1860-1925
1886 went to Newnham, aged 26
1895 Married Bernard Bosanquet
Organizer & Secretary of Shoreditch
Branch of Charity Organisation Society
Member of 1905 Royal Commission
COS stalwart

Braithwaite, William J
1875-1938
Treasury Civil servant
Inland Revenue 1898
Toynbee Hall 1898-1903
Worked with Lloyd George on
National Insurance 1910-1912

Bright, John
1811-1889
Politician; Free Trader; leader of the
movement against the Corn Laws
Quaker
MP for Durham 1843; Manchester
1847; Birmingham 1858
Beatrice meets at Chamberlain's house

Brooke, Emma Frances
1844-1926
Novelist
Early Fabian
Educated Newnham
LSE
Wrote Fabian Tracts
Research on women's employment

Brooke, Rupert Chawner
1887-1915

© National Portrait Gallery, London

Cambridge Fabian; Neo-pagan;
Apostle
Supports campaign for Minority
Report.
Poet
Enlists at start of WW1
1915 Died of septicaemia, Skyros

Bulkley, Mildred Emily
1906-9 Research Secretary to Beatrice
1909-1912, Secretary, National
Campaign for the Prevention of
Destitution
Afterwards Research Secretary to RH
Tawney

Burns, John Elliott
1858-1943

© National Portrait Gallery, London

Trade unionist and politician; 'The
Man with the Red Flag'.
Early 1880s member of Social
Democratic Federation (SDF)
A leader of the 1889 Dock Strike; key
figure in the New Unionism

LCC member from 1889; Lib Lab
MP for Battersea from 1892
Pro Boer
President, Local Government Board
1905-1913
First working class cabinet minister
Resigned from government in protest
at outbreak of First World War
Uneasy relationship with Webbs

Buxton, Charles Roden
1875-1942
Politician & philanthropist
1910 (Jan-Dec) Liberal MP
Founder member Union of
Democratic Control (UDC)
1917 Left Liberals; joined ILP
Strong critic of Versailles Treaty
1920 Secretary Labour Party delegation to USSR
1922-3 & 1929-31 Labour MP
1930-31 Member East Africa Select
Committee

Cameron, Sir Donald
1872-1948
Colonial governor
1924-1931 Governor, Tanganyika

Campbell-Bannerman, Sir Henry
1836-1908
Liberal MP from 1868
1905-1908 Prime Minister

Carpenter, Edward
1844-1929
Socialist, humanitarian and anarchist
Radical sexual politics
1870 Ordained; curate in Cambridge
1874 Relinquished orders
Ordained 1870; curate in Cambridge,
then relinquished orders, 1874
Radical sexual politics
Carpenter's ideas were one of the
inspirations for the Neo-pagans
1884 joined SDF
1886 wrote England Arise
1889 Fabian Lecture 'Civilization: its
cause and cure"
Pro Boer

Carr-Saunders, Sir Alexander Morris
1886-1966
Sociologist and academic
administrator
Biologist then sociologist
Sub Warden Toynbee Hall
1923-1937 Charles Booth Professor
of Social Science, University of
Liverpool
1937-1956 Director, LSE
Later worked with African universities

Chadwick, Edwin
1800-1890
Born Longsight, Manchester
Secretary of the Poor Law Royal
Commission of 1834
Wrote most of the report
Author of the principle of 'less
eligibility'
No further involvement in Poor Law
after 1839

Chamberlain, Austen (Sir)
1863-1937
Conservative Politician
Son of Joseph Chamberlain and 1st
wife, Harriet Kenrick
1892 Liberal Unionist MP
1903-1905 Chancellor
1924-1929 Foreign Secretary

Chamberlain, Beatrice
1862-1918
Eldest child of Joseph Chamberlain
and 1st wife Harriet
Sister of Austen; half -sister of Neville
Maintained friendship with Beatrice
Webb

Chamberlain, Clara (later Ryland)
1881-1915
Youngest sister of Joseph
Chamberlain. Like her niece Beatrice
Chamberlain, a close friend of
Beatrice Webb before her marriage.

Chamberlain, Joseph
1836-1914

© National Portrait Gallery, London

Businessman and politician; Liberal,
then Liberal Unionist
Unitarian/nonconformist
Born London (Camberwell); sent to
Birmingham to pursue family business
interests
1873 Mayor of Birmingham
1876 MP for Birmingham
1880-1885 President, Board of Trade
1886 President, Local Government
Board
1895-1903 Colonial Secretary
Twice widowed;
Long, unhappy courtship between
Beatrice and Chamberlain in the
1880s
Founded London School of Tropical
Medicine
1906 stroke leading to effective
retirement

Chamberlain, (Arthur) Neville
(1869-1940)
Coservative Politician; Prime Minister
Only son of Joseph Chamberlain &
2nd wife, Florence
In 1890s an unsuccessful sisal grower
in Bahamas
Birmingham City Councillor and
Lord Mayor
1918 MP
1923-4, 1931-37 Chancellor of
Exchequer
1924-9 Minister of Health
1937-40 Prime Minister

Champion, Henry Hyde
1859-1928
Leading member of the Social
Democratic Federation; its first
Honorary Secretary
Editor of *Justice*
For a while close to Margaret
Harkness
Implicated in Tory Gold scandal
Subsequently emigrated to Australia

Chancellor, John
1870-1952
Soldier and colonial governor
1911-1916 Governor of Mauritius
1916-21 Governor Trinidad &
Tobago
1923 -1928 Governor Southern
Rhodesia - *more than justified his
reputation as a capable and progressive
administrator*
1928-31 Governor of Palestine
Thought the Balfour Declaration 'a
colossal blunder'

Chandler, Francis
1849-1938
General Secretary, Amalgamated
Society of Carpenters and Joiners
Trade union member of 1905 Royal
Commission
Signatory of Minority Report

Charteris (*née* Wyndham), Mary
Constance, Countess of Wemyss (Mary
Elcho)
1862-1937
Soul. Hostess.
ODNB (Jane Ridley and Clayre Percy,
2005):
*Mary Elcho was the least rank-con-
scious of the great Edwardian hostesses.
At Stanway she mixed Fabians with
fashionable young men, working writers
with cabinet ministers; but most of her
closest friends were members of the group
known as the Souls, of which Arthur
Balfour (1848-1930) was the central
figure.*

Chesterton, Cecil
1879-1918
Political journalist
Brother of G K Chesterton
1901 Joined Fabian Society
1904-1907 Fabian Executive
Committee
Close to Belloc; by 1911 had aban-
doned socialism for distributism
Assistant Editor *Eye Witness*
Anti-Semitic; charged with criminal
libel over Marconi scandal; fined.

Chesterton, Gilbert Keith (GK)
1874-1936
Writer
Pro Boer
Close to Belloc; GBS coined the term
the Chesterbelloc
Active with Belloc in the Distributist
movement, which aimed for a middle
way between capitalism and socialism
by ensuring the widest possible distribution of property.

Churchill, Winston S (Sir)
1874-1965

© National Portrait Gallery, London

Politician; Prime Minister
1900 Conservative MP for Oldham
1903 First meets Webbs
1904 Crosses floor; joins Liberals
1905 Minister in Liberal Government
1908 President, Board of Trade;
responsible for Labour Exchanges
1910 Home Secretary
1919-21 Secretary of State for War
1921-22 Colonial Secretary

1924-29 Chancellor of Exchequer
Responsible for return to Gold
Standard
1940-45; 1951-55 Prime Minister

Citrine, Walter (Later Sir; later Lord)
1887-1983
Trade unionist
1926-1946 General Secretary, Trade
Union Congress

Clifford, Dr John
1836-1923

© National Portrait Gallery, London
Baptist Minister
Minister of the New Connexion of
General Baptists
At various times President of the
London Baptist Association and of the
Baptist Union.
1858-1915: Minister of Praed St
Baptist Church, Paddington
Key figure in Nonconformist resis-
tance to 1902 Education Act; Leader
of passive resistance movement against
paying rates for church schools...
Pro Boer; supported 1889 Dock
Strike, Progressive Party on LCC
Lifelong Liberal; member of Fabian
Society;
Made Companion of Honour by
Lloyd George in 1921

Clynes, John Robert
1869-1949
Trade unionist and politician
1891- district organizer for
Gasworkers Union

1892- President Oldham Trades
Council
1906- MP for Manchester NE
(Platting)
1906-31; 1935-45 Labour MP
1924 Minister in Labour
Government;
1929-31 Home Secretary

Cohen, Rose
1894-1937
Socialist and communist activist
Worked for the LCC Education Dept,
then the Fabian Research Dept, which
became the Labour Research Dept.
- approx. 1916-1923. Secretary to R
Page Arnot
Joined CPGB
Later went to Russia, where she married
Shot as a spy 1937

Cole, George Douglas Howard (GDH)
1889-1962

© LSE Library; Passfield III/8(ii)2
Guild Socialist; later academic
Worked for Fabian Research
Department (later Labour Research
Department) during WW1, and later
for ASE
1918 Married M Postgate (see below)
Fellow in Economics, University
College Oxford
The Coles gradually moved from a
syndicalist to a Fabian position. They
began as implacable critics of the
Webbs and ended as their heirs

Cole, Margaret (*née* Postgate)
 1893-1980

© LSE Library; Passfield III/8(ii)3
Webb biographer, political activist, and writer; joint editor of *Our Partnership*
Worked for Fabian Research Department during WW1
Leading figure among the Passfield Trustees; 1 of Webb executors

Colegate, Arthur (later Sir)
 1884- 1956
Joined Fabian Society 1905
Worked for National Campaign for Prevention of Destitution
Then 'talent spotted' by Churchill to go and run a Labour Exchange
Private Secretary to Addison as Minister of Munitions
Later career in civil service, business, (Director of Brunner Mond) Elected a Conservative MP in 1941 after first standing in 1929.

Costelloe, Benjamin Francis Conn (Frank)
 1855-1899
Solicitor
Early involvement with Toynbee Hall
1889-99 LCC Progressive member
Neighbour of Webbs on Grosvenor Road

Courtney, Catherine (Kate) (Potter)
 1847-1929

© National Portrait Gallery, London
Sister of Beatrice
Married Leonard Courtney 1883
Worked with Charity Organisation Society, at Toynbee, and on East London housing
Journal 1875: *After a particularly difficult year... I made up my mind to leave home and go to Miss Octavia Hill to be trained for her work in London*

Courtney, Leonard; later Lord Courtney; Baron Courtney of Penwith
 1832-1918

© National Portrait Gallery, London
Journalist and politician; supporter of Proportional Representation
1883 Marries Beatrice's sister Catherine (Kate) in
Originally a Liberal Unionist, became an independent Liberal pacifist; pro-Boer; argued for peace in 1st World War
1876-85 Lib MP Liskeard;

1882 Financial Secretary to Treasury
1885 MP Bodmin
1886 anti-Home Rule - so Liberal
Unionist
1900 Opposes South African war; not
stand for re-election
1906 July peerage
WW1 works with Union for
Democratic Control (UCD)

Cox, Katharine (Ka)
1887-1938
Cambridge Fabian
Neo-pagan

Crane, Walter
1845-1915
Illustrator, designer, and painter
1884 joined SDF; then followed
Morris into Socialist League
1888 a founder of Arts and Crafts
Exhibition Society,

Creighton, Louise
1850-1936
1872 Married Mandell Creighton
Originally anti-suffrage; changed
1906
1st Pres Nat U Women Workers
After husband's death lectured at LSE

Creighton, Mandell
1843-1901
Bishop of London and historian
1884-91 Professor of Church History
at Cambridge
1885 Canon of Worcester
1891-7 Bishop of Peterborough
1897-1901 Bishop of London,
Old friend of Beatrice

Cripps, (Charles) Alfred; later Lord
Parmoor
1852-1941

© National Portrait Gallery, London
Lawyer
Married B's sister Theresa, who died
in 1893
1895 elected Conservative MP
1914 Peerage
1914 Resigned from Conservative
Party on pacifist grounds
Lord President in Labour
Governments of 1924 and 1929

Cripps, (Richard) Stafford (Sir)
1889-1952

© National Portrait Gallery, London
Barrister and politician
Son of Alfred and Theresa Cripps;
nephew of Beatrice
1931 Labour MP; Solicitor General
in MacDonald Government; survives
1931 election
1939 Expelled from Labour for advo-
cating popular front against Fascism;
(readmitted 1945).
June 1940 - February 1942 British

Ambassador to USSR,
February - November 1942 member
of War Cabinet
1945 President, Board of Trade
1947- 1950 Chancellor of the
Exchequer,
Beatrice's preferred candidate for the
Labour leadership

Cripps, William Harrison
1850-1923
Surgeon; brother of Alfred
Married Beatrice's sister Blanche

Curzon, George Nathaniel; later
Marquess
1859-1925
Conservative politician; Soul
Viceroy of India, 1899-1905
Foreign Secretary, 1919-1924
My name is George Nathaniel Curzon,
I am a most superior person.
My cheek is pink, my hair is sleek,
I dine at Blenheim once a week

Dalton, Hugh (later Lord Dalton)
1887-1962

© National Portrait Gallery, London
Politician
Cambridge Fabian
Active in campaign for Minority Report
Taught at LSE
War service in WW1 - Italian front
1924, 1929-31, and 1935-59 Labour
MP
Minister in second MacDonald
Labour government and in wartime
coalition
1945-47 Chancellor of Exchequer

Darling, Carrie (later Browne)
d.1900
Close friend of Beatrice

Davies, Margaret Caroline Llewelyn
1861-1944
1899-1921 General Secretary,
Co-operative Women's Guild
Pacifist/peace campaigner. Attends No
Conscription Fellowship conference
1916

Davy, James Stewart (Sir)
1848-1915
Civil servant
Poor Law Chief Inspector from 1905
Stern upholder of the principles of
1834

Delamere, Lord (Hugh Cholmondeley);
3rd Baron Delamere
1870-1931
Political leader of Kenya settlers
After military service began to organize big game hunting expeditions in
east Africa
1897 - 1st Briton to enter Kenya from
North; visited again 1899; settled
1902
1st bought 100,000 acres on 99 year
lease; more land later...
ODNB - (Clayton, 2011):
Above all he believed that Kenya was
destined to be developed as a 'white
man's country'

Dent, John James
1856-1936
Co-operator
1883-1909 Secretary, Club and
Institute Union
1909-1922 President, Club and
Institute Union

Desborough, Ettie (Grenfell)
1867-1952
Hostess; Soul; last of the Whig
hostesses
Chatelaine of two great houses,
Panshanger and Taplow

Despard, Charlotte
1844-1939
Feminist, socialist, and Irish
nationalist
Active in Nine Elms, Battersea
Supporter of the Social Democratic
Federation, the Independent Labour
Party, and the Women's Social and
Political Union (WSPU)
Later President of the Women's
Freedom League
Active in WW1 peace movement
In the 1918 Coupon Election she
displaced John Burns as the Labour
candidate in Battersea; members of
Beatrice's sister Kate Courtney's family
canvassed for her.

Lawson Dodd, Frederick
1868-1962

© LSE; GBS Photos Vol 24 no 115
Fabian, dentist, writer
1907 proposed the establishment of
the Fabian Summer Schools

Drake, Barbara (*née* Meinertzhagen)
1876-1963
Political activist and writer
Niece of Beatrice - daughter of
Georgina
London County Council member
Accompanied Sidney on second
USSR trip
Joint editor of *Our Partnership*; 1 of
Webb executors

Duckham, Sir Arthur McDougall
1879-1932
Gas engineer
1915 Deputy Controller, Munitions

Supply
1919 Member, Sankey Commission;
submitted Minority Report

Duff, Robert
1871-1946
Civil servant
Secretary to 1905 Royal Commission
1 of drafters of Majority Report
Later Secretary to Maclean
Committee on Local Government

Dukes, Ashley
1885-1959
Playwright & theatre critic
Graduated in science from
Manchester, 1905
Then to Munich & Zurich to study
modern theatre
1909 returns to London; theatre critic
of *New Age*

Edgeworth, Francis Ysidro
1845-1926
Economist and statistician
1888 Professor of Political Economy,
Kings College London
1891 Drummond professor of political economy at Oxford

Edwards, John Passmore
1823-1911
Newspaper proprietor, philanthropist,
and major benefactor of the LSE
1880-1882 Liberal MP for Salisbury
Chair, Transvaal Committee

Elcho, Lady
See Charteris [*née* Wyndham], Mary
Constance

Engels, Friedrich
1820-1895
Businessman and revolutionary leader
Born Westphalia
1842 moved to England to work in
his father's Manchester textile firm
1844 first meeting with Marx
1845 Publication of *The Condition of
the Working Class in England*
1849 Marx & Engels settle in

London; Engels resumes work with
textile firm
1869 Retires from textile firm

Ensor, Robert; later Sir
1877-1958
Journalist, barrister, Fabian and
historian
1907-11; 1912-19 Fabian Executive
Committee
1909 ILP National Administrative
Council
1910-1913 LCC member

Fawcett, Dame Millicent Garrett [née
Millicent Garrett]
1847-1929
Leader of the constitutional women's
suffrage movement, author

Fisher, Bella (Arabella; née Buckley)
1840-1929
Writer and popularizer of science
Childhood friend of Beatrice

Gaitskell, Hugh Todd Naylor
1906-1963
Labour Party Leader
Taught by GDH Cole
Worked for WEA in Notts coalfield
New Fabian Research Bureau
1945 Labour MP
1950 Chancellor of Exchequer
1955 Leader of Labour Party

Galsworthy, John
1867-1933
Novelist and playwright

Galton, Frank
1867-
1891 Joined Fabian Society
1892-98 Secretary to the Webbs,
1920-1939 General Secretary, Fabian
Society

Gardiner, Alfred George
1865-1946
Newspaper editor and journalist
Pro-Boer
1902-1919 editor, *Daily News,* oldest,
most widely read Liberal newspaper

Garnett, William
1850-1932
1882-Professor, Nottingham
1884-Principal Durham Coll Science
- forerunner Newcastle University
1893-1904 Secretary/Adviser, London
Technical Education Board
2 sons killed in 1st World War

George, David Lloyd; later first Earl
Lloyd-George of Dwyfor
1863-1945

© National Portrait Gallery, London
Prime Minister
Solicitor. Nonconformist. Pro Boer
1890-1945 MP (Liberal) Caernarfon
Boroughs
Opposed 1902 Education Act
1905 President of Board of Trade;
1908 Chancellor of Exchequer
1909 People's Budget
1916-1922 Prime Minister

Gill, (Arthur) Eric Rowton
1882-1940
Artist, craftsman, and social critic
Attended Central School of Arts and
Crafts as LCC scholar
February 1906 joined Fabian Society;
supported H G Wells

Gillies, William
1884-1958
Glasgow Fabian
Head of Labour International Dept c
1920-1944

Gladstone, Herbert John, Viscount
Gladstone
  1854-1930
  Liberal politician
  Youngest child of WE Gladstone
  1880 elected Liberal MP , Leeds
  1899 Liberal Chief Whip
  1903 negotiated Gladstone-
  MacDonald pact, giving some Labour
  candidates a clear run
  1905-1910 Home Secretary
  1910-1914 Governor-general of
  South Africa

Gould, Barbara Bodichon Ayrton
  1886-1950
  Suffragist and politician
  1910 married Gerald Gould (d. 1936)
  1932 Labour Party National Women's
  Officer
  1945-1950 Labour MP, Hendon North

Graham, Robert Bontine Cunninghame
  (1852-1936)
  Traveller, author, and politician
  1886-1892 Liberal MP for North-
  West Lanarkshire
  Arrested, tried and imprisoned for
  6 weeks with John Burns following Bloody Sunday demonstration,
  13.11.1887

Graham, William
  1887-1932
  Journalist and civil servant
  1908 joined ILP
  1918-1931 MP Edinburgh Central
  1924 Financial Secretary Treasury;
  close to Snowden
  1924-1929 Chair, Public Accounts
  Committee
  1929-1931 President Board of Trade

Green, Alice
  1847-1929
  Historian and Irish nationalist; friend
  of Beatrice; neighbour on Grosvenor
  Road
  Widowed 1883; husband J R Green,
  academic

1922 appointed to Irish Free State
Senate

Greenwood, Arthur
1880-1954

© National Portrait Gallery, London

Labour MP; Deputy Leader
Born Leeds; pupil teacher; then Leeds
University
Taught economics at Huddersfield
Tech College
Secretary Leeds Branch National
Campaign for the Prevention of
Destitution
1910 attends Fabian/NCPD Summer
School
1914 Moves from Leeds to London.
Close to Fred Keeling.
1916 Civil Servant, Ministry of
Reconstruction
1927-1943 Head, Labour Party
Research Department
1922-31 MP Nelson & Colne
1924 Junior Minister
1929-31 Minister of Health
1932-1954 MP Wakefield
1935-53 Labour Deputy Leader
1940-42 Member of War Cabinet;
Lord President
Sets up Beveridge Committee
1945-47 Lord Privy Seal in Attlee
government
Beatrice notes as heavy drinker from
1925

Grigg, Edward (Ned); later Sir
Edward; later Lord Altrincham
1879-1955

© National Portrait Gallery, London

Colonial administrator & politician
Disciple of Chamberlain & Milner;
before 1ˢᵗ World War, *Times* and
Milner Kindergarten
1ˢᵗ World War Guards; MC 1917
1919,1920, Advisor/Military
Secretary to Prince of Wales
Later private secretary to Lloyd George
Lloyd George Liberal MP 1922-25
1925-30 Governor of Kenya
Sent to Kenya by Amery to promote
ever closer union of Kenya/Uganda/
Tanganyika

Haldane, Elizabeth
1862-1937
Writer and public servant
Sister of Richard Haldane

Haldane, Richard (later Viscount Haldane)
1856-1928

© National Portrait Gallery, London

1885 elected MP for Haddingtonshire
Lawyer; QC 1890; Liberal MP;
educated Gottingen
Liberal Imperialist ('Limp');
Coefficient; close to, but not wholly
part of, the 'Souls'
1905 Secretary of State for War
1911 peerage
1912 Lord Chancellor
1924 Lord Chancellor in Labour
Government
Long term friend of Sidney & Beatrice
Heavy eater, drinker, smoker; diabetic

Hamilton, Lord George
1845-1927

© National Portrait Gallery, London

a Disraeli favourite ODNB
1868-1905 Conservative MP
1894 -95 Chair, London School Board,
1895-1903 Secretary of State for India
1905 Chair, Poor Law Commission

Hamilton, Mary Agnes (Molly) (*née*
Adamson)
1882-1986

© Blackburn public library

Writer, Labour MP, and civil servant; first biographer of the Webbs: 1933
Educated Newnham
1st woman journalist on *The Economist*
Supported campaign against the Poor Law
1914 Joined ILP; early member of Union for Democratic Control
1929-1931 MP for Blackburn
1937 LCC Alderman
1941 Civil servant member of Beveridge Committee
Later Foreign Office
1949 CBE
Remained in civil service to1952

Hammond, Barbara (*née* Bradby)
1873-1961
Historian
With her family, lived at Toynbee Hall from age of 10
Pro-Boer, a suffragist, and a pillar of the Women's Industrial Council
1901 Married J L Hammond

Hammond, (John) Lawrence Le Breton
1872-1949
Historian and journalist
Oxford contemporary and friend of Belloc and Gilbert Murray
Liberal; pro Boer
Member of WW1 Reconstruction Committee
With Barbara, author of *The Village Labourer, Town Labourer, Skilled Labourer.*
Gilbert Murray compared the Hammonds to the Webbs

Hankey, Maurice Pascal Alers, first Baron Hankey
1877-1963)
Civil servant
Royal Marines
1902 Naval Intelligence Department
1908 Asst Secretary, Committee on Imperial Defence
1916 Secretary to War Cabinet

Hankinson, Mary ('Hanky')
1868-1952

© LSE Library Fabian Society M 2.8.6.1

Gym teacher, St Paul's School
1905-1948 Fabian member
Strict manager of Fabian Summer School - *...no panky with Hanky...*
1913 President of the Gymnastics Teachers' Suffrage Society.
Possibly the model for Shaw's St Joan

Harben, Henry
1874-1967
Fabian; Member Fabian Society Executive, 1911-1920;
Leading shareholder in Prudential Insurance, and in *New Statesman*
Strong supporter of women's suffrage

Hardie, James Keir
1856-1915
Miner, trade unionist, politician
Secretary, Ayrshire Miners Union
1888 contested Mid Lanark byelection
Launched monthly paper, *The Labour Leader*
1892-1895 Ind Lab MP for West Ham South
1893 a founder of ILP
1900 First Chair of LRC
Elected MP for Merthyr Tydfil
1914 Opposed war
1915 Died

Harkness, Margaret Elise (John Law)
1854-1923

© *The Queen* magazine, via *The Harkives* website

Novelist, journalist, and political activist
2nd cousin to Beatrice; at school with
Beatrice in 1875
1885-1887 close to SDF
Very close to Beatrice between about
1875 and 1890; nurses Lawrencina in
her last illness; introduces Beatrice to
Sidney in 1890.
Spends time with Beatrice during the
relationship with Chamberlain. One of
Harkness's novels is written partly while
living at Cheyne Walk with Beatrice.
Novels:
1887 *A City Girl*
1888 *Out of Work*
1889 *Captain Lobe: a story of the
Salvation Army*
1890 *A Manchester Shirtmaker*

Hartshorn, Vernon
1872-1931
Trade union leader and politician
Primitive Methodist
ILP
1905 elected miners' agent for
Maesteg district, South Wales Miners'
Federation
1911 elected to executive council,
SWMF and to the national executive
council of the MFGB
1918-1931 Labour MP
1929 member, Simon Commission
on India
1930 Lord Privy Seal

Hatry, Clarence
1888-1965
Company promoter
Promoted industrial mergers and
restructuring through his company,
the Austin Friars Trust.
1929 used forged share certificates to
cover dealings; admitted all to DPP;
1930 sentenced to 14 years in prison

Headlam, Stewart
1847-1924
Clergyman & Christian Socialist
Influenced by F D Maurice
1873-78 curate St Matthews, Bethnal
Green - developed radical social views
Guild of St Matthew; stood bail for
Oscar Wilde
DNB (Jeremy Morris, 2004):
*though he served on the executive
committee of the Fabian Society for
three periods between 1890 and 1911
he was impatient of its gradualism.*
London School Board & LCC
member - Progressive

Henderson, Arthur
1863-1935

© National Portrait Gallery, London

Labour MP; Labour Party General
Secretary
Minister in 1st World War coalition
1924 Home Secretary
1929-31 Foreign Secretary
1931-1932 Labour leader
1934 awarded Nobel Peace Prize
Sidney close to Henderson from 1914

Henderson widely known as 'Uncle Arthur' or just 'Uncle'

Hewins, William A S
1865-1931
Economist and politician;
1895-1903 1st Director of LSE
Resigned in 1903 on conversion to Tariff Reform
1912-1918 Conservative MP

Heyworth, Lawrencina, (later Potter)
1821-1882
Beatrice's mother

Hill, Octavia
1838-1912

© National Portrait Gallery, London

Housing and social reformer; pioneer of housing management
Christian Socialist background
Secretary to Women's Classes at Working Men's College
Influenced by Ruskin
Copying for Ruskin at Dulwich & National Galleries
1st housing scheme, with Ruskin, Paradise Place 1864
Involved with Charity Organization Society - but later in life began to think over harsh
Member of 1905 Poor Law Commission - signed Majority Report

Hirst, Francis Wrigley
1873-1953
Journalist; liberal
1907- 1916: Editor, *The Economist*
Pro-Boer; opponent of 1st world war

Hobhouse, Emily
1860-1926
Social activist and charity worker
Pro-Boer
Author of report on British conduct in S African war

Hobhouse, Henry
1854-1937
Somerset landowner; Liberal Unionist MP; married to Beatrice's sister Margaret

Hobhouse, Stephen
1881-1964
Son of Henry & Margaret Hobhouse;
1st World War Conscientious Objector

Hobson, John Atkinson
1858-1940
Social theorist and economist
University extension lecturer; occasionally taught at LSE
Member, Rainbow Circle
'New liberalism'
1899 Manchester Guardian correspondent on South African war
1900 Book on South African war; presents war as fought in the interests of a confederacy of international financiers and capitalists
1902 book *Imperialism*; praised by Lenin; anti-Semitic overtones
Worked for *Nation*
1st World War - in UDC
1924 joined Labour Party

Hodges, Frank
1887-1947
Miners' leader and Labour MP
1909 Went to Ruskin College; involved in Ruskin strike and breakaway
1918 elected fulltime Secretary, S Wales Miners Federation
1923-4 Labour MP
Later Secretary International Mineworkers Federation
Later career in business

Hogg, Quintin
1845-1903
Merchant and philanthropist
1882 Re launched the Regent Street
Polytechnic as a publicly managed
institution , providing artisan and
lower-middle-class young men and
women with instruction, recreation,
and social opportunities, so contributing to the increased educational
opportunities for women.
1889-1895 LCC Alderman; member
of Technical Education Board (TEB)

Holt, Robert
1832-1908
Liverpool shipowner; married
Beatrice's sister Laurencina ('Lallie')

Hubback, Bill (Francis William)
1884 -1917
Cambridge Fabian
Poor Law Campaigner
1917 Killed Western Front

Hubback, Eva (Eva Spielman)
1886-1949
Cambridge Fabian
Poor Law Campaigner
1911 Married Bill Hubback ;
widowed 1917
1927 Principal Morley College
1946-1949 London County Council
member (Labour)

Hudson, James Hindle
1881-1962

© National Portrait Gallery, London

ILP Politician
Teacher, Manchester and Salford
Active in Poor Law Campaign
1st World War WW1 Conscientious
Objector; imprisoned. Quaker.
1923-31; 1945-55 Labour MP
1924 PPS to Philip Snowden
Member of 1930-31 East Africa Select
Committee

Hutchinson, Henry
-1894

© LSE Library; Passfield III/8 (ii) 4

Derby Solicitor; left £10k to Fabian
Society, half of which was used to
found LSE

Huysmans, Camille
1871- 1968
Belgian Socialist Politician & secretary
of Socialist International
In exile in Britain during 1st World
War

Hyndman, Henry Mayers
1842-1921
Socialist leader
Barrister & journalist
1881- presided over inaugural meet-
ing of Democratic Federation
1884- DF becomes Social Democratic
Federation; Morris secedes & forms
Socialist League
Member of War Emergency Workers
National Committee during 1st World
War

Hyndman, Henry Mayers
1842-1921

© National Portrait Gallery, London
Socialist leader
Barrister & journalist
1881- presided over inaugural meeting of Democratic Federation
1884- DF becomes Social Democratic Federation; Morris secedes & forms Socialist League Member of War Emergency Workers National Committee during 1st World War

Jackson, Cyril (Sir)
1863-1924
Educationalist
1885-1895 Toynbee Hall
1891-1896 member, London School Board
1888-96 Secretary Children's Country Holiday Fund
1896-1903 Chief Inspector Schools Western Australia
1903- Chief Inspector Elementary Schools, Board of Education - but resigned 1905 after dispute with Morant
1907-13 LCC member (Municipal Reform - i.e., Conservative)
Poor Law Commission investigator

Jackson, (George)Holbrook
1874-1948
Journalist, writer and publisher
Co-founder, with A R Orage, of first the Leeds Arts Group, and then (1907) the Fabian Arts Group

Also in 1907, with Orage, bought the weekly *New Age*

Jackson, Martha (Mills)
Beatrice's old nurse, and a distant cousin; known in the family as Dada

Joad, Cyril Edwin Mitchinson
1891-1953
Philosopher; broadcaster
1917- joined Fabian Society
Subsequently banned from Fabian Summer Schools, and expelled from Fabians, for sexual misbehaviour.
According to Beatrice, Mary Hankinson (no panky with Hanky) said that she: ... *would not allow the Fabian Summer School to be turned into a brothel.*
BW Diary 21.05.1939
Joad was briefly involved with Mosley's New Party in the 1930s; readmitted to Fabian Society in 1943. In 1948 he was convicted of rail travel without a ticket.

Johnston, Thomas
1881-1965
Politician and journalist
ILP;
1922-4; 1924-31; 1935-45 Labour MP
1929 Under Secretary for Scotland
1931 Lord Privy Seal;
1941-1945 Secretary of State for Scotland in wartime coalition

Jones, Benjamin
1847-1942
Cooperative movement activist and manager
Worked as an errand-boy and book-keeper before joining the Co-operative Wholesale Society (CWS) in 1866. Jones was successively assistant bookkeeper, bookkeeper, assistant salesman, departmental manager, and assistant buyer of butter and cheese for the CWS in Manchester
1874: established London branch of

the CWS, the first enduring co-operative wholesaler to serve southern England. By his retirement in 1902 the London branch had an annual turnover of £3.25 million.

Assisted Beatrice Webb with research for her book *The Co-Operative Movement in Great Britain* (1891)

Jones, Thomas 'TJ'
1870-1955

© National Portrait Gallery, London

Civil servant and diarist
Born Rhymney; left school at 14 to work as a clerk in the iron works; originally expected to enter ministry; studied at recently established University College of Wales at Aberystwyth. Then to Glasgow to study Economics.
1900 Spent a term at LSE, 1900; came to know Webbs
1901 Graduated from Glasgow with 1st in Economics; at Glasgow joined ILP & Fabian Society.
1906 Special commissioner for Poor Law Commission
1909 first professor of political economy at Queen's University, Belfast.
1910: secretary to a new philanthropic initiative: the King Edward VII Welsh National Memorial Association, financed by David Davies MP, the millionaire coal owner, and designed to reduce the incidence of tuberculosis. Came to the attention of David Lloyd George
1912: Secretary of the Welsh National

Insurance Commission, which was responsible for the implementation of the Liberal government's new health insurance scheme
1916: Cabinet Secretariat
Officially, T.J. was first assistant and then deputy secretary to the cabinet, responsible for domestic issues while Maurice Hankey, as secretary, concentrated on military and foreign affairs. He took and circulated cabinet minutes, acted as secretary to many cabinet committees, and deputized for Hankey on his frequent absences abroad.
1930 retired from civil service; appointed Secretary of Pilgrim Trust. In the late 30s close to the appeasers

Keeling, Frederick Hillersdon (Ben)
1886-1916

© LSE Library Shaw Photographs 2-3-36-1; Reproduced by kind permission of the National Trust.

Cambridge Fabian
Trinity College 1904-7
After graduating moves to Walworth, reads for bar, joins LCC care cttee
1909 marries Rachel Townshend - son, daughter; do not live together; later divorced
1910 manager Leeds Labour Exchange
1912 resigns from Civil Service
Works for *New Statesman*
08.1914 enlists as private soldier; promoted to sergeant-major

18.08.1916 killed on Somme
Ted Hatherleigh in *The New Machiavelli* based on Keeling.

Keeling, Rachel Susanna (*née* Townshend)
1885-1969

© LSE Library Shaw Photographs 2 3 40;
Reproduced by kind permission of the National Trust.

Daughter of Emily Townshend
Fabian and suffrage campaigner
1908 Imprisoned for 2 months during suffrage campaign
1909 Married Ben Keeling
2 children - Joan and Bernard Sidney
1934-1941   Labour LCC member

Keynes, John Maynard; <u>later</u> Baron Keynes
1883-1946

© National Portrait Gallery, London
Economist
Fierce critic of Versailles Treaty, and of British return to Gold Standard
Came to know Webbs in 1920s
1930 Appointed to Economic Advisory Council by 2nd Labour Government; his advice not taken
Nominated Beatrice as first woman

Fellow of British Academy
Keynes remained a Liberal, never joining Labour

Kollontai, Alexandra
1872-1952
Russian; Bolshevik and feminist
Soviet diplomatic representative in Sweden, 1930-1945
Met Beatrice in London ?1903 and in Moscow 1932

Kropotkin, Peter
1842-1921
Russian anarchist
Came to England 1886
Earned a living as a scientific journalist but also continued to develop and expound his social and political philosophy. This was a combination of biological evolution, naturalistic ethics, populist historiography, integral education, economic decentralization and self-management, political anarchy, and self-government, the final stages to be inaugurated through mass insurrection and popular revolution.

Lang, Cosmo Gordon
1864-1945
Clergyman; Archbishop of Canterbury
Early supporter of Toynbee Hall
1901-1908 Bishop of Stepney
1908- 1928 Archbishop of York
1928-1942 Archbishop of Canterbury

Lansbury, George
1859-1940

© National Portrait Gallery, London
Labour Party Leader

Pacifist, feminist, politician
1892-94 leading figure in the Social
Democratic Federation; its National
Organiser 1895-96
By 1904 joined ILP
Poplar Borough Councillor; Poor Law
Guardian; LCC member
1906-09 Member of Poor Law
Commission; signatory of Minority
Report
Supporter of National Campaign for
the Prevention of Destitution
1910(Dec) Labour MP Bow and
Bromley
1912 resigned as MP to fight byelec-
tion on Suffrage issue; defeated
1912-22 editor-proprietor of the
Daily Herald
1921 a leader of Poplar Borough
Council revolt; imprisoned for 6
weeks
1922-35 Labour MP Bow and
Bromley
1929-1931 Cabinet Minister; First
Commissioner of Works
1932-35 Leader of Labour Party
Resigned over rearmament
Dies day before the Norway debate,
May 1940
*…the most lovable figure in modern
politics* A. J. P. Taylor

Laski, Harold
1893-1950
Political theorist
1914 Graduated from Oxford;
Temporary work on Daily Herald;
Volunteered for military service;
rejected on medical grounds; spent
war in Canada & USA.
1920 Returned to UK; lectureship at
LSE; joined Fabian Society
Moved to left; 1930s - conflict with
Beveridge at LSE
1945 disagreements with Attlee

Law, Andrew Bonar
1858-1923

© National Portrait Gallery, London

Conservative politician
Born Canada; came to Scotland 1870;
business career
1900 elected a Glasgow MP
Early commitment to Chamberlain &
tariff reform
1906 Lost Glasgow seat; re-elected for
Camberwell (Dulwich) in May 1906
Involved with Leo Amery & Fabian
Ware in developing Conservative
social reform programme
1911-21; 1922-1923: Conservative
Leader
1915 joins Asquith Coalition
1916 Chancellor of Exchequer under
Lloyd George
1919-22 Leader of Commons/Lord
Privy Seal - effectively Deputy PM
1922-23 Prime Minister
2 sons killed in war

Lawrence, Susan
1871-1947

© National Portrait Gallery, London

Politician
Prosperous London background
Newnham 1895. Conservative as
a student; committed to Charity
Organisation Society
1910 elected a Conservative
(Municipal Reform) London County
Council member (Marylebone).
1912 resigned from Conservative
Party & LCC
Joined Fabian Society; thereafter close
to Webbs
1913-45 Fabian Society Executive
Committee
1913 elected Labour LCC member
for Poplar
1914-1918 Fabian representative on
War Emergency Workers' National
Committee
1919 Alderman on Poplar Borough
Council
1921 imprisoned with Poplar
Councillors
1923-24 and 1926-31 MP, East Ham
North
1929-31 Under Secretary, Ministry of
Health
Tenant of 41 Grosvenor Road after
Webbs move to Passfield, until it was
bombed in 1941

Lawson, Jack
1881-1965
Miner, Labour MP, and Minister; later
Lord Lawson
Attended Ruskin
1918 contested Seaham Harbour
1919-49 MP for Chester le Street
1924 PPS to MacDonald
1945 Secretary of State for War.
Contributor to *The Webbs and their
Work*

Levy, Amy
1861-1889
writer and poet
1879 1st Jewish woman to attend
Newnham College Cambridge (left
after 2 years)
1881-4 travelled in Europe (Germany,
Switzerland)
Lived in London with parents;
frequented British Museum Reading
Room; friends included Clementina
Black, Eleanor Marx, Dollie Radford,
and Olive Schreiner
1889 suicide

Leys, Norman
1875-1944
Doctor; medical officer in Kenya
Studied at Glasgow with Thomas
Jones
Fabian; Christian socialist

Lindsay, Alexander Dunlop (Sandy);
later Lord Lindsay of Birker
1879-1952
Educationist
Friend of Temple & Tawney as
undergraduates
Attended Fabian Summer Schools pre
1st World War
1924-1947 Master of Balliol
1938 Ind Progressive (i.e.pro popular
front) candidate in Oxford byelection
Later 1st head of Keele University

Litvinov, Maxim
1876-1951
Bolshevik
Exile in London
Married Ivy Low, (1889-1977);
English; *née* Ivy Teresa Low; daughter
of Walter Low, Fabian and friend of
HG Wells
1918 first official Bolshevik diplomatic representative in London
1930-1939 Soviet People's Commissar
for Foreign Affairs
1941-1943 Ambassador to
Washington

Lloyd, Charles Mostyn
1878-1946

© LSE Library; Image Library /972

Academic and journalist; Fabian; a
founding member of both the Fabian
Research Bureau and the New Fabian
Research Bureau
1909-14 Secretary, National
Campaign for the Prevention of
Destitution
Army in First World War
1922 Head of LSE Dept of Social
Science & Administration
1928-31 (Acting) Editor, *New
Statesman*

Loch, Charles Stewart (Sir)
1849-1923
1879-1914 Hon Secretary of the
Charity Organisation Society
friend of Bernard Bosanquet
1905-09 Member of Poor Law
Commission; signatory of majority
report;
1915 knighted
*Loch and the C.O.S. were almost inter-
changeable* terms Mowat
DNB (HCG Mathew, 2004):
*The poor law, even with its spirit of
deterrence, was by its existence, Loch
believed, 'a permanent obstacle to thrift
and self-reliance' ... He thought that
'degraded pauperism' had been a significant cause of the decline of the Roman
empire*

Lodge, Oliver
1851-1940
Physicist & psychical researcher

Lough, Thomas
1850-1922
London tea merchant and Liberal MP
1892-1918 MP for West Islington
1888-1892 employs J R Macdonald as
private secretary
1905-08 junior education minister

Lugard, Frederick; later Lord Lugard
1858-1945

© National Portrait Gallery, London

Colonial administrator; developed
concept of 'dual mandate'
1876-1886 army
1888-92 East Africa
1894-95 West Africa
1896-97 South Africa
1897-1906 and 1912-18 Governor
General of Nigeria
1907- 12 Governor of Hong Kong,
where the Webbs meet him in 1911
1928 peerage
1930-31 Member of 1931 Select
Committee on East Africa

Macarthur, Mary
1880-1921
Trade Union organizer
Honorary secretary of the Women's
Trade Union League (WTUL)
1906 founded National Federation of
Women Workers
1907 began (and edited) the monthly
paper the *Woman Worker*, which was

soon transformed into a weekly with a
circulation of about 20,000.
A tireless campaigner on behalf of
sweated workers, Mary Macarthur sat
on the executive of the Anti-Sweating
League.
1909-12 Member, Nat Council ILP
1911- married William Anderson -
MP 1914-18
Anderson died 1919, Macarthur 1920
Beatrice: Mary Macarthur was 'the
axle round which the machinery
moved'.

MacCarthy, Desmond; later Sir
1877-1952
Literary reviewer and critic
Apostle
1913: drama critic, *New Statesman*
1920: Literary Editor
Chapter in 'The Webbs and their
work'

McCleary, George
1867-1962
1890 (Nov) joins Fabians
Doctor; public health expert and
campaigner; Fabian
Medical Officer of Health for
Battersea and later for Hampstead
Worked for National Health
Insurance Commission and Ministry
of Health

MacDonald, James Ramsay
1866-1937

© National Portrait Gallery, London
Prime Minister

1884 joined Social Democratic
Federation; after split joined Socialist
League
21.05.1886 accepted as F Soc
member
1887 present at Bloody Sunday,
13.11.1887
1888-92 Private secretary to Tommy
Lough, tea merchant and, from 1892,
Liberal MP for West Islington
1892 Joined Independent Labour
Party (ILP)
Member of Fabian Society (resigned
1900); Fellowship of the New Life;
Rainbow Circle
Secretary of the London committee of
the Scottish Home Rule Association
Pro Boer
1900 founding secretary of Labour
Representation Committee
1901-04 member, London County
Council
1906-18; 1922-37 MP
1914-1918 Opposed First World War.
MP 1906-18; 1922-37
1924 and 1929-1931 Labour Prime
Minister
1931-1935 Prime Minister, National
Government
Russell thought Beatrice always hated
MacDonald

MacDonald, Malcolm
1901-1981
Politician, then diplomat
2nd son of Ramsay MacDonald
1927-30 member, London County
Council
1929-1931 Labour MP
Worked with Weizmann over
Palestine during second Labour
government
Stayed with his father after 1931 split
1931-35 and 1936-45 National
Labour MP
Minister in national governments to
1940
1941: High Commissioner to Canada
1946: Governor General of Malay

States & Singapore
1955-60 High Commissioner to India
1963 last Governor of Kenya

McKenna, Reginald
1863-1943
Politician and banker
1895-1918 Liberal MP
1905 Financial Secretary to Treasury
1907 President Board of Education
1908 Admiralty
1911 Home Secretary in exchange
with Churchill
1915 Chancellor of Exchequer
1916 out of office when Lloyd George
PM
1919 Chair Midland Bank

Mackinder, Halford; later Sir
1861-1947
Geographer and politician
Coefficient
1903-08 Second director of LSE
Linked to Michael Sadler/University
Extension
1910-22 Conservative MP
Imperialist. Geopolitics
*Who rules East Europe commands the
Heartland:*
*Who rules the Heartland commands the
World-Island:*
*Who rules the World-Island commands
the World*

Maclean, Donald
1864-1932
Politician
1906-10; 1910-22; 1929-32 Liberal MP
Supporter of Asquith rather than
Lloyd George
1917 Chair of Reconstruction
Committee on local government
1931 President, Board of Education,
in National Government
Father of spy Donald Maclean

Macmillan, Hugh Pattison, Baron
Macmillan
1873-1952,
Judge

Lord Advocate in 1924 labour
Government, despite previous
Conservative affiliation
1929-1931 chaired committee on
Finance and Industry, tho' report
largely written by Keynes

Mair, Janet (Jessie); later Beveridge
1876-1959
Married to a cousin of Beveridge,
David Mair.
Meets Beveridge early 1900s
Works with Beveridge as civil servant
during 1st World War, and at LSE,
where her role is resented by some
academic staff
1942 death of David Mair; Janet
marries Beveridge

Maisky, Ivan
1884-1975

© National Portrait Gallery, London
Soviet diplomat, historian, and
politician
1912-1917: in exile in London
Menshevik before 1917
1921 joined Bolshevik Party
1929 envoy to Finland
1932-1943 USSR ambassador to
London

Mallon, James Joseph (Jimmy)
1874-1961
Social reformer
Born Manchester
1903 Joined ILP & Fabian Society
1906 Moved to London; based at
Toynbee Hall

1917 appointed (by Lloyd George; recommended by Thomas Jones) commissioner for industrial unrest, dealing with the grievances of munitions workers
1919-54 Warden, Toynbee Hall
Secretary of the National League to Establish a Minimum Wage
Member, Romney Street Group

Mann, Tom
1856-1941
Trade Unionist; engineer. Joined ASE
1881 joined Amalgamated Society of Engineers
1885 joined Social Democratic Federation, Battersea Branch
1889 with John Burns, an organizer of Dock strike
1894-97 Secretary, Independent Labour Party
1901- 1910 In Australia
1910 returned to London; supported syndicalism before 1st World War
1912 6 month prison sentence for sedition (served 7 weeks)
1917 Spoke at Leeds convention to welcome Russian revolution
1919-21 Secretary, Amalgamated Society of Engineers
Foundation member Communist Party

Manning, Leah (*née* Perrett); Dame
1886-1977
Educationist and politician;
Cambridge Fabian
1906 Homerton College Cambridge
Subsequently taught in Cambridge; active NUT member
1924 National Executive, NUT
1930 President NUT
1931 (Feb-Oct) Labour MP, Islington East
1945-1950 Labour MP, Islington East
1966 DBE

Mant, Sir Reginald
1870-1942
Civil servant
Born Australia

1894 Indian Civil Service
1920 Finance Secretary, Government of India
1927-1929 Member, Hilton Young Commission

Marsh, Edward Howard, (Eddie); later Sir Edward
1872-1953
Civil Servant
Apostle
Colonial Office
Intermittently Private Secretary to Winston Churchill from 1905
…his apartments had become the rendezvous of poets as well as painters and, from 1913, a virtual second home for Rupert Brooke.
Author of 1918 memoir of Brooke
Literary executor of Brooke

Marshall, Alfred
1842-1924
Economist
1884 -1924 Professor of Economics, Cambridge

Martin, (Basil) Kingsley
1897-1969
Academic, journalist and editor
Son of a nonconformist minister
First World War Conscientious Objector
Cambridge 1919
1924 LSE Politics Lecturer
Uneasy relationship with Beveridge
1927 *Guardian* Leader writer
1931-60 Editor, *New Statesman*

Marx, Eleanor
1855-1898

Socialist writer and activist
6th child of Karl Marx
'Literary piecework' : worked at
British Museum Reading Room on
editing and translation
Early member of SDF;
1884 (Dec) left with Morris for
Socialist League
From 1884 lived with Edward Aveling
1889 supported London gas and dock
strikes
1893 attended ILP founding conference, Bradford
1898 suicide following Aveling's
deceptions

Massingham, Henry William
1860-1924
Journalist
1888 worked for *The Star,* London
evening paper
1890 briefly editor, *The Star*
Then joins *Daily Chronicle*
1895 Editor, *Daily Chronicle*
1907 Editor of *The Nation* - radical, loss-making Liberal journal
- supported by Rowntree trust
Opposed to Liberal foreign policy
before 1st World War
Supported moves for peace during 1st
World War
1923 Joined Labour

Masterman, Charles
1873-1927
Writer and politician
Politics influenced by Christian
socialism
1906 Liberal MP West Ham North
1908 Under-secretary, Local
Government Board, working with
Burns
1910 Under-secretary, Home Office
1911 Chairman, National Insurance
Commission
1912 Financial Secretary, Treasury
1914 Chancellor of Duchy of
Lancaster.

Lost consequent byelection
Failed to find another seat, so resigned
as Chancellor in February 1915
1914-17 in charge of Government
war propaganda
1923-24 Liberal MP for Manchester
Rusholme

Maxton, James
1885-1946
Clydeside ILP MP
politician
1922-1946 MP (Labour, then ILP)
for Glasgow Bridgeton

May, George (later Baron May)
1871-1946
Insurance official & government
adviser
1915-1931 Company Secretary,
Prudential,
1931 Chair, Committee on National
Expenditure,:
*'So heavily loaded are the dice in favour
of expenditure that no representation
we can make is more important than
to emphasise the need for caution in
undertaking any commitments of a
continuing character'*
(Committee on national expenditure
report, *Parl. papers,* 1930-31, 16.12,
Cmd 3920)
JM Keynes: May report *...not fit to be
published*

Meinertzhagen, Daniel
1842-1910
Banker
Married Beatrice's sister Georgina

Melchett, Lord; Alfred Moritz Mond,
later first Baron Melchett
1868-1930
Industrialist, financier, and politician
Built up Brunner-Mond chemical
company to become ICI
1906-1923; 1924-1928 Liberal MP
1921-1922 Minister of Health
1921 visited Palestine with
Weizmann; became enthusiastic

Zionist
1926 joined Conservatives
Started Mond-Turner talks to rebuild relationships between employers and TUs after General Strike
1928 peerage

Mellor, William
1888-1942
Journalist; guild socialist
1912 Secretary, Fabian Research Department, which became the Labour Research Department
1915 founded National Guilds League, with GDH Cole
1st World War Conscientious Objector
1920 Foundation member of Communist Party (resigned 1924)
1926-1930 Editor, *Daily Herald*, Later worked with Stafford Cripps; editor of *Tribune*

Middleton, James (Jim)
1878-1962
Political organizer
1902- Assistant Secretary Labour Party
Close to Macdonald
Helped establish War Emergency Workers National Committee
1934-44 Labour Party General Secretary

Mond see Melchett

Money, Leo Chiozza; later Sir
1870-1944
Politician and writer
1906-10 (January); and 1910 (December) -1918 Liberal MP
1918 Stood unsuccessfully as Labour Candidate
1919 member, Sankey Commission
Later, twice arrested for indecent behaviour; convicted on second occasion

Montagu, Edwin
1879-1924
Liberal politician
1906-1922 Liberal MP

PPS to Asquith as Chancellor and PM
Junior minister from 1910
1916 (July-December) Minister of Munitions
1917 Minister for Reconstruction
1917-1922 Secretary of State for India

Moore, George Edward
1873-1958
Philosopher
1893 Trinity College Cambridge
1903 Published *Principia Ethica*

Morant, Robert (Sir)
1863-1920

© National Portrait Gallery, London

Civil servant
1886 tutor to Crown Prince of Siam
1894 returned to England - lived & worked at Toynbee Hall
1895 assistant director of special inquiries and reports in the office of special inquiries and reports at the education department of the Privy Council.
1903 Permanent Secretary, Board of Education
1907 Knighted
1911 Chairman National Insurance Commission
1919 Permanent Secretary Ministry of Health
Beatrice, 1917
Morant is the one man of genius in the Civil Service, but he excites violent dislike in some men and much suspicion in many men. He is public spirited in

his ends but devious in his methods …

Morel, Edmund Dene
1873-1924
Campaigner on international issues
and journalist
From 1900 campaigned against forced
labour in Belgian Congo
1912 Liberal candidate for
Birkenhead
1914 Initially campaigned for
neutrality
Subsequently established Union of
Democratic Control (UDC), which
opposed annexationist war aims and
later also called for a negotiated peace.
1917 served 6 months hard labour for
breach of the Defence of the Realm
Act
1918 joined Labour Party
1922 Labour MP for Dundee, defeating WS Churchill

Morrell, Lady Ottoline Violet Anne
1873-1938

© National Portrait Gallery, London
Literary hostess
Married Phillip Morrell, Liberal MP
from 1906
Friendship/relationship with Bertrand
Russell from 1911
Home at Garsington a refuge for
Conscientious Objectors during
WW1

Morris, William
1834-1896
Designer, author, and visionary
socialist
Early member of Social Democratic
Federation
1884 Morris and his followers split
the SDF to found the Socialist League
Close to George Bernard Shaw

Morrison, Herbert; later Lord Morrison
1888-1965

© National Portrait Gallery, London
Labour politician
1906 Joined ILP
1908 joined SDF
Conscientious Objector during 1st
World War
1915 Secretary London Labour Party
1923-4;1929-31;1935-59 Labour MP
1934 Leader London County Council
Minister in 1929-31 Labour
Government; Wartime Coalition;
1945-51 Labour Government

Mosley, Oswald, Sir
1896-1980

© National Portrait Gallery, London
Politician; fascist leader

Known in family as Tom
1918 Conservative MP
1920 Crossed floor; independent
1924 Joined Labour Party
1929 Chancellor of the duchy of
Lancaster, one of three Ministers,
under J H Thomas, responsible
for coming up with solutions to
unemployment
1930 resigned when his own radical
proposals ('the Mosley Memorandum'
were neither supported by Thomas,
nor accepted by Cabinet
*"Over the next two years Mosley
dissipated his hard-won political
achievement by a series of catastrophic
misjudgements."*
(DNB - Skidelsky)
1931 Founded New Party, supported
by 5 Labour and 1 Tory MP
1932 Started British Union of Fascists
Interned during 2nd World War

Murby, Millicent
1873-1951
Socialist activist; Fabian
1901 joined Fabian Society
1907-13 Fabian Society Executive
Committee
1908 wrote Fabian pamphlet, *The
Common Sense of the Woman Question*
Founder member of the Fabian
women's group
1911 'Explainer' for National
Assistance Act

Murray, Gilbert
1866-1957
Classical scholar and internationalist
Friend of G B Shaw; model for
Adolphus Cusins in *Major Barbara*
1908 Regius Professor of Greek,
Oxford
Chaired meetings for National
Campaign for the Prevention of
Destitution
Detested Lloyd George, who vetoed
him for Order of Merit in 1921
During 1st World War worked for

Board of Education
Cooperated with Beveridge over
German refugee scholars in 1930s

Namier, Lewis
1888-1960
Historian and Zionist campaigner
Born in Russian Poland
1907 arrived London; studied at LSE;
joined Fabian Society
1908 Balliol
Attends Fabian summer schools before
1st World War
1915 adviser to Foreign Office
1920 met Chaim Weizmann,
president of the World Zionist
Organization
1929 political secretary of the Zionist
Organization
1931 History Professor, Manchester

Nash, Vaughan
1861-1932
Journalist/Civil Servant
1887-89 Toynbee Hall resident
Co-author of book on 1889 Dock
Strike, with Llewellyn Smith
1905 Assistant Private Secretary to
Campbell Bannerman at No 10
1908 Principal Private Secretary
1916 Secretariat Reconstruction Cttee

Nesbit, Edith
1858-1924

© National Portrait Gallery, London
Writer; Fabian
Married to Hubert Bland

Nevinson, Henry
1856-1941
Social activist & journalist
Toynbee Hall
Both Nevinsons live in Wentworth
Buildings for some time
Wrote novel *Neighbours of Ours* about
E London life
By 1889 joined Social Democratic
Federation - but closer to Carpenter
& Kropotkin
War correspondent in 1st World War

Nevinson, Margaret
1858-1932
m. Henry Nevinson
DNB - Angela John, 2006:
Margaret Nevinson ...*taught French
evening classes at Toynbee Hall and
helped with St Jude's Girls' Club. She
then became a rent collector in artisans'
dwellings*
Women's suffrage campaigner
Rent collector

Newman, George; later Sir
1870-1948
Medical Officer of Health
1900 MoH Finsbury
1907 after contact with Beatrice &
Morant - offered post of Chief Med
officer to Bd of Education
1911 knighted
1919 Chief Medical Officer, Ministry
of Health

Nicolson, Harold George
1886-1968
Diplomat and politician
1909 joined British Diplomatic
Service
1913 married Vita Sackville-West
1916 One of team involved in drafting Balfour Declaration
1929 left Foreign Office
1931-1932 in Mosley's New Party
1935-1945 National Labour MP

Norman, Montagu (later Baron Norman)
1871-1950

© National Portrait Gallery, London
1920-1944 Governor of the Bank of
England (longest in the history of the
Bank)

Oldham, Joseph Houldsworth
1874-1969
Missionary
1921: Secretary, International
Missionary Council (IMC)
Member of 1928 Hilton Young
Committee; drafted report
Worked effectively with Lugard

Olivier, Noel (later Richards)
1892-1969

© National Portrait Gallery, London
Doctor
Youngest daughter of Sydney Olivier
Pursued by Rupert Brooke

Olivier, Sydney; later Lord Olivier
1859-1943

© National Portrait Gallery, London
Civil servant, politician
Early Fabian, Sidney, GBS and G Wallas
Colonial Office in 1880s with Sidney
1900 to 1904; Colonial secretary of
Jamaica, on three occasions acting as
governor.
1907: appointed captain-general and
governor-in-chief of Jamaica.
1924: Peerage; Secretary of State for
India
1885 married Margaret Cox (c. 1862-
1953) 4 daughters Noel, Brynhild,
Daphne and Margery
Ollivant, Alfred
1874-1927

Ollivant, Alfred
1874-1927
Novelist
Supported Poor Law Campaign

Orage, Alfred Richard
1873-1934
Journalist; editor, *The New Age*
ILP member
1903 Founder, with Holbrook
Jackson and A J Penty, of the Leeds
Arts Club
1905 moved to London
1907 bought New Age, encouraged
by GBS - syndicalist; Guild Socialist
Established Fabian Arts Group
Later Gurdjieff; Major Douglas; Social
Credit

Osmaston, Dorothy (later Lady Layton)
1887-1959
Suffragist and politician
Cambridge Fabian
1906 Newnham
1910 married Walter Layton,
economist

Parker, Gilbert (Sir)
1860-1932
Politician
Born Canada
1900-1918 Conservative MP Gravesend
Imperialist. Supported Poor Law
campaign

Parker, John
1906-1987

© LSE Library Fabian M2 89
Politician
1935-1983 Labour MP
1933 General Secretary New Fabian
Research Bureau
1939-1945 General Secretary, Fabian
Society

Paul, Maurice (Eden)
1865-1944
Doctor and writer
As a student worked alongside
Beatrice and Ella Pycroft at Katherine
Buildings
Worked on Booth Study
In early 20th century a member of
Independent Labour Party and the
People's Suffrage Federation
With 2nd wife, Cedar Paul, a founda-
tion member of CPGB

Translators

Payne-Townshend, Charlotte; later Shaw
  1857-1943
  1898 Married GBS
  Fabian. Generous benefactor towards
  LSE, Fabian Society, and suffrage
  movement.

Pease, Edward Reynolds
  1857-1955

Public Domain, https://commons.wikimedia.
org/w/index.php?curid=653406
  Quaker. Early Fabian
  1889-1913, and 1915-1918 Secretary
  of the Fabian Society; historian of the
  society
  Member of Fabian Executive
  Committee until 1939

Penty, Arthur Joseph
  1875-1937
  Architect and social thinker, guild
  socialist
  1890s: joined ILP and Fabian Society
  In partnership with A R Orage, set up
  Leeds Arts Club
  Supported arts and crafts movement
  and Fabian Arts Group
  Wrote for New Age; attended 1908
  Fabian Summer School
  ODNB: ...original but ultimately
  marginal figure in the history of guild
  socialism
  Penty was ...one of the two or three
  truly original minds of the modern
  world (GK Chesterton)

Phelps, Lancelot
  1853-1936
  Academic; lectured on classics and
  political economy
  COS member
  1880- Poor Law Guardian, Oxford
  Member, Executive committee
  Toynbee Hall
  1905 member, Royal Commission on
  Poor Law; signed Majority Report
  1914-1929 Provost, Oriel College
  Oxford

Phillips, Marion

© National Portrait Gallery, London
  1881-1932
  Labour MP; 1st Labour Party women's
  national organiser
  Born Australia
  1904-7 LSE Doctorate in economics
  Researcher for Poor Law Commission
  1907 joined the Fabian Society and
  the Independent Labour Party
  1908 joined Women's Labour League,
  whose executive committee she joined
  in the following year.
  1911 LSE lecturer
  1912 Fabian Reform Cttee
  1912 Labour Councillor Kensington
  1916 member of Reconstruction
  Committee
  1918 Labour Party Chief Women's
  Officer
  1929-31 Labour MP Sunderland

Playne, Arthur
  1845-1923
  Married to Beatrice's sister Mary

Plumer, Herbert Charles Onslow, first
Viscount Plumer
  1857-1932
  Army officer
  1902 Major General
  1915-1918 a commander on Western
  Front
  1919-1924 Governor of Malta
  1925-1928 High Commissioner
  Palestine

Plunkett, Horace
  1854-1932
  Irish agricultural reformer and
  politician
  Co-operator
  Ambivalent towards Irish nationalism

Podmore, Frank
  1856-1910
  Writer on psychical research
  Involved with Pease in Fellowship
  of New Life, a precursor of Fabian
  Society

Pollitt, Harry
  1890-1960
  Political organiser
  1929-56 General Secretary,
  Communist Party of Great Britain,
  (with a break 1939-41)
  Twice proposed marriage to Rose
  Cohen

Ponsonby, Arthur, (later first Lord
Ponsonby of Shulbrede)
  1871-1946
  Politician and peace campaigner
  1908-18 Liberal MP
  A founder of the Union of
  Democratic Control with MacDonald
  Joined Labour after 1918
  1922-30 Labour MP
  Junior Minister in 1st & 2nd Labour
  governments
  Peerage in 1930
  1931-35 Labour leader in Lords
  1 of founders of Peace Pledge Union
  Later close to appeasers
  1940 left Labour Party

Postan, Michael (Mouna) (Sir)
  1899-1981
  Economic historian
  Born Bessarabia
  1920 moved to UK
  1921 LSE student
  1937 married Eileen Power
  1938 Professor economic history,
  Cambridge
  1939-1942 Head, Russian section of
  the Ministry of Economic Warfare

Power [*married name* Postan], Eileen
Edna Le Poer
  1889-1940)
  Economic historian
  1907-1910 Girton
  1911-1913 Shaw research student, LSE
  1913-1921 Director of studies in
  history at Girton
  1921-1940 Lecturer in Economic
  History, LSE
  1937 married Michael Postan

Pritt, Denis Nowell
  1887-1972
  Barrister and politician
  1927 KC
  1932 Went to USSR with New
  Fabian Research Bureau
  1933 President International inquiry
  into Reichstag fire (Muenzenberg)
  1935-1950 MP N Hammersmith
  1940 Expelled from Labour (unlike
  Cripps, never readmitted)
  Defended Kenyatta in 1952 trial

Provis, Samuel; later Sir
  1845-1926
  Civil servant
  1872 Joined Local Government Board
  (LGB)
  1899-1910 Permanent Secretary, LGB
  Member of Poor Law Royal Commission

Pycroft, Ella
  Fellow housing manager with Beatrice
  at Katherine Buildings
  Later Domestic Economy organiser
  for Technical Education Board

Raverat, Jacques
  1885-1925
  Painter
  Neo-pagan
  Bedales
  Studied at Emmanuel College
  Cambridge
  1925 dies of multiple sclerosis

Reading, Marquess of; Rufus Daniel
Isaacs
  1860-1935
  Politician and judge
  Barrister
  1904 Liberal MP
  1910 Solicitor General
  Attorney General
  1912 Implicated in Marconi scandal
  1913 Lord Chief Justice
  1918 Ambassador to USA
  1921-1926 Viceroy of India
  1931 Foreign Secretary in National
  Govt (August-October)

Reeves, Amber (later Blanco White)
  1887-1981

© The Principal and Fellows, Newham College,
Cambridge
  Cambridge Fabian
  Relationship with H G Wells
  Civil servant during 1st World War
  Lectured at Morley College after 1928
  (Eva Hubback, the Principal, a friend
  from Newnham)

Reeves, Maud Pember
  1865-1953

(Maud and Pember Reeves with - right-
Charlotte Shaw, 1900.) © LSE Library
Shaw Photographic prints: vol 15 no 1427.
Reproduced by kind permission of the National
Trust.
  Suffragist, socialist, Fabian
  Married to William Pember Reeves
  Mother of Amber Reeves
  Active in Fabian Women's Group
  Author of *Round About a Pound a week.*

Reeves, William Pember
  1857-1932
  University administrator, diplomat,
  and politician
  Born New Zealand; political career
  in NZ; came to UK 1896 as Agent
  General for NZ (post later known as
  High Commissioner)
  Coefficient
  1908-19 Third Director of LSE;
  appointed by Sidney in May 1908;
  pressed to resign (again by SW) in
  1919
  1 son killed in 1st World War

Ribbentrop, Joachim von
  1893-1946
  1936-1938 German Ambassador to
  Britain
  1938- German Foreign Minister
  1946 Executed following trial at
  Nuremberg

Robson, William Alexander
  1895-1980
  Jurist and reformer
  Introduced to the Webbs by GBS

Studied at LSE. Later Professor of
Public Administration there
Barrister in Slessor's chambers
1 of the founders of Political Quarterly
Married the cellist Juliette Alvin, who
played to Beatrice in her last years

Rosebery, Lord
1847-1929
Politician
Liberal Imperialist
1889 1st Chairman, London County
Council (LCC)
1894-5 Prime Minister
President LSE

Rowntree, Benjamin Seebohm
1871-1954
Businessman, researcher,
philanthropist
Influenced by Booth, studied poverty
in York
1917 member, Reconstruction
Committee

Rowse, Alfred Leslie
1903-1997
Historian
Born Cornwall; local schools and
Oxford
1925 Fellow, All Souls
1931, 1935 Labour candidate
1956 left Labour over Suez

Russell, Bertrand; 3rd Earl Russell
1872-1970

© National Portrait Gallery, London
Mathematician, philosopher, politician, and peace campaigner

Apostle. Coefficient (but not for long)
1890-1893 Trinity College
Cambridge
Opposed 1st World War; Union for
Democratic Control member
Long affair/friendship with Ottoline
Morell
Supported No Conscription
Fellowship; fined, and sacked from
Cambridge
1917 supported Guild Socialism and
Russian Revolution
1918 6 months in prison
1920 visited Russia; disillusioned
1931 became Earl Russell on the
death of his brother
1949 Nobel Prize for Literature
1958 one of founders of Campaign
for Nuclear Disarmament
1961 again imprisoned for peace
campaign activities, at age of 89

Sadler, Michael Ernest; later Sir
1861-1943
Educationalist
Friend of Austen Chamberlain and
Arthur Acland
1885 Secretary, Oxford Delegacy for
extramural studies, following Acland
1895 Head of Office of special
inquires and reports, Education
Department
Barnett recommends Morant to Sadler
1903 resigns after conflict with Morant
1911-1923 Vice Chancellor, Leeds
University
1923-1934 Master, University College
Oxford

Saleeby, Caleb Williams Elijah
1878-1940
Writer and eugenicist
Trained as a doctor; became freelance
writer & journalist
1907 involved in launch of Eugenics
Education Society
Temperance reformer
Leading spokesman for what scholars
later called 'reform eugenics'.

ODNB:
*…many of the causes he espoused had
become widely accepted by the time of
his death: for example, his advocacy of
clean air legislation, his warnings of the
dangers of tobacco, his commitment to
preventive medicine, and his calls for the
training of parenthood*

Salisbury, Lord
    1830-1903
    1895-1902 Prime Minister

Samuel, Herbert, later Viscount Samuel
    1870-1963

© National Portrait Gallery, London
Close to Fabians as a young man; on
friendly terms with Webbs.
1902-1918; 1929-1935 Liberal MP
1916 and 1931-1932 Home Secretary
1920-1925 Palestine High
Commissioner
1937 Peerage

Sanders, William Stephen
    1871-1941

© National Portrait Gallery, London

The secretarial monopolist
Secularist; studied in Germany
Married Beatrice Martin, (1874-
1932) who was Financial Secretary
of the Women's Social and Political
Union, 1904-1910
1888 Social Democratic Federation
member - Battersea Branch
Subsequently secretary of Battersea
Labour league - J Burns' electoral vehi-
cle; later Secretary London ILP
18.07.1890 accepted as Fabian member
Worked closely with Burns
Hutchinson lecturer
1905-1906: F Soc organiser for local
Fabian Societies
1904-1910 London County Council
Alderman
1914-1920 Secretary Fabian Society
Military service WW1; later
International Labour Organisation
1929-1931; 1935-40 Labour MP for
North Battersea
Autobiography, *Early Socialist Days*,
on early SDF

Sankey, John; later Viscount
    1866-1948

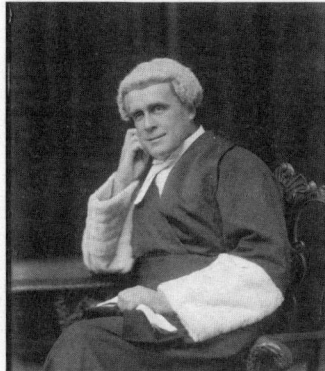

© National Portrait Gallery, London
Lawyer; politician
1919 Chair of Commission on Coal
Industry
1928 Court of Appeal
1929 Lord Chancellor in Labour
Government
1931 stayed with Macdonald, remaining Lord Chancellor until 1935

Schreiner, Olive
1855-1920

© National Portrait Gallery, London
Writer
Born South Africa
1881 came to London
1883 2nd novel, *The Story of an African Farm ...secured her reputation as an evocative storyteller, a daring and perceptive freethinker, and feminist.*
ODNB
formed close ties with pioneering authors and reformers, notably Havelock Ellis, Edward Carpenter, Karl Pearson, and Eleanor Marx
1889 returned to Africa following nervous breakdown

Schuster, Sir George
1881-1982
Government adviser
Army in 1st World War
1922-1927 Financial Secretary, Sudan
1928 member, Hilton Young Committee on East Africa
Economic and Financial Advisor to the Colonial Office
1928-1934 Finance Member, Viceroy's Council, India
1938-1945 National Liberal MP

Shackleton, David; later Sir
1863-1938
Trade unionist, Labour MP, civil servant
1902 Elected Labour MP for Clitheroe
1908,1909 President TUC
1910 Re-elected, but then appointed Senior Labour Adviser, Home Office
1911 A Nat Health Insurance Commissioner
1916 Permanent Secretary, Ministry of Labour

Sharp, Clifford Dyce
1883-1935

© LSE Library Shaw Photos 1-13-1007-1: Reproduced by kind permission of the National Trust.
Journalist and editor
Studied engineering at UCL
Worked with Orage at *New Age*
1909-1913 Editor of *The Crusade*, monthly paper of the Campaign against the Poor Law.
1913-1931 1st editor of *New Statesman*
ODNB (Adrian Smith), 2004:
Sharp tolerated Shaw, but genuinely loathed David Lloyd George. The prime minister reciprocated by orchestrating Sharp's conscription into the Royal Artillery early in 1917
...chronic alcoholism...

Shaw, George Bernard (GBS)
1856-1950

© National Portrait Gallery, London
Writer; Fabian; lifetime friend of the
Webbs
Born Dublin
1876 moved to London
Worked in British Museum Reading
Room, trying to establish himself as
a writer
Becomes vegetarian
Inspired by Henry George. Reads
Marx. Close to Social Democratic
Federation. Friend of William Morris
1879/80 meets Sidney
*In the mid-1880s Shaw became a
socialist, a polemicist, a journalist, a
spellbinding speaker, a critic of the arts
- even, tentatively, a playwright. - DNB
- Stanley Weintraub*
Works as theatre/music/arts critic
Emerges as playwright; champions Ibsen
1898 marries Charlotte Payne
Townshend
1925 Nobel Prize for literature

Shaw, Thomas
1872-1938
Started work in textile factory aged 10
Secretary, Colne Weavers Association
Posts in regional, national, and international textile trade unions
1918-1931 Labour MP Preston
1924 Minister of Labour
1929-1931 Secretary of State for War

Shaw, Walter
1863-1937
Judge
1921-25: Chief Justice of the Straits
Settlements
1929: Shaw chaired the Commission
on the Palestine Disturbances
of August 1929, (the Shaw
Commission), which looked into the
causes of the August 1929 riots

Shiels, (Thomas) Drummond; later (Sir)
1881-1953
Doctor and politician
Joined Fabian Society before 1st World
War
Soldier in war
1924-31 Labour MP, Edinburgh East
1929 Under-secretary of State, India
Office
1929-31 Under-secretary of State,
Colonial Office - and thus Sidney's
junior minister
1930 met Jomo Kenyatta
Author of chapter in '*The Webbs and
their work*' on Sidney as Minister

Shove, Gerald
1887-1947
Cambridge Fabian
Attended pre-1st World War Fabian
Summer Schools
1st World War Conscientious Objector
Economics Fellow at Kings College
Cambridge

Simon, Ernest; later Lord Simon
1879-1960

© National Portrait Gallery, London

Industrialist, politician, and public servant
Close friend of Webbs from 1909
Supporter of Poor Law campaign; attended summer schools
1912 married Shena Potter
elected to Manchester City Council as a Liberal
1923-24; 1929-31 Liberal MP, Manchester Withington
1931 accepted post in National Government, but defeated at October 1931 election
1932 knighted
1946 joined Labour Party; Labour Peer
1947 Chair BBC

Simon, Shena (*née* Potter)
1883-1972
Newnham College Cambridge; Cambridge Fabian
1912 Married Ernest Simon

Simpson, John Hope (Sir)
1868-1961
Civil servant & colonial administrator
Nonconformist; Indian Civil Service; Balliol
Webbs met him on 1912 tour
1922-1924 Liberal MP for Taunton
1930 - appointed by SW to do report on Palestine land issues

Slesser [formerly Schloesser], Sir Henry Herman
1883-1979
Judge and politician
1906 barrister
Joins Fabian Society on advice of Ensor
1910 drafted Prevention of Destitution Bill
1912 Standing Counsel to Labour Party
1914 changes name by deed poll
WW1 advised War Emergency Workers National Committee
1924 Solicitor General in 1st Labour government
1924-1929 Labour MP
1929 Appeal Court Judge

Smart, William
1853-1915
Economist
1896 Adam Smith Chair of Political Economy, Glasgow
Interested in temperance and housing reform
1905 member, Royal Commission on Poor Law

Smillie, Robert
1857-1940
Trade unionist and politician
Started work age 9
Miner from 17
1879 checkweighman
1888 founder member of the Scottish Labour Party
1893 founder member Independent Labour Party
1894 President Scottish Miners Federation
1909 President, Miners Federation of Great Britain
1914 Chair, War Emergency Workers National Committee
1919 member, Sankey Commission
1923-1929 Labour MP for Morpeth

Smith, Sir Allan MacGregor
1871-1941
Solicitor; employers' leader and politician
1910 Secretary, Engineering Employers Federation
1919 member Sankey Commission (December) Conservative MP
1919-1922 Chairman, National Confederation of Employers Organisations

Smith, Frederick Edwin, later Sir, later Earl of Birkenhead
1872-1930
Lawyer and Conservative politician
Liverpool Conservative MP 1906-1918
Attorney General 1915-1918
Lord Chancellor 1919-1922
Secretary of State for India 1924-1928

Smith, Hubert Llewellyn
1864-1945

© National Portrait Gallery, London

Civil servant & social investigator
Student contemporary of M Sadler
An early patron of W H Beveridge
1886 graduates from Oxford
After graduating lives at Toynbee Hall
and works as a lecturer for the Oxford
University Extension Delegacy
Worked on first Booth study
Involvement in trade union activity;
match girls; dock strike; history of
dock strike with Vaughan Nash
Knew both Sidney and Beatrice before
their marriage
1890s- Secretary of the National
Association for the Promotion of
Technical and Secondary Education.
1892 Works for Sidney in LCC election
Writes report for Sidney on technical
and secondary education, leading to
establishment of Technical Education
Board
1893 appointed as the first labour
commissioner of the Board of Trade,
in charge of a newly established
Labour Department
Later deputy comptroller-general and
comptroller-general of the commercial, labour, and statistical branch
1907-19 Permanent secretary of the
Board of Trade
1924 Again Permanent Secretary
when Sidney is President in 1924
In retirement led the successor to the
Booth study of London

Snell, Harry; later Lord Snell
1865-1944

© National Portrait Gallery, London

Secularist; Labour politician
Child of agricultural workers; started
work in fields aged 8
Hired as an indoor farm servant at
Newark hiring fair, aged 12.
Joins Fabian Society June 1890
Secretary to 1st Director of LSE
ILP, SDF
LCC member, then MP for Woolwich
1929
Chair, PLP
On Shaw Commission in Palestine,
1930
Peerage 1931
Chair, LCC, 1934

Snowden, Philip; later Viscount
Snowden
1864-1937

© National Portrait Gallery, London

Labour Politician
Civil Service (Inland Revenue) 1886;

Polio 1891
Nonconformist; ILP; anti-drink
Labour MP 1906
WW1 opponent of conscription
Chancellor 1924; 1929-31
Went with MacDonald 08.31
Viscount Snowden Nov 1931

Sokolnikov, Grigory
1888-1939
Russian revolutionary
Old Bolshevik
1917 People's Commissar for Finance
1929-1932 Ambassador to London
1937 Arrested
1939 killed in prison, probably by
NKVD
UK special Branch file; security
services thought S was sent to London
because Stalin wanted him out of
Russia

Spencer, Frederick
-1946
Webb research secretary from March
1899
Worked on history of Local
Government
Later LCC Chief Inspector of Schools

Spencer, Herbert
1820-1903

© National Portrait Gallery, London)
Philosopher, social theorist, sociol-
ogist, friend, mentor and teacher to
Beatrice and her sisters

Squire, Jack (Sir John Collings Squire)
1884-1958
Writer, poet, parodist, editor
Cambridge Fabian; original secretary,
Cambridge Fabians
Wrote for New Age
1913- Literary Editor *New Statesman*
Later Acting Editor
1919 established *London Mercury*,
monthly literary magazine
Later alcoholic; flirtation with fascism

Stamp, Josiah Charles, Baron Stamp
1880-1941
Statistician and business administrator
Inland Revenue clerk
Studied for London University BSc
Econ; 1st Class; 1910
Invited by Wallas to LSE, where he
did a PhD
1919 moved to business; Nobel, then
ICI, then LMS railway
1925-1935 Governor& Vice
Chairman, LSE
1929 member, Econ Advisory
Council
1935-1941 Chair, LSE Governors
Close to Neville Chamberlain before
war

Stanley, Arthur Lyulph; Lord Stanley of
Alderley, Lord
1875-1931
1904 LCC member
1906-1910 Liberal MP
1914-1920 Governor of Victoria
1925 inherited peerage
1930-1931 Chair, East Africa Joint
Committee

Stead, William Thomas
1849-1912
Newspaper Editor and social reformer
Editor, *Pall Mall Gazette* 1883-1890
Pro Boer
Drowned when Titanic went down

Steel-Maitland, Arthur (later Sir)
  1876-1935
  Conservative politician
  1907: Assistant Commissioner, Poor
  Law Commission; studied casual labour
  1910-1929; 1929-1935: Conservative
  MP
  1911: Chair, Conservative Party
  1924-1929 Minister of Labour
  1916-35 Chair, LSE Governors

Strauss, George Russell; later Strauss
  1901-1993
  Politician
  1925-1931 and 1932-1946 LCC
  member
  1934-1979 Labour MP
  1947-1951 Minister of Supply
  1979 Life Peer

Tawney, R H
  1880-1962

© National Portrait Gallery, London
Historian and political thinker
Adult educationist; lifelong friend
of William Temple and William
Beveridge; brother in law of Beveridge
Toynbee Hall
Children's Country Holiday Fund
Gave evidence to Poor Law
Commission
LSE
Member of Sankey Commission

Thesiger, Frederick John Napier, first
Viscount Chelmsford
  1868-1933
  Politician; Viceroy of India
  1900-1904 Member, London School
  Board
  1904- Member, LCC
  1905-1909 Governor, Queensland
  1910-1913 Governor, New South
  Wales
  1916-1921 Viceroy, India
  1924 1st Lord Admiralty

Thomas, James H (Jimmy)
  1874-1949

© National Portrait Gallery, London
Trade unionist and politician
Joined Great Western Railway as a
cleaner in 1889
Soon active in railway trade union
1910- Labour MP Derby
Prominent in pre WW1 Lab unrest
DNB: Thomas was 'never a socialist'
1916: National Union of Railwaymen
General Secretary
1924   Colonial Secretary
1929   Lord Privy Seal, leading on
unemployment
1930   Dominions Secretary
1931- went with MacDonald
Drinking and gambling after 1931
1936 budget leak

Thomson, Christopher Birdwood, Baron
Thomson
  1875-1930
  army officer and politician

1919 left army as Brigadier General;
joined Labour Party
Labour candidate 1922, 1923
1924 Peerage - Secretary of State for
Air
1929 again S of S, Air
1930 killed in R101 Airship crash

Tillett, Ben
1860-1943
Trade unionist and politician
Involved in 1889 Dock Strike and in
1893 ILP foundation conf
Present at 02.1900 LRC foundation
conf
MP after 1917

Townshend, Caroline
1878-1944

© LSE Library ILP/6/21/2
Stained glass artist, Fabian and
suffrage campaigner
Designer of Fabian window

Townshend, Emily (*née* Gibson)
1849-1934
Fabian and suffrage campaigner
Cousin of Charlotte Payne
Townshend (Charlotte Shaw)
1869-1872 - one of the first students
at Girton College, then at Hitchin
1873   Married Chambrey Corker
Townshend, architect. 4 children,
including Caroline and Rachel.
1907   Imprisoned for 2 weeks during
suffrage campaign
Author of Fabian Tracts on
school nurseries (1909); Charity

Organisation Society (1911); and
William Morris (1912)
1915   resigned from Fabian Society
1918   edited memorial volume from
Ben Keeling
Later sympathetic to Mussolini

Townshend, Rachel Susanna (Keeling)
1885-1969
See Keeling, Rachel

Trevelyan, (Sir) Charles
1870-1958
Politician - Lib then Lab
Goes to N America & Australia &
New Zealand w S + B In 1898 to 9
(The Trevelyan brothers appear in H.
G. Wells's novel *The New Machiavelli*
as the Cramptons.)
WW1 - involved in UDC
1918- joins Labour
Minister of Education in 1924, 1929
governments

Turin, Lucia
Russian émigré
Secretary to William Beveridge at LSE
and at Oxford
Married to S P Turin

Turin, SP
Russian émigré; economist and writer
Taught at School of Slavonic Studies
and at LSE

Wake, Egerton
1871-1929
Labour Party Official
ILP; UDC
1919-1929 Labour National Agent

Wakefield, Russell
1854-1933
Clergyman
Member of Poor Law Commission
Bishop of Birmingham (1911); signa-
tory of Minority Report
Member of London School Board and
of St Marylebone Borough Council
President of NCPD

Wallas, Graham
1858-1932

© LSE Library, Fabian archive M/2/16
Political scientist. Early Fabian
Differed from Sidney over education
policy (schoolboards; church schools)
Early lecturer at LSE

Ward, Dudley
1885-1957
Civil servant and banker
Cambridge Fabian

Watson, Alfred, Sir
1870-1936
Actuary and civil servant
Advised on National Insurance from
1910
Later Government Actuary

Wedgwood, Josiah Clement, first Baron
Wedgwood
1872-1943
Politician
Soldier during Boer War
1906 Liberal MP
1919 joined Labour Party
1924 Chancellor, Duchy of Lancaster
1942 Baron Wedgwood
Supporter of Jewish National Home
in Palestine

Weizmann, Chaim
1874-1952

© National Portrait Gallery, London
Zionist leader; President of Israel
Scientist. Came to work at
Manchester, 1904
1910- naturalized British subject
1913; Reader in Biochemistry
During WW1 worked for British
Govt as a scientific adviser
Also lobbied for Zionist cause - 1917
- secured Balfour Declaration
1930 battles over Passfield White
Paper

Wellock, Wilfred
1879-1972
Socialist; Labour MP; later Gandhian
Independent Methodist and vegetar-
ian; ILP
WW1 Conscientious objector; impris-
oned. Member, No Conscription
Fellowship
Guild Socialist sympathiser
Labour MP 1927-31
Member East Africa Joint Select
Committee

Wells, Herbert George
1866-1946

© National Portrait Gallery, London
Novelist and social commentator
Fabian. Coefficient. Satirist of the
Webbs in *The New Machiavelli*

Wernher, Julius
1850-1912
Businessman & philanthropist
Born Germany
To UK, then to S Africa for diamond
interests; Kimberley
Then gold - Witwatersrand
British citizen 1879
Bought Luton Hoo 1903

West, Julius (born Rapoport)
1891-1918
Writer; Fabian; Russian origin
Worked for Fabian Society

Wheatley, John
1869-1930
Politician
Born in Ireland
Moved to Scotland as a child
Started work as a miner at 11 yrs old
United Irish League
Catholic Socialist Society
1910 Lab Councillor - from 1912 on
Glasgow Council
UDC member
Supported Conscientious Objectors
1922-1930 MP Glasgow Shettleston
1924 Minister of Health
Wheatley Housing Act

White, George Rivers Blanco
Lawyer; later judge
Fabian
Married Amber Reeves 1909

Wilkinson, Ellen
1891-1947

© National Portrait Gallery, London
Politician
1912 Secretary, Manchester University
Fabian Society
Fabian, ILP; early member CPGB
(but soon left)
Supported Poor Law Campaign
MP 1924-31;1935-47
Junior minister in wartime coalition
Minister of Education 1945-47

Williams, Glynne
Argentine ranch owner
New Statesman shareholder
'progressive' rather than Labour

Wilson, Charlotte
1854-1944
Anarchist, feminist, early Fabian
1884 joined SDF & Fabian Society
Only woman elected to 1st Fabian EC,
12.84
She withdrew from the Fabian
executive in April 1887 and concentrated on work within the anarchist
movement, returning to activity in the
Fabian Society twenty years later
1908 founded Fabian Women's group
Fabian EC 1911-14

Wilson, Horace; <u>later</u> (Sir)
1882-1972
Civil Servant
LSE night school graduate 1904-8
Joined civil service as a boy clerk 1898
Labour Dept Board of Trade, 1907
1921 Permanent Secretary, Ministry
of Labour
Nov 1930- Chief Industrial Advisor
Advised Neville Chamberlain on
appeasement
1939: Permanent Secretary to
Treasury; Head of Civil Service

Wilson, Samuel; <u>later</u> (Sir)
1873-1950
Colonial Governor & Civil Servant
Permanent Secretary, Colonial Office,
1925-33

Woolf, Leonard
1880-1969

© National Portrait Gallery, London
Author and publisher
Apostle. Bloomsbury
1904-11: 7 years a colonial civil
servant in Ceylon
DNB:
'He had become', he wrote later,
'a socialist of a rather peculiar sort'
(Beginning Again, 105).
1912 marries Virginia Stephen
Secretary, Labour Party International
and Imperial Cttee

Woolf, Virginia (*née* Stephen)
1882-1941

© National Portrait Gallery, London
Novelist and diarist; Bloomsbury
Daughter of Leslie Stephen, first
editor of *Dictionary of National
Biography*
1912   Married Leonard Woolf
1915   Publication of 1st novel, *The
Voyage Out*
Knew Webbs from 1913
BW: *I think we liked them better than
they liked us.*
After V's death in 1941:
*I am pained by the thought of that
beautiful and brilliant Virginia, yield-
ing to the passion for death, rather than
endure the misery of continued life*

Wootton [*née* Adam], Barbara Frances,
Baroness Wootton of Abinger
1897-1988
Economist and social scientist
Girton
1919 1st in Economics
Worked for LRD, TUC
1926 Principal Morley College
1958 Life Peer

Yarrow, Alfred (Sir)
1842-1932
Shipbuilder
1906-8 moved business from Thames
to Clyde
Glasgow supporter of Poor Law
campaign

Young, (Edward) Hilton (Sir) (Lord
Kennet)
   1879-1960
   Politician & writer
   On the fringes of the Neo-pagans and
   Bloomsbury
   Liberal MP after 1918; chief
   whip Lloyd George Liberals; later
   Conservative
   1927-1929 Hilton Young mission to
   East Africa on ever closer union

Annexe Three: Bibliography

ARCHIVAL MATERIAL

British Library of Political and Economic Science (LSE)
- Booth papers
- Braithwaite Diary
- Coefficients Minutes (ASSOC 17)
- Colegate Diaries (Coll Misc 741)
- Fabian Society - including:
  · Minutes of the Executive Committee and other minutes.
  · Correspondence
  · Schools and Conferences, including Summer School
- Independent Labour Party papers (Coll Misc 0314)
- Passfield Papers
The main collection of the Webbs' own papers - includes complete manuscript and typescript versions of Beatrice's diary (1873-1943) The diaries are also now available on line, with the financial support of the Webb Memorial Trust.
- Tawney Papers
- Webb East Africa (Coll Misc 156)
- Webb Local Government Collection
- Coll Misc 0043 WEBB St Katherine Buildings
Bodleian Library
- Greenwood Papers
Kings College Cambridge
- Brooke papers
- Keynes papers
People's History Museum Manchester:
- Labour Party Archive
- Records of the War Emergency National Workers Committee
British Library
- John Burns Diary Add ms 46323
- Bernard Shaw papers Add ms 50508-50743: [1995-1956]
London Metropolitan Archives
- Papers of the LCC Technical

Education Board
- London Picture Archive
National Archives (TNA)
- PREM Prime Ministers series
- CAB (Cabinet) files
- CO (Colonial Office)
- KV2 (Security Services)
The Harkives (https://harkives.com/) is an on-line collection of material about the life and work of Margaret Harkness.

OFFICIAL PUBLICATIONS

Closer Union in East Africa, Joint Committee on; Vol I, Report; Vol II, Minutes of evidence; Cmd 156, 1931
Palestine; Report by Sir John Hope Simpson, CIE; Cmd 3686, 1930
Report of the Commission on Closer Union of the Dependencies in Eastern and Central Africa (Hilton Young Report) Cmd 3234 1929
Report of the Commission on the Palestine Disturbances of August 1929. (Shaw Report) Cmd. 3530 1930
Report of the Royal Commission on the Poor Laws and Relief of Distress; Cd 4499 1909
Social Insurance and Allied Services; Report by Sir William Beveridge; Cmd 6404 1942

WORKS BY BEATRICE AND SIDNEY WEBB

AUTOBIOGRAPHICAL

Webb, B;
- *My Apprenticeship*; London, Longmans, 1926
- *Our Partnership*; ed. Cole, M & Drake, B; London, Longmans, 1948

DIARIES

LSE Library holds both the manuscript and typewritten diaries, which are also on line.

There is a 4 volume edited edition:
Webb, B; *The Diary of Beatrice Webb*; edited by Norman and Jeanne Mackenzie
  Vol I 1873-1892
  Vol II 1892-1905
  Vol III 1905-1924
  Vol IV 1924-1943
  London; Virago, in association with LSE, 1982-1985

LETTERS
Three-volume collection of the Webbs' letters, edited by Norman Mackenzie. *The Letters of Sidney and Beatrice Webb*, edited by Norman Mackenzie
  Vol I   1873-1892
  Vol II   1892-1912
  Vol III   1912-1947
Cambridge, Cambridge University Press in cooperation with the London School of Economics, 1978
Margaret Cole edited two other collections of extracts from Beatrice's Diary
Cole, Margaret, Editor;
- *Beatrice Webb's Diaries 1912-1924*; introduction by Lord Beveridge; London, Longmans Green, 1952
- *Beatrice Webb's Diaries 1924-1932*; London, Longmans Green, 1956.

OTHER
Potter, B
- *The Cooperative Movement in Great Britain*; London, Swan Sonnenschein & Co, 1891
Webb, S;
- *Socialism in England*; London, Swan Sonnenschein & Co; 1893
- *How to Pay for the War*; London, Fabian Research Department 1916
- *The Story of the Durham Miners*, 1662-1921, London, Fabian Society, 1921
- *The Labour Party on the Threshold*, Fabian Tract no 207; London, the Fabian Society, June 1923
- *What happened in 1931*: a Record.;

Fabian Tract No 237; London, 1932
Webb, S; editor; *How to Pay for the War*; London, Fabian Research Department 1916
Webb, S & B
- *The History of Trade Unionism*; London; Longmans Green; 1894, 1920
- *Industrial Democracy*; Vol I; Vol II; London, Longmans, Green & Co; 1897
- *Problems of Modern Industry*; London, Longmans Green; 1902
- *Constitution for the socialist commonwealth of Great Britain, A*; London; Longmans; 1920
- *English Poor Law Policy*; London, Longmans, 1910
- *English Local Government*
  Vol 1, *The parish and the county* (1906)
  Vol 2, *From the Revolution to the Municipal Corporations Act: The manor and the borough, Part One* (1908)
  Vol 3, *From the Revolution to the Municipal Corporations Act: The manor and the borough. Part Two* (1908)
  Vol 4, *Statutory authorities for special purposes* (1922)
  Vol 5, *The story of the king's highway* (1913)
  Vol 6, *English prisons under local government* (1922) with preface by George Bernard Shaw
  Vol 7, *English poor law history. Part I: The old poor law* (1927)
  Vol 8, *English poor law history. Part II: The last hundred years, vol 1*
  Vol 9, *English poor law history. Part II: The last hundred years, vol 2*
- *Methods of Social Study*; London, Longmans Green, 1932
- *Soviet Communism: A New Civilisation*; London, Longmans, 1935, 1937, 1941

Previous Biographies

Cole, M. *Beatrice Webb* London, Longmans, 1945

Cole, M ed. *The Webbs and their Work* London, Frederick Muller, 1949

Hamilton, Mary Agnes (Molly); *Sidney and Beatrice Webb* London, Sampson Low, 1933

Harrison, R J *The Life and Times of Sidney and Beatrice Webb; 1858-1905: the formative years* London, Macmillan, 2000

MacKenzie, J *A Victorian Courtship: The story of Beatrice Potter and Sidney Webb* London, Weidenfeld & Nicolson, 1979

Muggeridge, K & Adam, R *Beatrice Webb: A life 1858-1943* London, Secker & Warburg, 1967

Nord, D E *The Apprenticeship of Beatrice Webb* New York, Cornell University Press, 1989

Radice, L *Beatrice and Sidney Webb: Fabian Socialists* London, Macmillan, 1984

Reisman, D *Sidney and Beatrice Webb, An academic biography*; Cham, Switzerland, Palgrave Macmillan, 2022

Seymour-Jones, C *Beatrice Webb, Woman of conflict* London, Pandora, 1992

Fabian Society Publications

Shaw, G B, ed. Fabian Essays London 1889
And 1920 edition with preface by Sidney Webb

Fabianism and the Empire, a manifesto for the Fabian Society; London, Grant Richards, 1900

Journals

The Crusade
The New Age

Other secondary sources

Abdy, Jane and Gere, Charlotte; *The Souls;* London, Sidgwick & Jackson, 1984

Ablett, Noah and others The Miners' Next Step; in Coates, Ken, Editor; Democracy in the Mines; Nottingham, Spokesman Books, 1974

Adams, R J Q; *Balfour, the last grandee;* London, Thistle Publishing, 1913

Allen, Bernard M
- *Down the Stream of Life* ,London, The Lindsey Press, 1948
- *Sir Robert Morant, A great public servant*; London, 1934
- *William Garnett, a memoir*; Cambridge, W Heffer & Sons, 1933

Amery, Leopold S;
- *The Leo Amery Diaries; Vol 1 1896-1929*; London, Hutchinson, 1980
- *The Empire at bay The Leo Amery Diaries; Vol 2 1929-1945*; Ed John Barnes & David Nicholson; London, Hutchinson, 198

Armstrong, George, ed. *London's Struggle for Socialism*; London, Thames Publications, 1948

Arnot, Robin P; *South Wales Miners*; Cardiff, Cymric Federation Press, 1975

Attlee, Clement R
- *As it happened*; London, Heinemann, 1954
- *Blue Stocking in action; in* Field, F, ed; *Attlee's Great Contemporaries: the politics of character*; London, continuum, 2009

Barnett, Henrietta; *Canon Barnett, His life, work and friends*; London, John Murray,1918

Beckerman-Boys, Carly;
- *British Foreign Policy Decision-making Towards Palestine During the Mandate (1917-1948): A Poliheuristic Perspective;* Birmingham PhD thesis, 1913
- *The Reversal of the Passfield White Paper, 1930-31: A Reassessment.* Journal of Contemporary History 51(2) (2016): pp 213-233

Belloc, Hilaire; *The Servile State*; London,

T N Foulis, 1912

Beveridge, W
- *Power and Influence*; London; Hodder and Stoughton, 1953
- *Unemployment, a problem of industry*; London, Longmans Green & Co, 1912

Bew, John; *Citizen Clem; A biography of Attlee*; London, Riverrun, 2017

Bogdanor, Vernon; *The Strange Survival of Liberal Britain; politics and power before the First World War*; London; Biteback Publishing Ltd, 2022

Booth, Charles; *Life and Labour of the People in London*, Third Edition; London, Macmillan, 1902-1903 First Series, Poverty; Volumes i - iv

Booth, Mary; *Charles Booth - A Memoir*; London, Macmillan, 1918

Bouverie, Tim; *Appeasing Hitler*; London, Vintage, 2020.

Bowle, John E; *Viscount Samuel, A biography*; London, Victor Gollancz, 1957

Braithwaite, William J; *Lloyd George's Ambulance Wagon*; <u>ed</u> H N Banbury; Bath, 1957

Brennan, E J T, <u>Ed</u>; *Education for National Efficiency: the contribution of Beatrice and Sidney Webb*; London, The Athlone Press, 1975

Briggs, Asa; and Ann Macartney; *Toynbee Hall, The first Hundred Years*; London, Routledge, 1984

Briggs, Asa and Savile, John; editors; *Essays in Labour History 1886-1923*; London; Macmillan; 1971

Briggs, Asa *The Welfare State in historical perspective*; <u>in</u> Collected Essays, Vol II; Brighton, Harvester Press, 1985

Britain, Ian; *Fabianism and Culture; a study in British Socialism and the arts; 1884-1918*; Cambridge, CUP, 1982

Brooke, Rupert
- *The Collected Poems, with a memoir by Edward Marsh;* London, Sidgwick & Jackson, 1918
- *The Letters of Rupert Brooke*, <u>ed</u> Geoffrey Keynes, London, Faber,

1968

Brown, Gordon *Maxton*; Edinburgh, Mainstream Publishing, 1986

Brown, Kenneth D; *John Burns*; London, Royal Historical Society, 1977

Bruce, Maurice, <u>ed</u>.; *The rise of the welfare state*; London, Weidenfeld and Nicolson, 1973

Bryant, Chris; *Stafford Cripps, The first modern Chancellor*; London, Hodder and Stoughton, 1997

Bullock, Alan; *The Life and Times of Ernest Bevin; I Trade Union Leader 1881-1940*; London, Heinemann; 1960

Burgess, Joseph; *John Burns: the rise and progress of a Right Honourable*; Glasgow, The Reformers Bookstall, 1911;

Caine, Barbara; *Destined to be wives; the sisters of Beatrice Webb*; Oxford, OUP, 1986

Campbell, John; *Haldane, The forgotten statesman who shaped modern Britain*; London, Hurst, 2020

Castle, Barbara; *Fighting all the way*; London; Macmillan; 1993

'Cato'; *Guilty Men*; London, Victor Gollancz; 1940

Checkland, SG & EOA, <u>eds</u>.; *The Poor Law Report of 1834*; London, Penguin, 1973

Churchill, Randolph S; *Winston S Churchill 1901-14*; London, Minerva, 1991

Churchill, Winston S
- *Great Contemporaries*; London; Leo Cooper; 1990
- The Gathering Storm; Vol 1 of *The Second World War*; London, Cassell; 1948

Clarke, Joan S; *The break-up of the Poor Law;* <u>in</u> Cole, M, <u>ed</u> The Webbs and their work, 1949

Clegg, Hugh A; *A History of British Trade Unions since 1889; Vol II 1911-1933*; Oxford; OUP, 1987

Clements, Keith; *Faith on the Frontier, A*

life of J R Oldham; Edinburgh, T&T Clark,1999

Coates, K and Topham, T; *The making of the labour movement*; Nottingham, Spokesman, 1994

Cohen, Michael J; *Britain's Moment in Palestine; Retrospect and Perspectives,1917-1948*; London, Routledge, 2014

Cole, George Douglas Howard (GDH)
- *John Burns* Fabian Biographical Series no 14; 1943
- *The World of Labour*; London, G Bell and Sons, 1913

Cole, Margaret
- *Beatrice Webb*; London, Longmans, 1945
- *Growing up into revolution*; London, Longmans, 1949
- *The story of Fabian Socialism*; London, Heinemann, 1963
- *The Social Services and the Webb Tradition* Webb Memorial Lecture, 1946
- (Ed) *The Webbs and their Work*; London, F Muller, 1949

Cole, George Douglas Howard (GDH) and Cole, Margaret, editors;
- *The Bolo Book*; London; 1921; The Labour Publishing Company Ltd, and George Allen and Unwin

Courtney, Katherine; *Extracts from a diary during the war*; Printed for private circulation, December 1927

Craig, FWS, Ed; *British General Election Manifestos1900-1974*, London, Macmillan, 1975

Crosland, Susan; *Tony Crosland*; London, Coronet Books (Hodder and Stoughton); 1982

Dalton, Hugh
- *Call Back Yesterday, Memoirs 1887-1931*; London, F Muller, 1953
- *The Political Diary of Hugh Dalton, 1918-40;1945-60*; ed Pimlott, B; London, Jonathan Cape, 1986
- *The Second World War Diary of Hugh Dalton 1940-1945;* ed Pimlott, B;

London, Jonathan Cape, in association with the London School of Economics and Political Science, 1986

Dangerfield, George; *The strange death of Liberal England, 1910-1914*; New York, Capricorn Books, 1961

Davenport-Hines, Richard; *Ettie; The intimate life and dauntless spirit of Lady Desborough*; London, Weidenfeld and Nicholson, 2008

Delany, Paul; *The Neo-Pagans; friendship and love in the Rupert Brooke circle*; London, Hamish Hamilton, 1988

Egremont, Max; *Balfour; A life of Arthur James Balfour*; London, Collins, 1980

Ellenberger, Nancy; *Balfour's World; Aristocracy and political culture at the fin de siècle*; Woodbridge, The Boydell Press, 2015

Ellis, Edward L; *TJ, A life of Dr Thomas Jones, CH*; Cardiff, 1992

Ensor, Robert; *England 1870-1914*; Oxford, OUP, 1936

Estorick, Eric; *Stafford Cripps, a biography*; London, William Heinemann Ltd, 1949

Evans, Richard J; *Eric Hobsbawm, a life in history*; London, Little Brown, 2019

Finlayson, Geoffrey; *Citizen, State and Social Welfare in Britain 1830-1990*; Oxford, Clarendon Press, 1994

Foot, Michael; *The History of Mr Wells*; Counterpoint, Washington DC; 1995

Fox, James; *White Mischief*; London, Penguin, 1984

Freeden, M; *The coming of the welfare state* in Ball, T and Bellamy, R, Eds, The Cambridge History of Twentieth Century Political Thought, Cambridge 2003.

Fremantle, Anne; *This Little Band of Prophets*; the British Fabians; London, Allen and Unwin; 1960

Fry, R; *Maud and Amber; A New Zealand Mother and Daughter and the Women's Cause 1865-1981*; Christchurch NZ

1992, Canterbury University Press

Gardiner, Alfred George;
- *Pillars of Society*; London; J M Dent;1916
- *Prophets, Priests, and Kings;* London; J M Dent;1914

Gibbon, G, and Bell, R; *History of the London County Council, 1889-1939*; London, Macmillan, 1939

Gilbert, Bentley; *Evolution of National Insurance in Britain*; London, Michael Joseph, 1966

Gilmour, David; *Curzon*; London, John Murray, 1994

Goldman, Lawrence; *The life of R H Tawney*; London, Bloomsbury, 2013

Gregory, Roy G; *Sidney Webb and East Africa; Labour's Experiment with the doctrine of native paramountcy*; University of California Press, Berkeley and Los Angeles, 1962

Grubb, Arthur Page; *From Candle Factory to British Cabinet; The life story of the Right Hon John Burns, PC, MP*; London, Edwin Dalton, 1908

Gupta, P S; *Imperialism and the British Labour movement, 1914-1964*; London, Macmillan, 1975

Haldane, Richard B; *An Autobiography*; London, Hodder and Stoughton, 1929

Hale, Keith, <u>editor</u> *Friends and Apostles: the correspondence of Rupert Brooke and James Strachey, 1905-1914* London, Yale University Press, 1998

Hamilton, Mary Agnes (Mollie)
- *Mary Macarthur, a biographical sketch*; London, Leon and Parsons, 1925
- *Remembering my good friends*; London, Jonathan Cape, 1944
- *Up-hill all the way; a third cheer for democracy*; London, Jonathan Cape, 1953

Harkness, M (John Law)
- *A City Girl*; Brighton, Victorian Secrets, 2015
- *In Darkest London*; Black Apollo

Press 2003; originally published by Hodder and Stoughton, 1889

Harris, Jose
- *Unemployment and Politics: A study in English Social Policy, 1886-1914*; Oxford, Oxford University Press, 1972
- *Private Lives, Public Spirit; social history of Britain 1870-1914*; Oxford, OUP, 1993;
- *William Beveridge, a biography;* Oxford, OUP, 1977

Harris, Kenneth; *Attlee*; London, Weidenfeld and Nicolson, 1982

Harris, Pippa, <u>editor</u> *Song of Love: The letters of Rupert Brooke and Noel Olivier, 1909-1915*; London, Bloomsbury, 1991

Hassall, Christopher; *Rupert Brooke*; London, Faber, 1964

Healey, D; *The Time of my Life*; London, Michael Joseph, 1989

Hennessy, Peter; *Never Again*; Britain 1945-51; London, Jonathan Cape, 1992

Hewins, William A S; *Apologia of an Imperialist*; London, Constable, 1929

Hirshfield, Claire; *The Anglo-Boer War and the issue of Jewish Culpability*; Journal of Contemporary History, Vol 15, No 4 (Oct 1980; pp619-31

Holmes, R *Eleanor Marx, A life*; London, Bloomsbury, 2014; p 232

Holroyd, M
Bernard Shaw;
- *Volume 1, The Search for Love, 1856-1898;* London, Penguin, 1990
- *Volume 2, The Pursuit of Power, 1898-1918*; London, Penguin, 1991
- *Volume 3, The Lure of Fantasy,* London, Chatto and Windus, 1991

Honeyball, Mary
- *Parliamentary Pioneers; Labour Women MPs 1918-1945*;
- Chatham, Urbane Publications, 2015

Hopkinson, Diana; *Family Inheritance, a life of Eva Hubback*; London, Staples

Press, 1954

Howarth, Patrick; *Squire: Most generous of men*; London, Hutchinson, 1963

Hunt, Tristram; *Building Jerusalem; The rise and fall of the Victorian City*; London; Weidenfeld & Nicolson, 2004

Hutt, Allen; *The Post War History of the British Working Class*; London, Gollancz, 1937

Hyams, Edward; *The New Statesman; the history of the first fifty years*; London, Longmans, 1963

Hynes, Samuel; *Edwardian Occasions; Essays on English Writing in the early Twentieth Century*; London, Routledge, 1972

Jackson, Ben; *Equality and the British Left 1900-64*; Manchester MUP 2007

Jenkins, Roy *Asquith*; London, Collins, 1964

Jones, Gareth Stedman; *Outcast London*; Oxford; Clarendon Press; 1971

Jones, Nigel; *Rupert Brooke; Life, death and myth*; London, Richard Cohen Books, 1999

Jones, Thomas
- *A Diary with Letters, 1931-1950*; Oxford, OUP, 1954
- *Lloyd George*; London, OUP, 1951
- *Welsh Broth*; London, W Griffiths & Co 1951
- *Whitehall Diary; Volume I 1916-1925*; ed. K Middlemas; Oxford, OUP, 1969
- *Whitehall Diary; Volume II 1926-1930*; ed. K Middlemas; Oxford, OUP, 1969

Katanka, Michael, Editor; *Radicals, Reformers, and Socialists*; from the Fabian Biographical Series; London; Charles Knight & Co; 1973

Keeling, Ben; *Letters and recollections*, edited by ET; with an introduction by H G Wells; London, George Allen and Unwin, 1918

Kent, William; *John Burns: Labour's Lost Leader*: London, Williams and

Norgate, 1950

Keynes, John Maynard
- *Collected Writings; Vol IX; Essays in Persuasion*; London; Macmillan, for Royal Economic Society, 1972
- *The economic consequences of Mr. Churchill*; London, The Hogarth Press, 1925

Khrushchev, Nikita; *The dethronement of Stalin; full text of the Khrushchev speech*; Manchester Guardian, June 1956

Klugmann, James; *History of the Communist party of Great Britain; Vol I; Formation and Early Years 1919-1924*; London; Lawrence & Wishart, 1968

Koss, Stephen; *Fleet Street radical; A G Gardiner and the Daily News*; London, Allen Lane, 1973

Koss, Stephen Ed; *The Pro-Boers; The Anatomy of an Antiwar Movement*; Chicago & London, University of Chicago Press, 1973

Kynaston, David
- *The City of London; Vol I A World of Its Own 1815-1890;* London, Pimlico; 1994
- *The City of London; Vol III Illusions of Gold 1914-1945;* London, Pimlico, 2000

Labour Party *Labour and the New Social Order*, London, 1918

Lansbury, George
- *My Life*; London, Constable & Co, 1928
- *What I saw in Russia*; London; Leonard Parsons; 1920

Laski, Harold J
- *The Webbs and Soviet Communism*; Webb Memorial Lecture 1947
- *Parliamentary Government in England*; London, Allen and Unwin, 1938

Layton, Lord (WT); *Dorothy*; London, Collins, 1961

Lee, Hermione; *Virginia Woolf*; London, Vintage Books, 1997

Lehmann, John; *Rupert Brooke, His life and his legend*; London, 1980

Leys, Norman *Kenya*; London, Hogarth Press, 1926;

London Congregational Union, The; *The bitter cry of outcast London*; London, James Clarke & Co; 1883

Longford, Elizabeth; *The Pebbled Shore*; Stroud, Sutton Publishing, 2004

McBriar, Alan
- *Fabian Socialism and English Politics, 1884-1918*; Cambridge, Cambridge University Press, 1966
- *An Edwardian Mixed Doubles; The Bosanquets versus the Webbs; a study in British Social Policy, 1890-1929*; Oxford, Clarendon Press, 1987

MacCarthy, Fiona; *Eric Gill*; London, Faber and Faber; 1989

MacKenzie, Jeanne and MacKenzie, Norman
- *The Fabians*; New York, Simon and Schuster, 1977
- *The life of H G Wells*; London, Hogarth Press, 1987

McKibbin, Ross
- *The evolution of the Labour Party*; Oxford, Clarendon Press, 1974
- *Parties and People*, Oxford, OUP; 2010

Maisky, Ivan
- *Memoirs of a Soviet Ambassador; The War 1939-43*; London; Hutchinson; 1967
- *The Maisky Diaries*; ed Gorodetsky, G; London, Yale UP, 2015
- *The Complete Maisky Diaries*; ed Gorodetsky, G; New Haven & London, Yale University Press, 2017

Manning, Leah; *A life for education*; London, Victor Gollancz, 1970

Mansfield, Peter; *A History of the Middle East*; London, Penguin Books, 1992

Marquand, David
- *Britain since1918*; London, Weidenfeld & Nicholson; 2008;
- *Ramsay MacDonald*; London, Richard Cohen Books, 1997

Martin, Basil Kingsley
- *Editor*; London, Penguin, 1968
- *Father Figures,* London, Penguin, 1969

Marwick, Arthur; *Clifford Allen, The Open Conspirator*; London, Oliver and Boyd, 1984

Masterman, Lucy; *C F G Masterman, a biography*; London, Nicholson & Watson; 1939

Meinertzhagen, Georgina; *From Ploughshare to Parliament; a short memoir of the Potters of Tadcaster*; London, John Murray; 1908

Michalos, Alex C & Poff, Deborah C; eds; *Bernard Shaw and the Webbs*; Toronto, University of Toronto Press, 2002

Micklethwait, John and Wooldridge, Adrian; *The Fourth Revolution: the global race to reinvent the state*; London, Penguin Random House, 2014

Milne-Bailey, W, Editor; *Trade Union Documents*; Compiled and edited with an Introduction; London, G Bell & Sons; 1929

Morgan, Kenneth O; *Labour People*; Oxford, OUP,1992

Morgan, K; *The Webbs and Soviet Communism*; Bolshevism and the British Left; Part 2; London, Lawrence and Wishart, 2006

Mowat, Charles Loch; *The Charity Organisation Society 1869-1913*; London, Methuen, 1961

Mutch, Deborah & Terry Elkiss Biography of Margaret Harkness; in Harkness, M, *A City Girl* (ed. Mutch, D); Brighton, Victorian Secrets, 2015

Nord, D E; *Walking the Victorian Streets: Women , representation, and the city*; New York, Cornell University Press, 1995

Nunn, Thomas Hancock; *The life and work of a social reformer*; London, Baines and Scarisbrooke, 1942

Oakley, Ann; *Forgotten Wives; How*

women get written out of history;
Bristol, Polity Press, 2021

Olivier, Sydney; *Letters and Selected
Writings;* Ed. with a memoir by
Margaret Olivier London, George
Allen and Unwin, 1948

Pakenham, Thomas; *The Boer War*;
London; Weidenfeld and Nicholson,
1979

Parmoor, Lord (Alfred Cripps); *A
Retrospect*; London, Heinemann, 1936

Pease, Edward R; *The History of the
Fabian Society*; London, Fabian
Society and Allen and Unwin; 1925

Pelling, Henry; *A short history of the
Labour Party*; London; Macmillan,
1961

Perham, Margery; *Lugard, The Years
of Authority, 1898-1945*; London,
Collins, 1960

Pimlott, Ben
- *Hugh Dalton*; London; Jonathan
Cape, 1985
- *Harold Wilson*; London; Harper
Collins; 1992
- *Labour and the Left in the 1930s*;
Cambridge; CUP; 1977

Qualter, Terence H; *Graham Wallas and
the Great Society*; London, Macmillan,
1980

Reckitt, Maurice; *As it happened, an
autobiography*; London; J M Dent,
1941

Renton, Claudia; *Those wild Wyndhams*;
London, William Collins, 2014

Riddell, Neil; *Labour in Crisis: The second
Labour Government, 1929-1931*;
Manchester, Manchester University
Press, 1999

Ross, William McGregor; *Kenya from
Within; a short political history*;
London, Frank Cass, 1968 (reprint of
1927 edition)

Rowse, Alfred Leslie; *All Souls and
Appeasement*; London; Macmillan;
1961

Russell, Bertrand
- *Autobiography*; London, George

Allen and Unwin, 1978
- *Collected Papers*; London, George
Allen and Unwin, 1985; Vol 12
- *Portraits from Memory*; London,
George Allen and Unwin, 1956
- *The Selected Letters of Bertrand
Russell; Vol I The Private Years, 1884-
1914;* Edited by Nicholas Griffin.
London, Allen Lane, The Penguin
Press; 1992

Saint, Andrew, Ed; *Politics and the
People of London; The London County
Council 1889- 1965*; London, The
Hambledon Press, 1986)

Samuel, Viscount (Herbert Samuel);
Memoirs; London, the Cresset Press;
1945

Schuster, George; *Private Work and
Public Causes; A personal record, 1881-
1978*; Cowbridge, G Brown and Sons,
1979

Searle, Geoffrey R *A; new England? Peace
and War 1886-1918*; Oxford, OUP,
2004

Semmel, Bernard; *Imperialism and Social
Reform*; London, George Allen and
Unwin, 1960

Shaw, George Bernard
- *Sixteen Self-Sketches*
- *Bernard Shaw: The Diaries*;
ed Stanley Weintraub London;
Pennsylvania State University Press;
1986
- *Bernard Shaw and the Webbs; Selected
correspondence of Bernard Shaw*; ed
Alec C Michalos and Deborah C Poff;
Toronto, University of Toronto Press,
2002

Shepherd, John; Jonathan Davis; and
Chris Wrigley, eds; *Britain's Second
Labour Government,1929-31: a reap-
praisal* Manchester, MUP, 2011

Shiels, Drummond; *The East Africa
Report*; In *Political Quarterly*, Vol III,
no 1, Jan-Mar 1932

Shove, Fredegond; *Fredegond and Gerald
Shove*; privately printed, 1952

Simey, Thomas & Simey, Margaret;

Charles Booth, Social Scientist; Oxford, OUP, 1960

Simon, Brian; *Education and the Labour Movement 1870-1920*; London, Lawrence and Wishart, 1974

Sinclair, K; *William Pember Reeves; New Zealand Fabian;* Oxford, Clarendon Press, 1965

Skidelsky, Robert
- *Oswald Mosley*; London, Macmillan,1975
- *John Maynard Keynes: Hopes Betrayed 1883-1920*; London, Macmillan, 1983
- *John Maynard Keynes: The economist as saviour: 1920-1937;* London, Macmillan, 1992

Smith, Adrian; *The New Statesman; Portrait of a political weekly 1913-31*; London; Frank Cass, 1996

Snell, Lord (Harry Snell); *Men, Movements, and Myself* London, J M Dent, 1936

Sommer, Dudley; *Haldane of Cloan*; London, Allen and Unwin; 1960

Squire, Rose; *Thirty Years in the Public Service*; London, Nisbet & Co; 1927

Stears, Marc; *Progressives, Pluralists and the problems of the state*; Oxford, OUP, 2002

Stocks, Mary; *Ernest Simon of Manchester*; Manchester University Press, 1963

Stringer, Arthur; *Red wine of youth: a life of Rupert Brooke*; Indianapolis and New York, Bobbs Merrill, 1948

Tawney, Richard H
- *R H Tawney's Commonplace Book*; edited and with introduction by J M Winter and D M Joslin; Cambridge; Cambridge University Press; 1972
- *The Webbs and their Work ; Webb Memorial Lecture No 1;* Published for the Webb Memorial Trust by Fabian Publications Ltd, 1945
- *The Webbs in Perspective*; Webb Memorial Lecture 1952; University of London Athlone Press, 1952

Taylor, AJP
- *The Trouble Makers*; London, Panther, 1957
- *English History 1914-1945* Oxford, OUP, 1965
- (editor) *Lloyd George: A diary* by Frances Stevenson; London; Hutchinson; 1971

Taylor, George R S; *Leaders of Socialism Past and Present*; London, the New Age Press; 1908

Thane, Pat
- *Old Age in English History*; Oxford, OUP, 2000
- *Foundations of the Welfare State*; London, Longman, 1996

Thompson, Edward P; *The Making of the English Working Class;* London, Penguin, 1968,

Tsuzuki Chushichi; *H M Hyndman and British socialism*; Oxford, OUP, 1961

Ward, Maisie; *Gilbert Keith Chesterton*; London, Sheed and Ward, 1944

Wells, Herbert G
- *Ann Veronica*; London Penguin; 2005
- *Experiments in Autobiography; Vol I*; London, Gollancz; 1934
- *Experiments in Autobiography; Vol II*; London, Gollancz; 1937
- *Faults of the Fabian, The*; London, Fabian Society, 1906
- *H G Wells in Love; postscript to an experiment in autobiography;* edited by G P Wells; London; Faber & Faber; 1984
- *The New Machiavelli; London,* Penguin, 2005
- *This Misery of Boots*; Boston; The Ball Publishing Co; 1908

Wilkinson, Ellen; *The Town That was Murdered*; London; Victor Gollancz Ltd; 1939

Williamson, Philip; *National Crisis and National Government; British Politics, the economy and Empire, 1926-1932*; Cambridge, CUP, 1992

Winter, Jay M; *Socialism and the*

*Challenge of War; Ideas and Politics
in Britain 1912-1918*; London,
Routledge and Kegan Paul, 1974
Woolf, Leonard
- *Beginning Again; An autobiography
of the years 1911-1918*; London,
Harvest; Harcourt Brace Jovanovich;
1972;
- *Downhill all the way, an autobiogra-
phy of the years 1919-1939*; London,
Hogarth Press, 1967
Woolf, Virginia
- *Selected Diaries*; <u>abridged and
edited by</u> Anne Olivier Bell; London,
Vintage, 2008
- *Letters, Volumes I - VI*; London,
Chatto & Windus, 1980
- *Selected Letters*, <u>ed</u> J T Banks,
London, Vintage, 2008

Annexe Four: The Potter Sisters

NAME	BORN	MARRIED	DIED
Lawrencina	1845	Robert Holt, Shipowner; 1867	1906
Catherine (Kate)	1847	Leonard Courtney, Politician; 1883	1929
Mary	1849	Arthur Playne, Gloucestershire landowner; 1870	1923
Georgina	1850	Daniel Meinertzhagen, Banker; 1873	1914
Blanche	1851	William Cripps Surgeon; 1877	1905
Theresa	1852	Charles A Cripps Politician; 1881	1893
Margaret	1854	Henry Hobhouse; 1880	1921
Beatrice	1858	Sidney Webb	1943
Rosalind (Rosy)	1865	Arthur Dyson Williams George Dobbs	1949

Annexe Five: Abbreviations and acronyms

ASE	Amalgamated Society of Engineers
ASRS	Amalgamated Society of Railway Servants;(later NUR)
BSP	British Socialist Party (SDF renamed as BSP)
COS	Charity Organisation Society
CPGB	Communist Party of Great Britain
EAC	Economic Advisory Council
GBS	George Bernard Shaw
ILP	Independent Labour Party
JRM	James Ramsay MacDonald
LCC	London County Council
LGB	Local Government Board
LMA	London Metropolitan Archives
LRC	Labour Representation Committee
LSE	London School of Economics
MFGB	Miners Federation of Great Britain
NEC	National Executive Committee
NFRB	New Fabian Research Bureau
NKVD	USSR secret police (People's Commissariat for Internal Affairs)
NUR	National Union of Railwaymen (before 1913, Amalgamated Society of Railway Servants)
NUT	National Union of Teachers

ODNB	Oxford Dictionary of National Biography
PLP	Parliamentary Labour Party
SDF	Social Democratic Federation (Later British Socialist Party -BSP)
SSIP	Society for Socialist Inquiry and Propaganda (ZIP)
SWMF	South Wales Miners Federation
TGWU	Transport and General Workers Union
TJ	Dr Thomas Jones
TUC	Trades Union Congress
UDC	Union for Democratic Control
WEA	Workers Educational Association

INDEX

Illustrations are in *italics*. Sidney Webb is SW and Beatrice Webb is BW throughout.

Ablett, Noah, 305, 314, 334, 581
Abyssinia Crisis (1935), 512, 536
Academic Assistance, 538
Acland, Arthur (Sir), 161, 581
Acland, Richard (Sir), 71, 552, 581
Adams, Annie, 75–6
Adamson, William, 357, 581
Addison, Christopher, 307, 323, 343, 346, 581
Admiralty, the, 207, 431, 468–9
Alexander, A V, 565
Allen, Clifford (*later* Lord Allen of Hurtwood), 243, 265, 306, 581
Alvin, Juliette, 27, 562
Amery, Leopold (Leo), 415–21, 426–7; Coefficients member, 20, 200; Minority Report, 226; Palestine and, 434; calls for Chamberlain's resignation, 553; biography, 581–2; portrait, *581*
Anderson, William Crawford (W C), 334, 347, 582
Apthorpe, Alfred, 64–5
Apostles, Cambridge, 241
Arab communities, 431–47
Argyle, Jesse, 582
Arnold, Sydney, first Baron Arnold, 418, 452, 537, 582
Arnot, Robin Page, 324, 326, 383, 582

Arundel, Sussex, eighteenth century municipal corruption, 187, *187*
Asquith, Herbert Henry (*later* Earl of Oxford & Asquith): social reform, 71; Key Limp, 177, 197, 198, 208; becomes PM, 206, 220; Webbs and, 211; Burns and, 220–1, 262, 272, 274, 315; Poor Law Commission, 225; BW and, 273, 381; Masterman and, 273; pensions and, 275; MacDonald and, 282; Irish Home Rule Bill, 304; forms coalition, 315; Sharp and, 365; Jones on, 381; biography, 582; portrait, *582*
Asquith, Margot (Emma Margaret) (*née* Tennant), 178, 347, 582
Astor, Nancy, 493, 539
Atkinson, Mabel, 243, 267, 582
Attlee, Clement Richard (*later* Earl Attlee): biography, 6, 583; helps at boys' club, 205–6; Webbs and, 232, 395–6; Break Up of the Poor Law (propaganda), 255, 256; NCPD and, 270; National Insurance 'explainer, 284; LSE lecturer, 306, 367, 395; *War on Poverty* campaign, 306; First World War, 318; SW and, 366, 566, 567, 568; Chancellor of the Duchy of Lancaster, 457–8; economic policy

paper, 458; Labour deputy Leader, 470, 507; *Problems of Industry*, 490; NFRB Chairman, 505; S Cripps and, 506–7, 543; BW on, 512–13, 551; acting Labour Leader, 512; Labour Leader, 513; Maisky and, 552; Lansbury and, 553; Norway expedition debate, 553; Lord Privy Seal, 554; Russia and, 556; opens Beatrice Webb House, 565; Webbs' internment of ashes, 568; portrait, *583*

Attlee family, 318

Attlee, Thomas (Tom), 232, 318, 396

Austria, 111, 334, 462, 511, 540

Aveling, Edward, 67, 80

Bailey, Altiora and Oscar, 370

Baldwin, Stanley, 367–9, 402–3; MFGB and, 390; Jones and, 394, 539; Jones on, 402, 413; Passfield White Paper and, 443; as PM, 512, 538; biography, 583

Balfour, Arthur (*later* Earl Balfour): as PM, 26, 171; Webbs and, 175, 177–81, 190, 246, 307; Education Acts and, 188, 189; SW and, 193; resigns, 206; loses seat, 207; Poor Law Commission, 209–10, 225; Minority Report, 226; Prevention of Destitution Bill, 262, 281; BW and, 270; Jones on, 402; Foreign Secretary, 431; biography, 583; portrait, *583*

Balfour, Betty (Elizabeth), 179, 260, 583

Balfour Declaration, 431–45

Balfour, Gerald William, 178–9, 207, 209–10, 222, 260, 583

Bank of England, 448, 462, 464, 465, 466, 469

Barker, Ernest, 464

Barker, Harley Granville-, 26, 233, 244, 583

Barnato, Barney, 194

Barnes, George Nicoll, 282, 584

Barnett, Dame Henrietta (*née* Rowlands), 49, 52, 98, 530, 584

Barnett, Samuel (*later* Canon): COS and, 49, 51–3, 57–8, 98; dock strikers and, 101; Hewins and, 166; Beveridge

and, 175, 221, 530; Boer War and, 196; Hamilton and, 211; BW and, 222; pensions and, 274; biography, 584; portrait, *584*

Battle of Britain (1940), 559

Beatrice Webb House, 565

Beatrice Webb Memorial Trust Fund, 565

Beckerman-Boys, Carly, 447

Beehive, The, 156

Beit, Alfred, 194

Belgium, 552, 554

Bell, Clive, 408

Bell, Vanessa (*née* Stephen), 319, 330, 387

Belloc, Hilaire: background, 17; Boer War and, 196–7; moves to the right, 233, 305; as influence, 241, 318; *The Servile State*, 262; poetry, 310, 364; biography, 584; portrait, *584*

Bennett, Arnold, 366, 380

Bentham, Frank, 212

Beresford, Lord Charles, 178

Besant, Annie, 70–2, 100–1; BW and, 28, 121; Fabian Society, 73, 97, 102; biography, 584–5; portrait, *584*

Betts, Barbara (*later* Castle), 514, 515, 585

Bevan, Aneurin, 459, 543, 545, 550

Beveridge Report (1942), 526–8, 530

Beveridge, William (*later* Lord): on the Webbs, 6, 220; 'Beveridge-Mair dictatorship' at LSE, 31–2, 409–11, 517, 518; LSE Director, 165, 363–4, 383, 503; Webbs and, 175–6, 219, 383, 409–10, 516; labour exchanges and, 219, 228, 258; Churchill and, 221; Fabian Society Summer Schools, 244, 245; government posts, 322; BW asks for advice, 343; Royal Commission (mining industry), 388; economy and, 450; leaves LSE, 516–20; Unemployment Insurance Statutory Committee Chairman, 518; Master of University College Oxford, 520, 524, 528–9; Webbs' eightieth birthday party, 521; 'one man disguised as a committee', 524–31; Wilson on,

524; manpower survey, 525–6; ill health, 525, 541; Keynes and, 525; Second World War, 525; marries Janet Mair, 528; later life, 529–30; MP for Berwick on Tweed, 529; Academic Assistance, 538; biography, 585; portrait, *585*

Bevin, Ernest: Gold Standard, 449, 451; NFRB and, 505, 506; SSIP and, 506; on Lansbury, 512; Minister of Labour, 525; Beveridge and, 526; Norway expedition debate, 553; biography, 585

Bevir, Anthony, 566–7

Black, Clementina Maria, 80, 100, 585

Black Tuesday (1929), 449

Blanco White, George Rivers 230, 244, 245, 247–51, 248, 260, 630

Bland, Hubert: Fabian Society Treasurer, 29, 70, 73, 231; Shaw on, 70; *New Age* magazine, 233; Colegate and, 235; Wells and, 250; biography, 585–6; portrait, *585*

Bland, Rosamund, 230

Bloomsbury Group, 239

Bodkin, Minnie, 257

Boer War, Second (1899-1902), 19–20, 177, 193–9, 511

Bolsheviks, the, 6, 336–7, 393

Bolton, Ivy, 508

Bondfield, Margaret, 307, 370, 398, 566, 586, *586*

Booth, Charles, 57–9; *Life and Labour of the People of London*, 11, 58, 72, 96; 'The Webbs' and, 12; J Chamberlain and, 92; BW and, 96, 214, 386; does not approve of SW, 105, 117, 119; correspondence with BW, 117; Royal Commissioner, 207, 210; MOHs and, 215; pensions and, 274; biography, 586; portrait, *586*

Booth, Mary (*née* Macaulay), 48, 57–9, 88, 105, 117, 119, 386, 586

Bosanquet, Bernard, 207, 586

Bosanquet, Helen (*née* Dendy), 207, 214, 215, 216, 224, 228–9, 586

Braithwaite, William J, 209, 278–80, 282, 586

Break Up of the Poor Law (propaganda), 253–71

Bright, John, 586

British Association, Leeds, 113–14

British Socialist Party (BSP), 236, 331, 334

Brooke, Emma Frances, 130, 234, 586

Brooke, Rupert Chawner: Dangerfield on, 7; CUFS member, 24, 239–43, 256, 264–5; Wells and, 230; Carbonari Society, 240–1; Cambridge Apostles, 241; Ka Cox and, 242, 318; Noel Olivier and, 242, 243, 318; BW on, 244, 268; Fabian Society Summer Schools, 244; Keynes and, 256–7; Webbs and, 257, 268; NCPD and, 263; Dalton and, 264, 569; Shove and, 268; poetry, 310, 364; Spencer and, 318–19; antisemitism, 318; First World War, 319; fear of growing old, 320–1; death, 321; biography, 587; portrait, *587*

Browning, Robert, 64, 104

Bryant and May, 100–1

Buchanan, George, 377

Bulkley, Mildred Emily, 587

Burns, Delisle, 339

Burns, John Elliott, 66–7, 71–2, 98–102, 273–4; LCC and, 72, 121–2, 160; Eight Hour Day rally, 107; SW and, 124, 208–9; as MP, 147; BW on, 150, 155–6; Wells salon and, 183; pro-Boer, 195–6; on Boer War, 196; LGB President, 208, 271–3; on Provis, 212; visits colonies, 218; labour exchanges and, 219; Asquith and, 220–1; Haldane on, 222–3; Prevention of Destitution Bill, 262; BW and, 272–3; Mastermans and, 272; Lloyd George and, 279–80, 283; Braithwaite on, 280, 282; resigns as president of Board of Trade, 315; biography, 587; portrait, *587*

Butt, Clara, 334

Buxton, Charles Roden, 422, 424, 426, 438, 587

Cambridge University Fabian Society

(CUFS), 24, 238–47, 256, 257, 264–5, 308
Cameron, Sir Donald, 587
Campbell-Bannerman, Sir Henry, 177, 197–8, 206, 220, 440, 587
Campbell, John, 177
Campbell, John Ross, 376–7
Carpenter, Edward, 69, 72, 239, 306, 334, 566, 587
Carr-Saunders, Sir Alexander Morris, 520, 588
Central Authority Poor Law, policy (1834–1907), 203, 204, 213, 215
Chadwick, Edwin, 588
Chamberlain, Austen (Sir), 207, 359, 414, 588
Chamberlain, Beatrice, 77, 84, 86, 91, 588
Chamberlain, Clara (later Ryland), 83, 87, 89, 91, 588
Chamberlain family, 24, 29
Chamberlain, Hilda, 125
Chamberlain, Joseph: BW and, 11–12, 29–30, 75, 81–93, 103, 110–12, 116, 118, 125, 171–2, 195, 386; SW and, 75–132; background, 82; LGB President, 89, 90, 217; resigns, 90; marriages, 93, 94, 103, 118, 172; Colonial Secretary, 170–1, 194; tariff campaign, 182; on Gorst, 187; effigy of, 198–9; Amery and, 200; ill health and death, 207; re-elected, 207; biography, 588; portrait, 588
Chamberlain, Mary (née Endicott), 93, 125
Chamberlain, (Arthur) Neville: Minister of Health, 391–2, 466; as PM, 538, 546; Eden and, 540; Munich Agreement, 540; S Cripps on, 544, 546–7; Maisky and, 545; Churchill on, 546; BW on, 553; Lansbury and, 553; Norway expedition speech, 553; Party Leader, 554; biography, 588
Champion, Henry Hyde, 98, 99, 100, 101, 121, 589
Chancellor, Sir John, 433–6, 439, 446, 589
Chandler, Francis, 207, 223, 227, 589

Charity Organisation Society (COS), 48–53, 212–15; BW on committee, 11, 48, 50, 90; Barnett and, 98; Poor Law Commissioners, 207, 222, 224; state pensions and, 275
Charteris (née Wyndham), Mary Constance, Countess of Wemyss (Mary Elcho), 178, 180–1, 589
Chesterton, Cecil, 231, 589
Chesterton, Frances, 182
Chesterton, Gilbert Keith (GK), 17, 182, 233, 305, 568, 589
China, 283, 548, 550–1
Christian Socialists, 49
Churchill, Winston S (Sir), 181–2, 219–21, 416–17; as PM, 13, 561, 563; government posts, 209, 221; Webbs and, 209, 261, 275; SW and, 219; dines with the Webbs, 258; labour exchanges and, 258, 276; Simon on, 266; BW on, 277, 553, 554; homes, 340; coal crisis and, 352; on Snowden, 373, 470; Chancellor, 388; coal industry and, 390; Beveridge and, 409, 525; Jones on, 413; Colonial Secretary, 433; Keynes and, 470; on N Chamberlain, 538, 546; Maisky and, 545, 549; S Cripps and, 546, 547; becomes PM, 554; biography, 589–90; portrait, 589
Citrine, Walter (later Lord), 451, 503, 552, 553, 590
Clarke, William, 73, 151
Clay, Henry, 450
Clifford, Dr John, 189, 192, 195, 196, 590
Cliveden Set, 539
Closer Union, East Africa, 417–20, 423, 429–31
Clyman, Rhea, 496, 500
Clynes, John Robert, 590
coal crisis, 349–58
coal industry, and the General Strike, 388–91
Coal Inquiry Commission, 349–58
Cockerton case (1901), 188
Coefficients, the, 20, 199–201
Cohen, Rose, 534–5, 590

Cole, George Douglas Howard (GDH), 312–14, 324–7, 525–6; Guild Socialist, 17, 18; Fabian Society, 74, 505; BW on, 327, 340; marriage, 327; Labour Party trade and finance secretary, 339–40; Webbs and, 339, 383, 404, 405, 560; *New Statesman* and, 366, 379; Economic Advisory Council, 450–1; discusses Russia with the Webbs, 494; stays at Passfield, 494; renewal of socialist ideas, 505; Bevin and, 506; launches SSIP, 506; on the NFRB, 506; visit to Russia, 506; Beveridge and, 520; Second World War, 529; Social Security League, 529; biography, 590

Cole, Margaret (*née* Postgate): on Russia 6, 494; edits BW books, 8; Webbs and, 8, 12, 18, 186, 383, 404, 405, 563; on BW, 23–5, 27, 326, 393, 405; on 'the workhouse', 205; 'Wellsian Socialist', 230; Fabian Society, 325–7, 505; BW on, 327, 405; marriage, 327; on BW and Chamberlain, 386; stays at Passfield, 399, 400, 494; launches SSIP, 506; on the Labour Party, 511; on Spanish civil war, 513; manpower survey, 526; Social Security League, 529; Webb trustee, 560; Beatrice Webb Memorial Trust Fund, 565; biography, 591; portrait, *591*

Colegate, Arthur (*later* Sir), 230–1, 234–5, 247–51; on Sanders, 231; Fabian Nursery, 232; holidays with the Webbs, 245, 260; Sharp and, 2, 254–5; Break Up of the Poor Law (propaganda), 254; Labour Exchange post, 258, 259–60; *New Statesman* and, 310; BW on, 323; First World War, 323; biography, 591

communism, 22–3, 360–1; Webbs and, 16, 403, 488–520, 521, 542; *Workers' Weekly*, 376; British Communist Party, 380, 505, 537, 548, 557

conscription, 17, 316, 321, 324, 332–3

Cook, A J, 459

cooperative conferences, 109, 122

Cornwall, Edwin, 192

Costelloe, Benjamin Francis Conn (Frank), 148, 151, 591

Cotterill, Erica, 257, 264

county councils, 160, 187–8, 193, 223, 224, 392

Courtney, Catherine (Kate) (*née* Potter) (BW sister): Barnetts and, 49, 52; Katherine Buildings, 52, 53; marriage, 52; BW stays with, 54, 55; on Chamberlain, 88; stays with BW, 94, 104; Webbs and, 127, 176, 385; on 41 Grosvenor Road, 148; E Hobhouse and, 197; supports nephew as conscientious objector, 317–18; Russian Revolution and, 334; Litvinov and, 337; illness and death, 408; biography, 591; portrait, *591*

Courtney, Leonard (*later* Lord; Baron Courtney of Penwith): marriage, 52; BW and, 54; J Chamberlain and, 88; Browning and, 104; South Africa Conciliation Committee, 195; E Hobhouse and, 197; death, 317, 408; Litvinov and, 337; Amery and, 415; biography, 591–2; portrait, *591*

Cox, Katharine (Ka), 239, 242, 257, 265, 268, 318, 330, 592

Coxon, William, 470

Crane, Walter, 71, 73, 199, 592

Cranworth, Lord, 425, 426

Creighton, Louise, 592

Creighton, Mandell, 592

Cripps, Blanche (*née* Potter) (BW sister), 32, 44, 174, 558

Cripps, (Charles) Alfred (*later* Lord Parmoor): marriage, 44–5, 151, 174; on SW, 128; Lord President, 371, 413; Stafford Cripps and, 513, 514; SW writes to, 515; League of Nations, 540; biography, 592; portrait, *592*

Cripps, Isabel (*née* Swithinbank), 509, 550, 561

Cripps, John (great nephew), 501

Cripps Memorandum (1939), 542

Cripps, (Richard) Stafford (Sir), 511–15, 541–7, 549–51; becomes MP, 460–1; NFRB and, 505; Socialist League

Chairman, 506–7; BW and, 509, 514, 542, 543; League of Nations, 512, 513; resigns from NEC, 513; funds *Tribune*, 514; Maisky and, 515, 552; Webbs and, 515, 561, 562; on Keynes and Beveridge, 527; Leader of the House of Commons, 527; on Munich Agreement, 541; expelled from NEC, 542–3; Keynes writes to, 543; Left Book Club speech, 544; appeal against Labour Party expulsion, 545, 550; N Chamberlain and, 546–7, 553; independent MP, 546; travels to India and China, 550; Russia and, 551, 556–7; Halifax and, 556; SW burial suggestion, 566–8; Chancellor, 568; biography, 592–3; portrait, *592*

Cripps, Theresa (*née* Potter) (BW sister), 42, 44–5, 128, 151, 174

Cripps, William Harrison (Willie), 32, 44, 45, 129, 174, 593

Crooks, Will, 160

Crosland, Anthony, 23

Crusade newspaper, 254, 255–6, 265, 267, 281, 308, 311

Curzon, George Nathaniel (*later* Marquess), 352, 593

Czechoslovakia, 540–1, 543–4, 548

Daily Herald, 313, 503

Daladier, Édouard, 540

Dalton, Hugh (*later* Lord), 238–42; BW on, 22, 394, 508; CUFS member, 238–9, 240, 265; Carbonari Society, 240–1; Fabian Society Summer Schools, 244; Break Up of the Poor Law (propaganda), 257; Brooke and, 257, 264; on BW, 268; LSE lecturer, 306, 394; First World War, 319; loses seat, 370; stays with the Webbs, 400, 508, 510; on Henderson, 444; deputy Foreign Secretary, 447; Attlee and, 458; on Mosley Manifesto, 459; visit to Russia, 506; on Attlee, 507; on the Webbs, 508–9; on S Cripps, 510, 514, 543, 556; Minister of Economic Warfare, 554; SW eulogy, 566;

Chancellor, 568; Lord Privy Seal, 568; biography, 593; portrait, *593*

Dalton, Ruth, 508

Dangerfield, George, 7, 304

Darling, Carrie (*later* Browne): BW and, 11, 45, 47, 77–8, 87, 104; moves to Australia, 47, 84, 104; marriage, 95; death, 173; biography, 593

Darwin, Gwen, 239

Davidson, Marjorie (*later* Pease), 76

Davies, Margaret Caroline Llewelyn, 407, 593

Davy, James Stewart (Sir), 210, 593

Dawson, Geoffrey, 539

de la Mare, Walter, 364

Delahaye, Victor, 66

Delamere, Lord (Hugh Cholmondeley); 3rd Baron Delamere, 416, 593

Democratic Federation, 66

Denmark, 552

Dent, John James (JJ), 72–3, 105, 593

Derbyshire Miners, 157

Desborough, Ettie (Grenfell), 178, 593

Despard, Charlotte, 594

destitution, disease of, 202–85

Devonshire, Duke of, 187, 417

Dickens, Charles, *Oliver Twist*, 205

Distributist League, 17–18

Dobbs, George, 26, 33

Dobbs, Rosalind (Rosie) (*earlier* Dyson Williams, *née* Potter) (BW sister): on BW, 23, 26, 29, 76–7; marriages, 26, 32–3, 94, 95, 129; Potter family and, 42, 568; on Spencer, 42; family holidays, 47, 75, 519; on J Chamberlain, 82–3, 85, 86; BW and, 87, 521, 563; J Chamberlain and, 89, 92; BW looks after, 93–4; Webbs and, 128, 569; son killed in WW1, 318

Dock Strike (1889), 101–2, 175

Dockers Union, 121

Don, Alan, Dean of Westminster, 567, 569

Drake, Barbara (*née* Meinertzhagen) (BW niece), 8, 501, 508, 510, 543, 553, 560, 594

Duckham, Sir Arthur McDougall, 350, 354, 594

Duff, Robert, 210, 224, 594
Dukes, Ashley, 245, 594
Dyson Williams, Arthur, 32, 33, 94, 129

East Africa, 415, 416, 467
East African Standard, 426
Eckstein, Hermann, 194
Economic Advisory Council (EAC), 21, 451, 457–8, 489–90
Eden, Anthony, 538, 540, 546, 547, 554
Edgeworth, Francis Ysidro, 69, 594
Education Acts (1901–3), 188–93
Edward VII, King, 220
Edwards, John Passmore, 195, 594
Eight Hour Day rally (1890), 107–8
Elcho, Lady. *See* Charteris (*née* Wyndham), Mary Constance, Countess of Wemyss (Mary Elcho)
Elgar, Edward, 494
Employment White Paper (1944), 228, 490
Engels, Friedrich, 98, 107–8, 594–5
Ensor, Robert (*later* Sir), 177, 188, 193, 230, 319, 595
Eugenics Education Society (*later* Eugenics Society), 201
eugenics movement, 201, 266

Fabian Society: 1905–12, 229–53; Annual Report, 312; Belfast, 147; bequests, 164–7; BW speech, 558; divisions in, 17–18, 198–9; Executive Committee, 12, 26, 29, 68, 70, 166, 169, 170, 230–2, 236–8, 306–7, 311, 312, 313, 328; Fabian Arts Group, 232–3; Fabian Basis, 233, 236, 238, 285; Fabian Nursery, 232, 247, 251; Fabian Research Department, 307, 312–14, 323–8, 534; Fabian Women's Group, 68, 70, 170, 233–4; Finance and General Purposes Committee, 367; first Tract, 70; growth of, 12; Labour Research Department, 327–8, 340; leading members, 70, 150, 229; lecture series, 73–4; *London Programme*, 160; at a low ebb, 505; LRC and, 189; members, 69, 153; National Insurance Bill and, 281;

National Minimum, 19, 20; New Fabian Research Bureau (NFRB), 494, 495; *New Statesman* and, 310; pensions and, 275; Sharp on, 285; Special Committee (Wells), 235, 236; Summer Schools, 243–5, 257–8, 265–8, 313–14, 438, 468, 491, 493; SW joins, 11; tracts, 187; Trustees, 164, 165–6, 168–9; WEWNC and, 331; young recruits, 30–1; *Fabianism and the Empire*, 199; . *See also* Cambridge University Fabian Society (CUFS)
Fairfield, Letitia, 234
Fawcett, Dame Millicent Garrett (*née* Garrett), 234, 595
Federal Reserve, 466, 467
Fellowship of the New Life, 69, 70
female genital mutilation (FGM), 427
feminism, 28, 40, 70, 80, 267, 499, 534
Financial News, 449
Finland, 551, 552
First World War, 16–17, 21, 315–23, 511
Fisher, Bella (Arabella; *née* Buckley), 595
Fisher family, 56
Foot, Michael, 514
Foot, Paul, 9
France, 161, 319–20, 432, 551, 554–6; Britain and, 13, 513–14, 538, 540, 544–5, 547
Franco, General, 513, 544, 556
French Socialists, 334

Gaitskell, Hugh Todd Naylor, 505–6, 595
Galsworthy, John, 26, 595
Galton, Frank, 130, 131, 149, 156, 505, 595
Gardiner, Alfred George (A G), 3, 146, 206, 212, 595
Garnett, William, 595
Garvin, James Louis, 539
Geddes, Auckland, 354
general elections: 1880s–1890s, 89, 100, 147; 1900s–1910s, 171, 194, 207, 234, 271, 277, 347–8; 1920s–1930s, 13, 374, 377, 381, 412–13, 470,

512–13

General Strike, coal industry and the, 388–91

George, David Lloyd (*later* first Earl Lloyd-George of Dwyfor). *See* Lloyd George, David (*later* first Earl Lloyd-George of Dwyfor)

George, Henry, 66, 68, 69

George V, King, 372, 377–8, 403, 413, 415, 417, 467

George VI, King, 554, 568

Gill, (Arthur) Eric Rowton, 163, 232–3, 565–6, 595

Gillespie, H J, 339

Gillies, William, 339, 340, 595

Gladstone, Herbert John, Viscount Gladstone, 89, 171, 181, 596

Gold Standard, 388, 449–50, 469–70

Gollancz, Victor, 503, 548

Gorst, Sir John, 187, 188

Gould, Barbara Bodichon Ayrton, 32, 596

Graham, Robert Bontine Cunninghame, , 99–100, 596

Graham, William, 392, 463, 596

Grant, Corrie, 75–6

Grant, Duncan, 387

Grant, Mrs (SW nurse attendant), 523–4, 548, 559, 565

Gray, Dr, 522, 523

Green, Alice: BW and, 110–11, 121–2, 148, 161; SW and, 115; Webbs and, 151, 383; biography, 596

Greenwood, Arthur, 266–7, 339–40; Webbs and, 261, 383; NCPD and, 270; Keeling and, 319; biography, 323, 596; BW on, 342, 394–5; Laski and, 509; deputy Labour Leader, 513; Beveridge and, 526; Minister without Portfolio, 526; Maisky and, 551–2; Norway expedition debate, 553; War Cabinet, 554; portrait, *596*

Grey, Edward, 71, 197, 200, 208

Grigg, Edward (Ned) (*later* Sir Edward; *later* Lord Altrincham), 417, 419, 424–5, 429, 597, *597*

Guild Socialism, 17, 18, 305, 311–15, 325, 327, 389

Hailsham, Lord, 443

Haldane, Elizabeth, 434–5, 597

Haldane, Richard (*later* Viscount Haldane), 19–20, 177–81; Liberal MP, 12, 147; biography, 71, 597; Webbs and, 118, 147, 172, 275, 307, 344, 349, 371, 383; Pycroft on, 126; BW on, 128, 170, 269, 401; LSE bequest, 164–5; Education Acts and, 188; SW and, 193; Key Limp, 197, 198, 208; Coefficients member, 200; on Burns, 222–3; BW and, 222, 374; Poor Law Commission, 225; on Poor Law reports, 277; dropped from Cabinet, 315; Machinery of Government Committee Chairman, 343; Lord Chancellor, 371–2, 378, 384; *My Apprenticeship* review, 387; on the Webbs, 387; Jones on, 402; East Africa and, 418; portrait, *597*

Halifax, Edward, Lord, 540, 544, 547, 550, 552, 554

Hamilton, Lord George: BW and, 206, 210–12, 214–17, 222–4; SW and, 217; Poor Law and, 222–5; H Bosanquet and, 224–5, 228; Webbs and, 226–7; Burns and, 262; on BW, 345–6; Local Government Committee, 345; BW praises, 346; biography, 597; portrait, *597*

Hamilton, Mary Agnes (Molly) (*née* Adamson): Webbs' first biographer, 14, 64, 211, 312, 496; Webbs and, 182–3; on *History of English Local Government*, 186; Break Up of the Poor Law (propaganda), 255; 'Anti Beatrice Society', 361; BW and Chamberlain, 386; Greenwood and, 526–7; portrait, *597*; biography, 598

Hammond, Barbara (*née* Bradby), 598

Hammond, (John) Lawrence (J L) Le Breton, 196, 598

Hankey, Maurice Pascal Alers, first Baron Hankey, 450, 598

Hankinson, Mary ('Hanky'), 243, 314, 325, 598, *598*

Harben, Henry, 309, 383, 598

Hardie, (James) Keir: Harkness pays expenses, 100, 102; Independent Labour MP, 147; LRC and, 171; pro-Boer, 195; CUFS lecture, 242; against Insurance Bill, 282; biography, 598

Harkness, Margaret Elise (John Law): BW cousin, 11, 29–30, 41, 46–7, 79, 93, 121; writer, 25, 103, 156; Besant and, 28; *A City Girl*, 54–5, 81, 98; travels with BW, 87; BW on, 96, 97, 102–3, 113; *A Manchester Shirtmaker*, 97; socialist movement contacts, 98; SDF and, 99; *Out of Work*, 99; Hardie and, 100, 102; introduces BW to Besant, 100; Dock Strike and, 102; London politics, 103; introduces BW to SW, 104; trade unions, 105; end of friendship with BW, 114, 125; *In Darkest London*, 114; on Burns, 156; biography, 599; portrait, *599*

Harmsworth, Lord, 190

Harrison, Royden, 8–9, 158–9, 200

Hartshorn, Vernon, 357, 457, 599

Hastings, Patrick, 377

Hatry, Clarence, 448–9, 599

Headlam, Stewart, 187, 599

Helsby, Laurence, 566

Henderson, Arthur: SW and, 13, 412, 444, 446; Webbs and, 276, 347; Labour Leader, 315, 332, 469; WEWNC and, 331; Russian Revolution and, 334–5; *Memorandum of War Aims* (contributor), 335; BW on, 338, 340, 404, 507; rewrites Labour constitution with SW, 338; Lloyd George on, 344; loses seat, 348, 359, 369, 370, 470; Home Secretary, 372; stays with the Webbs, 391; BW and, 394; awarded Nobel Peace Prize, 413, 511; Foreign Secretary, 413, 443–7, 452, 472, 510; Treasury and, 449; May Report, 463; biography, 599–600; portrait, *599*

Henderson, Hubert, 367

Hennessy, Peter, 530

Hewins, William A S, 166, 167, 182, 200, 600

Heyworth, Elizabeth (*née* Aked) (BW grandmother), 39, 50

Heyworth family, 39, 50

Heyworth, Lawrence (BW grandfather), 39

Heyworth, Lawrencina, (*later* Potter). *See* Potter, Lawrencina (*née* Heyworth) (BW mother)

Hill, Octavia, 48–9, 51, 52, 56, 207, 215, 600, *600*

Hills, Jack, 341

Hirst, Francis Wrigley (F W), 196, 600

Hitler, Adolf, 13, 511, 536, 537–41, 544, 546, 553

Hoare, Samuel, 556

Hoatson, Alice, 29, 236

Hobhouse, Emily, 197, 600

Hobhouse, Henry, 45, 600

Hobhouse, Margaret (*née* Potter) (BW sister), 45, 127–9, 131, 151, 317–18, 358, 382

Hobhouse, Paul (BW nephew), 318

Hobhouse, Stephen (BW nephew), 317–18, 600

Hobsbawm, Eric, 8

Hobson, John Atkinson (J A), 196, 600

Hodges, Frank, 350, 600

Hodgkinson, Dr, 560, 562–3

Hogg, Quintin, 162, 601

Holland, 553, 554

Holman Gregory Commission, 461–2

Holt, Lawrencina (Lallie) (*née* Potter) (BW sister), 32, 44, 58, 128, 129, 131–2, 151, 558

Holt, Robert, 44, 58, 131–2, 601

Hope Simpson, Sir John, 281, 285, 412, 438–41, 446, 624

Horne, Robert, 354

Horner, Frances, 178, 180

House of Lords, 207–8, 277–8; members, 13, 196, 460; Committees, 96; clashes with MPs, 192, 271, 506; Bills and, 281, 283; hearings, 351; MacDonald and, 371; SW and, 412, 414, 427; debates, 420, 425; Secretaries of State in, 457

Hubback, Bill (Francis William), 261, 264, 308–9, 319, 320, 321, 601

Hubback, Eva (*née* Spielman): at Newnham, 242; Fabian Society Summer Schools, 244; Colegate and, 245; dines with the Webbs, 254; Hubback and, 261; engagement, 265; marriage, 309; First World War, 319; Social Security League, 529; biography, 601

Hudson, James Hindle, 426, 429, 601

Hugo, Victor, 277

Al-Husseini, Hajj Amin, Mufti of Jerusalem, *see* Mufti of Jerusalem

Hutchinson, Constance, 163–4

Hutchinson, Henry, 115, 163–4, 168, 601, *601*

Huysmans, Camille, 335, 601

Hyndman, Henry Mayers: *England for All*, 66; SDF leader, 67, 71, 99, 196, 208; on conscription of riches, 332–3; on SW, 333; biography, 602; portrait, *602*

Independent Labour Party, The (ILP), 149, 165, 171, 195, 207, 236, 261, 264, 265, 281, 283, 306, 325, 331, 334, 336, 339, 347, 358, 359, 372, 373, 376, 395, 404, 406, 407, 422, 424, 425, 426, 448, 458, 460,462, 466, 470, 489, 506, 514, 515, 566, 581, 582, 584, 585, 587, 594, 595, 596, 598, 599, 601, 602, 603, 605, 608, 609, 610, 611, 613, 616, 617, 621, 624, 625, 626 628, 639, 630 633, 645

India, 285, 412, 418, 504, 550

Ireland, 226, 304, 504

Irish Home Rule Bill (1914), 304, 315

Irish Nationalists, 207, 208, 282

Irwin, Gabrielle, 521, 522

Isaacs, Rufus, 278

Italy, 512, 536

Jackson, Cyril (Sir), 176, 218, 602

Jackson, (George) Holbrook, 232–3, 602

Jackson, Martha 'Dada' (*née* Mills), 39, 40, 43, 50–1, 602

Jerred, Walter Tapper, 273

Jesuits, the, 22–3, 393

Jewish communities, 196, 431–47, 537

Jewish Times, 445

Joad, Cyril Edwin Mitchinson (C E M), 32, 602

Johnston, Thomas, 413, 447, 451, 453–4, 602

Jones, Benjamin, 97, 602–3

Jones, Thomas 'TJ', 167–8, 212–13, 265–8, 368–9; Welsh Commission Secretary, 229, 284, 323; Lloyd George and, 335, 341–2, 350; Reconstruction Committee Chairman, 341; BW and, 342, 343–4, 407; coal crisis and, 352; Webbs and, 372–3, 383, 402–3, 412–13; SW and unemployment, 375; King's Speech, 378; on Asquith, 381; Baldwin and, 394; stays at Passfield, 399, 400; on Leys, 417; on Oldham and Schuster, 419; Amery and, 420; on Kenya, 423; Namier and, 438; Thomas and, 447–8, 454; Economic Advisory Council, 450–1; on Attlee, 457; does not vote Labour in 1931, 470; on Hitler, 538–9; biography, 603; portrait, *603*

Kamenev, Lev, 491

Karl Marx Society, 68

Katherine Buildings, London, 52–7

Keeling, Frederick Hillersdon (Ben), 319–20; CUFS member, 230, 238, 242, 244; Keynes on, 239–40; Colegate and, 245; SW and, 245; BW on, 251; Break Up of the Poor Law (propaganda), 254; Labour Exchange post, 258–9; marriage, 259; Shaw and, 259; *New Statesman* assistant editor, 308, 310, 319; Brooke and, 320; death, 321; Mallon and, 322; Dalton and, 569; biography, 603–4; portrait, *603*

Keeling, Rachel Susanna (*née* Townshend): Fabian Society, 230, 244–5; marriage, 251, 259; on Shaw, 259; LCC Councillor, 508; biography, 604; portrait, *604*

Kell, Vernon, 324

Kenya, 416–31
Kenyatta, Johnstone (Jomo), 427–8
Kerensky, Alexander, 334, 336, 337
Kerr, Philip, Marquess of Lothian, 539
Keynes, John Maynard (*later* Baron),
    362–3, 406–8; Webbs and, 21,
    406–7, 469; Keeling and, 239–40;
    on Moore, 239; Cambridge Apostles,
    241; Brooke and, 256–7; *Economic
    Consequences of the Peace*, 364;
    Nation and, 367, 406; reads *My
    Apprenticeship*, 387, 406; *Economic
    Consequences of Mr Churchill*, 388;
    Liberalism and Labour, 406; BW
    on, 407; advises Lloyd George, 448;
    Macmillan and, 449; Economic
    Advisory Council, 450–1, 456,
    489–90; MacDonald writes to,
    463–4; on the May Report, 463;
    'going off gold', 469; Churchill and,
    470; BW writes to, 488–9; Beveridge
    and, 517, 525; *General Theory of
    Employment, Interest and Money*, 519;
    Second World War, 525; writes to S
    Cripps, 543; biography, 604; portrait,
    604
Khrushchev, Nikita, 497
Kikuyu Central Association, Kenya, 427
King, Anthony, 567
Kirkwood, David, 359–60
Kirov, Sergei, 503–4
Kisch, Colonel, 439
Koinange, Chief, 429
Kollontai, Alexandra, 534, 604
Koss, Stephen, 195
Krassin, Leonid, 491
Kropotkin, Peter, 68, 114, 490–1, 604

labour exchanges, 219–21, 224, 228,
    258, 275–6, 322–3
Labour Party: BW on, 12–13, 340;
    taxation, 17; National Minimum,
    19, 159; in government, 21,
    367–81, 412–72; *Labour and the
    New Social Order*, 21; Labour
    Representation Committee, 171;
    National Executive Committee,
    315, 331, 358, 361, 369, 459, 465,

513, 515, 542–3, 553; Russian
    Revolution and, 334; *Memorandum
    of War Aims*, 335–6; conferences,
    337–8, 362, 368, 392, 407, 449,
    458, 488, 512, 536; Local, 338–9;
    post-war reconstruction, 340–8;
    Local Government Committee, 345;
    Advisory Committee chairmen, 347;
    unemployment and, 374–6; housing
    programme, 375; Labour Research
    Department, 383; *Labour and the
    Nation*, 392–3; Imperial Advisory
    Committee, 418; *Statement of War
    Aims*, 431, 510, 536; economy,
    unemployment, and the fall of the
    government, 447–72; international
    policy, 510–15
Labour Representation Committee
    (LRC), 171, 189, 207
Lamb, Henry, 318
Lang, Cosmo Gordon, 425, 604
Lansbury, George, 451–5; speeches,
    107, 267; Poor Law Commissioner,
    207, 210, 218, 223, 227; Prevention
    of Destitution Bill, 262; Simon and,
    266; NCPD and, 270; C Masterman
    and, 280; against Insurance Bill, 282,
    283; *War on Poverty* campaign, 306;
    launches *Daily Herald*, 313; Russian
    Revolution and, 333–4; Webbs and,
    347, 361, 383; First Commissioner
    of Work, 413; addressing unemploy-
    ment, 447, 452; BW on, 450; pledge
    to improve pensions, 451; agree with
    Mosley, 453; denounces Snowden's
    report, 455; Labour Leader, 470,
    507; visit to Russia, 490; League of
    Nations, 512; resigns, 512; meets
    Hitler, 537; death, 553; biography,
    604–5; portrait, *604*
Laski, Harold: Tawney and, 8; Martin
    and, 183–4; LSE lecturer, 364, 410,
    503; Webbs and, 413; NFRB and,
    505; on Greenwood, 509; Beveridge
    and, 517, 518; Beatrice Webb
    Memorial Trust Fund, 565; biogra-
    phy, 605
Law, Andrew Bonar: Conservative leader,

304, 348; coal nationalization and, 352–3, 356; coal crisis and, 355; ill health, 358–9; as PM, 367–8; biography, 605; portrait, *605*

Lawrence, D H, 495

Lawrence, Susan, 384–5, 389, 395, 397, 491, 494, 512, *605, 606*

Lawrence, TE, 432

Lawson Dodd, Frederick, 243, 594, *594*

Lawson, Jack, 358, 606

League of Nations, 510–13; arbitrator, 336; refugee issues, 412, 438; mandates, 415–16, 430, 431, 436, 440; policies, 443; Woolf on, 536–7; Abyssinia Crisis, 536; A Cripps and, 540; Munich agreement and, 541

Left Book Club, 503, 543, 544

Lenin, Vladimir, 372, 488, 490

Levy, Amy, 80, 81, 103, 558, 606

Leys, Norman, 417–18, 606

Liberal Imperialists (Limps), 177–8, 180, 197–8, 200, 208

Liberal Industrial Inquiry (1928), 407

Liberal Unionist Party, 207

Lindsay, Alexander Dunlop (Sandy) (*later* Lord Lindsay of Birker), 422, 606

Litvinov, Maxim, 336–7, 544, 545, 606

Llewellyn Smith, Hubert. *See* Smith, Hubert Llewellyn

Lloyd, Charles Mostyn: CUFS member, 230; Poor Law campaign, 254, 306; holidays with the Webbs, 260, 307; NCPD and, 263, 264, 266, 270; First World War, 322; Webbs and, 364, 560; *New Statesman* and, 365, 379; LSE lecturer, 366, 367, 503; on the Zinovieff letter, 381; *Political Quarterly* and, 470; NFRB and, 505; biography, 607; portrait, *607*

Lloyd George, David (*later* first Earl Lloyd-George of Dwyfor): Keynes advises, 21, 448, 489; Boer War and, 177; BW on, 182, 280, 342; pro-Boer, 195–6; People's Budget, 207; government posts, 208, 315; Webbs and, 209, 279, 344, 349, 402; Chancellor, 275–84;

Burns and, 279–80; Insurance Bill and, 282–3; Sharp on, 284, 321; National Insurance Act, 307; leads War Cabinet, 315; Minister of Munitions, 316; First World War, 322–3; Russian Revolution and, 334–5; Reconstruction Committee Chairman, 341; on the Webbs, 341; 'Coupon' election candidates, 347–8; coal crisis, 349–57; Paris Peace Conference, 352; Liberal Industrial Inquiry (1928), 407; as PM, 433; Passfield White Paper and, 443; on Passfield White Paper, 445; meets Hitler, 539; Left Book Club speech, 544; Maisky and, 551, 555; biography, 595; portrait, *595*

Local Government Act (1929), 392

Local Government Board (LGB), 89, 208–9, 212, 226, 271, 275, 279–80, 344–5

local government, history of, 184–7

Loch, Charles Stewart (C S) (Sir), 49, 207, 212, 214, 215, 607

Lodge, Oliver, 607

London Central Unemployed Body, 218, 219

London Congregational Union, 48

London County Council (LCC), 129–30, 159–63, 189–93; secondary education, 12; public services, 16; Burns and, 72, 121–2, 160; members, 148, 231; Progressives, 160, 190, 191–2; NAPSTE on, 161; care committees, 245; BW and, 508

London education authority, 159, 190, 191

London Mercury, 364

London School Board, 160, 187, 188, 190

London School of Economics (LSE): Webbs found, 12, 164–9; 'Beveridge-Mair dictatorship', 31, 409–11, 517; Library, 167; Rosebery and, 197; post-war, 362–7; Webbs look for land, 383; *Soviet Communism, A new civilisation?* lunch, 503; Beveridge leaves, 516–20; governance reform, 518;

governors, 519–20; Passfield Corner left to, 560
London University, 180, 348, 409
Longford, Elizabeth, 125
Lopokova, Lydia (*also* Keynes), 406–7, 469
Lough, Thomas, 607
Lugard, Frederick (*later* Lord), 284–5, 420, 421, 423, 425, 607, *607*
Lyons, Lewis, 96

Macarthur, Mary, 307, 347, 607–8
McCarthy, Bill, 4
MacCarthy, Desmond (*later* Sir), 365, 608
McCleary, George, 253, 608
MacDonald, Ishbel, 391
MacDonald, James Ramsay, 369–73, 376–8, 463–72; as PM, 13, 413, 452, 454, 455, 468, 510, 538; biography, 69–70, 608; Bloody Sunday demonstration, 99; Rainbow Circle, 151; 'Hutchinson Lecturer', 166; lectures, 167; and Fabian Trustees, 168–9; BW on, 168, 393, 469; Gladstone and, 171; LRC and, 171, 189; Martin and, 184; LCC member, 191; Boer War and, 198, 199; resigns from Fabian Society, 199; Prevention of Destitution Bill, 262; Prevention of Destitution speech, 281; Insurance Bill and, 282–3; Sharp on, 284; *War on Poverty* campaign, 306–7; resigns as party leader, 315; Russian Revolution and, 334; *Memorandum of War Aims* (contributor), 335; machinery of government committee secretary, 340; Machinery of Government Committee, 344; Webbs and, 347, 360, 361, 370; loses seat, 348; returns as MP, 359; prospect of power, 369, 370; *Workers' Weekly* prosecution, 376; King's Speech, 377–8; Foreign Secretary, 378, 380–1, 510; SW and, 384, 415; reads *My Apprenticeship*, 387–8; becomes Seaham MP, 391; Webbs' garden party, 398, 399; London University and, 409; letter from Lindsay, 422; Jewish communities and, 437; party leaders and, 437, 465; Weizmann lobbies, 438; *A Socialist in Palestine*, 445; Passfield White Paper and, 447; Economic Advisory Council, 450; complaint about Thomas, 453; Mosley and, 453, 456; addressing unemployment, 456; conference speeches, 458–9; Webbs on, 459–60; May Report, 463; Seaham Labour Party disown, 470; portrait, *608*
MacDonald, Malcolm, 438, 444, 608–9
McKenna, Reginald, 275, 449, 609
Mackenzie, Norman and Jeanne, 8, 9, 246, 249
Mackinder, Halford (*later* Sir), 182, 200, 246, 609
Maclean, Donald, 345, 346, 609
Macmillan, Hugh Pattison, Baron Macmillan, 449, 609
Mactaggart, Miss, 364
McVail, Dr John, 215, 216
Main, John, 75
Mair, David, 31, 175–6, 517, 528
Mair family, 516
Mair, Janet (Jessie) (*later* Beveridge): 'Beveridge-Mair dictatorship' at LSE, 31–2, 364, 409–11, 517, 518; Beveridge and, 176; Ministry work, 322–3; LSE and, 383, 519–20; Turins and, 516; ill health, 525; unpopularity at Oxford, 528–9; marries Beveridge, 528; Social Security League, 529; death, 530; biography, 609
Maisky, Agniya, 501–3, 534–6, 544–5; stays with the Webbs, 500, 523, 529; Webbs and, 549, 551, 552, 562, 563
Maisky, Ivan, 534–6, 544–57, 564–5; stays with the Webbs, 500–3, 515, 529; Webbs and, 523, 549, 551, 552, 555, 561, 562, 563; Beveridge and, 528; ambassador, 538; death, 564; Stalin and, 564; biography, 609; portrait, *609*
Mallon, James Joseph (Jimmy), 322, 339, 340, 493, 609–10
Manchester Guardian, 38

Mann, Pattie, 99
Mann, Tom, 98, 99, 101, 108, 121, 155, 610
Manning, Cardinal, 101, 102
Manning, Dame Leah (*née* Perrett), 242, 610
Mant, Sir Reginald, 418, 610
Marquand, David, 186
marriage and the moral code, 29–33, 250–1
Marsh, Edward Howard, (Eddie) (*later* Sir Edward), 610
Marshall, Alfred, 28, 96–7, 111, 114, 610
Martin, (Basil) Kingsley, 183, 192, 399–400, 410–11, 470, 526, 563, 610
Marx, Eleanor (Tussy), 29, 66, 67, 80, 107, 250, *610*, 611
Marx, Karl, 66, 68, 69, 71, 73, 108
Massingham, Henry William, 366, 369, 611
Masterman, Charles, 176, 220, 271–3, 276, 278, 280, 611
Masterman, Lucy, 271–2, 273, 278
Matchgirls' Strike (1888), 100–1
Maxton, James, 377, 458, 611
May Report (1931), 462–5
May, George (*later* Baron), 461, 611
Medical Officers of Health (MOHs), 215–16, 279
Meinertzhagen, Daniel, 44, 128, 611
Meinertzhagen, Georgina (*née* Potter) (BW sister), 44, 128, 257–8, 316
Melchett, Lord; Alfred Moritz Mond (*later* first Baron Melchett), 437, 442, 611–12
Mellor, William, 312–13, 314, 324, 327, 506, 514, 612
Micklethwait, John, 15
Middleton, James (Jim): WEWNC Secretary, 331; Henderson and, 332; SW and, 333, 335, 338, 339; BW on, 340; S Cripps and, 542; biography, 612
Mill, John Stuart, 62
Milton, Mary, 267
Miners Federation (MFGB), 349–58,

388–91
Miners Union, 331
Molotov–Ribbentrop Pact (1939), 536–48
Molotov, Vyacheslav, 544, 545, 551
Mond. *See* Melchett, Lord, Alfred Moritz Mond (*later* first Baron Melchett)
Money, Leo Chiozza (*later* Sir), 209, 350, 353, 356, 612
Monro, Horace, 273
Montagu, Edwin, 307, 341, 342–3, 345, 355–6, 612
Moor, Ethel, 325
Moore, George Edward (G E), 239, 241, 612
Morant, Robert (Sir), 187–9, 272–3; Health Ministry, 182, 346; BW on, 190, 343; Minority Report, 222, 226; Burns and, 273; Insurance Commission Chairman, 284; Machinery of Government Committee secretary, 343, 344; Local Government Committee, 345; biography, 612–13; portrait, *612*
Morel, Edmund Dene, 613
Morgan, Kenneth, 503
Morgan, Kevin, 488
Morley, John, 197, 315
Morrell, Lady Ottoline Violet Anne, 319, 613, *613*
Morris, May, 73
Morris, William: BW and, 24; *Dream of John Ball*, 25, 114; Democratic Federation, 66; on Hyndman, 67; on Socialists, 72; *Fabian Essays* critic, 73; Shaw and, 99; *March of the Workers*, 334; spirit of, 362; biography, 613
Morrison, Herbert (*later* Lord): Fabian Basis, 325; Mosley and, 451; BW on, 507–8; on S Cripps, 509–10; possible Labour Leader, 512; stays at Passfield, 514; BW on Cripps, 543; S Cripps and, 543; Norway expedition debate, 553; Webbs and, 560; Beatrice Webb Memorial Trust Fund, 565; biography, 613; portrait, *613*
Mortimer, Raymond, 563
Mosley, Cynthia, 394, 456

Mosley, Sir Oswald, 452–61; Webbs and, 393–4, 406; stays with the Webbs, 394, 455–6; Chancellor of the Duchy of Lancaster, 413; addressing unemployment, 447, 452, 461; Treasury and, 449; BW on, 450, 456–7; Morrison and, 451; pledge to improve pensions, 451; 'Mosley Memorandum', 453–4, 459; complains about Thomas, 453; sees MacDonald, 455; resigns, 456; at Labour conference, 458; elected to NEC, 459; BW and, 461; expelled from Party, 461; biography, 613–14; portrait, *613*

Mostyn Lloyd, Charles. *See* Lloyd, Charles Mostyn

Mufti of Jerusalem, The, (Al-Husseini, Hajj Amin,), 432,434,436,437, 439, 440

Muggeridge, Kitty (*née* Dobbs), 9, 497

Muggeridge, Malcolm, 497, 499–500

Munich Agreement (1938), 540

Murby, Millicent, 234, 284, 614

Murray, Gilbert, 196, 261, 316, 614

Namier, Lewis, 265, 438, 444, 614

Nash, Vaughan, 101, 109, 121, 342, 614

Nation magazine, 310, 366–7, 406

National Assistance Bill (1948), 568

National Association for the Promotion of Secondary and Technical Education (NAPSTE), 160–1

National Campaign for the Prevention of Destitution (NCPD), 262, 266, 268, 304, 308, 568. *See also* Break Up of the Poor Law (propaganda)

national efficiency, 20, 199–201

National Government (1931–1935), 468–70, 488

National Guilds League, 312

National Health Service Act (1946), 568

National Insurance Act (1911), 17, 275–84, 307

National Insurance Act (1946), 530, 568

National Union of Railwaymen (NUR), 352

National Unity Campaign Committee,

515

Nazi-Soviet pact, 536–48

Nehru, Jawaharlal, 514

Neo-pagans, 239, 242, 320

Nesbit, Edith, 29, 70, 236, 614–15, *614*

Nevinson, Henry, 615

Nevinson, Margaret, 615

New Age magazine, 17, 233, 262, 305, 308

New Fabian Research Bureau (NFRB), 494, 495, 505–6

New Poor Law (1834). *See* Poor Law Amendment Act (1834)

New Republic magazine, 338

New Statesman, 364–7, 378–80; founded, 12, 308–11; sponsors, 309, 366; staff, 312; articles, 319, 522; Sharp and, 321, 369; Pease and, 322; Colegate and, 323; review of *Soviet Communism*, 503

Newman, George (*later* Sir), 615

Newsholme, Arthur, 280

Nicholson, William, 409

Nicolson, Harold George, 546, 615

Nineteenth Century, 96, 106

Norman, Montagu (*later* Baron), 449, 450, 615, *615*

Norris, Jessie, 383, 397–8, 521

Norway, 552, 553

Observer, The, 503, 539

Oldham, Joseph Houldsworth, 418, 421, 615

Oliver (gardener), 398

Oliver, Mrs, 398

Olivier, Brynhild, 230, 242, 245, 320

Olivier, Daphne, 242, 244, 245

Olivier, Margery, 230, 242, 244, 245, 320, 321

Olivier, Noel (*later* Richards): Brooke and, 242–3, 263, 265, 318, 319; Fabian Society Summer Schools, 245; biography, 615–16; portrait, *615*

Olivier, Sydney (*later* Lord): Fabian Society and, 11, 69, 73, 235, 238; S Webb and, 65–6; Rainbow Circle, 151; Boer War and, 198–9; family, 230, 242; Brooke and, 256, 318;

Webbs and, 307, 402; Secretary of State for India, 372; East Africa and, 418, 420, 425; Kenya and, 423; biography, 616; portrait, *616*

Ollivant, Alfred, 268, 616

Orage, Alfred Richard, 17, 232, 233, 305, 616

Ormsby-Gore, David, 426

Osborne Judgement (1909), 282

Osmaston, Dorothy (*later* Lady Layton), 240, 616

Ovey, Sir Edmund, 492, 498

Owen, Robert, 362

Palestine, 431–47

Pankhurst, Mrs Emmeline, 199

Paris Peace Conference, 323, 334, 349, 352

Parker, Gilbert (Sir), 616

Parker, John, 560, 563, 616, *616*

Parliamentary Labour Party (PLP), 281, 282, 370, 456, 461

Passfield Trustees, 8–9, 560

Passfield White Paper (1930), 440–7

Patch, Blanche, 533

Paul, Maurice (Eden), 78, 108, 109, 616–17

Payne-Townshend, Charlotte (*later* Shaw), 617

Pease, Edward Reynolds: Fabian Society and, 69, 70, 73, 238, 285, 402; Fabian Secretary, 76, 168; 1914,replaced as Fabian Secretary by Stephen Sanders 321; 1915, returns as Secretary; SW and, 147, 332; on MacDonald, 199; on BW, 311; on guild socialism, 311; *New Statesman* acting editor, 322; BW on his stroke, 524; biography, 617; portrait, *617*

Pelling, Henry, 74, 338

pensions, 98, 207, 276, 448, 451; introduction of, 48, 49, 274–5

Penty, Arthur Joseph, 17, 305, 617

Pepler, Hilary, 18

Perham, Magery, 431

Phelps, Lancelot (L R), 219, 223, 345, 617

Phillips, Dr Marion: report on children,

214; Fabian Women's Group, 234; Fabian Executive Committee, 285, 306; WEWNC and, 331; Russian Revolution and, 334; Labour Party and, 339, 340; Lloyd George and, 341; biography, 617; portrait, *617*

Picture Post, 561

Playne, Arthur, 44, 45, 128, 617

Playne, Mary (*née* Potter) (BW sister): Darling and, 11; marriage and children, 11, 44–5, 77; BW writes to, 52, 54; BW on Chamberlain, 84, 88; stays with BW, 94; Pycroft and, 126, 162; BW on Churchill, 220; BW on Majority Report, 224; Webbs stay with, 226; BW on Dalton, 238–9; BW stays with, 317, 383; death, 382

Plumer, Herbert Charles Onslow, first Viscount Plumer, 433, 618

Plunkett, Horace, 122, 147, 618

Podmore, Frank, 618

Poland, 544, 549

Political Quarterly, 470–2

Pollitt, Harry, 376, 514–15, 544, 548, 550, 557, 618

Ponsonby, Arthur, (*later* first Lord Ponsonby of Shulbrede), 522, 618

Poor Law Amendment Act (1834), 50, 202–6

Poor Law history, 185, 202, 568

Poor Law medical service, 215–16

Poor Law Royal Commission (1905–09): Minority Report, 12, 17, 28, 212, 222, 225–9, 265, 267, 281, 312, 345, 490, 530, 531; Tawney and, 15; reports, 202–5, 276; 'that nasty old Poor Law', 202–29; principles, 203–4; Commissioners, 206–7; Special Investigators, 212–13, 217–18; work on unemployment, 212, 217–21, 224, 225–8; Evidence Committee, 214; Majority Report, 217, 224, 225–6, 227–9, 265; endgame, 271–85

Poor Relief Act (1601), 202

Popular Front, 544, 545

Ponsonby, Arthur, 403–4, 512, 521, 537–8

Postan, Michael (Mouna) (Sir), 557, 618
Postgate, Raymond, 325
Postmaster-General post, 15, 74
Potter, Beatrice. *See* Webb, Beatrice (*née* Potter)
Potter, Blanche. *See* Cripps, Blanche (*née* Potter) (BW sister)
Potter, Catherine (Kate). *See* Courtney, Catherine (Kate) (*née* Potter) (BW sister)
Potter family, 32–3, 38–43, 93–4; musical household, 26–7; holidays, 47, 307; cousins, 57–8, 80; BW in charge of, 76; Chamberlain and, 81, 83, 84, 88; Christmas and, 104; Webbs and, 128–9; brothers-in-law, 195; First World War, 317–18, 511; ageing, 521–2
Potter, Georgina. *See* Meinertzhagen, Georgina (*née* Potter) (BW sister)
Potter, Lawrencina. *See* Holt, Lawrencina (Lallie) (*née* Potter) (BW sister)
Potter, Lawrencina (*née* Heyworth) (BW mother), 38, 39, 40, 46–7, 50, 600
Potter, Margaret. *See* Hobhouse, Margaret (*née* Potter) (BW sister)
Potter, Mary. *See* Playne, Mary (*née* Potter) (BW sister)
Potter, Richard (brother), 39
Potter, Richard (BW father), 38–43, 46–7; no ear for music, 26; feminist, 28; BW writes to, 30, 54; sons-in-law and, 45, 104, 174; BW looks after, 47, 92, 93, 101, 102, 103, 121, 126–7; family holidays, 47, 75, 91; ill health and death, 55–6, 76, 89, 103, 104, 105, 126–7; Harkness and, 81; Chamberlain and, 84–5; servants and, 397
Potter, Richard (BW grandfather), 38
Potter, Rosalind (Rosie). *See* Dobbs, Rosalind (Rosie) (*earlier* Dyson Williams, *née* Potter) (BW sister)
Potter, Shena. *See* Simon, Shena (*née* Potter)
Potter, Theresa. *See* Cripps, Theresa (*née* Potter) (BW sister)
Potter, Thomas (BW uncle), 38

Potter, William (BW uncle), 38
Power, Eileen Edna Le Poer (*later* Postan), 518, 618
Prevention of Destitution Bill (1910), 262
Prevention of Destitution conference, 281
Pringle, John, 218
Pritt, Denis Nowell, 618
Progressive Party, 190
Provis, Sir Samuel, 212, 226, 272–3, 345, 618
Pryse, Spencer, 263
public services, 16, 215, 453
Pycroft, Ella: friendship with BW, 11, 12, 77, 94–5, 125–6; Katherine Buildings collector, 52–7, 59–60; engagement, 78, 108, 109; London politics, 103; Eight Hour Day rally, 108; BW and, 111; stays with BW, 113; 'Domestic Economy', 162; reads *My Apprenticeship*, 387; biography, 618

Radice, Lisanne, 5, 6
Rainbow Circle, 151, 166
Randlords (SA mine owners), 194
Raverat, Jacques, 239, 264, 318, 319, 320, 321, 619
Ravogli, Julia, 174
Reading, Marquess of, Rufus Daniel Isaacs, 437, 619
Reading Room, British Museum, 11, 46, 64, 67, 79–80, 492
Reading, Rufus Isaacs, Lord, 437, 442
Reeves, Amber (*later* Blanco White): Wells and, 31, 243, 245–51, 246–9; Fabian Society Summer Schools, 230, 232, 244; at Newnham, 242; stays with the Webbs, 245–6; BW on, 247, 249; holidays with the Webbs, 260; biography, 619; portrait, *619*
Reeves, Maud: women's suffrage, 151–2; Fabian Society, 233, 235, 238; *Round About a Pound a Week*, 234; Wells and, 246; BW and, 249; dines with the Webbs, 251; biography, 619
Reeves, Pember: biography, 151–2, 230,

619; LSE Director, 200, 362; Wells and, 246, 248; BW and, 249, 250; dines with the Webbs, 251; pensions and, 275

Ribbentrop, Joachim von, 539, 547–8, 619

Robbins, Lionel, 517

Roberts, John, 366

Robeson, Paul, 544

Robson, William Alexander (W A): Webbs and, 27, 527, 562; *Political Quarterly* and, 470, 471; NFRB and, 505; Social Security League, 529; biography, 619–20

Roosevelt, Franklin D, 517, 563

Rosebery, Lord, 177, 178, 197, 620

Rosenberg, Rose, 338–9

Ross, McGregor, 418

Rossetti, Dante Gabriel, 24

Rowntree, Benjamin Seebohm, 211, 328, 341, 366–7, 620

Rowse, A L (Alfred Leslie), 509, 539, 620

Ruskin, John, 49

Russell, Alys (*née* Pearsall Smith), 19, 151, 173, 185, 398

Russell, Bertrand; 3rd Earl Russell, 19–20, 151–2; Webbs and, 13, 15, 173, 316, 382; on the Webbs, 3, 146; stays with the Webbs, 151; cycling with the Webbs, 152, 173; LSE and, 167; Webbs stay with, 185; Coefficients member, 200; Moore and, 239; Russian Revolution and, 334; visit to Russia, 490; biography, 620; portrait, *620*

Russell, John Francis Stanley, 2nd Earl Russell, 389

Russia, 13, 551, 556, 561

Russian Revolutions (1917), 333–7

Ryland, Frederick, 87

Sackville-West, Vita, 408

Sadler, Michael Ernest (*later* Sir), 200, 620

Saleeby, Caleb Williams Elijah, 266, 310, 620–1

Salisbury, Lord, 82, 88, 170, 194, 621

Salter, Arthur, 456

Salvation Army, 22, 114, 218–19, 393

Samuel, Herbert (*later* Viscount Samuel): on the Webbs, 10, 146; stays with the Webbs, 151; Webbs and, 183, 307, 409; BW asks for advice, 343; Royal Commission Chairman (mining industry), 388, 389; Liberal Industrial Inquiry (1928), 407; High Commissioner of Palestine, 432–3; Kisch and, 439; on BW, 563–4; biography, 621; portrait, *621*

Samuel Memorandum, 390

Samurai, the, 22, 175, 393

Sanders, William Stephen: Battersea SDF, 67; Fabian Society, 72, 231, 321–2, 325; NEC Fabian member, 315, 331; biography, 621; portrait, *621*

Sankey Commission, 350–8

Sankey, John (*later* Viscount), 468, 621, *621*

Sarolea, Charles, 491

Sassoon, Siegfried, 364

Schacht, Hjalmar, 517

Schloesser, (*later* Slesser), Sir Henry Herman. *See* Slesser (*formerly* Schloesser), Sir Henry Herman

Schloss, Arthur, 244

Schreiner, Olive, 80–1, 622, *622*

Schuster, Sir George, 416, 418, 419, 622

Scurr, John, 376

Second World War, 13, 525, 532–3, 548–57, 559, 561–2

Seymour-Jones, Caroline, 107

Shackleton, David (*later* Sir), 276, 622

Sharp, Clifford Dyce: Fabian Society, 230–1, 234–5; *The New Age*, 233; Colegates and, 2, 236, 248, 254–5; dines with the Webbs, 254; *Crusade* editor, 255, 308; holidays with the Webbs, 260; correspondence with BW, 281, 282–3, 284, 285; *New Statesman* editor, 308, 321, 366–7, 364, 369, 379–80; Shaw and, 310–11, 321; First World War, 321; influence of Asquith, 365; Webbs and, 365, 380; alcoholism, 378;

MacDonald and, 378; biography, 622; portrait, *622*

Sharp, Rosamund (*née* Bland), 236

Sharp, William, 223

Shaw, Charlotte (*née* Payne-Townshend): marriage, 153, 167; Fabian Society, 233; Fabian Women's Group, 234; reads *My Apprenticeship*, 386; stays at Passfield, 401; Webbs' eightieth birthday party, 521; Webbs and, 531–4; ill health and death, 531, 532–4; Hitler and, 539; biography, 619

Shaw Commission (1929), 435–7

Shaw, George Bernard (GBS), 493–4; on the Webbs, 10; friendship with SW, 11, 12, 73, 75, 76; on Chesterbelloc, 17; *On the Rocks*, 26; philanderer, 29; on SW parents, 62; on Olivier, 65; BW and, 67–71, 113, 321; joins Zetetical Society, 67; Morris and, 67; on Bland, 70; on Fabian Society, 71; Fabian Society and, 72; on the Reading Room, 79; writes to Morris, 99; Eight Hour Day rally, 107; speeches, 115, 147; holidays with the Webbs, 131, 150, 151, 163; Webbs and, 147, 149–50, 261, 382, 387, 409, 531–4; BW on, 150, 152–3, 340; cycling with the Webbs, 152, 153; and *History of Trade Unionism*, 154–5; marriage, 154; Mrs Warren's Profession, 155; stays with the Webbs, 156, 157, 401; works on *Industrial Democracy*, 158; and Fabian Trustees, 168; Wells and, 175, 234, 236–7; Boer War and, 199; *Fabianism and the Empire*, 199; Coefficients member, 200; on Hamilton, 206; *Major Barbara*, 206, 533; Webbs stay with, 219, 307; CUFS and, 238, 242; Fabian Society Summer Schools, 243–4; Colegate and, 250; *War on Poverty* campaign, 306; *New Statesman* and, 308–11, 365, 366; Sharp and, 310–11; on Sharp, 321, 379–80; Cole and, 325; V, Woolf on, 330; Lloyd George and, 341; on BW *My Apprenticeship*, 386; *The Apple*

Cart, 401; *Saint Joan*, 401; Passfield White Paper and, 446; visit to Russia, 493; LSE lunch, 503; Webbs' eightieth birthday party, 521; *Spectator* article on BW, 522; advises BW, 523; manpower survey, 526; ill health, 531; letter objecting to war with Russia, 552; BW article in *Picture Post*, 561; writes to SW, 565, 566; SW burial suggestion, 566–7; proposes BW memorial, 566; biography, 623; portrait, *623*

Shaw, Sir Walter, 435, 436, 623

Shaw, Thomas (Tom), 392, 623

Shiels, (Thomas) Drummond (*later* Sir), 424, 426, 427, 429, 430, 438, 445, 447, 623

Shinwell, Emmanuel, 394

Shipton, George, 102

Shove, Gerald, 244, 265, 268, 319, 623

Simon, Ernest (*later* Lord): Webbs and, 266, 308, 309, 380; Fabian Basis, 285; *New Statesman* sponsor, 309, 310, 366; *Nation* and, 367; Liberal Industrial Inquiry (1928), 407; portrait, *623*; biography, 624

Simon family, 309

Simon, Shena (*née* Potter), 242, 309, 503, 624

Simon, Sir John, 281, 443

Simpson, Sir John Hope. *See* Hope Simpson, Sir John

Slesser (*formerly* Schloesser), Sir Henry Herman: Fabian Society, 18, 231, 306; Wells and, 230; Fabian Nursery Committee, 232; Prevention of Destitution Bill, 262, 264; Solicitor General, 372; biography, 624

Smart, William, 213, 224, 624

Smillie, Robert, 331, 334, 350, 353–4, 624

Smith, Allan, 350, 353

Smith, Frederick Edwin (*later* Sir, *later* Earl of Birkenhead), 390, 624

Smith, Hubert Llewellyn: BW on, 60–1; Fabian Society, 72; Dock Strike and, 101; cooperative conference, 109; Webbs and, 122, 124; TEB and, 161;

Board of Trade, 175, 221; coal crisis and, 354; Chief Economic Adviser, 372–3; Unemployment Cabinet Committee, 374; biography, 625; portrait, *625*

Smith, Sir Allan MacGregor, 624

Smuts, General, 425, 437

Snell, Harry (*later* Lord): biography, 72, 205, 625; LSE administrator, 166; Fabian Executive Committee, 306; Labour MP, 424; Inquiry Commission, 435, 437; LCC Chairman, 508; Lords Labour Leader, 512; BW on, 513; Webbs' eightieth birthday party, 521; portrait, *625*

Snowden, Ethel, 403, 464–5

Snowden, Philip (*later* Viscount Snowden), 454–6, 463–8; Chancellor, 21, 372, 373, 413, 448–50, 452, 465, 468, 470, 490; lectures, 261; against Insurance Bill, 282, 283; BW on, 307; Russian Revolution and, 334; loses seat, 348; prospect of power, 369; *Labour and the Nation*, 392; Webbs and, 403, 459–60; Palestine and, 440, 441; addressing unemployment, 454; May Report, 463; lunches at Passmore, 464–5; Churchill on, 470; biography, 625–6; portrait, *625*

Social Democratic Federation (SDF), 67, 68, 69, 72, 90, 98–9

Social Security League, 529

Socialist International, 334, 335, 361

Socialist League, 67, 72, 506–7, 514

Society for Socialist Inquiry and Propaganda (SSIP), 506

Sokolnikov, Grigory, 492, 493, 495, 500, 534, 626

Souls, the, 147, 176–80

South Wales Miners, 305

Soviet Union, 16, 22, 393, 488–520

Spain, 548, 556

Spanish civil war (1936–39), 513–14, 514, 544

Spencer, Frederick, 626

Spencer, Herbert: Potter family and, 42–3, 47, 83; BW and, 45, 129, 174; Webbs lodge with, 124; SW and, 129;

death, 173; biography, 626

Spencer, Stanley, 318–19

Spielman, Eva. *See* Hubback, Eva (*née* Spielman)

Spoor, Ben, 376, 395

Squire, Jack (Sir John Collings Squire): on the Webbs, 18; CUFS member, 242, 308; Fabian Nursery, 247; *New Statesman* acting editor, 310, 321–2; Keeling and, 319; founds *London Mercury*, 364; biography, 626

Squire, Rose, 213

Stacey family, 62

Stalin, Joseph, 13, 493, 497, 534–5, 544–5, 549, 564

Stamp, Josiah Charles, Baron Stamp, 519–20, 626

Stanley, Arthur Lyulph; Lord Stanley of Alderley, 426, 430, 626

Stead, William Thomas (W T), 196, 626

Steel-Maitland, Arthur (*later* Sir), 213, 363, 627

Stein, Leonard, 445

Stephen, Leslie, 558

Stevenson, Frances (*later* Lloyd George), 277, 352

Stockholm Conference (1917), 334

Stocks, Mary, 309

Strachey, James, 244, 265

Strachey, John, 548

Strachey, Lytton, 239–40

Strauss, George Russell (*later* Baron), 543, 545, 550, 627

strikes, industrial, 101–2, 175, 304–5, 388–91, 405

suffragists/suffragettes, 28, 113, 230, 233–4, 267, 304

syndicalism, 305, 311–15, 389

Talbot, Edward, bishop of Rochester, 188

Tawney, R H: Webbs' biographer, 8, 9; social policy issues, 15; on portrait of Webbs, 18; Beveridge and, 175; on the Webbs, 182; Webbs and, 183, 341, 352, 364, 383, 496; LSE lecturer, 213, 410; *Morning Post* editor, 221; Fabian Society Summer

Schools, 245; Jones and, 265; NCPD and, 270; First World War, 322; BW and, 339, 422; MFGB and, 390; *Political Quarterly* and, 470; on S Cripps, 542; biography, 627; portrait, *627*

Taylor, AJP, 198, 416, 448, 530, 546

Technical Education Board, (TEB), 161–3

Technical Instruction, Royal Commission on, 160

Temple, William, Archbishop of Canterbury, 528

Terry, Ellen, 153

Thesiger, Frederick John Napier, first Viscount Chelmsford, 372, 627

Thomas, Edward, 264, 310

Thomas, James H (Jimmy), 451–7; Local Government Committee, 345; Webbs and, 347; NUR General Secretary, 352; Campbell and, 377; Lord Privy Seal, 413; Dominions Secretary, 415, 457; Amery and, 416; addressing unemployment, 447–8, 538; Treasury and, 449; BW on, 450, 452, 469; economic policy, 451; Henderson on, 452; Mosley on, 453; Mosley and, 456; May Report, 463; leaves government, 468; biography, 627; portrait, *627*

Thompson, Edward, 202

Thomson, Basil, 324

Thomson, Christopher Birdwood, Baron Thomson, 458, 627–8

Three Choirs Festival, Gloucester, 26–7, 84, 396, 494

Tillett, Ben, 101, 108, 628

Times, The, 539, 566

Tobinson, Mrs, 503

Townshend, Caroline, 230, 245, 628, *628*

Townshend, Emily (*née* Gibson), 233, 245, 259, 319–20, 628

Townshend, Rachel Susanna. *See* Keeling, Rachel Susanna (*née* Townshend)

Toynbee, Arnold, 339

Trade Disputes Act (1927), 391, 392

Trades Union Congress (TUC): National Minimum, 19, 159; conferences, 21, 102, 147, 152, 281; Germany insurance delegation, 276; General Council, 389, 390, 465; post-General Strike, 405; Secretary, 451; unemployment benefit cuts, 465; 'going off gold', 469; League of Nations, 512

Trevelyan, (Sir) Charles, 151, 157, 394, 552, 628

Tribune, 514

Trotsky, Leon, 412, 492, 497, 504

Turin, Lucia, 516, 517, 518, 628

Turin, SP, 503, 516, 518, 628

Uganda, 428–30

Uitlanders, 194

Ukraine, 496, 497, 498

unemployment, 447–9, 452–6, 459, 461–2, 465–6, 468

United Front (Unity Campaign), 514–15, 542

USA, 489, 517

Versailles Treaty (1919), 431

Victoria, Queen, 82

Wailing Wall, Jerusalem, 434, 439–40

Wake, Egerton, 370, 398, 628

Wakefield, Russell, 227, 628

Wallas, Ada (*née* Radford), 154, 386–7

Wallas, Graham: Olivier and, 11, 65–6; SW and, 62, 65–6, 76, 120, 130; Fabian Society, 69, 71, 73; Eight Hour Day rally, 107; stays with BW, 113; Webbs and, 121, 307, 364; holidays with the Webbs, 123, 131, 150, 151, 163; BW and, 147; BW on, 150, 152; Rainbow Circle, 151; stays with the Webbs, 151, 156; Payne-Townshend and, 153; and *History of Trade Unionism,* 154–5; marriage, 154; LSE and, 166, 402; Wells and, 175; London School Board, 187; reads *My Apprenticeship,* 386–7; J Mair and, 411; biography, 629; portrait, *629*

War Cabinet: First World War, 315, 335;

Second World War, 553, 554, 556
War Emergency Workers National
    Committee (WEWNC), 16–17, 316,
    331–3
Warburg, Felix, 442, 445
Ward, Dudley, 244, 263, 320, 323, 629
Ward, Mrs Humphrey, 233
Watson, Sir Alfred, 275, 629
Webb, Ada, 63
Webb, Beatrice (*née* Potter)
    ARTS, MUSIC AND CULTURE:
        poetry, 24–5, 111; literature, 25–6;
        music, 26–7, 396–7, 494–5, 522
    CAREER: social investigator,
        10, 95–6; Poor Law Royal
        Commissioner, 12, 202–29; early
        career, 14; at TUC conference,
        21; founds *Political Quarterly*, 27;
        Committee on Women in Industry,
        28; housing manager, 30; London
        and, 47–8; social apprentice,
        47–61; COS committee, 48, 50,
        90; research for *Life and Labour
        of the People of London*, 58–9, 60,
        72, 96; gives evidence to House of
        Lords Committee, 96; writes for
        Nineteenth Century, 96, 106; trade
        union study, 101–2, 120, 121,
        124, 130; cooperative conference,
        Glasgow, 109, 122; Fabian Society,
        121, 233, 244, 257–8, 306, 311,
        312, 313; research for *Industrial
        Democracy*, 157–8; Commission
        visits, 212, 218; health report, 216;
        CUFS and, 238; *War on Poverty*
        campaign, 306–7; joins ILP, 306;
        women in industry committee, 346;
        coal crisis and, 349–51, 354–5;
        writes to Seaham women, 373, 390,
        391, 470; Labour Party, 340–8, 449,
        450, 460, 466, 489–90
    CHILDHOOD AND
        EDUCATION, 10, 11, 26–7,
        38–43
    FRIENDSHIPS: 'glorified spinsters',
        11, 28, 29, 94–5, 104, 107; . *See
        also* Darling, Carrie (*later* Browne);

Green, Alice; Harkness, Margaret
Elise (John Law); Pycroft, Ella
OPINIONS AND ATTITUDES:
    Communist Party, 22–3; political
    leadership, 22–3; Salvation Army,
    22; Chamberlain family home,
    24; on sexual code, 26, 29–33, 42,
    250, 410, 495, 516; as feminist,
    28; suffrage and, 28, 113, 233–4;
    marriage and the moral code, 29–
    33, 250–1; on marriage, 30, 118–
    19; on Wallas, 65; on cooperation,
    96–7; on Lloyd George, 182; on
    Manchester and Liverpool, 184–5;
    on Campbell-Bannerman, 197;
    on 'Limp' friends, 198; on young
    intellectuals, 230; health insurance,
    275–6; First World War and,
    316–17; on Labour, 331–2; on trade
    union MPs, 332; on the Russian
    Revolution, 333; on Henderson,
    335; on Permanent Secretaries,
    343–4; on unemployment, 376,
    528; on the Zinovieff letter, 381;
    on Royal Commission (mining
    industry), 388; opposes General
    Strike, 389; on the next generation,
    393–6; on 'Beveridge-Mair
    dictatorship' at LSE, 409; on Kenya,
    422; on Palestine, 435, 443; on
    SW and Palestine, 445–6; on the
    Cabinet, 463; on the Communist
    Party, 495–6; on Viennese socialists,
    511; on Spanish civil war, 513–14;
    on Beveridge Report, 527–8; on
    National Insurance, 528; on Munich
    Agreement, 540–1; on France, 556;
    on life and death, 558–9
PERSONAL: preoccupied with
    religion, 22, 43, 45–6, 173; fellow
    of the British Academy, 28; ill
    health, 40, 41, 172, 214, 216–17,
    269, 316, 320, 342, 382, 498, 500,
    501, 516–17, 559–64; 'irresponsible
    girlhood', 44–7; on the Webb
    family, 62; family inheritance, 127,

160; dieting, 172–3; domestic servants and, 397–8, 521, 523, 548–9, 559, 562; ageing, 521–4; death, 529, 534, 564

PUBLICATIONS: *My Apprenticeship*, 44, 47, 91, 146, 340, 385–8; *The co-operative movement in Great Britain*, 113, 122, 123; *Our Partnership*, 192, 522, 559

RELATIONSHIPS: Chamberlain, 11–12, 29–30, 75, 81–93, 103, 110, 111, 116, 125, 171–2, 195, 386, 414; Main, 75

TRAVELS: before marriage, 40, 45, 47, 51, 75, 87, 110–11

Webb, Charles (SW brother), 63

Webb, Charles (SW father), 62, 127

Webb, Elizabeth (*née* Stacey) (SW mother), 62, 65

Webb family, 10, 62

Webb, James (SW grandfather), 62

Webb, Sidney

CAREER: Fabian Society, 11, 12, 69, 71–4, 115, 167, 187, 257–8; MP and Minister, 13; early career, 63–5; 'the ablest man in England', 66–74; joins Zetetical Society, 67; speaking tour, 115, 116; TEB Chairman, 161–2, 191; Liberal Party, 170; *New Age* magazine, 233; CUFS lecture, 242; *War on Poverty* campaign, 306; LCC, 313, 187–93, 148, 159–63, 160–2, 157, 12, 122, 129–31, 16; WEWNC and, 331–3; Labour Party 'intellectual leader', 346, 348; Sankey Commission, 350–8; offered peerage as 'Lord Passfield', 414; Labour Party, 13, 16–17, 21, 316, 337–9, 358–62, 368, 372–6, 378, 381, 388, 391–2, 414–47, 457, 467–8; Order of Merit, 565

EARLY LIFE AND BACKGROUND, 11, 14, 62–3

OPINIONS AND ATTITUDES: on trade union MPs, 332; on conscription of riches, 333; on taxation, 338; on benefits cuts, 459; on Mosley Manifesto, 459; on MacDonald, 472; on France, 556

PERSONAL: ill health, 26, 119, 270, 382, 522–4, 531; ageing, 521–4; BW death, 564; death, 560, 565;

PUBLICATIONS: *Fabian Essays in Socialism* (contributor), 15, 73–4, 105; *The Necessary Basis of Society*, 20; *Facts for Socialists*, 73; *The War and the Workers*, 331; *Memorandum of War Aims* (major contributor), 335; *The Labour Party on the Threshold*, 361–2; '*What happened in 1931: a Record*', 471

RELATIONSHIPS: Annie Adams, 75; Potter family, 128–9

TRAVELS: Ukraine, 498–9; Russia, 501

'The Webbs'

ARTS, MUSIC AND CULTURE, 23–7

FRIENDSHIPS: the Souls, 176–80; Beveridge, 219, 383, 409–10, 516, 524–31; Woolfs, 328–30, 346, 422; Sokolnikovs, 493, 495; Maiskys and, 534–6, 549, 551, 552, 555, 561–4; . *See also* Shaw, Charlotte (*née* Payne-Townshend); Shaw, George Bernard (GBS)

HOMES AND HOUSES, 12; 41 Grosvenor Road, 24, 147–9, 167, 170–201, 206, 208–9, 211, 220, 235, 246, 251, 254, 258, 328, 336–7, 341, 347, 369–70, 384–5; Passfield Corner, 24, 27, 382–411, 452, 455–6, 458, 464–5, 492, 494–6, 500–2, 508–10, 518–19, 521, 534–6, 542–7, 560–3; Madehurst Vicarage, Arundel, 304, 308; Artillery Mansions, 385; Passfield Corner, 396–408

IDEAS, 14; permeation, 12, 19, 145–285, 305–6, 347, 365; and the State, 15–19; The National Minimum, 19–21, 159, 200, 231,

306, 406; political leadership, 22–3,
150, 308, 313, 369, 393–6, 490,
506–7; Russia, 488–96, 516
INSTITUTIONS: London School
of Economics, 12, 31, 164–9, 191,
306, 362–7, 383, 410, 517; Fabian
Society, 229–53, 323–8
LABOUR PARTY, 343, 358–62;
belief in gradual change, 6, 12–13,
349–81, 496, 505, 508; host dinner
for, 347; host reception for, 374;
conferences, 407, 449, 488, 512;
asked to draft programme, 469; after
MacDonald, 504–10
LATER YEARS: 'phoney war',
548–57
NETWORKS, 322, 339, 365–7, 372,
382–3, 568–9; the Coefficients, 20,
199–201; Webbs salon (cross-party
network), 176–84; dining club, 199;
and the war, 317–23; Half Circle
Club, 361, 363–4; Passfield Corner
weekends, 399–400; Morrison LCC,
508–10
OPINIONS AND ATTITUDES:
Russia, 13; political leadership, 22–
3; differing views on suffrage, 28,
234; influence of Wells, 174–5, 234;
differing views on Boer War, 194–5;
health insurance sceptics, 275–84;
differing views on First World War,
316; appeasement and the Nazi-
Soviet pact, 536–48; international
affairs and, 537–48; letter objecting
to war with Russia, 552
PARTNERSHIP, 14; Minority
Report, 12, 17, 28, 212, 222,
225–7, 265, 345–6, 490, 531;
cooperative conference, Glasgow,
109–10; lectures, 122; trade union
study, 124; BW pays LCC expenses,
130; 'firm of Webb', 146–69; 'the
Webbs' year', 150–4; 'solid work in
economic and political principles',
163–9; 'Webb myth', 170–6;
research projects, 213–14; Break Up

of the Poor Law (propaganda), 253–
71; BW reflects on, 261; NCPD
and, 262–3; Poor Law endgame,
271–85; reviewing priorities, 305,
348; challenging syndicalism and
Guild Socialist ideas, 311–15;
remaking Labour, 337–40; as SW
becomes MP, 360
PERSONAL: library, 5; wills, 77,
560; joint portrait of, 409–10
PUBLICATIONS, 4–5; *New
Statesman*, 12, 308–11, 364–7,
379–80; *Constitution for the Socialist
Commonwealth of Great Britain*,
15–16; *History of Trade Unionism*,
18, 148, 150, 154, 156–7, 502;
Industrial Democracy, 4, 19, 157–9,
174; *Soviet Communism: a new
civilisation*, 23, 519, 522; trade
union books, 154–9; *History of
English Local Government*, 184–7;
English Poor Law Policy, 203, 213;
History of the English Poor Law,
392; *Soviet Communism, A new
civilisation?*, 496, 497, 500–1,
502–4
RECREATION: walking, 24, 85,
154, 245, 260, 268, 307, 384, 386,
396, 402–3, 560; holidays, 33, 131,
150–1, 163, 169, 173, 185, 219,
253, 260–1, 385–6, 457, 492, 519,
523, 524; cycling, 152, 153, 173,
180
RELATIONSHIP: meet each other,
12, 104–5, 106; early days, 104–32;
first impressions of each other, 106–
7; crisis in, 120–1; resume contact,
121–2; engagement, 123, 126, 127,
128; wedding and honeymoon, 124,
131–2, 146–7; marriage, 3, 12, 30,
116; correspondence between, 14,
23, 24, 108–9, 110, 111–13, 115–
17, 119–20, 124–5; later life, 557–
69; ashes interred at Westminster
Abbey, 10, 566–8, 569
TRAVELS: Russia, 16, 23, 488,

534; European, 27, 123, 412, 511; North America, New Zealand and Australia, 152, 170; round-the-world trip, 271, 279, 281, 283, 284–5, 304; Russia and Ukraine, 496–9
Wedgwood Benn, William, first Viscount Stansgate, 423
Wedgwood, Josiah Clement, first Baron Wedgwood, 435, 629
Weizmann, Chaim, 431, 434, 437, 438, 441–7, 629, *629*
Wellock, Wilfred, 426, 629
Wells, Herbert George (H G): *The New Machiavelli*, 3, 23, 183, 200, 240, 251–3, 279; Coefficients member, 20, 200; Samurai model, 22, 175, 393; *A Modern Utopia*, 22, 175; Webbs and, 25, 146, 174–5; influence of, 30, 230; Reeves family and, 31, 246–7; on 41 Grosvenor Road, 149; *Anticipations*, 174; on *History of English Local Government*, 186; Eugenics Society member, 201; BW writes to, 214, 491; Attlee on, 232; *New Age* magazine, 233; Fabian Society lectures, 234–5; Fabian Society and, 2, 234–8; BW on, 235–6, 237, 370; Blands and, 236; lectures, 241; CUFS lecture, 242; A Reeves and, 246–9; SW and, 250; *Ann Veronica*, 251–2; Burns and, 274; on Minority Report, 305–6; Lloyd George and, 341; visit to Russia, 490; *New Statesman* article on BW, 522; biography, 630; portrait, *630*
Wells, Jane, 174, 175, 235–6, 237, 246
Wernher, Julius, 194, 226, 630
West, Julius (born Rapoport), 312, 630
Westminster Abbey, 10
Wheatley, John, 372, 373, 375, 630
Whisky Money (tax), 160, 161
Whiston, William Harvey, 164
Whitley, Edward, 309, 366, 367
Wilde, Oscar, 71–2, 81
Wilkinson, Ellen, 32, 325, 395, 554, 569, 630
Williams, Caroline, 81, 83, 94

Williams, Constance, 213
Williams, Glynne, 366, 367, 630
Williams, Noel (BW nephew), 318
Wilson, Charlotte, 68–9, 71, 72, 233, 630
Wilson, Harold, 524
Wilson, Horace (*later* Sir), 452, 538, 568, 631
Wilson, Sir Samuel, 420–2, 425, 428, 631
Wise, Frank, 506
Women's Social and Political Union, 238
Wooldridge, Adrian, 15
Woolf, Leonard: on liberty, 14; writer, 25; *Political Quarterly* editor, 27, 470; Fabian Society, 328–9; Webbs and, 328–30, 346, 422, 536, 557–8; Russian Revolution and, 334; Labour Party secretary, 339; Keynes and, 388; publisher, 388, 418; Coles and, 404–5; stays at Passfield, 408; Imperial Advisory Committee, 418; Kenya and, 422; on Grigg, 425; on BS as Colonial Secretary, 430; and Labour's international policy, 510; on League of Nations, 536–7; International and Imperial Advisory Committee Chairman, 537; biography, 631
Woolf, Virginia (*née* Stephen): BW and, 25–6, 27, 30, 408; SW and, 63; Neo-pagans and, 239; on Ka Cox, 242; Fabian Society, 328–9; Webbs and, 328–30, 346, 422, 557–8; ill health, 329; *Night and Day*, 364; reads *My Apprenticeship*, 387; Coles and, 404–5; on the Keynes, 407; stays at Passfield, 408; publisher, 418; death, 558; biography, 631
Wootton, Barbara Frances, Baroness Wootton of Abinger (*née* Adam), 364, 529, 631
Wordley, Emily, 397
Wordsworth, Elizabeth, 229
Workers' Weekly, 376–7, 380
workhouses, 202–5, 212, 215

Yarrow, Alfred (Sir), 270, 631

Yeats, WB, 81, 310
Young, (Edward) Hilton (Sir) (Lord
    Kennet), 418–22, 428, 429, 632

Zetetical Society, 67–8
Zinoviev letter (1924), 380–1
Zionist Organization, 432–5, 442, 445